COMPUTER ENGINEERING HANDBOOK

OTHER COMPUTER ENGINEERING BOOKS OF INTEREST

COMPUTER ENGINEERING HANDBOOK

C. H. Chen, Editor-in-Chief

Department of Electrical and Computer Engineering
University of Massachusetts Dartmouth

McGRAW-HILL, INC.

New York   St. Louis   San Francisco   Auckland   Bogotá
Caracas   Lisbon   London   Madrid   Mexico   Milan
Montreal   New Delhi   Paris   San Juan   São Paulo
Singapore   Sydney   Tokyo   Toronto

Library of Congress Cataloging-in-Publication Data

Computer engineering handbook / C. H. Chen, editor.
   p.   cm. — (Computer engineering series)
  Includes index.
  ISBN 0-07-010924-9 :
  1. Electronic digital computers—Handbooks, manuals, etc.
2. Computer engineering—Handbooks, manuals, etc.   I. Chen, C. H.
(Chi-hau), date.   II. Series.
TK7888.3.C652 1992
621.395—dc20
                                     92-6203
                                       CIP

  2 3 4 5 6 7 8 9 0 DOC/DOC 9 8 7 6 5 4 3 2

ISBN 0-07-010924-9

*The sponsoring editor for this book was Daniel A. Gonneau, the editing
supervisor was Ruth W. Mannino, and the production supervisor was Suzanne W.
Babeuf. It was set in Times Roman by Clarinda Company.*

Printed and bound by R. R. Donnelley & Sons Company.

CONTENTS

v

Chapter 4. Computer Arithmetic   *Earl E. Swartzlander, Jr.*   4.1

Chapter 5. Computer Architecture   *Robert B. K. Dewar*   5.1

Chapter 6. Reliability of Digital Systems   *Arden R. Helland*   6.1

Chapter 11. Computer Vision Principles and Applications
Giovanni Garibotto and Stefano Masciangelo   **11.1**

Chapter 12. Architectures for Image Processing and Computer Vision
Giovanni Garibotto   **12.1**

Chapter 13. VSLI Systems Design *Donald W. Bouldin*   13.1

Chapter 14. Application-Specific VLSI Processors
Earl E. Swartzlander, Jr.   14.1

Chapter 15. Attached Vector Processors in Signal Processing
Richard C. Borgioli   15.1

Chapter 16. Parallel Computing Systems *Tse-yun Feng, A. R. Hurson, and Chuan-lin Wu*   **16.1**

Chapter 17. Parallel Supercomputers *Geoffrey C. Fox*   **17.1**

Chapter 18. Neural Network Computing *Pietro G. Morasso*   18.1

Chapter 19. Optics in Computers *Henri H. Arsenault and Yunlong Sheng*   19.1

Chapter 20. Computer Networks (LAN, MAN, and WAN): An Overview   *Gurdeep S. Hura*   20.1

CONTRIBUTORS

Edward Angel *Department of Computer Science, University of New Mexico, Albuquerque* (CHAP. 8)

Henri H. Arsenault *Departement de Physique, Université Laval, Quebec, Canada* (CHAP. 19)

Richard C. Borgioli *CSPI Western Regional Office, Newbury Park, California* (CHAP. 15)

Donald W. Bouldin *Department of Electrical and Computer Engineering, University of Tennessee, Knoxville* (CHAP. 13)

James E. Buchanan *Electronic Systems Group, Westinghouse Electric Corporation, Baltimore, Maryland* (CHAP. 7)

C. H. Chen *Department of Electrical and Computer Engineering, University of Massachusetts Dartmouth, North Dartmouth* (CHAP. 1)

José G. Delgado-Frias *Department of Electrical Engineering, State University of New York at Binghamton* (CHAP. 10)

Robert B. K. Dewar *Courant Institute of Mathematical Sciences, New York University*

Tse-yun Feng *Department of Electrical and Computer Engineering, Pennsylvania State University, University Park* (CHAP. 16)

Geoffrey C. Fox *Northeast Parallel Architecture Centers, Syracuse University, New York* (CHAP. 17)

Giovanni Garibotto, *Research and Development, Elsag Bailey spa, Genoa, Italy* (CHAPS. 11 & 12)

Arden R. Helland *Electronic Systems Group, Westinghouse Electric Corp., Baltimore, Maryland* (CHAP. 6)

Paul T. Hulina *Department of Electrical and Computer Engineering, Pennsylvania State University, University Park* (CHAP. 3)

Gurdeep Hura *Department of Computer Science and Engineeering, Wright State University, Dayton, Ohio* (CHAP. 20)

A. R. Hurson *Department of Electrical and Computer Engineering, Pennsylvania State University, University Park* (CHAP. 16)

Hsi-Ho Liu *IBM Development Laboratory, Boca Raton, Florida* (CHAP. 2)

George F. Luger *Department of Computer Science, University of New Mexico, Albuquerque* (CHAP. 9)

Stefano Masciangelo *Research and Development, Elsag Bailey spa, Genoa, Italy* (CHAP. 11)

Pietro G. Morasso *Dipartimento di Informatica, Sistemistica, e Telematica, Università di Genoa, Italy* (CHAP. 18)

Yunlong Sheng *Departement de Physique, Université Laval, Quebec, Canada* (CHAP. 19)

William A. Stubblefield *Department of Computer Science, University of New Mexico, Albuquerque* (CHAP. 9)

Earl E. Swartzlander, Jr. *Department of Electrical and Computer Engineering, University of Texas, Austin* (CHAPS. 4 & 14)

Chuan-lin Wu *Department of Electrical and Computer Engineering, University of Texas, Austin,* (CHAP. 16)

PREFACE

After nearly 50 years of rapid development, modern computers are still experiencing a vigorous growth, and the trend will likely continue well into the twenty-first century. Building better and more powerful computers is certainly the main direction of the computer engineering field. Computer engineers, however, should be more knowledgeable about the many roles of computers in order to design computers more suitable to the expanding information-intensive society.

The area of computer engineering now encompasses so many topics that it is not possible to cover all of them in one handbook. This single-volume handbook focuses on the basics and new developments in computer engineering. The topics presented include digital logic and design, computer arithmetic, computer architecture, digital system design and reliability, and computer graphics. Topics on recent computer hardware development include VLSI systems and processors, vector processors, parallel computing systems, supercomputers, neural network computing, optical computing, and computer networks. A major emphasis is placed on intelligent processing of numeric and nonnumeric data and information by computers as reflected by Chapters 9 through 12 and 18 on artificial intelligence expert systems and neural networks as well as computer vision. It is now increasingly difficult to draw a fine line between computer hardware and computer software, and Chapter 2, which presents software issues in hardware development, is thus unique and important.

The book is written with computer professionals in both industry and academia as well as computer engineering students in mind, and should serve as a key reference book in the field. The composition of chapters reflects our view that computers will be playing an ever more dominant role in intelligent information processing in the next century, and thus future design of computer components and systems will emphasize meeting such demands.

In preparing this book it has been my great fortune to work with some of the leaders in computer engineering. I wish to thank all the contributors of the volume for their important work, and Daniel Gonneau for his continuous encouragement and insistence on publishing the highest quality book in the field.

C. H. Chen

CHAPTER 1

INTRODUCTION

C. H. Chen

Department of Electrical and Computer Engineering
University of Massachusetts Dartmouth

1.1 EVOLUTION OF COMPUTER ENGINEERING EDUCATION

Although computers have been around for almost 50 years, until about 30 years ago, computer engineering education had been limited to courses in logical design and circuits and a general introduction to computers in the electrical engineering curriculum. References 1 to 7 are some texts published in the early 1960s. A formal computer engineering program as an option or degree program in electrical engineering education was started only about 20 years ago and became popular in the late 1970s. Thus, in spite of the continued and tremendous progress in computers, a structured computer engineering educational program has been developed much more recently and updated at a slower pace. In the twenty-fifth anniversary issue of the *IEEE Transactions on Computers* in 1976 [8], the issue of computer science and engineering education was addressed at length. The distinction between computer science and computer engineering was defined. The computer scientist is more interested in the theory and science of computation while the computer engineer is more involved in the design and implementation of data processing systems including both hardware and software. Such a distinction is still valid today, but there is greater emphasis on computer hardware and systems in the current computer engineering curriculum. Undoubtedly there is a significant overlap between computer engineering and computer science programs, especially at the undergraduate level.

Typical courses now required in an undergraduate computer engineering program include digital logic and design, computer arithmetic, data structure, programming languages, microprocessors, operating systems, software engineering, digital system design, microprogrammed design, *very large-scale integration* (VLSI) circuits and systems, etc. The curriculum has remained essentially the same for a number of years.

Two points can be made from the above discussions. The first is the pressing need for continued and professional education in computer engineering. This is a field which experiences constant changes. Both fresh computer engineering graduates and practicing professionals must keep up with the progress through publications and by attending seminars or short courses. The second point, as indicated by slow curriculum changes, is that computer engineering has now reached a stage of maturity. Both points suggest that now is the time for a computer engineering handbook which presents not only the most up-to-date progress but also the fundamentals of the computer engineering topics. This single-volume comprehensive handbook is prepared exactly with these objectives in mind, with an emphasis on computer hardware and systems.

1.2 ORGANIZATION OF THE BOOK

Computer hardware design now greatly depends on the software systems. Chapter 2 deals with software issues such as computer-aided design using the *hardware design language* (HDL) tool. The basic computer engineering topics are covered in Chaps. 3 to 8. The remaining chapters deal with specific topics in computer systems and applications. Chapter 3 on digital logic and design provides an overview of the basic elements and methods in the design process. Chapter 4 on computer arithmetic discusses binary fixed-point number systems and implementations of both fixed-point and floating-point arithmetic. Chapter 5 on computer architecture describes the basic high-level design of modern processors and associated memory systems, with specific reference to the basic debate between the older *complex instruction set computers* (CISC) and the newer *reduced instruction set computer* (RISC) designs. Chapter 6 on the reliability of digital systems and Chap. 7 on digital system design complement each other by presenting in detail the models, specifications, requirements, and systems-level issues for designing reliable digital systems. With increased miniaturization and extensive use of digital components, the importance of digital system reliability simply cannot be overemphasized. Chapter 8 surveys a few of the most important aspects of computer graphics.

It is now evident that the future of computer engineering lies in the intelligent computer systems which perform, though in a much limited scale, some intelligent tasks as performed by humans. This book has placed great emphasis on such development. Chapter 9 on rule-based expert systems and Chap. 10 on computer architectures for *artificial intelligence* (AI) and neural networks complement each other in discussing both the systems and architectures of this AI area of interest to computer engineers. Chapter 11 on computer vision principles and applications and the accompanying Chap. 12 on architectures for image processing and computer vision present another area of intelligent computer system, which is the use of computers to process and interpret image and scene data, similar to the function of the human vision system. One application of such a system is in intelligent robots which will be used much more extensively as we enter the twenty-first century. The VLSI systems have been the single most important development in computer engineering in recent years. Chapter 13 on VLSI system design and Chap. 14 on application-specific VLSI processors also complement each other by starting with the discussion of microelectronic technology with emphasis on digital *complementary metal-oxide semiconductor* (CMOS) circuits and design methodology for VLSI systems and extending to VLSI architectures and application-specific processors such as the fast Fourier transform (FFT) processor. The major role of computers will still be in data and signal processing, and thus Chap. 15 on attached vector processors in signal processing has emphasized the importance of the array processor to speed up the computation. Chapter 16 on parallel computing systems and Chap. 17 on parallel supercomputers again complement each other on the needs for and the use of parallelism to achieve high throughput and supercomputing. The future of high-speed computing definitely lies in parallel computing systems.

The revitalization of neural network study in the last 5 years has had a great impact on almost all areas of science, engineering, business, and other disciplines. For computer engineers, neural networks represent a parallel computer system on distributed representations, which promises to reach the computing capability of biological systems especially in pattern classification and functional synthesis. Chapter 18 on neural network computing presents the basic neural network models and their principles. Optical computing has long been recognized as important for its speed and storage capability, and thus optics will play some role in all future supercomputers. Chapter 19 on optics in computers provides an extensive discussion of optical computer architectures, components, and technologies as well as optical interconnects. The final chapter, Chap. 20 on computer networks, explores another important topic in computer development, computer networking, which has become vital to utilize effectively the computer resources. It is remarked that although individual chapters are self-contained and complete with careful introduction of a topic and extensive references for further reading, the chapters as presented represent different but correlated and vital aspects of computer engineering for many years to come.

REFERENCES

1. T. C. Bartee, *Digital Computer Fundamentals,* 3d ed. New York: McGraw-Hill, 1972.
2. T. C. Bartee, I. L. Lebow, and I. S. Reed, *Theory and Design of Digital Machines.* New York: McGraw-Hill, 1962.
3. E. J. McCluskey and T. C. Bartee, *A Survey of Switching Circuit Theory.* New York: McGraw-Hill, 1962.
4. Y. Chu, *Digital Computer Design Fundamentals.* New York: McGraw-Hill, 1962.
5. H. J. Gray, *Digital Computer Engineering.* Englewood Cliffs, N.J.: Prentice-Hall, 1963.
6. H. T. Torng, *An Introduction to the Logic Design of Switching Systems.* Reading, Mass.: Addison-Wesley, 1964.
7. M. A. Harrison, *Introduction to Switching and Automata Theory.* New York: McGraw-Hill, 1965.
8. C. V. Ramamoorthy, "Computer Science and Engineering Education," *IEEE Transactions on Computers,* C-25(12):1200–1206, December 1976.

CHAPTER 2
SOFTWARE ISSUES IN HARDWARE DEVELOPMENT

Hsi-Ho Liu
IBM Corporation, Boca Raton, Florida

2.1 INTRODUCTION

Today's hardware design is facing pressure from two fronts. One is the rapid increase in the density and complexity of *very large-scale integration* (VLSI) and computer systems. The other is the decrease of design cycle times. A successful design can be achieved only by using advanced *computer-aided design* (CAD) tools. Hardware design using CAD tools is heavily dependent on software. Most CAD tools are software systems that create and manipulate design data. *Hardware description languages* (HDLs) even describe hardware design as programs. As the complexity of hardware design increases, many software-related issues need to be addressed. Tool compatibility is one example. Managing a large design database and the design process is another important issue.

To meet today's and tomorrow's challenges in hardware design, we need a set of powerful CAD tools. In addition, we need a well-structured framework for these tools to operate. The framework must also support the management of the design database and the design process. This chapter discusses typical design processes, some of the available tools, and some open issues in hardware design. The topics include design process, design entry, synthesis, simulation and verification, test, and the framework. We focus mainly on digital design. The development of technology and CAD tools for analog design is still quite primitive and lagging way behind that of digital design.

2.2 DESIGN PROCESS

Computer hardware design, like the design of any complex system, is often characterized by a hierarchical approach. The design process usually starts with a high-level system design, then subsystem design and *printed-circuit board* (PCB) design, and finally, chip design. Bell and Newell divided computer hardware into five levels of abstraction [2]. The levels are processors-memories-switches (system), instruction set (algorithm), register transfer, logic, and circuit. Hardware systems at any level can also be described by their behavior, structure, and physical implementation. Walker and Thomas combined these

TABLE 2.1   Levels of Abstraction versus Domains of Description

Level	Behavioral domain	Structural domain	Physical domain
Architectural level (system level)	Performance specification	CPUs Memories Switches Controllers Buses	Physical partitions
Algorithmic level	Algorithms (manipulation of data structures)	Hardware modules Data structures	Clusters
Functional block level (register transfer level)	Operations Register transfer State sequencing	ALUs MUXs Registers Microsequencer Microstore	Floor plans
Logic level	Boolean equations	Gates Flip-flops Latches	Cell estimates
Circuit level	Differential equations	Transistors Capacitors Resistors	Cell estimates Cell details

Source: © 1985 IEEE.

two views and proposed a model of design representation and synthesis [21]. Table 2.1 shows this model of three domains and five levels in each domain. McFarland et al. [18] also proposed a similar model. Others have used a *Y* chart to represent similar information [9, 22].

Behavioral design describes the behavior or function of the hardware using such notations as behavioral languages, register transfer languages, and logic equations. *Structural design* specifies functional blocks and components such as *arithmetic logic units* (ALUs), registers, gates, flip-flops, and their interconnections. *Physical design* describes the implementation of a design idea in a hardware platform, such as the floor plan of a circuit board and layout of transistors, standard cells, and macrocells in an *integrated-circuit* (IC) chip. The final goal of hardware design is to have a physical description at the circuit level. Hierarchical design starts with high-level algorithmic or behavioral design. These high-level designs are then converted to the circuits at the physical domain. Various CAD tools are available for design entry and conversion. For example, schematic entry tools allow input of logic in the structural domain. Logic synthesis tools convert behavioral descriptions at the register transfer level to structural descriptions at the logic level.

2.2.1 Design Entry

The first step in CAD is to enter design ideas and store them in computer format. Because design ideas can be described at different levels of abstraction and in various domains, we must be able to enter the design at any level or domain. One of the early applications of CAD tools is in schematic entry. The core representation of digital systems is the logic circuit. For computers, a logic circuit is typically described by a list of gates and their connections, called *netlist*. However, for human beings, a graphical representation of the circuit is more conceivable. Schematic entry tools provide graphic capabilities to create, display, and change the design. They also provide a syntax check and therefore prevent many human errors such as unconnected gates. With proper support, schematics can be converted to executable form, so that the logic can be simulated.

Figure 2.1 shows a typical design process with schematic entry where the gate-level designs are entered by using graphical interface. The design of a large system is usually divided into several modules that are created and simulated separately and then merged into a complete system. The simulation verifies both the functions and the timing of the design. A feedback loop is generally needed for design iteration. After verification of the design, test patterns are generated either manually or automatically. Physical design, the final step, completes the layout of the chips or the boards and then the design is sent to manufacturing. The major drawback of gate-level schematic-based design is that the functions of the entire circuit cannot be tested until all the modules are completed. Functional errors will not be discovered until several months into the design cycle. Debugging functional errors at the gate level is a difficult and time-consuming task. A hierarchical design process where the functions can be simulated at high level will alleviate this problem.

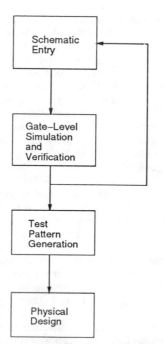

FIGURE 2.1 Typical design process with schematic entry.

Schematic entry is a useful tool for creating small- or medium-size circuits and for changing existing circuits. However, it would not be practical to create a 50,000-gate or larger circuit from scratch, using traditional schematic entry tools. Because of the advances in synthesis tools, design entry using HDL description is becoming popular, particularly in *application-specific integrated-circuit* (ASIC) design. Many ASIC designs use high-level behavioral or structural descriptions as design entry. After that, these high-level designs can be simulated and verified before being converted to a lower level by using synthesis tools.

A typical HDL-based design process is shown in Fig. 2.2. The design is described by HDL constructs. The functions of the design can be simulated at the HDL level. Functional errors can be discovered as early as a few weeks into the design cycle. Debugging of functional errors at the HDL level is also much easier and quicker. After verification of all the functions, HDL constructs are then synthesized into gate-level circuits. Gate-level simulation verifies the functions as well as the timings of the design. Two feedback loops for design iteration are provided to the HDL and the gate levels. The advantage of this design approach has been shown on several products that hit the market at record-breaking times. The most popular HDLs today are the very-high-speed integrated circuit (VHSIC), VHSIC hardware description language (VHDL), and the Verilog. A simple

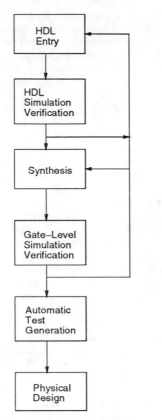

FIGURE 2.2   Typical HDL-based design process.

design example using VHDL is given in Sec. 2.2.4. VHDL is now IEEE Standard 1076 and is quickly becoming the industry standard.

2.2.2 Design Synthesis

Hardware design for complex systems and circuits usually proceeds in three phases: high-level design, logic design, and physical design. At high level, the design is described by either a behavioral or a structural model. Hardware description languages are a popular choice for high-level design. Some HDLs can describe only behavioral models. Some can describe only structural models. Others, like VHDL, can describe both. High-level design, whether behavioral or structural, can be simulated and verified before it is converted to a lower level. The conversion from high- to low-level description is called *synthesis*. If the conversion is from an abstract behavioral specification to a logic specification, it will require two steps. First, high-level synthesis converts abstract behavioral specifications to register transfer specifications. Next, logic synthesis maps register transfer specifications to logic specifications.

Logic synthesis, particularly for combinational logic, has been well studied and is relatively mature. It provides automatic synthesis of near-optimal logic circuits with either minimum delay or minimum area. Logic synthesis for combinational circuits can be divided into two types: two-level synthesis for *programmable logic array* (PLA) and multilevel synthesis for random logic. Synthesis for two-level logic is easy because of its regular structure and because it has already matured. Synthesis for multilevel logic, which includes both data path and control, is more complicated. Two approaches have been successfully used in multilevel logic synthesis: the algorithmic approach and the rule-based approach. The algorithmic approach is based on algorithmic transformation and hence has a global perspective. One such example is the MIS developed at the University of California, Berkeley [4]. The rule-based approach uses a set of heuristic rules for local transformation and optimization. One example is the logic synthesis system (LSS) developed at IBM [7]. A recent development has been a combination of the algorithmic approach in technology-independent transformation and the rule-based approach in technology mapping. Automatic synthesis for sequential circuits usually deals with the combinational circuits and the memory devices separately. The synthesis for memory devices is not as well developed as that for combinational circuits.

Large companies such as IBM, AT&T, and NEC have in-house synthesis programs that have been used routinely in chip design. Many CAD vendors such as Synopsys,

Mentor Graphics, and Recal-Redac are also offering advanced synthesis tools. The recent increase in circuit complexity has made hardware testing more difficult and critical. Area and performance are no longer the only concerns in chip design. Design for testability is becoming a criterion in logic synthesis just as the area and performance are. Many synthesis tools produce logic that is 100 percent testable for stuck-at faults. Some also automatically generate test patterns.

2.2.3 Simulation and Verification

One major advantage of using CAD tools is that the design can be simulated before any hardware is actually built. Through simulation design, errors can be detected and corrected much more quickly and easily. Simulation also allows experimentation with different design ideas. This is especially useful at high-level design.

A design is not complete until the final behavior or function of the physical circuit meets the design specification. In a hierarchical, multilevel approach, we must ensure that the high-level design is correct and that no discrepancies or errors are introduced during the conversion from high- to low-level design. Most synthesis tools accomplish the second requirement automatically because they maintain the equivalence of the design before and after conversion. This is called *correctness by construction*. Hand-constructed circuits are more susceptible to human error. Since there is no automatic tool to generate behavioral or structural descriptions at high level, the only way to ensure design correctness is by running some test cases in simulation.

In simulation test, a set of test cases is used to verify that the design meets the specification. Since a finite number of test cases cannot cover a virtually infinite number of possible situations, good engineering judgment and reasoning are required to supplement this shortcoming. Test coverage analysis and automatic test generation for high-level functional test are still primitive and need more study. Because there is no better method, the simulation test remains the primary tool for design verification. Formal proof has recently emerged as a promising method for design verification [5]. However, it needs to demonstrate that it can handle complex, real-world designs. Also, since this technology is still immature, there is no dominant technique, so tools are needed to fill the gap between the current CAD systems and the formal verification systems.

In general, two types of simulation are conducted in digital design. First, based on behavioral and structural models, high-level simulation verifies that the functionality of the design meets the specifications. It is technology-independent. Most HDL simulators can serve this purpose. In the past, various HDL simulators, such as ISPS (Carnegie Mellon University), CDL (the University of Maryland), etc., have been used. Since VHDL is becoming the standard HDL in industry and everywhere else, the VHDL simulator is becoming the natural choice for VHDL-based designs. Second, low-level timing simulation considers all timing parameters and verifies that the timing of the circuit also meets the specification. It is technology-dependent. A discrete event simulation model is used at this level [13]. Many vendor tools, such as LASAR (Teradyne) and HILO4 (GenRad), are available for logic simulation.[†] Some vendors, such as Zycad, also supply hardware simulators which are much more powerful than software simulators. If analog design is involved and circuit simulation is needed, then the most popular tool is SPICE [19] and its variations. SPICE uses a detailed device model to create accurate simulation for transistor-level circuits.

[†]LASAR and HILO are registered trademarks of Teradyne, Inc., and of GenRad, respectively.

2.2.4 VHDL-Based Design

The development of VHDL was initiated and sponsored by the U.S. government to address a number of recurrent problems in the development, exchange, and documentation of digital hardware. The language VHDL Version 7.2, developed by a team from Intermetrics, IBM, and Texas Instruments, was completed in August 1985. The IEEE subsequently took on the effort of standardizing VHDL, and the new language standard, now known as IEEE-1076, was approved in December 1987.

VHDL is making a great impact on digital hardware design because of the IEEE standard and the U.S. government's support. Now an industry standard, VHDL models will run on any system that conforms to that standard, just as programs written in ANSI Standard Fortran or C can run on almost any computer system. This will encourage exchange and reuse of designs. VHDL has more desirable features than any other existing HDLs [1]. VHDL supports different design methodologies; e.g., it supports both top-down and library-based design. VHDL is also independent of implementation technology and process. A system can be designed and verified at high level and then mapped to selected implementation technology such as CMOS, NMOS, or GaAs. This greatly increases the flexibility and efficiency. The Department of Defense is making VHDL a requirement on all contracts that develop ASICs.

VHDL can describe a system by using a combination of descriptions at different levels. It can also describe a system by using a mixture of behavioral and structural models. This allows great flexibility because the design can be simulated without a complete structural model. The following example from Lipsett et al. [14] shows how to design a simple circuit, a full adder, using VHDL and some of its features.

```
--The entity declaration
entity Half_adder is
  port (
    X: in Bit;
    Y: in Bit;
    Sum: out Bit;
    Carry: out Bit);
end Half_adder;
```

Readers are referred to the reference manual [10] for a full account of VHDL and the book by Lipsett et al. [14] for more design examples. In VHDL a component, the half adder here, is represented by the *design entity*. A port is the component's point of connection to the world. The direction of data flow can be input (in), output (out), or bidirectional (inout). The data type can be two-level (Bit) or three-level (TriState). Figure 2.3 shows the entity declaration of a half adder. "--" marks a comment in VHDL.

The following architecture body describes the behavior of the half adder.

```
--The architecture body;
architecture Behavioral_description of Half_adder is
begin
  process
    Sum <= X xor Y after 5 ns;
    Carry <= X and Y after 5 ns;
    Wait on X, Y;
  end process;
end Behavioral_description;
```

The first assignment statement says that the signal connected to the port Sum will obtain the "exclusive or" of the signal values of ports X and Y after 5 ns of delay. The wait

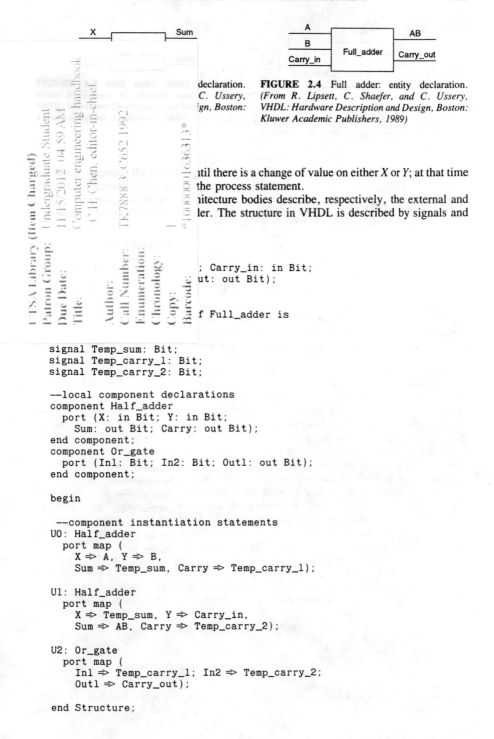

declaration.   **FIGURE 2.4** Full adder: entity declaration.
C. Ussery,   *(From R. Lipsett, C. Shaefer, and C. Ussery,*
ign, Boston: *VHDL: Hardware Description and Design, Boston:*
              Kluwer Academic Publishers, 1989)

ntil there is a change of value on either *X* or *Y*; at that time
the process statement.
nitecture bodies describe, respectively, the external and
ler. The structure in VHDL is described by signals and

```
; Carry_in: in Bit;
ut: out Bit);


f Full_adder is

signal Temp_sum: Bit;
signal Temp_carry_1: Bit;
signal Temp_carry_2: Bit;

--local component declarations
component Half_adder
  port (X: in Bit; Y: in Bit;
    Sum: out Bit; Carry: out Bit);
end component;
component Or_gate
  port (In1: Bit; In2: Bit; Out1: out Bit);
end component;

begin

 --component instantiation statements
U0: Half_adder
  port map (
    X ⇒ A, Y ⇒ B,
    Sum ⇒ Temp_sum, Carry ⇒ Temp_carry_1);

U1: Half_adder
  port map (
    X ⇒ Temp_sum, Y ⇒ Carry_in,
    Sum ⇒ AB, Carry ⇒ Temp_carry_2);

U2: Or_gate
  port map (
    In1 ⇒ Temp_carry_1; In2 ⇒ Temp_carry_2;
    Out1 ⇒ Carry_out);

end Structure;
```

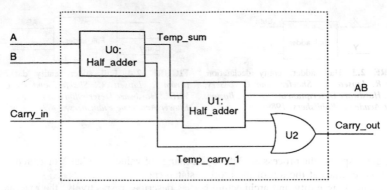

FIGURE 2.5 Full adder: architecture body. *(From R. Lipsett, C. Shaefer, and C. Ussery, VHDL: Hardware Description and Design, Boston: Kluwer Academic Publishers, 1989)*

connections of signals to subcomponents. Three signals—temp sum, temp carry 1, and temp carry 2—are needed for the full adder. Two types of component—the half adder and OR gate—are also required. The component instantiation statement shows how to connect, using signals, two half adders, U0 and U1, and one OR gate, U2, to make a full adder. Figures 2.4 and 2.5 show the entity declaration and architecture body of a full adder.

Design with VHDL at its current stage is not without problems. The biggest problem is compatibility since each vendor implemented only a subset, and often a different subset, of VHDL. A design running perfectly on one VHDL simulator may not run on another because some of the language constructs are not supported. This poses a problem in using library models from other vendors. Another serious problem is that the simulators and the synthesizers from different vendors are not always compatible. That is, some constructs supported by one simulator may not be synthesizable at another synthesizer. Fortunately, solutions are available. Those vendors who offer integrated design solutions guarantee that their simulation and synthesis tools are compatible even though they may use other vendors' tools in their systems. A partial list of the systems vendors include Cadence Design Systems, Mentor Graphics, Recal-Redac, and Valid Logic Systems. Some simulator vendors, such as Vantage Analysis Systems, and synthesizer vendors, such as Synopsys, are also forming partnership and associate programs with other vendors to make sure that their tools are compatible with other tools.

Engineers who are used to graphics-oriented design tools will need to adjust to master language-oriented design tools. Many vendors provide tools that accept both graphics-oriented schematic entry and text-oriented language entry. A tool such as Concept[†] from Valid Logic Systems also provides automatic conversion from graphic schematic entry to VHDL text.

[†]Concept is a trademark of Valid Logic Systems.

2.3 TEST TOOLS

Simulation test as discussed in Sec. 2.3 is aimed at design verification. Its goal is to make sure that the circuit is designed correctly. Another type of test is to verify that the hardware is manufactured correctly. The design is assumed to be correct, and the test is to determine whether the hardware is free of manufacturing defects. Common manufacturing defects include open and short circuits, etc. Such a test has garnered much attention and studies because manufacturing yield, for VLSI fabrication and for card assembly alike, is by no means perfect. The *defect level* (DL), defined as the percentage of bad parts that pass the test, can be calculated from the equation

$$DL = 1 - Y^{1-T}$$

where Y is the manufacturing process yield and T is the test coverage [23]. This equation indicates that to keep the defect level low, we need high test coverage and that the lower the yield, the higher the coverage.

Instead of using transistor-level circuits, the test generation here is based on logic circuits. Such a test usually specifies the type of fault to be covered and then generates test patterns to detect if that fault exists. The most common fault for investigation is the single stuck-at fault. Automatic algorithms are available for generating test patterns for these faults. However, some faults in complex circuits are not detectable from the external inputs and outputs for lacking controllability and observability. *Design for testability* (DFT) is a solution to achieve better test coverage and to ease test generation. It has gained much attention lately despite its overhead in circuit costs and performance.

2.3.1 Test Pattern Generation

Test pattern generation for the stuck-at fault has been studied quite extensively. It has become a routine in most design processes. A stuck-at fault occurs when a logic net, such as the output of a gate, is stuck at a permanent value of either 0 or 1. Test patterns are generated in such a way that if stuck-at faults exist, the outputs of the circuit will be different from the correct outputs. The algorithm (from [12]) for test pattern generation consists of three steps:

1. Select a fault that has not been detected.
2. Construct the search graph for the chosen fault.
3. Search the search space until either a test is found or the space is exhausted.

To find a test, we need to sensitize the fault and propagate the fault to the output. Fault sensitizing means finding a set of inputs that will cause a good circuit to have different values at the faulty location. The D algorithm [21] is the most popular and widely used one for *automatic test pattern generation* (ATPG).

When the search space is exhausted and no test can be found, we have an undetectable fault, also called a *redundant fault*. Many logic synthesis programs generate a logic circuit that has no redundancy; that means it is 100 percent testable. Test generation time is spent searching the search space and backtracking during the search to resolve conflicts. The size of the search space, the search strategy, and the heuristics differentiate the ATPG algorithms. As the size and the complexity of VLSI circuits increase rapidly, we need better ATPG algorithms to increase fault coverage and reduce generation time. Recently, expert-system technology has been applied to test generation to increase test coverage. ExpertTest offers an ATPG system for sequential circuits that uses high-level behavioral information and knowledge-based reasoning.

Most of the ATPG algorithms used today are designed for single stuck-at faults and combinational circuits. Other types of faults, such as multiple faults and bridging faults, are more difficult to detect. Further, there is often no one-to-one correspondence between a physical defect and a stuck-at fault model. Some physical defects cannot be represented by any logic model. Other physical defects correspond to more than one logic model. Nevertheless, statistical data showed that if we can detect a large percentage of single stuck-at faults, we can detect a high percentage of all failures [23]. The stuck-at faults are static (logic) faults. Other faults such as dynamic faults and parametric faults will also cause the circuit to fail. Dynamic faults, such as delay-time faults, are timing-related. Parametric faults are incorrect voltage and current levels. A functional at-speed test is needed to detect these faults. That is, we need to run the test at the circuit's operational speed and check the timing and electrical parameters. This requires more sophisticated *automatic test equipment* (ATE). Most test programs for dynamic faults are created manually; more study is needed in automatic test generation and test coverage analysis for dynamic faults.

As the circuits become more complicated, they require more test generation time, longer test patterns, and more time to execute those tests. This leads to the development of the *built-in self-test* (BIST) [16, 17]. Instead of receiving the test patterns from the testers, BIST uses test patterns generated internally from the circuit under test. The tests are generated using pseudo-random or weighted random pattern generators. The test results are then compressed, or compacted, for analysis. Since the results are compacted, a problem called *aliasing* exists; i.e., a faulty circuit may have the same output as the good circuit. BIST requires extra circuits for test generation and output compaction; however, it relieves the pain of test generation and investment in costly testers.

2.3.2 Design for Testability

Because of quality requirements and rapid expansion in the size and complexity of VLSI, testability has become a major issue in design. Design for testability (DFT) is a methodology to ensure that the design is testable. *Level-sensitive scan design* (LSSD) is one of the most popular techniques for DFT, which is also IBM's discipline for structural DFT. The LSSD is implemented by linking, with additional circuits, all the latches in a circuit into a shift register. By doing so a sequential circuit can be divided into several combinational circuits separated by the shift registers. Test vectors can be scanned into, and the results scanned out of, the shift registers. The LSSD makes test generation much easier and increases test coverage but adds some area overhead and a little performance overhead.

The typical approach at board-level test is called the *in-circuit test* (ICT) where a bed-of-nails fixture is used to test the input and output of the components and the interconnections. As the components get denser and the surface-mounted technology proliferates, it becomes more difficult to probe the test points. A new approach called a *boundary scan* was developed to deal with this problem. In this approach, all the primary inputs and outputs of an integrated circuit (IC) are connected into a shift register, and the shift registers on all the ICs of a board are connected into a large shift register. A single scan-in and a scan-out path for this large shift register are provided at the card edge. With boundary scan test, vectors can be scanned into those nodes that are hard to reach for ICT. Boundary scan architecture was first proposed by the Joint Test Action Group (JTAG) and later became IEEE Standard 1149.1 in 1990. This standard defines the architecture for test-access port and boundary scan test. An IEEE subcommittee is now reviewing a proposal for the *boundary-scan description language* (BSDL). This language will be used to describe the boundary scan test logic added to an IC. It is very likely that the future board design will use a mixture of scannable and nonscannable components. Therefore, efficient ATPG algorithms and test coverage study must be developed to deal with this situation. Again, boundary scan will add extra circuits to the chips but will improve test coverage and reduce test costs at the card level.

DFT in current practice is often a postdesign process. A testability test is conducted after the design is completed. Several rule-based systems are available for testability check and recommendation [3]. However, testability check as a postdesign process usually achieves only suboptimal results. A different approach, called *synthesis for testability,* considers testability as one of the design constraints just as performance and area are. Testability is considered from the very beginning of the design, especially at high-level design. By treating testability, performance, and area from a global perspective, this approach will achieve better results in balancing the three.

2.4 CAD FRAMEWORK

Hardware design involves very large design databases, complex and heterogeneous CAD software, many participating groups, and constant revision of the design. Therefore, design tool integration and design data/process management pose great challenges to the CAD/CAE community. CAD frameworks address these problems by providing a common operating environment for various CAD tools and management of the design database and process. CAD tool developers, CAD tool integrators, and end users will all benefit from a standard, well-defined framework. A CAD framework usually includes

1. A common user interface that provides a consistent, graphical, and easy-to-use front end
2. A design database containing design and library information that may actually be stored across a network
3. A design data and process manager to control design information and the design process
4. A communications manager for tool integration

Managing a large design database is a critical issue. Hierarchical representation provides multiple levels of abstraction and hence is a preferred method for design. However, it is not always easy or automatic to derive information from different levels. Consequently, redundant representations usually exist. Moreover, a traditional database is record-oriented. While adequate for business applications, it is not suitable for engineering design. Engineering data are much more complicated. The object-oriented system is becoming popular lately in engineering design because of its abilities in data abstraction, data encapsulation, inheritance, and reusability. The object-oriented system will play a major role in future engineering database design.

Intertool communication is another important issue. Since different tools use different data formats, translators are necessary for transferring design data between tools. A tool-to-tool translator is not efficient when there are large numbers of tools. For example, N tools require $N(N - 1)$ translators, for both directions. Each additional tool would need $2N, 2(N + 1), \ldots$ translators. A better solution is to use a common exchange format for all tools. With a common exchange format, N tools require only $2N$ translators. Each additional tool would need only two translators. There are some emerging industry-standard data formats such as *electronic data interchange format* (EDIF) and VHDL. The CAD Framework Initiative (CFI) is a cooperative effort to develop industrial guidelines for a design automation framework. This will enable the coexistence and cooperation of a variety of tools. The Engineering Information System (EIS) program of the Department of Defense is focused on a framework standard for *computer-aided engineering* (CAE) tool integration. Considerable research and development activities in CAD frameworks are underway in universities, government, and industry [6].

2.5 CONCLUSIONS

Hardware design, to a large degree, relies on software tools for synthesis and verification of the design and on the framework for management of design tools, databases, and processes. As design becomes more complex and design tools proliferate, more advanced design technologies and a standard framework are desperately needed. Among the design technologies, some are quite mature, such as schematic design capture and logic design verification. Others are near maturity, such as physical design and process and device modeling. Still others are still emerging, such as behavioral synthesis and verification [6]. CAD Framework Initiative is now receiving strong support from industry. Universities and government are also active in doing and supporting research in CAD frameworks. The future design environment will include a standardized framework, advanced design tools, an efficient user interface, and an intelligent, knowledge-based assistant for design.

Design automation is a relatively young field (less than 30 years old). Major conferences in this area include the Design Automation Conference (sponsored by IEEE and ACM), the IEEE International Conference on Computer-Aided Design (ICCAD), the International Test Conference (ITC), and several others. These conferences are good sources for the latest commercial CAD/CAE products and new research results. Other sources for research and development and application results include *IEEE Transactions on Computer-Aided Design of Integrated Circuits and Systems, IEEE Design and Test of Computers,* and several other publications.

REFERENCES

1. J. H. Aylor, R. Waxman, and C. Scarratt, "VHDL—Feature Description and Analysis," *IEEE Design and Test of Computers,* 3(2):17–27, April 1986.

2. C. G. Bell and A. Newell, *Computer Structure: Readings and Examples.* New York: McGraw-Hill, 1973.

3. M. Bidjan-Irani, "A Rule-Based Design-for-Testability Rule Checker," *IEEE Design and Test of Computers,* 8(1):50–57, March 1991.

4. R. K. Brayton, R. Rudell, A. L. Sangiovanni-Vincentelli, and A. Wang, "MIS: Multiple-Level Interactive Logic Optimization System," *IEEE Transactions on Computer-Aided Design of Integrated Circuits and Systems,* CAD-6(6):1062–1081, November 1987.

5. P. Camurati and P. Prinetto, "Formal Verification of Hardware Correctness: Introduction and Survey of Current Research," *Computer,* 21(7):8–20, July 1988.

6. R. K. Cavin and J. L. Hilbert, "Design of Integrated Circuits: Directions and Challenges," *Proceedings of the IEEE,* Special Issue on the Future of Computer-Aided Design, 78(2):418–435, February 1990.

7. J. Darringer, D. Brand, J. Gerbi, W. Joyner, and L. Trevillyan, "LSS: A System for Production Logic Synthesis," *IBM Journal of Research and Development,* 28(5):537–545, September 1984.

8. J. Donnell, "Boundary Scan Puts Tomorrow's Devices to Test," *Electronic Design*, 39(12):75–86, June 1991.

9. D. Gajske and R. Kuhn, "Guest Editors' Introduction: New VLSI Tools," *Computer*, 16(12):11–14, December 1983.

10. *IEEE Standard VHDL Language Reference Manual—Std. 1076-1987.* New York: IEEE, 1988.

11. IEEE Standard 1149.1-1990, *IEEE Standard Test Access Port and Boundary-Scan Architecture*. New York: IEEE, 1990.

12. T. Kirkland and M. R. Mercer, "Algorithms for Automatic Test Pattern Generation," *IEEE Design and Test of Computers*, 5(3):43–55, June 1988.

13. M. R. Lightner, "Modeling and Simulation of VLSI Digital Systems," *Proceedings of the IEEE*, 75(6):786–796, June 1987.

14. R. Lipsett, C. Schaefer, and C. Ussery, *VHDL: Hardware Description and Design*. Boston: Kluwer Academic Publishers, 1989.

15. L. Maliniak, "Synthesis Tools Move into the Mainstream," *Electronic Design*, 39(16):51–66, August 1991.

16. E. J. McCluskey, "Built-in Self-Test Techniques," *IEEE Design and Test of Computers*, 2(2):21–28, April 1985.

17. E. J. McCluskey, "Built-in Self-Test Structures," *IEEE Design and Test of Computers*, 2(2):29–36, April 1985.

18. M. C. McFarland, A. C. Parker, and R. Camposano, "The High-Level Synthesis of Computer Systems," *Proceedings of the IEEE*, Special Issue on the Future of Computer-Aided Design, 78(2):301–318, February 1990.

19. L. W. Nagel, "SPICE2: A Computer Program to Simulate Semiconductor Circuits," ERL-Memo M520, Electronics Research Laboratory, University of California, Berkeley, May 1975.

20. K. P. Parker, "The Impact of Boundary Scan on Board Test," *IEEE Design and Test of Computers*, 6(4):18–30, August 1989.

21. J. P. Roth, "Diagnosis of Automata Failures: A Calculus and a Method," *IBM Journal of Research and Development*, 10(4):278–291, July 1966.

22. R. A. Walker and D. E. Thomas, "A Model of Design Representation and Synthesis," *Proceedings of the 22d Design Automation Conference*, pp. 453–459, 1985.

23. T. W. Williams and N. Brown, "Defect Level as a Function of Fault Coverage," *IEEE Transactions on Computers*, C-30(12):987–988, December 1981.

24. T. W. Williams and K. P. Parker, "Design for Testability—A Survey," *IEEE Transactions on Computers*, C-31(1):2–15, January 1982.

CHAPTER 3
DIGITAL LOGIC AND DESIGN

Paul T. Hulina

Pennsylvania State University, University Park

3.1 INTRODUCTION

Available design components and tools are constantly changing due to advances being made in both the solid-state and computer areas. The digital designer must be able to take advantage of these new developments in order to remain competitive in the marketplace. However, basic concepts remain important in spite of new technologies.

This chapter on digital logic and design provides a brief overview of the basic elements and methods involved in the design process. It is assumed that the reader is familiar with the binary number system and has had exposure to some aspects of digital design.

3.2 BOOLEAN ALGEBRA

In 1854, George Boole postulated an algebraic system for symbolizing the fundamental laws of reasoning. In the 1930s, Claude Shannon of Bell Laboratories adapted this boolean algebra to specify the behavior of relay circuits which performed various logical operations. This adaptation was the foundation of a two-valued switching algebra presented next.

Switching Algebra. A set of elements $\{0, 1\}$ and two associated operations $+$ and $\cdot$ form a switching algebra if and only if:

(P1)   An inverse is defined:

$$a + a' = 1$$
$$a \cdot a' = 0$$

(P2)   Identity elements exist for the $+$ and $\cdot$ operations:

$$0 + a = a$$
$$1 \cdot a = a$$

(P3)   The + and · operations are commutative.

$$a + b = b + a$$

$$a \cdot b = b \cdot a$$

(P4)   The + and · operations are distributive.

$$a(b + c) = a \cdot b + a \cdot c$$
$$a + b \cdot c = (a + b) \cdot (a + c)$$

From these rules or postulates, the following relationships can be formulated.

Associative	$a + (b + c) = (a + b) + c$	$a \cdot (b \cdot c) = (a \cdot b) \cdot c$
Complement	$(a + b)' = a' + b'$	$(a \cdot b)' = a' + b'$
Idempotent	$a + a = a$	$a \cdot a = a$
Absorption	$a + a \cdot b = a$	$a \cdot (a + b) = a$
Combination	$a \cdot b + a \cdot b' = a$	$(a + b) \cdot (a + b') = a$
Null	$a + 1 = 1$	$a \cdot 0 = 0$
Involution	$(a')' = a$	

Observe that this algebra adheres to the principle of duality. Each expression has a dual that can be formed by interchanging + with · , · with + , 0 with 1, and 1 with 0.

It is possible to mathematically formalize and express in equation form logic statements that describe some process or situation by using switching algebra postulates and relationships. To illustrate, suppose that we wish to turn on a front door light when it is dark and a key has been inserted into the front door. Assume that sensors are in place that indicate when it is dark (D) and a key is in the door (K). When the light should be on is described by the equation

$$F(D, K) = D \cdot K$$

Here D and K are termed *switching variables* such that $D = 1$ indicates that it is dark while $D = 0$ represents the not-dark, or light, condition. And F is a switching function of the two variables (D and K), and $F = 1$ (the light is on) only when both D and K are 1.

To physically realize or construct these functions, it is necessary to have actual devices that can emulate the various operations and expressions required to specify a given set of logic conditions and constraints. Devices are available that implement the basic AND and OR operations as well as a number of other operations such as NAND (AND-NOT) and NOR (OR-NOT).

3.3 LOGIC TYPES

Presently, logic devices are fabricated from gallium arsenide (GaAs) or silicon (Si). Gallium arsenide technology is relatively new and produces devices which are extremely fast but expensive. For this reason, they are employed only in the relatively few applications where ultra-high-speed operation is essential. All other applications employ devices that are fabricated with silicon. Thus, we limit the coverage to devices using this material.

All silicon devices are made up of transistors, and two different types are employed to produce the various commercial digital logic circuits. These two types are the bipolar and *metal-oxide semiconductor* (MOS) transistors. Bipolar technology is in general faster than MOS technology but is also more costly for a given digital circuit. For a given transistor, basic logic gates can be implemented in a number of ways. A given gate circuit implementation along with a number of function implementations defines what is termed a *digital integrated-circuit logic family*. Examples of *integrated-circut* (IC) families are *transistor-transistor logic* (TTL), *emitter-coupled logic* (ECL), MOS, and *complementary MOS* (CMOS).

Shown in Fig. 3.1*a* is a symbolic representation for a two-input NAND gate, which is the most basic digital building block. A truth table is included in Fig. 3.1*b*. The truth table is simply a tabular representation obtained by evaluating the function ($F = A \cdot B$) for all possible input values, using the switching algebra postulates. Finally, a typical circuit representation is given in Fig. 3.1*c* to show the complexity involved. Here transistor Q1 provides the AND function while Q2 serves as a phase splitter. Transistors Q3 and Q4 serve as output drivers with Q3 functioning as an active pull-up resistor to speed up circuit

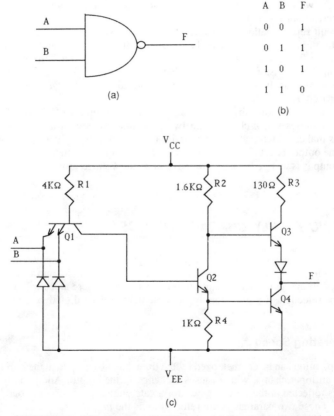

(a)

A	B	F
0	0	1
0	1	1
1	0	1
1	1	0

(b)

(c)

FIGURE 3.1 TTL two-input NAND gate. *(a)* Functional representation. *(b)* Truth table. *(c)* Typical circuit representation.

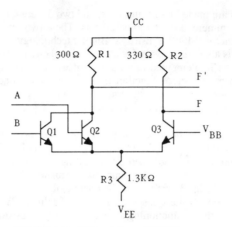

FIGURE 3.2   ECL two-input OR/NOR gate.

operation. As we will see, a number of different TTL circuit implementations give rise to different performance features.

The circuit representation of a two-input ECL OR/NOR gate is depicted in Fig. 3.2. This structure employs current mode logic to prevent transistor saturation, which allows ECL to be the fastest-operating silicon gate. The name is derived from the use of the emitter coupled transistor in the circuit realization. Notice that this family of devices produces both the function and its complement, thus allowing the gate to serve in both an OR and/or a NOR capacity.

Finally, Fig. 3.3 shows the circuit diagram for a two-input CMOS NAND gate. The device just requires two *n*-channel and two *p*-channel transistors and no other components. This makes IC fabrication much easier than the other gate types just discussed. In one state the output is at V_{CC} minus only the voltage drop of the on transistor. In the other state, the output is at V_{EE} (usually ground) minus the voltage drop across transistors Q2 and Q3.

3.4 LOGIC FAMILY CHARACTERISTICS

Important characteristics of a logic family are its speed of operation, power consumption, noise immunity, cost, and variety of functions available in single-chip form. For a particular application, device performance in one (or more) of these areas will usually be the criterion for selection of a logic family to implement a given digital system.

3.4.1 Operating Speed

Speed of operation can be characterized by the time that a basic gate in the family requires to react to an input change which causes a change in the output. Additionally, speed of operation is reflected in the time required for a gate output to switch from one logic level to another. These two parameters are referred to as the *propagation delay* and *transition time* and are defined as follows:

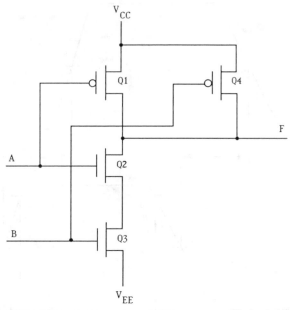

FIGURE 3.3 CMOS two-input NAND gate.

Propagation delay time, low to high, t_{PLH}: The time between specified reference points (usually 50 percent of the total voltage change) of the input and output voltage waveforms with the output changing from a low to high level.

Propagation delay time, high to low, t_{PHL}: The time between specified reference points (usually 50 percent of the total voltage change) of the input and output voltage waveforms with the output changing from a high to low level.

Propagation delay time, t_{PD}: The average delay time, which is given by $(t_{PLH} + t_{PHL})/2$.

Transition time, low to high, t_{TLH}: The time between two specified reference points (usually 10 and 90 percent of the total voltage change) of the output voltage waveform with the output changing from a low to high level.

Transition time, high to low, t_{THL}: The time between two specified reference points (usually 90 and 10 percent of the total voltage change) of the output voltage waveform with the output changing from a high to low level.

Shown in Fig. 3.4 is an illustration of the above definitions for a noninverting-type gate. The same timing diagram applies to an inverting gate with the parameters again referenced to the output waveform. To ascertain the propagation delay of a digital signal, the total number of gates between the input and output must be determined. If a number of input-output paths exist, then the longest one (in terms of time) must be used. Additionally, unless it has been determined that for certain gates only low-to-high (high-to-low) transitions need to be considered, then worst-case gate propagation times should be used.

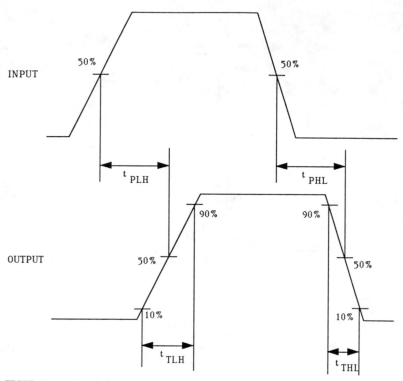

FIGURE 3.4 Waveform propagation and transition time.

3.4.2 Noise

All digital signal lines consist of a voltage that can be defined only within prescribed limits. This voltage level can be considered to be made up of some static level with a superimposed random voltage, which is referred to as *noise*. In a digital system, noise is generated in the following manner:

1. External coupling through a power line
2. External radiation from a nearby device that is switching a high-current load
3. Internal noise caused by ringing on signal and power lines due to improper or no termination of signal lines
4. Internal noise induced onto a signal line from adjacent signal lines
5. Internal noise generated by the gates themselves, due to the high-speed current switching

Logic families are classified in terms of the amount of noise that they themselves generate and the amount of noise that they can tolerate, referred to as their *noise immunity*, or *noise margin*. High-speed TTL generates the most noise, followed by ECL, and then CMOS. Noise margin is a measure of the amount of noise (change in actual signal level) that a gate can tolerate and still operate correctly. That is, if a logic 1 is supposed to be a certain voltage level, how much of a voltage change from that level can exist and still have the

TABLE 3.1 Typical Family Characteristics

Family	Prop delay, ns	Power, mW	Speed-power, pJ
TTL			
74	10	10	100
74S	3	20	60
74L	30	1	30
74LS	10	2	20
74AS	2	10	20
74ALS	5	1	5
ECL			
10K	2	25	50
100K	1	40	40
CMOS			
74HC	20	$0.6^{\dagger}$	12
74AC	5	$0.7^{\dagger}$	3.5

†Represents the power dissipation at 1 MHz.

gate recognize the voltage as a logic 1? Assuming a 5-V supply, the following are typical noise margins:

ECL	0.15 V	Low
TTL	0.4 V	Medium
CMOS	1.25 V	High

3.4.3 Power Dissipation

The amount of power consumed by individual gates of a logic family is important for two reasons. First, the more power required, the larger and more expensive the power supply must be. Second, and even more important, all the dissipated power is converted to heat that must be removed from the circuitry in order for it to operate correctly. With the constant desire to shrink the size of digital equipment, it is imperative that logic devices require less and less power to operate.

Table 3.1 shows three important parameters used in selecting a logic family for use in a given application: propagation delay, power, and the speed-power product. The speed-power product gives a figure of merit for a logic family by indicating its speed in terms of power consumed. Obviously, a low speed-power value is desirable, assuming that all other system requirements are met. Notice that there are six TTL circuit variations, each offering something different in the way of speed and power.

3.5 COMBINATIONAL CIRCUIT DESIGN

Logical expressions corresponding to a descriptive statement defining various logical conditions and constraints can be realized by a combinational circuit as depicted in Fig. 3.5. Here we have p circuit outputs that are functions of the n input variables. Notice that

FIGURE 3.5   Combinational circuit—functional representation. $F_i = f_i(X_{n-1} X_{n-2} \cdots X_1 X_0)$ for $i = 0, 1, \ldots, p - 1$.

the outputs directly follow the inputs, constantly changing after some delay, to reflect the present input combination. Inside the box we have a number of gates appropriately interconnected to implement the defined function.

To determine the internal gate arrangement so that any arbitrary function can be implemented, we need to form an equation that will allow a general switching function to be expressed. With n variables, we have 2^n possible input combinations, since each of the variables can assume one of two values. For each of the input combinations we must specify a functional value of either 1 or 0. A complete enumeration of the functional values for each possible input combination is known as the function *truth table*. For a function with n input variables, there will be 2^n entries in the truth table. The functional values will be 1, 0, or X, where X represents a don't-care condition. Don't-care conditions arise when we literally don't care what value the function assumes since the corresponding input combination will not occur for the application being considered.

3.5.1 Function Specification

We can express the truth table in equation form, and this reasoning leads to the following general form, often referred to as the *Shannon expansion*.

$$F(X_{n-1}, \ldots, X_0) =$$

$$a_{2^n-1}X_{n-1} \cdots X_0 + \cdots + a_1 X'_{n-1} \cdots X'_1 X_0 + a_0 X'_{n-1} \cdots X'_1 X'_0$$

Each of the 2^n terms of the form $X_{n-1} \cdots X_1 X_0$ is called a *minterm* or *standard product*. That is, a minterm of an n-variable function is the AND of each of the n variables either complemented or uncomplemented. If one or more of the variables are not represented, then the AND term is referred to as simply a *product term*. Choosing an $a_i = 1$ makes $F = 1$ for this input combination, while making $a_i = 0$ automatically forces $F = 0$. By assigning appropriate values to the a's, any arbitrary function can be implemented. The implementation will require an AND gate for each $a_i = 1$, with the AND gate outputs all connected to an OR gate that generates the final function output. Using the minterm notation, we can rewrite the above equation in shorthand form:

$$F(X_{n-1}, \ldots, X_0) = \Sigma a_i m_i \qquad \text{where } i = 0, 1, \ldots, 2^n - 1$$

Here m_i represents the ith minterm such that substituting 1 for an uncomplemented variable and 0 for a complemented variable in the minterm produces the binary value i.

The above equation is in a sum-of-products form, but a dual expression which is in a product-of-sums form can also be used.

Now that we have a standard form for expressing any arbitrary switching function, the next step is an attempt to simplify or minimize the function before actual circuit implementation. Cost can be defined in several ways, but the most severe is to let the circuit cost equal the sum of all gate inputs. Minimal circuits are not only less costly, but also, in general, more reliable since there are fewer devices to malfunction. There are three methods commonly used to effect function minimization.

3.5.2 Algebraic Simplification

Here the function is minimized by rearranging and simplifying the function, using boolean postulates and relationships. As an example, consider the following four-variable function:

$$F(w, x, y, z) = \Sigma(m_1 + m_3 + m_5 + m_7 + m_{14} + m_{15})$$
$$= w'x'y'z + w'x'yz + w'xy'z + w'xyz + wxyz' + wxyz$$
$$= w'x'z + w'xz + xyz + wxy$$
$$= [x'(w'z) + x(w'z)] + xyz + wxy$$
$$= w'z + xyz + wxy$$
$$= w'z + w(xy) + z(xy)$$
$$= w'z + wxy$$

The above function has had a cost reduction from 16 (12 AND inputs and 4 OR inputs) to 7. With this procedure, however, there is no way of knowing if the rearranged expression is indeed minimal cost except for very simple functions.

3.5.3 Karnaugh Map

Here a graphical presentation is used that allows the function to be viewed in its entirety. The map permits the user to more easily see where simplification is possible. Function minimization by the map technique is based on continually applying the boolean relationship $A \cdot B + A \cdot B' = A$. An illustration of a four-variable Karnaugh map with the above function inserted into the map is given in Fig. 3.6. Notice that the map is just a rearrangement (of the function truth table) to allow application of the identity $A \cdot B + A \cdot B' = A$. The group of four 1s is "factored" to produce the term $w'z$, while the group of two 1s is factored to produce wxy. The map is similar to a Venn diagram in the presentation of information.

wx \ yz	00	01	11	10
00	0	1	1	0
01	0	1	1	0
11	0	0	1	1
10	0	0	0	0

FIGURE 3.6 Four-variable Karnaugh map.

3.5.4 Quine-McCluskey Method

Karnaugh maps can produce minimal functions if one has keen eyes and can spot the correct patterns of 1s for grouping. However, as the map size increases, this becomes an impossible task. The Quine-McCluskey method still employs the identity $A \cdot B + A \cdot B' = A$, but consists of an algorithm that can be easily programmed on a computer. The technique is to generate all possible different groupings of 1s. In addition, these groupings must be as large as possible. Groupings of 1s that satisfy these constraints are known as *prime implicants*. The reasoning is that a minimal function will consist of a subset of these terms. Choosing a suitable set of prime implicants is referred to as the *covering problem*. Minimizing individual functions will not necessarily give a minimal cost implementation in the multiple-function case since product terms may be shared among functions. The Quine-McCluskey algorithmic procedure is well suited to handle this situation.

3.6 LOGIC CONVENTIONS

Having briefly touched on methods for function minimization, we are now ready to draw the logic diagrams necessary for final circuit implementation. There are two ways to represent the logic. To see this, we must first consider the following definitions.

Active high: A logic signal line is active high if it represents the named signal action when the signal value is HIGH.

Active low: A logic signal line is active low if it represents the named signal action when the signal value is LOW.

Assert: A signal line is asserted when it is at its active level.

Negate: A signal line is negated, or deasserted, when it is not at its active level.

Positive logic: A logic convention whereby the more positive of the two voltage levels is assigned the logic HIGH.

Negative logic: A logic convention whereby the more negative of the two voltage levels is assigned the logic HIGH.

Mixed logic: A logic convention whereby both positive and negative logic are used interchangeably to specify and implement a logic function.

To incorporate these ideas into a methodology for specifying and analyzing logic circuits, consider the following situation. Suppose that we have an error signal (ERROR) coming from some process, which indicates whether that particular process has executed correctly. That is, ERROR = 1 represents an erroneous condition, while ERROR = 0 indicates that the process has satisfactorily terminated. We now want to signal a GO condition when two different processes have successfully executed. Shown in Fig. 3.7a is a NOR gate implementation for the desired GO signal. GO is 1 whenever ERROR1 and ERROR2 are both 0. This is a logically correct implementation, but at first glance the structure gives the impression that functionally we are looking for the two signals to be ORed. A more meaningful representation of the operation is presented in Fig. 3.7b. Here the functional implementation suggests that both ERROR1 and ERROR2 must be at the low level to produce a GO signal. Bubbles (signifying level inversion) now appear at the gate inputs, implying that we are looking for the AND of two low logic levels to produce the desired high GO level. Stated another way, the desired input signals are ACTIVE LOW while the desired output is ACTIVE HIGH. To convey this information, the signal designations or names have been appended with (L) or (H) to specify the desired active signal level.

The use of mixed logic also makes the analysis of logic circuits easier. As an example, consider the circuit diagram shown in Fig. 3.8a. To generate the switching function $F(H)$ defined by the circuit, it will be necessary to perform a number of complementations of intermediate expressions. Under these circumstances, the final expression for $F(H)$ will

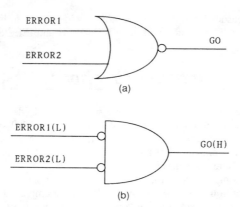

FIGURE 3.7 Logic notation. *(a)* Standard logic. *(b)* Mixed logic.

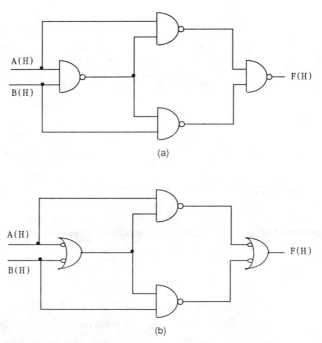

FIGURE 3.8 Logic circuit representation. *(a)* NAND implementation. *(b)* Mixed logic form.

require some manipulation before it is in a sum-of-products (AND-OR) form. The same circuit is shown redrawn in Fig. 3.8*b,* using a mixed logic notation. We start from the circuit output and make the gate output level the same as the named signal level. This process continues toward the circuit inputs, while trying to make the gate input-output levels match, i.e., bubbles on both input and output or bubbles on neither. Determining a boolean equation for $F(H)$ is a much easier task for the diagram in Fig. 3.8*b*.

For the above reasons, mixed logic notation is widely used in industry and government. The rules are addressed in detail in Mil-Std-806B and IEEE Standard 91-1984.

3.7 BASIC COMBINATIONAL FUNCTIONS

The first pair of combinational functions we will discuss is decoding and encoding. Decoders are frequently employed in the control section of digital systems to determine when some event has occurred or when some command has been issued. The encoding function is the inverse companion of the decoding operation; it puts the existing data or information into a more compact form. The second pair of basic functions we will examine is multiplexing and demultiplexing. These operations are primarily utilized to route, or direct, data in digital systems. Multiplexers are employed to channel multiple streams of data into a single stream. Conversely, demultiplexers select only one source, out of many, to receive common data.

3.7.1 Decoding

This operation allows us to separate and uniquely identify the 2^n combinations of n variables. A higher-level representation of the decoding function is illustrated in Fig. 3.9a. This shows the decoding operation as transforming the n input lines into 2^n output lines. More specifically, Fig. 3.9b gives a functional representation of a decoder with inputs x_i ($i = 1, 2, \ldots, n$) and Z_j ($j = 0, 1, \ldots, 2^n - 1$) such that

$$Z_i = x_{ni} \cdots x_{ji} \cdots x_{2i} x_{1i}$$

where each x_{ji} is either complemented or uncomplemented to make the product term produce minterm i.

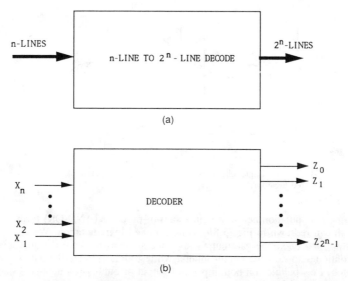

(a)

(b)

FIGURE 3.9 Decoding. *(a)* Block representation. *(b)* Functional representation.

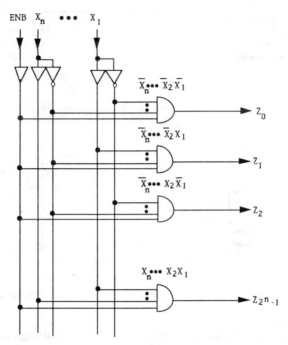

FIGURE 3.10 Logical representation of a decoder with enable.

The circuit realization of the decoder is shown in Fig. 3.10. The implementation includes 2^n gates each with n inputs corresponding to the 2^n minterms. Thus, only one output can be active at any time. Notice that buffers, both inverting and noninverting, are used so that the inputs x_n through x_1 present only one unit load to the signal source. Knowing the decoder structure, we can now determine the propagation delay between inputs and any output to be $2T_{PG}$, where we assume that T_{PG} represents the propagation delay of each gate used in the implementation.

Individual decoder chips have a fixed size with an upper limit determined by available input-output pins. To construct larger decoders, one must use several of the existing decoders to achieve the desired size. Interconnecting decoders to achieve a larger size requires the addition of an input to the standard decoder implementation. This is not an inherent part of the decoding function but a required feature when larger decoders are constructed. This ENB line appears at the input of all gates. The ENB input allows the entire decoder to be deactivated regardless of the x inputs. We now require $n + 1$ inputs to each of the 2^n AND gates.

3.7.2 Encoding

The encoding function is the companion and inverse of the decoding operation. Here, existing data or information is put into a more compact form. Figure 3.11a shows the encoding operation transforming the 2^n input lines into n output lines. The data on these lines represent a binary number corresponding to positional information for the active input. Initially, we assume that one and only one of the 2^n inputs is active at any given instant of time. Figure 3.11b gives a functional representation of an encoder with inputs

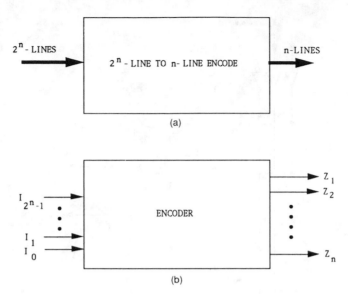

FIGURE 3.11   Encoding. *(a)* Block representation. *(b)* Functional representation.

I_k ($k = 0, 1, \ldots, 2^n- 1$) and outputs Z_i ($i = 1, 2, \ldots, n$) such that each Z_i is an OR function with exactly 2^{n-1} inputs. An example of an encoder for $n = 3$ is shown in Fig. 3.12*a*. Notice that each OR gate has four inputs and, further, that all inputs which have a 1 in the least significant bit of their binary representation appear as an input to the OR gate implementing Z_1. Similarly, all inputs which have a 1 in the next-least-significant bit of their binary representation appear as an input to the OR gate implementing the Z_2 function. The same reasoning applies for the OR gate which realizes the Z_3 function.

Using this example, we can generalize the implementation for the 2^n-to-n encoder which appears in Fig. 3.12*b*. Again each Z_i is made up of the OR of 2^{n-1} inputs. The function Z_1 is the OR of all Ij ($j = 1, 3, 5, \ldots, 2^n - 1$) whose binary representation has a 1 in the least-significant-bit position. And Z_2 consists of the OR of all input pairs I_{2j} and I_{2j+1} ($j = 1, 3, 5, \ldots, 2^n-2$) whose binary representation has a 1 in the second least-significant-bit position. Then Z_3 would be made up of the OR of all input quadruples $I_{4j}, I_{4j+1}, I_{4j+2},$ and I_{4j+3}. Finally, Z_n consists of the OR of the last 2^{n-1} inputs, as shown at the bottom of Fig. 3.12*b*.

As previously mentioned, it has been assumed that only one input is active at any given time. Consider again the 8-to-3 encoder depicted in Fig. 3.12*a*, and assume that inputs I_1 and I_2 are both active simultaneously. It is clearly seen that the end result ($Z_3Z_2Z_1 = 011$) is erroneous.

In many instances where encoders are employed, typically it is the rule rather than the exception to have multiple inputs active simultaneously. An example is the situation where events external to a computer must be allowed to signal the computer that they require immediate attention. These inputs are known as *interrupts* because they are capable of interrupting normal computer operation. Here, it is entirely possible for several inputs to be active, and it is therefore mandatory for the encoder to provide a correct indication of the input number of one of the active inputs. Since the encoder can only generate one binary value corresponding to some input, it is necessary to establish a priority for inputs. That is, the encoder (now termed a *priority encoder*) must output a

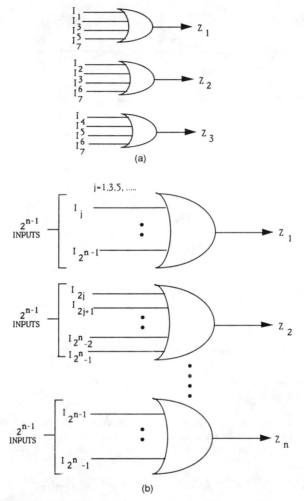

FIGURE 3.12 Logical representation of encoders: *(a)* An 8-to-3 encoder, *(b)* 2^n-to-n encoder.

binary value corresponding to the currently active input having the highest priority (the input that is judged to be the most critical in terms of being recognized). The standard encoder detailed in Fig. 3.12 can still be used to implement a priority encoder if an additional circuit is added to the front of the encoder. This additional circuitry must accept 2^n inputs (where multiple inputs can be active) and generate 2^n outputs (where one and only one output can be active).

3.7.3 Multiplexing

The third basic combinational function is multiplexing. This consists of n control inputs which are used to select one of 2^n inputs to be connected to a single output line. A block

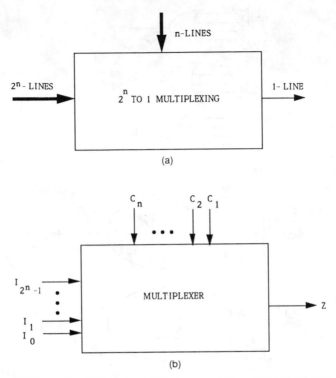

FIGURE 3.13   Multiplexing. *(a)* Block representation. *(b)* Functional representation.

representation is shown in Fig. 3.13a, and a more detailed functional representation is given in Fig. 3.13b. As can be seen, the circuit has I_i $(i = 0, 1, \ldots, 2^n - 1)$ inputs and C_j $(j = 1, 2, \ldots, n)$ control lines and an output Z. The function being implemented is given by

$$Z = I_0 C_n' \cdots C_2' C_1' + I_1 C_n \cdots C_2' C_1' + \cdots + I_{2^n-1}^n C_n \cdots C_2 C_1$$

with the circuit shown in Fig. 3.14. Here we have 2^n AND gates each with $n + 1$ inputs and a single OR gate with 2^n inputs. Again, buffers are used to present a single-unit load to the source. Assuming a gate delay of T_{PG}, the multiplexer has a total propagation delay of $3T_{PG}$.

As with decoders, there is an upper limit on the size of multiplexers due to input-output pin limitations. However, similar to the decoder case, it is possible to cascade existing multiplexers to construct larger devices. An example of a 16-to-1 multiplexer implemented with 4-to-1 multiplexers illustrates this point. The initial set of 4-to-1 multiplexers each simultaneously select one input (out of four) based on the two least-significant control bits. These four inputs are now available to the final multiplexer which then makes the final selection, using the two most significant control inputs. Basically, C_4 and C_3 determine which fourth of the inputs will be considered. Other arrangements of input and control lines are possible. Note that a multiplexer implemented in this fashion will exhibit twice the delay compared to that of an individual unit due to the cascading effect.

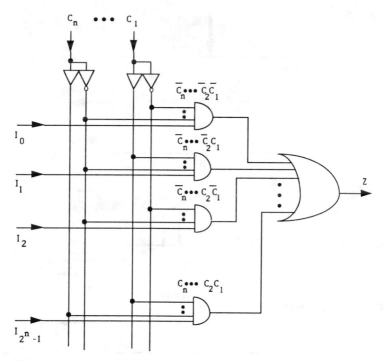

FIGURE 3.14 Logical representation of a multiplexer.

3.7.4 Demultiplexing

The fourth basic combinational function or operation is a companion to and the inverse of multiplexing. Shown in Fig. 3.15a is the block representation of the demultiplexing operation which consists of connecting a single input data line to one of 2^n output lines. Figure 3.15b gives a more detailed functional representation of a demultiplexer with input I, outputs Z_i ($i = 0, 1, . . . , 2^n - 1$), and control inputs C_j ($j = 1, 2, . . . , n$). The function defining the outputs is given by

$$Z_i = IC_nC_{n-1} \cdot \cdot \cdot C_j \cdot \cdot \cdot C_2C_1$$

where C_j is either complemented or uncomplemented so as to make the C variables produce minterm i. The implementation in Fig. 3.16 is composed of 2^n AND gates, each with $n + 1$ inputs. Basically, the demultiplexer routes common information to one of 2^n destinations under control of the C inputs. An example could be a computer which has information for a particular output display (one of many) on some display console. Comparing the demultiplexer implementation in Fig. 3.16 and the decoder with enable in Fig. 3.10, we see that they are identical if we equate I with ENB and the C's with the X's. For this reason, the demultiplexer as a device receives little attention. However, it does play an important role as a basic combinational function or operation. Again, physical input-output pins limit the size of demultiplexers, but larger sizes can be constructed by using fixed-size demultiplexers.

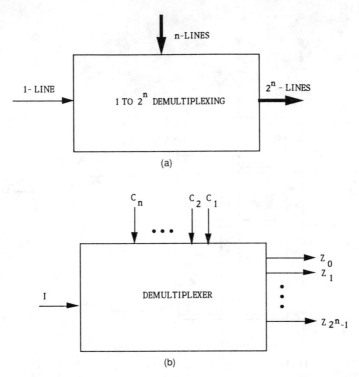

FIGURE 3.15 Demultiplexing. *(a)* Block representation. *(b)* Functional representation.

3.8 INTEGRATED CIRCUITS

Initial logic devices were built by using discrete components. These individual transistors, resistors, and diodes were interconnected on a printed-circuit board to implement various digital functions. Present-day technology implements these same devices or functions on a single silicon chip. This is referred to as a *monolithic integrated circuit*. Another arrangement that places multichip circuits and/or components in a single package is known as a *hybrid integrated circuit*. Hybrid integrated circuits predominantly find use in analog circuit implementation. Here there is a stronger need to mix different technologies in a single package. Digital circuits, on the other hand, are almost exclusively monolithic.

Single digital integrated circuits are typically classified in terms of the number of gates as follows:

Small-scale integration (SSI):   Chip complexity is 1 to 10 gates. Available in TTL, ECL, and CMOS.

Medium-scale integration (MSI):   Chip complexity is 10 to 100 gates. Available in TTL, ECL, and CMOS.

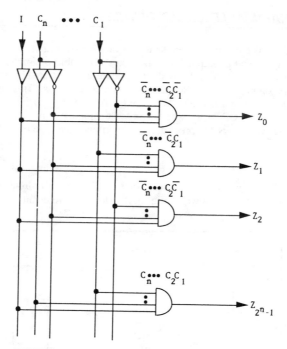

FIGURE 3.16 Logical representation of a demultiplexer.

Large-scale integration (LSI): Chip complexity is 100 to 1000 gates. Available in NMOS and CMOS.

Very large-scale integration (VLSI): Chip complexity is more than 1000 gates. Available in NMOS and CMOS.

Once a particular realization exists, this circuit does not have to be designed again. In effect, the circuit becomes part of a circuit library much like an existing computer program that can be used over and over. As we have just seen, some combinational functions are more important than others and therefore have now become basic in the design of digital systems. In fact, as chip density has increased, a number of options have become available to the digital designer. These IC design options can be classified as follows:

Standard: Consists of standard circuit functions immediately available from the manufacturer.

Programmable: Consists of user-definable and user-configurable functions.

Semicustom: Consists of user-definable and manufacturer-configurable functions using a predefined structure.

Full custom: Consists of user-definable and manufacturer-configurable functions which are specific to the user application.

3.9 PROGRAMMABLE LOGIC DEVICES

Shown in Fig. 3.17 is a functional representation of a *programmable logic device* (PLD). The IC has n inputs and p outputs, which makes it capable of implementing up to p functions of the same n variables. Individual functions are generated by allowing the user to easily specify or program the internal gate interconnections. This figure details an internal structure used in many PLDs. We have the AND array which generates k product terms, followed by the OR array which sums the product terms to produce the final outputs. How the two arrays are programmed determines the type of PLD.

3.9.1 ROMs

Probably the best known and most widely used PLD is the *read-only memory* (ROM) whose gate array structure is shown in Fig. 3.18. Here a more detailed view of both the

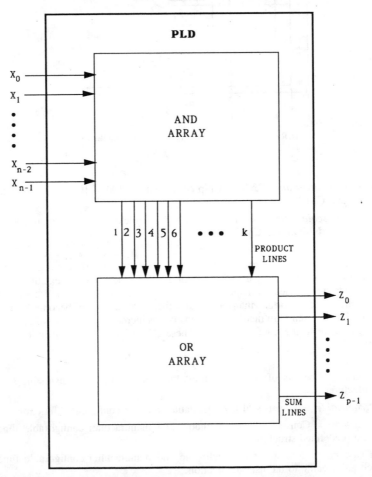

FIGURE 3.17 Programmable logic device (PLD)—array representation.

AND and OR arrays is given. Notice that the AND array is actually a large n-to-2^n decoder which generates all minterms of n variables. The solid, dark circles indicate a fixed electrical connection between inputs and AND gates. For this reason, the array is termed a *fixed AND array*.

As before, we have one OR gate per function with each OR gate having up to 2^n inputs. The interconnections between the product term outputs and OR inputs are user-specified via the unshaded programming cells which appear at the product output–OR input intersections. Unlike the fixed AND array, the OR array is programmable. The programmable nature of the cell can best be understood by considering the expanded view also included in Fig. 3.18. Basically, the cell consists of a switch which can be specified as either open or closed. Closing the switch includes the corresponding product term in the final sum, thus making the function 1 for the input combination. Conversely, with the switch open the product term is not included, and the function is 0 for this particular input.

As might be imagined, since the ROM generates all minterms, any n-variable function can be implemented. Because of the complete decoding of n variables, this capability is not without cost. In many cases functions will require the generation of only a fraction of the minterms, therefore wasting minterms that were already generated.

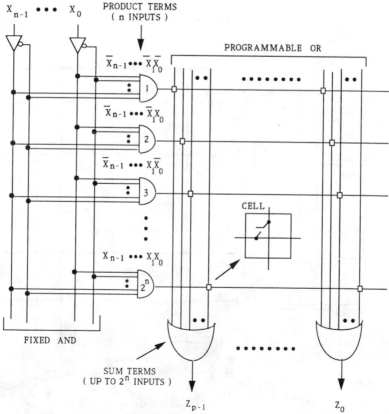

FIGURE 3.18 Gate array structure of ROM.

3.9.2 PALs

The second arrangement of AND-OR arrays shown in Fig. 3.19 details the structure of a *programmable array logic* (PAL). The PAL makes use of the fact that in realizing a number of functions of the same variables, not all minterms will be required. Here we have k product terms, where $k < 2^n$, and the number of inputs into each AND gate can be less than n. Thus each product term is not necessarily a minterm.

Unlike the ROM, the PAL AND array is completely programmable and can be electrically connected, or not connected, to each variable or its complement. On the other hand, the OR array is fixed by a predefined number of product terms making up each function. Figure 3.19 assumes that each output is made up of k/p or fewer product terms. Due to the fixed nature of the OR array, the PAL does not allow sharing of product terms. However, some function minimization, such as combining minterms, is encouraged since only a limited number of product terms exist.

3.9.3 PLAs

We have just examined the ROM (fixed AND, programmable OR) and the PAL (programmable AND, fixed OR). The final AND-OR array structure is the *programmable*

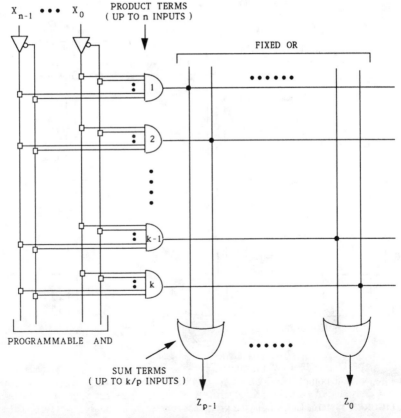

FIGURE 3.19 Gate array structure of PAL.

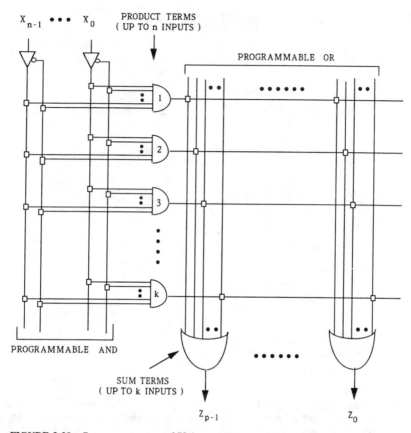

FIGURE 3.20   Gate array structure of PLA.

logic array (PLA) where both the AND and OR arrays are programmable, as shown in Fig. 3.20. This arrangement allows complete flexibility in specifying the chip internal gate connections. Like the PAL, this structure also allows k product terms, where $k < 2^n$, with up to n inputs per AND gate. We could, if desired, generate any k out of the 2^n possible minterms. In this sense, the PLA mimics a ROM without complete variable decoding. As we previously discussed, in many cases implementing a group of functions will not require all minterms. This is when a PLA is most useful.

3.9.4 PGAs

In addition to the three AND-OR array structures we just studied, certain chips are available that contain various gate configurations which can be programmed. One possible arrangement of a *programmable gate array* (PGA) is shown in Fig. 3.21. This IC includes k product terms making up the programmable AND array, as in the PAL and PLA. As can be seen, there is no OR array but rather a programmable mechanism (exclusive OR) for providing output complement. This type of PLD would be used whenever the desired function consisted of a single product term. A situation where this occurs is in the design of a computer system. Lines from the processor represent, in binary, the locations in the computer memory where information is stored. The total memory is composed of a

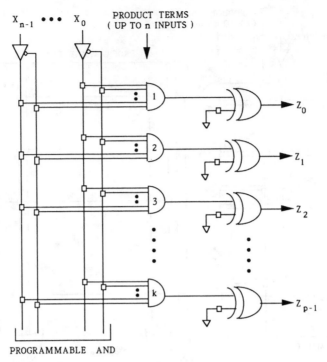

FIGURE 3.21   Structure of PGA.

number of memory chips, each containing a contiguous set of locations. Some subset of these processor lines is then decoded by an AND gate to enable communication with the desired chip corresponding to this memory area.

3.9.5 Programming PLDs

There are several ways in which a PLD can be customized to suit a particular application. In Fig. 3.18 we looked at a detailed view of a programming cell. A switch in the cell can be programmed so that any intersecting line in both the AND array and the OR array can be electrically connected. As we will now see, the type of programming can be either mask or field programmable.

In a mask programmable PLD, the connections (programming cells) are specified as part of the manufacturing process. That is, the desired array connections are specified as a template or mask during the final production step of the chip. Making the initial mask is expensive, but then chips are relatively inexpensive. However, the user cannot quickly and inexpensively change the IC structure. Masked PLDs are employed where volume is required, such as in television circuitry.

In many situations, the user would like to be able to specify and program the PLD connections in the field. Looked at another way, users want to do programming at their facilities, and they want to be able to do it quickly. In this case a field programmable PLD is chosen. As might be imagined, this approach is more expensive than the mask programmable one and is therefore intended for a small-quantity environment. Here all switches (typically known as *programming links,* or *fuses*) are initially closed, making an electrical connection. A programming mechanism built into the chip then allows the user to open individual switches by passing a current through the corresponding link or fuse.

There are several PLD programming languages available to assist in formally specifying the design and then for translating this design into a fuse pattern for the PLD. Two such languages are ABEL by the Data I/O Corporation and PALASM by AMD, Inc.

3.9.6 Cost of PLDs

We have seen that any of the three gate array arrangements (ROM, PLA, PAL) can be used to implement functions of a given number of variables. The primary determining factor in choosing which organization to employ will be cost. Given a specific device technology, the total cost will consist of chip cost and programming cost. Assuming that the other factors for the three arrangements are similar, the total cost will be proportional to the number of programmable fuses or links. For the three arrays, we assume n input variables and p output functions. In addition, for the PLA and PAL we assume that each device has k product terms.

In a ROM where only the OR array is programmable, we have 2^n AND outputs connected to p OR gates (representing the p functions), so the number of links can be represented as

$$ROM = 2^n \times p$$

In the PLA where both AND and OR arrays are programmable, the number of AND gates is k and always less than 2^n. The k gates must be connected to $2n$ inputs (complemented and uncomplemented values of each variable) and p OR gates, so the number of links can be represented as

$$PLA = k(2n + p)$$

In the PAL, where only the AND array is programmable, the number of AND gates is again k. The k gates must be connected to $2n$ inputs (complemented and uncomplemented values of each variable), so the number of links can be represented as

$$PAL = k(2n)$$

When the numbers of circuit inputs and circuit outputs are approximately the same, the cost of the PLA is only 1.5 times the cost of the more rigid PAL structure. As the number of inputs becomes much greater than the number of outputs, the costs of the PAL and PLA become equal. Thus, the PLA with its flexible structure is usually preferred over the PAL in most applications. However, the PAL is most useful in an environment where there is little or no sharing of product terms among the functions to be implemented. The PAL is best viewed as a set of independent AND-OR gates with programmable connections to a large number of common input variables.

Again, when the numbers of circuit inputs and circuit outputs are roughly the same, for $k = 2^n/3$ the costs of the ROM and PLA structures are equal. This cost equality represents the situation where the number of product terms (AND gates) is equal to one-third the number of minterms. When the number of AND gates is less than this value, then the PLA is more cost-effective than the ROM. The ROM is ideal when the functions being implemented require that most of the minterms be generated. Compared to the PAL, both the ROM and PLA are more cost-effective when there is a good deal of AND gate sharing in realizing multiple output functions.

To illustrate, consider the realization of a BCD (binary-coded decimal) to a seven segment code converter. To realize the seven segment outputs, all 16 minterms are required since each minterm will be used in one or more of the seven functions. In this situation, the ROM is clearly preferable to a PLA implementation.

As a final example, consider implementing a combinational circuit with 10 inputs that represent the numbers from 0 to 1000 in binary notation. The circuit is to have one output which equals 1 whenever the input is divisible by 10. To realize this function, we will need 100 minterms out of the 1024 possible minterms. Here a PLA implementation is preferable since a ROM realization would pay a heavy cost penalty in producing 924 minterms which would never be used.

3.10 SEQUENTIAL CIRCUITS

In many instances, the requirements imposed by an application simply cannot be satisfied by a combinational circuit. As an example, something other than a combinational circuit is needed to produce an output corresponding to a lock where a predetermined sequence of numbers must be entered for the lock to open. Here the output is not only a function

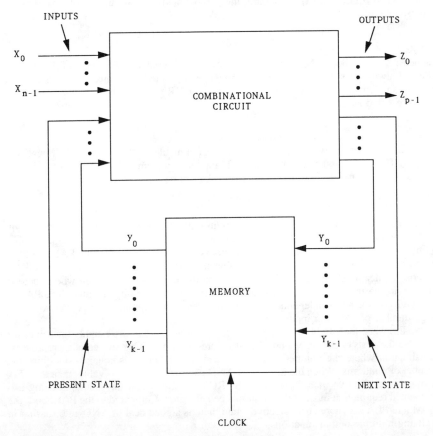

FIGURE 3.22 Sequential circuit—functional representation.

of the immediate input but also a past history of inputs. This is precisely the definition of a sequential circuit. Shown in Fig. 3.22 is a functional representation of a sequential circuit which consists of a combinational circuit and an additional block labeled MEMORY. The memory portion, typically referred to as flip-flops, provides storage for the past history of the circuit. At a specific instant of time, the sequential circuit reflects all prior inputs that have occurred. The sequential circuit is constrained to only process information or change its state at well-defined instances of time as determined by CLOCK. Circuits of this type are referred to as *synchronous sequential circuits*. Sequential circuits that are not clocked and continuously react to input changes are called *asynchronous sequential circuits*. For a sequential circuit with n inputs, p outputs, and k memory elements, the following definitions apply:

State variable: The output of a sequential circuit flip-flop that provides 1 bit of information y_i about the condition of the circuit.

State: The present condition of the sequential circuit. The state or present state $s_i = y_{k-1} \cdots y_1 y_0$ is defined by the k state variables. With k state variables, it is possible to define 2^k states.

Next state: The new present state that the sequential circuit will assume whenever a CLOCK arrives to update the circuit. The next state $S_j = Y_{n-1} \cdots Y_1 Y_0$ is a function of the present state and the present inputs.

3.10.1 Clocks

Figure 3.23 shows the type of waveforms that appear as clock inputs to the system memory devices. Figure 3.23a and b shows periodic waveforms with period T. The waveform in Fig. 3.23a is symmetric because it is 1 and 0 for the same amounts of time

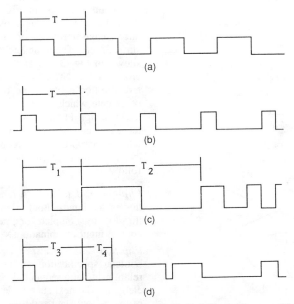

FIGURE 3.23 Clock waveforms. *(a)* Periodic and symmetric. *(b)* Periodic but nonsymmetric. *(c)* Nonperiodic but symmetric. *(d)* Nonperiodic and nonsymmetric.

in a period. This symmetric waveform is said to have a 50 percent duty cycle. In turn, the signal in Fig. 3.23b is nonsymmetric because the high and low times are not equal. Last, Fig. 3.23c and d shows, respectively, signals that are nonperiodic but symmetric and nonperiodic and nonsymmetric. These two clocks are used to drive synchronous sequential circuits because the clock represents, in certain cases, an event which is nonperiodic. There are applications where a periodic clock is unnecessary. The only requirements are that all flip-flops be clocked simultaneously and that the clock satisfy minimum high and low times for the memory elements being used.

3.10.2 Memory Devices

A functional representation of a generalized flip-flop is shown in Fig. 3.24a. The flip-flop produces both complemented and uncomplemented output. Associated with the CLOCK input is a carrot signifying that this input responds only to a positive level change. There are two control inputs associated with the CLOCK. That is, CONTROL1 and CONTROL2 can affect the flip-flop contents only during the CLOCK transition. Two other inputs, SET and CLEAR, not associated with the CLOCK can cause a change in flip-flop contents any time there is a change in either of the two inputs. That is, they act in an asynchronous manner. These two inputs are normally used for initializing the memory element.

There are several different types of flip-flops, and they may or may not contain all the inputs depicted in Fig. 3.24a. Flip-flops are usually categorized as being a latch, edge-sensitive, or of the master-slave variety. The basic latch mechanism is shown in Fig. 3.24b and consists of two cross-coupled NOR gates. The edge-sensitive flip-flop contains the basic latch and other gate which allow it to respond only during a signal transition. Finally, the master-slave consists of two of the basic latches appropriately interconnected. However, all flip-flops can be defined by the following:

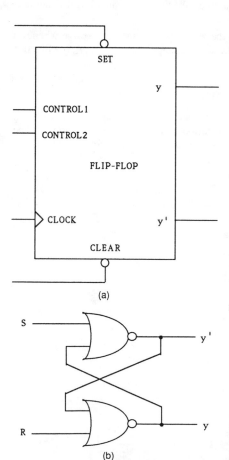

(a)

(b)

FIGURE 3.24 General flip-flop representation. *(a)* Functional representation. *(b)* Basic latching mechanism.

Flip-flop truth table: A tabular presentation of the input-output relationship of the flip-flop by complete enumeration of all control input combinations.

Flip-flop characteristic equation: A boolean specification of the input-output relationship of a sequential circuit memory element. The next state is defined in terms of the present state and flip-flop control inputs. The characteristic equation is derived from the flip-flop truth table.

Flip-flop transition table: A tabular representation that specifies the required control input values for all combinations of flip-flop in the present and next state.

Setup time: The time that signal levels on the control inputs must be established and maintained before an active transition occurs on the CLOCK input.

Hold time: The time that signal levels must be maintained after an active transition on the CLOCK input.

There are four different, commonly used clocked flip-flops. The D and T flip-flops each have one control input, while the SR and JK flip-flops each have two. The characteristic equation, truth table, and transition table for each of these flip-flops are given below.

D Flip-Flop

$Y = D$

D	Y
0	0
1	1

y	Y	D
0	0	0
0	1	1
1	0	0
1	1	1

T Flip-Flop

$Y = T'y + Ty'$

T	Y
0	y
1	y'

y	Y	T
0	0	0
0	1	1
1	0	1
1	1	0

SR Flip-Flop

$Y = S + R'y$

S	R	Y
0	0	y
0	1	0
1	0	1
1	1	—

y	Y	S	R
0	0	0	X
0	1	1	0
1	0	0	1
1	1	X	0

JK Flip-Flop

$Y = J'_y + K'_y$

J	K	Y
0	0	y
0	1	0
1	0	1
1	1	y'

y	Y	J	K
0	0	0	X
0	1	1	X
1	0	X	1
1	1	X	0

3.10.3 Sequential Circuit Definitions

By using the flip-flop truth or transition tables, it is possible to either analyze or synthesize sequential circuits. To see how this is accomplished, we first introduce some standard definitions used to discuss sequential circuit theory.

State diagram: A directed graph consisting of nodes and line segments that defines the input-output behavior of a sequential circuit. Named states are represented by nodes with directed line segments between nodes reflecting circuit response to inputs.

State table: A tabular representation of the information contained in the state diagram. Each row represents a state of the sequential circuit, and each column represents one of the possible input combinations to the circuit. The entries denote the next state and output behavior of the circuit.

State transition table: A tabular representation of the information contained in the state table with each named state replaced by a unique binary code. Next-state entries are similarly replaced by coded values corresponding to the named-state entry.

Excitation table: A tabular representation of information that defines the required behavior of each of the flip-flop control inputs. This table is formed by using both the state transition table and the flip-flop transition table.

Transition equations: A formal boolean specification of the next-state mapping defined by the transition table. There is one equation for each state variable.

Excitation equations: A formal boolean specification that defines each of the flip-flop control inputs such that the desired state table is realized.

Output equations: A formal boolean specification of the output mapping defined by the transition table. There is one equation for each circuit output.

3.10.4 Sequential Circuit Analysis Procedure

Starting with a circuit diagram, all sequential circuits can be formalized into a state table by applying the following four steps.

1. Working from the sequential circuit implementation, determine the excitation equations for each of the flip-flop inputs, along with sequential circuit output equations.

2. Obtain the transition equations by substituting the excitation equations into the flip-flop characteristic equations.

3. Using the transition and output equations, construct a state transition table which contains both next-state and output behavior. This table may have up to 2^n rows, where n is the number of flip-flops, and 2^m columns, where m is the number of sequential circuit inputs.

4. Obtain a state table representation, consisting of next-state and output information, by giving an arbitrary state name to each row of the state transition table.

To show the analysis procedure, consider the circuit diagram shown in Fig. 3.25. The four steps detailed above yield the following results.

Step 1. The excitation equations are a function of the inputs and present-state variables, while the output is strictly a function of the present-state variables. For the D flip-flops shown, the appropriate equations are

$$D1 = x'y2 + xy1$$
$$D2 = x$$
$$Z = y1y2$$

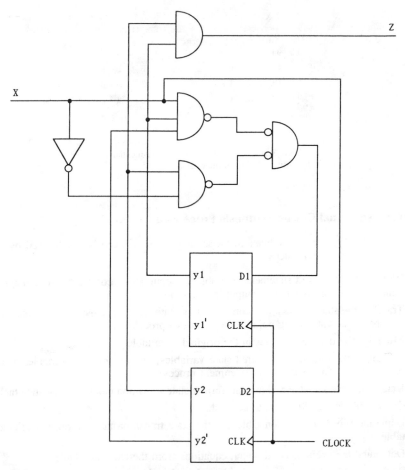

FIGURE 3.25 Four-state synchronous sequential circuit.

Step 2. Since D flip-flops are used, we have $Y = D$ and the transition equations are identical to the excitation equations.

Step 3. Shown in Fig. 3.26a is the state transition table corresponding to the circuit we have been analyzing. The table is just another way of expressing the information contained in the above three equations. Notice that the output Z appears as a separate column, instead of being associated with each next-state entry, since the output is a function of only the present state.

Step 4. By arbitrarily assigning letters to the four rows of the state transition table, the state table is formed. Using the assignment $A = 00$, $B = 01$, $C = 11$, and $D = 10$, the table in Fig. 3.26b results.

	X		
y1 y2	0	1	Z
0 0	00	01	0
0 1	10	01	0
1 1	10	01	1
1 0	00	11	0
	Y1 Y2		

(a)

	X		
s	0	1	Z
A	A	B	0
B	D	B	0
C	D	B	1
D	A	C	0
	S		

(b)

FIGURE 3.26 Tables for four-state sequential circuit. (a) Transition table. (b) State table.

3.10.5 Sequential Circuit Synthesis Procedure

Starting with a problem specification, all sequential circuits can be synthesized by applying the following nine steps.

1. Working from a word statement or problem specification, construct a state diagram which includes next-state and output information.
2. Translate the state diagram to a corresponding state table. In some cases, a state table may be the actual starting point in the synthesis process.
3. Minimize the number of states in the original state table.
4. Determine the number of required state variables, and assign these variables to the named states. This is the state assignment process.
5. Using this state variable assignment, form a state transition table from the state table.
6. Choose the type of flip-flops to be used.
7. Using the flip-flop transition table and the state transition table, form an excitation table.
8. Determine the excitation and output equations from the excitation table.
9. Realize the desired sequential circuit, using the chosen flip-flops and the derived excitation and output equations.

The above procedure can be illustrated by considering the design of a sequential circuit whose description follows.

Design a circuit that will detect, on an input X, the sequence 1, 0, 1 and produce, on an output Z, a 1 whenever this sequence is detected.

Step 1. Working from the above word statement, we construct the state diagram shown in Fig. 3.27a. Once an initial 1, 0, 1 sequence occurs, an additional 0, 1 sequence will again produce a 1 output.

Step 2. Figure 3.27b gives the state table, which is just a duplication of the state diagram information, but presented in tabular form.

Step 3. In this step we attempt to remove unnecessary states that may have been formed when the original state diagram was constructed. Well-known techniques are available for arriving at a minimal state machine. In our case, no further state minimization is possible.

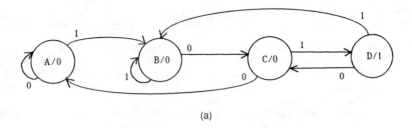

(a)

s	X 0	1	Z
A	A	B	0
B	C	B	0
C	A	D	0
D	C	B	1

S

(b)

y1 y2	X 0	1	Z
0 0	00	01	0
0 1	10	01	0
1 0	00	11	0
1 1	10	01	1

Y1 Y2

(c)

y1 y2	X 0	1	Z
0 0	0x,0x	0x,1x	0
0 1	1x,x1	0x,x0	0
1 0	x1,0x	x0,1x	0
1 1	x0,x1	x1,x0	1

J1K1,J2K2

(d)

FIGURE 3.27 Synthesis example. *(a)* State diagram. *(b)* State table. *(c)* Transition table. *(d)* Excitation table.

Step 4. With four states, two state variables (flip-flops) will be required to uniquely identify each of the four states. We choose the state assignment $A = 00, B = 01, C = 11$, and $D = 10$.

Step 5. By using the assignment in step 4, the state transition table is constructed, as shown in Fig. 3.27c.

Step 6. To illustrate the use of the flip-flop transition table, we choose JK (instead of D) flip-flops for the circuit implementation, so that we will not simply have $Y = D$.

Step 7. The excitation table is formed by using both the state and the flip-flop transition tables. For each entry in the state transition table, we determine one of four present-state – next-state combinations. Based on this combination, we choose the appropriate flip-flop control excitation required to produce this combination. For example, if we desire $yY = 00$, then we must have $JK = 00$ or 01 which combines to $JK = 0X$.

Step 8. Next the excitation table results are minimized and written in equation form. For the excitation table in Fig. 3.27d, the equations are

$$J1 = x'y2 \qquad\qquad J2 = x \qquad Z = y1y2$$
$$K1 = x'y2' + xy2 \qquad K2 = x'$$

Step 9. Finally, the circuit is implemented by using two JK flip-flops and gates interconnected as prescribed by the equations generated in step 8.

3.11 BASIC SEQUENTIAL FUNCTIONS

The counter is an important sequential function that is primarily used as part of the system control, but it can be and often is employed as a mechanism to operate on data as well.

The functional representation of a universal counter appears in Fig. 3.28a with a corresponding function table detailed in Fig. 3.28b. It should be mentioned that other simpler variations of this functional representation exist. Here we have n lines (A_{n-1}, . . . , A_0) with which we can preset each individual flip-flop to a specific binary value. Also included is an enable input (ENB), which must be active to allow the counter to respond to the other control and counting inputs. According to the function table, either loading or counting occurs on the positive edge of CLK, depending on the value of load (LD). This, of course, assumes that ENB = 1; otherwise the CLK input has no effect on the counter and the present flip-flop values remain until enabling (ENB = 1) occurs. Loading is synchronized with the clock so that even if LD = 1, the A inputs will not be transferred to the flip-flops until a positive transition of CLK. The U/D' line specifies the counting direction. Here U/D' = 1 specifies up (0, 1, 2, . . .) while U/D' = 0 specifies down (3, 2, 1, . . .). The U/D' line can be changed at any time as long as it adheres to the timing relationship between this control line and CLK. In addition, the carry output is implemented to produce CO = 1 for a counter value of $2^n - 1$ when counting up and CO = 1 for a counter value of 0 when counting down. This is to let the user know when counter rollover (up or down) is going to occur.

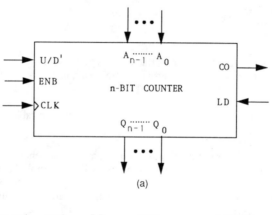

(a)

U/D'	ENB	LD	CLK	ACTION
X	0	X	X	HOLD
1	1	0	_⌐	COUNT UP
0	1	0	_⌐	COUNT DOWN
X	1	1	_⌐	LOAD

(b)

FIGURE 3.28   General model of an n-bit counter. *(a)* Functional representation. *(b)* Function table.

It should also be mentioned that the counter may have a reset line which allows controlled resetting of all flip-flops. We choose not to include a reset here since we can easily load the flip-flops with 0s. Finally, the required setup times between the CLK and other inputs (data and control) must be satisfied.

3.11.1 Binary Counters

With n flip-flops, we have the capability of constructing any counter with k states where $2^{n-1} < k \leqq 2^n$. For example, if $n = 3$, then it is possible to build a counter with five, six, seven, or eight states. It is assumed here that we would not use three flip-flops to implement a four-state counter. If $k = 2^n$ and the counter generates the binary sequence from 0 to $2^n - 1$, then we denote this as a full binary counter.

3.11.2 Decimal Counters

Decimal counters have an abbreviated count (less than 2^n states for n memory devices) and are referred to as *truncated binary counters*. More specifically, when the counter is modulo 10, it is commonly referred to as a *BCD counter*. The 10 states are in correspondence with the integers 0 through 9.

3.11.3 Programmable Counters

Consider a full binary counter which continuously sequences through the states S_1, S_2, . . . , S_{k-1}, where $k = 2^n$. To change the counter modulus, we must be able to truncate the count. Instead of allowing the count to proceed from S_{k-1} to S_0, we can force the next state to be, say, S_j. In doing so, we have altered the modulus of the counter. In effect, we can "program" whatever modulus is desired by forcing a particular next state.

Using the general counter just discussed in Fig. 3.28, there are three possible arrangements which will yield a variable modulus design. The configurations appear in Fig. 3.29a and b.

In Fig. 3.29a we have a truncated binary counter since the count sequence is 0, 1, . . . , N. When the counter reaches N, the output of the AND gate becomes 1, which in turn makes LD = 1. Normally, the counter would increment to $N + 1$, but an active LD now causes loading (0) to occur on the next clock. With the counter at 0, the AND gate output and LD are inactive, and on the next clock, counting starts again.

Figure 3.29b demonstrates a truncated counter which produces the sequence N, $N + 1$, . . . , $2^n - 1$. To obtain this count sequence, the CO output is connected to LD. Here the next state would be 0, but at the maximum count (all 1s) CO = LD = 1. At the next positive edge of CLK the counter is preset to N instead of going to 0. Again LD is inactive, and normal counter incrementing returns.

Finally, Fig. 3.29c shows a truncated counter generating the sequence N_1, $N_1 + 1$, . . . , N_2. If we choose $N_1 = 0$ and $N_2 = N$, then we have the counter in Fig. 3.29a. If we choose $N_1 = N$ and $N_2 = 2^n - 1$, then we have the counter in Fig. 3.29b.

3.11.4 Ripple Counters

Appearing in Fig. 3.30 is an arrangement for constructing larger counters from existing counting units. Here we have enabled all counter units (ENB1 = ENB2 = ENB3 = 1),

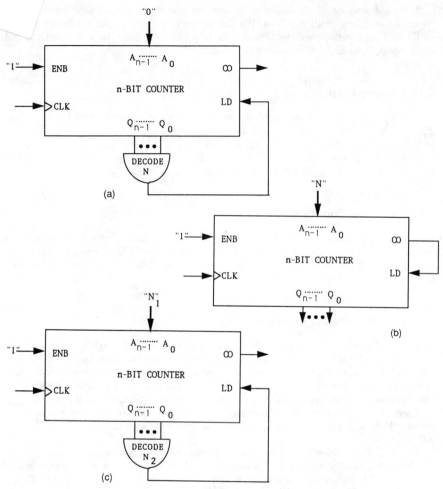

FIGURE 3.29 Three n-bit variable-modulus counters. *(a)* Counting from 0 to N. *(b)* Counting from N to $2^n - 1$. *(c)* Counting from N_1 to N_2.

but CLOCK IN is only connected to the leftmost counter. Therefore, all flip-flops will not change state simultaneously, making this configuration a nonsynchronized or asynchronous cascade of counter units. CO1 becomes 1 for a count of $2^n - 1$ and returns to 0 when the counter rolls over to 0. Since the next counter unit is to increment on this rollover, the negative of CO1 must be connected to CLK of the middle counter. By the same rationale, the middle and rightmost counter units are interconnected in an identical manner. With this implementation, the count ripples through the entire counter from input to output.

Consider the situation where the counter must roll over from a maximum count to 0, and assume a propagation delay from CLK to CO of T_{CP}. With respect to CLOCK IN the least significant counter unit's CO output will change after T_{CP} second(s), the middle unit's CO output will change after $2T_{CP} + T_{GP}$ (inverter delay) s, and the most significant unit's CO output will change after $3T_{CP} + 2T_{GP}$ s. Thus, not all bits of the counter change

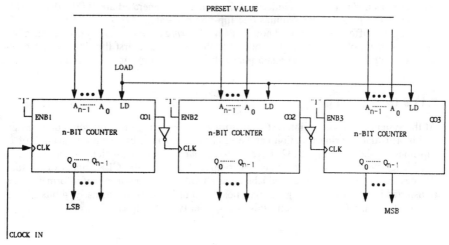

FIGURE 3.30 Cascading counters asynchronously.

simultaneously, as in the synchronous case. Because of this ripple effect, asynchronous counters, or *ripple counters* as they are often called, typically cannot operate as rapidly as their synchronous counterpart, but in general require less logic to implement.

3.11.5 Nonbinary Counters

Up until now we have considered only full or truncated binary counters, i.e., a modulo-k counter whose count sequence corresponds to the integers $0, 1, \ldots, k - 1$. To illustrate a nonbinary counter, consider the circuit shown in Fig. 3.31 which consists of four flip-flops. They are configured so that the last output is connected to the first flip-flop input in a ring arrangement. Assume that, initially, the pattern 1000 was loaded into the flip-flops by using direct-current (dc) sets and resets, which are not shown. Now as the single 1 is moved from one flip-flop to another, identical time-shifted waveforms will be produced on T_0 through T_4. This well-known circuit for producing multiphase clocks is

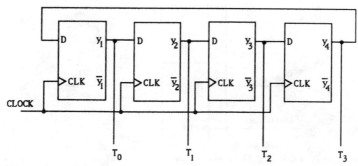

FIGURE 3.31 Ring counter.

referred to as a *ring counter*. Notice that the four states generated are 1000, 0100, 0010, and 0001. The ring counter requires one flip-flop per state.

A slightly different structure, known as a *twisted ring counter,* results from connecting the complement of the last flip-flop output to the input of the first flip-flop. Now we get 2^n states with n flip-flops, and again phase-shifted waveforms are produced.

3.11.6 Data Storing

At the system level we are interested in storing and operating on data words of a certain width. This data-storing function can be easily implemented by using a collection of D flip-flops, as shown in Fig. 3.32. Here we have four D flip-flops, which are referred to as a 4-bit register, with separate input and output. However, the CLK inputs of all four devices are connected together and labeled as a LOAD input. Four bits of information are transferred in parallel to the register on a positive transition. More basically, 4 bits of data is loaded into the register. Again, this is a special type of sequential circuit.

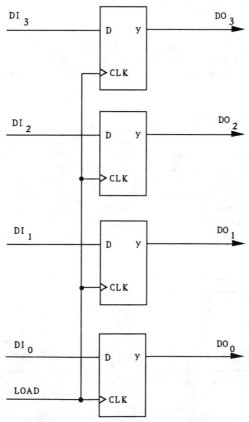

FIGURE 3.32   A 4-bit register.

3.11.7 Registers

There are four basic ways that data can be stored and retrieved. The four configurations are shown in Fig. 3.33a through d. The heavy lines indicate a multiple-signal input or output. In Fig. 3.33a we have the case of parallel data in and parallel data out. This is, in fact, the implementation in Fig. 3.32 with CLK equated with LOAD and n equal to 4.

The functional representation in Fig. 3.33b allows parallel data in and serial data out under control of the LD/SHT' line. If LD/SHT' = 1, data are loaded into the register in parallel when a positive transition occurs on the CLK input. If LD/SHT' = 0, parallel data already in the register are moved one bit position in the direction of DO. DO is directly

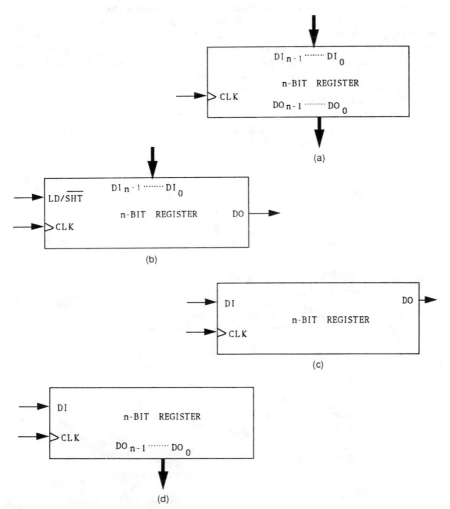

FIGURE 3.33   Register data operations. *(a)* Parallel in, parallel out. *(b)* Parallel in, serial out. *(c)* Serial in, serial out. *(d)* Serial in, parallel out.

connected to either DI_0 or to DI_{n-1}, depending on whether information is being moved (shifted) to the right or left. In either case, this arrangement allows parallel information to be retrieved or accessed serially on a bit-by-bit basis.

The n-bit register in Fig. 3.33c has a single input and output, therefore permitting serial storing and serial retrieval of data under control of CLK. As an example, n bits could be moved in, temporarily stored, and then serially shifted out.

Finally, Fig. 3.33d illustrates the last arrangement where n serial bits are moved into the register and are now available in parallel as an n-bit word of data. The registers in Fig. 3.33a and c basically provide temporary storage for parallel and serial data, respectively. In addition to providing data storage, the registers in Fig. 3.33b and d allow the data to be converted from one form to another.

These four configurations can be combined into one general register, shown in Fig. 3.34a. This general register is capable of performing all the data-storing operations just discussed. In addition to the n parallel lines in and out (CLK and LD/SHT$'$), this device has an L/R$'$ line to control right or left shifting as well as serial data inputs DIR and DIL. Examining the function table in Fig. 3.34b, we see that with LD/SHT$'$ = 1, parallel data ($DI_{n-1}, \ldots, DI_0$) will be loaded on the next positive edge of CLK. With LD/SHT$'$ = 0, on a positive transition of CLK, either right or left shifting will occur. Specifically, with L/R$'$ = 0, data will be moved right within the register with the serial data on DIR being shifted into the register. Each positive clock transition will shift the data one bit position to the right. It would require n clock transitions to completely shift the existing n bits out of this n-bit register. Exactly the same thing occurs when shifting left except that DIL is used.

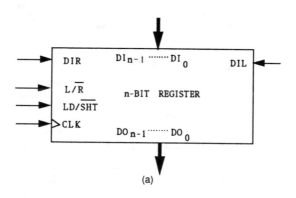

(a)

LD/$\overline{\text{SHT}}$	L/$\overline{\text{R}}$	ACTION
1	X	LOAD REGISTER
0	0	SHIFT DATA RIGHT
0	1	SHIFT DATA LEFT

(b)

FIGURE 3.34 General model of an n-bit register. (a) Functional representation. (b) Function table.

3.12 CONCLUDING REMARKS

There is no doubt that design is becoming more mechanized. Systems that were once being implemented with catalog items are now being realized with either programmable or semicustom devices. In fact, semicustom devices are moving from final-state processing by the manufacturer to user-programmable. This trend will continue with the development of CAD tools to support this type of design process. Whether the design is combinational or sequential, the procedure is still formal specification, design minimization of some type, and finally implementation. Typically implementation and design minimization are closely coupled.

In this short space, we have attempted to summarize and define some of the more important topics and aspects of digital design. The reader is advised to consult the references for a more expanded discussion of any of the topics addressed here.

REFERENCES

1. K. Breeding, *Digital Design Fundamentals*. Englewood Cliffs, N.J.: Prentice-Hall, 1989.
2. D. Dietmeyer, *Logic Design of Digital Systems*. Boston: Allyn and Bacon, 1978.
3. W. Fletcher, *An Engineering Approach to Digital Design*. Englewood Cliffs, N.J.: Prentice-Hall, 1980.
4. J. Hill and G. Peterson, *Introduction to Switching Theory and Logic Design*. New York: Wiley, 1981.
5. E. McCluskey, *Logic Design with Emphasis on Testable Semicustom Circuits*. Englewood Cliffs, N.J.: Prentice-Hall, 1986.
6. M. Mano, *Digital Design*. Englewood Cliffs, N.J.: Prentice-Hall, 1991.
7. *MECL Data Book,* Motorola Inc., Phoenix.
8. Monolithic Memories Technical Staff, *Designing with Programmable Array Logic*. New York: McGraw-Hill, 1978.
9. *PAL Device Handbook,* AMD Inc., Sunnyvale, Calif.
10. C. Roth, *Fundamentals of Logic Design*. St. Paul, Minn.: West Publishing, 1979.
11. M. Shoji, *CMOS Digital Circuit Technology*. Englewood Cliffs, N.J.: Prentice-Hall, 1988.
12. *TTL Data Book,* Texas Instruments Inc., Dallas.
13. J. Wakerly, *Digital Design Principles and Practices*. Englewood Cliffs, N.J.: Prentice-Hall, 1990.

CHAPTER 4
COMPUTER ARITHMETIC

Earl E. Swartzlander, Jr.
Department of Electrical and Computer Engineering,
University of Texas, Austin

4.1 INTRODUCTION

The speeds of memory and of arithmetic units are the primary determinants of the speed of a computer. While the speed of both units depends directly on the implementation technology, arithmetic unit speed also depends strongly on the algorithms employed to realize the basic arithmetic operations (add, subtract, multiply, and divide) and on the logic design. Even for an integer adder, speeds can easily vary by an order of magnitude while the complexity varies by less than 50 percent.

This chapter begins with a discussion of binary fixed-point number systems in Sec. 4.2. Section 4.3 provides examples of fixed-point implementation of the four basic arithmetic operations (i.e., add, subtract, multiply, and divide). Finally Sec. 4.4 describes algorithms to implement floating-point arithmetic.

Regarding notation, capital letters represent digital numbers (i.e., words), while lowercase letters represent bits of the corresponding word. The lowercase letters are subscripted with numbers ranging from 0 to $n - 1$ to indicate bit position within the word (x_0 is the least significant bit of X, x_{n-1} is the most significant bit of X, etc.).

4.2 FIXED-POINT NUMBER SYSTEMS

Most arithmetic is performed with fixed-point numbers which have constant scaling (i.e., the position of the binary point is fixed). The numbers can be interpreted as fractions, integers, or mixed numbers depending on the application. Alternatively, pairs of fixed-point numbers can be interpreted as floating-point numbers as discussed in Sec. 4.4.

Fixed-point binary numbers are generally represented by using the 2's complement number system. This choice has prevailed over the sign magnitude and 1's complement number systems, because the frequently performed operations of addition and subtraction are easiest to perform on 2's complement numbers. Sign magnitude numbers are more efficient for multiplication, but the lower frequency of multiplication and the development of Booth's multiplication algorithm for 2's complement numbers have resulted in the nearly universal selection of the 2's complement number system for most contemporary applications.

Fixed-point number systems represent numbers, such as A, by n bits: a sign bit (a_{n-1}) and $n - 1$ data bits ($a_{n-2}, a_{n-3}, \ldots, a_1, a_0$). By convention the sign bit a_{n-1} is a 1 for negative numbers and a 0 for positive numbers.

Although negative numbers are represented differently in the 2's complement, sign magnitude, and 1's complement number systems, positive numbers are represented identically in the three systems. Fractional numbers are used in this section.

$$A = \sum_{i=0}^{n-1} a_i 2^{i-n+1} \tag{4.1}$$

Note that since the sign bit a_{n-1} is a 0, it has no effect in determining the value of A. The summation in Eq. (4.1) can be performed either from $i = 0$ to $i = n - 1$ or from $i = 0$ to $i = n - 2$ without affecting the value of A.

2's Complement. In the 2's complement fractional number system (occasionally called the *radix complement number system* [1]), negative numbers are represented by subtracting their absolute value from 2, hence the name. Equivalently, the number may be viewed as a sign bit with a weight of -1 and $n - 1$ positive binary fractional bits:

$$A = -a_{n-1} + \sum_{i=0}^{n-2} a_i 2^{i-n+1} \tag{4.2}$$

The negative of a 2's complement number is formed by inverting all bits and adding 1 to the least significant position. For example, to form $-\frac{5}{8}$:

$$
\begin{array}{lll}
+\frac{5}{8} & = & 0101 \\
\text{Invert all bits} & = & 1010 \\
\text{Add 1 lsb} & & \underline{0001} \\
& 1011 & = \quad -\frac{5}{8}
\end{array}
$$

Sign Magnitude. Sign magnitude numbers consist of a sign bit and $n - 1$ bits that express the magnitude of the number:

$$A = (1 - 2a_{n-1}) \sum_{i=0}^{n-2} a_i 2^{i-n+1} \tag{4.3}$$

The negative of a sign magnitude number is formed by simply inverting the sign bit. For example, to form $-\frac{5}{8}$:

$$
\begin{array}{lll}
+\frac{5}{8} & = & 0101 \\
\text{Invert sign bit} & = & 1101 \quad = \quad -\frac{5}{8}
\end{array}
$$

1's Complement. The 1's complement representation (occasionally called the *diminished radix complement* [1]) of a negative number is obtained by complementing each bit of the corresponding positive number:

$$A = \sum_{i=0}^{n-2} (a_i - a_{n-1}) 2^{i-n+1} \tag{4.4}$$

TABLE 4.1 Example of 4-Bit Fractional Fixed-Point Numbers

Number	2's complement	Sign magnitude	1's complement
$+\frac{7}{8}$	0111	0111	0111
$+\frac{3}{4}$	0110	0110	0110
$+\frac{5}{8}$	0101	0101	0101
$+\frac{1}{2}$	0100	0100	0100
$+\frac{3}{8}$	0011	0011	0011
$+\frac{1}{4}$	0010	0010	0010
$+\frac{1}{8}$	0001	0001	0001
$+0$	0000	0000	0000
-0	N/A	1000	1111
$-\frac{1}{8}$	1111	1001	1110
$-\frac{1}{4}$	1110	1010	1101
$-\frac{3}{8}$	1101	1011	1100
$-\frac{1}{2}$	1100	1100	1011
$-\frac{5}{8}$	1011	1101	1010
$-\frac{3}{4}$	1010	1110	1001
$-\frac{7}{8}$	1001	1111	1000
-1	1000	N/A	N/A

In Eq. (4.4), the subtraction in the first term $a_i - a_{n-1}$ is an arithmetic operation that produces values of -1, 0, or $+1$.

The negative of a 1's complement number is formed by inverting all bits. For example, to form $-\frac{5}{8}$:

$$+\frac{5}{8} \qquad = 0101$$

$$\text{Invert all bits} = 1010 \quad = \quad -\frac{5}{8}$$

Table 4.1 compares 4-bit fractional fixed-point numbers in the three number systems. Note that both the sign magnitude and the 1's complement number systems are symmetric and have two 0s and that only the 2's complement number system is capable of representing -1. The 2's complement has a unique representation for 0.

A significant difference between the number systems lies in their behavior under truncation. Truncation of 2's complement numbers never increases the value of the number (i.e., numbers are always rounded toward $-\infty$). This bias can cause difficulty for computations that involve summing many truncated numbers (which often occurs in signal processing applications). In both the sign magnitude and 1's complement number systems, truncation is equivalent to rounding toward 0.

4.3 FIXED-POINT ARITHMETIC OPERATIONS

This section presents typical fixed-point algorithms for addition, subtraction, multiplication, and division. The algorithms presented in this section assume the use of 2's complement numbers.

TABLE 4.2 Full Adder Truth Table

Inputs			Outputs	
a_k	b_k	c_k	s_k	c_{k+1}
0	0	0	0	0
0	0	1	1	0
0	1	0	1	0
0	1	1	0	1
1	0	0	1	0
1	0	1	0	1
1	1	0	0	1
1	1	1	1	1

4.3.1 Fixed-Point Addition and Subtraction

Addition is performed by summing the corresponding bits of two n-bit numbers, including the sign bit. Subtraction is performed by summing the corresponding bits of the minuend and the 2's complement of the subtrahend. Overflow is detected in a 2's complement adder by comparing the carry signals into and out of the most significant adder stage (i.e., the stage which computes the sign bit). If the carries disagree, the arithmetic has overflowed and the result is invalid.

Full Adder. The full adder is the fundamental building block of most arithmetic circuits. Its operation is described by the following equations:

$$s_k = a_k \bar{b}_k \bar{c}_k + \bar{a}_k b_k \bar{c}_k + \bar{a}_k \bar{b}_k c_k + a_k b_k c_k \tag{4.5}$$

$$c_{k+1} = \bar{a}_k b_k c_k + a_k \bar{b}_k c_k + a_k b_k \bar{c}_k + a_k b_k c_k = a_k b_k + a_k c_k + b_k c_k \tag{4.6}$$

where a_k, b_k, and c_k are the inputs to the kth full adder stage and s_k and c_{k+1} are the sum and carry outputs, respectively. For some applications, Eq. (4.5) is alternately represented as $a_k \oplus b_k \oplus c_k$, where $\oplus$ denotes the EXCLUSIVE-OR logic operation. Table 4.2 shows the truth table of a full adder. The block diagram of a nine-gate full adder (constructed from two half adders and an OR gate) is shown in Fig. 4.1.

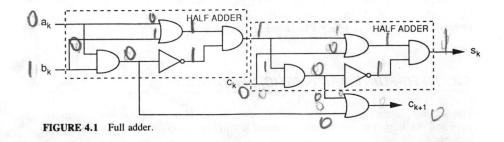

FIGURE 4.1 Full adder.

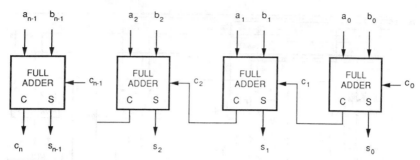

FIGURE 4.2 Ripple carry adder.

Ripple Carry Adder. A ripple carry adder for n-bit numbers is implemented by concatenating n full adders as shown in Fig. 4.2. At the kth bit position, the kth bits of operands A and B (a_k and b_k) and a carry signal from the preceding adder stage (c_k) are used to generate the kth bit of the sum s_k and a carry c_{k+1} to the $(k + 1)$st adder stage. This is called a *ripple carry adder,* since the carry signals "ripple" from the least-significant-bit position to the most-significant-bit one. If the ripple carry adder is implemented with the full adders of Fig. 4.1, an n-bit adder requires $2n + 4$ gate delays to produce the most significant sum bit and $2n + 3$ gate delays to produce the carry output.

Carry Completion Adder. Analysis has shown [2] that the average maximum carry chain length when n-bit numbers are added is approximately $\log_2 n$. Thus it is feasible to construct a carry completion adder by providing circuitry to determine when carry propagation is complete. This approach can provide excellent average addition times [1], but is not widely used, since it exhibits variable (data-dependent) timing which generally impacts the interface complexity. It can be useful in applications where variable timing is acceptable.

Carry Save Adder. An alternative approach for the summation of several n-bit numbers A_i is to apply the first three numbers A_1, A_2, and A_3 to a set of full adders, producing a sum and a carry word. Both the sum and carry words are "saved" in latches, as shown in Fig. 4.3. Subsequent numbers are added by applying the next number A_i and the previous sum S and twice the previous carry C (i.e., each bit of C is moved to the next-most-significant position) to the full adders, producing a new sum S and carry C, which are again "saved" in latches. After all input numbers A_i have been "added," additional (up to $n - 1$) sum, save, and shift cycles are performed where the shifted carry is added to the sum. The addition is complete when all carries are 0s. Alternatively, the S and upshifted C words may be added with a conventional carry propagate adder. It is important to note that the adder needs to be wide enough to accommodate growth in word size as multiple numbers are summed.

Carry save addition has been used to implement relatively simple high-speed multipliers since only a full adder delay and a latch setup time must be allowed between successive inputs A_i and A_{i+1}.

Carry Lookahead Adder. Another adder approach is the carry lookahead adder [3, 4]. Here specialized carry logic computes the carries in parallel with the sum computation. The carry lookahead adder uses modified full adders (the carry out OR gate is eliminated)

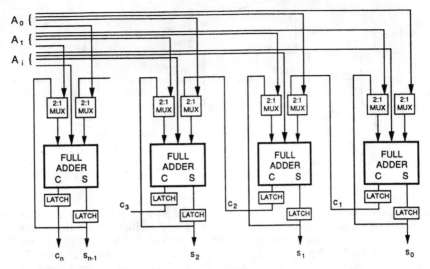

FIGURE 4.3   Carry save adder.

for each bit position and carry lookahead modules, whose outputs indicate that a carry has been generated within that module or that a lower-order carry would be propagated across that module. This is seen by rewriting Eq. (4.6) with $g_k = a_k b_k$ and $p_k = a_k + b_k$:

$$c_{k+1} = g_k + p_k c_k \tag{4.7}$$

This helps to explain the concept of carry generation and propagation: A given stage *generates* a carry if g_k is true (that is, $a_k = b_k = 1$) and *propagates* an input carry (to its output) if p_k is true (i.e., either a_k or b_k is a 1). Extending this definition to a 4-bit-wide module, we get

$$c_{k+2} = g_{k+1} + p_{k+1}c_{k+1} = g_{k+1} + p_{k+1}(g_k + p_k c_k)$$
$$= g_{k+1} + p_{k+1}g_k + p_{k+1}p_k c_k \tag{4.8}$$

Equation (4.8) results from evaluating Eq. (4.7) for the $(k+1)$st stage, giving $c_{k+2} = g_{k+1} + f_{k+1}c_{k+1}$ and substituting c_{k+1} from Eq. (4.7). Carry c_{k+2} exits from stage $k+1$ if (1) a carry is generated there or (2) a carry exits from stage k and propagates across stage $k+1$ or (3) a carry enters stage k and propagates across both stages k and $k+1$, etc. Extending to subsequent stages gives

$$c_{k+3} = g_{k+2} + p_{k+2}c_{k+2} = g_{k+2} + p_{k+2}(g_{k+1} + p_{k+1}g_k + p_{k+1}p_k c_k)$$
$$= g_{k+2} + p_{k+2}g_{k+1} + p_{k+2}p_{k+1}g_k + p_{k+2}p_{k+1}p_k c_k \tag{4.9}$$

$$c_{k+4} = g_{k+3} + p_{k+3}c_{k+3}$$
$$= g_{k+3} + p_{k+3}(g_{k+2} + p_{k+2}g_{k+1} + p_{k+2}p_{k+1}g_k + p_{k+2}p_{k+1}p_k c_k) \tag{4.10}$$
$$= g_{k+3} + p_{k+3}g_{k+2} + p_{k+3}p_{k+2}g_{k+1} + p_{k+3}p_{k+2}p_{k+1}g_k + p_{k+3}p_{k+2}p_{k+1}p_k c_k$$

Equation (4.10) can be expressed in terms of block generate and block propagate signals g_b and p_b, respectively, as

$$c_{k+4} = g_b + p_b c_k \tag{4.11}$$

where

$$g_b = g_{k+3} + p_{k+3}g_{k+2} + p_{k+3}p_{k+2}g_{k+1} + p_{k+3}p_{k+2}p_{k+1}g_k \tag{4.12}$$

and

$$p_b = p_{k+3}p_{k+2}p_{k+1}p_k \tag{4.13}$$

Equation (4.11), which is Eq. (4.7) extended over the 4-bit block, shows that the carry out from a 4-bit-wide block can be computed in only four gate delays [the first to compute p_n and g_n for $n = k$ through $k + 3$, the second to evaluate p_b, the second and third to evaluate g_b, and the third and fourth to evaluate c_{k+4} by using Eq. (4.11)]. This compares with 11 delays to compute the carry from a four-stage ripple carry adder implemented with the full adders of Fig. 4.2.

Although the carry lookahead approach can be extended to larger blocks, the number of inputs to the logic gates increases in direct proportion to the block size. Industry practice has standardized on 4-bit-wide blocks which are implemented with logic gates with at most four inputs. The carry lookahead block is a direct implementation of Eqs. (4.7) to (4.9), (4.12), and (4.13) with 14 logic gates.

Figure 4.4 shows the interconnection of 16 adders and 5 lookahead logic blocks to realize a 16-bit carry lookahead adder. The sequence of events which occur during an add operation is as follows: (1) Apply a, b, and carry in signals; (2) each adder computes p and g; (3) carry lookahead logic computes the carries; and (4) each adder computes the sum outputs. This process may be extended to larger adders by subdividing the large adder into 16-bit blocks and using additional levels of carry lookahead (a 64-bit adder requires three levels).

The delay of carry lookahead adders is evaluated by recognizing that a single-level carry lookahead adder (for 4-bit words) has six gate delays, and that each additional level of lookahead increases the word size by a factor of 4 and adds four gate delays. Because of the performance gain achieved by use of carry lookahead logic, it is quite widely accepted for bit slice microprocessors. More generally [5, pp. 83–88], the number of carry lookahead levels for an n-bit adder is $\lceil \log_r n1 \rceil$, where r is the maximum number of inputs per gate. Since an r-bit carry lookahead adder has six gate delays and there are four additional gate delays per carry lookahead level after the first, the delay of an n-bit carry lookahead adder is $2 + 4 \lceil \log_r n1 \rceil$. The Manchester carry chain [6] is an effective technique for the implementation of carry lookahead logic in CMOS implementations.

Carry Skip Adder. The carry skip adder divides the words to be added into blocks (as the carry lookahead adder does). From Eq. (4.11), the carry in to each block is the carry out from the previous block ORed with (the carry in to the previous block ANDed with the propagate signal) computed with a single gate from Eq. (4.13) for the block. The basic structure of a 16-bit carry skip adder is shown in Fig. 4.5. Within each block, ripple carry is used to produce the sum and generate the block carry output. The first and last blocks are simple ripple carry adders. The delay of a carry skip adder is the sum of the delay to generate the carry in the first block ($2k + 3$ gate delays), two gate delays through each of the $n/k - 2$ intermediate blocks, and $2k + 1$ gate delays to generate the most significant bit of the sum in the last block. If the block width is k,

$$D_{\text{total}} = 2k + 3 + 2\left(\frac{n}{k} - 2\right) + 2k + 1 \tag{4.14}$$

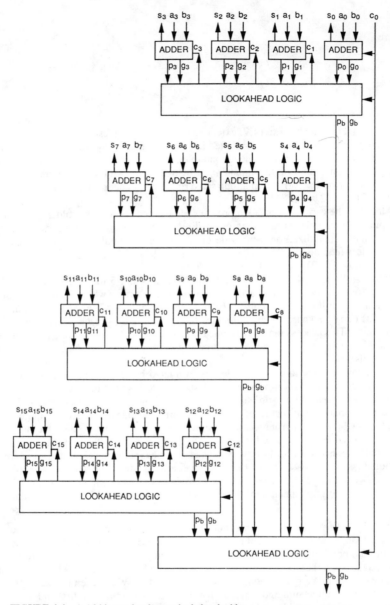

FIGURE 4.4 A 16-bit two-level carry lookahead adder.

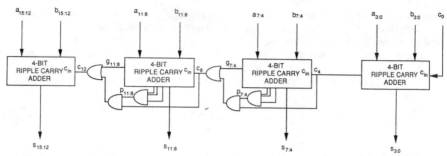

FIGURE 4.5 Carry skip adder.

where D_{total} is the total delay. The optimum block size is determined by taking the derivative of D_{total} with respect to k, setting it to 0, and solving for k. The resulting optimum values for k and D_{total} are

$$k = \sqrt{\frac{n}{2}} \tag{4.15}$$

$$D_{total} = 4\sqrt{2n} \tag{4.16}$$

Better results can be obtained by varying the block width, so that the first and last blocks are smaller and the intermediate blocks are larger, and by using multiple levels of carry skip [7, 8].

The complexity of the carry skip adder is only very slightly greater than that of a ripple carry adder because the first and last blocks are ripple carry adders and each intermediate stage is a ripple carry adder with three gates added for carry skipping.

Carry Select Adder. The carry select adder divides the words to be added into blocks and forms two sums for each block in parallel (one with a carry in of 0 and the other with a carry in of 1). As shown for a 16-bit carry select adder in Fig. 4.6, the carry out from the previous block controls a multiplexer that selects the appropriate sum. The carry into a block is

$$c_{in}(m + 1) = c_{out}^0 (m) + c_{out}^1 (m) c_{in}(m) \tag{4.17}$$

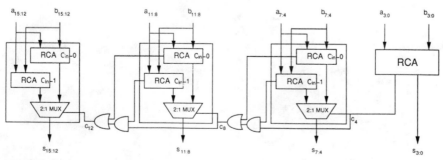

FIGURE 4.6 Carry select adder.

where $c_{in}(m + 1)$ is the carry in to the $(m + 1)$st block, $c_{out}^0(m)$ is the carry out of the mth block (assuming $C_{in} = 0$), $c_{out}^1(m)$ is the carry out of the mth block (assuming $C_{in} = 1$), and $c_{in}(m)$ is the carry in to the mth block.

If a constant block width of k is used, there will be n/k blocks, and the delay to generate the sum is $2k + 3$ gate delays to form the carry out of the first block, two gate delays for each of the $n/k - 2$ intermediate blocks, and three gate delays in the final block. The total delay is thus

$$D_{total} = 2k + \frac{2n}{k} + 2 \tag{4.18}$$

The optimum block size is determined by taking the derivative of D_{total} with respect to k, setting it to 0, and solving for k. The result is

$$k = \sqrt{n} \tag{4.19}$$

$$D_{total} = 2 + 4\sqrt{n} \tag{4.20}$$

Better results can be obtained by varying the block width so that the two least-significant blocks are the same size and each successively more significant block is 1 bit larger. For this configuration, the delay for each block's most significant sum bit will equal the delay to the multiplexer control signal [9, p. A-38].

The complexity of the carry select adder shown in Fig. 4.6 is $2n-k$ ripple carry adder stages plus $n - k$ 2-to-1 multiplexers. This is somewhat more than twice the complexity of a ripple carry adder. It is possible to simplify the design by designing an integrated adder that produces the two sums with fewer gates, but the total complexity of the carry select adder is still high.

4.3.2 Fixed-Point Multiplication

Multiplication is generally implemented either via a sequence of addition, subtraction, and shift operations or with direct logic implementations.

Booth Multiplier. Booth's algorithm [10] is widely used for 2's complement multiplication, since it is easy to implement. Earlier 2's complement multipliers (e.g., [11]) required data-dependent correction cycles if either operand was negative. To multiply $A \cdot B$, the product P is initially set to 0. Then the bits of the multiplier, A, are examined in pairs of adjacent bits, starting with the least significant bit (that is, a_0a_{-1}) and assuming $a_{-1} = 0$:

If $a_i = a_{i-1}$,

$$P = \frac{P}{2}$$

If $a_i = 0$ and $a_{i-1} = 1$,

$$P = \frac{P + B}{2}$$

If $a_i = 1$ and $a_{i-1} = 0$,

$$P = \frac{P - B}{2}$$

No division is performed on the last stage (i.e., when $i = n - 1$). All the divide-by-2 operations are simple arithmetic right shifts (i.e., the word is shifted right one position, and the old sign bit is repeated for the new sign bit), and overflows in the addition process are ignored. The algorithm is illustrated in Fig. 4.7, in which products for all combinations of $\pm\frac{5}{8} \cdot \pm\frac{3}{4}$ are computed for 4-bit operands. Booth's method requires n cycles to form the product of a pair of n-bit numbers, where each cycle consists of an n-bit addition and a shift, an n-bit subtraction and a shift, or a shift without any other arithmetic operation.

Modified Booth Multiplier. The modified Booth multiplier developed by MacSorley [4] uses $n/2$ cycles where each cycle examines 3 adjacent bits, adds B or $2B$ and shifts 2 bits

i	a_i	a_{i-1}	OPERATION	RESULT
	$A = \frac{5}{8} = 0.101$		$B = \frac{3}{4} = 0.110$	
0	1	0	$P = (P - B)/2$	1.1010
1	0	1	$P = (P + B)/2$	0.00110
2	1	0	$P = (P - B)/2$	1.101110
3	0	1	$P = P + B$	0.011110
	THUS: $P = 0.011110 = \frac{15}{32}$			
	$A = \frac{-5}{8} = 1.011$		$B = \frac{3}{4} = 0.110$	
0	1	0	$P = (P - B)/2$	1.1010
1	1	1	$P = P/2$	1.11010
2	0	1	$P = (P + B)/2$	0.010010
3	1	0	$P = P - B$	1.100010
	THUS: $P = 1.100010 = \frac{-15}{32}$			
	$A = \frac{5}{8} = 0.101$		$B = \frac{-3}{4} = 1.010$	
0	1	0	$P = (P - B)/2$	0.0110
1	0	1	$P = (P + B)/2$	1.1010
2	1	0	$P = (P - B)/2$	0.010010
3	0	1	$P = P + B$	1.100010
	THUS: $P = 1.100010 = \frac{-15}{32}$			
	$A = \frac{-5}{8} = 1.011$		$B = \frac{-3}{4} = 1.010$	
0	1	0	$P = (P - B)/2$	0.0110
1	1	1	$P = P/2$	0.00110
2	0	1	$P = (P + B)/2$	1.101110
3	1	0	$P = P - B$	0.011110
	THUS: $P = 0.011110 = \frac{15}{32}$			

FIGURE 4.7 Example of Booth multiplication.

TABLE 4.3   Modified Booth's Algorithm

a_{i+1}	a_i	a_{i-1}	Operation
0	0	0	$P = P/4$
0	0	1	$P = (P + B)/4$
0	1	0	$P = (P + B)/4$
0	1	1	$P = (P + 2B)/4$
1	0	0	$P = (P - 2B)/4$
1	0	1	$P = (P - B)/4$
1	1	0	$P = (P - B)/4$
1	1	1	$P = P/4$

to the right, subtracts B or $2B$ and shifts 2 bits to the right, or shifts 2 bits to the right. Table 4.3 shows the operations as a function of the 3 bits a_{i+1}, a_i, and a_{i-1}. The modified Booth algorithm takes half as many cycles as the "standard" Booth algorithm, and the operations performed during a cycle are no more complex (although more selection is required). Extensions that examine more than 3 bits [12] are generally not attractive because the addition/subtraction operations involve non-power-of-2 multiples (such as 3, 5, 6, and 7) of B, which raises the complexity.

Array Multipliers.   An alternative approach to multiplication involves the combinational generation of all bit products and their summation with an array of full adders. The block diagram of a 6×6 array multiplier is shown in Fig. 4.8. It uses an $n \times n - 1$ array of adders ($n^2 - 2n$ full adders and n half adders) to sum the n^2 bit products. Summing the bits requires $2n - 2$ adder delays.

Modification of the array multiplier to multiply two's complement numbers requires inverting the most significant bit of the multiplier and multiplicand before forming the bit product matrix and adding a few correction terms [13, 14]. Array multipliers are easily laid out in cellular fashion, making them suitable for VLSI implementation, where minimizing the design effort may be more important than maximizing the speed.

Wallace Tree/Dadda Fast Multiplier.   A method for fast multiplication was developed by Wallace [15] and refined by Dadda [16, 17]. With this method, a three-step process is used to multiply two numbers: (1) The bit products are formed, (2) the bit product matrix is "reduced" to a two-row matrix where the sum of the rows equals the sum of the bit products, and (3) the two numbers are summed with a fast adder to produce the product. Although this may seem to be a complex process, it yields multipliers with delay proportional to the logarithm of the operand word size, which is "faster" than Booth's algorithm, the modified Booth algorithm, or array multipliers which all have delays proportional to the word size.

The second step in the fast multiplication process is shown for an 8×8 multiplier in Fig. 4.9. An input 8×8 matrix of dots (each dot represents a bit product) is shown as matrix 0. Columns having more than six dots (or that will grow to more than six dots due to carries) are reduced by the use of half adders (each half adder takes in two dots and outputs one in the same column and one in the next-more-significant column) and full adders (each full adder takes in three dots and outputs one in the same column and one in the next-more-significant column) so that no column in matrix 1 will have more than six dots. In the succeeding steps reduction to matrix 2 with no more than four dots per column, matrix 3 with no more than three dots per column, and finally matrix 4 with no

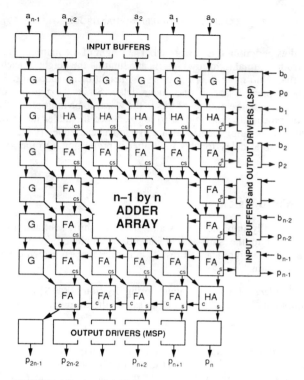

FIGURE 4.8 Array multiplier.

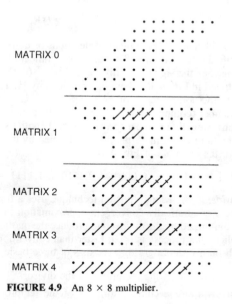

FIGURE 4.9 An 8 × 8 multiplier.

more than two dots per column is performed. The height of the matrices is determined by working back from the final (two-row) matrix and limiting the height of each matrix to the largest integer that is no more than 1.5 times the height of its successor. Each matrix is produced from its predecessor in one adder delay. Since the number of matrices is logarithmically related to the number of bits in the words to be multiplied, the delay of the matrix reduction process is proportional to log n. Since the adder that reduces the final two-row matrix can be implemented as a carry lookahead adder (which also has logarithmic delay), the total delay for this multiplier is proportional to the logarithm of the word size.

4.3.3 Fixed-Point Division

Division is traditionally implemented as a sequence of shift, subtract, and compare operations, in contrast to the shift-and-add approach employed for multiplication. The comparison operation is significant: It results in a serial process which is not amenable to parallel implementation.

Nonrestoring Divider.   Traditional nonrestoring division [18, 19] is based on selecting digits of the quotient Q (where $Q = A/B$) to satisfy the following equation:

$$R^{(i+1)} = rR^{(i)} - q_{n-i-1}B \qquad \text{for } i = 0, 1, \ldots, n - 1 \qquad (4.21)$$

where $R^{(j)}$ is the partial remainder after selection of the jth quotient digit, $R^{(0)} = A$ (subject to the constraint $|R^{(0)}| < |B|$), r is the radix ($= 2$ for binary nonrestoring division), q_{n-i-1} is the ith quotient digit to the right of the binary point, and B is the divisor. In nonrestoring division, the quotient digits are constrained to be either $+1$ or -1. The digit selection and resulting partial remainder are given for the jth iteration by the following relations:

$$\text{If} \quad 0 < R^{(j)}, \text{ then} \qquad q_{n-i-1} = 1 \quad \text{and} \quad R^{(j+1)} = 2R^{(j)} - B \qquad (4.22)$$

$$\text{If} \quad 0 > R^{(j)}, \text{ then} \qquad q_{n-i-1} = -1 \quad \text{and} \quad R^{(j+1)} = 2R^{(j)} + B \qquad (4.23)$$

This process continues either for a set number of iterations or until the partial remainder is smaller than a specified error criterion. The ith most significant bit of the quotient is a 1 if the sign of $R^{(j)}$ matches the sign of the divisor and is a $\bar{1}$ (-1) if the signs disagree. The algorithm is illustrated in Fig. 4.10 where $5/16$ is divided by $3/8$. The result ($13/16$) is the closest 4-bit fraction to the correct result of $5/6$.

The signed digit number (comprised of ± 1 digits) can be converted to a conventional binary number by subtracting N, a number formed by the $\bar{1}$ (with 0s where there are $+1$s and 1s where there are $\bar{1}$s in Q) from P, the number formed by the $+1$s (with 0s where there are $\bar{1}$s in Q). For the example of Fig. 4.10,

$$Q = 0.111\bar{1} = 0.1110 - 0.0001 = 0.1110 + 1.1111 = 0.1101$$

Newton-Raphson Divider.   A second division technique uses a form of Newton-Raphson iteration to derive a quadratically convergent approximation to the reciprocal of the divisor which is then multiplied by the dividend to produce the quotient. In systems which include a fast multiplier, this process is often faster than conventional division [20].

The Newton-Raphson division algorithm consists of three basic steps:

1. Calculate a starting estimate of the reciprocal of the divisor $X^{(0)}$.
2. Compute successively more accurate estimates of the reciprocal by the following iterative procedure:

$R^{(0)} = A = \frac{5}{16} = 0.0101$

$B = \frac{3}{8} = 0.0110$

$R^{(0)} = A$

Since $R^{(0)} > 0$, then $q_{n-1} = 1$ and $R^{(1)} = 2R^{(0)} - B$

$$
\begin{array}{rl}
2R^{(0)} = & 0.1010 \\
-B = & \underline{1.1010} \\
R^{(1)} = & 0.0100
\end{array}
$$

Since $R^{(1)} > 0$, then $q_{n-2} = 1$ and $R^{(2)} = 2R^{(1)} - B$

$$
\begin{array}{rl}
2R^{(1)} = & 0.1000 \\
-B = & \underline{1.1010} \\
R^{(2)} = & 0.0010
\end{array}
$$

Since $R^{(2)} > 0$, then $q_{n-3} = 1$ and $R^{(3)} = 2R^{(2)} - B$

$$
\begin{array}{rl}
2R^{(2)} = & 0.0100 \\
-B = & \underline{1.1010} \\
R^{(3)} = & 1.1110
\end{array}
$$

Since $R^{(3)} < 0$, then $q_{n-4} = \overline{1}$ and $R^{(4)} = 2R^{(3)} + B$

$$
\begin{array}{rl}
2R^{(3)} = & 1.1100 \\
+B = & \underline{0.0110} \\
R^{(4)} = & 0.0010
\end{array}
$$

$Q = 0.111\overline{1} = 0.1101 = \frac{13}{16}$

FIGURE 4.10 Example of nonrestoring division.

$$X^{(i+1)} = X^{(i)} - \frac{F(X^{(i)})}{F'(X^{(i)})} \tag{4.24}$$

3. Compute the quotient by multiplying the dividend by the reciprocal of the divisor.

If $F(X^{(i)}) = 1/X^{(i)} - B$ and the initial value $X^{(0)}$ is close enough, then $X^{(i+1)}$ produced by Eq. (4.24) will converge to $X^{(i)} = 1/B$. If the divisor B is normalized (that is, $\frac{1}{2} \le B < 1$), the following estimate of the reciprocal of the divisor gives an initial value that is within 0.085 of the correct value.

$$R^{(0)} = 2.915 - 2B \tag{4.25}$$

Equation (4.25) is developed by noting that in the interval $0.5 \le B < 1$, $R^{(0)} = 3 - 2B$ exactly computes $1/B$ at $B = 0.5$ and $B = 1$ and exhibits maximum error (0.17 high) at $B = \sqrt{\frac{1}{2}}$. Adjusting $R^{(0)}$ downward to $R^{(0)} = 2.915 - 2 \cdot B$ gives an initial estimate that is within 0.085 of the correct value for all points in the interval.

$$R^{(i+1)} = R^i (2 - B \cdot R^{(i)}) \qquad \text{for } i = 0, 1, \ldots, k \tag{4.26}$$

$$Q = A \cdot R^{(k)} \tag{4.27}$$

where i is the iteration count and A is the numerator. Figure 4.11 illustrates the operation of the Newton-Raphson algorithm. For this example, three iterations (one shift, four subtractions, and seven multiplications) produce an answer accurate to nine decimal digits (approximately 30 bits).

A = .625

B = .75

$R^{(0)}$ = 2.915 − 2 • B   1 Shift, 1 Subtract
      = 2.915 − 2 • .75
$R^{(0)}$ = 1.415

$R^{(1)}$ = $R^{(0)}$ (2 − B • $R^{(0)}$)   2 Multiplies, 1 Subtract
      = 1.415 (2 − .75 • 1.415)
      = 1.415 • .95875
$R^{(1)}$ = 1.32833125

$R^{(2)}$ = $R^{(1)}$ (2 − B • $R^{(1)}$)   2 Multiplies, 1 Subtract
      = 1.32833125 (2 − .75 • 1.32833125)
      = 1.32833125 • 1.00375156
$R^{(2)}$ = 1.3333145677

$R^{(3)}$ = $R^{(2)}$ (2 − B • $R^{(2)}$)   2 Multiplies, 1 Subtract
      = 1.3333145677 (2 − .75 • 1.3333145677)
      = 1.3333145677 • 1.00001407
$R^{(3)}$ = 1.3333333331

Q   = A • $R^{(3)}$ 1 Multiply
Q   = .83333333319

FIGURE 4.11 Example of Newton-Raphson division.

With this algorithm, the error decreases quadratically, so that each approximation's error is a constant times the square of the error of the previous approximation. In practice, this means that the number of correct bits in each approximation is roughly twice the number of correct bits on the previous iteration. Thus, from a 4-bit initial approximation, two iterations produce a reciprocal estimate accurate to 16 bits, four iterations produce a reciprocal estimate accurate to 64 bits, etc.

The efficiency of this process is dependent on the availability of a fast multiplier, since each iteration of Eq. (4.26) requires two multiplications and a subtraction. The complete process for the initial estimate, two iterations, and the final quotient determination requires six addition operations and five multiplication operations to produce a 16-bit quotient. This is a factor of two to three times faster than a conventional nonrestoring divider if multiplication is roughly as fast as addition, a condition which is usually satisfied for systems which include hardware multipliers.

4.4 FLOATING-POINT ARITHMETIC

Recent advances in VLSI have increased the feasibility of hardware implementation of floating-point arithmetic units. The main advantage of floating-point arithmetic is that its wide dynamic range virtually eliminates overflow for most applications.

Floating-Point Number Systems. A floating-point number A consists of a significand (or mantissa) S_a and an exponent E_a. The value of a number A is given by

$$A = S_a r^{E_a} \tag{4.28}$$

where r is the radix (or base) of the number system. Use of the binary radix ($r = 2$) gives maximum accuracy, but may require more frequent normalization.

The IEEE Standard 754 single-precision (32-bit) floating-point format, which is widely implemented, has an 8-bit biased integer exponent which ranges between 1 and 254 [21]. The exponent is expressed in excess 127 code so that its effective value is determined by subtracting 127 from the stored value. Thus, the range of effective values of the exponent is -126 to 127, corresponding to stored values of 1 to 254, respectively. An exponent value of 128 (E_{min}) serves as a flag for 0 (if the significand is 0) and for denormalized numbers. An exponent value of -129 (E_{max}) serves as a flag for infinity (if the significand is 0) and for "not a number." The significand is a 25-bit sign magnitude mixed number (the binary point is to the right of the most significant bit which is always a 1, except for denormalized numbers). More details on floating-point formats and on the various considerations that arise in the implementation of floating-point arithmetic units can be found in the literature [9, 22–24].

Floating-Point Addition. A flowchart for floating-point addition is shown in Fig. 4.12. For this flowchart (and those that follow for multiplication and division), the operands are assumed to be "unpacked" and normalized with magnitudes in the range $(1.0, \frac{1}{2})$.

On the flowchart of Fig. 4.12, the operands are (E_a, S_a) and (E_b, S_b), the result is (E_s, S_s), and the radix is r ($r = 2$ for IEEE Standard 754 implementations). In step 1 the operand exponents are compared; if they are unequal, the significand of the number with the smaller exponent is shifted right in step 3 or 4 by the difference in the exponents to properly align the significands. For example, to add 0.867×10^5 and 0.512×10^4, the latter would be shifted right and 0.867 added to 0.0512 to give a sum of 0.9182×10^5. The addition of the significands is performed in step 5. Steps 6 to 8 test for overflow and correct, if necessary, by shifting the significand one position to the right and incrementing the exponent. Step 9 tests for a zero significand. The loop of steps 10 and 11 scales small significands (but nonzero) upward to normalize the result. Step 12 tests for underflow.

Floating-Point Subtraction. Floating-point subtraction is implemented with a similar algorithm. Many refinements are possible to improve the speed of the addition and subtraction algorithms, but floating-point addition will, in general, be much slower than fixed-point addition as a result of the need for preaddition alignment and postaddition normalization.

Floating-Point Multiplication. The algorithm for floating-point multiplication is shown in Fig. 4.13. In step 1, the product of the operand significands and the sum of the operand exponents are computed. Step 2 tests for overflow. Steps 3 and 4 normalize the product significand if necessary. For radix 2 floating-point numbers, if the operands are normalized, at most a single left shift is required to normalize the product. Finally, step 5 tests the exponent for underflow.

Floating-Point Division. The basic steps of a floating-point division algorithm are shown in Fig. 4.14. The quotient of the significands and the difference of the exponents are computed in step 1. The second step tests for underflow. The quotient is normalized (if necessary) in steps 3 and 4 by right-shifting the quotient significand while the quotient exponent is incremented. For radix 2, if the operands are normalized, only a single right

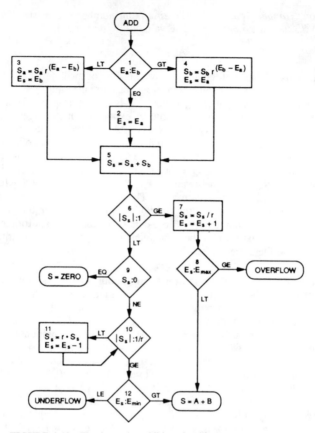

FIGURE 4.12 Floating-point addition algorithm.

shift is required to normalize the quotient. Finally, the computed exponent is tested for overflow in step 5.

Floating-Point Rounding.   All floating-point algorithms may require rounding to produce a result in the correct format. A variety of alternative rounding schemes have been developed for specific applications. Round to nearest, round toward ∞, round toward $-\infty$, and round toward 0 are available in implementations of the IEEE floating-point standard. Selection should be based on both static and dynamic performance [25] although round to nearest is appropriate for most applications.

4.5 CONCLUSIONS

This chapter has presented an overview of binary number systems, algorithms for the basic integer arithmetic operations, and a brief introduction to floating-point operations. When arithmetic units are implemented, there is often an opportunity to optimize the

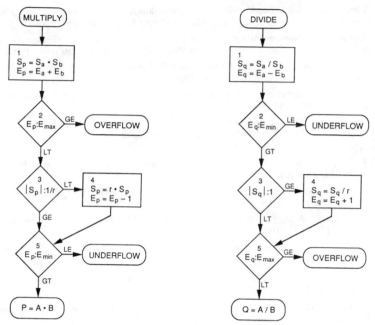

FIGURE 4.13 Floating-point multiplication algorithm.

FIGURE 4.14 Floating-point division algorithm.

performance and the area to the requirements of the specific application. In general, faster algorithms require more area or more complex control: it is often useful to use the fastest algorithm that will fit the available area.

REFERENCES

References 2–4, 10, 11, 13–20, and 25 are reprinted in Ref. 26.

1. H. L. Garner, "Number Systems and Arithmetic," in F. L. Alt and M. Rubinoff (eds.), *Advances in Computers,* vol. 6. New York: Academic Press, 1960, pp. 148–149.

2. B. Gilchrist, J. H. Pomerene, and S. Y. Wong, "Fast Carry Logic for Digital Computers," *IRE Transactions on Electronic Computers,* EC-4:133–136, 1955.

3. A. Weinberger and J. L. Smith, "A Logic for High-Speed Addition," *National Bureau of Standards Circular 591,* pp. 3–12, 1958.

4. O. L. MacSorley, "High-Speed Arithmetic in Binary Computers," *Proceedings of the IRE,* 49:67–91, 1961.

5. Shlomo Waser and Michael J. Flynn, *Introduction to Arithmetic for Digital Systems Designers.* New York: Holt, Rinehart and Winston, 1982.

6. T. Kilburn, D. B. G. Edwards, and D. Aspinall, "A Parallel Arithmetic Unit Using a Saturated Transistor Fast-Carry Circuit," *Proceedings of the IEE,* Part B, 107:573–584, 1960.

7. P. K. Chen and M. D. F. Schlag, "Analysis and Design of CMOS Manchester Adders with Variable Carry Skip," *IEEE Transactions on Computers,* C-39:983–992, 1990.

8. S. Turrini, "Optimal Group Distribution in Carry-Skip Adders," *Proceedings of the 9th Symposium on Computer Arithmetic*. Santa Monica, Calif.: IEEE, 1989. Pp. 96–103.

9. D. Goldberg, "Computer Arithmetic," in D. A. Patterson and J. L. Hennessy, *Computer Architecture: A Quantitative Approach*. San Mateo, Calif.: Morgan Kauffmann, 1990, app. A.

10. A. D. Booth, "A Signed Binary Multiplication Technique," *Quarterly Journal of Mechanics and Applied Mathematics*, 4(2):236–240, 1951.

11. R. F. Shaw, "Arithmetic Operations in a Binary Computer," *Review of Scientific Instrumentation*, 21:687–693, 1950.

12. H. Sam and A. Gupta, "A Generalized Multibit Recoding of Two's Complement Binary Numbers and Its Proof with Application in Multiplier Implementations," *IEEE Transactions on Computers*, C-39:1006–1015, 1990.

13. C. R. Baugh and B. A. Wooley, "A Two's Complement Parallel Array Multiplication Algorithm," *IEEE Transactions on Computers*, C-22:1045–1047, 1973.

14. P. E. Blankenship, "Comments on 'A Two's Complement Parallel Array Multiplication Algorithm,'" *IEEE Transactions on Computers*, C-23:1327, 1974.

15. C. S. Wallace, "A Suggestion for a Fast Multiplier," *IEEE Transactions on Electronic Computers*, EC-13:14–17, 1964.

16. L. Dadda, "Some Schemes for Parallel Multipliers," *Alta Frequenza*, 34:349–356, 1965.

17. L. Dadda, "On Parallel Digital Multipliers," *Alta Frequenza*, 45:574–580, 1976.

18. J. E. Robertson, "A New Class of Digital Division Methods," *IRE Transactions on Electronic Computers*, EC-7:218–222, 1958.

19. D. E. Atkins, "Higher-Radix Division Using Estimates of the Divisor and Partial Remainders," *IEEE Transactions on Computers*, C-17:925–934, 1968.

20. D. Ferrari, "A Division Method Using a Parallel Multiplier," *IEEE Transactions on Electronic Computers*, EC-16:224–226, 1967.

21. *IEEE Standard for Binary Floating-Point Arithmetic*, IEEE Standard 754-1985, Reaffirmed 1990.

22. J. B. Gosling, *Design of Arithmetic Units for Digital Computers*. New York: Macmillan Press, 1980.

23. K. Hwang, *Computer Arithmetic: Principles, Architecture, and Design*. New York: Wiley, 1979.

24. E. E. Swartzlander, Jr., *Computer Arithmetic*, vol. 2. Los Alamitos, Calif.: IEEE Computer Society Press, 1990.

25. D. J. Kuck, D. S. Parker, Jr., and A. H. Sameh, "Analysis of Rounding Methods in Floating-Point Arithmetic," *IEEE Transactions on Computers*, C-26:643–650, 1977.

26. E. E. Swartzlander, Jr., *Computer Arithmetic*, vol. 1. Los Alamitos, Calif.: IEEE Computer Society Press, 1990.

CHAPTER 5

COMPUTER ARCHITECTURE

Robert B. K. Dewar

Courant Institute of Mathematical Sciences
New York University

In this chapter, we describe the basic high-level design of modern processors and associated memory systems. We will be concerned with those design aspects which directly affect the functionality and performance of computer systems, as seen by applications programs and by operating systems and other systems software, rather than with the detailed hardware approaches used to realize these designs.

An important underlying theme in any such examination is the tension (sometimes devolving into outright squabbling) between two schools of thought. Historically, there was an attempt to provide rich instruction sets, containing all sorts of specialized instructions, including ones intended specifically to simplify the implementation of high-level languages. More recently, the *reduced instruction set computer* (RISC) designers have pointed out that this kind of development is not only unnecessary (empirical studies show that these fancy instructions have little effect on the overall performance of programs, since they are executed infrequently), but also actively harmful (because implementing these fancy instructions introduces a level of complexity that slows down all instructions).

Older designs, called, somewhat derisively, *complex instruction set computers* (CISCs), typically require several processor clocks to complete the execution of each instruction. By streamlining the instruction sets in RISC machines, execution throughputs can approach or even exceed the rate of one instruction per clock, greatly increasing the overall performance. Interestingly, often as a result of this basically faster performance, RISC machines can beat CISC machines at their own game, in the sense that implementing fancy functions as a sequence of RISC instructions is often as fast as, or even faster than, the execution of the comparable single fancy instruction on a CISC machine.

Still, the basic debate is far from resolved, especially since recently several manufacturers of CISC processors have shown that they can use RISC techniques to achieve RISC-like throughput while retaining fancy complex instruction sets. Some RISC manufacturers have also produced chips with large instruction sets that have a definite CISC flavor. As we will see in this chapter, the dividing line between RISC and CISC is not entirely clear. Certainly the basic techniques of RISC design, in particular the notion of

This chapter is adapted from Robert Dewar and Matthew Smosna, *Microprocessors: A Programmer's View*. New York: McGraw-Hill, 1990.

pipelining, are of great importance and will play an important role in any future processor designs.

5.1 DATA REPRESENTATION

Manipulation of data is at the heart of any computer program, so the manner in which data are represented is an important issue. Historically, all sorts of peculiar data representations have appeared in processors, but there seems at this stage to be a general convergence, and even RISC and CISC designers are pretty much in agreement on the basic approaches. Compatible representations are particularly important in facilitating transfer of data between different processors. In this section we will look at how the various types of data are represented, and we note the few areas where there still are annoying differences, which do indeed cause major problems in data interoperability.

5.1.1 Representation of Character Data

Historically, characters have been represented by using a fixed number of bits, where a separate bit combination is used to represent each distinct character. Early on, when output devices were limited to uppercase letters, the character sets were quite limited, and 6 bits was sufficient, but now the use of 8 bits is almost universal. Indeed, it is this general agreement on the use of 8-bit coding for character data that has led almost all modern processor designs to be based around a design with 8-bit bytes.

The actual correspondence between graphic characters and binary codes does not typically affect the design of the instruction set, since there are usually no instructions which are specifically sensitive to particular 8-bit codes. Some exceptions to this rule are found on older CISC designs (e.g., the edit instruction of the IBM 370, which inserts characters such as the dollar sign into the output field), but no modern RISC designs depend on the character set. Consequently such processors can perfectly well be used with any of the 8-bit character sets in use. Some examples of such character sets are laid out in ISO Standard 8859, which describes a number of different sets suitable for various Western languages. Of these the most important is Latin-1, an extended version of the familiar ASCII code, in which the upper half characters are used to represent the accented letters and other special symbols required by Western European countries.

All the 8859 character sets reserve the first 32 positions as *control characters*, with specialized functions (e.g., the code hexadecimal 0D is designated as the *carriage return* function). However, once again, this assignment has essentially no effect on processor design, since the meaning of control characters, like all other characters, is only relevant for I/O interfaces. Of course, programs must be aware of the character set in use, and differences in character sets often present major portability problems for both programs and data. These portability problems are aggravated by the widespread use of nonstandard character sets, including EBCDIC (the native character set of IBM mainframes, which bears no relation to ASCII), and the extended ASCII set found on IBM personal computers (PCs), where both the control character space and the upper half are used for such idiosyncratic purposes as "smiling face," musical notes, integral signs, and box drawing characters. Furthermore, in the typographical world, specialized character sets such as Sonata and Zapf Dingbats, both copyrighted fonts marketed by Adobe systems, have completely different interpretations of these 8-bit codes, in one case as musical notes and in the other as various randomly designed symbols such as decorative bullets.

In the above discussion, we specifically noted that the 8-bit character sets were appropriate for representation of Western alphabets, which are typically small. The increased prominence in the computer field of countries whose writing is based on the ancient Han characters from China (including Japan, Korea, Taiwan, and China itself) means that the problem of representing these character sets has recently become an important issue. Obviously 8-bit character coding cannot be used to represent such character sets (where there are literally thousands of distinct characters). Two approaches are in common use. First, these characters can be encoded by using a stream of 8-bit codes, where the number of codes used to represent each character is not necessarily fixed. ISO Standard 2022 specifies several such standards. Second, simply use larger codes. In several countries 16-bit codes have come into wide use.

Recently, there has been an attempt to devise a 32-bit standard, ISO 10646, that is intended to provide enough space for all the characters in all languages in the world. An ambitious project, involving delicate political as well as technical issues, ISO 10646 failed on the first ballot and is thus not yet accepted. A competing 16-bit approach, called Unicode, pushed particularly by U.S. companies, attempts to squeeze all needed characters into the smaller 16-bit space. At the time this chapter was written, an attempt was being made to unify the two approaches by setting aside a 16-bit section of the full 32-bit 10646 space called the *basic multilingual plane* (BMP), which would correspond to a modified version of Unicode.

In any case, once again, these character set controversies do not affect processor design, since all typical modern processors are perfectly capable of handling 16-bit and 32-bit data as well as 8-bit data. The programmer's problem in trying to write programs suitable for use in an international marketplace is often severe, but the processor neither helps nor hinders this endeavor.

5.1.2 Representation of Integer Data

Integer values may either be signed or unsigned. Unsigned values are simply represented in binary in the obvious manner. A number of different systems for representation of signed values have been used in the past, but now the use of *two's complement* form, in which negative numbers are represented by complementing the bits and adding 1, is now essentially universal. In this notation, the first, or most significant, bit is the sign bit (0 = plus, 1 = minus), and an important property is that addition and subtraction operations are carried out exactly as for unsigned values, avoiding the need for separate signed and unsigned logic.

Other operations are a little more complicated. Multiplication of a 32-bit quantity by a 32-bit quantity to give a 32-bit result (a common operation in high-level languages) gives the same result for signed and unsigned operands. However, if a 64-bit result is produced, a common machine operation (and one that is important in implementing multiple-precision arithmetic) *does* give different results for signed and unsigned operands, so we typically find two sets of multiply instructions. In the case of division, the results are different even in the case of single-length operands, so here again we usually find two sets of instructions.

The only other representation for integers that is sometimes used is *packed decimal,* where the integer value is represented in decimal, using 4 bits for each decimal digit (i.e., two digits per 8-bit byte). This format is supported at the hardware level to varying degrees. On some CISC mainframes, notably those from IBM, there is a full implementation of arithmetic operations, to the high precision required for Cobol implementations. Other machines simply provide a few specialized instructions to assist in writing software arithmetic packages for this format, while most RISC machines provide no support at all

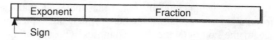

FIGURE 5.1 Typical floating-point format.

for packed decimal. Nevertheless this format is sometimes used on RISC machines where input and output conversions (obviously more efficient since no decimal-to-binary transformation is required) are more common than computations. RISC machines can, of course, process data in this (or any other) format, and indeed such manipulations often provide a demonstration of the basic RISC creed since we find examples where software implementations of packed-decimal arithmetic operations using fast RISC instruction sets are more efficient than built-in operations on slower CISC designs.

5.1.3 Representation of Floating-Point Data

The basic idea used in all systems of representing floating-point data is to divide the value into two parts, an exponent and a fraction, each of which is represented in binary format. The fraction is signed, and usually a sign-and-magnitude representation is used (some machines do use two's complement representation for the fraction, but there are rather obscure technical reasons for preferring sign and magnitude in this case). The basic format of floating-point data is shown in Fig. 5.1. Within this basic format, many variations are possible: The size (and hence the precision) of the fraction can vary, the size (and hence the range) of the exponent can vary, and the exact method of representing each component can also vary. Historically, a large set of incompatible idiosyncratic floating-point formats have arisen, with all sorts of variations on the basic theme. For example, the IBM 370 mainframes use a format in which the exponent uses a hexadecimal base instead of the more usual binary base.

In addition to the variation in representation formats, further uncertainty arises from the fact that there are significant differences from one machine to another in exactly how floating-point operations are performed. For example, one might expect that dividing 84.0 by 3.0 would give a result of exactly 28.0, since all three values are exactly representable. However, on some hardware, the result will be 1 bit different, because division is done by multiplication by the reciprocal.

IEEE Standard 754 represents an attempt to specify a single uniform approach which specifies both the floating-point formats and the required results of floating-point operations. This standard specifies the support of two formats, as shown in Fig. 5.2. Figure 5.2

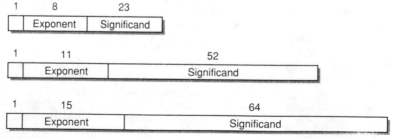

FIGURE 5.2 IEEE floating-point formats.

also shows a typical implementation of the extended format, an additional optional representation providing extra precision for intermediate calculations. The IEEE standard also specifies exact required results for floating-point operations. In particular, the result must be exact if possible, so the behavior we described above of getting the wrong result when dividing 84.0 by 3.0 would not be permitted.

Recent processor designs, including virtually all the RISC processors, have provided an essentially complete implementation of the IEEE 754 standard, so where there was once complete chaos, order is beginning to emerge, and the previously difficult task of transferring floating-point data from one machine to another is often greatly simplified when both machines implement this standard. A full description of the issues of floating-point representation is beyond the scope of this chapter. For more information, see chapter 5 of *Microprocessors: A Programmer's View*, by Robert Dewar and Matthew Smosna (New York: McGraw-Hill, 1990).

5.2 MEMORY ORGANIZATION

Physical memory is organized as a linear sequence of *addressing units* of a fixed number of bits, with each unit having a unique address, which is an integer value starting at 0 and incrementing sequentially. These addressing units are typically called either *words* or *bytes*, depending on the size (byte always means 8 bits). Historically, a number of machines were built using word-addressed memory (e.g., the Unisys 1100 series has 36-bit words). However, at this point, byte-addressed memories have become so universal that we concentrate only on this model.

5.2.1 Virtual Memory

In early machines, a memory address developed by a load or store instruction corresponded directly to a hardware address in memory. Now on most machines, there is at least the option of using a virtual memory address translation technique to map addresses generated by instructions (virtual addresses) into actual hardware memory addresses (physical addresses). Figure 5.3 shows the approach used in a virtual memory system to map virtual addresses into physical addresses. The top part of the virtual address supplies a page number, and the lower part of the virtual address is the address within this page. The page number is translated by some mechanism to give an actual physical address of the corresponding page in memory, and then the desired byte or bytes are selected. This virtualization of addresses has two important advantages. First, it allows separate programs running on the same machine to have a completely independent view of memory addressing. Second, it allows implementation of *demand paging*, in which the program addresses a virtual memory larger than the physical memory and the translation takes care of moving pages to and from disk as needed.

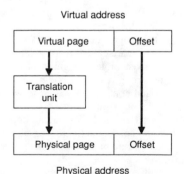

FIGURE 5.3 Mapping a virtual address into a physical address.

The translation approach is usually a two-level one. First there is a table, called the *translation lookaside buffer* (TLB), in the processor which contains a fairly small table (32 to 128 entries are typical) mapping virtual page numbers to physical page numbers. If the desired page is in the TLB, then the processor can perform the translation immediately without any speed penalty. If the TLB does not contain the desired page (a TLB miss), then a secondary mechanism uses a table in memory to find the desired entry and updates the TLB accordingly.

This secondary mechanism may be either a combination of hardware and software or entirely software. In the combination approach, the format of the memory tables is specified by the hardware, and the processor automatically conducts the search in this table. If the desired entry is found, then the program continues uninterrupted, with the TLB update occurring automatically. If the entry is not found, a *page fault* is signaled, and the operating system must take appropriate action (e.g., by swapping a page from disk). In the all-software approach, a TLB miss causes an immediate trap to the operating system.

The page table can be organized in many different manners. Two common approaches in hardware are the use of a multilevel tree (e.g., Dec and Intel processors) or the use of a hash table (IBM RISC processors). Of course, if the handling of TLB misses is done entirely in software, then the format of the table is an operating systems issue rather than a hardware issue. The issue of whether to perform this function in hardware is a typical CISC versus RISC issue, since we are talking about a function which is executed relatively infrequently. The MIPS RISC processors have always used a software-only approach, arguing in the typical RISC style that this complex function is equally well done by using sequences of RISC instructions instead of fancy built-in logic. Still, most other processors, including most other RISC processors, choose to implement the table lookup in hardware. The AMD29000 is an example of a processor which gives the system designer a choice. There is a hardware lookup capability, but it can be disabled.

Finally, we should mention that there are application areas in which paging is generally considered undesirable. In hard real-time systems, the possibility that any memory reference might cause a TLB miss, and hence take longer than usual, is unpleasant to deal with. Consequently many embedded processors, notably the Intel i960, do not provide virtual memory capability, and if other processors are used, this feature is often turned off for embedded real-time systems.

5.2.2 Big-Endian versus Little-Endian Ordering

When a value requires more than 1 byte in memory, the issue arises of the order of these bytes. There are two possible decisions. Suppose that the 4-byte value hexadecimal 12345678 is to be stored starting at address 1000, so the 4 bytes occupy addresses 1000 to 1003. Figure 5.4 shows the two possible orderings, which are called, respectively, big- and little-endian ordering, depending on whether the most or least significant byte is stored "first" (i.e., in the lowest address). There is no strong reason to prefer one order over the other. If you are used to writing left to right and consequently used to writing numbers with the most significant digit first, then the big-endian order seems more familiar, and that has caused some observers to characterize the little-endian choice as "backward." However, an Arab writing right to left and consequently writing numbers with the least significant digit first will have exactly the opposite predilection. In any case, the choice has no significant influence on the hardware.

What *is* significant is that different machines make different choices. In the big-endian camp, we find all IBM processors and the Motorola 680x0. In the little-endian camp are all Dec processors and the Intel 80x86. This causes severe difficulties in data interoper-

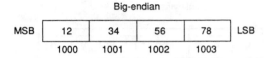

FIGURE 5.4 Big- and little-endian orderings of a 4-byte integer.

ability between machines where the endian choice is different. Some processors have been built so that the endianness of the processor can be changed, either at start-up time or even dynamically at execution time (the Intel i860 and the MIPS R4000 implement such dynamic switching). This increases the flexibility, but at the expense of significant extra complexity in the operating system. Another approach to the problem is found on the IBM RIOS processor which provides load and store instructions that switch the order of the bytes as they are transferred to or from memory.

A related problem arises in numbering the bits in a single word. In big-endian bit ordering, the most significant bit is called bit 0, and in little-endian bit ordering, the least significant bit is called bit 0. The bit-numbering convention is only a documentation issue on most RISC machines, since no instructions involve bit numbers, but on some CISC machines there are bit manipulation instructions which make this a hardware issue as well. Usually the choice for bit and byte ordering should be consistent, or else significant problems in addressing bit fields occur. An exception to this rule is the Motorola 68030, where the byte ordering is big-endian, the documentation uses little-endian bit ordering, and the bit instructions use sometimes one order and sometimes the other—a very confusing mess that results from ignoring the consistency rule.

5.2.3 Partial Word Accesses

From a logical point of view, memory is typically organized as a series of bytes, each with a unique address. A 32-bit word in memory occupies 4 consecutive bytes. However, at the hardware level, the memory is typically organized into words that contain several bytes. A typical organization for most RISC processors is that the memory is organized into 32-bit words (4 bytes per word). This means that at the memory level, the smallest unit of data that can be read or written is 32 bits.

At the instruction level, the issue is whether it is possible to read and write smaller units, in particular 8-bit bytes and 16-bit halfwords. For a read, this means obtaining the appropriate 32-bit word containing the data to be read and then discarding the unneeded bits. For a write, the process is a little more complex; the word must be read from memory, partially modified, and then written back. Despite this added complexity, even the RISC machines provide the capabilities for partial word access. One exception is the AMD29000, where only 32-bit words can be read and written and bytes must be extracted by using special instructions in the registers.

Although RISC machines limit partial word access to bytes and halfwords, there are CISC machines which go even further in this direction. Both the Motorola 680x0 and the

Load bytes 3 to 6

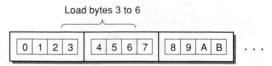

FIGURE 5.5   An unaligned access from memory.

Vax architectures permit general loading and storing of an arbitrary-sized bit string into or from a register. Interestingly these instructions are in some cases examples of excessive CISC complexity at work. If you look at the timings of these partial word instructions, you often find that it is quicker to do the operation ''manually,'' i.e., with a sequence of appropriate load, shift, and mask instructions, even on the CISC machine itself, and of course on a RISC machine the speed gain is even greater.

5.2.4 Alignment Requirements

Given a typical design in which memory is organized into 32-bit words, another issue that arises is whether *unaligned* accesses are allowed. Obviously it is easier to load a 32-bit word if the byte address corresponds to an actual word boundary in the memory. An unaligned access violates this rule. Figure 5.5 shows an example of an unaligned access. On many RISC processors such an access is disallowed, and either it causes an error trap or the lower-order bits are silently ignored (so that the ''wrong'' data are loaded). One difficulty with permitting such accesses is that a single load may cross cache boundaries or virtual page boundaries, complicating both the hardware and the software for managing caches and virtual memory.

Nevertheless, most CISC machines permit such unaligned access with a small time penalty, and among the RISC machines both the IBM RIOS and the HP Precision architectures provide support for unaligned accesses. This can be an important feature in commercial programming, since the Cobol language dictates that certain data will definitely be unaligned in practice. Fortran Common can also generate similar problems.

5.2.5 Segmented Addressing

Although most RISC machines provide a linear address space, in which the bytes in either physical or virtual memory can be seen as one long vector with increasing addresses, there are other possible arrangements. The most notable example is the segmented addressing of the original Intel 8086. This machine had 16-bit registers, so normal indexing and addressing were limited to 64K bytes. However, the machine allowed a maximum of 1 Mbyte to be addressed. This was achieved by the use of separate segment registers, designating a 64K region of memory to be addressed. In Fig. 5.6, we see that there are four segment registers (for code, stack, data, and extra data), and each of these registers can point to a separate 64K region. The program can thus address up to 256K at any one time. To address outside this region, segment registers must be modified. Instructions are available for doing this modification, but of course the process is significantly more complicated than just changing the value in an index register.

Since most modern processors are at least 32 bits, the need for segmentation is considerably reduced. The Intel 80386 is a 32-bit design which retains segmentation for compatibility with earlier designs, but now the segments are up to 4 Gbytes in length, so

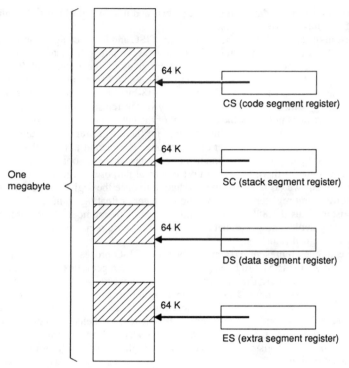

FIGURE 5.6   Segmentation on the Intel 8086.

the need for them from an addressing point of view has essentially gone away, although Intel has added a complex protection mechanism in which the segmentation continues to play a role. Among RISC processors, the RIOS provides a form of segmentation to increase the virtual address space from 32 to 52 bits (without increasing the register size). In the relatively near future, it seems likely that we will see many more 64-bit machines, and the residual utility of segmentation will essentially vanish.

5.3   REGISTER ORGANIZATION

An important characteristic of any processor is the configuration of the processor register set. Since memory references are relatively slow compared to operations in the registers, the performance of a processor will depend on the extent to which needed data can be held in the registers and operations carried out on register data, avoiding references to memory.

At the simplest level, it is clearly desirable to have a large number of registers, since this allows more data to be held in registers. In practice there is a tradeoff, because a large number of registers means that the instruction fields specifying register numbers increase in length. The other factor that is important is the uniformity of the register set. Ideally we prefer a set of *general registers* with the characteristic that any operation can be performed in any register. This uniformity eases the job of the compiler or human programmer in assigning data values to registers, and it avoids problems of conflict over the use of special-purpose registers.

The design of register sets is one point where CISC and RISC designs show significant differences. To compare two extremes, let's look at the integer register sets on the Intel 80386 and on the Motorola 88000 as representatives of the CISC and RISC design extremes. Figure 5.7 shows the register set of the 80386. There are two notable points. First, there are several distinct kinds of register (8-bit, 16-bit, and 32-bit registers and separate floating-point registers); second, many of the registers have special functions. Indeed the figure does not show the full extent of the latter phenomenon. If we look at the 80386 instruction set in detail, we find out that for the integer registers, there are no two registers which support the same set of operations. The second point is that the number of any particular kind of register is small. For example, there are only eight 32-bit integer registers, and some of them get taken up for special purposes (e.g., the stack pointer).

For the 88000, we do not even need a diagram, since the register set consists simply of 32 uniform 32-bit registers. Any operation, integer or floating-point, can be performed in any register. Thus the 88000 significantly increases the number of available registers and completely avoids the phenomenon of special-purpose registers and instructions tied to specially assigned registers.

These examples represent extremes. There are CISC processors with more uniform register sets (e.g., the IBM 370 has 16 general-purpose integer registers), and many RISC processors at least separate the integer and floating-point registers. Still the general rule is that RISC processors have a large number of uniform registers. The most common choice for the number is 32, since empirical research has shown that there is relatively little gain in going beyond this number, and 5-bit register fields are convenient in designing instruction sets. One interesting exception is the AMD29000 which has 256 registers, but the 8-bit register fields that result from this choice do limit the flexibility in instruction set design.

The reason that RISC processors take this approach to register set design is that if typical operations take one clock, then there is a much more severe mismatch between register operation speed and memory operation speed on RISC processors. This means it is relatively much more important to ensure that operands are in registers wherever possible, and indeed a large number of uniform registers are often cited as a fundamental characteristic of the RISC design approach. In any compiler, the allocation of registers is important, but in RISC compilers it becomes a critical aspect of code optimization, and many RISC compilers implement complex global optimization algorithms to ensure the best possible allocation of registers.

5.3.1 Length of Registers

The characterization of processors as 8-bit, 16-bit, 32-bit, and so on refers to a number of different characteristics, including the length of registers, the number of bits accessed from memory on the bus, the length of addresses, and the length of integer operations that can be performed. These three values do not always match; e.g., the Motorola 68000 has 32-bit registers, 16-bit access to memory, mixed 16- and 32-bit addressing, and mixed 16- or 32-bit limits on integer arithmetic length. Most current RISC machines are basically 32-bit processors, and consequently the integer registers are typically 32 bits, allowing 32-bit integer operations and 32-bit addressing.

Recently, we have seen processors where the width of accesses to memory has been increased (Intel i860 has a 64-bit memory path, and on the high-end models of the IBM RS6000 workstations 128-bit memory paths are implemented). The MIPS R4000 is a 64-bit design throughout (64-bit registers, 64-bit addressing, 64-bit integer operations,

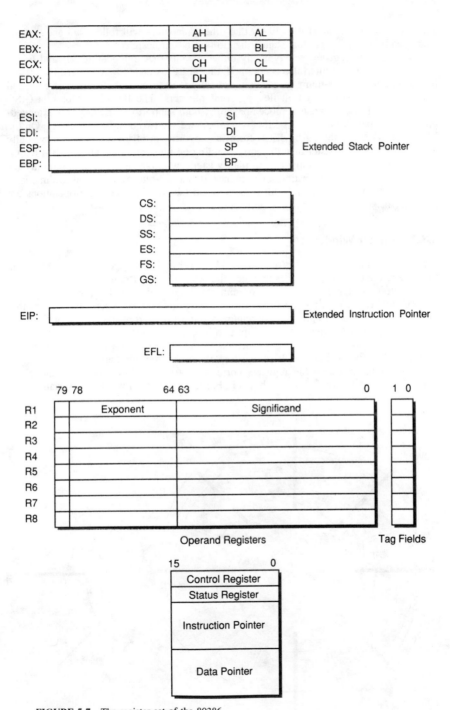

FIGURE 5.7 The register set of the 80386.

and 64-bit memory width). It is likely that other companies will follow suit and that the next decade will see a gradual standardization on 64-bit designs.

Floating-point registers are typically either 64 bits (accommodating 32- and 64-bit IEEE formats), or 80 bits (also accommodating IEEE extended precision). Since RISC machines aim for maximum speed, they typically tend to omit the support of extended precision and implement 64-bit floating-point registers. The Intel and Motorola CISC designs, which use separate coprocessor chips, both support the IEEE 80-bit extended-precision format. In the case of RISC machines, we see two design approaches. On the MIPS and SPARC, the 32-bit IEEE form is supported in all operations, and typically 32-bit operations are faster than the corresponding 64-bit operations. On the IBM RIOS, only the 64-bit format is supported in the registers, with the short format used only for memory storage. An interesting consequence is that 32-bit floating-point arithmetic is actually slightly slower than 64-bit arithmetic on the RIOS, since extra operations are required for storing 32-bit floating-point results.

5.3.2 Register Windows

Although most RISC processors only allow 32 integer registers to be addressed at any one time, there are design approaches in which the total number of registers is much greater. The simplest example is the provision of multiple sets of registers. One common approach is to provide two sets of registers, one for user state and one for supervisor state, so that the transition between states does not require register save and restore operations. This is particularly useful in improving interrupt performance.

A more extensive scheme is implemented on the SPARC processors, which typically provide 120 registers. Eight of these registers, the global registers, are always accessible. The remaining 24 accessible registers correspond to a window that slides along the remaining set of 112 registers. As shown in Fig. 5.8, the seven windows overlap so that

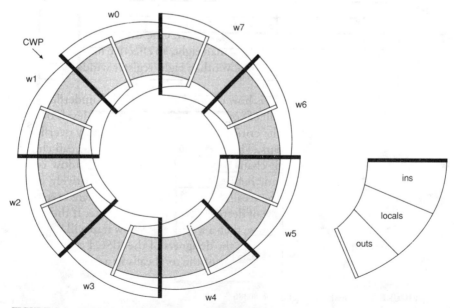

FIGURE 5.8 The register window organization of the SPARC.

adjacent windows have eight registers in common. Two instructions, SAVE and RE-STORE, allow the window to be moved in either direction. The idea is to do a SAVE on entry to a procedure and a RESTORE on exit. This provides a fresh set of registers for the new procedure without needing to explicitly save and restore registers. Only if all seven levels are in use (and the window pointer circles around on itself) does an interrupt occur, requiring the operating system to intervene and save registers. The overlapping registers between two adjacent windows can be used to pass parameters in registers and receive results.

How useful is the register window approach? This is a matter of energetic controversy. It seems clear that at least in some cases the window approach can save loads and restores. The counterargument is that a good optimizing compiler can in any case minimize the number of register saves and restores with a conventional design, and the implementation of register windows requires extra chip space (for the extra registers) and slows down execution (because of the slightly more complex access path to get at registers).

Relatively few microprocessors have implemented the windows approach. The only other commonly available chip with windows is the AMD29000, which has an even more complicated approach involving variable-length windows. It remains to be seen whether the improved efficiency resulting from the use of register windows justifies the additional complexity.

5.3.3 Condition Code Flags

Most, but not all, processors, both RISC and CISC, use condition code flags to indicate the result of arithmetic and comparison instructions. Typical flag sets include a *carry flag,* indicating whether an add causes a carry out; an *overflow flag,* indicating if a signed integer operation caused arithmetic overflow; a *sign flag,* indicating if the result of an arithmetic operation is negative; and a *zero flag,* indicating if the result of an operation is all 0 bits. A comparison instruction is typically a subtract instruction which sets these flags. Subsequent conditional branch instructions test these flags to implement the usual comparison conditions (greater than, less than, etc.).

One problem with this approach is that there is only one set of condition flags in many designs, meaning that it is not possible to interleave two sets of comparison operations. The IBM RIOS deals with this problem by providing eight separate sets of condition flags, with individual instructions specifying which set is to be used. The MIPS takes a completely different approach; the result of comparison instructions is placed in a general-purpose register, so that no specially dedicated flags are required.

5.4   INSTRUCTION SETS

The design of instruction formats and instruction sets is the point at which CISC and RISC designs most obviously diverge. Generally we expect CISC designs to have much larger instruction sets than RISC designs, and when it comes to instruction formats, we see an even more dramatic contrast. Figure 5.9 shows some of the 80386 instruction formats. It is, in fact, deceptively simplified in two respects. First, not all the specialized formats are shown. Second, the field labeled MODRM itself has eight separate formats, ranging in length from 1 to 6 bytes. Clearly there is not much attempt at uniformity in the instruction set design. If there is any design principle involved here, it is to make each instruction as short as possible by designing specialized formats optimized for each different style of instruction. In contrast to this complexity, Fig. 5.10 shows the *complete* set of instruction formats of the MIPS RISC design. There are very few distinct instruction formats, and all

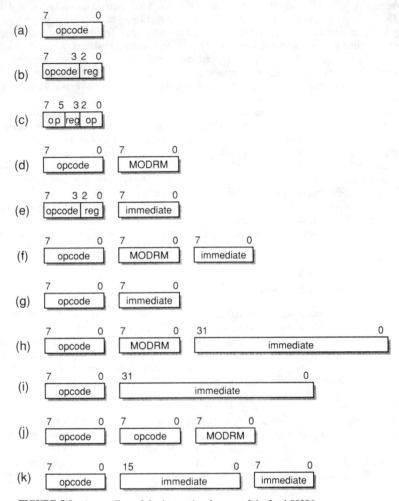

FIGURE 5.9 A sampling of the instruction formats of the Intel 80386.

instructions have the same length. It is this uniformity (rather than the raw count of numbers of instructions) that is one of the fundamental design characteristics of RISC processors.

5.4.1 Memory Reference and Addressing Modes

Memory reference instructions are a specific area where the differences between CISC and RISC designs are apparent. There are two important points of divergence. First, in RISC designs, the only instructions that reference memory are loads and stores, whereas typical CISC machines have much more extensive memory reference instructions (including,

I-Type Format (Immediate)

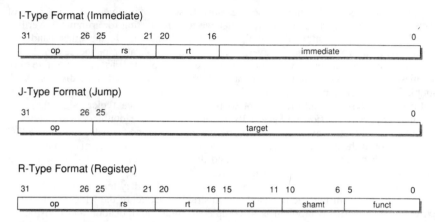

FIGURE 5.10   The instruction formats of the MIPS R4000.

e.g., arithmetic to and from memory and memory-to-memory move instructions). As we will see later, memory references are tricky in pipelined designs, so limiting their appearance simplifies the design of a pipeline.

Second, CISC machines tend to implement a large number of *addressing modes,* intended to simplify memory addressing. For example, on the 68030, if an array is passed by reference to a procedure, then a single instruction with a complex addressing mode can be used to locate the pointer to the array in the procedure's stack frame, load the pointer, multiply an index register by an appropriate scale factor, add the result to the pointer to obtain the address of the desired array element, and finally load the array element into a register. RISC machines avoid complex addressing modes and would need several instructions to access the array element of this example. On the 80386, the eight different MODRM formats relate to the provision of a complex set of addressing modes, whereas on the MIPS only the I-type format is used for memory addressing, and the only mode available is simple indexing with a 16-bit offset. The AMD 29000 carries this principle to extreme. The only addressing mode on this processor is register indirect, and even simple indexing with a short offset requires a sequence of two instructions.

One addressing mode typically present on CISC machines, and missing on RISC machines, is *direct addressing,* which allows a memory access instruction to reference an absolute location in memory. In RISC machines, this means that base registers must be established to access global data. However, this is not a severe problem, because there are plenty of registers available for this purpose and because often in modern operating system designs such indirect reference to global data is desirable in any case. In particular, if the operating system supports shared code modules, indirect addressing is typically necessary so that a given code module can operate on distinct sets of global data.

5.4.2 Integer Arithmetic Instructions

CISC and RISC processors typically provide a similar set of arithmetic operations, including integer addition, subtraction, multiplication, division, negation, and comparison. One issue is the handling of arithmetic overflow. Some machines provide automatic trapping on overflow, while others require explicit testing of flags. There is no particular CISC-RISC division here (the MIPS provides traps, but the RIOS does not, while the IBM

370 provides traps and the Intel 80386 does not). In some environments, the provision of traps is valuable. In particular, the Ada language requires testing for arithmetic overflow on all operations, so automatic trapping is highly desirable. On the other hand, the requirement for providing precise overflow traps can complicate pipeline design.

Multiplication and division operations pose special problems. First, it is useful to have double-length results on a multiplication and double-length dividends for a division. Such double-length operations are of critical importance in performing multiple-precision operations, and it seems unfortunate not to provide them, since typical algorithms for multiplication and division will naturally accommodate these double-length operands. However, providing them upsets the uniform nature of operand formats, and some RISC processors omit them for this reason. Since most high-level languages give no access to double-length operands for multiplication and division, this omission is less serious in environments where assembly language is avoided.

Another problem with multiplication and division is that they tend to be slow operations which do not fit into the one-clock-per-instruction model of the RISC pipeline. An extreme reaction to this problem is to completely omit multiplication and division instructions. The original SPARC design provides only a multiply step instruction (32 of which are needed to do a full 32-bit multiply) and has no support whatsoever for division (instead a software routine must be used). This approach is consistent with the general RISC philosophy of not providing complicated instructions for seldom-used functions, but it may be carrying this philosophy a little too far, and new SPARC designs include multiply and divide. In the case of the MIPS chip, the problem of multiplies and divides is dealt with by using special registers for the operands (a violation of the normal general register approach we expect on RISC machines).

5.4.3 Logical and Shift Instructions

Logical instructions typically include OR, NOT, AND, and XOR, although some machines have chosen slightly different sets of operations (the Dec Vax, e.g., implements NAND rather than AND). Shifts include rotations in either direction, logical shifts in either direction (in which 0 bits are introduced), and often, but not always, an arithmetic right shift which extends the sign. Note that the arithmetic shift is not quite the same as dividing by a power of 2, because the result for negative dividends may be 1 bit different (for example, -5 divided by 2 gives -2, but -5 arithmetically shifted right 1 bit gives -3 on a two's complement machine).

One important use of logical instructions is in constructing sequences of masking and shifting instructions for manipulating partial word quantities (such as appear in packed records in Pascal programs). Some processors (both RISC and CISC designs) provide additional specialized instructions to streamline this kind of processing. For example, the RIOS provides an instruction that can construct an arbitrary-length mask, arbitrarily positioned in a register, in a single instruction.

5.4.4 Branch Instructions

Branch instructions come in three basic varieties. *Unconditional jumps* simply specify a target address and unconditionally cause control to pass to the specified address. *Conditional jumps* test the outcome of some comparison or other condition to determine whether the branch should be taken. Finally, *counting jumps* use a counter to jump a fixed number of times (corresponding to the implementation of Fortran DO loops).

The jump target may be specified either within the instruction or (the case of an indirect jump) by use of a value in a register. In the case of a directly specified target, a common approach is to specify a relative displacement in the instruction, specifying the distance of the target from the jump instruction itself. This allows the common case of short jumps (i.e., jumps to a location nearby) to use a format with a relatively short offset.

5.4.5 Subroutine Call Instructions

The basic requirement for a subroutine call is to transfer control to another point in the program (the subroutine entry point) in a manner similar to a jump instruction and to save the return point so that a subsequent branch instruction can return to the call point. The simplest implementation is an instruction that stores the return point in either a standard or a designated register and a corresponding return instruction that uses the address stored in this register to return to the call point.

This simple approach is what is implemented in most RISC machines. However, in practice many other functions must be performed on a general procedure call, including saving and restoring registers, dealing with exception propagation, and arranging for up-level addressing of nested procedures. On RISC machines, these functions are expected to be handled by appropriate specialized code, but many CISC machines implement fancy CALL instructions that incorporate some of or all these auxiliary functions. For example, on the Vax, the CALLG (call general) instruction takes care of all these aspects of a call. One problem with this approach is that such fancy call instructions tend to be slow. The performance of programs on early Vax machines was significantly harmed by system conventions that required the use of CALLG for all calls, even when not all its fancy functions were needed.

Unlike jump instructions, which can reasonably be restricted to close-by targets, it is important for CALL instructions to be able to specify a wide range of addresses, meaning that it is desirable to have an instruction format that accommodates this wide range. An example of this approach is found on the SPARC, which has a special format for CALL instructions with a 2-bit opcode field and a 30-bit address field (enough to address all a 32-bit memory, given that the procedure address always has two low-order bits).

5.4.6 Floating-Point Instructions

The IEEE standard specifies a set of arithmetic operations that are to be supported, including not only the standard addition, subtraction, multiplication, and division operations but also specialized operations including square root, remainder, and conversion operations. However, it is specifically recognized in the standard that support of this set of operations may be achieved by a combination of hardware and software support.

A viable IEEE implementation must at least include fast hardware support for the basic arithmetic operations. Some CISC implementations extend the hardware support to cover all the defined IEEE operations (and even add a complete set of elementary trigonometric and logarithmic functions). However, most RISC implementations omit the specialized operations, leaving these to be done in software.

Another requirement of the IEEE standard is the full support of *denormal* numbers. These are very small values used in the implementation of gradual underflow. Again they may be supported in either hardware or software. Some RISC processors and all CISC IEEE processors fully support denormals at the hardware instruction level, but other RISC processors simply trap on encountering or generating denormal values, leaving the handling of denormals up to software trap routines. Since denormals are rarely encountered, this approach is consistent with the general RISC philosophy of supporting infrequently used operations in software.

5.4.7 System Control Instructions

All modern processor designs include the notion of separate user and system modes of operation (although the terminology varies). The idea is that a certain subset of operations should be restricted to the operating system in order to protect system integrity. Some kind of explicit trap instruction is provided to allow an application program (running in user mode) to make a transition into system mode by calling an operating system function with a specific request. The operating system will validate the parameters and then perform the requested operation, using privileged instructions where necessary.

On RISC processors, the set of privileged instructions is typically quite small, including only basic interrupt and I/O operations and operations for controlling the virtual memory mapping. CISC processors often implement much more extensive system-level capabilities. For example, the Intel 80386, which implements four levels of protection rather than the usual two, has a complete hardware implementation of multitasking, with an associated set of system control instructions for establishing and accessing the tasking control structures.

5.4.8 Specialized Instructions

In this category we see the most dramatic differences between the CISC and RISC design approaches. CISC machines have implemented all sorts of complex specialized instructions. The following is a small sampling, intended to give the flavor of the meaning of the first C (for complex) in CISC:

- The IBM 370 has an instruction *translate and test* (TRT) that scans a byte string, using an auxiliary table to categorize characters and search for a character with a specific characteristic (e.g., the first vowel in a string).

- The Motorola 68030 has an instruction *compare and exchange double* (CAS2) which can be used to remove an item from a doubly linked list as a protected atomic operation, including all necessary pointer updates.

- The Intel 80386 has an operation Enter Procedure (ENTER) that copies a multilevel display to implement up-level addressing for nested procedures in high-level programming languages and allocates the stack frame for the new procedure with a check for stack overflow.

Needless to say, these instructions do *not* take a single clock. Indeed, usually such instructions correspond to the execution of complex microprograms internal to the chip. One instruction on the 80386, the jump that automatically switches from one task to another, can take as long as 300 clocks. It is often the case that RISC machines, although they lack specific special function instructions of the kind we illustrate, can in fact perform the same functions much more rapidly with sequences of appropriate RISC instructions. Indeed, there is no particular reason to expect that a program of RISC instructions should execute any more slowly than a specialized microprogram on a CISC chip, and avoiding such microprogramming is one of the goals of the RISC design approach.

5.5 PIPELINING

The goal of the RISC design approach is to achieve a basic throughput of one instruction per clock. It is not, in fact, possible to construct a machine that will completely execute a single instruction in a single clock pulse, because too many sequential operations must be performed. To achieve the necessary throughput, the concept of pipelining is used. The basic idea is similar to an assembly line in a factory. A required operation (in this case the execution of a single instruction) is divided into a series of distinct steps. Each instruction passes through this sequence of steps, but the important point is that while one instruction is at a given step, the next instruction can follow along immediately behind. An individual instruction may take several steps (i.e., clock cycles), but one instruction is completing on every clock, so the throughput goal is achieved. Figure 5.11 shows the pipeline of the MIPS R2000. The five stages have the following basic functions:

1. The *instruction fetch* (IF) stage calculates the instruction address and loads the instruction.
2. The *read* (RD) stage reads any necessary register operands and performs initial instruction decoding.
3. The *arithmetic logic unit* (ALU) stage actually performs the requested operation.
4. The *memory* (MEM) stage performs memory accesses if any are required.
5. The *write-back* (WB) stage writes the result of the operation back to the appropriate result register.

One point at which our assembly-line analogy breaks down is that the successive instructions are not entirely independent. If an instruction requires the result of a previous instruction, it may have to wait for the result to be available. This is a particularly important factor in the case of floating-point pipelines, where the pipelines are typically longer since the operations to be performed are more complex.

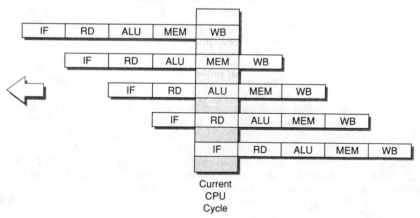

Current
CPU
Cycle

FIGURE 5.11 The five-stage pipeline of the MIPS R2000.

5.5.1 Dealing with Memory References

The pipeline model works smoothly if all operands and results are in registers, but memory references cannot be avoided entirely. When an operand is loaded from memory, there may be a significant delay in obtaining the necessary data (since memory units are slow compared to the basic processor cycle time, a single load can require several clocks to complete). Two approaches are commonly used to address this. One approach, typified by the original MIPS designs, is to simply stall the pipeline if a memory delay occurs. The other approach (implemented, e.g., on the IBM RIOS) is to mark the particular register being loaded as busy. In this case it is not necessary to stall the pipeline unless and until a subsequent instruction needs the data in this particular register before they are available.

Store instructions pose less of a problem since the store operation can overlap subsequent operations. The one tricky point is that it is important that any subsequent load operations which address the same location get the newly stored result and not what was there before. This can be achieved by extra logic which ensures that a load looks at the pending stores before going to memory. However, a simpler approach is to delay stores to make sure they are complete before proceeding. The initial SPARC implementations took this approach (and consequently stores on these processors could take up to 3 clocks). This compromise is not as serious as it might sound, since stores are much less frequent than loads.

5.5.2 Dealing with Jump Instructions

Another source of embarrassment to the pipeline model is the occurrence of jump instructions. The problem with a jump is that the following instruction may not be the sequentially next instruction; but by the time this is discovered, it is too late—the next instruction has already been loaded and is steaming on through the pipeline.

The usual approach for solving this problem is to implement *jump delay slots*. A jump instruction is always followed by an instruction which will be unconditionally executed whether or not the jump occurs. This means that the logical sequence of the program is not strictly sequential, since from the programmer's point of view the order of execution is the instruction *before* the jump, followed by the instruction *after* the jump, followed by the jump itself. On the Clipper C400, there are two jump delay slots, so this effect is even more pronounced. The delay slot approach allows the pipeline to proceed unimpeded on jump instructions, since the next instruction can now follow on through the pipeline unconditionally, and the jump gets recognized and interpreted early enough to ensure that the subsequent instructions come from the right place.

5.5.3 Programming Considerations

The pipelining approach involves instruction-level concurrency at execution time. To varying degrees this concurrency is visible to a programmer. At the very least, the ordering of instructions can have very significant effects on performance. An important consideration on RISC machines is understanding the situations which will cause the pipeline to be held up and avoiding them by reordering instructions. Compilers for RISC machines typically have a phase called the *scheduling phase* which shuffles instructions (being careful to preserve the intended meaning) in a manner that optimizes performance of the pipeline. This can be quite a complicated task and is better left up to compilers than done by hand.

On some processors, notably the Intel i860, the visible concurrency from the pipelining is even more extensive. On the i860, a floating-point add instruction has two input registers and one output register, which is typical. What is *not* typical is that the input registers feed the starting stage of a three-stage pipeline, and the output register gets its value from the output of the last stage of this pipeline. This means that the result of a floating-point add instruction corresponds to the inputs fed into the floating-point add issued three adds before. Although this approach facilitates the efficient control of multiple parallel pipelines, it greatly complicates the programming task. It remains to be seen whether compilers can manage to generate efficient code for this complex architecture.

Another important aspect, from the programmer's view, involves register management. Since loads potentially disrupt the pipeline, it is important to keep data in registers as much as possible. Allocating a large set of registers is another task best performed by an optimizing compiler. The RISC design approach, which depends heavily on optimizing the performance of the pipeline, typically depends on optimizing compilers, and it is no accident that companies that have produced RISC designs have also invested heavily in the development of technology for optimizing compilers.

5.5.4 Pipelining CISC Processors

Keeping the pipeline flowing is the main goal of a pipelined design. If we look at the main characteristics we associate with RISC, we see that they are all oriented to this goal.

- The large number of registers allows the minimization of memory loads, since more operands can be maintained in registers.
- The uniform instruction formats simplify the job of early pipeline stages, which must quickly complete instruction decoding.
- The fixed-length instructions mean that instruction fetch is simplified, since you can fetch an instruction without knowing anything about it, something that is certainly not practical with CISC designs, where the instruction length can vary widely.

Nevertheless, CISC manufacturers have recently shown that RISC-style pipelining techniques can be applied to CISC architectures to substantially increase performance. Notable examples of this approach are the Intel 80486 and the 68040 which are heavily pipelined versions of their precursors (the 80386 and 68030). Interestingly, these processors maintain complete compatibility with previous chips, including all the complicated, variable-length instruction formats and the complicated addressing modes.

Despite these impediments, a high degree of success seems to have been achieved. If we look at the 80486, most common operations take a single clock, including load instructions (as long as the data are found in the cache). There are some unsolved problems. In particular, jumps take 3 clocks, since there are no jump slots (remember that complete compatibility with previous nonpipelined designs is required), and there are still far too few registers. Still, the overall performance is quite impressive and rivals that of RISC chips operating at the same clock speed. Intel promises still faster implementations of this CISC design in the future, and it will be interesting to see how well they can keep up with the purer RISC approaches in the future.

5.6 CACHES

As we have described, loads from memory are a potential menace to the goal of keeping the pipeline flowing. If every memory fetch had to be done from main memory, then the pipeline approach would fail completely, because every instruction load would incur a long delay. To solve this problem, a crucial design element is the implementation of *caches,* which are high-speed secondary memories built from fast expensive technology (typically fast static RAM chips) that can keep up with the fast clock time of the processor. The cache attempts to keep the most recently referenced data around, so that most memory references can be satisfied from the cache and only relatively rarely will the full penalty of a real memory access be incurred. If the cache is large enough (the most recent RISC designs can accommodate caches of several megabytes), then in practice this goal can usually be achieved, although there are certain ill-behaved programs, e.g., ones that chase pointers around in memory, that have much more frequent cache misses.

As long as the data for a load are found in the cache, the operation of the pipeline can continue unimpeded. For example, on the MIPS, there is a rule that a program may not access loaded data in the immediately following instruction. Given this rule, as long as a load is satisfied from the cache, the MIPS pipeline keeps going. If a cache miss occurs, either for fetching an instruction or for fetching loaded data, then the pipeline *does* stall, but the hope is that this is an infrequent occurrence.

In practice, cache performance can be a crucial factor in the performance of algorithms, particularly numerical algorithms which involve calculations on large arrays. Take matrix multiplication of large arrays as an example. A naive approach has an inner loop that crosses an entire column of one array and an entire row of another array. If the arrays are too large to fit in the cache, practically every memory reference in this inner loop will involve a cache miss, and the performance can be a substantial factor less than what might be expected from a one-instruction-per-clock assumption. To approach this problem efficiently, entirely different algorithms should be used which do the multiplication of the matrices in sections, where each section is small enough to fit entirely into the cache.

Paying Attention to Caching in Compilers.   Generally it is hard for compilers to deal effectively with the caching problem. We certainly cannot expect compilers to generally recognize inefficient algorithms and replace them with algorithms that are more efficient in the use of caches. For one thing, a compiler often cannot tell how large an array is, since the dimensions may be symbolic at run time.

However, in some cases, compiler techniques have been developed which allow huge efficiency increases due to better use of caches. An interesting example is found in the Matrix 300 component of the Spec benchmark suite, commonly used for assessing the performance of engineering workstations. Executed naively, this test, which involves operations on large matrices, is very unfavorable from the point of view of cache performance. However, a special preprocessing transformation on the Fortran code yields an equivalent program that is much more efficient—so much more efficient that the overall performance rating of a system is substantially affected (one might almost say distorted) by this one optimization. How generally useful such transformations are in practice remains to be seen.

5.7 INTERRUPTS AND EXCEPTIONS

All modern processors have hardware support for interrupts and traps. This includes a mechanism (usually available only in supervisor state) to control whether individual hardware interrupts are recognized. When an interrupt (from an external device) or an exception (from an error condition during execution of some instruction) occurs, the usual action is to save a minimal component of the machine state and transfer control to an operating system routine. This routine is then responsible for saving any additional state information and servicing the interrupt or trap in an appropriate manner (using supervisor-state-only instructions where needed).

The particular mechanisms provided vary from one processor to another. On most RISC processors, the actions performed by the hardware are minimal, and the work is left up to operating system software routines. CISC processors often have much more complex mechanisms, and in the case of IBM mainframes, there are completely separate processors, called *I/O channels,* which perform most of the complex operations involved in servicing I/O operations entirely independently of the main processor.

5.8 INCREASING INSTRUCTION THROUGHPUT

A processor built around the pipeline model we have described cannot exceed a throughput of one instruction per clock, since the instruction decoding step acts as a bottleneck. In this section we look at some techniques for pushing beyond this barrier.

5.8.1 Very-Long-Instruction-Word (VLIW) Approach

The idea here is to increase the instruction length so that it has room to specify more than one operation. The operations in a single long instruction are then interpreted by hardware operating in parallel. An example of this approach was pioneered by the Multiflow Company which designed a machine with a 242-bit word, long enough to hold seven 32-bit Vax-type instructions. Assuming that useful work can be found for each of the seven component instructions, then clearly the throughput could approach the equivalent of seven instructions per clock. In practice, it is not so easy to find the seven instructions, given the requirement that they be completely independent. Multiflow devised a special compilation approach, called *trace compilation,* that attempted to maximize the degree of parallelization by looking forward past conditional branch points. After all, it is better to execute both branches of a conditional if you have nothing better to do. At least when you finally find out which way the conditional branch goes, you have done some of the necessary work in advance. In this approach, an example of *speculative execution,* you have to ensure that the instructions executed in the "wrong" branch can be undone. For example, no stores to permanent memory can be performed until the outcome is determined.

Among current processors in production, one that at least partially qualifies as a VLIW machine is the Intel i860. This processor has a mode, called *dual-instruction mode,* which can be switched on and off under program control. In this mode, the processor executes 64-bit instructions which contain one integer operation and one floating-point operation (i.e., two separate 32-bit instructions can be executed on each clock). Interestingly, Intel purchased the rights to the trace compiler when Multiflow closed its doors, so this interesting compilation technology may see further use.

5.8.2 Superscalar Approach

A related approach attempts to obtain the same effect (simultaneous dispatch of separate instructions) but with the dispatch control being done on the fly, so that no special compilation techniques are required. An important example of this approach is represented by the RIOS processor used in the IBM RISC-System 6000 workstations. Figure 5.12 shows the logical organization of the RIOS. There are three separate functional units. The branch unit reads instructions in 128-bit chunks (four instructions per clock) and categorizes them into integer instructions [which are queued for the *arithmetic-logic unit*

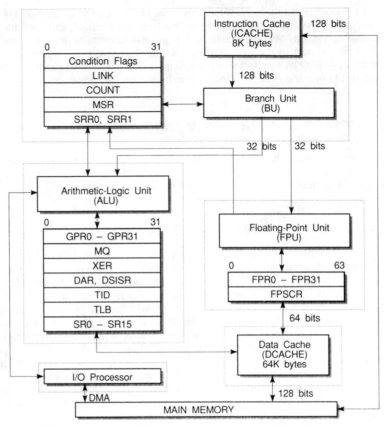

FIGURE 5.12   The RIOS architecture.

(ALU)], floating-point instructions [which are queued for the *floating-point unit* (FPU)], and branch instructions, which it handles internally. In the case of unconditional jumps, the branch unit can immediately determine where to get subsequent instructions, and the ALU and FPU pipelines are not disturbed. For conditional jumps, an assumption is made that the jump is not taken. A jump taken incurs up to 3 clocks (6 clocks for the floating-point case) of extra delay. However, a special form of count loop jump, suitable for implementing Fortran-type DO loops, is handled internally in the branch unit (as shown, the COUNT register is internal to this unit) and does not incur any penalty. An interesting consequence of this design is that it is *not* necessary to implement the usual RISC jump delay slot approach—instructions are logically executed in strict sequence.

While the branch unit is interpreting the instruction stream, the ALU and FPU can steam ahead, using independent pipelines, executing instructions from the queues built by the branch unit. Given a favorable mix of instructions (evenly divided between ALU, FPU, and branch instructions), the throughput on the RIOS can approach three instructions per clock. Actually there is a fourth category of instruction, which manipulates the flags, which can also be overlapped, so carefully constructed examples can achieve four clocks per instruction. In practice, the mix is not so favorable. Still, observed instruction execution frequencies of about two instructions per clock are frequently observed in real code.

Theoretically, additional ALU and FPU units could be added to this design to increase the potential parallelism. However, in practice, the inability to schedule past conditional jumps would limit the improvement obtained. Suggestions have been made for implementing speculative execution at the hardware level that might help to get past this limitation, but no standard microprocessors implement this approach.

5.8.3 Superpipelining

Strictly speaking, this subject does not belong here, because we said that we would be talking about methods for achieving more than one instruction per clock. Superpipelining attacks the other half of this equation, by attempting to reduce the clock period. Since we are really interested in the instruction throughput in instructions per second, this has the potential of being equally helpful.

The idea behind superpipelining is to increase the number of pipeline stages so that less work needs to be done on each stage. This should permit the use of higher clock speeds, since obviously there is a relation between the maximum clock speed and the amount of work that has to be done on each clock cycle. The exact definition of what constitutes a superpipeline is a matter of controversy. One definition is that the actual operation phase of the pipeline occupies more than one stage. By this definition, most floating-point processors are superpipelined, since it is impractical to carry out an operation such as a floating-point addition in a single clock, and typical designs use two or three clocks for operations of this type. Some observers have suggested that superpipelining is not a well-defined concept and that it is more of an advertising term than a definite technical characteristic. Still, the basic idea that increasing the pipeline length can lead to a shorter clock period is reasonable, and the choice of the pipeline length is clearly an important design parameter.

The most significant use of this approach is found in the recently delivered MIPS R4000 processor. This processor extends the integer pipeline to eight stages (previous versions had only five stages). What MIPS has done is to double most of the pipeline stages. For example, the cache fetch operations are now spread out over two pipeline stages (and hence two clocks), allowing a smoother match between fast processors and relatively slower caches. This may be quite important in practice, since the speed of caches is often a limiting factor in how much the clock speed can be scaled up. In the R4000, the clock period is doubled internally, so a nominal 50-MHz chip is operating its superpipeline at 100 MHz. MIPS is the first company to deliver a production microprocessor chip running this rapidly (the fastest comparable chip from the competition was running at 66 MHz at the time of the MIPS announcement), so the claim that extending the pipeline can shorten the clock period seems credible. Time will tell whether MIPS retains this speed advantage over the competition.

MIPS observes in its advertising literature that superpipelining of degree 2 (i.e., a doubling of the clock speed) has the same speed-up effect as superscalar dispatching where two instructions are dispatched on each clock. Of course, there is nothing to stop both approaches being used at the same time, and it is likely that the future will bring a number of designs that are both superpipelined and superscalar. Of course, the ultimate speedup will still be limited by the amount of parallelism that can be extracted from the code.

5.9 MULTIPROCESSING

We have looked at a number of techniques for speeding up the performance of a single processor, but these techniques are ultimately limited by fabrication technology and by the inherent microparallelism of the code. An entirely different approach is to simply increase the number of processors.

From a simpleminded point of view, it seems possible for a machine with a thousand processors to run a thousand times faster than a machine with one processor. In practice, there are difficult problems in achieving substantial speedups. First, we have *Amdahl's law,* which observes that the speedup is limited by the inherent parallelism of the task. If half the time for a given computation is spent on serial code that is not susceptible to parallelization, then no increase in the number of processors can do better than speed up the program by a factor of 2. In practice, it is often possible to restructure a computation so that more can be done in parallel. In some cases this involves using what appear to be less efficient algorithms, in that the total number of operations is increased, but ones which are more susceptible to parallelization.

The second major problem involves working out how to hook up massive numbers of processors. For a small number of processors, up to perhaps 16, all processors can be attached to a common bus, so that any processor can communicate with any other processor directly. However, this does not scale up, since the use of a single bus would result in a bottleneck for bus communications. Instead various communication networks have been designed so that communication is possible, though not necessarily direct, without bottlenecks. One popular arrangement of this kind is the *hypercube.* Figure 5.13 shows a hypercube arrangement of degree 4, in which 16 processors are attached together. In this design, a message can be sent from one processor to any other in no more than four steps. In general, the maximum number of steps is the logarithm to the base 2 of the number of

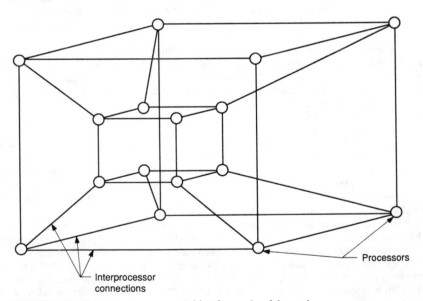

FIGURE 5.13   Sixteen processors arranged in a hypercube of degree 4.

processors. This scales up in quite a manageable manner. For example, a hypercube of degree 10 has 1024 processors and no more than 10 communication steps. Assuming that each communication step takes 2 clocks, the total time for an interprocessor access, 20 clocks, compares reasonably favorably with the time to access main memory. An interesting processor in this connection is the INMOS Transputer, which is distinguished by having four very high-speed communication channels on the processor chip, specially intended for connections of this type. Not surprisingly, the Transputer has found its most popular applications in multiprocessor machines.

Many different designs have been proposed for multiprocessor systems. One important division is between SIMD (single-instruction multiple-data) and MIMD (multiple-instruction multiple-data) machines. SIMD machines execute the same operation on separate data. For example, in a single clock, a SIMD machine might add two matrices, with each processor executing the same add instruction, but on separate elements of the matrix. In a MIMD machine, the separate processors execute separate instructions simultaneously. A MIMD machine is essentially executing multiple separate programs, although in practice these executions will be tightly linked together as the processors cooperate to solve a single problem.

Another important division is shared-memory machines versus local memory machines. In a shared-memory machine, the processors share a single memory, at least from a logical point of view (in practice, access to this shared memory must also use a complex communication network). Local memory machines have a separate memory for each processor, so access to some other processor's memory is achieved by explicit message passing. Shared-memory machines are harder to design, but tend to be easier to program. Of course, hybrid designs with some shared memory and some local memory are also possible.

Despite the formidable hardware and software problems posed by highly parallel multiprocessors, there is a gathering consensus that this direction is the one that makes sense for the future of extremely high-performance computers. An interesting article appeared in November 1991 in *The New York Times,* describing the latest supercomputer released by Cray, which is a 16-processor design. This article commented that Cray indicated that future Cray supercomputers would be of the very highly parallel variety with a large number of processors. Many other companies, including Intel and Thinking Machines, had been manufacturing highly parallel machines before this, but Cray had been seen as a holdout for the approach with a smaller number of very powerful processors. The fact that Cray is indicating a change of direction in such a public forum is highly significant.

5.10 SUMMARY

Some 10 years ago, it seemed as if innovation in computer architecture were slowing down. Some observers expected a world in which only a very small number of processor designs—the IBM 370, the Vax, the Intel 80x86, and perhaps one or two others—would survive.

For a number of reasons, this prediction has turned out to be completely false. The RISC revolution has made it worthwhile to investigate completely new architectural approaches. Furthermore, the development of VLSI technology has made it practical to design processors with a much smaller investment than was once required. An interesting example of this effect in practice can be found in the Intergraph company, which is primarily a manufacturer of packaged application systems. Intergraph maintains a small division, Intergraph APD, involving less than 3 percent of its workforce, which designs its own unique RISC processor for its own workstations. Ten years ago, it would have been unimaginable that such an approach could make economic sense.

At the same time, an important development is the increasing importance of *open systems,* which stress the use of portable programming techniques, allowing software to be moved from one processor to another with a minimal amount of work. For many users buying Unix workstations, the processor chip used is not nearly so important an issue as the software support and the basic level of performance.

These developments have combined to produce an environment in which new processor designs flourish. At some point, there will presumably be a shakeout in the market which will reduce the number of viable designs, but we have not seen much sign of this happening yet, and it is likely that the next decade will produce a number of interesting and innovative designs.

CHAPTER 6
RELIABILITY OF DIGITAL SYSTEMS

Arden R. Helland

Westinghouse Electric Corporation, Baltimore, Maryland

Reliability is a significant indication of the quality and usefulness of a system to those expecting to benefit from its application. Product quality provides customer satisfaction, which is the foundation for business success, employment security, and job satisfaction. Basic reliability concepts are described in this chapter with a concurrent design engineering perspective.

6.1 RELIABILITY DEFINITIONS

Reliability is the characteristic of being useful and dependable, especially when needed. The meaning may depend on the application; a user may consider a product reliable if it consistently achieves a desired objective. Product quality may include more than the description of reliability as a measure of the absence of failures. A product may be considered unreliable if it is not suited to the application, or if it is difficult to maintain. A product may be unavailable because it is waiting for maintenance—or idle if the user perceives that it is likely to require difficult maintenance.

Reliability usually refers to the ability of a product to operate in accordance with some description of "proper performance." Failures can be categorized according to several levels, from a negligible reduction in performance capability to permanent loss of all operation. It is convenient to divide failures into two categories: permanent and temporary. A permanent failure is an irreversible loss of performance capability; it is typically caused by changes in physical properties of materials. Temporary failures may be intermittent, or proper operation may be restored under less rigorous operating conditions.

6.1.1 Examples

Examples of permanent failures include dielectric breakdown (short circuits), corrosion of dissimilar metals, discontinuity of connections (open circuits), or a degradation in electrical properties (gain, threshold, leakage) that results in permanent malfunction. These failures remain after the initial occurrence; successful diagnosis is likely. Records of failure diagnosis typically include photographs or samples of the failure.

In contrast, temporary failures cause a malfunction only under some conditions. The causes of temporary failures may include some that also cause permanent failures. The conditions under which malfunction may occur are usually considered more severe than those for proper operation. Some examples of temporary failures include intermittent connections which open (or short-circuit), degradation in electrical properties, and inadequate design. Inadequate design includes incompatibility of replacement parts that are intended to be interchangeable, but may not be compatible under all conditions. Malfunction under severe operating conditions is often a result of inadequate testing which did not detect deficiencies in design, parts, or process controls.

6.1.2 Environmental Conditions

The conditions in which the product operates are usually referred to as the *environment*. Severe environmental conditions such as mechanical, electrical, or thermal limits of performance capability are considered environmental stresses. Some environmental stresses may cause immediate, but reversible, effects to operating performance. Exposure to some environmental stress may result in long-term reduction of performance capability. This is referred to as *degradation* and may eventually result in the lack of proper performance capability during the use of a product. The utility of a product generally deteriorates with use and age. It is highly unusual for defective parts to return to entirely proper operation without some corrective action.

Few products improve with the aging processes (the formation of diamonds and pearls is noteworthy, but sand does not naturally become computer chips). In most cases where aging actually improves products, it should be included in the production process so that the useful operating life begins with the best product. Although the apparent effect is similar, stress screening and early-life operation to remove "infant mortality" latent defects or to correct design defects are not examples of improvement with age. The distinction is that the original defects did not improve; the modified product has a lower proportion of defects after corrections which tend to improve future reliability. Similarly, if design and/or process improvements are incorporated into newly produced products to prevent defects, the observed reliability of the entire group of otherwise equivalent products should improve as the proportion of improved products increases. The population of products may improve, but it is not normal for the elements in it to improve with age.

Examples of mechanical stress include acceleration, shock, and vibration. Cracks, corrosion, and metal fatigue are examples of long-term degradation of mechanical performance capability. Examples of electrical stress include voltage, frequency, and data patterns. Thermal stress includes temperature extremes and thermal cycling (fast rates of temperature change are called *thermal shock*). Thermal stress may cause mechanical stress due to expansion and contraction of different materials. Temperature is one of the environmental conditions that tends to affect many semiconductor performance parameters.

6.2 THE ARRHENIUS PRINCIPLE

Thermal conditions influence the rate at which components degrade. The exponential model predicts the failure rate as a function of temperature. A general equation which expresses the relationship of the failure rate F to temperature T is

$$F = Ae^{-B/T} \tag{6.1}$$

Here A is a scaling constant that is considered to be independent of temperature, B is a physical constant, T is absolute temperature, and e is the base for natural logarithms (approximately 2.718). The scaling constant B is generally considered to be the ratio of activation energy (in electronvolts) to Boltzmann's constant when this equation is applied to semiconductors. The activation energies in semiconductors are typically within an order of magnitude of 1 electronvolt (eV). An equation of the form of (6.1) is called the *Arrhenius principle*. It is named for Svante Arrhenius, a Swedish physical chemist who advanced the theory of activation energy in 1889.

A significant result of the Arrhenius principle is that the failure rate is sensitive to temperature. This can be used to advantage in several ways. When failures are undesired, reducing the temperature will increase the time before failure is likely to occur. Increasing temperature will reduce the time to failure.

6.2.1 Defect Acceleration

Latent defects may degrade more rapidly than failures occur in normal parts. A short exposure to temperatures significantly more severe than normal operation may accelerate any latent defects so they become observable faults. Exposure to thermal stress is often called *burn-in,* and may be a part of *environmental stress screening* (ESS). Once a failure is observed, corrective action can be taken to improve reliability at normal operating temperatures. One basic form of corrective action is to subject all parts and/or products to appropriate ESS for a short time. Failures are scrapped or reworked before delivery to the user. ESS improves reliability because latent defects can be removed without significantly affecting the useful life of the surviving parts. This is sometimes referred to as moving the early-life failures from the field back to the factory; ESS is effective because the equivalent of the early-life operation is conducted during accelerated testing before product delivery.

> ESS is a process using greater than operational stress to stimulate latent defects. ESS applied to digital systems includes mechanical, thermal, and electrical aspects.

A more cost-effective corrective action than simply scrapping defective parts may be to determine the original cause of the defect and to prevent such defects in future products. It is even more effective to require new designs to survive severe ESS before release to production. Design derating and process controls can achieve robust designs that tolerate ESS for a short time, can be brought to market quickly, can be produced at low cost, and can operate for a long service lifetime without failure.

6.2.2 Accelerated Life Test

The Arrhenius principle is useful in reducing the time to estimate the failure rate of new products. A conventional life test method is to observe parts for degradation at maximum rated conditions. There are serious disadvantages to this method, including the number of parts and the time required before statistically valid results are available. Furthermore, such results are likely to include the early-life latent defect rates in addition to the rates applicable to useful life. If the test temperature is raised beyond operating temperatures, the time to obtain results is accelerated. Results may be obtained at different temperatures to estimate the constants in the Arrhenius equation. Significant acceleration may be obtained with reasonable increases in temperature. Statistically valid data may be obtained with minimum resources (including time) expended.

6.2.3 Performance Margin

A significant conclusion from the Arrhenius principle is that the time before a failure occurs is a function of the amount of degradation that can be tolerated. In this case, A in Eq. (6.1) is a scaled constant that is normalized to the amount of degradation that can be tolerated. The difference between actual capability and required performance is the performance margin. The actual failure rate of a product is inversely proportional to the performance margin. A product that has a high performance margin can continue to operate correctly, despite some degradation of component capability and/or more severe environmental conditions. A product designed only for worst-case conditions and operated near its performance capability may fail when any degradation or slightly worse operating condition occurs.

6.2.4 Design Margin

The design margin determines the performance characteristics of the design. Design derating requires the design to be capable of performance that exceeds the worst-case operating requirements by a minimum amount. For example, a design may be capable of performing properly at a semiconductor junction temperature of up to 150°C, but the application results in a maximum of 120°C in actual use. For this case, it would be described as thermally derated to 80 percent of maximum temperature (in degrees Celsius), or that it has 20 percent or 30°C of thermal design margin.

It is reasonable to achieve a significant reduction in the failure rate by increasing the performance margin. Much greater improvement factors can often be achieved with increased performance margin than is practical with reduced absolute temperature. The influence of the performance margin would be more apparent if the constant A in Eq. (6.1) were divided by the performance margin, so that $A' = A/(100 - D)$, where D is the derating in percent. The design margin sets the upper limit on capability, which limits the nature and strength of the ESS that can be used to verify performance capability, which determines reliability during service lifetime. Superior products have a greater design margin; they cost less to produce and provide greater satisfaction to the user. Guidelines for design and production of superior products should include the following:

1. Design standards for derating, verification, test, producibility, reliability, and maintainability
2. Design process controls to ensure timely, effective, and efficient product designs
3. ESS during product development to verify performance margin capability or identify corrections for any design weakness
4. Accelerated life test to identify reliability limits
5. ESS and process control during production to deliver high product quality
6. ESS during use to maintain high operating reliability
7. Corrective action and product warranty to eliminate defects and provide continuous product improvement

6.2.5 ESS for Margin Verification

Even though there is an intention to design a product to a minimum design margin, there is little confidence that the margin exists unless the actual performance margin is verified. In addition, high reliability may be difficult to maintain unless the actual margin can be verified (and restored if necessary). ESS is a test that can verify that minimum design margins are present. All the stress parameters should be increased beyond the worst operating levels until they represent the minimum design capability, or at least the derating requirement. Proper operation indicates that the design margins have been achieved.

It may be difficult to directly stimulate some types of stress parameters (e.g., fan-out and noise margin in digital systems) in operation. It is usually reasonable to stimulate other stresses that infer performance margins. For example, capacitance (or ac) fan-out affects the frequency capability of synchronous digital systems; increasing the clock frequency infers the fan-out margin on critical paths. Similarly, varying the dc power supply voltage affects system performance, so it is a convenient method to infer margin in several areas, including noise margin, fan-out, frequency, and temperature.

6.3 THE POISSON MODEL

The occurrence of failures is a statistical event if it cannot be predicted with certainty. The preceding descriptions of failure rates should be considered as averages that might be observed over a very large number of opportunities, but subject to uncertainty. Although the statistical model is based on an average rate, estimation of failure rates is also subject to uncertainty. Include a generous allowance for uncertainty when you are predicting performance. Changes in the underlying causes of failures may alter the results. For an example from the preceding description, a change in the average temperature will shift the failure rate. A change in a production process may shift the average product performance capability and defect rate.

A common statistical model for the chance of the occurrence of n discrete events with respect to an interval in which the events may occur is as follows:

$$P(n) = C(n)e^{-Fu} \qquad (6.2)$$

This function is called the *Poisson distribution,* after its discoverer. In this equation, $P(n)$ is the probability of n occurrences, $C(n)$ is a scaling factor that varies with the number of occurrences, F is the failure rate, u is the unit of measure, and e is the base for natural logarithms. The product Fu is a ratio that defines the average number of expected events, so e^{-Fu} is a characteristic of the distribution that depends only on the average rate. The factor $C(n) = (Fu)^n/n!$ for any nonnegative n. However, $n = 0$ is the case of interest when success or failure is defined by the absence of an event. Since $C(0) = 1$, the constant of unity is usually omitted in consideration of only the probability of 0 events.

The unit of measure is whatever provides the opportunity for events to occur. For events occurring over time, any convenient unit of time such as hours, years, or million hours may be used. If the events occur over physical space, then distance, area, or volume is the appropriate unit of measure. For example, events may be traffic fatalities per million kilometers of travel or defects per square centimeter of a semiconductor wafer. For many cases the unit of measure is simply the parts count itself; F is the proportion of parts in which the event occurs. Then Fu is the average number of defects in a group of u single units. For example, a group may be a production lot of identical parts, die from a semiconductor wafer, or an assembly containing components. If the group consists of different part types, the individual defect rates for each type are added for a total average number of defects.

6.3.1 Addition of Defect Rates

Applying Eq. (6.2) to the sum of the defect rates is equivalent to the product of the probabilities that each individual unit does not fail. The exponential model is convenient to use because the defect or failure rates are simply added when parts and/or production processes are combined. Addition of small numbers is more convenient (and accurate) than multiplication of numbers close to unity. This may be simplified when the total average number of defects is much less than unity, so the chance of any defects is simply Fu.

Equation (6.2) is applied to a variety of discrete events that occur randomly at some reasonably consistent rate if averaged over a large number of events. Some examples include the chance of failures in electronic equipment as a function of the number of parts and operating time, the chance of a defective production part, and the chance that a test fails to detect a random defect. The Poisson distribution is widely applied to arrivals at points of service as well as the time to complete a service. Queues, or waiting lines, result from statistical relationships between the service rate and arrival rate.

6.3.2 Normal Limit of the Poisson Model

The Poisson model is equivalent to the discrete binomial distribution, or the familiar "normal" distribution if the average number of events is large. The normal distribution is a symmetric continuous distribution with the bell-shaped curve which predicts results with equal probability above and below the average. However, it is not applicable to the analysis of high-quality products because the chance of failures must be very low. The Poisson and binomial models both tend to approximate the normal when more than several events are expected. The standard deviation for the Poisson model is the square root of the mean, so when the expected number of events is 1, the mean, variance, and standard deviation are all unity.

6.4 DESIGN AND PRODUCTION QUALITY

The preceding sections considered models for which the degradation rate, failure rate, and defect rate are essentially interchangeable according to the application. This section is concerned primarily with the production issues of defect rates, production yields, test effectiveness, and how these relate to production costs and defects that escape to the user. It is important for the entire production team, including initial design, test, and manufacturing, to establish a total-quality attitude that strives continuously to drive all defect rates toward zero. Most product quality analysis as well as scrap, repair, and warranty costs are based on the defect and escape rates. It may be comfortable to think in terms of parameters that are mostly "good stuff" like reliability, test coverage, and yield because the numbers tend to be near unity—but that leads to a false sense of well-being. A figure of 90 percent good may sound acceptable, but 10 percent defective products or services is intolerable. Even 1 percent defective would not be tolerated if an alternative with better performance were available. Consider that 1 percent of time is more than 1 h per week. It would not be considered satisfactory if any of the routine public services such as water, electricity, telephone, each TV channel, traffic lights, or every airline flight randomly failed for 1 h each week. To emphasize the challenge of complex systems, consider the combined effect if all the major components of each of the services listed above were to individually fail randomly for 1 h per week. For example, consider a product of just 10 major subsystems. So one failure per week per subsystem results in an average of 10 failures per week. If an average failure requires 10 h to repair, more time is spent in repair than is available for operation.

6.4.1 The Complexity Challenge

If complex systems contain more than 1000 individual parts, the defect rates of the parts must be much lower than 1 percent to avoid significant test and repair costs. Since no test is perfect, a proportion of the defects will be delivered to the user. The defects that escape are likely to result in failure during operation, degrading the observed system reliability. Repair costs will be high, whether paid by the dissatisfied user or by the producer as warranty costs. Some integrated circuits may contain several hundred thousand parts in a single chip. Extremely low defective rates and test escape rates are required to achieve acceptable yields and defect escape rates.

6.4.2 Production Yield

Defect-free production yield is of the same form as operational reliability; it is the probability of no defects, or e^{-Fu}. If all defects can be repaired, the probability of no defects is called the *first-time yield*. The total defect rate is simply the sum of all the defect rates. If defects are repaired, the rework cost is proportional to the total defect rate. Rework costs can be very high and tend to increase as the level of complexity increases. The cost of locating a defect, repairing, and retesting may increase by an order of magnitude at each level of product assembly. The cost to repair defects includes the labor skill levels and facilities required to perform diagnosis and rework, material inventory (both for a substitute for the removable assembly sent for repair and to replace any nonreparable defects), as well as the cost of retest, the risk of rework damage, and the cycle time cost due to the delay in shipment while diagnosis, repairs, and retest are conducted.

For example, consider an example of the total cost of repair at 10 times the cost of initial production and a defect rate of 10 percent (90 percent first-time yield). The cost of failures would be about equal to the cost of initial production, so the total cost of production at 90 percent yield is double what it would cost if no defects were produced. Furthermore, test adds no value when there are no defects, so most of the test cost is also due to defect production. A competitor that controls defects to a lower rate can produce a similar product at lower cost, retain higher profit, and deliver a superior product in less time to a satisfied customer.

Alternatives to repair of defective parts are seldom attractive. If the defect can be isolated to an inexpensive part that can be replaced easily, scrap may be cost-effective. However, this requires diagnosis costs, a design that adds complexity to facilitate replacement of parts, and a significant inventory of replacement parts and assemblies to support the repair and scrap effort. Although it may seem that it is only required to produce sufficient additional parts and assemblies to compensate for average defect rates, the actual inventory levels must be many times that to avoid the risk of stopping production due to shortage of critical parts. For example, considering that the variance of the Poisson distribution is equal to the average, it is reasonable to plan for at least three or more times the standard deviation (the square root of variance), to allow for uncertainty in the initial estimate, the statistical variability, ordering delays, high unit costs for ordering small quantities for replacement of parts used and to minimize the risk of delay of an entire production line when critical shortages occur (bad luck is likely to happen somewhere). Scrap of entire systems is not cost-effective because the ratio of the cost of the entire system to the cost of the defective part is very high, and the total defect rate at the system level is likely to be high. For example, a system with 10,000 parts and a defect rate of only 100 parts per million (ppm) per part reaching final assembly results in an average system defect rate of 100 percent.

6.4.3 Screening Effectiveness

Screening (testing to detect defective product) to reduce defect rates is seldom cost-effective, but may be necessary to detect defects that may occur. Screening is usually costly, tends to introduce some defects itself, is typically less effective at the higher assembly levels (where it is needed most), and allows defects to escape because no test is perfect. Screening may be used when cost-effective and as part of a corrective action process that prevents further production of defects. Zero defects should be the only acceptable quality level.

Screening effectiveness usually means the proportion of single defects that a screen is capable of detecting. It is normally assumed that all rejects are defective (false positives are usually ignored for screening of digital systems). If the proportion of single defects that the screen does not detect is defined as the *escape rate,* that proportion of the defects entering the screen will be passed to the next user. Therefore, the proportion of the input that escapes the screen as defects is approximately the input defect rate multiplied by the screening escape rate. There is an interaction between the input defect rate and the test escape rate because output defects increase the observed output yield, multiple defects in one unit increase test effectiveness, and rejected defects reduce the yield. The discrepancy is not significant for reasonable test effectiveness (less than 10 percent escape rate) and random defects. An estimate of the output defect rate $F(\text{out})$ is as follows:

$$F(\text{out}) = F(\text{in}) \times T(\text{escape}) \tag{6.3}$$

The output defect rate for low yields (about 40 percent) may be approximately equal to the test escape rate. If the input defect rate is unknown, it may be estimated from the observed screen yield and the screen effectiveness as $F(\text{in}) = -\ln(\text{yield})/\text{effectiveness}$, since yield is the negative exponential of the defect rate detected by the screen. Defect rates can often be derived from scrap and/or repair records and early-life failure reports. Test reject rate and user defect rates together provide a measure of test effectiveness. A strong warranty provides both customer satisfaction and useful feedback to the producer.

6.4.4 Test Integration Issues

A note of caution is that multiplication of the input defect rate and test escape rate is valid only when they are statistically independent—repeating a test on defects that previously escaped the same test should result in the same defects escaping again. Test effectiveness is a measure that is valid only with respect to the distribution of the incoming defects.

However, if repeating essentially the same test under the same conditions results in additional detections, this indicates that the test is not completely repeatable. Test repeatability is a concern when testing is done at several assembly levels and tests are repeated during maintenance. Tests should be conducted under the most severe conditions (and tightest tolerances if applicable) at the lowest levels where repair and/or scrap is least costly and to reduce defect rates to the higher assembly levels. However, the temptation to skip testing at the final assembly because a similar test has been previously performed at a lower level can be risky—latent defects that degrade to failures during the final assembly and test operation should not be delivered. Test environments at lower levels may not adequately represent the operating environment. It may be cost-effective to apply some of the ESS once at a higher assembly level, rather than to attempt to simulate extreme operating conditions at lower levels. Electrical stress (e.g., dc voltage, clock rate) may be more cost-effective at the system level than mechanical or thermal stress. Maintenance testing must be very effective to detect failures that occur during operation. If final test is less effective than user testing, there is the risk that the user will detect defects that existed at delivery and consider them as failures of an unreliable product.

System BIT and BIST. It is usually difficult to achieve high test effectiveness at the final assembly level of complex systems. Functional testing is usually time-consuming and/or ineffective at detecting low-level faults. It is important that testability be integrated into the initial design to support both production and user testing. Integrated test structures should be designed into complex architectures so that *built-in test* (BIT) may be performed at various levels of production integration as well as maintenance tests during the lifetime of the equipment. Complex systems may be difficult to test unless *built-in self-test* (BIST) has been integrated into the design. Local test control performs a test when commanded, then returns the result to the central controller to confirm correct operation. Test generators capable of long pseudo-random patterns and compressed signatures are commonly used in BIST applications. One effective technique to verify the test resources is to stimulate faults during a test sequence. The proper response confirms correct operation of the fault stimulation and detection. Digital system design often includes the challenge of incorporating BIST into the test controller itself. It is often difficult for the design team to understand how the controller will respond to internal faults. Integrating BIST into the initial design is essential, but it may be difficult. Simulation of an adequate set of faults, verifying the proper response, and achieving acceptable test effectiveness (low escape rate) can be time-consuming.

6.5 ESTIMATION

The mathematical models described in the previous sections tend to be based on an assumption that models already exist which simply need manipulation to find the optimal result. However, the digital system designer considering the requirements for a quality design that provides high performance, producibility, testability, and reliability may need to estimate some of the parameters and/or develop some of the models. There may be a limited opportunity to obtain data, so it is important that the parameters be estimated with a minimum amount of data. Common concerns are either what estimate can be made with available data or how much data is needed to obtain a desired estimate.

One of the common issues is how to estimate what the underlying rate might be, given that results have been observed. A corresponding issue is how much data is required to provide adequate confidence that an objective has been achieved. This may be considered a "what-if" question, or probabilities in reverse. The probability associated with an estimate is referred to as *confidence*. The concern is this: For an estimate made from specific data, what is the chance that the actual rate is no worse than the estimate? This is equivalent to the chance that the estimate might give results at least as good as the observed data. The "plus-one" method for estimating rates for the Poisson process makes an allowance for uncertainty by adding 1 to the number of observed events. The estimated rate is the ratio of 1 more than the number of observations to the interval of measurement, or $(n + 1)/u$, using the same notation as Eq. (6.2). The estimated rate may be multiplied by an appropriate factor to obtain higher confidence levels if desired.

For the common case of no failures observed for an interval of time or number of units, the estimated rate is simply the inverse of the failure-free interval. The average failure-free interval is commonly referred to as the *mean time between failures* (MTBF) when applied to reliability. Therefore, a failure-free interval of time at least equal to the MTBF to be demonstrated is needed for an estimate that the MTBF has been achieved. If one failure is observed, double the MTBF interval is needed; for two failures, triple the interval; etc. Similarly, 100 units defect-free would support an estimate of a 1 percent defect rate; fault detection of all 100 gates randomly selected from a custom integrated-circuit design would support an estimate of a 1 percent test escape rate (99 percent fault coverage).

The confidence of the plus-one estimate may be calculated from Eq. (6.2). When the average number of failures is 1, the probability of observing none is $e^{-1} = 0.368$, so there is almost a 37 percent chance of a result this low. Therefore, there is 63 percent confidence that the actual rate is less than the estimate.

For the case of one observed failure, the plus-one estimate of the average number is 2. The probability of observing no failures is $e^{-2} = 0.135$. Since $C(1) = Fu = 2$, the chance of one failure is twice the chance of none, or 0.271. The chance of either none or one failure is almost 41 percent. Therefore, there is 59 percent confidence that the actual rate is less than the estimate for this case. This can be extended to greater numbers of failures, which would show that confidence approaches 50 percent for larger numbers. The 1 that is added to the number of events actually observed can be considered an allowance for uncertainty due to the limited observation interval. The added 1 may be considered as an "impending event" that might occur just after the end of the observations. The plus-one estimate is slightly conservative compared to a most-likely estimate, especially for low numbers when the uncertainty is worst. The plus-one estimate is adequate and convenient for most engineering purposes.

Add 1 to the number of events observed to estimate the average rate over an interval of observation.

Since the standard deviation of the Poisson model is equal to the square root of the mean, the estimated standard deviation for the special case of no observed failures is also 1. Therefore, a reasonable estimate of the range of uncertainty is ± 1, or a range from approximately 0 to 2 per the failure-free interval. Therefore, the failure-free interval needed to estimate the failure rate with moderate confidence (1σ) is double the average to be demonstrated. Likewise, approximately 4 times the average is required for a confidence of 2 times the standard deviation (a 2σ confidence estimate). These approximate failure-free interval multiplication factors are summarized as follows:

Confidence of estimate	Interval factor
Mean estimate (60 percent)	1
Moderate (85 percent, 1σ)	2
High (98 percent, 2σ)	4

6.6 DESIGN OF EXPERIMENTS

This section introduces structured techniques to analyze a response to various conditions. These techniques are appropriate for a variety of systems (e.g., electrical, chemical, industrial, medical, biological, agricultural, environmental, financial) and are applicable to several areas of engineering, including initial design evaluation and production performance evaluation. Of course, initial design and improvement design are typically iterative processes; designs are seldom based on perfect knowledge, and experimentation is necessary to diagnose limitations. Tests that simply verify that performance is within acceptable limits may be structured to provide high confidence with low test complexity. Analysis should be designed to be effective and efficient [1]. A well-designed analysis is as desirable as a well-designed product or process.

The techniques described in this section are particularly suited to the analysis of digital systems and include concepts familiar to digital design. A typical activity in digital systems analysis is to determine performance over a defined range of various conditions. A related design issue is to determine which conditions are the worst case, or which design parameters or design alternatives result in the best system performance. The range of conditions is defined by the high and low limits of each parameter. Determining the best combination of conditions, or the worst combination of requirements, is a class of problems sometimes referred to as *linear programming* [3].

If the response to the parameters is reasonably consistent, extremes of performance should occur at a combination of the extremes of the parameters. If the performance is not affected by one (or more) of the parameters, the same performance may occur at more than one combination. If the range of parameter extremes is considered a geometric shape, the combinations of extremes are the corners. A two-parameter analysis has $2^2 = 4$ corners, a three-parameter analysis has $2^3 = 8$, etc. A worst-case analysis determines performance at a corner which has the worst performance. Examples of parameters affecting the performance of digital systems include temperature, voltage, propagation delay, dc load current, load capacitance, dynamic impedance, timing adjustments, and component tolerances. A complete worst-case analysis would consider all the combinations of the applicable parameters at their high and low extremes.

6.6.1 Undesirable Methods

Before we describe the binary combination method of analysis, it is worth considering analysis methods that may be inferior. One that seems attractive when there is motivation to indicate better performance than can be demonstrated over the worst combination is to conduct analysis only for the nominal (or typical) case. The hope is that most of the time, everything will tend to "average," so that acceptable operation will usually be achieved. Obviously this is not adequate to ensure reliable operation under all conditions, and a design based only on typical analysis is not likely to be cost-effective in production, where the parameters are likely to vary. Even if some of the units produced can be delivered based on an acceptance test at nominal conditions, the product is not likely to be reliable under operating conditions which are more severe than the acceptance test.

Little improvement is achieved by an analysis which can be best described as haphazard in which one "worst" condition or only a few combinations are analyzed, but there is no rigorous basis for selecting the proper combination. Either a design analysis or a failure diagnosis based on an inadequate analysis of the appropriate combinations is risky because the worst combination may not be discovered.

A classical method which may be common, but ineffective and inefficient, avoids the combinations and investigates each variable "one at a time." This is sometimes used in the haphazard approach in an attempt to discover sensitivity to parameters. Even if all parameters are investigated, the one-at-a-time method does not analyze the combinations, ignores parameter interactions, is vulnerable to selection of the starting conditions and measurement uncertainty, and may require more tests to get less data than is achieved by the binary method described below [3].

6.6.2 Analysis of Binary Combinations

This method is an effective technique to design a structured test that will permit analysis of the effects of combinations of parameters, including nonlinear effects called *interactions*. The structure of the design is fairly simple and is based on the binary counting sequence and binary arithmetic familiar to most digital designers. This testing is called *factorial experimentation*. It will be shown that when the number of parameters is large, only a small fraction of the total number of combinations need to be included in the analysis, especially for initial exploratory analysis. Although the basic analysis is performed for the two limits of the range for each parameter, it will be shown that it is conveniently adapted to include a third level between the two limits. The analysis at the third level is particularly important to the determination of best or worst cases that occur between the two limits of a parameter.

The binary combination method performs one-half of all the tests being run with each parameter at a low level and the other half with each parameter at the high level. The test is run for all combinations of the primary parameters. Additional parameters may be introduced into the test design without increasing the number of tests being run. Any effects of these parameters are added to the results, subject to the limitations that the results include aliases of the interactions of parameters.

The description of the structure of the binary combination method is based on parameters that have upper and lower extremes. It is convenient, but not necessary, that there is considered to be a midpoint halfway between the extremes, which is called the *center value*. It is usually convenient to select a range for the parameters which is symmetric with respect to the nominal, so that the test average represents nominal conditions. The standard convention used will determine the overall average and the effects of the parameters (and any interactions) with respect to the average of the parameter (one-half of the range of the parameter). If the resulting effects are doubled, this will give the result for changing the parameters from the low extreme to the high extreme (the total range).

The overall average is computed by averaging the results from each combination tested. If all the effects are perfectly linear (no interaction between parameters and no higher-order effects from any individual parameter), then the overall average should be the same as the result from all parameters at their average level (called a *center run*). It is usually appropriate to perform the center run for comparison to the overall average for the binary tests. This comparison is used to detect nonlinear effects from individual parameters. The use of the center run is important when the worst or best case occurs between the parameter limits. This is sometimes applicable to design optimization if the design requirements allow selection of a best value for a parameter that is not at either limit. Examples of digital design parameters that might have best center values include nominal resistor values, clock phase adjustments, or dynamic transmission line impedance.

Computing the Effects.   The effect for each parameter may be computed by adding the results from the half of all the cases where the parameter was high, subtracting the results from the other half of the cases where the parameter was low, then dividing by the number of cases to obtain the average effect. The two-way interaction effects may be calculated by adding the results from the half of the cases where both are alike and subtracting those that are not alike. Similar rules apply to higher-order effects according to the number of parameters that are high and low.

An algorithm due to Yates is a more structured routine for both calculating and identifying the effects. Calculations are either a pairwise sum or difference; the number of stages is one for each primary parameter. Although the actual data may be taken in any appropriate order, the results are arranged in the binary counting sequence, called *standard order*. The algorithm for *analysis of binary combinations* (ABC) is illustrated in Table 6.1. The parameters may be listed in any column order, but they are listed in reverse order (the least significant to the right) to emphasize the relationship to binary counting. The parameters are designated by column numbers (beginning with 1) in the table. Once assigned to actual parameters, it may be more convenient to replace them with symbols or more meaningful characters to represent actual names, such as T for temperature, V for voltage, D for delay, etc. Each entry in the Effect column is the product of those primary parameters that are high for that line. The first effect is designated 0 for the overall average. Column R0 is for the data input (the test results). The following columns are for calculating the intermediate results; one stage for each primary parameter. The rightmost column is for computing the averages from the results of the last calculating stage. There are different conventions for the division factor to be used for the average: either the total number of inputs to the analysis or one-half the number of inputs. The convention that is more appropriate for using the results to define response models with respect to a center value (plus or minus a tolerance limit) is to divide the results by the total number of data inputs. Dividing by only one-half of the number of inputs provides the total effect for a change from the low to high limits.

The calculations above the dividing line are pairwise sums; the calculations below the line are pairwise differences, where the upper value is subtracted from the lower (upside-down subtraction). The numbers in parentheses in the Calc. column refer to the line (case, test, or run) numbers in the table. The SS data at the bottom of the table indicate the *sum of squares* (SS) for each column. These are used to check the arithmetic; the sum of squares doubles at each stage. The SS check tends to verify that the magnitudes of the results are correct, but it is not sensitive to sign errors. Additional checks may be performed; one that is not shown is that line 1 of the last stage should be the total of the R0 column data inputs (a statistical algorithm is convenient for these computations).

TABLE 6.1 Analysis of Binary Combinations for Three Parameters

No.	3	2	1	Effect	Calc.	R0	R1	R2	R3	Avg.
1	0	0	0	0	(1+2)					
2	0	0	1	1	(3+4)					
3	0	1	0	2	(5+6)					
4	0	1	1	12	(7+8)					
5	1	0	0	3	(2−1)					
6	1	0	1	13	(4−3)					
7	1	1	0	23	(6−5)					
8	1	1	1	123	(8−7)					
					SS					
					2∗SS				SE	

Source: Adapted from George E. P. Box, William G. Hunter, and J. Stuart Hunter, *Statistics for Experimenters*, p. 342. Copyright © 1978, John Wiley & Sons, Inc. Adapted with permission of John Wiley & Sons, Inc.

Two checks of the final Avg. column are indicated. The actual sum of squares for the data in the Avg. column is multiplied by the divisor used to compute the averages. If the divisor is the total number of data inputs, the sum of squares for the Avg. column data multiplied by the divisor should be equal to the SS of the R0 column. The last entry in the Avg. column is labeled *SE* for the sum of effects (the sum of the results in the Avg. column). The SE in the Avg. column should be equal to the last data input in the R0 column. If any of the parameters are low for the last line (this may occur for fractional designs), then the sign for the effects of those parameters that are low for the last line is not reversed before SE is completed, although the sign of the actual effect is reversed. A divisor of one-half the number of inputs doubles the effects and SE.

Manual calculations should be checked carefully (the signs are easily confused by the upside-down subtraction). Normalization may be performed at each stage to eliminate the increase of magnitude and the final averaging step; the sum of squares will be reduced by 2 (instead of doubled) at each stage.

6.6.3 Fractions of Binary Combinations

Many tests with more than a few parameters do not need to be performed at all combinations of the parameters both high and low. The number of runs (and potential data) increases exponentially as the number of parameters if all combinations are performed. Many results are sensitive to only a few main parameters and possibly one or more interactions. Higher-order effects are usually not expected. What is important is to provide the capability to detect the presence of interactions; if any are detected, they can be analyzed further. The analysis of binary combinations allows a relatively large number of parameters to be investigated at once to determine which parameters and any interactions may be significant.

There is little distinction between which primary parameters are used to define the structure of the test and which are generated as interactions of the primary parameters. For example, eight combinations can completely define all the possible effects of any three parameters when combined for a total of up to seven parameters. In general, N binary combinations can define an average and up to $N - 1$ other significant effects. If there are no interactions (linear effects only), the significant main effects of up to $N - 1$ separate parameters can be determined.

If the number of significant effects is greater than the number of primary parameters and there are interactions between them, the results may be ambiguous. These are called *aliases* because there is more than one possible contribution to the same result [3]. Aliases are caused by the same basic effect as time sampling a signal at a rate less than twice the maximum frequency components. The following sections describe how to generate the additional parameters from interactions and how to determine the set of all possible aliases.

6.6.4 Half Fractions of Binary Combinations

A half-fraction binary combination adds just one parameter to the primary parameters that define a complete test. The added parameter is identified with the interaction of all the primary parameters. Therefore, the added parameter is an alias of the highest-order interaction of all the primary parameters. The identifying word that introduces the generated parameter into the analysis is called a *generator*.

A generator is the "product" of the associated interaction with the generated parameter. For example, $G(4) = 123 * 4 = 1234$. The binary operation called *product* is similar to ordinary algebraic multiplication of symbols. It is the equivalent of multiplication of plus and minus signs, or parity generation (modulo 2 addition, or binary sum without carry) of 1s and 0s, each representing the high and low parameter values. The product of a parameter by itself (a parameter squared) is unity and is deleted from the identifying word; if the operation is considered binary sum, the sum of any parameter with itself is 0 and is deleted. This is also equivalent to parity generation; if the same parameter is included twice, it will not affect the result. Therefore, when two words are combined, any common parameters are deleted from the result.

A generator is identified with another interaction for each generated parameter. The complete set of identifying words is composed of all the generators and all cross products of the generators. The identifying words are aliases of effect 0, the overall average. An illustration of the binary product of two words with some common parameters is $2345 * 123 = 12^2 3^2 45 = 145$. The alias pattern of a half fraction is the product of the generator (the only identifying word) with each effect. The alias pattern is simply the parameters that are missing from each effect because the generator contains all the parameters.

The data response for the example of Table 6.2 is the line number for the units digit, plus 10 if the generated parameter is high. The state of the generated parameter is defined as high or low for each effect as the product (or parity) of those parameters in the generator—for a half fraction it is parity over all the parameters. Either odd or even parity convention may be chosen; each defines one of the two halves of the complete binary combination of all the parameters. The convention was selected so that parity over all the parameters is even, so all four parameters are low for number 1 and all are high for number 8. All parameters high concurrently is convenient because the data response for the last line is the SE in the Avg. column. If the test needs to be rerun to resolve ambiguities, the opposite convention is used to obtain the other half of the binary combinations. When the generated parameter is low for the interaction which introduced it into the analysis, it is low when all the primary parameters are high, and the sign of the actual effect is reversed from the sign of the analysis.

TABLE 6.2 Half-Fraction Analysis for Four-Parameter Example[†]

No.	(4)	3	2	1	Effect + alias	Calc.	R0	R1	R2	R3	Avg.[‡] {Effect}
1	0	0	0	0	0 + 1234	(1+2)	1	13	30	76	19
2	1	0	0	1	1 + 234	(3+4)	12	17	46	4	1{1}
3	1	0	1	0	2 + 134	(5+6)	13	21	2	8	2{2}
4	0	0	1	1	12 + 34	(7+8)	4	23	2	0	
5	1	1	0	0	3 + 124	(2−1)	15	+11	+4	+16	4{3}
6	0	1	0	1	13 + 24	(4−3)	6	−9	+4	0	
7	0	1	1	0	23 + 14	(6−5)	7	−9	−20	0	
8	1	1	1	1	123 + 4	(8−7)	18	+11	+20	+40	10{4}
						SS	964	1928	3856	7712	1928
						2*SS	1928	3856	7712	SE	36

[†]Parameter 4 generator = 1234 (alias of effect 0). Response: R0 = line no. + 10 if parameter (4) = high.

[‡]The divisor was 4, so the Avg. column effects are twice the average. Effect 0 is the sum of minimum and maximum. SS is multiplied by 4 for comparison to 2*SS of column R0. SE is twice the R0 run 8 data.

TABLE 6.3 Half-Fraction Analysis for Binary Counting Example

No.	(4)	3	2	1	Effect + alias	Calc.	R0	R1	R2	R3	Avg.[†] {Effect}
1	0	0	0	0	0 + 1234	(1+2)	0	9	22	60	15
2	1	0	0	1	1 + 234	(3+4)	9	13	38	4	1{1}
3	1	0	1	0	2 + 134	(5+6)	10	17	2	8	2{2}
4	0	0	1	1	12 + 34	(7+8)	3	21	2	0	
5	1	1	0	0	3 + 124	(2−1)	12	+9	+4	+16	4{3}
6	0	1	0	1	13 + 24	(4−3)	5	−7	+4	0	
7	0	1	1	0	23 + 14	(6−5)	6	−7	−16	0	
8	1	1	1	1	123 + 4	(8−7)	15	+9	+16	+32	8{4}
						SS	620	1240	2480	4960	1240
						2*SS	1240	2480	4960	SE	30

[†]The divisor was 4, so the Avg. column effects are twice the average. SS is multiplied by 4.

The parameters selected for these examples are real integers, not upper and lower limits with respect to an average, so the results of the last stage of calculation were divided by only one-half the total number of runs. The results are the total effects from the low level (0) to the high level (1) instead of the one-way effects from center. This doubles all results in the Avg. column. The SE is twice the last line of data input, the SS multiplied by the divisor of 4 will match the 2*SS of column R0, and effect 0 is the sum of the minimum and maximum if there are no interactions. The minimum for the example of Table 6.3 is 0, so effect 0 is also equal to the last line of data input.

Tables 6.3, 6.4, and 6.5 illustrate half-fraction analysis based on binary counting. Table 6.3 results are exactly the binary weights with bit 1 the least significant. For the interaction example of Table 6.4, bit 3 in the low state inhibits the normal effect of bit 2. (This reduces the value when bit 2 is high and bit 3 is low.) The changes in the results columns are indicated by a dagger. The final results indicate that the sum (average) has been reduced, the suppression of bit 2 reduces its average effect, but the additional control by bit 3 enhances the effect it has on the response. The interaction effect of parameters 2 and 3 is identified on line 7 and indicates the bit 3 increase and the bit 2 reduction. Although the aliases cannot be resolved with this analysis, parameters with lower main effects are less likely to have interaction effects. The product of main effects is a convenient indicator of the relative likelihood of aliases in real systems. Bit 4 controlling bit 1 provides similar results for this example.

The data response of Table 6.5 indicates the results of a higher-order interaction effect or a single data error. Most real systems tend to be fairly regular, so that higher-order interactions are insignificant. The response for Table 6.5 was selected to be consistent with a "saturation" limit; the maximum value is less than normal binary counting. This reduces the sum and the response of each of the parameters by one-fourth of the difference from the correct value. Each of the interactions indicates the average deviation of 0.5 from the linear response.

If the minimum were increased (instead of the maximum reduced), the interaction signs would be positive. Test results with many significant interaction terms should be checked very carefully for inconsistent data input. However, the experimenter should be aware that higher-order effects may indicate an interior extreme. If higher-order effects exist, more complex models and/or a revised region of interest may be appropriate [1].

TABLE 6.4   Half-Fraction Analysis with Interaction* of Parameters 2 and 3 Example

No.	(4)	3	2	1	Effect + alias	Calc.	R0	R1	R2	R3	Avg.[†] {Effect}
1	0	0	0	0	0 + 1234	(1+2)	0	9	18*	56*	14
2	1	0	0	1	1 + 234	(3+4)	9	9*	38	4	1{1}
3	1	0	1	0	2 + 134	(5+6)	8*	17	2	4*	1{2}
4	0	0	1	1	12 + 34	(7+8)	1*	21	2	0	
5	1	1	0	0	3 + 124	(2−1)	12	+9	0*	+20*	5{3}
6	0	1	0	1	13 + 24	(4−3)	5	−7	+4	0	
7	0	1	1	0	23 + 14	(6−5)	6	−7	−16	4*	1{23}
8	1	1	1	1	123 + 4	(8−7)	15	+9	+16	+32	8{4}
						SS	576	1152	2304	4608	1152
						2*SS	1152	2304	4608	SE	30

[†]The divisor was 4, so the Avg. column effects are twice the average. SS is multiplied by 4.

6.6.5 Analysis of Data with Center Values

The previous examples used binary counting for illustration. Many actual problems have center (nominal or average) values with high and low limits. Table 6.6 illustrates some typical characteristics, using integer values for convenience. Every parameter has a significant response (the parameter number for this illustration), but this is neither necessary nor typical. Parameter 1 has a negative response; an increase of that parameter reduces the output, the others increase the output. An example of different response signs is logic device propagation delay, which may increase with temperature but decrease with voltage.

The divisor for the Avg. column is the number of data inputs, so the effects are with respect to the center value. The sum of effects and the sum of squares times the divisor

TABLE 6.5   Half-Fraction Analysis with Interaction or Data Error* Example

No.	(4)	3	2	1	Effect + alias	Calc.	R0	R1	R2	R3	Avg.[†] {Effect}
1	0	0	0	0	0 + 1234	(1+2)	0	9	22	58*	14.5
2	1	0	0	1	1 + 234	(3+4)	9	13	36*	2*	0.5{1+}
3	1	0	1	0	2 + 134	(5+6)	10	17	2	6*	1.5{2+}
4	0	0	1	1	12 + 34	(7+8)	3	19*	0*	−2*	−0.5{34+}
5	1	1	0	0	3 + 124	(2−1)	12	+9	+4	+14*	3.5{3+}
6	0	1	0	1	13 + 24	(4−3)	5	−7	+2*	−2*	−0.5{24+}
7	0	1	1	0	23 + 14	(6−5)	6	−7	−16	−2*	−0.5{23+}
8	1	1	1	1	123 + 4	(8−7)	13*	+7*	+14*	+30*	7.5{4+}
						SS	564	1128	2256	4512	1128
						2*SS	1128	2256	4512	SE	26

[†]The divisor was 4, so the Avg. column effects are twice the average. SS is multiplied by 4.

TABLE 6.6 Half-Fraction Analysis with Center Values

No.	(4)	3	2	1	Effect + alias	Calc.	R0	R1	R2	R3	Avg.[†] {Effect}
0	C	C	C	C	Center		30			DIFF	$0\ \{Sx^2\}$
1	0	0	0	0	0 + 1234	(1+2)	23	50	108	240	30
2	1	0	0	1	1 + 234	(3+4)	27	58	132	−8	−1{1}
3	1	0	1	0	2 + 134	(5+6)	33	62	−4	+16	2{2}
4	0	0	1	1	12 + 34	(7+8)	25	70	−4	−8	1{34}
5	1	1	0	0	3 + 124	(2−1)	37	+4	+8	+24	3{3}
6	0	1	0	1	13 + 24	(4−3)	25	−8	+8	0	
7	0	1	1	0	23 + 14	(6−5)	31	−12	−12	0	
8	1	1	1	1	123 + 4	(8−7)	39	+8	+20	+32	4{4}
						SS	7,448	14,896	29,792	59,584	7,448
						2*SS	14,896	29,792	59,584	SE	39

[†]The divisor was 8, so the Avg. column effects are with respect to the center values. SS is multiplied by 8 for comparison to SS of column R0. SE is compared to the R0 run 8 data.

(8) match the run 8 data input and the sum of squares in the R0 column. An exercise to demonstrate the checks at the bottom of the table is to change the algorithm to normalize (divide the sums and differences by 2) at each stage. The last line may be changed to SS/2 to compare the sum of squares which decrease by one-half at each stage. The last stage produces averages directly.

Although not typical, this analysis includes an example of an interaction of parameters 3 and 4. The response may increase (or be unaffected) if both parameters change in the same direction but may decrease when they are different. The logic function exclusive-OR (modulo 2 addition or parity) is a typical example of an interaction function. The response of this effect only is a curved (nonlinear) surface shaped like a saddle and is called a *minimax*. An electrical example of this effect may result from two digital signals connected together; there is no effect if both signals are the same state. However, if the signals are opposite states, one state may control, or dominate. Examples of signals connected together include logical "wired-OR" or wire bridging faults.

Further analysis would be needed to resolve the alias of the 12 interaction effect with the 34 interaction effect. However, it is usually reasonable to estimate that the alias with a greater product of main effects is the more likely interaction effect. In this example, the product of the effects of parameter 3 and parameter 4 is 12; the product of the effects of parameter 1 and parameter 2 is only 2. However, the actual interaction effects are not distinguishable in this half-fraction analysis.

The Center-Run Difference Effect.   The binary analysis may be supplemented by an additional center run, with all parameters at their center values (usually the average of the high and low limits). The difference between the center-run response on line 0, column R0, and the overall average on line 1 is indicated by DIFF for the last column. The difference effect (designated Sx^2) is the sum of squared terms of one parameter, not the interaction products. For this example, the center-run response matched the overall average. This indicates that there are no second-order effects of one parameter, which are coefficients of x^2 terms in a polynomial expansion that represent a local maximum or minimum. Any difference is the sum for all the parameters, so all squared effects are an alias set (similar to the two-way alias sets for resolution 4 designs). Significant squared effects may be analyzed by one-at-a-time tests at three levels or other techniques.

Polynomial Response Functions. The results in Table 6.6 indicate that the response is adequately defined by the binary analysis. If the nth parameter is designated x_n, then for analysis of the response at either the limits or center values, x_n is -1 for the lower limit, 0 at the center value, and $+1$ at the upper limit. If a quantitative model over the region of interest is to be defined, then the center value must be subtracted from the parameter value, and the parameter scaled to the units from the center value to the limits. It is usually convenient to collect the center response and the scaled center values for the parameters into a single constant term. The polynomial describing the response is as follows:

$$\text{Response} = 30 - x_1 + 2x_2 + 3x_3 + 4x_4 + x_3 * x_4$$

The response function indicates a linear effect for each parameter and a two-way interaction effect between parameters 3 and 4. However, the magnitude of the interaction is relatively small compared to both of the linear effects involved. It may be more convenient to evaluate the interaction effect in factored form with one of the parameters as follows:

$$\text{Response} = 30 - x_1 + 2x_2 + 3x_3 + (4 + x_3)x_4$$

The signs of the response function indicate that the upper extreme value of the response (at the limits of the range of the parameters) is 41 when x_1 is at its lower limit and the other parameters are at their upper limit. Similarly, the lower extreme value of the response is 21 when the signs are reversed. Note that these extremes were not included in the combinations evaluated in this half fraction, but the extremes can be computed from the results of the analysis. It can be shown by separation of the interaction effect from the linear effects that although the interaction has an effect on the response, the magnitude is not large enough to alter the combination at which the extremes of response occur, or to cause a local extreme to exist inside the limits for the parameters.

The magnitudes of the effects may be compared to evaluate the relative sensitivity to each of the parameters, either over the range or per scaled units. Evaluation of the results indicates which parameters should be changed for maximum response. Of course, it is important to be aware of the proper function to optimize. For example, a design team may be motivated to maximize performance (e.g., maximum clock rate possible), while the actual product objective is to maximize value for the customer. The best value may be a combination of performance, timely delivery, purchase cost, and maintenance cost. The parameters being evaluated should be converted to some common base (such as cost) so the analysis may determine the best combination.

The effects from the analysis of binary combinations (including interactions if significant) may be used to define low-order polynomial models of response functions that can be evaluated at the limits of a region of interest. The polynomials may be easier to evaluate for sensitivity or extremes of responses than the original function. Many complex functions are sufficiently smooth over a small region of interest for a particular application that they can be reasonably modeled as linear and two-way interaction terms. For example, in Chap. 7, Sec. 7.3 contains formulas that involve such mathematical functions as logarithms, square roots, and ratios. It may be more convenient to perform analysis with these functions if they are converted to low-order polynomials that apply over an appropriate region of interest. One of the benefits is that the relative magnitude of the effects (sensitivity) of various parameters becomes more obvious. Design alternatives and optimization can be simplified, particularly if some of the effects are not significant.

Summary of the Analysis of Binary Combinations.   These examples illustrated several characteristics of the analysis of binary combinations. Compared to one-at-a-time methods, analysis of binary combinations is less sensitive to an error in one of the data points and tends to average out noise because all the effects are based on all the data. If there are significant interactions, they can be detected separately from main effects. The example of Table 6.5 showed that if the one data input is considered an anomaly, the discrepancy is reduced by the ratio of the number of data inputs. In actual cases where the "correct" input is not known, the results may be investigated to indicate which input is likely to be anomalous. The pattern of the interaction effects for this example, which shows the same negative response for all the two-way interactions, is evidence that the response is suppressed when most of the parameters are high. If the results may be anomalous, it may be useful to construct the polynomial model as described above for the example of Table 6.6. The hypothesis that a linear model would describe most of the response can be investigated by deleting the interaction effects. If the results predicted by a linear model are compared to the observed results, it can be shown that all the data points except runs 1 and 8 are underestimated by the amount of the interactions for each parameter present. If the alias is subtracted from each of the main effects, it can be shown that the results of Table 6.5 are consistent with a linear model, with the exception of a single anomalous point for run 8.

6.6.6 Resolution of Fractions of Binary Combinations

The alias pattern for a half fraction is the product of each primary effect and the generator, which contains all the parameters. The sum of the number of parameters in each alias pair is the total number of parameters, so a half fraction provides the highest resolution possible for a fractional combination. For the half-fraction analysis shown in Table 6.6 (and earlier), the total number of parameters is four. Therefore, two-way interactions are the lowest-order effects that are aliases with each other. For example, the product of identifying word 1234 with primary effect 123 generates the alias with main effect 4; the product with primary effect 12 is the alias with effect 34.

The lowest sum of the number of terms in any alias pair is called the *resolution* of the analysis [1]. The resolution describes the lowest-order alias effects that can occur in the analysis. The terms in an alias pair result from the product of an identifying word and a primary effect. The lowest sum occurs when the identifying word contains all the primary parameters. The resolution is the shortest identifying word. For example, a word with p primary parameters and g generated parameters results in an alias of g with p (in addition to the other products). Both aliases contain the highest number of terms (the order of the alias) when they are within 1 of being equal. The following are examples of the lowest-order aliases:

Resolution 3: main effects with two-way interactions

Resolution 4: two-way interactions with each other

Resolution 5: two-way with three-way interactions

Resolution 6: three-way interactions with each other

6.6.7 Alias Patterns of Fractions

As previously described, a half fraction identifies the single additional parameter with the interaction of all the parameters. The generator is the product of the additional parameter and the associated primary interaction; the alias pairs are the product of the identifying word (the generator) with each of the effects. This basic process must be repeated for each additional parameter introduced into the analysis. Each additional parameter is identified with another primary interaction. The identifying word that generates each additional parameter is multiplied by all the previous identifying words to define a set of identifying words that includes all cross products.

Each additional parameter doubles the number of new identifying words and aliases for each effect. The single identifying word that generates the half fraction described previously is resolution 4 and has two aliases for each effect. Each main effect has a three-way alias; each two-way effect has another two-way alias as indicated in the Effect + Alias column of the half-fraction tables. There are four interactions (one three-way, plus three two-way) for three primary parameters, so there can be a maximum of $2^4 - 1 = 15$ identifying words and a set of 16 aliases (including the primary effect) for each of the eight effects. Introducing all four generated parameters into three primary parameters is a saturated resolution 3 analysis. Each of the seven main effects has three two-way aliases, four three-way aliases, and eight higher-order aliases.

Four three-way interactions can be identified with additional parameters for four primary parameters; this is a resolution 4 analysis with two-way aliases of each other. The analysis has $2^4 - 1 = 15$ identifying words and 16 aliases for each of the 16 effects. If all 11 interactions are identified with additional parameters, this results in a saturated resolution 3 analysis. Each of the 15 main effects has seven two-way aliases.

The Alias Matrix.   It is convenient to represent a set of aliases as a matrix where the first column is the primary effects in standard order. Each identifying word adds another column; each alias in the matrix is the product of the identifying word and the primary effect for that row and column. Each row is the aliases with each primary effect. The notation for the identifying words is that $I(x)$ for a single parameter designates the generator that introduced parameter x into the analysis; $I(xy \cdots)$ for multiple parameters designates the cross products of $I(x)$, $I(y)$, and the other parameters listed; $I(x)+$ designates the entire set of identifying words (including the cross products) that result from the introduction of parameter x, but the generator itself is the only identifying word entered in the effect 0 row for that column. A complete resolution 3 alias matrix for up to seven parameters with eight binary combinations is shown in Table 6.7. ID designates the row of column identifiers; the identifying words are entered in the effect 0 row. The main effects are noted in boldface print.

A Compressed Alias Matrix.   The complete alias matrix for only three primary parameters is rather complex and is shown primarily to illustrate the process of determining the alias set. An alias matrix that has been compressed to only the lower-order aliases is usually more convenient and useful. Higher-order aliases are usually insignificant in practical analysis. Table 6.8 indicates the compressed matrix of generators, main effects, and two-way aliases of three primary parameters. Each row has three two-way aliases of each main effect and contains each parameter once. All the two-way aliases resulting from the introduction of the generated parameter are listed in the same column. Each column contains the generated parameter once as a main effect and once as a two-way alias with each of the previous (to the left) main parameters. The rightmost column contains an entry in every row, indicating that the design is saturated with a main parameter for every effect.

Using the Alias Matrix for Test Design.   The alias matrix may be reviewed to determine an appropriate assignment of parameters to the actual test variables. Prior knowledge may be used to reduce the impact of aliases. These are examples of information that may be used: less than the maximum number of parameters is to be introduced into the analysis,

TABLE 6.7 Resolution 3 Alias Matrix for Eight Binary Combinations

			Part 1: Aliases of generated parameters 4, 5, 6 with 1, 2, 3			
ID:	$I(4)$	$I(5)$	$I(45)$	$I(6)$	$I(46)$	$I(56)$	$I(456)$
0	12 4	13 5	23 45	23 6	13 46	12 56	456
1	2 4	3 5	123 45	123 6	3 46	2 56	1 456
2	1 4	123 5	3 45	3 6	123 46	1 56	2 456
12	4	23 5	13 45	13 6	23 46	56	12 456
3	123 4	1 5	2 45	2 6	1 46	123 56	3 456
13	23 4	5	12 45	12 6	46	23 56	13 456
23	13 4	12 5	45	6	12 46	13 56	23 456
123	3 4	2 5	1 45	1 6	2 46	3 56	123 456

			Part 2: Aliases of generated parameter 7 with 1, 2, 3, 4, 5, 6			
ID:	$I(7)$	$I(47)$	$I(57)$	$I(457)$	$I(67)$	$I(467)$	$I(567)$	$I(4567)$
0	123 7	3 47	2 57	1 457	1 67	2 467	3 567	123 4567
1	23 7	13 47	12 57	457	67	12 467	13 567	23 4567
2	13 7	23 47	57	12 457	12 67	467	23 567	13 4567
12	3 7	123 47	1 57	2 457	2 67	1 467	123 567	3 4567
3	12 7	47	23 57	13 457	13 67	23 467	567	12 4567
13	2 7	1 47	123 57	3 457	3 67	123 467	1 567	2 4567
23	1 7	2 47	3 57	123 457	123 67	3 467	2 567	1 4567
123	7	12 47	13 57	23 457	23 67	13 467	12 567	4567

it is expected that some parameters are less significant, or some of the interactions are anticipated. For example, in Table 6.7, parameter 7 would be introduced for a half fraction; it has no two-way aliases with the primary parameters. Parameters 4, 5, and 6 are identified with two-way interactions. The aliases of these parameters involve those two primary parameters, but not the missing parameter in the generator for that parameter. Any parameters that are unused or do not have significant responses eliminate the poten-

TABLE 6.8 Compressed Two-Way Alias Matrix for Eight Binary Combinations Generators, **Main** Effects, and Two-Way Interactions

ID:	$I(4)$	$I(5)+$	$I(6)+$	$I(7)+$
0	12 4	13 5	23 6	123 7
1	2 4	3 5		6 7
2	1 4		3 6	5 7
12	4		5 6	3 7
3		1 5	2 6	4 7
13		5	4 6	2 7
23		4 5	6	1 7
123	3 4	2 5	1 6	7

tial alias terms of that parameter. The generated parameters were assigned numbers in these examples simply in the sequence in which they appear in standard order; the actual assignments should be based on any prior knowledge and the alias structure of the analysis.

Structure of Analysis for 16 Binary Combinations.   Tables 6.9 through 6.11 describe the alias structure of fractional analysis that provides resolution 4 performance for up to 8 parameters and resolution 3 performance for up to the full 15 parameters. Numbers above 9 use uppercase letters in hexadecimal (base-16) notation. Only the two-way aliases are shown for parameters 8 through F. The second row in the compressed matrix of Table 6.10 indicates the resolution (designated RES) of each of the parameters introduced into the analysis; the resolution is also the number of parameters in the generator. However, the cross products with other identifying words may reduce the resolution. For example, parameter 9 would be resolution 5 by itself, but cross products with resolution 4 parameters result in identifying words with only three parameters. The result is the two-way aliases involving each of the added parameters, as shown on the effect 1234 row for the main effect of parameter 9. The cross products of the resolution 4 generators with each other maintain resolution 4 performance. However, cross products of a resolution 4 generator with either the resolution 5 generator or any of the resolution 3 generators reduce the analysis to resolution 3.

Table 6.11 is both compressed and reordered to indicate all main effects in the first columns, with the two-way aliases following each main effect. The main effects are categorized according to whether they represent four primary parameters, the four resolution 4 parameters, or the seven resolution 3 parameters. The parameter that would comprise a half fraction if it were the only generated parameter is indicated by the number sign (#).

TABLE 6.9   Resolution 4 Alias Matrix for 16 Binary Combinations*

ID:	I(5)	I(6)	I(56)	I(7)	I(57)	I(67)	I(567)	I(8)+
0	123 5	124 6	34 56	134 7	24 57	23 67	1 567	234 8
1	23 5	24 6	134 56	34 7	124 57	123 67	567	
2	13 5	14 6	234 56	1234 7	4 57	3 67	12 567	
12	3 5	4 6	1234 56	234 7	14 57	13 67	2 567	7 8
3	12 5	1234 6	4 56	14 7	23 57	2 67	13 567	
13	2 5	234 6	14 56	4 7	1234 57	12 67	3 567	6 8
23	1 5	134 6	24 56	124 7	34 57	67	123 567	4 8
123	5	346 6	124 56	24 7	134 57	1 67	23 567	
4	1234 5	12 6	3 56	13 7	2 57	234 67	14 567	
14	234 5	2 6	13 56	3 7	12 57	1234 67	4 567	5 8
24	134 5	1 6	23 56	123 7	57	34 67	124 567	3 8
124	34 5	6	123 56	23 7	1 57	134 67	24 567	
34	124 5	123 6	56	1 7	23 57	24 67	134 567	2 8
134	24 5	23 6	1 56	7	123 57	124 67	34 567	
234	14 5	13 6	2 56	12 7	3 57	4 67	1234 567	8
1234	4 5	3 6	12 56	2 7	13 57	14 67	234 567	1 8

*All aliases of generated parameters 5, 6, 7 with 1, 2, 3, 4; generator, **main,** and two-way aliases of parameter 8 with 1 through 7.

TABLE 6.10 Compressed Two-Way Alias Matrix for 16 Binary Combinations*

ID: RES:	$I(5)$ 4	$I(6)+$ 4	$I(7)+$ 4	$I(8)+$ 4	$I(9)+$ 3/5.#	$I(A)+$ 3	$I(B)+$ 3	$I(C)+$ 3	$I(D)+$ 3	$I(E)+$ 3	$I(F)+$ 3
0	123 5	124 6	134 7	234 8	1234 9	12 A	13 B	23 C	14 D	24 E	34 F
1					8 9	2 A	3 B	5 C	4 D	6 E	7 F
2					7 9	1 A	5 B	3 C	6 D	4 E	8 F
12	3 5	4 6		7 8		A		B C		D E	9 F
3					6 9	5 A	1 B	2 C	7 D	8 E	4 F
13	2 5		4 7	6 8			**B**	A C		9 E	D F
23	1 5		6 7	4 8			A B	**C**	9 D		E F
123	**5**				4 9	3 A	2 B	1 C	8 D	7 E	6 F
4					5 9	6 A	7 B	8 C	1 D	2 E	3 F
14		2 6	3 7	5 8				9 C	**D**	A E	B F
24		1 6	5 7	3 8			9 B		A D	**E**	C F
124		**6**			3 9	4 A	8 B	7 C	2 D	1 E	5 F
34		5 6	1 7	2 8		9 A			B D	C E	**F**
134			**7**		2 9	8 A	4 B	6 C	3 D	5 E	1 F
234				**8**	1 9	7 A	6 B	4 C	5 D	3 E	2 F
1234	4 5	3 6	2 7	1 8	9#				C D	B E	A F

†Resolution, generators, **main,** and two-way aliases of parameters 5 through F with 1 through 4.

6.6.8 Saturated Fraction Designs

The design of an analysis of binary combinations is considered to be fully saturated when individual parameters have been identified with every effect of a binary combination except the overall average. Fully saturated designs are resolution 3.

TABLE 6.11 Two-Way Alias Summary for 16 Binary Combinations

P†	HS†	FS†							
1			89	2A	3B	5C	4D	6E	7F
2			79	1A	5B	3C	6D	4E	8F
		A	12	35	46	78	BC	DE	9F
3			69	5A	1B	2C	7D	8E	4F
		B	13	25	47	68	AC	9E	DF
		C	23	15	67	48	AB	9D	EF
	5		49	3A	2B	1C	8D	7E	6F
4			59	6A	7B	8C	1D	2E	3F
		D	14	26	37	58	9C	AE	BF
		E	24	16	57	38	9B	AD	CF
	6		39	4A	8B	7C	2D	1E	5F
		F	34	56	17	28	9A	BD	CE
	7		29	8A	4B	6C	3D	5E	1F
	8		19	7A	6B	4C	5D	3E	2F
		9#	45	36	27	18	CD	BE	AF

†Primary, half-, and fully saturated main effects.

Half-fraction designs as described previously add just one parameter to the primary parameters; resolution is equal to the total number of parameters (primary plus 1). A half fraction in three parameters (with only four runs) is also fully saturated and resolution 3. The half fraction in four parameters defined in Table 6.6 (and earlier) is resolution 4 and is considered half-saturated. Half-saturated designs are always resolution 4. A half-saturated design identifies parameters with the one-half of the effects that contain an odd number of primary parameters. Of course, the main effect of each primary parameter contains just that one parameter. The examples in Table 6.7 for four parameters and in Table 6.9 for eight parameters use all the three-way interactions of the primary parameters to introduce the new parameters.

Half-saturated designs are usually a reasonable compromise between the number of cases to be run and the number of variables to be investigated. One-half of the results measure main effects if three-way or higher aliases are not significant. The other half provide the overall average and collect sets of any two-way aliases.

Comparison to One-at-a-Time Methods.   We stated previously that one-at-a-time test methods are less effective than combination tests. A half-saturated binary design requires only twice the number of tests as parameters. This is the same as for the one-at-a-time method to test each parameter only once at two levels above and below the nominal level. Either method may include a center run with all parameters at their center value. The binary combination analysis provides much more information with greater precision.

A fully saturated design will provide the linear response at two levels for only one more test than the number of parameters. A test of each parameter one at a time at only one level, plus one test with all parameters at another level, may appear to achieve similar information with the same number of tests, but the results are vulnerable to the uncertainty of a single measurement and contain correlation due to the single measurement of the common reference for all the effects [3].

6.7   DESIGN TECHNIQUES

The previous sections described several of the basic definitions that characterize the relationship of such parameters as defect rate, production yield, test effectiveness, and reliability. Several of these indicated that the original responsibility for product quality lies with the design process. The design limits the performance capability that manufacturing can produce, which limits the performance that can be verified by test. Total product quality limits the profit which can be generated by sales of the product, by determining the total production and warranty costs as well as the customer satisfaction developed by use of the product. This section will summarize some of the basic design techniques that particularly apply to digital systems and that influence product quality. More of the system design guidelines are described in Chap. 7.

6.7.1 Digital Processing

Total quality is important for everything that influences the development, production, and use of products. This awareness is evidenced by the wide diversity of publications concerning various aspects of product improvement. One that primarily concerns applications to digital systems is *IEEE Design and Test of Computers*. The March 1991 cover feature is "Concurrent Engineering, Building Designs That Last" [4].

The following will be primarily concerned with the signal quality and noise suppression characteristics of digital processing that are required for error-free performance. A fundamental difference between digital and analog processing systems is the response to undesired signals. These undesired signals may be caused by a variety of sources, but they are called *noise* regardless of their heritage. Analog signals are generally processed in a linear fashion, which preserves the relationship of signals and noise. Analog processors are generally sensitive to power levels and refer to the relationship of signal power to noise power as the *signal-to-noise ratio*. However, each linear signal processing element generally adds some new source of noise, thereby degrading the signal-to-noise ratio.

Digital signals are processed by nonlinear methods which do not intend to preserve signal-to-noise ratios. Digital signals are intended to operate at discrete levels, with information contained in the transitions between states. Although binary logic levels are sometimes considered exact, with a fixed threshold that causes an input to be classified as one level or the other, it is more appropriate to consider operation to be defined by three regions. The two steady-state regions (generally called *High* and *Low* states) are characterized by nearly zero gain; small input signals that remain in this region have negligible effect on the output response. This is called *small-signal suppression;* small-amplitude noise is reduced at each processing element.

The two steady-state regions are separated by an intermediate region, usually called the *transition,* or *threshold,* region. The response in this region is characterized by greater-than-unity gain. Higher input levels are driven toward the High state; lower input levels are driven toward the Low state. This response is called *large signal gain,* or *strong signal capture.* If desired signals have valid transitions between the two states, each transition is amplified to the full level at each processing element. However, an input exactly at the threshold may remain there until some disturbance upsets this metastable condition.

Typical voltage transfer functions of digital devices are illustrated in Fig. 6.1. The illustration only indicates the function near the transition region. The small signal gain in the transition region is greater than unity and is indicated by T. Digital devices are considered vulnerable to noise in the transition region because noise is amplified. Some digital families may have very high gain in the transition region, so that the region is very small compared to the normal steady-state signal swing between levels. Some digital families may have high gain in the transition region, but the actual location of the region may be subject to significant uncertainty which is reflected in the specifications for the maximum Low and minimum High input levels. The performance of devices when their inputs are in the transition region is unspecified, generally undesirable, and to be avoided to the maximum extent practical. It is the principal objective of quality digital design to ensure that the operating signal levels are far from the transition region and that the possibility of malfunction when signals pass through the transition region is reduced to essentially zero. The steady-state signal gain is much less than unity, as indicated by SS; this provides noise suppression when signals are at valid levels.

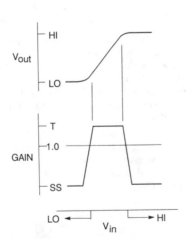

FIGURE 6.1 Voltage transfer and small-signal gain characteristics of a typical digital circuit.

Digital Magic.   Digital processing provides the "magic" of both noise suppression and strong signal capture, although this magic is neither guaranteed nor free. Careful attention to design and test of digital systems is required to achieve very low error rates for reliable signal processing in complex systems. Digital processing will suppress noise and respond to the desired signal only if noise is kept sufficiently low and the desired signals sufficiently strong. This characteristic has provided the basis for applications from digital computers and signal processors to digital audio, video, and radio-frequency processing.

Once a number or signal amplitude is represented by a pattern of *binary digits* (bits), they may be processed, stored, and retrieved virtually without limit without any significant risk of degradation. Unlike analog signal processing, where small signal levels and "quiet" levels must compete directly with noise, every digital bit (from most to least significant) has equal capability to suppress noise. Special techniques can reduce the vulnerability to any rare errors that might occur.

Synchronous design is critical to preserve the information content of signals when the speed of information transfers is pressed toward the limits of the technology applied in the design. Synchronous design is implemented to allow all data transitions to settle during a time interval in which the previous signal levels are preserved in temporary storage. All disturbances resulting from signal transitions are effectively ignored during the settling interval. This ensures that all signals have settled to their valid steady-state levels before being processed for the next time interval.

Additional signals (code bits) that represent characteristics of the intended data may be included to detect any errors, usually for purposes of correction. *Error detection and correction* (EDAC) may be achieved by a variety of codes; a common one is *parity* (modulo 2 addition without carry). A parity bit is added to a group of data bits according to whether the number of 1s in the data bits is odd or even. If an odd number of bits are changed during some processing, the parity will no longer match. The correction process may be accomplished by various methods, including in parallel with the coding processing or by repeating the data in which any errors are detected. EDAC prevents occasional errors from affecting subsequent data processing. EDAC also permits on-line error-rate monitoring. If the error rate is too high, a major review of the design and operation of the data processing system may be required.

Comparison of Digital and Production Processes.   There is a correlation between the concepts which can be used to achieve error-free digital processing and defect-free design, production, test, and maintenance of products. One basic foundation is that the design concept of the product and the architecture and technology base set the upper limit on performance for either system. Conservative design derating, which is used to minimize the chance that component degradation or severe conditions could result in errors, is comparable to the high *process capability* (C_P) index that is applied to production processes to minimize the chance that shifts in the process could result in production of defects. *Process capability* is the ratio of the acceptance specification limit to the variability of the production process. Process control and design derating are described further in Sec. 6.7.5. If the specification limit is greater than the variability and the process stays centered, defect rates can be kept low. Inner control limits are used for process control to ensure that the process remains reasonably centered. Process capability is the relationship of specification requirements to production performance; design derating is the relationship of specification requirements to the operating performance.

Undesired noise is added at digital processing elements in a manner similar to defects that are added at production processing steps. The suppression of noise corresponds to product screening that reduces defect rates (the analogy might be a little more obvious if production screening were called *defect suppression*). Note that noise suppression is an integral part of every digital process, not just a step inserted after serious degradation has

TABLE 6.12   Digital and Production Quality Control Comparison

Digital processes	Production processes
1. Design determines limit of capability	Design determines limit of capability
2. Derating reduces failure rate	Process capability reduces defect rate
3. Some noise added at each process	Some defects added at each process
4. Noise suppressed at each process	Defects detected in each process
5. Synchronization for minimum errors	Process control for minimum defects
6. ESS to verify performance margin	Inner controls to verify process capability
7. EDAC to prevent error propagation	CA to prevent defect production
8. Performance evaluation of EDAC	Performance evaluation of CA

occurred or only at the output stage. Likewise, production defect suppression is most effective when integrated into low-defect-rate process controls, not just added after defect rates are excessive or at final test.

Signal synchronization to ensure valid signal levels may be considered to correspond to *statistical process controls* (SPCs) that operate continuously to ensure that production processes are valid at all times, to minimize the chance of defects. The error detection rate of EDAC may be compared to the *corrective action* (CA) applied to prevent further defect production. The rate of defects requiring CA may be monitored to determine if the system is capable of quality production. If the rate of corrective action is too high, a review of the product design and the production system may be required. A comparison between digital processing and production is summarized in Table 6.12.

Other Nonlinear Processes.   It may be of interest that the nonlinear suppression of small signals in the presence of larger signals is characteristic of some other types of processing. The three-region response illustrated in Fig. 6.1 is sometimes called a *sigmoid transform* because of its S-shaped double-curved transfer characteristic. Sigmoidlike transforms with modest gain in the intermediate region are sometimes applied in an iterative manner called *relaxation* to enhance noisy video images. If the gain in the intermediate region is very high, the sigmoid response approaches the square threshold function. Related processing algorithms may be used in the processing nodes for artificial neural networks. It appears that biological neurons also use similar processing to suppress the less significant stimuli in the presence of more significant information. This seems to permit concentration on limited tasks without processing overload in the presence of numerous stimuli. However, it may also account for distraction and oversight of input that may be useful. The ability to separate the ''significant few'' from the ''insignificant many'' is an important part of problem identification and decision-making processes.

However, the tendency to overlook less significant information should be considered when evaluating human judgment. It is typical to underestimate the risks in ordinary tasks, as well as underestimate the chance of success on difficult tasks; this is called *cognitive bias* [5, pp. 80–81]. Experienced designers and managers may be especially susceptible to underestimating technical risks and cost overruns if actual quantitative data are not considered. Qualitative judgments of product quality may significantly underestimate defect rates or performance variability. Quality improvement teams should be aware that the tendency of management to underestimate or ignore the costs of defective products may make it difficult to obtain adequate support for corrective actions.

6.7.2 Noise Margin

The ability to accurately discriminate between high and low states is called the *noise margin*. An example of noise margin is illustrated in Fig. 6.2 for Schottky transistor-transistor logic (TTL). The specified noise margin is the difference between the specified worst-case output and the worst-case input which is processed correctly. The noise margin may be different for each logic state; many TTL-compatible families have less noise margin in the low state than for the high state. When many of the newer Schottky TTL families drive low-power Schottky (LS) TTL inputs, the low-state noise margin is only 200 mV [2]. Critical signals should be designed to be in the state with the greatest noise margin when operation is vulnerable to errors. For example, the active edge of TTL clock distribution should be low to high so it is less vulnerable to noise.

The noise margins may be different between logic families and sensitive to loading and temperature, in addition to the unit-to-unit variations. The specified noise margin is not the total worst-case noise margin; it includes only the conditions specified, usually a temperature and voltage range and unit-to-unit variations. Load variations or multiple signals in a dynamic environment are seldom included in the specifications. Most TTL families and the voltage-compensated ECL families are relatively insensitive to voltage tolerance. The input threshold for CMOS families is typically a proportion of the voltage, so increasing voltage tends to increase both high- and low-state noise margin. True CMOS outputs tend to drive signal levels "rail to rail," or essentially all the way to each power supply voltage for the low and high levels. This results in high steady-state noise margin but more switching noise, especially during high-low transitions. Some CMOS devices have high-state output levels that are similar to ordinary TTL to reduce transition noise.

Digital design must ensure that the maximum noise possible does not exceed the noise margin available at any time that proper input levels are required. Digital systems are vulnerable to internally generated noise that results from signal transitions. Although it may be difficult to model the amplitude of the noise with certainty, a design noise budget should be established so that requirements for characteristics such as ground offsets, power supply droop, and transient settling time can be defined. Significant derating should be included, especially considering the uncertainty of the modeling, the tendency to

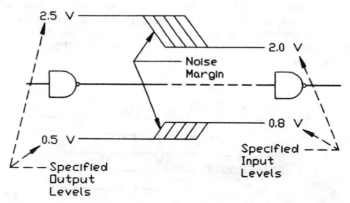

FIGURE 6.2   Schottky TTL noise margins. (*Source: James E. Buchanan, CMOS/ TTL Digital Systems Design. New York: McGraw-Hill, 1990. Used with permission of McGraw-Hill.*)

overlook some sources of noise, the likelihood that actual operation will be worse conditions than during design checkout, and the difficulty of fixing problems after production begins.

6.7.3 Synchronous Design

The concept of synchronous design as a signal quality-control technique is introduced in Sec. 6.7.1. Synchronous design involves signal quality, design derating, system timing, testability, signal distribution, and process control. Synchronous design partitions time into clock cycles. Clocked signals are allowed to transition only at a fixed point in the clock cycle. Digital signals are vulnerable to noise when they transition through the high-gain region between steady-state levels. Synchronous design uses the clock as a time gate so that disturbances cannot alter any storage device until the next clock cycle. Timing analysis determines if all transitions stabilize to valid input levels before the next active clock.

The input timing requirements to storage devices (flip-flops, memories, state machines, etc.) are referred to as *setup and hold time*. These define a timing window during which the input must remain stable and valid. The setup and hold time with respect to the active clock edge are illustrated in Fig. 6.3. The setup time is generally limited by the maximum delay of a transition initiated by a previous clock; hold time, by the minimum delay and clock skew. Timing analysis should be performed for derated worst-case actual conditions and to stable valid signal levels, not just the standard conditions at which parts are specified.

When both the levels and the times specified for inputs are met, this provides assurance that storage devices operate correctly. Little indication is provided to define how much degradation into the unspecified time or signal level region might be tolerated under particular conditions. Specifications define requirements for success; seldom is there a specification for failure. The consequence is that design verification by testing at nominal operating conditions is not effective. Adequate design ensures proper operation, but poor design only results in uncertainty. Malfunction is an indication of a design flaw, but proper operation proves little. Figure 6.3 does indicate that electrical ESS can be used to verify that the design has an actual performance margin. The clock cycle time can be reduced (or the propagation time increased) by an amount that represents setup time conditions for any operating condition. The farther beyond worst operating conditions that can be demonstrated without malfunction, the higher the confidence that other combinations of parts, worse operating conditions, and performance degradation can be tolerated without malfunction.

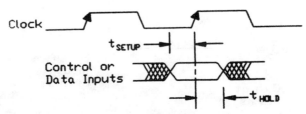

FIGURE 6.3 Signal setup and hold times. *(Source: James E. Buchanan, CMOS/TTL Digital Systems Design. New York: McGraw-Hill, 1990. Used with permission of McGraw-Hill.)*

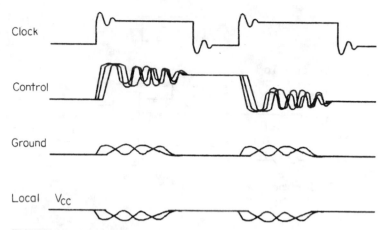

FIGURE 6.4 Noise and quiet times in a synchronous system. *(Source: James E. Buchanan, CMOS/TTL Digital Systems Design. New York: McGraw-Hill, 1990. Used with permission of McGraw-Hill.)*

Clock system design and distribution are important because signal transitions cause most of the noise in a digital system. Noise from clocked signals is illustrated in Fig. 6.4. The single-phase clock is in the high state after the active clock edge. Inputs are blocked from affecting storage devices until the next active clock edge. The single-phase clock divides time into distinct intervals that simplify analysis and test because time is divided into manageable sections. Actual performance margin can be measured by changing the clock rate when operation does not depend on critical nonsynchronous timing requirements.

A Summary of Synchronous Design Guidelines [2]

1. Use only the system clock to allow storage devices to change state. Avoid the use of control signals, decoded signals, and direct preset or reset to alter any storage devices.

2. Use only a single-phase continuous clock and fully registered storage devices. Avoid multiple clock phases or latches which allow transitions at more than one time within a clock cycle and result in critical timing that is difficult to test.

3. Use a single device with good metastable recovery to synchronize any asynchronous inputs to the lowest clock rate practical, and allow for recovery propagation delay.

4. Be sure the design is compatible with a variable clock rate to test critical timing functions. Provide a means to disable any internal clocks (automatic test equipment cannot test undefined functions) and operate on a test clock. A simple test control concept is shown in Fig. 6.5. Include controls to provide the capability for variable-clock-rate testing in the system.

5. Design the clock distribution to provide a fast transition through the threshold region. Verify that both clock generation and clock distribution have adequate large-signal gain and bandwidth to provide full noise margin at derated worst-case conditions. Test at higher assembly levels may be needed to ensure the performance margin if the bandwidth is not specified for logic devices.

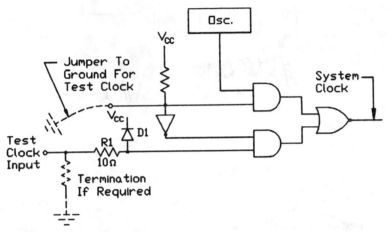

FIGURE 6.5 Test clock input port circuit. *(Source: James E. Buchanan, CMOS/TTL Digital Systems Design. New York: McGraw-Hill, 1990. Used with permission of McGraw-Hill.)*

6. When source series impedance is used for control of the rise time and waveshape, use lower resistance than line impedance and place the receivers close to the end of the line, so that the initial signal at the receivers crosses the threshold. Follow conservative loading derating to preserve waveshape and minimize clock skew.

7. Clock drivers should only share the same clock phase in the same package; never combine with any signal that may change near the active edge or when the clock is in the low state. Multiple clock rates should maintain the same phase, and the distribution should be separated to avoid timing uncertainty and interference.

6.7.4 Static Inputs

It is easy to overlook requirements for signals which do not change during normal operation. These include open, unused, preset, or reset inputs. Initialization or reset is a critical function that typically controls operation at power-on or when operation is recycled to the start-up condition. This function generally controls storage devices, so it is important that it operate reliably. Fault-tolerant systems may use the reset to recover from reconfiguration or serious transient upset. The reset function partitions time between a defined initialization state for storage devices and synchronous operating time.

The reset generator must respond to conditions including power up, power down, momentary interruptions, or any conditions that may affect storage devices, without any interference with normal operation. The reset function should be tested for proper response at the specified threshold, and the system should be capable of being tested for proper operation at just below the minimum reset threshold. Control logic should be provided for combining the voltage reset with any other logic signals for generating a system reset, as well as for inhibiting the reset to permit the system to be tested for proper operation down to below the minimum voltage threshold of the reset generator.

An example of a reset generator that operates from the 5-V logic supply is shown in Fig. 6.6. Here U1 is an analog comparator specified for low-voltage operation. The reset generator and distribution logic should be designed to operate well below the reset thresh-

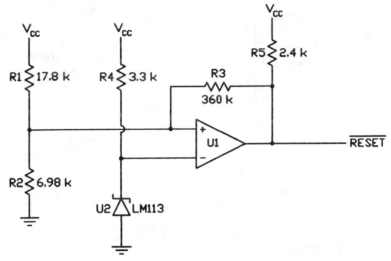

FIGURE 6.6   Reset signal generator using an analog comparator. *(Source: James E. Buchanan, CMOS/TTL Digital Systems Design. New York: McGraw-Hill, 1990. Used with permission of McGraw-Hill.)*

old. An LM193 comparator and CMOS specified for as low as 3 V are suitable for 5-V operation. The ratio of R1 and R2 sets the threshold, which is compared to the U2 precision voltage reference. The values shown provide a threshold of about 4.3 V. If a tolerance of ±200 mV can be achieved, the upper tolerance limit of 4.5 V allows system operation over the full specified TTL voltage range. The lower tolerance limit is 4.1 V, at which adequately derated designs should operate properly. If TTL-compatible designs are derated for fan-out, frequency, and temperature at 4.5 V, they should operate correctly at actual loads and nominal frequency below about 4 V. Most CMOS logic operates correctly at very low voltages, but at reduced frequency and noise margin. Correct performance of the reset generator should be verified by actual test before delivery to the user, and it should be testable in the system.

The distribution of the reset signal should use some of the same care as for the clock, to avoid interference with correct operation. Waveshape and bandwidth are not critical, so some of the guidelines for static inputs (logic or reset) apply. Reset should be in the high state during normal operation; a pull-up resistor or current source should be added to increase the noise margin for TTL outputs and to avoid interference with test if the input is open. Limit the number of points in the reset string, and separate the layout to reduce the chance of noise pickup.

TTL or CMOS inputs should never be allowed to float during operation or test conditions; an input bias source should provide a valid signal level. A logic low should be driven from a logic signal, not a resistor to ground. Although TTL inputs may tend to float to a high level due to the input current, it will be in the threshold region. CMOS inputs may tend to float to a level which allows both transistors to conduct, as illustrated in Fig. 6.7. All CMOS inputs that might be open during test or operation must have some bias to avoid undefined conditions or damage. Connect unused inputs to a logic signal or pull-up resistor (not power or ground) to provide current limiting during fault conditions and to allow control during in-circuit testing. Limit the number of points in any signal string to simplify possible redesign, troubleshooting, and in-circuit testing.

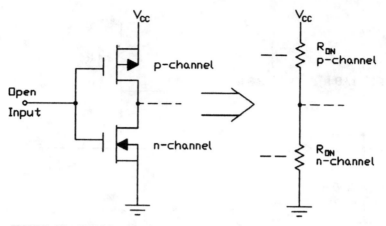

FIGURE 6.7   CMOS input state and open-circuit equivalent circuit. *(Source: James E. Buchanan, CMOS/TTL Digital Systems Design. New York: McGraw-Hill, 1990. Used with permission of McGraw-Hill.)*

Figure 6.7 also indicates what may happen if internal defects result in open-circuit or high-resistance connections. Defective connections internal to complex CMOS integrated circuits may be very difficult to detect with static tests because the state is undefined or may result in the correct state eventually. Dynamic switching and at-speed tests are required to achieve quality products. The resistive path from voltage to ground of an open CMOS stage suggests that some defective connections might be detectable as excess current draw. The symptoms may be easier to detect as a function of clock rate and temperature. Complex devices should be defect-free before assembly into systems where the defects may be much more costly to diagnose and repair.

Apply the System Reset without Delay.   Reset should be applied to the entire system without any analog delay or synchronization so that reset becomes active on power-up and as soon as any undervoltage condition occurs, without depending on an active clock to put the system in a safe condition. The system reset should be removed in synchronization with the clock so the transition to operation is performed correctly. Two examples of logic that will provide asynchronous application and synchronous removal of reset are shown in Fig. 6.8.

The basic logic shown can be augmented if additional turn-on delay is desired. The delay of a counter may be inserted into the *D* input of F1 or F2. Never use analog delays based on capacitors for synchronous digital logic designs; they are vulnerable to wide tolerances, aging degradation, and uncertain leakage currents that depend on environmental conditions, especially when long delay times are intended. Timing based on internal capacitors or oscillators is nearly impossible to test in system BIT or on automatic test equipment [2].

6.7.5 Design Derating and Verification

Design derating is the part of the design process that requires the design to be specified to exceed the worst-case performance requirements by a minimum amount. Design derating is usually expressed as the percentage ratio of actual operating stress to specified

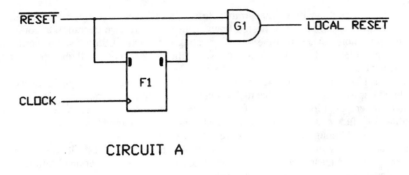

CIRCUIT A

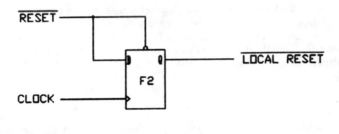

CIRCUIT B

FIGURE 6.8 Two circuits for asynchronously applying and synchronously removing reset signals. *(Source: James E. Buchanan, CMOS/TTL Digital Systems Design. New York: McGraw-Hill, 1990. Used with permission of McGraw-Hill.)*

capability. For example, a logic device rated at an absolute maximum of 7 V but operated at a maximum of 5.6 V is derated 80 percent; if it is specified for 10 percent voltage tolerance and regulated to within 7 percent, it is derated 70 percent for voltage tolerance. A design capable of 12.5 MHz and operated at 10 MHz is derated 80 percent for frequency. The purpose of derating is to provide several benefits, particularly the following:

1. Reduced design development cycle time
2. Reduced production costs
3. Reduced failure rate
4. Reduced operating costs

Establishing derating requirements improves the ability of the development organization to produce the first few units on schedule. The first units should work the first time and be ready for release to production without major redesign. Application and verification of derating requirements tend to result in more rigorous design analysis and fewer design errors. Even when the performance objectives are ambitious, derated designs are more tolerant of design deficiencies or less-than-ideal performance of critical parts which often occurs during technology development programs. Derating provides a margin, so that it is possible to support testing and integration in parallel with any performance improvements. The development organization also can learn what is needed to improve performance and reduce defects in both the product and the design processes.

Adequate derating allows the product to be produced with a minimum of defects, scrap, rework, or correction of design flaws. ESS is a short-term operation at conditions significantly more severe than the worst operating conditions. ESS is used to verify that the design is adequately derated so that the variability in production will remain within the requirements.

As described in Sec. 6.2.4, the presence of a performance margin in every unit produced improves the chance that the product will continue to operate properly for longer periods under conditions different from design verification and factory test. Different conditions include component degradation and more severe environmental conditions and data patterns. Although a reduced failure rate directly reduces operating costs, derating also reduces spares and repair-parts costs, cannot-duplicate and retest-OK test problems, improves interchangeability and system availability, and increases service lifetime before lack of available repair parts requires system replacement.

Process Capability Index.   The production performance margin is usually expressed as the ratio of the difference between the average performance and the performance requirement to the variability of the performance. This ratio is called the *process capability* (C_P) index and determines the defect rates as a function of statistical process control applied to design derating and production. A one-sided C_P index is defined as follows:

$$C_P = \frac{\text{Average performance} - \text{specification limit}}{3\sigma \text{ standard deviation}} \tag{6.4}$$

If the specification is two-sided, the maximum theoretical C_P uses the difference between the two specification limits for the numerator and double the 3σ deviation for the denominator. When C_P is applied to design capability, average performance is the worst-case performance objective. When Eq. (6.4) is corrected for the actual performance, or an allowance is made for the shift that may occur before SPC corrective action, it may be designated C_{PK} to indicate the correction.

A design to only the worst-case requirements with no derating has no design margin and a C_P of 0. The C_{PK} will be positive only if the actual performance can be maintained at better than the design. A C_P of 0 indicates an expected yield of 50 percent. A C_P of 1 indicates a design margin equal to the 3σ deviation. If the performance average is exactly as expected, the risk of failure is about 1 in 1000 for each critical element. However, if the average shifts 2σ toward the specification limit, the risk of failure jumps to about 15 percent. A standard for superior products and processes is $C_P = 2$. Even after an allowance for a 2σ shift, the risk of failure is only about 0.01 percent, or 1 in 10,000, or 100 parts per million (ppm).

The following illustrations are based on the example of frequency, with the units of megahertz dropped for convenience. The design specifies proper performance at 12.5 for worst-case conditions. The acceptance requirement is a minimum of 10, for a design derating of 80 percent. Although there are many engineering examples where nominal performance is the desired objective (voltage and dimension tolerances are examples), this illustration has a one-sided objective where more is better. The difference between the predicted performance and the specification limit is $12.5 - 10$, or 2.5. The uncertainty of the performance during production is often unknown. The statistical distribution of performance is assumed to be the normal distribution.

One sigma only represents a central tendency, since there is more than 15 percent probability to either side of a 1σ limit. A 1σ limit has a 15 percent reject rate just due to normal variability. It is difficult to attempt to control a process to within 1σ because a measurement sample is often outside the limit even when the actual mean is unbiased.

There is slightly more than 2 percent probability of an event beyond a 2σ limit, so it is a reasonable process control limit. If measured performance fails the inner limit, action is taken to determine if corrective action is needed. Delivery of acceptable product continues uninterrupted. A 2σ acceptance limit is not reasonable because there is more than a 2 percent reject rate for normal variability even if the distribution remains exactly centered. If the average (mean) shifts 2σ before corrective action is effective, the reject rate may exceed 50 percent.

From 2σ to 4σ, the one-sided tail probability, or reject rate, drops by a ratio of more than 10 to 1 per sigma. At 4σ beyond the actual mean, the defect rate is less than 100 ppm per part. This is generally considered acceptable for ordinary production. The acceptance limit needs to be 4σ beyond the control limit, for a total of 6σ beyond the ideal mean. If statistical process control is sufficiently effective to maintain a 1.5σ inner control limit, a 6σ acceptance limit results in less than a 10-ppm reject rate for normal variation.

If it is assumed that the 1σ uncertainty of the example is 0.8, a design margin of 2.5 is slightly more than 3σ. Compared to only a worst-case design with no derating, a 3σ margin seems rather comfortable, with less than 0.1 percent, or 1000 ppm, defect rate. However, consider what happens if there is a bias of 2σ in the difference between the initial performance estimate and the actual average achieved in production. This bias reduces the actual margin to only 1.13σ, which results in a defect rate of approximately 130,000 ppm, or 13 percent per part. Examples of bias include a design model which overestimated performance of a critical path or a critical component that did not achieve specified performance in actual application.

These reject rates apply to each individual opportunity for a problem to occur. If the uncertainty in the design model and the component performance is about one-third of the design margin, this represents a risk of about 1 in 1000 that each critical path or component will fail to meet the acceptance limit. A complex system might have about 1000 critical paths and critical components. The combined risk of failure of at least one of these critical elements is very high. The results may be low yield, high cost, schedule delays, and customer dissatisfaction.

Managing Design and Development Risk. The same analysis described above as reject rates in a factory environment can be applied to the risk of failure in the design process of developing a few initial units to meet performance requirements. The defect rates correspond to the risk of failure to meet the acceptance requirements. Unless the chance of each failure is much lower than the number of opportunities for failure, there is a high risk that some critical path or component will fail to meet the requirements. Failure is almost certain somewhere, but it is unknown where it will occur. A design policy is needed to significantly reduce the risk of failure.

There are three variables in the definition of C_P, so it can be improved by modifying one or any combination that provides acceptable results. First, the ratio involves the uncertainty or variability of the process. In the example, if the standard deviation can be reduced by a factor of 2, the same design has a 6σ margin. In many design and production applications, reduction of variability is the most cost-effective approach to improved product quality and reduced development risk. If the design is based on a 6σ objective and the actual results fall short of the objective by 2σ because one event with 1 chance in 100 happened, there is still a 4σ margin left. Even if no corrective action is taken to improve the performance to better than 4σ, this results in a chance of failure of 100 ppm, or 1 in 10,000.

This example indicated that some of the risks in achieving performance might be a design model that overestimated the actual capability or a vendor that was unable to supply a critical part with the intended performance. Examples of methods to reduce these risks are to improve the model to be more accurate and/or conservative, to perform preliminary evaluation of critical areas, and to cooperate with the vendor to develop a quality part that has been adequately proved to meet the requirements. Cooperating with a vendor to establish a $C_P = 2$ policy should virtually eliminate the risk of failure and produce parts that always exceed specifications. The impact of a vendor missing a $C_P = 2$ objective by 2σ or 3σ is negligible compared to missing an objective to only meet the specification ($C_P = 0$).

The second part of C_P improvement is that the specification limit might be reduced. If the 1σ uncertainty remains at 0.8 and the maximum design capability remains at 12.5, then a 6σ design margin is 4.8 and the specification limit should be reduced to 7.7. This performance reduction may be unpleasant but necessary if alternatives are unacceptable.

The third part of C_P improvement is the design performance. If the uncertainty and the specification remain unchanged, then a design performance of 14.8 is $C_P = 2$. This design derating of about 67 percent allows for constant uncertainty. This rather modest increase in the design objective, or the reduction in uncertainty described in the first part, or a lesser combination of both that provides $C_P = 2$ results in a dramatic reduction in risk without reducing the acceptance limit. For the example of just one critical path or component that falls short of the objective by one-third of the $C_P = 2$ design margin (about 10 percent), the risk of failure is reduced more than 1000 to 1 compared to $C_P = 1$.

The previous examples of risk reduction tend to be based on an assumed knowledge of the statistical distribution. Digital design teams may tend to be more comfortable with pass/fail than statistical distributions and defect rates. One way to become more familiar with quality processes is to be involved with a concurrent design team. Those representing test, production, reliability, maintenance, or logistic support responsibilities may be familiar with the relationship of design margin requirements to product quality attributes. Components and procurement specialists may provide information on the risk of achieving performance and the relative quality performance of vendors.

Design without Statistics.   Design margin requirements may be inferred and managed by ESS for process control without advance knowledge of statistical distributions. Inferred or managed process capability during design and development is discussed in the following examples. One method for considering design derating is based on queuing analysis using the Poisson distribution which does not have an independent parameter for variance. The Poisson distribution is appropriate when there are many opportunities but the expected number of events is low. This suggests that it is reasonable to plan for product quality without advance knowledge of the variance.

Many digital systems fail not because one element is far from the expected performance, but because two or three elements each are a little out of the expected performance and the combined effect exceeds the design margin under extreme conditions. The higher the risk that individual elements fail specifications, the greater the chance that a system problem may occur.

Queuing analysis considers the probability of the number of arrival events that are waiting for service as a function of the load derating, which is the ratio of the average arrival rate to the average service rate. The difference is the average idle time, which corresponds to design margin. On average, design margin and idle time are nonproductive and appear to be a waste of capability. However, this difference is needed to accommodate uncertainty. The average queue length increases the total time to complete the service. A dramatic difference occurs between 60 and 80 percent derating. Below 60 percent, the average queue length is less than 2; this means that the chance of a combination of two or more events is low. However, at 80 percent, the average queue length is 4 and rises rapidly to 10 as derating increases toward 90 percent [3]. Although a real system would not allow queues to grow beyond acceptable limits, the model for the waiting line grows rapidly toward infinity as derating increases above 90 percent.

Plan for Uncertainty — Win with Murphy.   The message from the queuing model is that an allowance for uncertainty is necessary; unless there is capability in reserve for uncertainty, when unlikely events happen, there is nothing to accommodate them. It is common to say, "Murphy wins." This means that if something can go wrong, it eventually will, possibly at a critical time. Statistical analysis confirms that if events are possible, some of them will happen. Random events are not regularly spaced, so they tend to cluster. Murphy wins if there are no resources in reserve when the unlikely happens.

The need to plan with an allowance for uncertainty is not limited to design and service queues. A design and development program must meet cost and schedule as well as performance requirements. If the plan is completely full of essential activities until the required delivery date, uncertainties will happen and cause the schedules to slip. Likewise, if the financial plan is to spend all available funds by the planned delivery date, either unplanned costs or schedule slippage will result in cost overruns. The plans must have an allowance for uncertainty, but progress must be controlled so that the margin is not wasted unless absolutely necessary. If all goes well, the program may be completed ahead of time and under the budget limit. This is the same principle as the inner limits of statistical process control that attempt to achieve a consistently superior product. If serious problems happen, there is margin available to meet the requirements.

The queuing model has a scheduling message that applies to a range of efforts from personal tasks to major programs. Because there is uncertainty, it will always take longer to complete a task than just the time to perform it. If we schedule (or allow) tasks to approach capacity, unplanned delays will cause slippage. We must schedule less work than the maximum that can be done, keeping some capacity in reserve [3, 6]. A planned hold in a launch countdown is an example of schedule reserve.

How much margin to allow is a tradeoff between efficiency and risk. Queuing analysis indicates that the maximum probability of an event's being serviced with no waiting occurs at 50 percent derating. Efficiency this low can be justified only when the cost of failure is very high. An objective of 2 in the waiting line occurs at about 75 percent derating. The application to design is that if a combination of two or three unlikely events can be accommodated, about 70 percent design derating is a good compromise.

Set Design Derating and Manage to $C_P = 2$.   It is important to set an achievable objective and make it happen. The objective may be an ambitious adventure in the unknown, but reasonable without being so risky that it is a reckless waste of resources. Process controls can manage risk by applying corrective action before failure becomes inevitable.

Selecting a derating of 70 percent and managing it as $C_P = 2$ is equivalent to managing the design, development, and production process so the 1σ uncertainty does not exceed 5 percent. This can be done without concern for what the uncontrolled uncertainty might have been. One-third of the design margin (about 10 percent) is allowed for SPC. The remainder is tested for performance verification; any shortfall is investigated for corrective action in a *test, analyze, and fix* (TAAF) program with the objective of product quality, not merely meeting requirements. When the design objective is 70 percent derating and the requirement is at 80 percent of the SPC limit, the product should pass an ESS test at $1/0.8 = 125$ percent of the requirement at worst-case conditions. The design objective should be about $1/0.7 = 140$ percent of the requirement to allow a reasonable chance of passing the 125 percent stress test.

Some of the various types of design derating parameters that should be considered include the following:

1. Absolute maximum ratings
2. The timing (ac) and static (dc) performance parameters and conditions
3. Design models for predicting unspecified performance

Absolute or maximum ratings are usually specified as those conditions beyond which permanent degradation or damage may occur. Although there may be a reasonable safety margin in the maximum rating, derating for operating conditions is a good practice for reliability improvement. Maximum ratings should not be exceeded in stress-testing of deliverable products.

It is important that ac and dc specifications be derated in the design and verified by ESS. Examples of specifications for digital components include input thresholds, output levels, input and output loading, propagation delay, temperature range, and power supply tolerance. Custom devices are often specified for additional parameters that should be derated, such as the number of ground pins, number of simultaneously switching outputs, and number of routable gates. There is often an equivalence between derating the conditions or the performance. For the example of propagation delay, it is approximately equivalent for synchronous design to meet a higher clock frequency at the specified propagation delays, or to meet the required frequency at higher propagation delays. Design policy should avoid derating essentially the same parameter more than once, while ensuring that all derating is met simultaneously.

6.7.6 Design Models

Design models are often used when actual conditions are not within component specifications. Although it is preferred to specify components for all operating conditions, cost and quality are improved when standard parts are used. Models are acceptable when adequately derated and appropriate and the performance margin is verified in the actual application. Examples of design models include increasing the maximum delay at greater than the test load or decreasing the minimum at less than the test load. Worst-case designs should not use models to predict improvements when operation is within the specified conditions.

Account for Derating and Actual Conditions. Models should account for actual operating conditions and maintain the derating requirements. For an example of 70 percent derating for loading, the model must predict a delay increase if actual loading exceeds 70 percent of the specification so that actual loading does not exceed 70 percent of the model because the model substitutes for the specification. If 80 percent derating applies to models, the delay increase must be 125 percent of the basic model. Models should be adjusted for actual worst-case load conditions, such as the following:

1. Line delay may increase and line impedance decrease by the factor $\sqrt{1 + C_l/C_o}$, where C_l is the lumped load capacitance and C_o is the total intrinsic line capacitance of a loaded short line.
2. Line impedance may increase or decrease by the factor $1 \pm K_b$. The initial backward crosstalk coefficient $K_b = C_m/(2C_o + C_m)$, where C_m is the mutual capacitance to adjacent short lines.
3. Rise and fall times may increase to approximately the line delay, including the loading allowance.

4. The intrinsic line capacitance loading may increase by a factor of approximately $1 \pm 2K_b$. The additional line capacitance is load capacitance for 1, above.

REFERENCES

1. George E. P. Box, William G. Hunter, and J. Stuart Hunter, *Statistics for Experimenters*. New York: Wiley, 1978.

2. James E. Buchanan, *CMOS/TTL Digital Systems Design*. New York: McGraw-Hill, 1990.

3. Charles C. Flagle, William H. Huggins, and Robert H. Roy (eds.), *Operations Research and Systems Engineering*. Baltimore, Md.: Johns Hopkins Press, 1960.

4. *IEEE Design and Test of Computers*, vol. 8, no. 1, March 1991.

5. Thomas J. Peters and R. H. Waterman, Jr., *In Search of Excellence*. New York: Warner Books, 1982.

6. Robert H. Roy, *The Administrative Process*. Baltimore, Md.: Johns Hopkins Press, 1958.

CHAPTER 7
DIGITAL SYSTEM DESIGN

James E. Buchanan
Westinghouse Electric Corporation, Baltimore, Maryland

7.1 INTRODUCTION

Digital system design is not confined to the functional definition of systems, as is often the perception. Many electrical, mechanical, test, and other issues must be addressed from a system-level standpoint. This chapter deals with some system-level electrical issues, namely, power distribution and signal interconnections.

System power distribution and the connection of signals between digital circuits, boards, and units are not simple tasks and must not be neglected when today's high-speed logic components are used. Most of today's digital circuits have very fast signal transitions, i.e., rise and fall times, which will cause problems unless a great deal of care is taken in their interconnection. The signal transition time, not the signal switching rate, establishes the high-frequency content of a signal [1, 2]. The signal high-frequency content, in turn, determines the onset of signal corruptio 1 due to transmission-line and crosstalk effects and power and signal distribution network bandwidth limitations.

7.2 POWER DISTRIBUTION

Power distribution networks for state-of-the-art digital systems must have the capability to supply large transient load and device switching currents, plus the capability to prevent noise generated by local load and device transient switching currents from propagating to other parts of the system. To meet those requirements, the power distribution network impedance must be as low as possible, and decoupling capacitors must be used in liberal quantities to compensate for unavoidable impedance, of which there is always some [3].

In the typical large digital system, possible voltage loss at each of the following power system interfaces must be controlled:

1. Logic device chip metallization, bond wires, and package leads
2. Logic device power and ground pin connections to circuit board power and ground planes

---

Some of the material in this chapter, including Figs. 7.1 to 7.4 and 7.6 to 7.24, is from James E. Buchanan, *BiCMOS/CMOS Systems Design*. New York: McGraw-Hill, 1990. Reproduced with permission of McGraw-Hill, Inc.

3. Circuit board power and ground planes
4. Circuit board–motherboard power and ground connections
5. Motherboard power and ground planes
6. Motherboard power and ground plane connections to power and ground feeder lines or busses
7. Power and ground lines or busses between motherboard and power supplies

Power distribution networks must be designed so that the total network loss plus the voltage tolerance of the power source plus an allowance for noise does not result in a voltage at the components that is below their minimum specified operating level. Both ac and dc losses are of concern at each interface, but power distribution problems are most often caused by ac losses in high-speed digital applications. Guidance for determining and controlling losses in each of the above-listed interfaces is provided below.

7.2.1 Logic Device Chip Metallization, Bond Wires, and Package Power and Ground Connections

The fast edges of today's logic devices cause large, high-frequency, transient load currents. Large load currents mean large currents in the device's power and ground connections. The inductance of package leads, bond wires, and chip metallization is significant at the frequencies contained in the switching edges of today's digital devices. The combination of large transient currents and significant inductance causes large shifts in chip power supply and reference levels [4]. These level shifts are called *power supply droop* and *ground bounce*. If the level shifts are large enough, they may cause

1. Logic errors in internal storage elements or at the inputs of devices connected to signals that originate from the switching device
2. Nonmonotonic transitions on outputs, which can cause double clocking if the outputs are used as clock signals
3. Degradation of propagation delays because the supply voltage across the device is reduced, which decreases the drive capability

Voltage loss due to the resistance and inductance of chip metallization is usually a difficult parameter for system designers to establish. The chip metallization inductance and resistance are usually not available (to system designers). Fortunately, most established integrated-circuit (IC) vendors are aware of the need to minimize on-chip power and ground losses, and they do so. When devices with less than optimum internal and package resistance or inductance must be used, the only recourse for the system designer is to limit the current.

Voltage losses due to bond wires (i.e., the connections between an integrated circuit and its package leads) are usually minor, but they tend to be more significant than on-chip losses. Fortunately, they are usually easier to evaluate. Table 7.1 shows typical bond wire resistance and inductance [5]. When the bond wire length is known, the bond wire resistance, or inductance, which is usually the more significant parameter, can be estimated by multiplying the inductance shown in Table 7.1 by the ratio of the actual length of the bond wire to 0.1 in. The bond wire inductance is then added to the package pin inductance, and the transient switching voltage drop across both is calculated as described below.

Package pin inductance is responsible for the major portion of any voltage loss at the chip and package level. Table 7.2 shows the range of typical pin inductances for several

TABLE 7.1 Bond Wire† Electrical Properties

Parameter	Aluminum	Gold
Resistance, Ω	0.142	0.122
Inductance, nH	2.621	2.621

†0.001-in diameter by 0.1-in-long bond wire

TABLE 7.2 Package Pin Inductance

	Self-inductance, nH	
Package	Upper value	Lower value
14-pin DIP	10	3
20-pin DIP	15	3
20-pin PLCC	5	4
28-pin DIP	17	5
44-pin PLCC	6	5
100-pin PLCC	15	12

common packages [6, 7]. The two values listed in Table 7.2 are representative of the inductance of the longer and shorter signal paths (pins) into or out of a given package style. Twenty-pin *plastic leaded chip carriers* (PLCCs) are nearly symmetric. Hence, there is little difference in the length, or inductance, of the pins. The actual worst-case pin inductance for the various listed package styles may vary considerably from that shown in Table 7.2, so actual package specifications should always be consulted. Note that surface-mounted packages such as LCCs and PLCCs have less lead inductance than *dual-in-line packages* (DIP) and offer an advantage where they can be used.

Ground bounce (or power supply droop) problems are compounded when several heavily loaded drivers in a common package switch simultaneously [8]. One observable manifestation of ground bounce or power supply droop is the appearance of transient voltage spikes on stable outputs when other heavily loaded devices in the (same) package switch [9].

Figure 7.1 shows a common situation where ground bounce spikes will be observable on a stable output of an octal driver (power supply droop will occur for the opposite switching conditions). A ground bounce spike will occur on the stable output when the other drivers switch from a *high* to a *low* level. High-to-low switching causes a large transient current to flow from the loads to ground through the package ground pin. The inductance of the pin and the large transient current cause a transient voltage drop (spike) across the ground pin. The transient voltage spike causes the reference level of the internal chip to shift in the positive direction, causing a positive voltage spike on the stable output, as shown in Fig. 7.1. The magnitude of the spike depends on the total load of the switched outputs. In many common situations, the magnitude of the spike will exceed the noise margin of the receiving device.

To find the magnitude of a transient ground bounce voltage spike for a given application, first the change in current in the package ground pin must be determined. The change in current ΔI is a function of the number N of output drivers in the package that switch simultaneously, their output voltage transitions ΔV, and the impedance of their

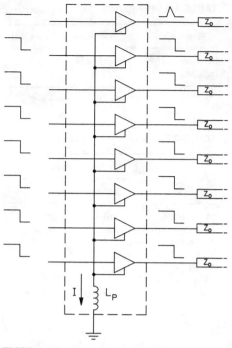

FIGURE 7.1 A static output will have a ground bounce spike (see top buffer output) when the other outputs of the package switch.

loads. In most situations, the interconnecting line characteristic impedance Z_o is the dominant dynamic portion of the load impedance (characteristic impedance is defined in Sec. 7.3.3). Where that is the case, the equation for ΔI is

$$\Delta I = N \frac{\Delta V}{Z_o} \qquad (7.1)$$

Typical level transitions ΔV for devices with the following interface levels are as follows:

ECL levels: 1 V

TTL levels: 3.5 V

CMOS levels: 5 V

Once ΔI is known, the transient ground bounce voltage V_{GB} can be calculated by using

$$v(t) = L \frac{di}{dt}$$

which for practical purposes is approximated by

$$V_{GB} = L \frac{\Delta I}{\Delta t} \qquad (7.2)$$

where Δt is the average transition time, i.e., rise or fall time, of the switching outputs.

Techniques for Minimizing Ground Bounce Effects. All devices have some ground bounce, even the new, improved second-generation advanced CMOS and BiCMOS devices. Even when all external connections are ideal, i.e., zero impedance, some package pin inductance remains, which may cause significant ground bounce depending upon the load and output slew rate. Ground bounce can be controlled on critical CLOCK and STROBE signals by carefully following the design practices that limit ground bounce, but it is impractical to follow those design practices for all signals. The only practical recourse for the system designer is to use logic techniques that negate the possible detrimental effects of ground bounce voltage spikes on most data and control signals [3]. Synchronous design practices are one means of limiting the possible detrimental effects of ground bounce [3]. Synchronous design prohibits the use of asynchronous inputs on storage elements (flip-flops) or cross-coupled gates for performing operational logic functions. Thus, short spikes, such as those generated by ground bounce, cannot directly upset synchronous systems.

To further limit the possible detrimental effects of ground bounce or power supply droop, the buffers used to drive critical signals, such as clocks and signals that go to asynchronous inputs, such as resets and presets, must be segregated into separate packages. The purpose is to prevent ground bounce from heavily loaded buffers from upsetting other buffers (in a common package). For example, different-frequency clock signals should not use buffers in a common package. Not all the buffers in an octal package should be used if all the buffers are driving heavily loaded lines and all the signals could switch at once; clock signal fan-out buffers are an example. When the number of buffers used in an octal package is limited due to ground bounce considerations, those used should be the buffers nearest the ground pin.

Ground bounce and power supply droop are of particular concern when *programmable logic devices* (PLDs), FIFOs, and other *large-scale integration* (LSI) devices are used. Most such devices have a large number of outputs that can switch at once. Yet, most LSI devices do not have sufficient ground or V_{cc} pins to support heavy simultaneously switched loads without severe output pin interaction. Some of the new high-speed PLDs have center ground pins to reduce ground bounce effects, but center ground pins only reduce ground bounce—they do not eliminate it. The only recourse system designers have is to limit output loads and to control the mix of signals in LSI devices, such as PLDs, where that is possible. In general, most of the rules for controlling ground bounce in *small-scale integration* (SSI) and *medium-scale integration* (MSI) devices covered above must be followed when PLDs and other LSI devices are used. For example, the following classes of signals should not be sourced from a common LSI device:

1. Signals going to asynchronous inputs and signals driving heavy loads
2. Clock enable signals and signals driving heavy loads
3. Write enable signals to random access memories (RAMs) and other heavily loaded signals
4. Clock signals of different frequencies

In general, PLDs should not be used as clock drivers because of potential ground bounce problems and other possible interaction.

To minimize the chance for ground bounce problems, outputs of byte-wide devices must not be heavily loaded. Byte-wide FIFOs and other LSI devices with byte-wide outputs (where it is possible for all bits to change at once) must not be used to drive heavily loaded busses. If outputs of byte-wide LSI devices must go to more than one or two loads, they should be buffered and redriven to prevent ground bounce from disrupting internal operation. FIFOs are of special concern; most FIFOs are asynchronous devices and are extremely sensitive to spikes on ground or V_{cc}.

In *application-specific integrated-circuit* (ASIC) applications, it is important to establish the number of package power and ground pins early in the design cycle. System speed is a function of ASIC output drive, and ASIC output drive capability is limited by the number of power and ground pins and the number of outputs that switch at once. Transient switching currents cause fluctuations in internal power and ground levels which cause spikes on unswitched outputs (which can cause system upsets) and may also disturb internal logic. It is easy to underestimate the number of power and ground pins required in high-performance applications. Often optimistic guesses are made that severely limit design options later on. High-speed high-current outputs (for example, 12 mA or higher) often require a ground and power pin per two outputs and in some cases may require a power and ground pin per output. Unless a proper allowance has been made for power and ground pins, a larger package may have to be used, which may cause a number of problems, or performance may have to be decreased. Slower, lower-current outputs that require fewer power and ground pins may have to be used, which means lower performance.

Most ASIC vendors have strict rules as to power and ground pin requirements and will not fabricate devices that do not meet these requirements. Thus, it is important to understand the requirements early in a design so that the proper number of power and ground pins is allocated. Vendor application information must be thoroughly studied. However, many system application issues also affect power and ground pin requirements. The ASIC vendor may not understand the system issues and should not be relied upon to establish the requirements. The system designer is in the best position to understand all the issues and must take responsibility for establishing the required number of power and ground pins. Even if the ASIC vendor takes the initiative to establish the number of pins, the system designer should check the results.

These important system application issues affect the number of power and ground pins required:

1. Number of simultaneously switching outputs
2. Output speed and current driver requirements
3. Package pin inductance
4. Ground bounce and power supply droop tolerance

Items 1 and 2 are system issues that the ASIC vendor has little knowledge of until the later stages of ASIC designs. They must be determined by the system designer. Package pin inductance is usually available from the ASIC vendor unless a custom package is used. If a custom package is used, it is important that either the user or the ASIC vendor determine the package lead inductance. The interconnection inductance between the package power and ground pins and circuit board power and ground planes must also be considered. Ideally, package power and ground pin connections should be made directly to power and ground planes so as to avoid adding more inductance, but that is sometimes not possible with certain surface-mounted techniques. If it is not possible to make a direct connection to circuit board power and ground planes, the inductance of interconnecting traces must be added to the package pin inductance, and the total used to calculate power and ground pin requirements.

7.2.2 Logic Device Power and Ground Pin Connections to Board Power and Ground Planes

The connections between component power and ground pins and board power and ground planes must be direct, to minimize ground bounce or power supply droop—there can be no wiring or long *printed-circuit* (pc) board tracks. The inductance of wired power or ground connections cannot be tolerated when high-speed logic components are used. Power and ground connections must be made directly to power and ground planes. Even sockets must be avoided in most applications, since they add inductance and increase ground bounce and power supply droop.

When prototyping boards (such as wire-wrap or welded-wire) are used, the package (or socket) power and ground pins must be connected directly to the power and ground planes, using solder washers or clips [11]. Often during the developmental phase of a project when wire-wrap or welded-wire universal boards are used, there is a temptation to wire ground and power connections. Yet, simple calculations [using Eq. (7.2)] of voltage loss as a function of transient switching currents (which are to be expected with most of today's logic devices) show the inappropriateness of wired power or ground connections. On wire-wrap boards, it is difficult to achieve connections that are much less than 1 in. The inductance of 1 in of no. 30 wire is in the range of 15 to 50 nH, depending upon how close the wire is to a ground plane or other return path [12, 13]. The transient voltage drop caused by 15 to 50 nH of additional inductance beyond that due to pin and bond wire inductance cannot be tolerated in most applications.

7.2.3 Voltage Loss across Circuit Boards and Motherboards

Low-impedance planes must be used to distribute power and ground on circuit boards and motherboards in high-performance digital systems. Planes are needed to keep the dc resistance and ac impedance as low as possible so that high dc and pulse current loads can be supplied with minimum loss. It is important when high-speed digital devices are used that board power and ground planes be continuous throughout all device and connector pin fields. Planes must not be interrupted except for clearance holes for vias (feedthroughs) and package leads. Boards with ground cutouts for pin rows must not be used in high-speed digital applications. Some board manufacturers' catalogs describe universal boards with the required continuous planes as "Schottky" boards.

Static (DC) Loss.   Power system voltage losses due to dc effects are usually not a major problem in today's digital systems. In most circuit board or motherboard applications where planes are used, dc losses are kept to negligible levels. However, in higher-current applications, possible dc losses across power and ground planes must be evaluated.

The dc drop across a circuit board or motherboard plane is difficult to calculate since currents in planes are not confined to known paths. One useful approach for estimating dc voltage drops across a plane is to segment the plane into squares, as shown in Fig. 7.2, and sum the more manageable and more easily determined drops across the individual squares. First, determine the current requirements of each square (i.e., the supply current requirements of components or circuit board connector pins that are located in that portion of the plane). Second, average the current for each row of squares, and make the as-

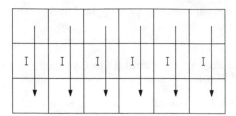

FIGURE 7.2 Segment ground or voltage planes into squares to calculate *IR* loss.

sumption that the current density is uniform in each square in a given row across the plane (i.e., from left to right in Fig. 7.2). Third, determine the cumulative current in each square in a column of the squares, working from the top of the plane to the bottom. Use the sheet resistance of the plane and the current in a given square to calculate the *IR* drop across each square. Sum the drops across the squares to arrive at the drop across the plane or points of interest.

Resistance of a Section of a Plane. For a section of a plane, with dimensions as shown in Fig. 7.3, the resistance is [14]

$$R = \rho \frac{l}{tw} = \rho \frac{l}{\text{area of cross-section}} \qquad (7.3)$$

where ρ is the resistivity of the plane. For a square section ($l = w$), the resistance is

$$R = \frac{\rho}{t(\text{thickness})} = \rho_s(\text{sheet resistance}) \qquad (7.4)$$

The approximate sheet resistance for three common weights of copper printed-circuit board conductive layers is [15]

0.5-oz copper plane $\approx$ 1.0 mΩ per square

1.0-oz copper plane $\approx$ 0.5 mΩ per square

2.0-oz copper plane $\approx$ 0.25 mΩ per square

Today most multilayer printed backplane and circuit boards are built with 1-oz copper planes. Two-ounce planes are used in very high-current applications. Half-ounce material is seldom used for backpanel or motherboard power and ground planes. Half-ounce material is used for signal layers and in a few cases for power and ground planes in low-current applications.

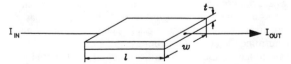

FIGURE 7.3 Square section of a plane showing dimensions used to define sheet resistance.

The sheet resistance used to calculate the drop across a plane should be derated from the solid plane based on the number and location of voids. In many applications, voids due to clearance holes for vias and package or connector pins will result in cross-sectional area losses in excess of 50 percent, in some cases as much as 70 percent. The cross-sectional loss must be determined and the sheet resistance adjusted as appropriate. In most applications, dc loss in power or ground planes is not significant when 1-oz or heavier copper planes are used.

Dynamic (AC) Loss.   The ac voltage loss in power and ground planes due to inductance is typically of much more concern than dc loss in high-speed digital systems [12]. The inductance of power and ground planes is kept low by the use of continuous planes with no cutouts except for feedthroughs (vias) and by keeping the power and ground planes as close together as possible. The basic equation for the inductance of two parallel plates or planes of equal width w, where the width is much greater than the separation h, is given by Matick [16] as

$$L = \left(4\pi\mu_r \times 10^{-7}\right)\left(\frac{h}{w}\right) \qquad \frac{\text{H}}{\text{m}} \qquad (7.5)$$

The relative permeability μ_r is approximately 1 for nonconducting materials [17] such as the epoxy glass used to separate planes in multilayer printed-circuit boards. Thus, in a parallel-plate model, the inductance of closely spaced power and ground planes on printed-circuit boards is given by (with the units changed to nanohenries per centimeter)

$$L = 4\pi\frac{h}{w} \qquad \frac{\text{nH}}{\text{cm}} \qquad (7.6)$$

The parallel-plate model assumes uniform current density, which is not the actual case in most local situations on a printed-circuit board. On a printed-circuit board the current is typically flowing to or from a point (the power or ground pin of a package). However, it seems reasonable to assume that most of the transient current flow, when a device switches, follows a relatively direct path between the nearest decoupling capacitor and the power and ground pins of the device. If that is the case, then the question is, How wide is the path over which the current flows relative to the separation of the power and ground planes? From Eq. (7.6) we see that if the width-to-separation ratio is on the order of 10:1, the inductance is on the order of 1 to 2 nH/cm. For most practical purposes, 1 to 2 nH can be used to estimate ac voltage loss in planes. Note that if the power and ground path is very long, 1 or 2 nH/cm quickly becomes significant with the edge speeds and transient load currents associated with today's digital devices.

7.2.4 Circuit Board–Motherboard Connections

Interfaces between the device and the pc board are not the only system interfaces where ground bounce or power supply droop is of concern. Any circuitry not connected to the ground or supply voltage by a continuous plane can experience ground bounce or power supply droop. For example, circuit board–motherboard or backplane connections by necessity (so that boards can be removed) are not continuous. To keep board ground bounce and power supply droop within limits that allow reliable transmission of single-ended signals, circuit board–motherboard connectors must have a sufficient and well-distributed number of ground and power connections.

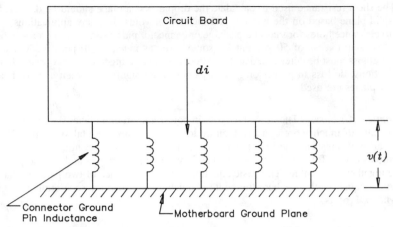

FIGURE 7.4 Circuit board–motherboard connectors must have sufficient ground pins to keep connector ground inductance low enough that board interface signal return currents do not significantly shift the board ground (reference) level.

The number of ground (or voltage) pins needed in a circuit board–motherboard connector (or in any connector) should be calculated based on an overall system noise budget [10] that defines the allowable ground bounce at the connector (see Fig. 7.4). The parallel inductance L_p of the ground or power pins

$$\frac{1}{L_p} = \frac{1}{L_1} + \frac{1}{L_2} + \cdots + \frac{1}{L_N}$$

must be small enough that the transient voltage drop $v(t)$ across the connector for the worst-case number of simultaneous switching outputs does not cause a transient voltage shift greater than that allowed in the error budget. As a rule of thumb, there should be a ground pin for every four to eight outputs (depending upon the output edge speed— faster edges require more ground pins), and they must be evenly distributed across the connector.

The magnitude of the possible voltage shift across a connector is found in a manner similar to that used to determine the ground bounce caused by package pin inductance (see Sec. 7.2.1). First the change in current in the connector ground pins is determined. The change in current ΔI is a function of the number N of signals in the connector that switch simultaneously, their output voltage transitions ΔV, and the impedance of their loads. In most situations, the interconnecting line characteristic impedance Z_o is the dominant dynamic portion of the load impedance (see Sec. 7.3.3 for the definition of Z_o). Where that is the case, ΔI is found by using Eq. (7.1). Once ΔI is known, the connector transient ground bounce voltage $v(t)$ in Fig. 7.4 can be estimated by using Eq. (7.2).

Static dc voltage loss across connectors is generally not a problem, but dc loss must be carefully evaluated. Some high-density connectors have relatively high resistance and very low current ratings (1 A or less). The connector manufacturer's data should always be consulted for connector pin current ratings. In high-reliability applications, actual connector pin currents are often limited to no more than 50 percent of the manufacturer's rating.

7.2.5 Power Supply–Motherboard Connections

The length of V_{cc} and ground conductors between power supplies and backpanels or motherboards must be as short as possible to keep transient voltage drops due to high-pulse-current loads as small as possible. The optimum arrangement is a dedicated power supply for each motherboard, with the supply located as close as possible to the motherboard. A local power supply for each unit keeps V_{cc} and ground connections as short as possible and minimizes the chance of circulating ground loop currents.

Remote Power Supply Connections. If it is not possible to directly connect power supplies to motherboard power and ground planes, then power connections should be made with twisted pair lines or low-impedance closely coupled bus bars [15]. Minimizing the inductance of remote power connections is as important as minimizing the resistance due to the pulsed-current nature of most digital systems. Minimum impedance is achieved by keeping the current path as short as possible and by minimizing the area enclosed by the current path (which twisting does) [12]. To help supply peak current demands, some local bulk capacitance should be located near where the power connects to the motherboard (see Sec. 7.2.7). However, the best solution is to eliminate the need for bulk decoupling capacitors. A local power supply with short low-impedance connections to low-impedance planes achieves that purpose.

When the power supply cannot be located near the load, overshoot at turn-on and undershoot at turn-off are common occurrences. Power supply overshoot and undershoot are enhanced by the amount of inductance in the supply path. Thus, it is essential to minimize the inductance of the power conductors to control overshoot and undershoot as well as to ensure a low-impedance path for transient load demands. The possibility of overshooting at turn-on, due to inductance between the supply and the load, can be minimized by mounting a 10- to 100-Ω resistor directly across the power supply terminals to provide a real (noninductive) load. A resistor at the source has additional benefits; it tends to reduce reflected noise by matching (terminating) the power lines. A power supply may have very low dc output impedance and be capable of sourcing and sinking large amounts of direct current, yet the output may reflect and enhance incident ac noise waveforms (see Sec. 7.3.4).

Power supply return or reference outputs should not be connected to chassis ground at both the point of use and at the supplies. Power supply reference lines and backpanel (or motherboard) ground planes should only be connected to earth, or chassis, ground at one central point [3]. In most applications, the best location for the central ground point is where the supply reference lines connect to the motherboard or backpanel. A single system ground point prevents circulating ground currents. Circulating ground currents introduce noise that can upset system operation [7].

Using a single power source for multiple units, e.g., backpanels, motherboards, chassis, etc., is undesirable. With a single unit feeding multiple units, grounding individual units creates multiple grounds and introduces the possibility of large circulating ground currents. When multiple units must be powered from a single source, the single-point earth ground must be located at the power source. Separate lines should be used to connect each unit to the supply. Units should not be serially connected, to limit unit-to-unit interference. In most situations, a supply for each unit, which allows each unit to be directly grounded, is the best configuration.

All electronic equipment, chassis, racks, test equipment, etc., must have a solid, direct connection to earth ground to protect personnel from electrical shock hazards and to prevent *electrostatic discharge* (ESD) or overvoltage damage to interface devices. If a unit is allowed to float, even if input-output devices are not damaged, they may not operate correctly.

TABLE 7.3   Resistance of Stranded Copper
Conductor

AWG	mΩ/ft
4	0.27
6	0.42
8	0.66
10	1.2
12	1.8
14	2.9
16	4.5
18	5.9
20	9.5
22	15
24	24
26	40
28	64
30	100
32	160
34	260
36	410

Voltage Loss in Power Conductors.   In all cases, dc voltage loss in power wiring or
bus bars must be evaluated. Many of today's digital systems have power supply current
requirements of 100 A or more. In high-current applications, very small resistances are
significant. Even in low-current applications, power conductor loss is often underestimated. When the power conductor loss is calculated, be sure to consider both power and
ground return lines.

When the power conductor loss is calculated, the actual resistance specification for the
conductor used must be known and used for voltage loss calculations. Manufacturer's data
should be consulted for actual resistance data. However, if stranded copper wire is used,
the voltage drop can be estimated from the data in Table 7.3. Table 7.3 lists the approximate resistance (in milliohms per foot) for several common sizes of stranded copper
conductor [11, 12].

Voltage Loss in Power Connectors.   Connector and power line junction losses are a
serious problem in high-power systems. Large high-speed digital processing systems
often require supply currents in the 100- to 200-A range. In such applications, a small
connector or junction resistance can result in large voltage losses. To minimize the voltage
loss, the power connections must be tight and clean and have sufficient contact area (to
limit the current density) [18]. In most large-current applications (greater than 100 A), it
is not practical to use a quick-disconnect power connector; bolted junctions are required.
If pins are paralleled in connectors to increase the current capacity, the per-pin current
must be derated. Due to varying resistance, connector pins tend not to share the current
equally.

Determining the resistance of power connections under all conditions is a difficult task.
The contact pressure, oxidation of mating surfaces, and actual mating surface area (there
may be high or low spots) are all critical parameters that are difficult to establish initially
and with aging. To compensate for these uncertainties, power connections should be
designed with a large safety margin.

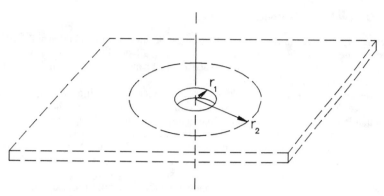

FIGURE 7.5 Variables used to determine the radial resistance of a plane.

Multiple power and ground connections to backpanel planes (backplanes) may be required in high-current applications, to limit the current density and voltage loss in backplanes in the vicinity of power connections. When multilayer printed-circuit motherboards with thin planes are used in high-current applications, the current density in the vicinity of power connections is of special concern. In such applications, the voltage loss in the plane in the vicinity of the connections must be evaluated, and corrective measures (such as multiple connections) taken if the loss is significant.

Radial Resistance of a Thin Plane from a Point. In high-current applications, where "point" power and ground connections are made to multilayer printed-circuit motherboards with thin planes, the voltage loss in the local vicinity must be evaluated to determine the needed plane thickness. The radial resistance R between r_1 and r_2 in a thin plane (see Fig. 7.5) with sheet resistance ρ_S is [3]

$$R = \frac{\rho_S}{2\pi} \ln \frac{r_2}{r_1} \tag{7.7}$$

See Sec. 7.2.3 for ρ_S for various weights of common copper planes.

Connections between Dissimilar Metals. Direct connections between current-carrying conductors of dissimilar metals, such as aluminum backplanes and copper bus bars or wires, must be avoided. Untreated aluminum quickly forms a thin oxide film, which causes a high-impedance joint. Power connections to aluminum backplanes must be made by using bimetallic transition joints, or contact surfaces must be coated with an appropriate joint compound [19, 20]. Joint compounds contain chemicals that dissolve surface oxide films and seal joints against moisture and further oxidation. A joint compound, such as Alcoa No. 2 Electrical Joint Compound, or an equivalent compound, should be used on all untreated aluminum-to-aluminum or aluminum-to-copper electrical connections. Transition joints are formed by creating a metallic bond between an aluminum backplane and some other metal, such as copper, that does not form a high-impedance oxide film. The metallic bond between the aluminum and the copper prevents an oxide layer from forming at the aluminum-to-copper junction, and the copper outer layer provides a low-impedance surface for power connections [21].

7.2.6 Overvoltage Protection

Power supply voltages at their point of use must be limited to levels that will not stress or instantly destroy devices. In most digital systems, all steady-state and transient supply voltage levels must be kept below 7 V, since 7 V is the absolute maximum rating for most logic components.

To ensure that supply voltages do not exceed device limits, all power supplies should be equipped with overvoltage shutdown circuits, which are often called *crowbars*. In addition, all systems should have a passive voltage-limiting or clamping device (i.e., one not dependent on other conditions to operate) located directly and permanently at the load (so that it will not be neglected or improperly connected). In most applications, passive clamps should be located where power is connected to motherboards or backpanels. Power zener diodes or power transient suppressors are typically used. The clamp must have sufficient standoff voltage to not conduct appreciable current during normal operation, but have a low enough breakdown voltage to effectively limit the supply voltage to below the absolute maximum rating of the logic devices in the system. The passive clamping device must also have the transient power-handling capability to last long enough to trip the circuit breaker or primary fuse in the power supply. Removing the primary source of power from the supply ensures that the faulty or improperly adjusted supply is taken off-line and that it will remain off until corrective action is taken [22, 23].

7.2.7 Decoupling Capacitors

High-speed logic devices require decoupling (also called *bypass*) capacitors to provide a local source of load-switching current to compensate for power and ground system inductance. *Local* decoupling capacitors are used to provide a nearby current source for individual components, and *bulk* decoupling capacitors are used to provide longer-term, lower-frequency, transient current replenishment for circuit boards and motherboards.

Local Decoupling.   All high-speed logic devices need local decoupling capacitors to supply the current demanded during switching intervals (i.e., when changing states). The fast edge rates of today's digital devices exacerbate the requirement for local decoupling. Local decoupling capacitors compensate for power distribution system inductance and prevent large transient shifts in local power or reference levels when large loads are quickly charged. When several devices in a given area switch at once, significant amounts of instantaneous current must be available to prevent large shifts in local power or ground levels. Planes alone, even when closely spaced, do not provide sufficient local storage of energy (charge—they are not good capacitors) to supply the instantaneous current (charge) demanded when a large number of devices in a given area switch at the same time [24]. Thus, even well-designed power and ground distribution systems may have local transient excursions of V_{cc} and ground that violate device power supply levels unless local decoupling is present. With low supply voltage, devices slow down, signal transitions slow down, and the potential system operating speed is reduced. Decoupling capacitors located near the power terminals of devices limit local power-level transient excursions to harmless levels.

Guidelines for Local Decoupling Capacitors.   A general guideline for the amount and the placement of decoupling capacitors for SSI or MSI devices mounted on conventional printed-circuit boards, wire-wrap or welded-wire boards, is one 0.1-μF high-frequency decoupling capacitor mounted as close as possible to the V_{cc} pin of each SSI or MSI device [11, 12]. In all applications, the device manufacturer's decoupling recommendation must be followed. In many cases, larger values, such as 0.22 μF, are recommended for LSI devices such as dynamic memories and programmable devices [25]. Devices in large packages with multiple power and ground pins have special decoupling requirements; again, the manufacturer's recommendations must be closely followed. It is extremely important to provide an adequate amount of local decoupling for octal drivers or for parts driving large-capacitance loads.

A typical design goal is to provide enough local decoupling capacitance to keep (support) the local dc supply voltage level within 1 percent of the nominal dc supply level under worst-case switching current demands. To meet that goal, the local decoupling capacitance C_d must be at least 100 times the maximum possible simultaneously switched load capacitance. That is,

$$C_d \geq 100\ C_{\text{load}}$$

where C_{load} is the signal track capacitance plus the input and output capacitance of all loads tied to the decoupled device's outputs that switch at a given time.

Device supply-level degradation during switching is not due to charge transfer alone. The actual transient supply voltage excursion seen by a switching device is a function of the total inductance and resistance between it and its decoupling capacitor plus the decrease in local supply level due to charge transfer. The inductance includes the internal *equivalent series inductance* (ESL) and lead inductance of the decoupling capacitor and the inductance of the interconnecting power and ground network and the package power and ground pins [26]. In most cases, the only significant resistance in the path is the *equivalent series resistance* (ESR) of the decoupling capacitor [26]. A reasonable design goal is to keep the transient supply voltage excursions seen by the switching device due to inductance, resistance, and charge transfer to below 0.2 V.

To keep transient supply excursions low, the decoupling capacitor must be mounted as close as possible to the device being decoupled, and the decoupling capacitor leads need to be as short as possible (to minimize the inductance between the capacitor and the device being decoupled) [27]. Either surface-mounted or radial leaded devices are best, but DIP profile packaged capacitors made especially for decoupling also have good high-frequency characteristics. Axially leaded capacitors should not be used since in most mounting arrangements their leads must be relatively long, which means higher inductance [28].

Bulk Decoupling.   Bulk decoupling capacitors help compensate for inadequate power or ground connections between circuit boards and motherboards or between motherboards and power supplies. Large bulk capacitors provide low-frequency replenishment of charge to local decoupling capacitors to help maintain V_{cc} at the proper level [28]. In addition,

1. Circuit board bulk capacitors reduce the transmission of board-generated noise to the motherboard.
2. Motherboard bulk capacitors help eliminate low-frequency ripple and ringing due to power supply conductor inductance.
3. Circuit board and motherboard bulk capacitors help reduce the transmission of digital switching noise back to the power source; thus bulk capacitors help in meeting emission requirements.

Bulk decoupling capacitors must be sized for worst-case low-frequency charge replenishment [29]. A good rule of thumb to follow is this: The value should be approximately 50 to 100 times the total worst-case simultaneous switched load capacitance. The simultaneous switched load capacitance is the total signal track capacitance plus the total device load for the worst-case combination of signals, within a unit, that could switch at one time.

When bulk decoupling capacitors are chosen, careful attention must be given to their operating voltage, ripple current, and in-rush current specifications. Most large capacitors are polarized, so care must be taken to not reverse leads during installation. Bulk decoupling capacitors, as well as the location where they are to be installed, should be clearly marked to reduce the opportunity for incorrect installation. Extra care must be taken to ensure that power connections are not reversed. Small power supply reversals at turn-on or turn-off, which often occur, will damage most polarized capacitors [30]. *Caution:* Many of the capacitor styles available in the size range needed for bulk decoupling are only rated for 0.5 V of reverse voltage—a difficult requirement to meet.

7.3 SIGNAL INTERCONNECTIONS

7.3.1 Signal Interconnection Categories

Signal interconnections fall into three basic categories in most large digital systems:

1. Interconnections within a circuit board (component-to-component)
2. Interconnections between circuit boards that are mounted on a common motherboard (board-to-board)
3. Interconnections between separate units such as boxes, chassis, racks, cabinets, etc. (unit-to-unit)

Fundamental issues that must be addressed at each interconnection level include interconnection propagation delays, transmission-line effects, and crosstalk [31, 32].

7.3.2 Physical Means of Interconnecting Signals

Large high-speed digital systems typically use the following means of physical interconnection for the three interconnection categories [18, 33, 34]:

1. Multilayer printed-circuit wiring boards for component-to-component connections
2. Multilayer printed-circuit or wire-wrap backpanels (motherboards) for board-to-board connections
3. Shielded twisted pair, *twinaxial cables* (twinex) or coaxial cables for unit-to-unit connections

Minimizing the signal line length is a fundamental requirement in all three categories. Reducing the signal line length reduces the capacitance load, minimizes the chance for crosstalk, and reduces transmission-line effects and signal interconnection propagation delays.

Component-to-Component Connections. Multilayer pc boards with multiple signal, voltage, and ground planes are required for most component-to-component connections because of signal density and electrical requirements [35]. It is usually impossible to interconnect high-performance circuits without multiple signal layers, and in most cases multiple voltage and ground planes are required to limit crosstalk and to control the interconnection impedance.

Continuous ground planes are essential and are a fundamental requirement for circuit boards when high-speed digital devices are used [35]. Ground planes must not be broken or interrupted by device and connector pin fields [35]. Ground planes must be arranged so they are below (or above) all signal runs, including signal traces going to connector pin fields. Ground planes provide low-impedance return paths for transient load currents. Voltage planes are important, but not as important as ground planes. Voltage planes must be continuous where boards are populated with circuits (to minimize signal return paths), but voltage planes do not have to be continuous in all connector pin fields.

Board-to-Board Connections.   Board-to-board connections are typically implemented by one of the following methods:

1. Multilayer pc motherboards with multiple signal layers and multiple ground and voltage planes
2. Wire-wrap signal connections above a multilayer backpanel with ground and voltage planes
3. Wire-wrap signal connections, bus bars for voltage connections, and a backpanel that serves as a ground plane

With attention to the basic concerns of a high-performance signal distribution system, any of the above structures can be used successfully for most moderate-speed applications. Very high-speed applications require multilayer mother-daughter pc boards with controlled impedance signal layers (instead of standard printed wiring interconnects that do not have controlled impedances), so that the response of signals can be accurately predicted and controlled. In all cases, daughterboard-to-motherboard connections must have sufficient ground pins that transient load currents do not cause significant shifts in the reference level of daughterboards [32, 36] (see Sec. 7.2.4).

At the board-to-board level, signal connections tend to be dominated by bus structures that have an increased probability of crosstalk due to long runs across backpanels or motherboards. Care should be taken in the assignment of daughterboard connector signal pins so as to minimize the length of signal lines. Also care must be taken to isolate signals that can be upset by cross-coupling (Sec. 7.3.5 discusses cross-coupling and its control). In general, busses should be grouped rather than intermingled. Control signals, such as enables and strobes, must be physically remote from busses to minimize the possibility of cross-coupling when a large number of bus signals change at once.

Unit-to-Unit Connections.   Unit-to-unit connections in high-speed digital systems are typically implemented by using some type of shielded twisted-pair connections. For very high-performance applications, controlled-impedance shielded twisted-pair, twinex, or coaxial interconnections are used so that terminations can be closely matched to cable impedance [37]. In all cable interconnections, the cable impedance, propagation delay, dispersion, and shielding factor must be considered [38]. Knowledge of cable impedance is needed so that proper terminations can be selected. The propagation delay must be known to predict the transport delay. Dispersion characteristics are important in long cables with high data rate; if dispersion is excessive, data and controls may be skewed sufficiently to cause errors. Sufficient shielding is needed to maintain data integrity and prevent excessive radiation. Cable manufacturers' data books and Ott [12] and Morrison [13] are recommended for guidance on these issues.

All unit-to-unit signal cables must include ground lines for signal return currents. When single-ended high-level interunit communication is used (low-level single-ended signals should never be used), ideally there should be one ground line per signal line. When balanced differential interunit communication is used, one ground line per four to

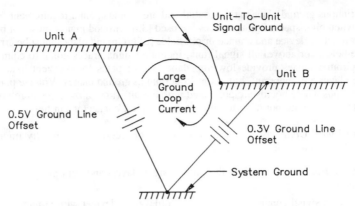

FIGURE 7.6 Large ground loop currents may flow in unit-to-unit ground connections because of reference-level offsets.

eight signal pairs is a good rule of thumb. If differential signals are perfectly balanced, no return ground lines are needed, but differential signals are never perfectly balanced. Thus, some ground lines are needed to provide a direct return path for the unbalanced portion of the signal currents. However, direct unit-to-unit ground connections offer the potential for large ground loop currents, as shown in Fig. 7.6. Thus, when unit-to-unit signal ground lines are required to ensure a low-impedance path for signal return currents, care must be taken to ensure that all units have low-impedance connections to a central ground point, to prevent large interunit reference-voltage offsets and large ground loop currents. If large offset voltages exist between units, the ground current in the signal return lines can be of such a magnitude to disrupt system operation by introducing noise [39] and in severe cases overheat and burn out the signal return lines.

Breadboard Interconnections. Often during the breadboard phase of a project, welded-wire or wire-wrap interconnections are used at both the component-to-component and the motherboard levels to expedite the completion of the initial breadboard unit and so that corrections or modifications can be easily incorporated.

When breadboarding with off-the-shelf welded-wire or wire-wrap boards, only those boards that are described as Schottky boards should be used when high-speed devices are being applied. Schottky boards have ground and voltage planes that are interconnected between all device and connector pins and provide low-impedance return paths for signals.

When high-speed digital devices are interconnected with wired boards, the signal response characteristics will not be representative of the final pc board system. Thus, wired breadboards should be used only to establish the functionality of a logic design; they should not be used to forecast the operating speed of the final pc board system. When the limits of the operating speed of a system must be demonstrated, the breadboard system must have the same physical dimensions and electrical characteristics as the final product.

Routing Guidelines. When state-of-the-art digital devices are used, signal routing (at any of the interconnection levels) cannot be left to chance or based on purely mechanical concerns. Specific routing instructions must be given to drafting departments or routing houses. Generalized statements lead to misunderstandings. Electrical (digital) designers and pc board designers tend to speak different languages [40]. Electrical designers think in terms of impedances, inductances, capacitances, and propagation delays, while pc board designers think in physical implementation terms such as widths, lengths, and layers. Statements such as "Keep all clock lines as short as possible" have little meaning to drafting departments or routing houses. Specific physical routing instructions with specific signal names must be called out.

To simplify the task of routing boards, signals should be grouped into categories based on waveshape control requirements, crosstalk limits, or other special requirements. For example, clocks, strobes, busses, memory address, data, chip select, write lines, asynchronous signals, *emitter-coupled logic* (ECL) signals, and analog signals have special routing requirements. Analog and ECL signals require special care when mixed with advanced Schottky transistor-transister logic (TTL), advanced CMOS, or BiCMOS devices. See below:

Clock signals: Clock signals have waveshape, skew, and crosstalk control requirements. To meet clock signal waveshape requirements, the clock signals must be routed on pc board layers with reasonably controlled impedance. Clock lines must not branch or have long stubs. Termination networks must be properly located. The location of the source and the locations of the loads must be controlled (see Buchanan [3, 10]). To control clock skew, clock lines may need defined maximum and minimum lengths. To meet crosstalk limits, the clock signals must be isolated and confined between reference layers. Other signals must not be mixed with clock signals. Clock signals on a given layer must have extra spacing between lines. Clock signals of different frequency must have extrawide spacing as must clock signals and other signals if they are to be routed on the same layer.

Strobes: Strobes typically have the same requirements as clocks (see above).

Busses: Signals in a given bus can generally run next to other signals in the bus (which may save space), but not with other busses or signals.

Memory address and data lines: High-speed memory address and data busses need to be isolated by reference planes to prevent interaction. Memory address signals can run next to each other, and memory data lines can run next to each other as bussed signals (see above).

Memory chip select lines: Generally memory chip select lines have the same routing requirements as address lines (see above) and in most cases can be grouped with address lines.

Memory write lines: Memory write lines require the highest possible degree of isolation from crosstalk. They must be isolated by reference planes and by extrawide line-to-line spacing from other signals, particularly other memory chip selects and address and data busses.

ECL and analog: ECL and analog signals require a high degree of isolation from TTL or CMOS signals. They must be physically isolated in separate board areas with separate ground and voltage planes that are isolated from TTL or CMOS switching currents.

Once the electrical requirements or limits of each signal category have been established (based on system performance requirements and error budgets), the requirements must then be translated to specific mechanical requirements for the pc board designer or routing house.

Routing Order.   Most pc board routers route signals from point to point and thus do not cause branches. However, if there are requirements for the location of loads or sources, their locations must be defined and relayed to the routing house. In general, in lower-performance applications, the locations of loads and sources on a signal line are not critical. As performance increases, the physical relationship of loads and sources becomes more important. Routing order must be specified in high-speed applications. Routing order is of particular importance for clock and other signals, such as strobes, that have waveshape requirements or settling-time requirements. Typically, when waveshape control or minimum settling time is required, the source is located at one end of the line and any parallel termination or clamping is located at the other end, with the loads grouped near the termination or clamped end of the line. Alternately, if series termination is used (see Sec. 7.3.4), the series termination network must be located very near the source.

In some applications where minimum settling time is needed, lines are often center-driven or made into loops. Center-driving the lines or looping the lines (back to the source) reduces the effective line impedance [26] seen by the driver to $\frac{1}{2} Z_o$ and more nearly matches the line impedance to the output impedance of most TTL or CMOS drivers, which in turn reduces ringing and signal settling times. Looping the lines back to the source also has an additional benefit; it typically reduces the worst-case distance between the source and the most remote load, and thus reduces the worst-case propagation time. Center-driving and looping techniques are often used on clock and memory address lines to improve waveshape and to reduce settling time. Loops may also be useful in some bus applications to reduce the settling time. The line impedance can be further lowered by connecting additional lines between loops to form grids. However, grids, loops, etc., are only beneficial where the effective line impedance (before being looped or gridded) is much greater than the driver output impedance (which is the typical situation when advanced Schottky TTL or advanced CMOS bus drivers are used). If the basic line impedance is much less than the driver worst-case output impedance, grids and loops are not beneficial. Lines may require numerous reflections to step up to the final value, and thus such an arrangement might degrade the response time. If such arrangements are considered, caution must be exercised since the CMOS device output impedance may change by a factor of 2 to 1 from nominal with process variations and the extremes of the military operating conditions [41]. An additional complication is that most routers will not automatically connect loops or grids, so manual intervention and layout are required.

7.3.3 Interconnection Impedance

The interconnection characteristic impedance Z_o is the key parameter that interrelates all aspects of high-speed system performance. An optimum range of Z_o exists which is a function of the electrical characteristics of the logic family used and mechanical limitations and requirements. This optimum range of Z_o is the best compromise between noise, delay, crosstalk, and mechanical constraints [42]. Lines with high Z_o are easier to drive, but high Z_o increases crosstalk (coupled signals are attenuated less), RC delays, and transmission-line ringing (advanced Schottky, advanced CMOS, and BiCMOS devices tend to have very low output impedance so there is greater mismatch). Mechanical constraints make it difficult to achieve high Z_o in high-density multilayer pc boards. Low Z_o attenuates signals which reduces signal-to-noise margins, increases delay (signals take longer to reach switching thresholds—first incident switching may not occur), and increases transient switching currents, which increases system noise. When the cumulative effects are considered, 50 to 60 Ω tends to be the optimum impedance for most digital components and the most practical range of Z_o to achieve from a mechanical standpoint.

The characteristic impedance Z_o of an ideal transmission line is defined as [16, 43]

$$Z_o = \sqrt{\frac{L}{C}} \tag{7.8}$$

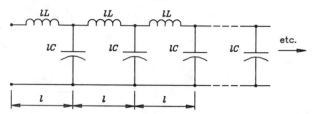

FIGURE 7.7   Equivalent circuit for an ideal transmission line.

and the propagation delay t_{pd} as

$$t_{\text{pd}} = \sqrt{LC} \qquad\qquad (7.9)$$

where L and C are as shown in Fig. 7.7. At a sufficiently high frequency, which is exceeded by the frequency components in the switching edges of most of today's digital devices (e.g., ECL, advanced Schottky TTL, CMOS, and BiCMOS devices), the inductive and capacitive effects cancel and a transmission line appears to the source and load as a pure resistance [16].

Interconnection impedance requirements for TTL, CMOS, and BiCMOS digital devices are not straightforward. High-speed TTL, CMOS, and BiCMOS circuits do not require the precise control of line impedance for waveshape control as ECL circuits do. In some but not all cases, TTL, CMOS, and BiCMOS circuits have input clamps for waveshape control. Signal response, when controlled by input clamps, can tolerate wide variations in line impedance, but input dynamic clamping characteristics are seldom specified and many parts do not have effective clamps, which means that predicting the signal response in TTL, CMOS, and BiCMOS systems is difficult, if not impossible. Practical experience has shown that a 2:1 line impedance range can be tolerated on signal lines that require waveshape control, such as clocks, and even more on lines that do not require waveshape control (assuming settling time is available). Thus, precise control of the impedance of the signal line is not a major issue relative to waveshape control. The main issues relative to pc board characteristics for TTL and CMOS level signals are minimum line impedance and control of crosstalk.

The impedance of signal lines must be high enough that the driving device can drive the signal lines in a timely manner. If the line impedance is too low, signals require too long to reach the final value, and the system operating speed is reduced. It is essential that certain signals, such as clocks, reach a level that exceeds the switching threshold of the receiving devices on the first trip down the line (this is called *first incident switching*) [41].

All digital devices have some finite amount of output impedance; when they switch, their output impedance forms a divider with the line impedance [44]. If the line impedance is too low, signals must step to new levels, as shown in Fig. 7.8. If the line impedance is very low, it may take a number of steps for signals to reach the final value [45]. In low-speed applications, stepping waveforms may not cause problems. For example, data and control signals with steps are not disruptive in synchronous systems if time is available for signals to reach valid logic levels (see chapter 8 of Buchanan [3] for a description of synchronous systems). However, the extra time that a stepping signal requires to reach a valid logic level reduces the potential system operating speed. In a few cases, a waveform with a step can cause secondary problems. If a step happened to be near the threshold level of a receiver, the receiver input circuitry could oscillate during the time the signal dwells in the threshold region. In some cases, the oscillation may generate enough noise to upset nearby circuits, but in most cases the time that signals dwell in the intermediate

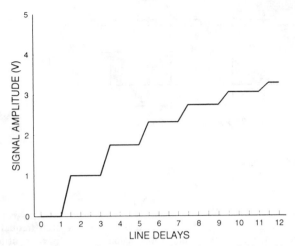

FIGURE 7.8 Interconnection impedance forms a divider with device output impedance that causes signal transitions to step up or down.

region is relatively short, and so there are no ill effects. However, signals with steps must not be used to clock devices; multiple clocking may occur. For example, signals with steps are inherent near the source end of lines driven with TTL, CMOS, or BiCMOS devices. To prevent steps from causing multiple clocking, clock lines must be routed so that the devices being clocked are located near the end of the lines. Alternately, the line impedance must be high enough that any steps are well above the threshold of the clocked devices.

In applications where devices have TTL output levels, minimum line impedance requirements are established by the dynamic high-state output impedance. The dynamic high-state output impedance is greater than low-state output impedance because most TTL-level output stages have a resistor in the pull-up circuit, but not in the pull-down [7]. For example, high-state output impedance for advanced Schottky TTL drivers is typically near 20 Ω and for standard logic function is near 45 Ω. For first incident wave switching and to prevent multiple clocking from steps dwelling in the threshold region, clock lines or other lines where wave edge shape is important must have an effective line impedance that is at a minimum on the same order as the device output impedance, and ideally the line impedance is much greater than the device output impedance. The voltage divider formed by the device output impedance and the line impedance must not attenuate the signal so much that it fails to exceed the switching threshold of the receiving devices. If the interconnection system minimum line impedance meets the needs of high-going signals, it will be more than adequate for high-to-low transitions since low-level output impedance for TTL-level devices tends to be much less than high-state output impedance (typically near 10 Ω for advanced Schottky and BiCMOS devices).

Also 40 Ω is near the minimum usable line impedance for CMOS-level signals that must switch on the first incident wave. Advanced CMOS input thresholds are at typically 30 and 70 percent of V_{cc}. Thus, both high and low initial signal transitions must equal or exceed $\frac{2}{3}V_{cc}$. Under nominal $+25°C$ conditions the output impedance of advanced CMOS devices is near 10 Ω. The worst-case output impedance over the extremes of military operating conditions is near 20 Ω. Thus, initial signal transitions on lines with 40 Ω or greater impedance will equal or exceed $\frac{2}{3}V_{cc}$.

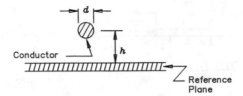

FIGURE 7.9 Wire over a reference plane with dimensions shown that are used to calculate line impedance and propagation delay.

Characteristic Impedance of Some Common Interconnection Structures. From a practical standpoint, the basic equations for characteristic impedance and propagation time, Eqs. (7.8) and (7.9), are of limited value since L and C are difficult to determine. However, empirically derived equations for determining the characteristic impedance and propagation delay time for most common physical interconnection structures are available. Some of the more common ones are given below. *Caution:* They are only valid for a limited range where the line width, spacing, and distance from the reference plane are in the same order.

For wire-wrap or welded-wire boards, the basic physical interconnection structure is a wire over a ground or voltage plane (voltage planes serve as *ac* references), as shown in Fig. 7.9.

For a wire above a reference plane, Z_o is [46]

$$Z_o = \frac{60}{\sqrt{\epsilon_r}} \ln \frac{4h}{d} \qquad (7.10)$$

where d = wire diameter and h = distance from ground to center of the wire, and t_{pd} is

$$t_{\text{pd}} = 1.017 \sqrt{\epsilon_r} \qquad (7.11)$$

where the constant 1.017 is the reciprocal of the velocity of light in free space [16]. In both Eqs. (7.10) and (7.11), ϵ_r is the effective dielectric constant of the material in the separation between the reference plane and the wire. For a wire in air, the dielectric constant is 1, but the case of a wire in air is of little interest. For an actual wire-wrap or welded-wire board, the separation consists of air, the insulation on the wire, and other conductors. Thus, the effective dielectric constant is difficult to determine, and Z_o and t_{pd} calculations are quite complex. Actual Z_o measurements of wire-wrap and welded-wire boards show Z_o to be in the range of 80 to 150 Ω and t_{pd} to be on the order of 1.5 ns/ft. The value of Z_o is dependent upon the distance between the wires and the reference plane. If the wires are not kept close to the reference plane, Z_o values higher than 150 Ω are possible.

For pc board interconnections, two basic physical arrangements of conductors relative to reference planes are possible:

1. Conductors may be located above a reference plane.

2. Conductors may be enclosed between two reference planes.

Printed-circuit board connections above a reference plane are called *microstrip conductors* (see Fig. 7.10). A microstrip conductor can be on the surface of a pc board (as shown in Fig. 7.10*a*) or buried in a board (as shown in Fig. 7.10*b*). The configuration in Fig. 7.10*a* corresponds to conductors on uncovered surface layers of pc boards, and the

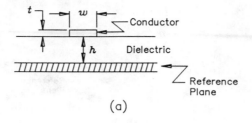

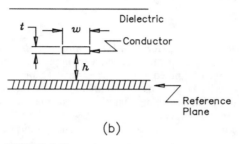

FIGURE 7.10 (*a*) Microstrip conductor on the surface of a dielectric. (*b*) Microstrip conductor buried in a dielectric with dimensions shown that are used to calculate line impedance and propagation delay.

configuration in Fig. 7.10*b* corresponds to conductors on internal layers of multilayer pc boards (that are not enclosed by reference planes). Figure 7.10*b* is more common today. Most present-day high-performance systems are built with multilayer pc boards with buried signal layers.

The equation for Z_o (in ohms) for a microstrip transmission line on the surface of a dielectric is

$$Z_o = \frac{60}{\sqrt{0.475\epsilon_r + 0.67}} \ln \frac{5.98h}{0.8w + t} \tag{7.12}$$

which is usually shown as [15, 47]

$$Z_o = \frac{87}{\sqrt{\epsilon_r + 1.41}} \ln \frac{5.98h}{0.8w + t}$$

and t_{pd} for a surface microstrip conductor (in nanoseconds per foot) is

$$t_{pd} = 1.017\sqrt{0.475\epsilon_r + 0.67} \tag{7.13}$$

where h, t, and w are in inches and are as shown in Fig. 7.10 and ϵ_r is the dielectric constant of the material between the conductor and the reference plane.

The equation for Z_o (in ohms) for a buried microstrip transmission line is

$$Z_o = \frac{60}{\sqrt{\epsilon_r}} \ln \frac{5.98h}{0.8w + t} \tag{7.14}$$

and t_{pd} for a buried microstrip (in nanoseconds per foot) is

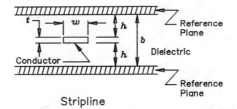

Stripline

FIGURE 7.11 Stripline conductor with dimensions shown that are used to calculate line impedance and propagation delay.

$$t_{pd} = 1.017\sqrt{\epsilon_r} \tag{7.15}$$

(the variables are as defined above).

Printed-circuit board connections with a reference plane above and below conductors are called *stripline conductors* (see Fig. 7.11).

The equation for Z_o (in ohms) for a stripline conductor is [15]

$$Z_o = \frac{60}{\sqrt{\epsilon_r}} \ln \frac{4b}{0.67\pi(0.8w + t)} \tag{7.16}$$

and

$$t_{pd} = 1.017\sqrt{\epsilon_r} \tag{7.17}$$

where b, h, t, and w are in inches and are as shown in Fig. 7.11.

The dielectric constant ϵ_r for epoxy glass pc board typically ranges from 4 to 5. For interconnection layers on most present-day multilayer pc boards, 1-oz copper plating is used. The thickness t in Eqs. (7.14) and (7.16) for 1-oz copper is approximately 0.0014 in (t of 2-oz copper is 0.0028 in). Today it is not uncommon to see production boards with 4- to 8-mil-wide conductors with similar line-to-line spacing and similar line-to-adjacent-voltage or ground plane spacing. Such boards typically have Z_o in the range of 30 to 70 Ω and t_{pd} in the range of 1.8 to 2.2 ns/ft.

The Z_o curves shown in Figs. 7.12 and 7.13 were generated from Eqs. (7.14) and (7.16). They are not exact because the equations lose their validity at the extremes and do not take into account effects of other nearby signal lines; but they are accurate enough for most engineering purposes and are useful for quick estimates of Z_o versus line width and dielectric thickness. Figure 7.12 shows the characteristic impedance Z_o of microstrip conductors in epoxy glass pc boards ($\epsilon_r = 4.5$) as a function of conductor width w and height h above a reference plane. Figure 7.13 shows the characteristic impedance of stripline conductors in epoxy glass pc boards ($\epsilon_r = 4.5$) as a function of conductor width w and distance h from the two reference planes.

In addition to wires over grounds, microstrip, and stripline conductor configurations, digital designers must often deal with coaxial cables and twisted pair interconnections. Cable parameters, such as Z_o and t_{pd}, are supplied in cable manufacturers' catalogs (which should be consulted when such interconnections are used). Coaxial cables are available with various Z_o values; typical values range from 50 to 90 Ω [23]. Twisted pair lines have a Z_o in the neighborhood of 120 to 150 Ω, and shielded-twisted pair lines range from 70 to 120 Ω [9].

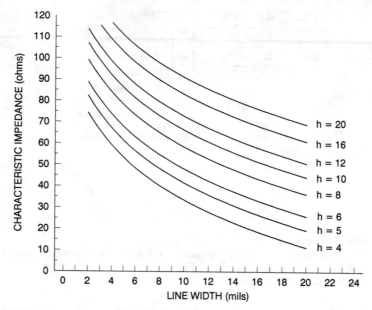

FIGURE 7.12 Characteristic impedance Z_o of microstrip conductors in epoxy glass pc boards ($\epsilon_r = 4.5$) as a function of conductor width w and height h above a reference plane (see Fig. 7.10 for dimensions).

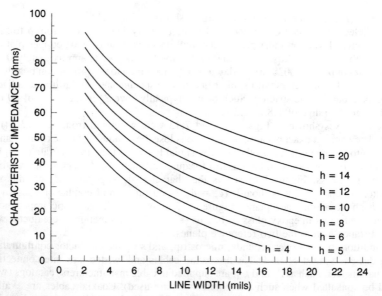

FIGURE 7.13 Characteristic impedance of stripline conductors in epoxy glass pc boards ($\epsilon_r = 4.5$) as a function of conductor width w and distance h from the two reference planes (see Fig. 7.11 for dimensions).

Loaded Transmission-Line Impedance.   Distributed lumped loading on lines lowers the effective impedance and increases the propagation delay. The effective characteristic impedance Z'_o and effective propagation time t'_{pd} of a line is a function of the total lumped load capacitance C_{LOAD} and the total intrinsic line capacitance C_{LINE}. The expressions for effective characteristic impedance and for effective propagation delay of loaded lines are [33]

$$Z'_o = \frac{Z_o}{\sqrt{1 + \dfrac{C_{LOAD}}{C_{LINE}}}} \qquad (7.18)$$

$$t'_{pd} = t_{pd} \sqrt{1 + \frac{C_{LOAD}}{C_{LINE}}} \qquad (7.19)$$

where C_{LOAD} is the total lumped capacitance (inputs and outputs) of each device connected to the line and C_{LINE} is the total line capacitance. Determining C_{LOAD} is straightforward; C_{LOAD} is the sum of the input (or output) capacitance (as the case may be) of all the devices connected to the line. Determining C_{LINE} requires the per-unit-length line capacitance C be known ($C_{LINE} = C$ per unit length $\times$ line length). However, deriving C (per unit length) is not a straightforward process.

The most practical means of determining the capacitance per unit length of a line is to measure the propagation delay of an actual unloaded pc board track of the configuration of interest and use the measured time (t_{pd} measured) and the calculated Z_o—from Eq. (7.12), (7.14), or (7.16)—in Eq. (7.20). Equation (7.20) is derived from Eqs. (7.8) and (7.9).

$$C = \frac{t_{pd}(\text{measured})}{Z_o(\text{calculated})} \qquad (7.20)$$

And the total capacitance of the line C_{LINE} is

$$C_{LINE} = C \times \text{line length}$$

where the line length is in the same units as those used with C.

It is important to note that lines with a number of loads will have an effective Z'_o much less than the unloaded Z_o and that the effective t'_{pd} will be much greater. It is not unusual for the effective impedance of bussed lines, or other lines that connect to numerous locations, to be reduced to one-half the intrinsic unloaded impedance. It is not uncommon for the effective Z'_o of a loaded pc track to be as low as 20 Ω, and the actual propagation delay as large as 3.5 ns/ft.

7.3.4 Transmission-Line Effects

Transmission-line effects, at the pc board or motherboard level, were of little concern with the older, slower TTL and CMOS families. The slow edge rates of early TTL or 4000 series CMOS devices (5 ns or greater) did not induce transmission-line effects, except on very long lines such as might exist between remote units. However, when advanced Schottky, advanced CMOS, ECL, or GaAs devices with 2-ns (or faster) edge rates are used, transmission-line effects are of concern at the pc board level. For all practical purposes, all signal lines are transmission lines, when today's logic components are used to implement digital designs.

Transmission-line effects (line response characteristics) are of concern when signal runs (the length from the driving point to the most remote load) are equal to, or exceed, one-half the signal rise time t_r divided by the loaded (actual) propagation delay time t'_{pd} of the signal through the conducting media [16, 33, 42]. That is,

$$\text{Critical line length} = \frac{1}{2}\left(\frac{t_r}{t'_{pd}}\right) \qquad (7.21)$$

The propagation delay for a typical pc board is 2 ns/ft. For a signal with a rise time of 2 ns (which is typical for today's devices), the critical line length is

$$\text{Critical line length} = \frac{1}{2}\left(\frac{2 \text{ ns}}{2 \text{ ns/ft}}\right)$$

$$= 0.5 \text{ ft}$$

Thus, in most applications where advanced Schottky or advanced CMOS devices are used, the transmission-line effect must be considered since most signal runs, even on small pc boards, exceed 0.5 ft.

Basic Transmission-Line Considerations.   Signals transmitted on a line are well behaved when the signal source impedance, signal line impedance, and load impedance are very closely matched (i.e., almost equal) and the line has only one source and one load with no discontinuities, branches, or stubs. In such cases, one line propagation delay (approximately 2 ns/ft if the line is in a pc board) after a signal is launched into a line at the source, a signal very much like the signal launched at the source can be observed at the load. If the signal source, line, and load are not matched, or the circuit topology does not consist of the ideal case of one source and one load, the signal quality will degrade due to transmission-line ringing and other effects. Signal sources, loads, and lines are not matched on a typical pc board, welded-wire, or wire-wrap logic device interconnection circuit board or motherboard. Thus, when signal runs are greater than the critical line length [see Eq. (7.21) for the definition of the critical line length], the signal quality will degrade due to transmission-line effects, and additional time, beyond the one-way propagation delay of the lines, will be required for signals to settle.

As unterminated signal lines increase in length beyond the critical length, signal quality progressively degrades and takes longer to stabilize. Depending upon where along a line a signal is observed, transmission-line effects will be apparent on lines longer than the critical line length under most conditions, even when lines are properly terminated. When signal lines are not significantly longer than the critical length, transmission-line effects may not be severe enough to impact normal operation. When TTL components are used, the possible detrimental response of lines may be controlled by the current-limiting resistors used in the pull-up section of TTL totem-pole output stages and the input clamp diodes that are built into the input-output circuits of most TTL devices [7]. When CMOS components are used, the situation is less clear. There is little uniformity in the input-output circuitry used or in the response of CMOS input-output circuits. Thus, when CMOS logic components are used and the interconnecting lines are longer than the critical length, additional time beyond one-way line propagation times must be allowed for signals to settle unless the lines are properly terminated. Properly terminating a line consists of matching the impedance of the source and the line, or the load and the line, or both. It is generally impractical to terminate all the signals in a digital system, since terminations require additional components and may dissipate additional power (depending upon the method of termination used).

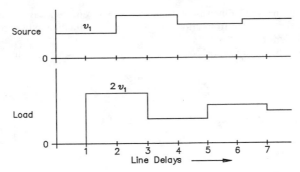

FIGURE 7.14 Idealized typical source and load waveforms for a long transmission line with one advanced Schottky TTL or advanced CMOS source and load.

Transmission-Line Response. A long transmission line, as shown in Fig. 7.14, with a one-way delay greater than the signal rise time, with one source and one load, responds to signal transitions approximately as follows [10]:

1. A signal transition is initiated at the source.
2. The signal travels along the transmission line with a delay time depending on the dielectric constant of the surrounding material.
3. The signal arrives as the first incident wave at the load after a delay that is a function of the line length and the dielectric of the material adjacent to the line.
4. Part of the energy of the first incident wave is absorbed by the load in establishing the initial signal level at the load.
5. The part of the energy of the first incident wave not absorbed due to mismatch between the line and the load impedance is reflected back toward the source.
6. When the reflection of the first incident wave arrives at the source, part of it may be absorbed by the source in establishing a new signal level; any mismatch is reflected back toward the load.
7. When the second incident wave arrives at the load, part of the energy is absorbed in establishing a new signal level; any mismatch is reflected back to the source as in item 5 above.
8. The cycles of reflections between load and source are repeated with part of the energy absorbed in each cycle; after some time, depending upon the characteristics of the source, line, and load, the reflected transient levels are so small that they are negligible.

Reflections. The amount of a signal that is reflected when an incident wave arrives at a load is determined by the mismatch between the impedance of the line and the load (or source). If a transmission line is terminated with an impedance that is equal to the characteristic impedance Z_o of the line, there will be no reflection from the end of the line, and the only signal appearing on the line will be the incident wave. If some other value of termination is used, a portion of the incident wave will be reflected, and the signal appearing on the line will be the sum of the incident and reflected waves. The magnitude and polarity of the reflection from a load or a source are quantitatively described by the reflection coefficient ρ.

The equation for the reflection coefficient ρ_L for the load end of a line is [26, 48]

$$\rho_L = \frac{R_L - Z_o}{R_L + Z_o} \tag{7.22}$$

and the reflection coefficient ρ_S for the source end of the line is

$$\rho_S = \frac{R_S - Z_o}{R_S + Z_o} \tag{7.23}$$

If either end of the line is exactly matched to Z_o, that is, $R_S = Z_o$ or $R_L = Z_o$, the reflection coefficient is 0, the incident wave is completely absorbed, and no reflection occurs.

There are a couple of cases of ρ that are of special interest:

1. $\rho = +1$ when $R_L = \infty$ or $R_S = \infty$ (an open-circuit line). When $\rho = +1$, the signal doubles when the incident wave arrives at the end of the line.

2. $\rho = -1$ when $R_L = 0$ or $R_S = 0$ (a short-circuited line). When $\rho = -1$, the incident wave reverses its polarity and subtracts an amount equal to the incident wave from the existing voltage at the load (or source), and the new voltage level is reflected back toward the other end of the line. The energy in an incident wave is *not* absorbed by a short circuit.

Case 1 above is the typical situation for TTL or CMOS input circuits; inputs are sensitive to voltage (not power) and require only a small proportion of the energy in the incident wave arriving from the transmission line to maintain steady-state operation (i.e., the load impedance is very large with respect to the line impedance). Therefore, the voltage at the load device is increased (up to double) compared to the incident wave, and a significant portion of the energy is reflected back toward the source.

Case 2 above is approximated by typical CMOS high and low outputs and TTL low outputs; their effective output impedance is not zero, but it is much less than the normal line impedance. Thus, low TTL outputs or CMOS high or low outputs have negative reflection coefficients. Energy is reflected with a reversal of voltage polarity. A negative reflection coefficient at the source end of a line will cause overshoot that may have occurred at the load end of the line to be converted to undershoot on alternate reflection cycles. The undershoot, when it arrives at the load, may cause the signal level to transition into the threshold region of the receiving device, upsetting the logic sense of the signal. Under such conditions, which are typical of advanced TTL or advanced CMOS devices, a number of round trips may be required for the excess energy in the signal to be absorbed and for the signal to achieve a steady-state value [10].

Transmission-Line Termination.   There are two basic ways of terminating transmission lines: series (source) termination or load termination. Either method can be used to achieve a stable signal at the far (load) end of a line after one line delay. However, the response at the source and at intermediate points is different for the two methods of termination. Series termination requires at least two line delays for signals to stabilize at the source end of a line; load-terminated lines can reach steady-state conditions at the source, at all points along the line, and at the load after one line delay.

Load Termination.   A line is defined as *load-terminated* when the load at the end of the line is matched to the impedance of the line. Figure 7.15a to d shows various means

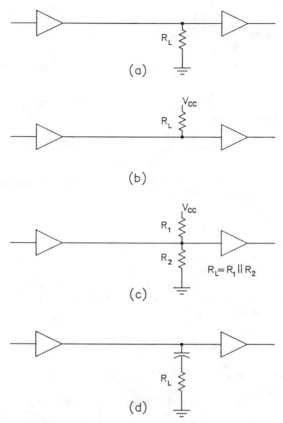

FIGURE 7.15   Load termination. (*a*) Termination to ground. (*b*) Termination to V_{cc}. (*c*) Split termination. (*d*) AC termination.

of load termination [33, 49]. The same dynamic results are achieved with each of the configurations.

When a line is load-terminated with a matching impedance (R_L of the load $= Z_o$ of the line), regardless of the dc circuit configuration of the terminating network, the signal at the source, at intermediate points, and at the load should appear as a well-behaved signal, as shown in Fig. 7.16. In such a case, the signal is launched into the line and at some later time (equal to the propagation time of the line t_{LINE}) arrives at the load. The energy in the wavefront is absorbed, and a steady-state level is established upon the arrival of the incident wave at the load (see Fig. 7.16). In Fig. 7.15 it is implied that the receivers have infinite impedance, and for all practical purposes, that is the case for TTL and CMOS device inputs, as long as the signal levels remain between ground and V_{cc}. Thus, the value of the load termination does not need to be adjusted to compensate for receiver input impedance.

Source Termination.   Source termination, which is often referred to as *series termination,* consists of matching the source impedance to the line impedance, as shown in Fig. 7.17. Figure 7.18 shows the idealized waveforms for a source-terminated circuit exactly matched to a line with an infinite load.

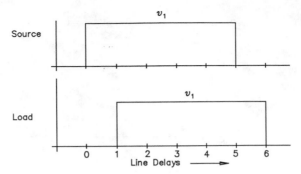

FIGURE 7.16 Idealized source and load waveforms in a load-terminated transmission line.

Series termination works best where there is one source and one load. The waveform at the load end of a series-terminated line is well behaved, but at the source and at intermediate points near the source, the leading edge of the waveform will step up rather than make a smooth transition (see Fig. 7.18). The initial step (or steps) occurs as a result of the divider formed by the source resistance R_S of the driving device and Z_o of the line. The amplitude of the initial step is

$$V_{t=0^+}(\text{at source}) = \frac{Z_o}{R_S + Z_o} \times V_{cc}$$

When R_S is matched to Z_o, the amplitude of the initial step is

$$V_{t=0^+}(\text{at source}) = \frac{1}{2}V_{cc} \qquad \text{when } R_S = Z_o$$

However, if Z_o of a line is very low relative to R_S, multiple energy injection and reflection cycles and steps may be necessary for the line to reach the final value.

The high-level and low-level output impedances of TTL devices are not the same, which complicates the selection of line-matching resistors. For standard (i.e., not drivers) advanced Schottky components, the high-level output impedance is near 40 Ω and low-level output impedance is near 10 Ω. Thus, an exact impedance match to a line cannot be achieved for both high- and low-going TTL signals. Hence, series termination of TTL circuits is by necessity a compromise. Since low TTL levels have the least noise margin, and since all TTL devices have higher drive in the low state, which increases the possibility of ringing, it is best to more exactly match the low-state output impedance.

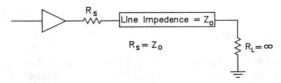

FIGURE 7.17 Source termination of transmission lines is accomplished by matching the signal source impedance to the transmission-line characteristic impedance.

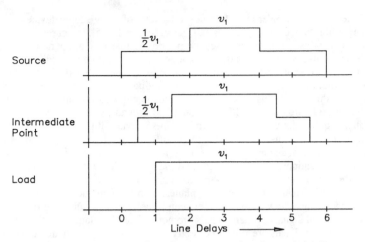

FIGURE 7.18 Idealized waveforms in a source-terminated transmission line.

The high- and low-state output impedances of CMOS devices tend to be more evenly matched than those of TTL devices, but CMOS output impedance changes on the order of 2:1 from nominal in both the positive and negative directions with processing, temperature, and voltage. Thus, it is impossible to closely match CMOS outputs to line impedances.

Real-world responses of TTL or CMOS signals, whether source-terminated or not, do not consist of nice single-level square-cornered transitions at sources or at intermediate points in lines. Actual signals tend to overshoot and undershoot, i.e., ring. Real TTL and CMOS devices have some finite amount of output impedance. Hence, signal waveforms with steps (that may ring around the step level) are common throughout TTL and CMOS systems; in most cases they do not cause a problem [26, 50, 51]. Such signal responses are of no concern in synchronous systems on data and control lines. In a few remote cases, a waveform with a step can cause problems at a secondary level. If a step happened to be near the threshold level of a receiver, the receiver input circuitry could oscillate during the time the signal dwells in the threshold region. In some cases, the oscillation may generate enough noise to upset nearby circuits, but in most cases the time that signals dwell in the intermediate region is relatively short, and as a result no ill effects are caused. However, such signals cannot be used to clock devices; multiple clocking may occur. Since signals with steps are inherent near the source of TTL or CMOS driven lines, high-speed TTL and CMOS clock lines must be arranged so that the clocked devices are near the ends of the lines (see Buchanan [3, 10] for clock distribution guidelines), or the impedance of the lines must be high enough that the level of the step is well above the threshold of the clocked devices.

7.3.5 Crosstalk

Crosstalk is the noise voltage developed on signal lines when nearby lines change state. Crosstalk occurs due to capacitive and inductive coupling between adjacent or nearby lines. It is a function of the separation between signal lines, the linear distance over which signal lines run parallel to each other, and the height above a ground, or other reference, plane.

The faster (relative to older logic families) edge rates of today's logic devices greatly increase the possibility of coupling or crosstalk between signals [35]. Increased coupling, plus faster device response, greatly increases the possibility that system operation will be degraded by crosstalk. Synchronous design practices [3] reduce the possibility of crosstalk disrupting system operation if time can be allotted for crosstalk to subside, but the goal in most modern digital systems is to achieve high operating speed. To maximize speed, crosstalk must be reduced to levels where no extra time is required for the signal to stabilize.

Multilayer pc boards with multiple voltage and ground planes are needed to achieve the isolation required for critical signals in high-performance digital systems [10]. In less critical applications, it is usually possible to get sufficient isolation of signals by arranging the signal layer so that signal runs (traces) are at right angles on adjacent layers; but in very critical applications, voltage and ground planes should be used to isolate all signal layers. For example, when very high-speed memory devices are used, address and data signals should be isolated by reference planes. Other techniques of isolating critical signals include using extrawide spacing between signal lines and running ground traces on each side of critical signals. When signals are not isolated by planes, care must be taken to ensure that noisy signals are not run directly above or below a critical signal for some length.

On welded-wire or wire-wrap boards or backpanels, the wiring should be as direct as possible between points so as to randomize the routing, and the wiring should be kept as close as possible to the ground (or voltage) plane. Care must be taken to ensure that wiring is not channelized. Particular care must be taken to ensure that the critical signals, such as clocks, do not get channelized with noisy signals.

On welded-wire or wire-wrap boards or backpanels, critical single-ended signals should be run twisted with a ground wire connected to ground at the source and at the load, as shown in Fig. 7.19. Twisting signal lines with ground lines provides the most direct path possible for return currents and provides some shielding effect. Return currents tend to flow in the nearby twisted ground line and not in the power or ground planes (see Fig. 7.20). Thus, transient current flow and noise are reduced in the power and ground system. In addition, twisted-pair signal lines provide better control of the line impedance, which allows more accurate terminations and helps control ringing and line reflections. Twisted-pair lines also tend to confine the magnetic fields of the two twisted conductors, which minimizes the chance for coupling into adjacent wiring.

In all but the most trivial of systems, some signal line inevitably must run close to and parallel with other signals. Where signals are close and parallel, two forms of crosstalk exist: forward and backward. Forward crosstalk is present on coupled lines in time coincidence with an active wavefront on a nearby driven line and exists for the duration of the edge transition of the driven line. Backward crosstalk on coupled lines flows away from the wavefront on the nearby active line and exists for twice the propagation delay of the coupled line length [52]. Both forms of crosstalk can cause circuit malfunctions. Backward crosstalk tends to be more detrimental, since it tends to be of a higher amplitude and lasts for a longer time; but either form can cause logic errors. The extent of the possible upset of a coupled-to line is dependent upon the polarity and amplitude of the coupled noise relative to the logic level of the signal that is disturbed and the physical topology of the lines. The signal flow may be such that the coupling is of little concern.

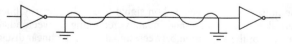

FIGURE 7.19   Twisted-pair signal lines with ground lines to reduce crosstalk.

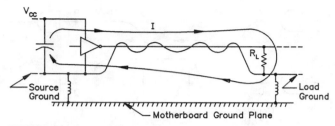

FIGURE 7.20 Twisted-pair lines provide direct low-impedance return current paths.

For example, backward crosstalk is of no concern at output node *C* in Fig. 7.21. However, backward crosstalk could be a major problem for a circuit with the topology shown in Fig. 7.22.

In a case as shown in Fig. 7.22, backward crosstalk may or may not cause a problem depending upon the polarity of the coupled signal. If the coupling adds to or subtracts from the existing level so that the resulting composite signal has more margin, then the coupling is of little concern (assuming that the coupled signal does not cause excessive ringing). Since it may be impractical to analyze all possible combinations, the safest approach is to assume that there will be some combinations of active and inactive signals such that some inactive signals will be degraded by crosstalk.

In those cases, where the interconnect topology and the polarity of the coupling are in the harmful direction, the crosstalk may or may not be harmful depending on the amplitude and duration of the coupled voltage. If the amplitude of the coupled voltage is less than the noise margin of the logic components used, then the coupling may not be detrimental. Likewise, if the duration of the coupled pulse is short enough, even though it exceeds the noise margin of the receiving devices, then the receiving devices may not

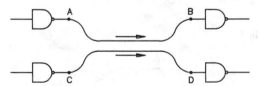

FIGURE 7.21 Coupled lines with the signal flow in the same direction.

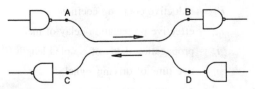

FIGURE 7.22 Coupled lines with the signal flow in the opposite direction.

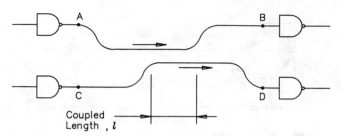

FIGURE 7.23 Coupling occurs where signal lines are in close proximity which may only be a small portion of the total signal length.

react to a narrow pulse. Some device manufacturers are specifying the pulse immunity of their devices to help designers evaluate the possible detrimental effects of ground bounce transients [41]. Such data are also useful for determining the sensitivity of devices to coupled pulses.

The general expressions for crosstalk voltage amplitude between two lines with coupled length l (see Fig. 7.23) are as follows [50, 51]:

Backward Crosstalk V_B:

$$V_B = \left(\frac{K_C + K_L}{4}\right)\left(\frac{2t_p}{t_r}\right)(\Delta V_S) \qquad (7.24)$$

for coupled line lengths from $l = 0$ to $l = t_r/(2t'_{pd})$, and

$$V_B = \left(\frac{K_C + K_L}{4}\right)(\Delta V_S) \qquad (7.25)$$

for coupled line lengths of $l = t_r/(2t'_{pd}))$ or greater.

Forward Crosstalk V_F:

$$V_F = \left(\frac{K_C - K_L}{2}\right)\left(\frac{t_p}{t_r}\right)(\Delta V_S) \qquad (7.26)$$

For Eqs. (7.24), (7.25), and (7.26),

$$\Delta V_S = \text{driving signal transition amplitude}$$
$$K_C = \text{capacitive coupling coefficient}$$
$$K_L = \text{inductive coupling coefficient}$$
$$t'_{pd} = \text{effective propagation delay of media}$$
$$t_p = \text{propagation delay of coupled length } (l \times t'_{pd})$$
$$t_r = \text{rise time of driving signal}$$
$$l = \text{coupled length}$$

and

$$K_C = \frac{C_m}{C}$$

$$K_L = \frac{L_m}{L}$$

where C_m = mutual capacitance between lines

C = capacitance between lines and ground

L_m = mutual inductance between lines

L = inductance of each line

In a homogeneous material K_C and K_L are equal, and no forward crosstalk exists [51]. However, conductors in typical digital applications are not surrounded by a pure homogeneous material. Welded-wire or wire-wrap interconnections, as well as pc board interconnections, are surrounded by a conglomerate of materials, other conductors, insulation, etc. Yet, for practical engineering purposes, forward crosstalk is of little concern in welded-wire or wire-wrap circuit board or motherboard interconnections or in embedded conductors in multilayer pc boards. The exception is when two lines have a long coupled length (relative to the active signal rise time); in those cases the t_p/t_r term in the forward crosstalk equation becomes significant. Where forward crosstalk exists, it consists of a pulse with a width equal to the rise time t_r of the driving source. The amplitude is proportional to the coupled length.

Equation (7.24) shows that backward crosstalk magnitude is a function of coupled line length for coupled line lengths from $l = 0$ to $l = t_r/(2t'_{pd})$. At $l = t_r/(2t'_{pd})$ (which is the *critical line length* [33]—see Sec. 7.3.4), backward crosstalk reaches a maximum amplitude; for longer coupled lengths, it increases in width but does not increase in amplitude [52]—see Eq. (7.25). The duration of backward crosstalk is equal to the two-way delay of the coupled length l.

Backward crosstalk reaches a maximum amplitude where the propagation delay (t_p) of the coupled length of line is equal to one-half the rise time t_r of the active signal, i.e., when the coupled line length is equal to the *critical line length* [33].

It is apparent from the limits of Eq. (7.24) that the coupled line length needed for maximum amplitude coupling is reduced as the signal rise time decreases. A signal trace adjacent to a trace driven with a signal with a 2-ns edge transition requires one-half the coupled length to achieve the limiting value of crosstalk, as is required for a signal with a 4-ns edge transition. It therefore follows that systems with signals with fast rise times will have significantly more crosstalk than systems with signals with slow rise times.

To calculate crosstalk from Eqs. (7.24), (7.25), and (7.26), the line capacitance C, inductance L, and propagation delay t_{pd}, as well as the mutual capacitance C_m and inductance L_m between lines, are needed. All are difficult to determine manually. Fortunately, today there are programs available, such as Quad Design's XTK Crosstalk Program [53], that calculate crosstalk based on conductor topology and driver-receiver input-output characteristics [54].

When crosstalk calculation tools are not available, the family of crosstalk plots for microstrip, dual-stripline, and stripline conductors (see Fig. 7.24) shown in Figs. 7.25 to 7.27 allows a quick estimation of the approximate amplitude of backward crosstalk [which is usually of greatest concern since it tends to be larger than forward crosstalk except where lines are very long—see Eq. (7.26)]. The crosstalk curves shown in Figs. 7.25 to 7.27 are for unit-level (1-V) signal transitions with 2-ns transition times (on the driven line). Faster or slower driving signal rise times move the knee of the curves in or out on the coupled length axis—the knee of the curves corresponds to the critical line length (see above). The curves are directly applicable for signals with ECL levels since most ECL signal transitions are approximately 1 V. Crosstalk amplitude estimates for TTL-level signals, which are typically in the 3- to 4-V range, should be proportionally increased (i.e., by 3 to 4 times the values shown). For CMOS signals, which typically have 5-V transitions, the crosstalk amplitudes shown in the curves should be multiplied by 5. The curves were generated by using data for 8-mil-wide, 2-mil-thick traces in a

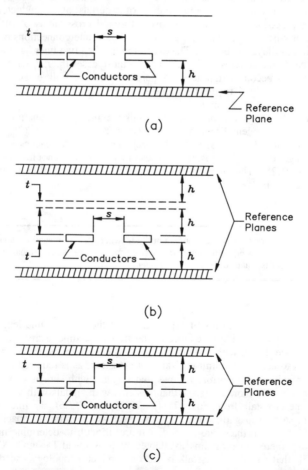

FIGURE 7.24 Typical pc board interconnection structures. (*a*) Microstrip. (*b*) Dual stripline. (*c*) Stripline.

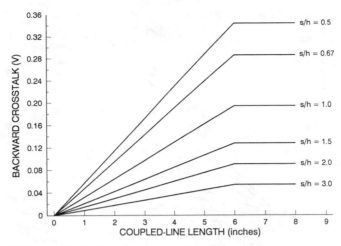

FIGURE 7.25 Backward crosstalk per volt of signal transition in 2 ns versus line length l, spacing s, and height h above a reference plane for buried microstrip conductors in epoxy glass pc boards with a dielectric constant ϵ_r of 4.5 (data calculated using Quad Design XTK crosstalk simulation program—see Fig. 7.24 for dimensions).

material with a dielectric constant of 4.5, which is typical for epoxy glass pc boards. The line thickness and width variation, within $2:1$ in either direction, have little effect on the results.

Backward crosstalk estimates based on the curves shown in Figs. 7.25 to 7.27 should be accurate enough for most engineering purposes, but one must remember that crosstalk is usually not a simple phenomenon. In most cases, it is the result of complex interactions

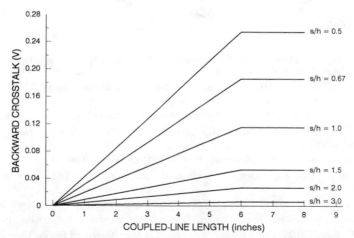

FIGURE 7.26 Backward crosstalk per volt of signal transition in 2 ns versus line length l, spacing s, and distance h from reference planes for stripline conductors in epoxy glass pc boards with a dielectric constant ϵ_r of 4.5 (data calculated using Quad Design XTK crosstalk simulation program—see Fig. 7.24 for dimensions).

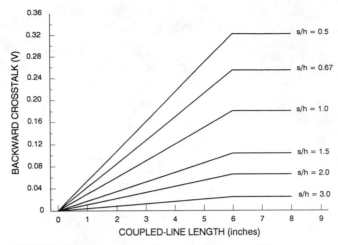

FIGURE 7.27   Backward crosstalk per volt of signal transition in 2 ns versus line length l, spacing s, and distance h from reference planes for dual stripline conductors in epoxy glass pc boards with a dielectric constant ϵ_r of 4.5 (data calculated using Quad Design XTK crosstalk simulation program—see Fig. 7.24 for dimensions).

between a number of signals and their reflections. Actual measurements are the most reliable source for determining crosstalk, but the practicing engineer seldom has the time or resources to make controlled measurements on final production configuration boards, and measurements ''after the fact'' are of little benefit except for educational purposes. Crosstalk is a major problem when high-speed digital devices are used; it will cause problems unless the interconnection system is designed to minimize it.

REFERENCES

1. IEEE Standard 181-1977, *IEEE Standard on Pulse Measurement and Analysis by Objective Techniques*. New York: IEEE, 1977.

2. Robert K. Southard, ''High-Speed Signal Pathways from Board to Board,'' 1981 WESCON Record, Session 18, paper no. 2, September 1981.

3. James E. Buchanan, *CMOS/TTL Digital Systems Design*. New York: McGraw-Hill, 1990.

4. David Shear, ''EDN's Advanced CMOS Logic Ground-Bounce Tests,'' *EDN*, pp. 88–97, March 2, 1989.

5. Joseph DiGiacomo, *VLSI Handbook*. New York: McGraw-Hill, 1989, chap. 23.

6. *Advanced CMOS Logic Design Considerations*, SCLA004, Texas Instruments Inc., Dallas, 1986.

7. *FAST Applications Handbook 1987*, National Semiconductor Corp., South Portland, Me., 1988.

8. *Simultaneous Switching Evaluation and Testing*, Texas Instruments Inc., Dallas, 1987.

9. *FCT—Fast, CMOS, TTL—Compatible Logic Tech Note*, Integrated Device Technology Inc., Santa Clara, Calif., December 1986.

10. James E. Buchanan, *BiCMOS/CMOS Systems Design*. New York: McGraw-Hill, 1990.

11. Anthony P. Visco, "Coaxing Top Bipolar Speeds from Prototyping Boards," *Electronic Products,* pp. 55–58, September 1, 1987.

12. Henry W. Ott, *Noise Reduction Techniques in Electronic Systems,* 2d ed. New York: Wiley, 1988.

13. Ralph Morrison, *Grounding and Shielding Techniques in Instrumentation,* 3d ed. New York: Wiley, 1986.

14. H. C. Lin, *Integrated Electronics.* San Francisco: Holden-Day, 1967.

15. William R. Blood, Jr., *MECL System Design Handbook,* 4th ed. Phoenix, Ariz.: Motorola Semiconductor Products Inc., 1988.

16. Richard E. Matick, *Transmission Lines for Digital and Communication Networks.* New York: McGraw-Hill, 1969.

17. John C. Truxal, *Control Engineers' Handbook.* New York: McGraw-Hill, 1958, p. 7–4.

18. Charles A. Harper, *Handbook of Wiring, Cabling and Interconnections for Electronics.* New York: McGraw-Hill, 1972.

19. *Aluminum Building Wire Installation Manual.* New York: The Aluminum Association.

20. *Bimetallic Electrical Transition Joints,* Aluminum Company of America, Pittsburgh.

21. Charles A. Harper, *Handbook of Materials and Processes for Electronics.* New York: McGraw-Hill, 1970.

22. Richard Klein, "Protecting Circuits from Over and Under Voltages," *The Electronic Engineer,* pp. 59–61, March 1969.

23. Richard W. Fox, "Six Ways to Control Transients," *Electronic Design,* no. 11, pp. 52–57, May 24, 1974.

24. Jock Tomlinson, "Avoid the Pitfalls of High-Speed Logic Design," *Electronic Design,* pp. 75–84, November 9, 1989.

25. *ATMEL Data Book 1989,* ATMEL Corp., San Jose, Calif., 1989.

26. *A Guide to Backplane Electrical Performance Measurements,* IEEE Standard P1194.0/D2. New York: IEEE, 1989.

27. Robert B. Cowdell, "Bypass and Feedthrough Filters," *Electronic Design,* no. 17, pp. 62–67, August 16, 1975.

28. Arch G. Martin and R. Kenneth Keenan, "Neater Decoupling on Surface-Mount Boards," *Electronic Products,* pp. 47–49, August 15, 1987.

29. Laudie Doubrava, "Bypass Supply Loads with Care for Optimum Transient Response," *EDN,* pp. 113–117, September 20, 1979.

30. Arthur F. Upham, "Failure Analyses and Testing Yield Reliable Products," *EDN,* pp. 165–174, August 8, 1985.

31. Robert Cutler, "Your Logic Simulation Is Only as Good as Your Board Layout," *VLSI System Design,* pp. 40–42, July 1987.

32. Tim Tripp and Bill Hall, "Good Design Methods, Quiet High-Speed CMOS Noise Problems," *EDN,* pp. 229–236, October 29, 1987.

33. Robert K. Southard, "High-Speed Signal Pathways from Board to Board," 1981 WESCON Record, Session 18, paper no. 2, September 1981.

34. Charles A. Harper, *Handbook of Electronic Packaging.* New York: McGraw-Hill, 1969.

35. Jock Tomlinson, "Avoid the Pitfalls of High-Speed Logic Design," *Electronic Design,* pp. 75–84, November 9, 1989.

36. Joseph DiCerto, "Poor Packaging Produces Problems," *The Electronic Engineer,* pp. 91–93, September 1970.

37. Ronald A. Crouch, "Choose Cable with Care to Optimize System Design," *EDN,* pp. 113–116, November 5, 1978.

38. Frank Timmons, "Wire or Cable Has Many Faces, Know Them All before Choosing, Part II," *EDN*, pp. 49–55, March 1, 1970.

39. H. C. Brown, "Get Rid of Ground-Loop Noise," *Electronic Design*, no. 15, pp. 84–87, July 19, 1969.

40. Shiv C. Tasker, "Making the Best Use of On-Board Interconnections," *Electronic Engineering Times*, pp. 41, 66, December 4, 1989.

41. *FACT Advanced CMOS Logic Databook*, National Semiconductor Corp., Santa Clara, Calif., 1989.

42. N. C. Arvanitakis and J. J. Zara, "Design Considerations of Printed Circuit Transmission Lines for High Performance Circuits," 1981 WESCON Record, Session 18, paper no. 4, September 1981.

43. H. R. Kaupp, "Characteristics of Microstrip Transmission Lines," *IEEE Transactions on Electronic Computers*, EC-16(2):185–193, April 1967.

44. William Heniford, "Muffling Noise in TTL," *The Electronic Engineer*, pp. 63–69, July 1969.

45. Joseph L. DeClue, "Wiring for High-Speed Circuits," *Electronic Design*, no. 11, pp. 84–86, May 24, 1976.

46. William K. Springfield, "Designing Transmission Lines into Multilayer Circuit Boards," *Electronics*, pp. 90–96, November 1, 1965.

47. *Applications Handbook*, Cypress Semiconductor Corp., San Jose, Calif., 1989, p. 1–12.

48. Ivor Catt, "Crosstalk (Noise) in Digital Systems," *IEEE Transactions on Electronic Computers*, EC-16(6): 743–768, December 1967.

49. John A. DeFalco, "Reflection and Crosstalk in Logic Circuit Interconnections," *IEEE Spectrum*, pp. 44–50, July 1970.

50. Tushar Gheewala and David MacMillan, "High-Speed GaAs Logic Systems Require Special Packaging," *EDN*, pp. 8–14, May 17, 1984.

51. John J. Kozuch, "A High Speed Approach to Controlled Impedance Packaging," Multiwire Division, Kollmorgen Corp., Glen Cove, N.Y., January 1987.

52. John A. DeFalco, "Predicting Crosstalk in Digital Systems," *Computer Design*, pp. 69–75, June 1973.

53. Richard Nass, "PC-Board Speeds Skyrocket," *Electronic Design*, pp. 31–32, 37–38, September 28, 1989.

54. Roderic Beresford, "How to Tame High-Speed Design," *High Performance Systems*, pp. 78–82, September 1989.

CHAPTER 8
COMPUTER GRAPHICS

Edward Angel

Department of Computer Science
University of New Mexico, Albuquerque

8.1 OVERVIEW

Computer graphics is concerned with all aspects of using a computer to generate images. Under this definition, computer graphics includes the design of hardware such as displays, the algorithms that are necessary to generate lines on these displays, the software that is used by both the graphics system programmer and the application programmer, and the applications of computer-generated images.

In this chapter we will survey a few of the most important aspects of computer graphics. After a brief survey of applications, we will introduce the hardware found in a graphics system. Then we will present a visualization model which includes both traditional imaging methods, such as the camera, and computer image formation. This model will lead us to the mathematical foundations of the field. Finally, we will survey the types of software currently available.

8.2 APPLICATIONS OF COMPUTER GRAPHICS

The use of computer graphics pervades many diverse fields. Applications range from the production of charts and graphs, to the generation of realistic images for television and motion pictures, to the interactive design of mechanical parts.

We can classify applications of computer graphics into four main areas:

- Display of information
- Design
- Simulation
- User interfaces

Although many applications span two, three, or even all these areas, the development of the field was based, for the most part, on separate work in each domain.

Some of this chapter is adapted from E. Angel, *Computer Graphics*. Reading, Mass.: Addison-Wesley, 1990.

8.2.1 Display of Information

Graphics has always been associated with the display of information. Examples of the use of orthographic projections to display floorplans of buildings can be found on 4000-year-old Babylonian stone tablets. Mechanical methods for creating perspective drawings were developed during the Renaissance. Countless engineering students have become familiar with interpreting data plotted on log paper. More recently, software packages that allow interactive design of charts incorporating color, multiple data sets, and alternate plotting methods have become the norm. In fields such as architecture and mechanical design, hand drafting is being replaced by computer-based drafting systems using plotters and workstations. Medical imaging uses computer graphics in a number of exciting ways. See Tufte [22, 23] and Carlbom and Paciorek [4] for many examples of both the history of and methods used in visualization.

Recently there has been great interest in problems of scientific visualization. Although researchers are now using supercomputers to solve formerly intractable problems in fields such as fluid flow and molecular biology, they need new display techniques to interpret the results of analyzing the vast quantities of multidimensional data generated.

8.2.2 Design

Professions such as engineering and architecture are concerned with design. Although their applications vary, most designers face similar difficulties and use similar methodologies. One of the principal characteristics of most design problems is the lack of a unique solution. Hence, the designer will examine a potential design and then modify it, possibly many times, in an attempt to achieve a better solution. Computer graphics has become an indispensable element in this iterative process.

Consider, e.g., how computer graphics might enter into the design of an electronic circuit. The designer is seated at a graphics workstation with a graphical input device, such as a mouse, with which she can indicate locations on the display. The initial display screen might consist of the various elements that can be used in the circuit and an empty area in which the circuit will be "constructed." The designer will then use the input device to select and move the desired elements into the design and to make connections between elements. Circuit elements are drawn and perhaps are moved about the screen. A graphical input device is used to indicate choices and positions. A number of aids may be used to help the designer position the elements accurately and to do automatically such tasks as routing of wires.

At this point, the designer probably will want to test her design. The circuit will be tested by an analysis program, which will display its results (e.g., graphs of voltage versus time) on the workstation. Now the designer can modify the design as necessary, try another design, or accept what has already been done.

8.2.3 Simulation

Some of the most impressive and familiar uses of computer graphics can be classified as simulations. Video games demonstrate both the visual appeal of computer graphics and the ability to generate complex imagery in real time. The insides of an arcade game reveal state-of-the-art hardware and software. Computer-generated images are also the heart of flight simulators, which have become the standard method for training pilots. The savings in dollars and lives realized from use of these simulators have been enormous. The computer-generated images we see on television and in movies have advanced to the point that they are almost indistinguishable from real-world images.

8.2.4 User Interfaces

The interface between the person and the computer has been radically altered by the use of computer graphics. Consider the electronic office. A secretary sits at a workstation, rather than at a desk equipped with a typewriter. This user has a pointing device, such as a mouse, that allows communication with the workstation. The display consists of a number of icons that represent the various operations the secretary can perform. For example, there might be an icon of a mailbox that, if pointed to and clicked on, causes any electronic-mail messages to appear on the screen. An icon of a wastepaper basket allows the user to dispose of unwanted mail, whereas an icon of a file cabinet is used to save letters or other documents.

A similar graphical interface would be part of our circuit design system. While engineers see these interfaces as being obvious uses of computer graphics, from the perspective of the secretary using the office automation system or of the circuit designer, however, the graphics is a secondary aspect of the task to be done. Although they never write graphics programs, multitudes of computer users use computer graphics.

8.3 A BASIC GRAPHICS SYSTEM

Let us consider the organization of a typical graphics system we might use. Since our emphasis will be on how the applications programmer sees the system, we omit details of the hardware. A block diagram of a system is shown in Fig. 8.1. There are four key types of elements in our system:

- Processor(s)
- Memory
- Output devices
- Input devices

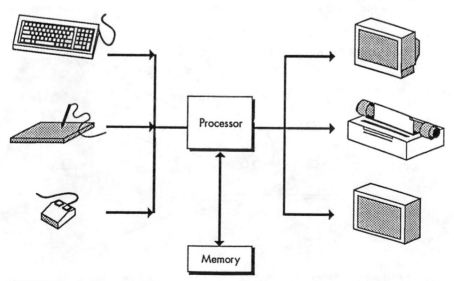

FIGURE 8.1 Graphics system.

The model is general enough to include workstations, personal computers, terminals attached to a central timeshared computer, and sophisticated image generation systems. In most ways, this block diagram is that of a standard computer. How each element is specialized for computer graphics will characterize this diagram as one of a graphics system, rather than one of a general-purpose computer.

8.3.1 Output Devices

Our basic system has one or more output devices. From the earliest days of computer graphics, the *cathode-ray tube* (CRT) has been the standard output device. A simplified picture of a CRT is seen in Fig 8.2. When electrons strike the phosphor coating on the tube, light is emitted. The position of the beam is controlled by two pairs of deflection plates. The output of the computer is converted, by digital-to-analog converters, to voltages across the x and y deflection plates. Light can be made to appear on the surface of the CRT by directing a sufficiently intense beam of electrons at the phosphor. If the voltages steering the beam change at a constant rate, the beam will trace a straight line, visible to a viewer. In this configuration, this device is known as the *random-scan* or *calligraphic* CRT because the beam can be moved directly from any position to any other position. Since most CRT phosphors emit light for a very short period after they are energized, the display must be redrawn or *refreshed* at least 50 times per second to prevent noticeable flicker.

During the 1970s, reductions in the cost of solid-state memory made it feasible to construct systems that used a raster scan CRT. In raster graphics, the image is stored as an array of picture elements, or *pixels* (Fig. 8.3), rather than as a set of line segments, as it is with simple random-scan displays. The pixels are stored in a special memory area, known as the *frame buffer*. The display hardware scans the frame buffer, usually at a rate of 50 to 70 scans per second, refreshing the display line by line. Many displays are still *interlaced,* displaying odd and even scan lines on alternate refresh cycles, much in the way commercial television images are produced. Graphical output primitives, such as line segments and text, are displayed by turning on or off pixels in the frame buffer that approximate the primitive. This process is known as *scan conversion,* or *rasterization.*

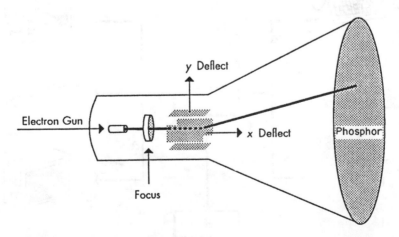

FIGURE 8.2   Cathode-ray tube.

 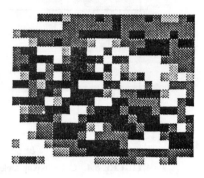

FIGURE 8.3   Rasterized image (left) with pixels around eye blown up (right).

Use of multiple bits for each pixel allows the display of color and density images. Other types of displays such as laser plotters are also raster devices.

8.3.2 Color

Virtually all graphics systems are based on a three-color *red-green-blue* (RGB) model. A given color is formed by mixing appropriate amounts of the three primary colors. Color CRTs have patterns of red, green, and blue phosphors arranged in triads or interleaved strips on their surface. Precisely controlled electron beams produce the desired mix of primary colors. This color model is additive. Other systems use a subtractive model based on the complimentary primary colors of *cyan, magenta, and yellow* (CMY) [24].

In terms of a frame buffer, there must be extra memory for the color information. In what is sometimes called a *true-color system,* 24 (or more) bits is allocated to each pixel. With 8 bits per primary color, we can display 2^{24} different colors. More typically graphics systems have fewer bits per pixel (most often 8) but use *color lookup tables* to give the benefits of a large palette. The bits stored for a pixel are used as an address into a (typically) 24-bit table (see Fig. 8.4). The entry in the table gives the amount of red, green, and blue to be used for that value in the frame buffer.

8.3.3 The Processor

Within the processor box, two types of processing take place. The first is *picture forma-tion* processing. In this stage, the user program or commands are processed. The picture is formed from the output primitives, e.g., lines and text, available in the system using the desired attributes, such as line color and text font. The picture can be specified in a number of ways, such as through an interactive menu-controlled painting program or via a C program using a graphics library. The physical processor used in this stage is often the processor in the workstation or host computer.

The second kind of processing is concerned with the display of the picture. In a raster system, the specified primitives must be scan-converted. The screen must be refreshed to

Input		Red	Green	Blue
0 1 . . . 2^8-1				

$\longleftarrow$ 8 bits $\longrightarrow$ $\longleftarrow$ 8 bits $\longrightarrow$ $\longleftarrow$ 8 bits $\longrightarrow$

FIGURE 8.4 Color lookup table.

avoid flicker. Input from the user might require objects to be repositioned on the display. The kind of processor best suited for these jobs is not the standard type of processor found in most computers. Instead, special boards and chips are often used.

8.3.4 Display Processors

From the early days of computer graphics, the major processing bottleneck has been keeping the display refreshed. The development of the *display processor* [8] allowed the generation of interactive real-time graphics. The display processor is a special-purpose computer with a limited set of instructions that it can execute quickly. Primary among its tasks is to keep the CRT refreshed at a rate that makes the display appear smooth and flicker-free. Graphical entities that are defined on the host are placed in a special memory, called the *display memory,* or *display file,* which is accessed by the *display processing unit* (DPU), as in Fig. 8.5. The host computer then needs to define graphical primitives only once. Once these primitives are sent on to the display processor, the host is free for other tasks. The functions of the display processor are incorporated in most present graphics systems, although advances in VLSI technology have allowed the functionality of the earliest systems to be reduced to one or two chips.

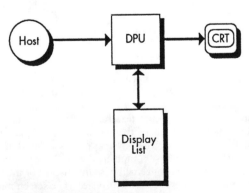

FIGURE 8.5 Display processor.

The present generation of display processors is characterized by a number of special-function chips sometimes called *application-specific integrated circuits* (ASICs). In addition to controlling the display, operations such as rasterization, transformations, hidden surface removal, lighting effects, and transparency are now hardware functions. Consequently, on high-end graphics systems, producing a realistic image is often no more difficult or time-consuming than producing a simple wire-frame image.

8.3.5 Memory

There are often two distinct types of memory employed in graphics systems. For the processing of the user program, the memory is similar to that of a standard computer, as the picture is formed by a standard type of arithmetic processing. Display processing, however, requires high-speed display memory that can be accessed by the display processor and, in raster systems, memory for the frame buffer. This display memory usually is different in both its physical characteristics and its organization from what is used by the picture processor. In a typical raster system, the display memory uses either *dynamic random-access memory* (DRAM) or *video random-access memory* (VRAM). This memory is organized so that it is refreshed (or reenergized) at the same rate as the display. It is also *dual-ported,* which allows independent reading and writing of its contents. The way the internals of the processor and memory boxes are organized distinguishes a slow system from a real-time picture-generating system, such as a flight simulator. However, from our present perspective, we emphasize that all implementations have to do the same kinds of tasks to produce output.

8.3.6 Input Devices

A simple system may have only a keyboard to provide whatever input is necessary. Most graphics systems will provide at least one other input device. The most common devices are the mouse, the light pen, the joystick, and the data tablet. Each can provide positional information to the system, and usually each is equipped with one or more buttons to provide signals to the processor.

In typical nongraphics programs, input is usually either a string of characters or a string of bits. Both modes are typically treated by user programs as logical input streams rather than as physical input. In computer graphics, logical input is used in more varied forms. A logical input device that provides a position is called a *locator;* if it provides the identifier of an object on the display, it is called a *pick.* If characters are provided, the device is a *string* device. A *choice* device provides one of a number of possible selections while a *valuator* allows the input of real numbers.

Physical input devices can operate in a variety of modes. In the simplest mode, *request* mode, the input is returned to the program after the user triggers the device by an action such as clicking a button. In *sample* mode, input is returned immediately to the program. In *event* mode, each triggering of a physical device causes the input from this device to be placed in an event queue. The queue can then be examined independently by the user program.

The Light Pen. The light pen was the first of the special devices available for interactive computer graphics. The light pen does not write (or emit) light, but rather reads (or senses) it. A threshold is set in the light pen so that if the light intensity exceeds this threshold, an interrupt is generated. The processor knows exactly when this event occurs and uses this time to compute the position of the light pen on the face of the CRT.

The handling of the triggering event is somewhat different in random-scan and raster scan systems. A raster scan system displays information line by line. Each refresh cycle begins at a precise time and proceeds line by line. By knowing when the triggering event occurred, the system can compute exactly where on the CRT face the light pen was located at that time, so the use of the light pen as a locator device is fairly easy. For a light pen to be used as a pick on a raster system, the processor must use a position on the display to determine a segment.

On a random-scan system, the light pen can be used most easily as a pick device. The displayed elements are stored and displayed in groups of elements or *segments* that comprise the display file. On each refresh of the display, which is initiated at a precise time, the system goes through the segments in the display file, displaying their primitives. When the trigger fires, we know which segment is being displayed, which provides the pick measure. Using the light pen as a locator involves further calculation based on which primitive caused the trigger. For example, if the threshold is exceeded while a line segment is being drawn, the processor can interpolate between the endpoints of the line segment to find the location of the light pen at the time of the trigger firing.

The Joystick.   The joystick (Fig. 8.6) is a device with 2 degrees of freedom. In the standard joystick, when the user moves the stick, the settings are changed on two potentiometers that provide the processor with two independent values which are stored in a pair of registers. Such a configuration makes the joystick a natural locator device. The trigger is usually provided by a button on the stick.

FIGURE 8.6   Joystick.

The joystick is often used in a manner which gives it unique advantages. When the joystick is constructed with mechanical elements such as springs, it can give the user a natural "feel," like the control stick in an airplane. The joystick is usually constructed so that there is increasing resistance as the user pushes it farther from its resting position. It returns to the resting position when the user releases it.

With these mechanical properties, the joystick does not lend itself to use as a direct positioning device. However, if the output of the internal sensors in the joystick is integrated before being made available to the user program, the joystick becomes an incremental or relative device. If the stick is in its resting position, the input values to the registers are unchanged. The device now has variable sensitivity. A small movement from the resting position causes small slow changes; a large movement from the resting position allows rapid but rough positioning.

The Track Ball and the Mouse.   Figure 8.7 shows a track ball, which, like the joystick, provides two independent values to the program. In this case, the user changes the settings of the potentiometers by rolling the ball. The track ball is thus a relative-positioning device, where the velocity of the ball determines the change in position value stored in the processor's registers.

If we take our track ball and turn it upside down, we have a device called a *mouse* (Fig. 8.8). The user grasps the device and rolls the ball along a surface. One or more buttons on the device allow the user to generate trigger signals. Since the mouse is a relative-positioning device, the user can pick it up and move it to a new position without signaling any change to the processor. The mouse in Fig. 8.8 is an electromechanical mouse; the

FIGURE 8.7 Track ball.

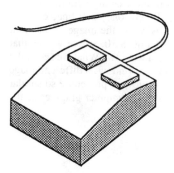

FIGURE 8.8 Mouse.

motion is mechanical (the ball), and the sensing device is electrical (the potentiometers). Other popular mice are electro-optical and optico-mechanical.

The mouse is probably the most popular of the presently available input devices. It is inexpensive, reliable, and easy to use. Implementing a locator and a pick with the mouse is similar to implementing the joystick for these uses. With all these devices, however, it is difficult to obtain absolute positioning, which is necessary for tasks such as entering data from a map or a hand drawing.

Data Tablets. The data tablet provides absolute positions to the processor. The user positions a stylus on the tablet. In a typical data tablet, the stylus can sense electromagnetic signals, which are sent out over finely spaced wires in the tablet. These signals can be decoded to determine the position of the stylus with extreme accuracy. A button is provided either on the side or on the tip of the stylus for triggering.

How we can use the data tablet as a locator or stroke device is clear. Like our other devices, with some calculation, it can also be used as a pick. The absolute positioning of this device allows us to set aside areas of the tablet for special purposes. For example, we can create a string device by laying out a keyboard on part of the tablet. Devices such as touch-pads are conceptually similar to the data tablet, but replace the stylus with the user's finger. Invisible touch screens can be placed over the face of a CRT, allowing the user to work directly on the screen image, albeit with resolution reduced to the size of the fingertip.

8.4 IMAGE FORMATION

Both traditional graphics and computer graphics are concerned with the creation of pictures. The connection between modern computer graphics and the more traditional methods of picture formation such as painting and photography is a strong one. Consider the making of a photograph. We have two distinct entities in the process: the world, which consists of objects such as the house, the trees, and grass; and the viewer of these objects, the camera. What is in our photograph will be determined only when we know everything about both the camera (where it is, what lens is on it, and in what direction it is pointing) and the objects (their positions, orientations, and surface properties). If we move the camera, the picture recorded on the film must change, as it will if we move any of the objects.

The result of the picture formation process is an image that appears on the film. A similar process will be involved in describing the image formed by a painter or what we find in the image plane of a telescope. The mathematics of how objects that exist in a three-dimensional world and a viewer who has to be positioned in this world are combined to form an image that is two-dimensional will be discussed later.

The image formation process for a human is almost identical. The optics of the eye replace those of the camera. The image is formed on the retina, a sensing structure located at the back of the eye. Both the retina and the film at the back of our camera have a finite size. The image that is formed cannot be infinite in extent. For human vision, what we see in the image is everything that lies in a cone whose apex is at the eye. For the camera, the cone of vision is replaced by a pyramid, since the back of the camera is a rectangle.

A slightly different conceptual view of image formation is seen in Fig. 8.9, where now the image plane has been moved in front of the camera. The major difference here is that the image is now right-side-up, which is often easier to conceptualize. The image can be thought of as being formed by lines drawn from the apex of the viewing pyramid, known as the *center of projection,* to all points on the object. Where one such line, called a *projector,* intersects the image plane, or *projection* plane, is where the image of the point on the object is located. An equivalent picture is shown in Fig. 8.10, where we see that this viewing procedure is similar to simply looking through a window. What we see in the window must be finite; when we move either the viewer or the window, a different image appears in the window. Making a picture with a computer follows a procedure so similar to the one we have just described that it has become known in computer graphics as the *synthetic camera analogy.*

8.4.1 The Synthetic Camera

When we think of taking a picture with a camera and of other picture formation processes (such as painting, using a telescope, or simply looking at something with the eye), we

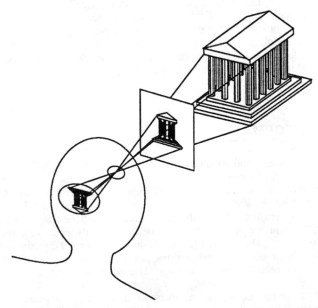

FIGURE 8.9 Image formation.

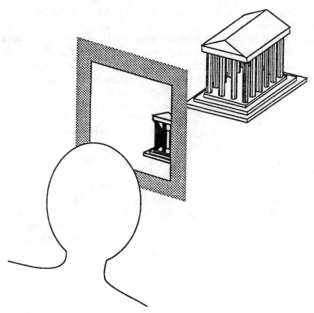

FIGURE 8.10   Windowing.

may think of imaging as combining objects with a viewer. It was not clear in the early days of computer graphics how to apply this notion to the writing of graphics programs. Early graphics programming languages required that the user specify the picture directly through functions that emulated the actual drawing of the picture.

This mechanism made programming a difficult job. The objects are in a three-dimensional world, as is the camera. To compute the positions, the programmer had to work through the mathematics of projection or image formation. Thus, to draw a simple line, she had to do complex trigonometric calculations. Leaving this calculation to the user not only required that the user add a considerable amount of code, but also was a conceptually poor way to go about developing graphics software. Consider, e.g., what happens if we move the camera in such a system. The application program has to calculate all new positions in units of the pen plotter. So the simple conceptual idea of letting the camera roam about the scene became potentially a laborious task.

The alternative is to use the synthetic camera analogy and to provide a graphics system that treats the viewer and the objects separately. Of course, the calculations will have to be done to find where on the pen plotter the lines will appear. In the modern systems, however, they are done within the graphics system. This is the importance of the synthetic camera analogy: The applications programmer specifies independent object and viewing conditions. Picture formation, which combines these specifications, is the job of the graphics system. We will discuss the mathematics of image formation later.

8.4.2 Device Independence

Another notion that follows from the synthetic camera analogy is *device independence*. Since the viewing and object specifications are separate, the user program can specify these entities in any desired coordinate system and let the graphics hardware and software take care of the coordinate conversions necessary to produce output on the display and to provide input to the user.

Users usually work in application coordinates such as meters for an architectural problem or micrometers for a VLSI layout. This system is called *world coordinates*. Often in *computer-aided design* (CAD) we work with models or simple objects which must be transformed as they are placed into a user model. These objects can be thought to be in *modeling coordinates*. Hence various transformations on objects in modeling coordinates produce a database in world coordinates, and the location of the viewer is also specified in world coordinates.

Graphics systems eventually produce output on or receive input from physical devices. The behavior of each physical device can be described in its own coordinate system, usually called *device coordinates*. For raster devices, device coordinates are specified as the (integer) addresses into the frame buffer, while for older devices such as a pen plotter the coordinates might be the voltages necessary to drive the device.

Graphics software systems often introduce one or two additional coordinate systems. The idea is to use a simple internal coordinate system for the graphics which is independent of both the application and any physical devices. In some systems, such as the *graphical kernel system* (GKS) [10], this coordinate system is called *normalized device coordinates* and corresponds to a virtual display device which is a unit square. in three-dimensional systems such as the *Programmer's Hierarchical Interactive Graphics System* (PHIGS), things are a bit more complex, as we shall see [16].

8.4.3 Three-Dimensional Viewing

Most three-dimensional viewing in graphics systems is based on a model which seeks to specify the projectors and the projection plane independently. The most common views are all *planar geometric projections* [4, 8]. Here all the projectors are lines which either meet at a single point, the *center of projection* (COP), or are parallel, which specifies a *direction of projection* (DOP). The two types of projection thus defined are called *parallel* and *perspective*. This information can be specified by a single function call whose parameters are the projection type and a point called the *projection reference point* (PRP). For parallel projections the direction of projection is determined by the vector from the view reference point (see below) and the PRP. For perspective projections the PRP is the COP.

The specification of the projection plane is somewhat more complex. The orientation of a plane can be specified by the normal to the plane, the *view plane normal* (VPN), as in Fig. 8.11. Since the projection plane is the place where the image will appear, we can form a new coordinate system, called *view reference coordinates* (VRC), two of whose coordinate axes lie in the plane and the other in the direction of the view plane normal n.

The origin of this coordinate system is specified by the user as a point called the *view reference point* (VRP). The up direction v in the projection plane is determined by projecting the user-specified *view up* (VUP) vector onto the plane. The final direction u can then be determined by requiring it to be orthogonal to both the up direction and the view plane normal. The transformation from the original coordinate system to viewing coordinates can be accomplished by a sequence of rotations and translations [2], as will be described be-

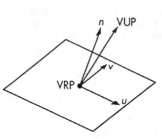

FIGURE 8.11   View reference coordinates.

low. The principal reason for transforming to this coordinate system is that projections can easily be carried out in viewing coordinates. For example, an orthogonal projection, the simplest parallel projection, is obtained by setting the coordinate value in the view plane normal direction to zero and leaving the other two values unchanged.

One additional step must be added—*clipping*. The projection plane is infinite in extent. Hence we must specify which part of it will be mapped to our physical device. We specify a rectangular region called a *window* in the plane which is eventually mapped to another rectangle called a *viewport* on the physical device. Objects are clipped to fit in this window. We can also have clipping in depth by specifying front and back clipping planes in the normal direction. The resulting view volumes for both parallel and perspective viewing are shown in Fig. 8.12. We can envision the image formation process in most graphics systems as a pipeline of transformations and clippers, as in Fig. 8.13.

8.4.4 Rendering

Up to this point, we have not discussed the details of the primitives that are to be viewed, nor have we discussed any notion of realism in the image. In most applications, we start

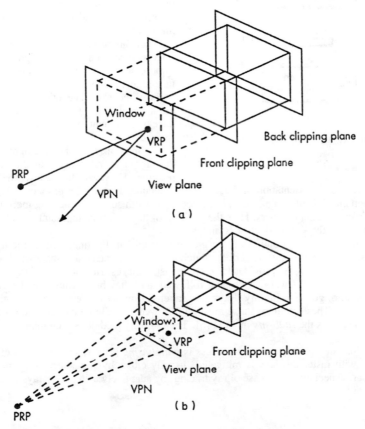

FIGURE 8.12 *(a)* Parallel and *(b)* perspective clipping volumes.

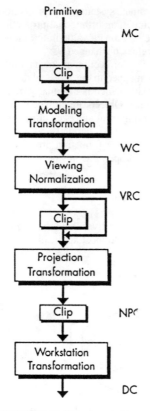

FIGURE 8.13 Viewing pipeline.

with a simple *wire-frame* image of our model and then work our way up to a realistic image which includes surface effects and light sources (see Fig. 8.14). The usual rendering process consists of three steps.

First, a hidden-surface algorithm is applied to the model. In this process, all surfaces which would not be visible to the viewer are eliminated. The low cost of solid-state memory has made hardware implementations of the z-buffer algorithm available in many workstations.

Second, add light sources and surface effects. The Phong model [15] is illustrated in Fig. 8.15. In this model, we make use of the local surface properties, e.g., absorption, the orientation of the surface as expressed by the surface normal **N**, the direction to the light source **L**, the direction of a perfect reflection **R**, and the direction to the viewer **V**. For color images, the model is applied independently for the three primary colors.

There are usually three types of lighting effects considered. Ambient light gives the same contribution at each point. The surface reflects some of this incident light and absorbs the rest. The other contributions are normally done for point sources to reduce the amount of calculation. Diffuse surfaces scatter the incoming light equally in all directions, and thus the light seen by the viewer is independent of the viewer's position. However, the relative height of the source and the orientation of the surface as calculated by the dot product of **V** and **N** are important. Specular highlights are caused by smooth surfaces reflecting more light in some directions than in others. Here the position of the viewer is important and enters the model through the dot product of **R** and **V**.

This model does not address more global problems in lighting such as multiple reflections, partially transmitting surfaces (such as glass and water), and shadows. For these situations, *ray tracing* [9] provides far more realistic images. Here individual rays are cast from the eye of the viewer or COP and followed until they hit an illuminated surface, a light source, or go off to infinity. Rays are scattered from a surface and thus can generate multiple rays. These child rays also must be followed. An alternative, also computationally expensive, is the *radiosity* method [6]. The radiosity method is preferable for diffuse surfaces.

The final step in the rendering process is *antialiasing* [19]. Here the jagged effect of working with raster displays is mitigated, usually either by some sort of a smoothing process or, especially in the case of ray tracing, by adaptively using more rays in areas of great detail.

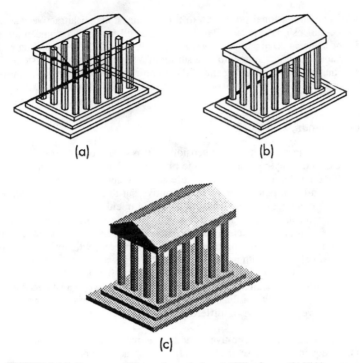

FIGURE 8.14 Sequence of images in rendering. *(a)* Wire frame. *(b)* Hidden surface removed. *(c)* Shaded.

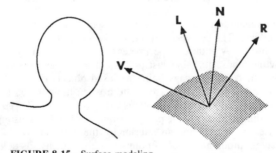

FIGURE 8.15 Surface modeling.

8.5 PRIMITIVES

Most graphics systems have been built upon two-dimensional primitives. Part of the reason is historical, part is that most output devices have two-dimensional displays. In addition, the almost infinite variety of possible three-dimensional primitives makes the extension of two-dimensional primitives to three dimensions an attractive way to start building three-dimensional systems. We will look at all two-dimensional primitives as existing in the plane $z = 0$ in a three-dimensional (x, y, z) world. This approach will allow a two-dimensional graphics system to be a subset of a three-dimensional system. We will define our primitives at the modeling end of the graphics process. Thus, our primitives can be thought of as existing in either world coordinates or modeling coordinates.

8.5.1 Points, Lines, and Curves

A *point* is a location in space. It has a dimension of 0, as it has no size. Some raster system designers chose to display a point as a single pixel even though the size of the displayed point will differ on different systems. The more common approach in device-independent systems is to not allow a point as an output primitive but to use the point to define other primitives. Let P denote a point which can be defined in either two or three dimensions.

Lines, line segments, curves, and curve segments have length but no width and are thus one-dimensional entities. Here again the dichotomy between an object and its rendered image is important. These primitives must be rendered with some width, or they would not be visible. Just as with points, we will refer to the mathematical entities we will allow the modeler to work with rather than to their rendering on a display.

One- (and zero-) dimensional objects can exist in both two- and three-dimensional worlds. A line is a perfectly reasonable entity in either two dimensions or three dimensions, although we might use a different mathematical representation in the two cases.

Our basic one-dimensional primitive is the line segment, the piece of a line connecting two points. A sequence of line segments can be used to define a *polyline* primitive in two or three dimensions. Given a sequence of points $P_1, P_2, \ldots, P_N$, a polyline consists of a line segment from P_1 to P_2, another from P_2 to P_3, and so on with the last segment connecting P_{N-1} to P_N. A polyline in three dimensions is not necessarily planar, although many graphics systems require the user to restrict polylines to lie in an arbitrary plane.

A *polygon* is an object formed by connecting a sequence of points (or vertices) with line segments (or edges). The last vertex in the list is connected to the first with an edge. For a polygon, defined by N points, its perimeter can be traced out by a polyline of $N + 1$ points, the polyline whose first and last points are the same. However, in computer graphics, the polygon, besides always being a closed object, is considered to have an interior which can be filled with a color or pattern when the polygon is rendered. This characteristic has led to many graphics systems using the name *fill area* to refer to this primitive. In a two-dimensional world, polygons may be simple, nonsimple, or convex. In any of these cases, we can define an interior for the polygon. When we go to three dimensions, we have a problem. A set of points in three dimensions defines a sequence of edges for a polygon. However, unless all the vertices lie in the same plane, it is not clear how we can define the interior of the polygon. For this reason, virtually all graphics systems define the polygon or fill area to be a planar object. The user is expected to ensure that all the vertices lie in the same plane.

Most graphics systems offer three additional planar primitives: *polymarkers, cell arrays,* and *text* (Fig. 8.16). Planar curves such as circles and ellipses are available in many systems since they are both useful and relatively easy to generate. Low-order polynomial curves, usually cubics, are increasingly available, especially in CAD-oriented systems. Of particular importance are families of smooth polynomials which can be joined in segments such as Bezier polynomials, B splines, and NURBS (nonuniform rational B splines) [7].

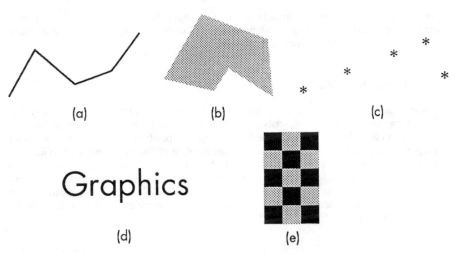

FIGURE 8.16 Graphics primitives. *(a)* Polyline. *(b)* Fill area. *(c)* Polymarker. *(d)* Text. *(e)* Cell array.

8.5.2 Extending Planar Primitives

The standard two-dimensional systems such as GKS have the five primitives of polyline, polymarker, text, fill area, and cell array. Since these are two-dimensional primitives, they must be planar. For the polyline and polymarker, whether the points are coplanar is not relevant since individual line segments and markers all make sense in three dimensions. The fill area, text, and cell array all extend to planar three-dimensional primitives which can lie in an arbitrary user-specified plane.

A richer set of three-dimensional primitives can be obtained by a number of techniques. One family, usually known as $2\frac{1}{2} D$, takes an arbitrary planar primitive and extends it to three dimensions by extruding it from the plane or revolving it about some axis. For example, a cylinder is an extruded circle, and a cone can be obtained by rotating a right triangle. Meshes of triangular or rectangular polygons (Fig. 8.17) are common three-dimensional modeling entities.

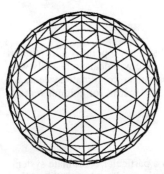

FIGURE 8.17 Sphere approximated by triangular mesh of polygons.

Curves are usually defined parametrically

$$x = x(t) \qquad y = y(t) \qquad z = z(t)$$

where x, y, and z are typically low-order polynomials in the parameter t. Polynomial curves are usually defined over short segments, and the segments are joined, maintaining continuity at the joints of the curve and the first few derivatives. For the Bezier and spline curves, the curves are easily obtained from data at a set of *control points*. Surfaces are also defined parametrically as functions of two parameters:

$$x = x(s, t) \qquad y = y(s, t) \qquad z = z(s, t)$$

For surfaces the functions are usually at worst bicubic polynomials, but more often they are quadrics. Surfaces are typically defined as small surface patches, and some continuity conditions are imposed between adjacent patches.

8.5.3 Hierarchical Models

In many modeling situations, the various parts of the model are related in such a way that their behaviors can best be described in terms of the relationships between them. For example, in describing a model of the human arm, the position of the fingers depends on the position of the hand, which depends on the position of the wrist, and so on. Graphics systems allow the description of such relationships through the use of transformations (to be discussed below) and *structures,* or *segments*. A structure is a collection of primitives and other elements. One of these elements is a structure call. Another is a matrix which positions subsequent elements in the structure. Hence a description of a bicycle might be something like

```
begin_structure(bicycle)
    execute_structure(chassis)
    set_position_matrix(front_wheel)
    execute_structure(wheel)
    set_position_matrix(rear_wheel)
    execute_structure(wheel)
end_structure(bicycle)
```

Such structures can describe a *directed acyclic graph* of relationships between groups of primitives.

8.6 MATHEMATICAL FOUNDATIONS

Computer graphics deals with a number of geometric entities. All can be developed by using points, lines, vectors, and planes. We will develop the mathematical underpinnings and hopefully avoid much of the confusion which seems to pervade the field. We will do our development in three dimensions, although it will be clear that virtually everything we present is equally valid in a space of arbitrary dimension.

8.6.1 Points and Coordinate Systems

Our fundamental entity is a *point*. In a three-dimensional system, a point is a location in space. A coordinate system provides a frame of reference. We will deal exclusively with orthogonal right-handed coordinate systems. Within a particular coordinate system, we can represent a point P by the triplet (x, y, z) or the column matrix (or column vector)

$$\mathbf{p} = \begin{bmatrix} x \\ y \\ z \end{bmatrix}$$

Note that both (x, y, z) and $\mathbf{p}$ are *representations* of P in a particular coordinate system. If we change coordinate systems, we change the representation of P, although P itself has not changed. Later we will see that a major use of transformations is to characterize changes in representations caused by changes in coordinate systems.

8.6.2 Vectors

A *vector* is a quantity with both direction and magnitude. Physical quantities such as velocity and force are vectors. A vector does not have a fixed position, and thus any two directed line segments with the same length and orientation are identical vectors regardless of their location. Note that a vector exists regardless of the coordinate system, but, as with the point, we most often work with the representation of a vector in a particular coordinate system. Unfortunately, a major source of confusion is the common use of the term *vector* both for the column vector representation of a point and to describe the "free" vector of length and magnitude.

Within a particular coordinate system, we can represent a vector in a number of ways. One way is to specify its magnitude as a scalar and to also give its direction. Specifying the direction could be done by specifying two of the three direction angles. More often we specify a vector by two points, as in Fig. 8.18, a representation which is independent of any coordinate system. If V is a vector and P_1 and P_2 are two points, then

FIGURE 8.18 Specifying a vector.

$$V = P_1 - P_2$$

Using the representation of the two points, we can obtain a magnitude and direction. Suppose, in some coordinate system,

$$\mathbf{p}_1 = \begin{bmatrix} x_1 \\ y_1 \\ z_1 \end{bmatrix} \qquad \mathbf{p}_2 = \begin{bmatrix} x_2 \\ y_2 \\ z_2 \end{bmatrix}$$

Then we have a column matrix $\mathbf{v}$

$$\mathbf{v} = \mathbf{p}_1 - \mathbf{p}_2 = \begin{bmatrix} x_1 - x_2 \\ y_1 - y_2 \\ z_1 - z_2 \end{bmatrix}$$

The magnitude of $\mathbf{v}$ is simply

$$\|\mathbf{v}\| = \sqrt{(x_1 - x_2)^2 + (y_1 - y_2)^2 \, (z_1 - z_2)^2}$$

and the direction can be computed in a simple manner. Unfortunately, we have two potential sources of confusion. First, the magnitude appears to depend on the representation; second, both vectors and points are now represented as column matrices, which might lead us to believe they are similar entities.

Affine Spaces.   An *affine space* is an extension of the familiar euclidean space. In this space, there are three types of entities: scalars, points, and vectors. These entities are defined independently of any representation or implementation.

The only scalars we will use are the real numbers. The scalar-scalar operations are thus ordinary addition and multiplication. Subtraction and division are defined by the existence of additive and multiplicative inverses.

Vectors and points are abstractions of the point and vector we defined above. The point has the single attribute of position, and the vector has the two properties of magnitude and direction. We will let α, β, γ denote scalars; P, Q, R define points; and u, v, w denote vectors. The magnitude of a vector v is a real number denoted by $|v|$. The operation of vector-scalar multiplication has the property that

$$\|\alpha v\| = |\alpha| \, \|v\|$$

and the direction of v is unchanged if α is positive. Note that there must be a special vector $\mathbf{0}$ with zero magnitude.

There are two operations which relate points and vectors. First, there is an operation of *point subtraction* such that the subtraction of two points P and Q yields a vector v:

$$v = P - Q$$

This operation has the property that given any point Q and vector v, there is a unique point P satisfying the above relationship. We can express this statement as follows: Given a Q and a v, there is a P such that

$$P = v + Q$$

Thus we define an addition operation. The second operation defines vector-vector addition through what is called the *head-to-tail axiom*, which states that for any three points P, Q, and R

$$(P - Q) + (Q - R) = P - R$$

Note this operation defines the result of adding two vectors as yielding a new vector.

While the addition of two vectors, the multiplication of a vector by a scalar, and the addition of a vector and a point make sense, the addition of two arbitrary points and the multiplication of a point by a scalar do not.

8.6.3 Coordinate Systems and Frames

So far we have considered vectors and points as abstract entities without any underlying coordinate system. In a three-dimensional euclidean space, we represent a vector in terms of three *basis* vectors, i.e.,

$$v = \alpha_1 v_1 + \alpha_2 v_2 + \alpha_3 v_3$$

The scalars α_1, α_2, and α_3 are the *components* of v with respect to the basis v_1, v_2, v_3. We usually write the representation of v as the column matrix

$$\mathbf{v} = \begin{bmatrix} \alpha_1 \\ \alpha_2 \\ \alpha_3 \end{bmatrix}$$

In a euclidean space, the origin (the point whose components are all zero) plays a special role. In affine spaces we get a more general representation by specifying a *frame* as a basis set of vectors and a particular point P. Loosely, this extension allows us to move the origin of the coordinate system to P_0. Given a frame, every vector can be written uniquely as

$$v = \alpha_1 v_1 + \alpha_2 v_2 + \alpha_3 v_3$$

and every point can be written uniquely as

$$P = P_0 + \alpha_1 v_1 + \alpha_2 v_2 + \alpha_3 v_3$$

8.6.4 Changes of Coordinate Systems and Frames

A common problem is to find how the representation of a vector changes when we change the basis vectors. Suppose v_1, v_2, v_3 and u_1, u_2, u_3 are two bases. Then each basis vector in the second set can be represented in terms of the first (and vice versa). Hence there exist scalar components such that

$$u_1 = \alpha_{11}v_1 + \alpha_{12}v_2 + \alpha_{13}v_3$$

$$u_2 = \alpha_{21}v_1 + \alpha_{22}v_2 + \alpha_{23}v_3$$

$$u_3 = \alpha_{31}v_1 + \alpha_{32}v_2 + \alpha_{33}v_3$$

Thus the 3×3 matrix

$$\mathbf{M} = \begin{bmatrix} \alpha_{11} & \alpha_{12} & \alpha_{13} \\ \alpha_{21} & \alpha_{22} & \alpha_{23} \\ \alpha_{31} & \alpha_{32} & \alpha_{33} \end{bmatrix}$$

represents the change in basis, and its inverse gives the matrix representation of the change from u_1, u_2, u_3 to v_1, v_2, v_3. If a vector v has the representation with respect to $\mathbf{v}$

$$\mathbf{v} = \begin{bmatrix} \beta_1 \\ \beta_2 \\ \beta_3 \end{bmatrix}$$

its representation $\mathbf{u}$ with respect to u_1, u_2, u_3 is

$$\mathbf{u} = \mathbf{M}\mathbf{v}$$

Such changes in basis leave the origin unchanged and can represent rotating and scaling a set of basis vectors to derive another basis set. However, a simple translation of the origin or change of frame cannot be represented in this way. The use of *homogeneous coordinates* [17] allows us to change frames and still use matrices to represent the change.

8.6.5 Homogeneous Coordinates

In the previous section, we did not give a representation of a point. The major difficulty is that, given a frame, if we attempt to represent a point by a three-dimensional column matrix of its coordinates, the point and vector will have the same representation. However, if we use homogeneous coordinates, we can avoid this source of confusion. In homogeneous coordinates, we use four-dimensional column matrices to represent both points and vectors in three dimensions.

A point is represented, in a given frame, by the column matrix

$$\mathbf{p} = \begin{bmatrix} \alpha_1 \\ \alpha_2 \\ \alpha_3 \\ 1 \end{bmatrix}$$

which expresses that given the frames specified by v_1, v_2, v_3, and P_0, we can express the point P as

$$P = \alpha_x v_1 + \alpha_2 v_2 + \alpha_3 v_3 + P_0$$

A vector v is represented by the column matrix

$$\mathbf{v} = \begin{bmatrix} \beta_1 \\ \beta_2 \\ \beta_3 \\ 0 \end{bmatrix}$$

which states that

$$v = \beta_1 v_1 + \beta_2 v_2 + \beta_3 v_3$$

While there are a number of ways to interpret this formulation geometrically, we simply note that all our operations on points and vectors work on their homogeneous coordinate representations by the rules of ordinary matrix algebra.

Changes of frames can now be expressed by using matrix algebra. If v_1, v_2, v_3, P_0 and u_1, u_2, u_3, Q_0 are two frames, we can express the second frame in terms of the first as

$$u_1 = \alpha_{11} v_1 + \alpha_{12} v_2 + \alpha_{13} v_3$$

$$u_2 = \alpha_{21} v_1 + \alpha_{22} v_2 + \alpha_{23} v_3$$

$$u_3 = \alpha_{31} v_1 + \alpha_{32} v_2 + \alpha_{33} v_3$$

$$Q_0 = \alpha_{41} v_1 + \alpha_{42} v_2 + \alpha_{43} v_3 + \alpha_{44} P_0$$

If $\mathbf{u}$ and $\mathbf{v}$ are the homogeneous coordinate representations of either two points or vectors in the two frames, then

$$\mathbf{u} = \mathbf{Mv}$$

where $\mathbf{M}$ is the 4×4 matrix

$$\mathbf{M} = \begin{bmatrix} \alpha_{11} & \alpha_{12} & \alpha_{13} & 0 \\ \alpha_{21} & \alpha_{22} & \alpha_{23} & 0 \\ \alpha_{31} & \alpha_{32} & \alpha_{33} & 0 \\ \alpha_{41} & \alpha_{42} & \alpha_{43} & \alpha_{44} \end{bmatrix}$$

8.6.6 Transformations

Transformations represent both changes in coordinate systems and operations on primitives such as rotation, translation, and scaling. For example, to rotate a polyline, we represent each of its points as a column vector in homogeneous coordinates and multiply each by a rotation matrix. A major advantage of homogeneous coordinates is that all the major transformations can be represented by 4×4 matrices. Translation can be represented as a vector addition

$$P' = P + v$$

where P is the original point, P' is the translated point, and v is the displacement vector. Hence, P is moved a distance $\|v\|$ in the direction of v. In the frame we are working, v has a representation $\mathbf{v} = (\Delta x, \Delta y, \Delta z)$. In homogeneous coordinates

$$\mathbf{p'} = \mathbf{Tp} = \begin{bmatrix} 1 & 0 & 0 & \Delta x \\ 0 & 1 & 0 & \Delta y \\ 0 & 0 & 1 & \Delta z \\ 0 & 0 & 0 & 1 \end{bmatrix} \mathbf{p}$$

where $\mathbf{T}$ is the translation matrix. In a similar manner, a generalized scaling matrix is obtained:

$$\mathbf{S} = \begin{bmatrix} s_x & 0 & 0 & 0 \\ 0 & s_y & 0 & 0 \\ 0 & 0 & s_z & 0 \\ 0 & 0 & 0 & 1 \end{bmatrix}$$

Rotation (about the origin) has 3 degrees of freedom. We can represent a general rotation by the concatenation of three independent rotations about the three axes as

$$\mathbf{R} = \mathbf{R}_x \mathbf{R}_y \mathbf{R}_z$$

We can derive the individual rotation matrices by noting that rotation about a given axis leaves the corresponding coordinate values unchanged. For example, rotation about the z axis by an angle θ yields the matrix

$$\mathbf{R}_z = \begin{bmatrix} \cos \theta & -\sin \theta & 0 & 0 \\ \sin \theta & \cos \theta & 0 & 0 \\ 0 & 0 & 1 & 0 \\ 0 & 0 & 0 & 1 \end{bmatrix}$$

More complex affine transformations are composed by concatenation. For example, rotation about a point other than the origin is a shift of the point (the *fixed point*) to the origin, a rotation, and a translation back to the original frame, yielding the matrix

$$\mathbf{M} = \mathbf{T}^{-1} \mathbf{R} \mathbf{T}$$

Homogeneous coordinate transformations are so powerful that direct hardware implementations are common.

8.6.7 Modeling and Viewing

With the exception of perspective projections, we can use homogeneous coordinates to express all the operations required by a basic graphics system. For example, the view plane normal, view up vector, and view reference point define a frame, as does the original user modeling system. Hence the transformations from modeling coordinates to view reference coordinates can be represented by a transformation matrix in homogeneous coordinates.

A simple orthogonal projection in VRC is characterized by the simple equations

$$x_p = x \qquad y_p = y \qquad z_p = 0$$

These equations lead to the homogeneous coordinate projection matrix

$$\mathbf{M} = \begin{bmatrix} 1 & 0 & 0 & 0 \\ 0 & 1 & 0 & 0 \\ 0 & 0 & 0 & 0 \\ 0 & 0 & 0 & 1 \end{bmatrix}$$

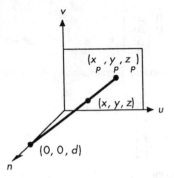

FIGURE 8.19   Perspective projection.

Oblique parallel projections also have a simple matrix representation.

Perspective projections pose a few difficulties. Consider a simple perspective projection in view reference coordinates with the COP at $(0, 0, d)$ (Fig. 8.19). The equations of projection are

$$x_p = \frac{x}{1 - z/d} \qquad y_p = \frac{y}{1 - z/d} \qquad z_p = 0$$

These equations do not describe an affine transformation. We can, however, consider *perspective transformations* [8], which can be viewed as a generalization of transformations in homogeneous coordinates. In practical terms, while it has become fairly standard to include hardware implementations of 4×4 transformations at the hardware level (even at the chip level), it is far less common to find perspective implemented in hardware.

8.7 SOFTWARE

Graphics software has become increasingly sophisticated as both hardware and algorithms have developed. Most users no longer have to worry about low-level device-dependent graphics functions. We will consider device-independent graphics libraries. However, it is important to note that an increasing number of turn-key packages are becoming available. In these systems, the user is presented a graphical interface which allows him or her to build up an application interactively, using as building blocks very sophisticated graphics programs. These underlying programs are constructed by using graphics libraries of the type we will discuss.

8.7.1 Graphics Standards

Efforts to develop a standard device-independent graphics library resulted in the adoption in 1984 of the graphical kernel system (GKS) [10] by the International Standards Organization (ISO). GKS has a number of important features, including

- Device-independent functionality
- Multiple logical workstations
- Request, sample, and event mode input
- Segments and transformations
- Sophisticated attribute handling
- Inquiry functions

Since GKS was designed so it could be implemented on virtually any system and is based on the state of computer graphics in the mid-1970s, it has a number of weaknesses. First, the collection of primitives (polyline, polymarker, text, fill area, cell array) is very limited. Second, GKS is purely two-dimensional. Third, GKS is designed for a single user rather than for a number of users sharing a common database. Finally, GKS does not allow for hierarchical modeling. There is now a three-dimensional extension to GKS, GKS-3D [11], but it does not solve all these problems.

Within the CAD community another standard arose: the programmer's hierarchical interactive graphics system (PHIGS). It is now an ISO standard. PHIGS allows the user to form a hierarchical database of two- and three-dimensional elements, independent of any viewer. Multiple independent views of any part of the database are allowed. While there is a large amount of commonality between GKS, GKS-3D, and PHIGS, there are fundamental incompatibilities between the viewing models.

The major weaknesses of PHIGS are that it contains a limited collection of primitives (essentially the same ones as in GKS) and, being over 10 years old, it does not contain rendering options such as hidden surface removal and surface modeling. PHIGS+ [14] addresses many of these problems. Additional primitives include polygonal meshes and NURBs. A variety of color models are available. Light sources and surface modeling are included in addition to hidden surface removal.

Probably the biggest problem in the way of universal graphics standards is how to handle raster. The very nature of a raster is device-dependent. However, almost all systems are raster, and at the high levels of rendering the algorithms are raster algorithms. For example, the z-buffer algorithm and ray tracing work on a pixel-by-pixel basis within the frame buffer. One solution to this problem is to allow raster algorithms such as the z-buffer algorithm to be accessed by a simple function call, e.g., hide(), which allows the implementation to use its own raster. Another is to allow users to have a raster primitive such as a pixel array which will be mapped directly to the display without coordinate transformations.

8.7.2 A Graphics Library

Most graphics libraries include functions of the following classes:

- Workstation and control
- Primitives
- Attributes
- Modeling and transformations
- Viewing
- Input
- Inquiry
- Metafile

The workstation and control functions are used to open and close logical workstations, connect them to physical devices, and set up various tables and parameters, e.g., color tables, refresh modes, error-handling routines. The primitive and input functions are as discussed previously and, of course, will vary to reflect the complexity of the system. A complex graphics system will also possess a large variety of attributes, allowing users a tremendous flexibility in how primitives are displayed. For example, a simple system will display its text at a single size and always in the same orientation. The better systems provide color text attributes, text sizing and orientation, alignment options, and multiple fonts.

Modeling functions include those which enable the user to define segments or structures and those which allow definition of hierarchical relationships. Since transformations are crucial for modeling, we will all expect to see functions for applying transformations and forming transformation matrices. The viewing functions usually allow the user to specify the viewing transformations directly or to build these transformations from specifications such as the view plane normal, view-up, and view reference point.

Inquiry functions allow the user to find out properties of the system being used, such as the number of colors supported or the state of the system. These functions allow the user to customize the display while still working in a device-independent mode. They also allow for detecting errors and handling them within the scope of the graphics application.

While device-independent graphics software leads to portability through programs, often we want to transport only the image. Metafiles [13] provide a device-independent method for describing the pictures produced by a graphics system.

8.7.3 Networked Graphics

It is difficult to consider the modern graphics workstation without considering it as part of a network of workstations, file servers, compute servers, output devices, and databases. Communicating text and binary information over networks involves multiple levels of protocols. However, only recently have the special problems of communicating graphical information across digital networks been considered.

One approach is through the use of the PostScript [1] *page description language* (PDL). A PDL allows a user or a graphics system to describe a page which can include both text and graphics in device-independent form. The PostScript language contains enough functionality to allow the description of high-quality pages with lines, curves, raster, color, transformations, and multiple fonts. A PostScript description of a page is actually a program which is executed (interpreted) by the output device, typically a laser printer or phototypesetter. The output device, in addition to being able to produce output, has to contain an independent computer. This computer can be a node on a standard communication network. Since the PostScript program is in character form, it can be communicated over the network with standard protocols.

The X Window system [20] is aimed at networks with both input and output devices distributed over a network and networks in which the workstations will normally display multiple independent windows (usually called viewports in the graphics literature). In its original form, X Window was aimed at the common transmission control protocol/internet protocol (TCP/IP) networks, but this is not crucial. X Window is based in a server-client relationship. A standard workstation has a display, a keyboard, and a pointing device such as a mouse and thus can provide input and output services to multiple clients located on the network. A client and the server may be on the same workstation. For example, a self-contained workstation with GKS and X Window will run an X Window server process. GKS will be a client program and will make requests to the server for input and to display output. The situation is essentially the same if the GKS process is on one machine and the input/output on another. The communication between the client and server processes is based on the X Window protocols which are at a level above the TCP/IP layers and hence can use these underlying protocols.

X Window is a two-dimensional system and has as primitives text, lines, fill areas, curves, and rasters (blocks of pixels). This is a very limiting restriction for three-dimensional graphics because the client is forced to do almost all the work and only the final two-dimensional image can be shipped over the network. Recently, X Window has been extended with PEX (PHIGS extensions to X) [21]. PEX allows the network to convey PHIGS functionality. Hence, a PHIGS client can send all its function calls and their parameters for execution on one or more PEX servers. A major advantage of this approach is that special three-dimensional workstations can be constructed that carry out these operations very rapidly.

8.8 CONCLUSION

In this brief survey, we have addressed many issues of computer graphics but have omitted many others. In particular, we have ignored almost all implementation issues. These issues cover some of the most interesting aspects of the field, ranging from how lines and other primitives are generated on displays, to hidden surface removal algorithms, to details of ray tracing. The references that follow discuss these issues in detail.

From the user's perspective, computer graphics has achieved great maturity. On the hardware side, systems can generate a million line segments or polygons per second. Hidden surface removal, antialiasing, and shading are hardware options.

Implementations of standard software such as GKS, PHIGS, and X Window are available for most architectures and devices. PHIGS+ and PEX are becoming available. Of perhaps equal interest are a number of high-level products which can be transported and implemented on many architectures. For example, AVS (Stardent Computer), NCSA Image (National Center for Supercomputer Applications), and Ape (Ohio Supercomputer Center) provide visualization tools on a number of platforms. PIXAR's Renderman interface provides an interface between modelers and renderers. A user can use a system such as PHIGS to build a model and then use Renderman to produce a photorealistic image, using the standard interface to pass information between the two systems.

REFERENCES

1. Adobe Systems Inc., *PostScript Language Reference Manual*. Reading, Mass.: Addison-Wesley, 1985.

2. E. Angel, *Computer Graphics*. Reading, Mass.: Addison-Wesley, 1990.

3. R. H. Bartels, J. C. Beatty, and B. A. Barsky, *An Introduction to Splines for Use in Computer Graphics and Geometric Modeling*. Los Altos, Calif.: Morgan Kaufmann, 1987.

4. I. Carlbom and J. Paciorek, "Geometric Projection and Viewing Transformations," *Computing Surveys*, 1(4):465–502, 1978.

5. J. E. Clark, "The Geometry Engine: A VLSI Geometry System for Graphics," *Computer Graphics*, 10(3):127–133, 1982.

6. M. F. Cohen, S. E. Chen, J. R. Wallace, and D. P. Greenberg, "A Progressive Refinement Approach to Fast Radiosity Image Synthesis," *IEEE Computer Graphics and Applications*, 6(3):26–35, March 1986.

7. G. Farin, *Curves and Surfaces for Computer-Aided Design*. New York: Academic Press, 1988.

8. J. D. Foley, A. van Dam, S. K. Feiner, and J. F. Hughes, *Computer Graphics, Principles and Practice*. Reading, Mass.: Addison-Wesley, 1990.

9. A. Glassner, *An Introduction to Ray Tracing*. New York: Academic Press, 1989.

10. *Graphical Kernel System*, ISO 7492, International Standards Organization, 1985.

11. *Graphical Kernel System for Three Dimensions*, ISO 8805, International Standards Organization, 1986.

12. K. I. Joy, C. W. Grant, N. L. Max, and L. Hatfield, *Computer Graphics: Image Synthesis*. Washington: Computer Society Press, 1988.

13. "Metafile for the Storage and Transfer of Picture Description Information," ISO/DP 8632, International Standards Organization, 1986.

14. PHIGS+ Committee, "PHIGS+ Functional Description, Revision 3.0," *Computer Graphics*, 22(3):125–215, 1988.

15. B. T. Phong, "Illumination for Computer Generated Scenes," *Communications of the ACM*, 18(6):311–317, 1975.

16. *Programmer's Hierarchical Interactive Graphics System*, ISO TC97 SC21/N819, International Standards Organization, June 1986.

17. R. F. Reisenfeld, "Homogeneous Coordinates and Projective Planes in Computer Graphics," *IEEE Computer Graphics and Applications*, 1(1):50–56, 1981.

18. D. F. Rogers, *Procedural Elements for Computer Graphics*. New York: McGraw-Hill, 1985.

19. D. F. Rogers and A. J. Alan, *Mathematical Elements for Computer Graphics*. New York: McGraw-Hill, 1989.

20. R. W. Scheifler and J. Gettys, "The X Window System," *ACM Transactions on Graphics*, 5(2):79–109, 1986.

21. H. C. K. Sung, G. Rogers, and W. Kubitz, "A Critical Evaluation of PEX," *IEEE Computer Graphics and Applications*, 10(6): 65–75, November 1990.

22. E. R. Tufte, *Envisioning Information*. Chesire, Conn.: Graphics Press, 1990.

23. E. R. Tufte, *The Visual Display of Quantitative Information*. Chesire, Conn.: Graphics Press, 1983.

24. G. Wyszecki, and W. S. Stiles, *Color Science*. New York: Wiley, 1982.

CHAPTER 9
RULE-BASED EXPERT SYSTEMS

George F. Luger and William A. Stubblefield
Department of Computer Science
University of New Mexico, Albuquerque

The first principle of knowledge engineering is that the problem solving power exhibited by an intelligent agent's performance is primarily the consequence of its knowledge base, and only secondarily a consequence of the inference method employed. Expert systems must be knowledge-rich even if they are methods-poor. This is an important result and one that has only recently become well understood in AI. For a long time AI has focused its attentions almost exclusively on the development of clever inference methods; almost any inference method will do. The power resides in the knowledge.

EDWARD FEIGENBAUM, Stanford University

I hate to criticize, Dr. Davis, but did you know that most rules about what the category of an organism might be that mention:
    the site of a culture and
    the infection
also mention:
    the portal of entry of the organism?
Shall I try to write a clause to account for this?

TEIRESIAS program helping a Stanford physician improve MYCIN knowledge base

An *expert system* is a knowledge-based program that provides "expert-quality" solutions to problems in a specific domain. Generally, its knowledge is extracted from human experts in the domain, and it attempts to emulate their methodology and performance. As with skilled humans, expert systems tend to be specialists, focusing on a narrow set of problems. Also, like humans, their knowledge is both theoretical and practical, having been perfected through experience in the domain. Unlike a human being, however, current programs cannot learn from their own experience; their knowledge must be extracted from humans and encoded in a formal language. This is a major task facing expert-system builders.

Expert systems should not be confused with cognitive modeling programs, which attempt to simulate human mental architecture in detail. Expert systems neither copy the

This chapter is adapted from George F. Luger and William A. Stubblefield, *Artificial Intelligence and the Design of Expert Systems*. Palo Alto, Calif.: Benjamin Cummings, 1989, with permission.

9.1

structure of the human mind nor are mechanisms for general intelligence. They are practical programs that use heuristic strategies developed by humans to solve specific classes of problems.

Because of the heuristic, knowledge-intensive nature of expert-level problem solving, expert systems are generally

1. Open to inspection, both in presenting intermediate steps and in answering questions about the solution process
2. Easily modified, in both adding and deleting skills from the knowledge base
3. Heuristic, in using (often imperfect) knowledge to obtain solutions

An expert system is "open to inspection" in that the user may, at any time during program execution, inspect the state of its reasoning and determine the specific choices and decisions that the program is making. There are several reasons why this is desirable. First, if human experts such as doctors or engineers are to accept a recommendation from the computer, they must be satisfied the solution is correct. "The computer did it" is not sufficient reason to follow its advice. Indeed, few human experts will accept advice from another human without understanding the reasons for that advice. This need to have answers explained is more than mistrust on the part of users; explanations help people relate the advice to their existing understanding of the domain and apply it in a more confident and flexible manner.

Second, when a solution is open to inspection, we can evaluate every aspect and decision taken during the solution process, allowing for partial agreement and the addition of new information or rules to improve performance. This plays an essential role in the refinement of a knowledge base.

The exploratory nature of *artificial intelligence* (AI) and expert system programming requires that programs be easily prototyped, tested, and changed. These abilities are supported by AI programming languages and environments and the use of good programming techniques by the designer. In a pure production system, e.g., the modification of a single rule has no global syntactic side effects. Rules may be added or removed without requiring further changes to the larger program. Expert-system designers have commented that easy modification of the knowledge base is a major factor in producing a successful program [17].

Third, expert systems use heuristic problem-solving methods. As expert-system designers have discovered, informal tricks of the trade and rules of thumb are often more important than the standard theory presented in textbooks and classes. Sometimes these rules augment theoretical knowledge; occasionally they are simply shortcuts that seem unrelated to the theory but have been shown to work.

The heuristic nature of expert problem-solving knowledge creates problems in the evaluation of program performance. Although we know that heuristic methods will occasionally fail, it is not clear exactly how often a program must be correct in order to be accepted: 98 percent of the time? 90 percent? 80 percent? Perhaps the best way to evaluate a program is to compare its results to those obtained by human experts in the same area. This suggests a variation of the Turing test for evaluating the performance of expert systems: A program has achieved expert-level performance if people working in the area could not differentiate, in a blind evaluation, between the best human efforts and those of the program. In evaluating the MYCIN program for diagnosing meningitis infections, Stanford researchers had a number of infectious-disease experts blindly evaluate the performance of both MYCIN and human specialists in infectious disease (see Sec. 9.4.4). Similarly, Digital Equipment Corporation decided that XCON, a program for configuring Vax computers, was ready for commercial use when its performance was comparable to that of human engineers.

Expert systems have been built to solve a range of problems in domains such as medicine, mathematics, engineering, chemistry, geology, computer science, business, law, defense, and education. These programs have addressed a wide range of problem types; the following list, adapted from Waterman [23], is a useful summary of general expert-system problem categories. Another excellent survey of expert-system applications is by Smart and Langeland-Knudsen [21].

1. *Interpretation:* Formation of high-level conclusions or descriptions from collections of raw data

2. *Prediction:* Projection of probable consequences of given situations

3. *Diagnosis:* Determination of the cause of malfunctions in complex situations based on observable symptoms

4. *Design:* Determination of a configuration of system components that meets certain performance goals while satisfying a set of constraints

5. *Planning:* Devising a sequence of actions that will achieve a set of goals given certain starting conditions

6. *Monitoring:* Comparing the observed behavior of a system to its expected behavior

7. *Debugging and repair:* Prescribing and implementing remedies for malfunctions

8. *Instruction:* Detecting and correcting deficiencies in students' understanding of a subject domain

9. *Control:* Governing of the behavior of a complex environment

9.1 OVERVIEW OF EXPERT-SYSTEM TECHNOLOGY

9.1.1 Design of Rule-Based Expert Systems

Figure 9.1 shows the most important modules that make up a rule-based expert system. The user interacts with the expert system through a user interface that makes access more comfortable for the human and hides much of the system complexity, e.g., the internal

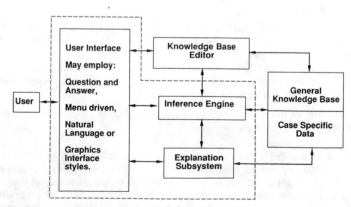

FIGURE 9.1 Architecture of a typical expert system.

structures of the rule base. Expert systems employ a variety of interface styles, including question-and-answer, menu-driven, natural language, or graphics interfaces.

The program must keep track of *case-specific data*—the facts, conclusions, and other relevant information of the case under consideration. This includes the data given in a problem instance, partial conclusions, confidence measures of conclusions, and dead ends in the search process. This information is separate from the general knowledge base.

The *explanation subsystem* allows the program to explain its reasoning to the user. These explanations include justifications for the system's conclusions (how queries, as discussed in Sec. 9.2.2), explanations of why the system needs a particular piece of data (why queries, as in Sec. 9.2.2), and, in some experimental systems, tutorial explanations deeper theoretical justifications of the program's actions.

Many systems also include a *knowledge-base editor*. Knowledge-base editors can access the explanation subsystem and help the programmer locate bugs in the program's performance. They also may assist in the addition of knowledge, help maintain correct rule syntax, and perform consistency checks on the updated knowledge base. An example of the Teiresias knowledge-base editor is presented in Sec. 9.4.5.

The heart of the expert system is the general knowledge base, which contains the problem-solving knowledge of the particular application. In a rule-based expert system, this knowledge is represented in the form of *if . . . then* rules, as in the automobile battery cable example of Sec. 9.2.

The *inference engine* applies the knowledge to the solution of actual problems. It is the interpreter for the knowledge base. In the production system [16, chap. 4], the inference engine performs the recognize-act control cycle. The procedures that implement the control cycle are separate from the production rules themselves. It is important to maintain this separation of knowledge base and inference engine for several reasons:

1. The separation of the problem-solving knowledge and the inference engine makes it possible to represent knowledge in a more natural fashion. If . . . then rules, e.g., are closer to the way in which human beings describe their own problem-solving techniques than a program that embeds this knowledge in lower-level computer code.

2. Because the knowledge base is separated from the program's lower-level control structures, expert-system builders can focus directly on capturing and organizing problem-solving knowledge rather than on the details of its computer implementation.

3. The separation of knowledge and control, along with the modularity of rules and other representational structures used in building knowledge bases, allows changes to be made in one part of the knowledge base without creating side effects in other parts of the program code.

4. The separation of the knowledge and control elements of the program allows the same control and interface software to be used in a variety of systems. The *expert-system shell* has all the components of Fig. 9.1 except that the knowledge base (and, of course, the case-specific data) contains no information. Programmers can use the "empty shell" and create a new knowledge base appropriate to their applications. The broken lines of Fig. 9.1 indicate the shell modules.

5. The modularity of the inference process also allows us to experiment with alternative control regimes for the same rule base.

The use of an expert-system shell can reduce the design and implementation time of a program considerably. As may be seen in Fig. 9.4, MYCIN was developed in about 20 person-years. EMYCIN (empty MYCIN) is a general expert-system shell that was produced by removing the specific domain knowledge from the MYCIN program. Using EMYCIN, knowledge engineers implemented PUFF, a program to analyze pulmonary problems in patients, in about 5 person-years. This is a remarkable savings and an important aspect of the commercial viability of expert-system technology. Expert-system shells have become increasingly common, with commercially produced shells available for all classes of computers.

It is important that the programmer choose the proper expert-system shell. Different problems often require different reasoning processes, goal-driven rather than data-driven search, for instance. The control strategy provided by the shell must be appropriate to the new application. The medical reasoning in the PUFF application was much like that of the original MYCIN work; this made the use of the EMYCIN shell appropriate. If the shell does not support the appropriate reasoning processes, its use can be a mistake and worse than starting from nothing. As we shall see, part of the responsibility of the expert-system builder is to correctly characterize the reasoning processes required for a given problem domain and to either select or construct an inference engine that implements these structures.

Unfortunately, shell programs do not solve all the problems involved in building expert systems. While the separation of knowledge and control, the modularity of the production system architecture, and the use of an appropriate knowledge representation language all help with the building of an expert system, the acquisition and organization of the knowledge base remain difficult tasks.

9.1.2 Selecting a Problem for Expert-System Development

Expert systems tend to involve a considerable investment in money and human effort. Attempts to solve a problem that is too complex, poorly understood, or otherwise unsuited to the available technology can lead to costly and embarrassing failures. Researchers have developed an informal set of guidelines for determining whether a problem is appropriate for expert-system solution:

1. *The need for the solution justifies the cost and effort of building an expert system.* For example, Digital Equipment Corporation (DEC) had experienced considerable financial expense because of errors in configurations of Vax and PDP-11 computers. If a computer is shipped with missing or incompatible components, the company is obliged to correct this situation as quickly as possible, often incurring added shipping expense or absorbing the cost of parts not taken into account when the original price was quoted. Because this expense was considerable, DEC was extremely interested in automating the configuration task; the resulting system, XCON, has paid for itself in both financial savings and customer goodwill. Similarly, many expert systems have been built in domains such as mineral exploration, business, defense, and medicine where there is a large potential for savings in money, time, or human life. In recent years, the cost of building expert systems has gone down as software tools and expertise in AI have become more available. The range of potentially profitable applications has grown correspondingly.

2. *Human expertise is not available in all situations where it is needed.* Much expert-system work has been done in medicine, e.g., because the specialization and technical sophistication of modern medicine have made it difficult for doctors to keep up with advances in diagnostics and treatment methods. Specialists with this knowledge are rare and expensive, and expert systems are seen as a way of making their expertise available to a wider range of doctors. In geology, there is a need for expertise at remote mining and drilling sites. Often geologists and engineers find themselves traveling large distances to visit sites, with resulting expense and wasted time. By placing expert systems at remote sites, many problems may be solved without needing a visit by a human expert. Similarly, loss of valuable expertise through employee turnover or pending retirement may justify building an expert system.

3. *The problem may be solved by using symbolic reasoning techniques.* This means that the problem should not require physical dexterity or perceptual skill. Although robots and vision systems are available, they currently lack the sophistication and flexibility of human beings. Expert systems are generally restricted to problems that humans can solve through symbolic reasoning.

4. *The problem domain is well structured and does not require commonsense reasoning.* Although expert systems have been built in a number of areas requiring specialized technical knowledge, more mundane commonsense reasoning is well beyond our current capabilities. Highly technical fields have the advantage of being well studied and formalized; terms are well defined, and domains have clear and specific conceptual models. Most significantly, however, the amount of knowledge required to solve such problems is small in comparison to the amount of knowledge used by human beings in commonsense reasoning.

5. *The problem may not be solved by using traditional computing methods.* Expert-system technology should not be used to reinvent the wheel. If a problem can be solved satisfactorily by using more traditional techniques such as numerical, statistical, or operations research techniques, then it is not a candidate for an expert system. Because expert systems rely on heuristic approaches, it is unlikely that an expert system will outperform an algorithmic solution if such a solution exists.

6. *Cooperative and articulate experts exist.* The knowledge used by expert systems is often not found in textbooks but comes from the experience and judgment of humans working in the domain. It is important that these experts be both willing and able to share that knowledge. This implies that the experts should be articulate and believe that the project is both practical and beneficial. If, however, the experts feel threatened by the system, fearing that they may be replaced by it or that the project cannot succeed and is therefore a waste of time, it is unlikely that they will give it the necessary time and effort. It is also important that management be supportive of the project and allow the domain experts to take time away from their usual responsibilities to work with the program implementers.

7. *The problem is of proper size and scope.* It is important that the problem not exceed the capabilities of current technology. For example, a program that attempted to capture all the expertise of a medical doctor would not be feasible; a program that advised MDs on the use of a particular piece of diagnostic equipment would be more appropriate. As a rule of thumb, problems that require days or weeks for human experts to solve are probably too complex for current expert-system technology.

Although a large problem may not be amenable to expert-system solution, it may be possible to break it into smaller, independent subproblems that are. Or we may be able to start with a simple program that solves a portion of the problem and gradually increase its functionality to handle more of the problem domain. This was done successfully in the creation of XCON. Initially the program was designed only to configure Vax 780 computers; later it was expanded to include the full Vax and PDP-11 series [2].

9.1.3 Overview of Knowledge Engineering

The primary people involved in building an expert system are the *knowledge engineer,* the *domain expert,* and the *end user.*

The knowledge engineer is the AI language and representation expert. His or her main task is to select the software and hardware tools for the project, help extract the necessary knowledge from the domain expert, and implement that knowledge in a correct and efficient knowledge base. The knowledge engineer may initially be ignorant of the application domain.

The domain expert provides the knowledge of the problem area. The domain expert is generally someone who has worked in the domain area and understands its problem-solving techniques, including the use of shortcuts, handling imprecise data, evaluating partial solutions, and all the other skills that mark a person as an expert. The domain expert is primarily responsible for spelling out these skills to the knowledge engineer.

As in most applications, the end user determines the major design constraints. Unless the user is happy, the development effort is wasted by and large. The skills and needs of the user must be considered throughout the design cycle: What level of explanation does the user need? Can the user provide correct information to the system? Is the user interface appropriate? Are there environmental restrictions on the program's use? An interface that required typing, e.g., would not be appropriate for use in the cockpit of a jet fighter. Will the program make the user's work easier, quicker, more comfortable?

Like most AI programming, expert-system development requires a nontraditional development cycle based on early prototyping and incremental revision of the code. This exploratory programming methodology is complicated by the interaction between the knowledge engineer and the domain expert.

Generally, work on the system begins with the knowledge engineers attempting to gain some familiarity with the problem domain. This helps in communicating with the domain expert. This is done in initial interviews with the expert or by reading introductory texts in the domain area. Next, the knowledge engineer and expert begin the process of extracting the expert's problem-solving knowledge. This is often done by giving the domain expert a series of sample problems and having her or him explain the techniques used in the solution.

Here, it is often useful for the knowledge engineer to be a novice in the problem domain. Human experts are notoriously unreliable in explaining exactly what goes on in solving a complex problem. Often they forget to mention steps that have become obvious or even automatic to them after years of work in the field. Knowledge engineers, by virtue of their relative naivete in the domain, should be able to spot these conceptual jumps and ask for clarification.

Once the knowledge engineer has obtained a general overview of the problem domain and gone through several problem-solving sessions with the domain expert, he or she is ready to begin actual design of the system: selecting a way to represent the knowledge, such as rules or frames; determining the basic search strategy, such as forward or backward; and designing the user interface. After making these design commitments, the knowledge engineer builds a prototype.

This prototype should be able to solve problems in a small area of the domain and provides a test bed for preliminary design assumptions. Once the prototype has been implemented, the knowledge engineer and domain expert test and refine its knowledge by giving it problems to solve and correcting its shortcomings. Should the assumptions made in designing the prototype prove correct, it can be built into a complete system.

Expert systems are built by progressive approximations, with the program's mistakes leading to corrections or additions to the knowledge base. In a sense, the knowledge base is "grown" rather than constructed. This approach to programming was proposed by Seymour Papert with his LOGO language [19]. The LOGO philosophy argues that watching the computer respond to the improperly formulated ideas represented by the code leads to their correction (being debugged) and clarification with more precise code. Other researchers have verified this notion that design proceeds through a process of trying and correcting candidate designs, rather than by such neatly hierarchical processes such as top-down design.

It is also understood that the prototype may be thrown away if it becomes too cumbersome or if the designers decide to change their basic approach to the problem. The prototype lets program builders explore the problem and its important relationships by actually constructing a program to solve it. After this progressive clarification is complete, they can often write a cleaner version, usually with fewer actual rules.

The second major feature of expert system programming is that the program need never be considered "finished." A large heuristic knowledge base will always have limitations. The modularity and ease of modification available in the production system model make it natural to add new rules or make up for the shortcomings of the present rule base at any time. For example, DEC has continued to add rules to the XCON program to extend its capabilities to the rest of their product line. In 1981, XCON had about 500 rules and could configure the Vax 780; it was progressively refined until, today with over 10,000 rules, it configured most of the DEC product line.

Furthermore, as DEC changed the specifications for its computers, previously correct rules needed updating. One report noted that up to 50 percent of the XCON rules were changed each year just to keep up with changes in the product line.

Figure 9.2 presents a schematic overview of the development cycle of expert-system software.

Even though expert systems of commercial quality have been available since 1980, research in the development of expert systems has gone on since the mid-1960s. In fact, the emergence of commercially viable expert systems in the present world market has been a direct result of this earlier research. Figure 9.3 shows the history of the programs now considered classic in this area.

The major development activity for these early programs took place at three universities: Stanford, Massachusetts Institute of Technology, and Carnegie Mellon. The main research and development thrust for the rule-based expert system was at Stanford, under

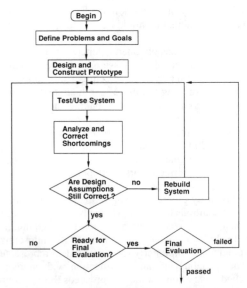

FIGURE 9.2 Exploratory development cycle for rule-based expert systems.

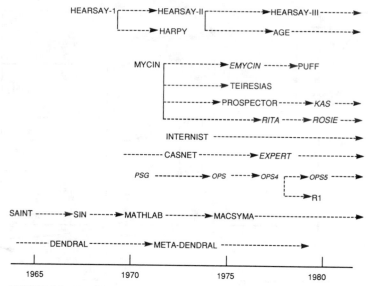

FIGURE 9.3 Development history for some classic expert systems. *(From P. H. Winston and K. A. Prendergast, eds., The AI Business. Cambridge, Mass.: MIT Press, 1984. Reprinted by permission.)*

the direction of Edward Feigenbaum, although other work in the area certainly took place at, for instance, Rutgers and the University of Pittsburgh. The early development of the production system model for problem solving, including the development of the OPS languages, took place primarily at Carnegie Mellon University.

Figure 9.4 presents another important aspect of the evolution of expert-system programs: The average development time for expert systems has been drastically reduced across the decades of evolution. The emergence of expert-system shells was instrumental in reducing the design time. This is perhaps the most important reason for current commercial successes.

9.2 A FRAMEWORK FOR ORGANIZING HUMAN KNOWLEDGE

9.2.1 Production Systems, Rules, and the Expert-System Architecture

The architecture of rule-based expert systems may be understood in terms of the production system model for problem solving [15]. In fact, the parallel between the two entities is more than a simple analogy: The production system was the intellectual precursor of modern expert-system architecture. This is not surprising; when Newell and Simon began developing the production system model, their goal was to find a way to model human problem solving.

If we regard the expert-system architecture in Fig. 9.1 as a production system, the knowledge base is the set of production rules. The expertise of the problem area is represented by the productions. In a rule-based system, these condition-action pairs are

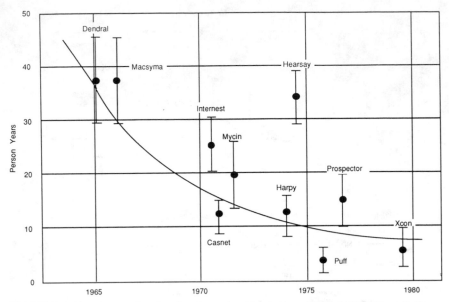

FIGURE 9.4 Development time for selected expert systems between 1965 and 1985. *(From F. Hayes-Roth, D. Waterman, and D. Lenat, Building Expert Systems. Reading, Mass.: Addison-Wesley, 1984. Reprinted by permission.)*

represented as rules, with the premises of the rules (the if portion) corresponding to the condition and the conclusion (the then portion) corresponding to the action. Case-specific data are kept in the working memory. Finally, the inference engine is the recognize-act cycle of the production system. This control may be either data-driven or goal-driven.

In a goal-driven expert system, the goal expression is initially placed in working memory. The system matches rule conclusions with the goal, selecting one rule and placing its *premises* in the working memory. This corresponds to a decomposition of the problem into simpler subgoals. The process continues, with these premises becoming the new goals to match against rule conclusions. The system thus works back from the original goal until all the subgoals in working memory are known to be true, indicating that the hypothesis has been verified. Thus, backward search in an expert system corresponds roughly to the process of hypothesis testing in human problem solving.

In an expert system, subgoals are often solved by asking the user for information. Some expert-system shells allow the system designer to specify which subgoals may be solved by asking the user. Other inference engines simply ask about all subgoals that fail to match with the conclusion of some rule in the knowledge base; i.e., if the program cannot infer the truth of a subgoal, it asks the user.

Many problem domains seem to lend themselves more naturally to forward search. In an interpretation problem, e.g., most of the data for the problem are initially given, and it is often difficult to formulate a hypothesis (goal). This suggests a forward reasoning process in which the facts are placed in working memory and the system searches for an interpretation in a forward fashion.

As a more detailed example, let us create a small expert system for diagnosing automotive problems:

```
Rule 1:
if
the engine is getting gas and
the engine will turn over,
then
the problem is spark plugs.

Rule 2:
if
the engine does not turn over and
the lights do not come on,
then
the problem is battery or cables.

Rule 3:
if
the engine does not turn over and
the lights do come on,
then
the problem is the starter motor.

Rule 4:
if
there is gas in the fuel tank and
there is gas in the carburetor,
then
the engine is getting gas.
```

To run this knowledge base under a goal-directed control regime, place the top-level goal, "the problem is X," in working memory, as in Fig. 9.5. Here X is a variable that can match with any phrase; it will become bound to the solution when the problem is solved.

There are three rules that match with the expression in working memory: rule 1, rule 2, and rule 3. If we resolve conflicts in favor of the lowest-numbered rule, then rule 1 will fire. This causes X to be bound to the value spark plugs and the premises of rule 1 to be placed in the working memory, as in Fig. 9.6. The system has thus chosen to explore the possible hypothesis that the spark plugs are bad. Another way to look at this is that the system has selected an OR branch in an AND/OR graph (Fig. 9.8).

Note that there are two premises to rule 1, both of which must be satisfied to prove the conclusion true. These are AND branches of the search graph representing a decompo-

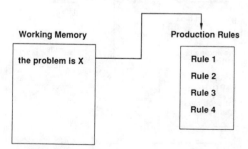

FIGURE 9.5 Working memory at the start of a consultation in the car diagnostic example.

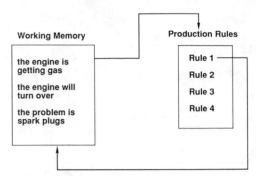

FIGURE 9.6 Working memory after rule 1 has fired.

sition of the problem (finding if the spark plugs are bad) into two subproblems—finding if the engine is getting gas and if the engine is turning over. We may then fire rule 4, whose conclusion matches with "engine is getting gas," causing its premises to be placed in working memory, as in Fig. 9.7.

At this point, there are three entries in working memory that do not match with any rule conclusions. Our expert system will query the user directly about these subgoals. If the user confirms all three of these as true, the expert system will have successfully determined that the car will not start because the spark plugs are bad. In finding this solution, the system has searched the AND/OR graph presented in Fig. 9.8.

This is, of course, a very simple example. Not only is its automotive knowledge limited at best, but a number of important aspects of real implementations are ignored. The rules are phrased in English, rather than a formal language. On finding a solution, a real expert system will tell the user its diagnosis; our model simply stops. Also we should maintain enough of a trace of the reasoning to allow backtracking if necessary; in our example, had we failed to determine that the spark plugs were bad, we would have needed to back up to the top level and try rule 2 instead. Notice that this information is implicit in the ordering of subgoals in working memory of Fig. 9.7 and in the graph of Fig. 9.8.

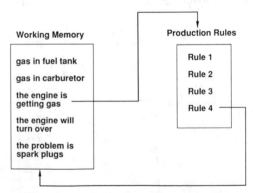

FIGURE 9.7 Working memory after rule 4 has fired.

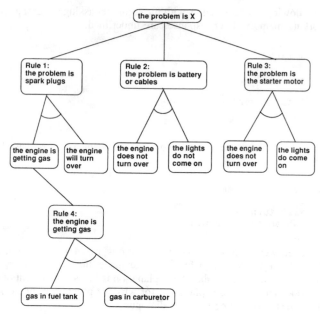

FIGURE 9.8 The AND/OR graph searched in the car diagnostic example.

This example of expert systems underscores their foundation in the production system and AND/OR graph search models of problem solving.

At the beginning of this chapter, we emphasized that an expert system needed to be open to inspection, easily modified, and heuristic. The production system architecture is an important factor in each of these requirements. Ease of modification, e.g., is made possible by the syntactic independence of production rules: Each rule is a chunk of knowledge that can be independently modified. The heuristic nature of these rules is in the knowledge obtained from the domain expert and, as seen in Sec. 9.3, from use of confidence measures. The next section discusses the way in which this architecture supports explanations and inspection of the reasoning process.

9.2.2 Explanation and Transparency

The production system implements a graph search; the explanation routines of Fig. 9.1 keep track of the graph search and use a trace of the search to answer user queries. The production rules themselves document each step of the reasoning process.

In general, the two questions supported by rule-based expert systems are why and how. In a why query, the user has been asked for information by the program and responds with why meaning "Why did you ask that?" The answer is the current rule that the production system is attempting to fire. The answer to "How did you get that result?" is the sequence of rules that were used to conclude a goal.

Suppose our automotive expert system has an explanation facility, and assume that the consultation has reached the stage represented by the working-memory configuration in

Fig. 9.7. The following dialogue begins with the computer asking the user about the goals present in working memory. User responses are underlined.

```
gas in fuel tank?
yes
gas in carburetor?
yes
engine will turn over?
why
```

Here the user enters a why query; i.e., why do you want to know that? It has been established that

```
1. Engine is getting gas,
therefore if
2. Engine will turn over,
then the problem is spark plugs.
```

Since the user answered yes to the first two questions, rule 4 was able to fire, verifying the first premise of rule 1. When the why query was made, the system was trying to solve the second premise of rule 1. Note that the explanation is just a restatement of the current rule, but it provides an adequate explanation for why the program wants to know if the engine will turn over. Continuing with the dialogue:

```
how engine is getting gas
```

Here the user asks how the program knew that the engine was getting gas. The response is a trace of the reasoning that led to this conclusion, working back from the goal along the rules that support it to the user responses:

```
This follows from rule 4:
if
gas in fuel tank and
gas in carburetor,
then
engine is getting gas.

gas in fuel tank was given by the user

gas in carburetor was given by the user
```

This simple example illustrates the explanations that expert systems provide to the user. Why queries are answered by showing the current rule that the system is attempting to fire. How queries are answered by giving a trace of the reasoning that led to a goal. Although the mechanisms are conceptually simple, they can exhibit remarkable explanatory power if the knowledge base is organized in a logical fashion.

The production system architecture provides an essential basis for these explanations. Each cycle of the control loop selects and fires another rule. The program may be stopped after each cycle and inspected. Since each rule represents a complete chunk of problem-solving knowledge, the current rule provides a context for the explanation. Contrast this with more traditional program architectures: If we stop a Pascal or Fortran program in midexecution, it is doubtful that the current statement will have much meaning.

If explanations are to behave logically, it is important not only that the knowledge base get the correct answer, but also that each rule correspond to a single logical step in the problem-solving process. If a knowledge base combines several steps into a single rule or if it breaks up the rules in an arbitrary fashion, it may get correct answers but seem arbitrary and illogical in responding to how and why queries. This not only undermines the user's faith in the system but also makes the program much more difficult for its builders to understand and modify.

9.2.3 Heuristics and Control in Expert Systems

Because of the separation of the knowledge base and the inference engine and the fixed control regimes provided by the inference engine, the only way that a programmer can control the search is through the structure of the rules in the knowledge base. This is an advantage, since the control strategies required for expert-level problem solving tend to be domain-specific and knowledge-intensive. Although a rule of the form if p, q, and r, then s resembles a logical expression, it may also be interpreted as a series of procedures for solving a problem: to do s, first do p, then do q, then do r.

This procedural interpretation allows us to control search through the structure of the rules. For example, we may order the premises of a rule so that the premise that is most likely to fail or is easiest to confirm will be tried first. This gives the opportunity of eliminating a rule (and hence a portion of the search space) as early in the search as possible. Rule 1 in the automotive example tries to determine if the engine is getting gas before it asks if the engine turns over. This is inefficient, in that trying to determine if the engine is getting gas invokes another rule and eventually asks the user two questions. By reversing the order of the premises, a negative response to the query "Engine will turn over?" eliminates this rule from consideration before the more involved condition is examined.

Also, from a semantic point of view, it makes more sense to determine whether the engine is turning over before checking to see if it is getting gas; if the engine will not turn over it does not matter if it is getting gas. Rule 4 asks the user to check for gas in the fuel tank before asking that the user open up the carburetor and look there. It is performing the easier check first.

In addition to the ordering of a rule's premises, the content of a rule itself may be fundamentally heuristic. In the automotive example, all the rules are heuristic; consequently, the system may obtain erroneous results. For example, if the engine is getting gas and turning over, the problem may be a bad distributor rather than bad spark plugs. In the next section, we examine this problem and some ways of dealing with it.

9.3 USING UNCERTAINTY MEASURES IN EXPERT SYSTEMS

9.3.1 Introduction

As mathematicians or scientists, we often want our inference procedures to follow the model presented with the predicate calculus: From correct premises sound inference rules produce new, guaranteed-correct, conclusions. In expert systems, however, we must often draw correct conclusions from poorly formed and uncertain evidence, using unsound inference rules.

This is not an impossible task; we do it successfully in almost every aspect of our daily survival. We deliver correct medical treatment for ambiguous symptoms; we mine natural resources with little or no guarantee of success before we start; we comprehend language statements that are often ambiguous or incomplete, and so on.

The reasons for this ambiguity may be better understood by referring once again to our automotive expert system example. Consider rule 2:

```
if
      the engine does not turn over and
      the lights do not come on,
then
      the problem is battery or cables.
```

This rule is heuristic in nature; it is possible, although less likely, that the battery and cables are fine but that the car simply has a bad starter motor and burned-out headlights. This rule seems to resemble a logical implication, but it is not: Failure of the engine to turn over and the lights to come on does not necessarily imply that the battery and cables are bad. What is interesting to note, however, is that the *converse* of the rule is a true implication:

```
if
      the problem is battery or cables,
then
      the engine does not turn over and
      the lights do not come on.
```

Barring the supernatural, a car with a dead battery will not light its headlamps or turn the starter motor.

This is an example of abductive reasoning. Formally, abduction states that from $P \rightarrow Q$ and Q it is possible to infer P.

Abduction is an *unsound* rule of inference, meaning that the conclusion is not necessarily true for every interpretation in which the premises are true. For example, if someone says, "If it rains, then I will not go running at 3:00 p.m." and you do not see that person on the track at 3:00 p.m., does it necessarily follow that it is raining? It is possible that the individual decided not to go running because of an injury or needing to work late.

Although abduction is unsound, it is often essential to solving problems. The "correct" version of the battery rule is not particularly useful in diagnosing car troubles since its premise (bad battery) is our goal and its conclusions are the observable symptoms that we must work with. Modus ponens cannot be applied, and the rule must be used in an abductive fashion. This is generally true of diagnostic (and other) expert systems. Faults or diseases cause (imply) symptoms, not the other way around, but diagnosis must work from the symptoms back to the cause.

Uncertainty results from the use of abductive inference as well as from attempts to reason with missing or unreliable data. To get around this problem, we can attach some measure of confidence to the conclusions. For example, although battery failure does not always accompany the failure of a car's lights and starter, it almost always does, and confidence in this rule is justifiably high.

Note that there are problems that do not require certainty measures. When one is configuring a computer, for instance, either the components go together, or they do not. The idea that "A particular disk drive and bus go together with certainty 0.75" does not even make sense. Similarly, if MACSYMA is attempting to find the integral of a function, a confidence of "0.6" that a result is correct is not useful. These programs may be either data-driven (Digital's XCON) or goal-driven (Massachusetts Institute of Technology's MACSYMA), but because they do not require abductive rules of inference or do not deal with unreliable data, they do not require the use of confidence measures.

In this section we discuss several ways of managing the uncertainty that results from heuristic rules: first, the bayesian approach and, second, the Stanford certainty theory. Finally, we briefly consider Zadeh's *fuzzy set theory,* the Dempster/Shafer theory of evidential reasoning, and nonmonotonic reasoning.

9.3.2 Bayesian Probability Theory

The bayesian approach to uncertainty is based in formal probability theory and has shown up in several areas of AI research, including pattern recognition and classification problems. The PROSPECTOR expert system, built at Stanford and SRI International and employed in mineral exploration (copper, molybdenum, and others), also uses a form of the bayesian statistical model.

Assuming random distribution of events, probability theory allows the calculation of more complex probabilities from previously known results. In simple probability calculations we are able to conclude, e.g., how cards might be distributed to a number of players.

Suppose that I am one person of a four-person card game where all the cards are equally distributed. If I do not have the queen of spades, I can conclude that each of the other players has it with probability $\frac{1}{3}$. Similarly, I can conclude that each player has the ace of hearts with probability $\frac{1}{3}$ and that any one player has both cards at $\frac{1}{3} \times \frac{1}{3}$, or $\frac{1}{9}$.

In the mathematical theory of probability, individual probability instances are worked out by sampling, and combinations of probabilities are worked out as above, using a rule such as

$$\text{probability}(A \text{ and } B) = \text{probability}(A) \times \text{probability}(B)$$

given that A and B are independent events.

One of the most important results of probability theory is Bayes' theorem. Bayes' results provide a way of computing the probability of a hypothesis following from a particular piece of evidence, given only the probabilities with which the evidence follows from actual causes (hypotheses).

Bayes' theorem states:

$$P(H_i|E) = \frac{P(E|H_i) \times P(H_i)}{\sum_{k=1}^{n}[P(E|H_k) \times P(H_k)]}$$

where $P(H_i|E)$ = probability that H_i is true given evidence E

$P(H_i)$ = probability that H_i is true overall

$P(E|H_i)$ = probability of observing evidence E when H_i is true

n = number of possible hypotheses

Suppose we desire to examine the geological evidence at some location to see if the location is suited to finding copper. We must know in advance the probability of finding each of a set of minerals and the probability of certain evidence being present when each particular mineral is found. Then we can use Bayes' theorem to determine the likelihood that copper will be present, using the evidence we collect at the location. This is the approach taken in the PROSPECTOR program, which has found commercially significant mineral deposits [9] at several sites.

There are two major assumptions for the use of Bayes' theorem: First, all the statistical data on the relationships of the evidence with the various hypotheses are known; second, and more difficult to establish, all relationships between evidence and hypotheses, or $P(E|H_k)$, are independent. Actually, this assumption of independence can be quite a tricky matter, especially when many assumptions of independence are needed to establish the validity of this approach across many rule applications. This represents the entire collected probabilities on the evidence given various hypothesis relationships in the denominator of Bayes' theorem. In general, and especially in areas like medicine, this assumption of independence cannot be justified.

A final problem, which makes keeping the statistics of the "evidence given hypotheses" relationships virtually intractable, is the need to rebuild all probability relationships when any new relationship of hypothesis to evidence is discovered. In many active research areas, such as medicine, this is happening continuously. Bayesian reasoning requires complete and up-to-date probabilities if its conclusions are to be correct. In many domains, such extensive data collection and verification are not possible.

Where these assumptions are met, bayesian approaches offer the benefit of a well-founded and statistically correct handling of uncertainty. Most expert-system domains do not meet these requirements and must rely on more heuristic approaches. It is also felt that the human expert does not use the bayesian model in successful problem solving. In the next section we describe certainty theory, a heuristic approach to the management of uncertainty.

9.3.3 A Theory for Certainty

Several early expert-system projects (besides PROSPECTOR) attempted to adapt Bayes' theorem to their problem-solving needs. The independence assumptions, continuous updates of statistical data, and other problems mentioned in Sec. 9.3.2 gradually led these researchers to search for other measures of "confidence." Probably the most important alternative approach was used at Stanford in developing the MYCIN program [3].

Certainty theory is based on a number of observations. The first is that in traditional probability theory the sum of confidence for a relationship and confidence against the same relationship must sum to 1. However, often an expert might have confidence 0.7, say, that some relationship is true and have no feeling about its being not true.

Another assumption that underpins certainty theory is that the knowledge content of the rules is much more important than the algebra of confidences which holds the system together. Confidence measures correspond to the informal evaluations that human experts attach to their conclusions, e.g., "It is probably true" or "It is highly unlikely."

Certainty theory makes some simple assumptions for creating confidence measures and has some equally simple rules for combining these confidences as the program moves toward its conclusion. The first assumption is to split "confidence for" from "confidence against" in a relationship:

Call $MB(H|E)$ the measure of belief of a hypothesis H given evidence E.

Call $MD(H|E)$ the measure of disbelief of a hypothesis H given evidence E.

Now either

$$1 > MB(H|E) > 0 \quad \text{while} \quad MD(H|E) = 0$$

or

$$1 > MD(H|E) > 0 \quad \text{while} \quad MB(H|E) = 0$$

The two measures constrain each other in that a given piece of evidence is either for or against a particular hypothesis. This is an important difference between certainty theory and probability theory. Once the link between measures of belief and disbelief has been established, they may be tied together again with the *certainty-factor* (CF) calculation:

$$CF(H|E) = MB(H|E) - MD(H|E)$$

As the certainty factor (CF) approaches 1, the evidence is stronger for a hypothesis; as CF approaches -1, the confidence against the hypothesis gets stronger; and a CF around 0 indicates that there is little evidence either for or against the hypothesis.

When experts put together the rule base, they must agree on a CF to go with each rule. This CF reflects their confidence in the rule's reliability. Certainty measures may be adjusted to tune the system's performance, although slight variations in this confidence measure tend to have little effect on the overall running of the system (again, the knowledge gives the power).

The premises for each rule are formed of the AND and OR of a number of facts. When a production rule is used, the certainty factors that are associated with each condition of the premise are combined to produce a certainty measure for the overall premise in the following manner.

For P_1 and P_2, premises of the rule,

$$CF(P_1 \text{ and } P_2) = \min(CF(P_1), CF(P_2))$$

and

$$CF(P_1 \text{ or } P_2) = \max(CF(P_1), CF(P_2))$$

The combined CF of the premises, by using the above combining rules, is then multiplied by the CF of the rule to get the CF for the conclusions of the rule.

For example, consider the rule in a knowledge base

$$(P_1 \text{ and } P_2) \text{ or } P_3 \rightarrow R_1(0.7) \text{ and } R_2(0.3)$$

where P_1, P_2, and P_3 are premises and R_1 and R_2 are the conclusions of the rule having CF values of 0.7 and 0.3, respectively. These numbers are added to the rule when it is designed and represent the expert's confidence in the conclusion if all the premises are known with complete certainty. If the running program has produced P_1, P_2, and P_3 with CF values of 0.6, 0.4, and 0.2, respectively, then R_1 and R_2 may be added to the collected case-specific results with CF values of 0.28 and 0.12, respectively.

Here are the calculations for this example:

$$CF(P_1(0.6) \text{ and } P_2(0.4)) = \min(0.6, 0.4) = 0.4$$

$$CF((0.4) \text{ or } P_3(0.2)) = \max(0.4, 0.2) = 0.4$$

The CF for R_1 is 7 in the rule, so R_1 is added to the set of true facts with the associated CF of $7 * 0.4 = 0.28$. The CF for R_2 is 0.3 in the rule, so R_2 is added to the set of true facts with the associated CF of $0.3 * 0.4 = 0.12$.

One further measure is required: how to combine multiple CFs when two or more rules support the same result R. This is the certainty theory analog of the probability theory procedure of multiplying the probability measures to combine independent evidence. By using this rule repeatedly, one can combine the results of any number of rules that are used for determining result R. Suppose $CF(R_1)$ is the present certainty factor associated with result R and a previously unused rule produces result R (again) with $CF(R_2)$; then the new CF of R is calculated by

$$CF(R_1) + CF(R_2) - (CF(R_1) * CF(R_2)) \text{ when } CF(R_1) \text{ and } CF(R_2) \text{ are positive}$$

$$CF(R_1) + CF(R_2) + (CF(R_1) * CF(R_2)) \text{ when } CF(R_1) \text{ and } CF(R_2) \text{ are negative}$$

$$CF(R_1) + CF(R_2) \text{ over } 1 - \min(|CF(R_1)|, |CF(R_2)|) \text{ otherwise}$$

where $|X|$ is the absolute value of X.

Besides being easy to compute, these equations have other desirable properties. First, the CFs that result from applying this rule are always between 1 and -1, as are the other CFs. Second, the result of combining contradictory CFs is that they cancel, as would be desired. Finally, the combined CF measure is a monotonically increasing (decreasing) function in the manner one would expect for combining evidence.

Certainty theory has been criticized as being excessively ad hoc. Although it is defined in a formal algebra, the meaning of the certainty measures is not as rigorously founded as in formal probability theory. However, certainty theory does not attempt to produce an algebra for "correct" reasoning. Rather it is the "lubrication" that lets the expert system combine confidences as it moves along through the problem at hand. Its measures are ad hoc in the same sense that a human expert's confidence in her or his results is approximate, heuristic, and informal. In Sec. 9.4, when MYCIN is considered, the CFs will be used in the heuristic search to give a priority for goals to be attempted and a cutoff point when a goal need not be considered further. But even though the CF is used to keep the program running and collecting information, the power of the program lies in the content of the rules themselves. This is the justification for the weakness of the certainty algebra.

9.3.4 Other Approaches to Uncertainty

Because of the importance of uncertain reasoning to expert-level problem solving and the limitations of certainty theory, work continues in this important area. In concluding this subsection, we mention briefly three other approaches to modeling uncertainty: Zadeh's *fuzzy set theory*, the Dempster/Shafer *theory of evidence*, and *nonmonotonic reasoning*.

Zadeh's main contention [25] is that although probability theory is appropriate for measuring randomness of information, it is inappropriate for measuring the *meaning* of information. Indeed, much of the confusion surrounding the use of English words and phrases is related to lack of clarity (vagueness) rather than randomness. This is a crucial point for analyzing language structures and can also be important in creating a measure of confidence in production rules. Zadeh proposes *possibility theory* as a measure of vagueness, just as probability theory measures randomness.

Zadeh's theory expresses lack of precision in a quantitative fashion by introducing a set membership function that can take on real values between 0 and 1. This is the notion of a *fuzzy set* and can be described as follows: Let S be a set and s a member of that set. A fuzzy subset F of S is defined by a membership function $mF(s)$ that measures the "degree" to which s belongs to F.

A standard example of the fuzzy set is for S to be the set of positive integers and F to be the fuzzy subset of S called "small integers." Now various integer values can have a "possibility" distribution defining their "fuzzy membership" in the set of small integers: $mF(1) = 1$, $mF(2) = 1$, $mF(3) = 0.9$, $mF(4) = 0.8, \ldots, mF(50) = 0.001$, etc. For the statement that positive integer X is a "small integer," mF creates a possibility distribution across all the positive integers (S).

Fuzzy set theory is not concerned with how these possibility distributions are created, but rather with the rules for computing the combined possibilities over expressions that each contain fuzzy variables. Thus it includes rules for combining possibility measures for expressions containing fuzzy variables. The laws for the OR, AND, and ¬ of these expressions are similar to those just presented for certainty factors. In fact, the approach at Stanford was modeled on some of the combination rules described by Zadeh [3].

Dempster and Shafer approach the problem of measuring certainty by asking us to make a fundamental distinction between uncertainty and ignorance. In probability theory we are *forced* to express the extent of our knowledge about a belief X in a single number $P(X)$. The problem with this, say Dempster and Shafer, is that we simply cannot always know the values of prior probabilities, and thus any particular choice of $P(X)$ may not be justified.

The Dempster-Shafer approach recognizes the distinction between uncertainty and ignorance by creating "belief functions." These belief functions satisfy axioms that are weaker than those of probability theory. Thus probability theory is seen as a subclass of belief functions, and the theory of evidence can reduce to probability theory when all the probabilities are obtainable. Belief functions therefore allow us to use our knowledge to bound the assignment of probabilities to events without having to come up with exact probabilities, when these may be unavailable.

Even though the Dempster-Shafer approach gives us methods of computing these various belief parameters, their greater complexity adds to the computational cost as well. Besides, any theory that has probability theory as a special case is plagued by the assumptions that have made probability theory already quite difficult to use. Conclusions using beliefs, even though they avoid commitment to a stronger (and often unjustified) assignment of probability, produce conclusions that are necessarily weaker. But as the Dempster-Shafer model points out quite correctly, the stronger conclusion may not be justified.

All the methods we have examined can be criticized for using numeric approaches to the handling of uncertain reasoning. It is unlikely that humans use any of these techniques for reasoning with uncertainty, and many applications seem to require a more qualitative approach to the problem. For example, numeric approaches do not support adequate explanations of the causes of uncertainty. If we ask human experts why their conclusions are uncertain, they can answer in terms of the qualitative relationships between features of the problem instance. In a numeric model of uncertainty, this information is replaced by numeric measures. Similarly, numeric approaches do not address the problem of changing data. What should the system do if a piece of uncertain information is later found to be true or false?

Nonmonotonic reasoning addresses these problems directly. A nonmonotonic reasoning system handles uncertainty by making the most reasonable assumptions in light of uncertain information. It proceeds with its reasoning as if these assumptions were true. At a later time, it may find out that an assumption was erroneous, either through a change in problem data or by discovering that the assumption led to an impossible conclusion. When this occurs, the system must change both the assumption and all the conclusions that depend on it.

Nonmonotonicity is an important feature of human problem solving and commonsense reasoning. When we drive to work, e.g., we make numerous assumptions about the roads and traffic. If we find that one of these assumptions is violated, perhaps by construction or an accident on our usual route, we change our plans and devise an alternative route to work.

Nonmonotonic reasoning contrasts sharply with the inference strategies we have discussed so far in the text. These strategies assume that axioms do not change and that the conclusions drawn from them remain true. They are called *monotonic* reasoning systems because knowledge can only be added through the reasoning process. Since information may also be retracted in a nonmonotonic reasoning system when something that was previously thought to be true is later shown to be false, it is important to record the justification for all new knowledge. When an assumed fact is withdrawn, all conclusions that depend on that fact must be reexamined and possibly withdrawn as well. This record keeping is the task of *truth maintenance systems* [7, 8].

9.4 MYCIN: A CASE STUDY

9.4.1 Introduction

Although our small automotive diagnostic example is useful in presenting some of the concepts of expert-system design, it is a toy system and ignores much of the complexity encountered in building large knowledge-based programs. For this reason, we end this chapter with a case study of an actual working expert system.

The MYCIN project was a cooperative venture by the Department of Computer Science and the Medical School at Stanford University. The main work on the project was done during the middle and late 1970s, and about 50 person-years were expended in the effort. MYCIN was written in INTERLISP, a dialect of the LISP programming language. One of the earliest expert systems to be proposed and designed, it has become an important classic in the field. Indeed, it is often presented as the archetype for the rule-based program, with many commercial systems essentially duplicating the MYCIN approach. One of the main reasons for the influence of the MYCIN program is the extensive documentation of the project by the Stanford research teams [3].

MYCIN was designed to solve the problem of diagnosing and recommending treatment for meningitis and bacteremia (blood infections). This particular domain was chosen largely because the program architects wanted to explore the way in which human experts reason with missing and incomplete information. Although there are diagnostic tools that can unambiguously determine the identity of the infecting organisms in a case of meningitis, these tools require on the order of 48 h (chiefly to grow a culture of the infecting organisms) to return a diagnosis. Meningitis patients, however, are very sick, and some treatment must begin immediately. Because of this need, doctors have developed considerable expertise, based on initial symptoms and test results, for forming a diagnosis that *covers* (i.e., includes as a subset) the actual infecting organisms. Treatment begins with this diagnosis and is refined when more conclusive information becomes available. Thus, the domain of meningitis diagnosis provided a natural focus for studying how humans solve problems by using incomplete or unreliable information.

Another goal of the MYCIN design team was to pattern the behavior of the program after the way in which human physicians interact in actual consultations. This was seen as an important factor in system acceptability, particularly since medical consultations tend to follow a standard set of protocols.

In the next subsections we examine the composition of the MYCIN rule and fact descriptions, including the syntax of MYCIN rules. Next, we present a trace of a MYCIN consultation, along with explanatory comments and a discussion of the design and structure of the dialogue. We then discuss the problem of evaluating expert systems and, finally, demonstrate the use of an experimental knowledge-base editor *Teiresias*. Editors such as Teiresias assist the domain experts (in this case the doctors) in correcting the MYCIN knowledge base without the need for a computer language expert. Although such tools are still mainly experimental, this is an important area of research and a potential key to increasing the range of applicability of expert-system technology.

9.4.2 Representation of Rules and Facts

Facts in MYCIN are represented as *attribute-object-value triples*. The first element of this structure is an attribute of an object in the problem domain. For example, we may wish to describe the identity of a disease organism or its sensitivity to certain drugs. The name of the object and the value of the attribute follow. Since information in this domain may be uncertain, a certainty factor is associated with MYCIN facts. Recall from Sec. 9.3.3 that this certainty factor will be between 1 and -1, with 1 being certain, -1 indicating certainty that the attribute is not true, and 0 indicating that little is known.

For example, MYCIN facts may be represented in English by:

```
There is evidence (0.25) that the identity of the organism is
Klebsiella.
```

and

```
It is known that the organism is not sensitive to penicillin.
```

These may be translated into the LISP s expressions:

```
(ident organism_1 klebsiella 0.25)
```

and

```
(sensitive organism_1 penicillin -1.0)
```

We next present an example MYCIN rule both in English and in its LISP equivalent. This sample rule is a condition-action pair in which the premise (condition) is the conjunction of three facts (attribute-object-value triples) and the action adds a new fact to the set of things known about the patient, the identity of a particular organism that is added to the "cover set" of possible infecting organisms. Because this is an abductive rule of inference (inferring the cause from the evidence), it has an attached certainty factor.

In English: IF (a) the infection is primary bacteremia, and (b) the site of the culture is one of the sterile sites, and (c) the suspected portal of entry is the gastrointestinal tract, then there is suggestive evidence (0.7) that infection is bacteroid.

This is rendered for MYCIN thus:

```
IF:    (AND (same_context infection primary_bacteremia)
       (membf_context site sterilesite)
       (same_context portal GI))

THEN:  (conclude context_ident bacteroid tally 0.7).
```

Syntactically, attribute-objective-value (A-O-V) triples are essentially a restriction of predicate calculus expressions to binary predicates. This restriction is not particularly limiting, since algorithms exist for translating predicates of any arity into a set of binary predicates.

There is a deeper difference between predicate calculus and the A-O-V triples used in MYCIN: Predicates may be either true or false. Predicate calculus uses sound rules of inference to determine the truth value of conclusions. In MYCIN, a fact has an attached confidence rather than a truth value. When the system is deriving new facts, it fails to fire any rule whose premise has a certainty value of less than 0.2. This contrasts with logic, which causes a rule to fail if its premise is found to be false.

This comparison of attribute-object-value triples and predicate calculus expressions is included here to emphasize both the similarities and the tradeoffs involved in different knowledge representations. At the highest conceptual level, the characteristics that define a rule-based expert system are independent of any commitment to a particular representational format. These characteristics have been discussed in the comparison of rule-based expert systems and the production system model of problem solving. At the level of an implementation, however, the selection of a particular representational formalism does involve a number of important tradeoffs. These issues include the clarity of the representation, expressiveness (what knowledge can the formalism effectively capture?), naturalness of expression, and ease of implementing and verifying the system.

The action of a MYCIN rule can perform a number of tasks once the rule is satisfied. It may add new information about a particular patient to the working memory. It may also write information to the terminal (or other output device), change the value of an attribute or its certainty measure, look up information in a table (where this representation is more efficient), or execute any piece of LISP code.

Although the ability to execute arbitrary LISP code gives unlimited added power, it should be used judiciously, since excessive use of escapes to the underlying language can lose many of the benefits of the production system formalism. As an absurd example of this, imagine an expert system with only one rule, whose action is to call a large and poorly structured LISP program that attempts to solve the problem!

MYCIN rule and fact descriptions, like all knowledge representation, are a formal language and have a formal syntactic definition. This formal syntax is essential to the definition of well-behaved inference procedures. Furthermore, the formal syntax of rules can help a knowledge-base editor, such as Teiresias, determine when the domain expert has produced an incorrectly formed rule and can prevent that rule from entering the knowledge base. Teiresias can detect syntactic errors in a rule and, to an impressive degree, automatically remedy the situation (see Sec. 9.4.5). This is possible only when the entire program is built on a set of formal specifications.

The syntax of MYCIN rules is given below. It is stated in *Backus-Naur form* (BNF) [20]. BNF is a form of context-free grammar that is widely used to define programming languages. In the notation, key words in the language are written in uppercase letters. These are terminals in the syntax. Nonterminals are enclosed in angle brackets (<>). The BNF grammar is a collection of rewrite rules; the nonterminal figure to the left of the ::= can be replaced with the expression on the right. If we begin with the nonterminal, anything that can be produced through a series of legal substitutions is a legal MYCIN rule.

```
<rule> ::= (IF <antecedent> THEN <action> [ELSE <action>])
<antecedent> ::= (AND {<condition>}+)
<condition> ::= (OR {<condition>}+ | <predicate><associative-triple>)
<associative-triple> ::= (<attribute><object><value>)
<action> ::= {<consequent>}+ | {<procedure>}+
<consequent> ::= (<associative-triple><certainty-factor>)
<certainty-factor> ::= ( ranges from -1 (false) to +1 (true))
<predicate> is any LISP predicate.
<procedure> is any piece of LISP code.
```

9.4.3 MYCIN Diagnosing an Illness

MYCIN is a goal-driven expert system. Its main action is to try to determine whether a particular organism may be present in the meningitis infection in the patient. A possible infecting organism forms a goal that is either confirmed or eliminated. It is interesting to note that the decision to make MYCIN a goal-driven system was not based exclusively on the effectiveness of the strategy in pruning the search space. Early in the design of the system, the MYCIN architects considered the use of forward search. This was rejected because the questions the system asked the user seemed random and unconnected. Goal-driven search, because it is attempting to either confirm or eliminate a particular hypothesis, causes the reasoning to seem more focused and logical. This builds the user's understanding and confidence in the system's actions. An expert system needs to do more than obtain a correct answer; it must also do so in an intelligent and understandable fashion. This criterion influences the choice of search strategies as well as the structure and order of rules.

In keeping with this goal of making the program behave as a doctor, MYCIN's designers noted that doctors ask routine questions at the beginning of a consultation (e.g., "How old are you?" and "Have you had any childhood diseases?") and ask more specific questions when needed. Collecting the general information at the beginning makes the session seem more focused in that it is not continually interrupted by trivial questions such as the name, age, sex, and race of the patient. Certain other questions are asked at other well-defined stages of a consultation, such as at the beginning of considering a new hypothesis.

Eventually the questions get more specific (questions 16 and 17 in the trace below) and related to possible meningitis. When positive responses are given to these questions, MYCIN determines that the infection is meningitis, goes into full goal-driven mode, and tries to determine the actual infecting organisms. It does this by considering each infecting organism that it knows about and by attempting to eliminate or confirm each hypothesis in turn. Since a patient may have more than one infecting organism, MYCIN searches exhaustively, continuing until all possible hypotheses have been considered.

MYCIN controls its search in a number of ways that have not been discussed yet. The knowledge base includes rules that restrict the hypotheses to be tested. For example, MYCIN concludes that it should test for meningitis when the patient has had headaches and other abnormal neurological signs.

Another feature of MYCIN's inference engine is the order in which it tries the backward chaining rules. After the general category of the infection (meningitis, bacteremia, etc.) is determined, each candidate diagnosis is examined exhaustively in a depth-first fashion.

To make the search behave more intelligently, MYCIN first examines all the premises of a rule to determine if any are already known to be false. This prevents the program from trying to solve several of the premises, only to discover that the rule could have been eliminated immediately by one of the later premises.

MYCIN also attempts to find a *unity path*. In trying to prove a goal, it looks for rules that can conclude that goal with a certainty of 1. If one of these rules succeeds, the system does not have to try other rules; the goal is known to be true. This increases both the efficiency and the rationality of the search procedure.

When the confidence measures for a rule premise get below a certain value, the depth-first search is terminated. As mentioned above, the certainty measure for each patient's data is combined with the measures resident in the rules to give the certainty of the new conclusions for the patient. When these get below 0.2, MYCIN abandons the search and goes back up the graph to try another branch of the search space.

When the user wants MYCIN to justify its request for some information, he or she can ask why. Initially, this is answered by the phrase "because I need the information as a necessary attribute of each patient." Once MYCIN begins its backward search for the causes of the patient's problems, however, the why question is answered by printing the rule that MYCIN is currently considering.

As mentioned earlier in this chapter, the "English-like" interaction that the computer offers the user is not a full English language understanding program. Appropriate forms for English language comments and questions are attached to each rule when it is created so that the proper query can be presented to the user when information is needed for use of the rule or so that a rule can be printed in response to a user query.

The following dialogue is a simulated run of the MYCIN program adapted from transcripts of actual MYCIN consultations. It is not necessary to understand either the medical terminology or the medical reasoning to appreciate MYCIN's problem solving.

Our comments on the MYCIN trace are reproduced in italics throughout the interaction. The MYCIN questions and answers are indented, with the user's responses underlined.

```
@mycin
   MYCIN 26-March....
   Instructions? (Y or N)
   N
   26-March 10:42
   -----PATIENT-1-----
```

Mycin has created an object (PATIENT-1) in its dynamic knowledge base or working memory. Certain attributes are immediately requested and are necessary for every patient. These make up the first four questions. . . .

```
   (1) Patient's name:
   Alan Apt
   (2) Age?
   34
   (3) Sex
   Why
```

MYCIN restates the question before answering. . . .

```
   [i.e., Why is it important to determine the sex of PATIENT-1?]
   [1.0] The sex of the patient is one of the four standard parameters
   that identify a patient. This may be useful later....
   [back to question 3...]
   Male
   (4) Race?
   Caucasian
   (5) Are there any cultures for Alan Apt that may be related to the
   present illness and from which organisms have been grown
   successfully in the laboratory?
   No
```

MYCIN is a program to analyze and treat infectious diseases, so before it gets into close questioning of the patient's present condition, it asks about any present or pending data (cultures) that are available. . . .

```
   (6) Are there any pending cultures for Alan Apt?
   Yes
   -----CULTURE-1-----
```

Another object (CULTURE-1) is created and linked to PATIENT-1. . . .

```
   (7) From what site was the specimen for CULTURE-1 taken?
   CSF
```

(8) Please give the date and time when the pending CSF culture was obtained?
<u>26-March-7:00</u>
(9) Was a smear examined at the time the specimen was obtained?
<u>Yes</u>
(10) Were any cultures seen on the smear of the specimen?
<u>No</u>

Indention indicates that MYCIN's attention has returned from consideration of the new object (CULTURE-1) back to the original object (PATIENT-1).

(11) Are there any other pending cultures?
<u>No</u>
.
.
.

(16) Has Alan Apt recently had symptoms of persistent headache or other abnormal neurologic symptoms (dizziness, lethargy, etc.)?
<u>Yes</u>
(17) Has Alan Apt recently had objective evidence of abnormal neurologic signs (nuchal rigidity, coma, seizures, etc.) documented by a physician?
<u>Yes</u>

With the answers of these last two questions in the affirmative, MYCIN decides to consider meningitis infections and goes into a full backchaining search to try to identify the organisms that might be causing the meningitis.

(18) Please give the date on which clinical evidence (symptoms, signs, or laboratory tests) of the meningitis first appeared.
<u>25 March 10:00</u>
.
.
.

(36) Has Alan Apt had neurosurgery?
<u>Why</u>
[i.e., Why is it important to determine whether PATIENT-1 has had neurosurgery?]
[6.0] This will aid in determining the organisms (other than those seen on cultures or smears) that might be causing the infection. It has already been established that
[6.1] the culture that requires therapy is meningitis, and
[6.2] organisms were not seen on the stain of the pending CSF culture (CULTURE-1), and
[6.3] the type of infection is bacterial
Therefore, if
[6.4] Alan Apt has had neurosurgery, and
[6.5] the time since the neurosurgical operation is less than 2 months, and
[6.5] the type of neurosurgery is not ventricular urethral shunt, then
there is evidence that the organisms that might be causing the infection are
    staphylococcus-coag-pos (0.75), staphylococcus-coag-neg (0.5),
      <u>E. coli</u> (0.4), <u>klebsiella</u>....
Author: Yu
    [RULE511]
[back to question 36...]
<u>How</u> <u>[6.3]</u>

The physician is concerned how MYCIN arrived at the conclusion that the infection is bacterial. MYCIN responds, after restating its interpretation of the question the doctor is asking, with the rules it used to determine that the infection was indeed bacterial. The answer to how is given as the rules used, as well as their (positive and negative) certainty factors, for determining this result. . . .

```
[i.e., How was it established that the type of infection is
bacterial?]
The following rules concluded about the likelihood that the type of
infection is bacterial

     Rule   Yes   No
     [6.7]   500  (0.4)
     [6.8]   501  (0.17)
     [6.9]   502  (0.1)
     [6.10]  524  (0.42)
     [6.11]  504  (0.28)

Thus it has been established that the type of infection might be
bacterial.
[back to question 36...]
No
     .
     .
     .
(42) Is Alan Apt a burn patient?
Yes
I have found evidence (RULE 507) that treatment should cover for
     Diplococcus pneumoniae causing meningitis.
I have found evidence (RULE 545) that treatment should cover for E.
     coli causing meningitis.
I have found evidence (RULE 545 RULE 578) that the treatment should
     cover for Pseudomonas aeruginosa causing meningitis.
```

MYCIN now attempts to prescribe appropriate therapies for these infections. First, it must be determined whether the patient has any allergies to antibody therapies. The height and weight of the patient are also requested to determine proper dosages . . .

```
(43) Does Alan Apt have focal neurological signs?
No
[Determining which dosages are desirable for use against the E.
coli ...]
[Determining which drugs are desirable for use ...]
INFECTION-1 is MENINGITIS
+ DIPLOCOCCUS-PNEUMONIAE (from clinical evidence only)
+ E. COLI (from clinical evidence only)
+ PSEUD...
     .
     .
     .
[REC-1] My preferred therapy recommendation is as follows:
In order to cover for items:
Give the following in combination:
(1) AMPICILLIN
Dose: 3.85 g (30.8 ml) q4h IV
(2) GENTAMICIN
Dose: 131 mg (3.2 ml) q8h IV
```

```
Comments:
    Monitor serum concentrations
    Since high concentrations of penicillins can inactivate
    aminoglycosides,
    do not mix these antibiotics in the same IV bottle.
Do you wish to see the next choice therapy?
No
```

If the physician did not like the recommended treatment, she or he could have asked for another, eliminating one of the drugs (ampicillin, for instance). MYCIN would then have attempted to find another treatment. . . .

9.4.4 Evaluation of Expert Systems

One of the difficult issues faced by expert-system design teams is to determine when the program is ready for actual use. This problem is all the more difficult when the program, like MYCIN, deals with life-threatening situations; here mistakes, such as overlooking an infecting agent, can be catastrophic. Many expert systems, including MYCIN [3], have been evaluated by using a form of the Turing test.

Ten randomly selected case histories of meningitis were rediagnosed by MYCIN and eight practitioners at the Stanford Medical School. These included five faculty members, one research fellow in infectious diseases, one resident physician, and one medical student. The actual therapy given by the original doctors on the case was also included, for a total of 10 diagnoses.

These 10 diagnoses were evaluated by eight other infectious-disease experts. The diagnoses were "blind" in that they were uniformly coded so that the experts did not know whether they were looking at the computer's diagnosis or that of the humans. The evaluators rated each diagnosis as acceptable or unacceptable, with a practitioner being given one point for each acceptable rating. Thus, a perfect score would be 80 points. The results of this evaluation are given in Table 9.1.

Table 9.2 presents the results of asking another important question in this "life-and-death" analysis: In how many cases did the recommended therapy fail to cover for a treatable infection? The results in both tables indicate that MYCIN performed at least as well as the Stanford experts. This is an exciting result, but it should not surprise us since

TABLE 9.1 Experts Evaluate MYCIN and Nine Other Prescribers

Prescriber	Score	Percent
MYCIN	55	69
Faculty-5	54	68
Fellow	53	66
Faculty-3	51	64
Faculty-2	49	61
Faculty-4	47	59
Actual RX	47	59
Faculty-1	45	56
Resident	39	49
Student	28	35

TABLE 9.2 Number of Cases in Which Therapy Missed a Treatable Pathogen

Prescriber	Number
MYCIN	0
Faculty-5	1
Fellow	1
Faculty-3	1
Faculty-2	0
Faculty-4	0
Actual RX	0
Faculty-1	0
Resident	1
Student	3

the MYCIN knowledge base represents the combined expertise of some of the best medical minds available. Finally, MYCIN gave fewer drugs than the human experts and thus did not overprescribe for the infections. Note: On the average MYCIN gave fewer drugs than the human experts.

Another noteworthy aspect of this evaluation is how little agreement there was among human experts concerning the correctness of diagnoses. Even the best of the diagnosticians failed to receive a unanimous endorsement from the evaluators. This observation underscores the extent to which human expertise is still largely heuristic.

These positive evaluation results do not mean that MYCIN is now ready to set up a medical practice and take on patients. In fact, MYCIN is not used for delivering medical care. There are several important reasons. First and most important, the rules (approximately 600 of them) did not give a speedy response in the doctor-computer interaction. Each session with the computer lasted about 0.5 h and required, as can be seen from the trace presented above, a good amount of typing.

Second, the program was "locked into" the particular part of its graph search for response to questions. It was not able to extrapolate to other situations or previous patients, but remained strictly within the nodes and links of the graph it was evaluating.

Third, MYCIN's explanations were limited: When the doctor expected a deep medical justification for some particular result—a physiological or antibacterial justification, say—MYCIN simply returned the "condition action plus certainty factor" relationship contained in its rule base. It is difficult for an expert system to relate its heuristic knowledge to any deeper understanding of the problem domain. For example, MYCIN does not really understand human physiology; it simply applies rules to case-specific data. Folklore has it that an early version of MYCIN, before recommending a particular drug, asked if the patient was pregnant, in spite of the fact that MYCIN had been told that the patient was male! Whether this actually happened or not, it does indicate the limitations of current expert-system technology. Attempting to give expert systems the flexibility and deeper understanding demonstrated by human beings is an important and open area of research.

Finally, unlike humans, who are extremely flexible in the way they apply knowledge, expert systems do not "degrade gracefully" when confronted with situations that do not fit the knowledge in their rule bases. That is, while a human can shift to reasoning from first principles or to intelligent guesses when confronted with a new situation, expert systems simply fail to get any answer at all.

All these issues have meant that MYCIN does not enjoy common use in the medical field. Nonetheless, it does serve as an archetype of this class of expert system, and many of its descendants, such as PUFF, are being used in clinical situations.

9.4.5 Knowledge Acquisition and the Teiresias Knowledge-Base Editor

Another one of the long-term goals of expert-systems research is to design software that will allow the human expert to interact directly with the knowledge base to correct and improve it. This is seen as a potential remedy for what has been called the *knowledge engineering bottleneck*. This bottleneck is caused by the fact that building an expert system generally requires a substantial commitment of time by both the domain expert and the knowledge engineer. This contributes to the expense and complexity of building expert systems. Both individuals tend to be highly paid professionals, and the loss in productivity caused by taking the domain expert away from other work during system development can add to the cost of the project. Additional cost and complexity come from the effort needed to communicate the domain expert's knowledge to the knowledge engineer, the logistics of getting these two people together, and the complexity of the programming required for an expert system.

The obvious solution to this problem is to automate as much of the process as possible. This has been done to a great extent through the development of expert-system shells and environments that reduce the amount of programming required by the knowledge engineer. However, these shells still require that the programmer understand the methodologies of knowledge representation and search. A more ambitious goal is to eliminate the need for a knowledge engineer entirely. One way to accomplish this is to provide knowledge-base editors that allow the domain expert to develop the program, interacting with the knowledge base in terms that come from the problem domain and letting the software handle the details of representation and knowledge organization. This approach has been explored in an experimental program called *Teiresias* [5, 6], a knowledge-base editor developed at Stanford University as part of the MYCIN project. We discuss the Teiresias project in this section.

Another approach to the problem is to develop programs that can learn on their own by refining their problem-solving efforts in response to feedback from the outside. These approaches have been explored with varying degrees of success by the machine learning community [16].

With the assistance of a knowledge-base editor, the domain expert can analyze the performance of a knowledge base, find missing or erroneous rules, and correct the problem in a language appropriate to the expert's way of thinking about the domain. The knowledge-base editor designed for MYCIN is called Teiresias, after the blind seer of the Greek tragedian Euripides. The name is altogether appropriate, as Teiresias was able to see and describe the relations of the world without the (literal) gift of sight; similarly, this software is able to understand relations in a knowledge base without (literally) understanding the referents of these relations.

Teiresias allows a doctor to step through MYCIN's treatment of a patient and locate problems with its performance. Teiresias also translates the doctor's corrections into the appropriate internal representations for the knowledge base. Thus Teiresias is able to maintain the syntactic consistency of the knowledge base by updating all appropriate program structures when new information is to be integrated into the knowledge base.

For example, MYCIN stores considerable knowledge in the form of tables. Certain rules include LISP code that retrieves information from these tables, such as characteristics of disease organisms. This improves the efficiency of the knowledge base, since a single table can capture information that would require numerous rules to encode. However, if a new object, such as a disease organism, is added to the knowledge base, then all tables that contain information about disease organisms must be updated to reflect this.

Semantic consistency is a more difficult problem, requiring knowledge of how well the knowledge base actually reflects the problem domain. Although Teiresias cannot be said to truly maintain semantic consistency, it does make an effort to ensure that rules appear consistent with one another. It does this by maintaining *rule models,* or statistical profiles of all the rules. If a new rule is added to the knowledge base, Teiresias compares this new rule with the rule model for all existing rules that draw the same conclusion. The assumption is that rules that draw similar conclusions should examine similar conditions in their premises. This enables Teiresias to detect potential inconsistencies in a new rule and to prompt the user for corrections.

To illustrate Teiresias, we analyze its interaction with the doctor after MYCIN has given its recommendations. The doctor disagrees with MYCIN's result and with Teiresias' help analyzes MYCIN's solution. The trace is a simulation taken from a session by Stanford researchers, where the analysis is in italics, Teiresias' questions are in regular type, and the doctor's responses are in boldface type.

When a conclusion is given with which the doctor disagrees, the rule that drew this conclusion is not necessarily wrong. A number of things could have happened, as Teiresias correctly shows: A fact of the rule could have been improperly concluded; the rule might, in fact, be wrong; or another rule might be missing from the knowledge base. Finding the cause of an error is a difficult problem that potentially requires examination of the entire line of reasoning. Teiresias assists the physician in determining the problem by maintaining an AND/OR graph of the solution process and working systematically through this trace.

All rules are translated into an English language syntax that assists the physician in understanding the trace. Once a problem is located, Teiresias lets the user add the missing rule in the same simplified syntax, translating the rule into an internal representation and checking the new rule for consistency with similar rules in the knowledge base.

MYCIN has reached a set of infections that it feels should be treated (as in the dialogue of Sec. 9.4.3). These are presented to the physician, who disagrees with MYCIN's analysis:

```
My therapy recommendation will be based on the following probable
infections and potential causative organisms:
        INFECTION-1 is PRIMARY BACTEREMIA
        <item-1>E. COLI
        <item-2>PSEUDOMONAS-AERUGINOSA
```

Now Teiresias steps in:

```
Are all these identities correct?
No
Are there any identities missing?
Yes
Which ones?
KLEBSIELLA PNEUMONIAE, PROTEUS-NON-MIRABILIS
Are there any identities which shouldn't have appeared?
Yes
Which ones?
PSEUDOMONAS-AERUGINOSA
Do you want to
(1) track down the problem yourself, or
(2) allow me to guide the debugging, or
(3) ignore it for now and fix it another time
        Type 1, 2, or 3
2
```

If the doctor had typed 1, he or she could have tried to sort out the problems with the traditional why and how queries on the preceding solution. Note that Teiresias has already begun to categorize the errors that appeared in the conclusions. Also note that the three problems could well be related (perhaps to one missing rule). Teiresias starts by trying to find out why the wrong organism appeared for treatment. . . .

```
The following rules were used in deducing that the identity of
ORGANISM-1 is PSEUDOMONAS-AERUGINOSA.
        RULE 184
        Since
                [1.1] The category of ORGANISM-1 is not known
                [1.2] The gram stain of ORGANISM-1 is gram-negative
                [1.3] The morphology of ORGANISM-1 is rod
                [1.4] The aerobicity of ORGANISM-1 is facultative
        There is weakly suggestive evidence (0.3) that the identity
        of ORGANISM-1 is PSEUDOMONAS-AERUGINOSA.
```

Is this rule correct?
<u>Yes</u>
Should its premise have failed in this case?
<u>Yes</u>
Which clause of the premise should have failed?
<u>Clause 1</u>

The expert feels the program should have been able to establish a category and that rule 184 should not have fired.

Should it have been possible to conclude a category?
<u>Yes</u>
Which one?
<u>ENTEROBACTERIACEAE</u>
There were no rules successfully called in the attempt to deduce this category. The following (potentially applicable) rules were NOT executed because the marked [++] clause failed:
    RULE 116
    If
      (1) the identity of ORGANISM-1 is not known
  ++(2) the gram stain of ORGANISM-1 is not known
      (3) the morphology of ORGANISM-1 is not known
      (4) the site of CULTURE-1 is CSF
      (5) the infection is meningitis
      (6) the age of the patient is less than or equal to 2 months
    Then
          there is weakly suggestive evidence (0.33) that the
          category of ORGANISM-1 is ENTEROBACTERIACEAE
    RULE 050
    If
      (1) the morphology of ORGANISM-1 is rod
      (2) the gram stain of ORGANISM-1 is gram-negative
      (3) the aerobicity of ORGANISM-1 is facultative
   ++(4) infection ORGANISM-1 was acquired while the
             patient was hospitalized
    Then
          there is suggestive evidence (0.7) that the category of
          ORGANISM-1 is ENTEROBACTERIACEAE
Are all these rules correct?
<u>Yes</u>
Should any of them have been successfully invoked?
<u>No</u>
Is there a rule missing?
<u>Yes</u>
Would you like to give me such a rule now?
<u>Yes</u>
Good ...
    If
        <u>1 ** THE PATIENT'S INFECTION IS PRIMARY-</u>
        <u>BACTEREMIA</u>
        <u>2 ** THE SITE IS ONE OF THE STERILE SITES</u>
     Then:
        <u>** THERE IS SUGGESTIVE EVIDENCE (0.8) THAT THE</u>
        <u>CATEGORY IS ENTEROBACTERIACEAE</u>

Teiresias parses this rule into its internal representation and then translates it back into English so the expert can check it. After the expert agrees on the parse, Teiresias attempts to integrate the new rule into the knowledge base. . . .

```
I hate to criticize, Dr. Davis, but did you know that most rules
about what the category of an organism might be that mention:
        the site of a culture, and
        the infection
also mention:
        the portal of entry of the organism?
Shall I try to write a clause to account for this?
Yes
How about:
  the portal of entry is gastrointestinal. OK?
Yes
```

Teiresias is itself a knowledge-based program with rules for reasoning about rules and objects in a MYCIN knowledge base. As the above trace illustrates, the program systematically searches back along the trace of the reasoning to find the source of the problem. Once this is done, it helps the user add to or correct the knowledge base. Using the rule models discussed at the beginning of this section, Teiresias is able to check the rule for consistency and to correct the missing premise.

To help the user add new information, Teiresias keeps a model of each class of object that appears in the system. The model for a MYCIN object is called a *schema*. Each schema describes how to create new instances of a class of objects such as a new disease organism, drug, or test. The schema for a class of objects also describes how information is to be obtained for rules of that class, e.g., to compute it from existing data, look it up, or ask the user.

Schemata record the interrelationships of all classes of objects in the MYCIN rule base. For example, if the addition of a new disease requires that a table of diseases and their sensitivities to various drugs also be updated, this is recorded in the disease schema. Schemata also include pointers to all current instances of each schema. This is very important if it is decided to change the form of the schema throughout the program.

Teiresias organizes its schemata into a hierarchy: A schema for describing bacterial infections may be a specification of a general class schema, which in turn is a specification of a general schema for MYCIN facts. Each schema includes pointers to its parents and children in this hierarchy.

Schemata also contain bookkeeping information. This includes the author and date of creation and addition of each instance to the program. It includes a description of the schema used to create it. Documentation of who created rules when is critical for discussion and analysis of the knowledge base; when rules are primarily condition-action pairs representing important aspects of an application domain and not full explications of these relationships, it is important to be able to trace the rules back to their authors for more complete discussion of the factors underlying their creation.

The top-level structure in the hierarchy of Teiresias' knowledge is the *schema-schema*. This structure is a schema for creating new schemata, when, e.g., the domain expert might wish to create a new category of objects. The schema-schema allows Teiresias to reason about its own knowledge structures, including creating new ones when appropriate. A schema-schema has the same basic structure as a schema itself and provides all the bookkeeping information to reconstitute the entire knowledge base.

Although the development of commercial programs to help with knowledge acquisition is still in the future, Teiresias has shown how AND/OR graph search and knowledge representation techniques provide a basis for automating knowledge-base refinement.

9.5 EPILOGUE

A number of references complement the material presented in this chapter; especially recommended is a collection of the original MYCIN publications from Stanford entitled *Rule-Based Expert Systems* by Buchanan and Shortliffe [2].

Other important books on general knowledge engineering include *Building Expert Systems* by Hayes-Roth et al. [12], *A Guide to Expert Systems* by Waterman [23], *Expert Systems: Concepts and Examples* by Alty and Coombs [1], *Expert Systems Technology: A Guide* by Johnson and Keravnou [13], *Expert Systems: Tools and Applications* by Harmon et al. [11], and *Expert Systems and Fuzzy Systems* by Negoita [18].

Because of the domain specificity of expert-system solutions, case studies are an important source of knowledge in the area. Books in this category include *Expert Systems: Techniques, Tools, and Applications* by Klahr and Waterman [15], *Competent Expert Systems: A Case Study in Fault Diagnosis* by Keravnou and Johnson [14], *The CRI Directory of Expert Systems* by Smart and Langeland-Knudsen [21], and *Developments in Expert Systems* by Coombs [4].

A pair of more general books that give an overview of commercial uses of AI are *The AI Business*, edited by Winston and Prendergast [24], and *Expert Systems: Artificial Intelligence in Business* by Harmon and King [10].

REFERENCES

1. J. L. Alty and M. J. Coombs, *Expert Systems: Concepts and Examples*. Manchester, Eng.: NCC Publications, 1984.

2. J. Bachant and J. McDermott, "R1 Revisited: Four Years in the Trenches," *AI Magazine*, 5(3):21–32, 1984.

3. B. G. Buchanan and E. H. Shortliffe (eds.), *Rule-Based Expert Systems: The MYCIN Experiments of the Stanford Heuristic Programming Project*. Reading, Mass.: Addison-Wesley, 1984.

4. M. J. Coombs (ed.), *Developments in Expert Systems*. New York: Academic Press, 1984.

5. R. Davis, "Applications of Meta Level Knowledge to the Construction, Maintenance, and Use of Large Knowledge Bases," in R. Davis and D. B. Lenat, *Knowledge-Based Systems in Artificial Intelligence*. New York: McGraw-Hill, 1982.

6. R. Davis and D. B. Lenat, *Knowledge-Based Systems in Artificial Intelligence*. New York: McGraw-Hill, 1982.

7. J. de Kleer, "An Assumption Based Truth Maintenance System," *Artificial Intelligence*, 28:127–162, 1986.

8. J. Doyle, "AAAA Truth Maintenance System," *Artificial Intelligence*, vol. 12, 1979.

9. R. O. Duda, J. Gaschnig, and P. E. Hart, "Model Design in the PROSPECTOR Consultant System for Mineral Exploration," in D. Michie (ed.), *Expert Systems in the Micro-Electronic Age*. Edinburgh, Scotland: Edinburgh University Press, 1979.

10. P. Harmon and D. King, *Expert Systems: Artificial Intelligence in Business*. New York: Wiley, 1985.

11. P. Harmon, R. Maus, and W. Morrissey, *Expert Systems: Tools and Applications*. New York: Wiley, 1988.

12. F. Hayes-Roth, D. Waterman, and D. Lenat, *Building Expert Systems*. Reading, Mass.: Addison-Wesley, 1984.

13. L. Johnson and E. T. Keravnou, *Expert Systems Technology: A Guide*. Cambridge, Mass.: Abacus Press, 1985.

14. E. T. Keravnou and L. Johnson, *Competent Expert Systems: A Case Study in Fault Diagnosis*. London: Kegan Paul, 1985.

15. P. Klahr and D. A. Waterman (eds.), *Expert Systems: Techniques, Tools, and Applications*. Reading, Mass.: Addison-Wesley, 1986.

16. G. F. Luger and W. A. Stubblefield, *Artificial Intelligence and the Design of Expert Systems*. Palo Alto, Calif.: Benjamin/Cummings, 1989.

17. J. McDermott, "R1, the Formative Years," *AI Magazine*, 2(2):21–29, 1981.

18. C. V. Negoita, *Expert Systems and Fuzzy Systems*. Menlo Park, Calif.: Benjamin/Cummings, 1984.

19. S. Papert, *Mindstorms*. New York: Basic Books, 1980.

20. T. W. Pratt, *Programming Languages: Design and Duplementation*. Englewood Cliffs, N.J.: Prentice-Hall, 1984.

21. G. Smart and J. Langeland-Knudsen, *The CRI Directory of Expert Systems*. Oxford, Eng.: Learned Information (Europe) Ltd., 1986.

22. E. Soloway, J. Bachant, and K. Jensen, "Assessing the Maintainability of XCON-in-RIME: Coping with the Problems of a Very Large Rule Base," *Proceedings of AAAI-87*. Los Altos, Calif.: Bowman Kaufmann, 1987.

23. D. A. Waterman, *A Guide to Expert Systems*. Reading, Mass.: Addison-Wesley, 1986.

24. P. H. Winston and K. A. Prendergast (eds.), *The AI Business*. Cambridge, Mass.: MIT Press, 1984.

25. L. A. Zadeh, "Commonsense Knowledge Representation Based on Fuzzy Logic," *Computer*, 16:61–65, 1983.

CHAPTER 10
COMPUTER ARCHITECTURES FOR ARTIFICIAL INTELLIGENCE AND NEURAL NETWORKS

José G. Delgado-Frias
Department of Electrical Engineering
State University of New York, Binghamton

Artificial intelligence (AI) applications and algorithms have grown steadily in many fields, such as computer vision, robotics, natural language understanding, and expert systems. As a consequence AI systems have increased in complexity. This in turn has created a need for high-performance computer architectures that can execute AI algorithms at reasonable speed. Since the conventional von Neumann computers are not well suited to artificial intelligence, novel architectures for AI are being investigated and developed in order to achieve the performance required.

In this chapter, issues on artificial intelligence and computer architectures for this application are presented. The AI issues have an impact on the design criteria, performance, and evaluation of the architectures. Within the AI field, there are a number of different computational requirements that a single computer architecture might not be able to meet. To provide a comprehensive study of computer architectures for artificial intelligence and neural networks, an introduction to AI concepts and languages is required. Each section begins with a brief description of key issues that affect the computer architecture design for that particular set of AI applications.

10.1 AI OVERVIEW

Due to the number of mechanisms that human beings have for information representation, processing, storage, retrieval, and discarding, a definition of natural intelligence seems almost impossible to agree upon. Defining artificial intelligence not only might be controversial and elusive but also depends heavily on the AI goals and models [102]. However, there are two generally acceptable goals in artificial intelligence [133]. The first is *to build an intelligent machine* that can perform tasks that so far only human beings have been able to do. The second goal is *to find out more about the nature of intelligence* by means of computer models. To achieve these two goals, artificial intelligence has become a multidisciplinary field [102]. AI involves disciplines such as computer science (computer programming techniques and languages), mathematics (predicate calculus and well-formed formulas), psychology (models of human thought), cognitive science (models of the human brain), philosophy (problem solving), linguistics (semantics and understanding), and engineering (mechanization of intelligence). Each of these fields has made contributions to achieve the current AI state of the art.

10.1.1 AI Areas of Application

AI major areas of application [121, 106, 104, 90, 116, 133, 101] include the following:

Knowledge-Based Expert Systems.   An *expert system* is usually defined as a computer system that incorporates a number of AI techniques to provide human users with expert conclusions about specialized subject areas. Knowledge-based approaches are generally used to manipulate and represent knowledge and to make inferences in these systems.

Natural Language and Speech Processing.   Natural languages allow human beings to communicate with one another. Its primary use is for transmitting a bit of mental structure among human beings under circumstances in which each human possesses a similar knowledge that serves as a common context. Natural language and speech processing is referred to as the *human-computer interaction* by means of a written and/or spoken natural language such as English. A computer system capable of understanding a message in natural language would require the context knowledge as well as the process to make the inferences assumed by the message generator.

Robotics.   This application deals with how computer programs create plans to satisfy goals. It involves two fields of AI: planning and search. Robotics applications require the generation of plans for action sequences as well as the monitoring of the execution of these plans. The world state changes constantly due to actions taken by the system or by human interaction with the system. Once a plan is put into action, the system should be able to dynamically change the plan if the world state changes do not fit the original plan. Planning a path of action involves AI searching techniques to find a viable route.

Theorem Proving.   Human beings make deductions from hypotheses and use intuitive skills to find a proof (or disproof) for a conjectured theorem in mathematics. A skilled mathematician has an accumulated knowledge from previously proved theorems in a subject area; this knowledge is useful for the present proof. Predicate logic, a formalization of the deductive process, is commonly used in this type of AI system.

Perception.   Perception applications deal with the understanding of complex input data, such as a scene. Knowledge about the set of things being observed as well as their environment plays an important role in perception. The main difficulty in perceiving a scene is the large number of possible descriptions of such a scene.

Knowledge Acquisition.   As AI systems grow, formalizing and implementing knowledge bases become a major task. A large AI system must have a knowledge-base editing system that allows it to modify the knowledge base.

Although there are many other AI applications that are not mentioned here, the application descriptions provide a background of AI capabilities. More applications, as well as a description of AI principles, can be found in Nilsson [90], Winston [133], Schalkoff [101], Barr [7], Shapiro [104], Kirsh [69], Genesereth and Nilsson [40], and Hecht-Nielsen [52].

10.1.2 AI Processing Features

Computational requirements for AI processing are different and more complex than those for other applications. In this section some of these requirements are presented [126, 57].

Symbolic Processing.   Most of the AI processing involves some sort of symbolic processing; i.e., in AI software many of the data are given in symbolic form. Primitive symbolic operations should include comparison, matching, logic set operations, selection, and sorting.

Nondeterministic Computations.   It is almost impossible to determine the execution path that an AI program would follow. The program execution depends heavily on the input. Exhaustive enumeration of all possible paths might be too costly or impossible. A *combinatorial explosion* problem is created when a program is run with no bounds. There is a need for a controlled search which could be achieved by heuristic approaches.

Dynamic Execution.   The execution path of many AI applications is modified at runtime. Functions may create new data to be processed by another function. Compilers, therefore, have little information on the size of the data that can be generated. The amount of space required and the type of communication required are not known in advance. Thus, resources have to be allocated and removed dynamically.

Parallel and Distributed Processing.   Many AI applications require parallel architectures in order to be executed at reasonable speed. There are various forms of parallelism in AI, such as OR parallelism, AND parallelism, semantic networks, and neural networks. However, these forms of potential parallelism usually present a number of challenges to computer architects.

Knowledge Representation, Manipulation, and Management.   Knowledge about an AI application can be represented in several ways, e.g., logic, semantic networks, and neural networks. The complexity of some problems is greatly reduced by proper representation. Highly specialized architectures may be needed to manipulate and manage a large knowledge base in an efficient manner.

Garbage Collection.   As a consequence of dynamic allocation of storage, garbage collection is required. Many processes are created at run time; such processes generate temporary data that soon after creation are no longer needed.

Load Balancing.   There is a need for a balanced load in multiprocessor architectures; i.e., every processing element in the architecture should have an equivalent computational load. An overload on a processing element might become the bottleneck of the architecture.

Computing requirements are usually different from one AI application to another. The requirements as well as the architectures for a set of AI applications are presented in this chapter.

10.1.3 Design Approaches for AI Machines

Designing a machine for AI applications spans from pure architectural concepts (such as data flow, reduction, etc.) through AI languages (such as LISP, Prolog, etc.) to knowledge representations (such as rules, semantic networks, etc.). There are three major

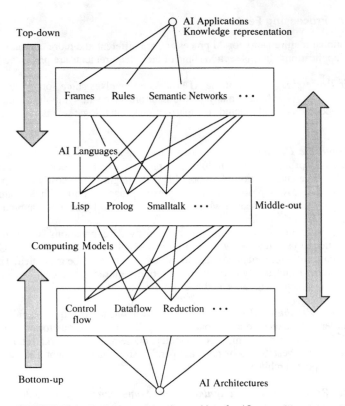

FIGURE 10.1 Design approaches for machines for AI.

approaches to the design of computer architectures for artificial intelligence [125, 62]; these are shown in Fig. 10.1 and described below.

Bottom-Up Approach. This approach begins with a study of the architectural issues that would affect the performance of an architecture for AI applications. These issues include parallel processing, fast technologies, level of control, and synchronization mechanisms. Computing models then can be implemented directly on the architecture. The AI applications may be modified to be efficiently implemented on the computing models. An example of this approach is Scheme-79 [114].

Top-Down Approach. This approach begins with the specification of the particular application requirements and works down toward the hardware implementation. This approach may lead toward very specialized machines. Examples of this approach include DADO [111] and FAIM-1 [4].

Middle-Out Approach. In this approach the starting point is a well-established language for artificial intelligence (such as LISP or Prolog). The language is modified (features that can be implemented in software are added) to accommodate the AI application. Then the implementation of the language on hardware is designed. Examples of this approach are SPUR [58] and Aquarius [33].

These three approaches represent basic design strategies. Other issues that should be considered in the implementation of computer architectures include the interprocessor communication scheme, memory structure, I/O strategies, and scaling. These issues are dealt with in Chap. 5 of this book.

10.2 FUNCTIONAL-PROGRAMMING-ORIENTED ARCHITECTURES

In this section the basic principles of functional programming languages are presented. Since LISP is the most widely used and mature functional language for AI applications, this section focuses on architectures for LISP.

10.2.1 Functional Programming Languages and LISP

Functional programming languages are based on the mathematical concept of a function [53]. A *function* is a rule of correspondence where for each member of a certain class there is a unique member of another class that corresponds to it. The correspondence can be denoted by a function $f(x)$. An individual of the range of f corresponds to an individual of x in the domain of f.

Functional languages have the following features: They are *history-insensitive,* where there is no notion of present state or storage, and there is *referential transparency* (the values of an expression depend *only* on its context, not on any computational history). These types of programming languages offer some advantages: (1) There are no side effects; the function output depends only on the inputs. (2) Programs are easy to verify; they can be mathematically verified. (3) There is a potential for parallelism; several functions can be run at the same time. There are, however, some problems with functional programming: (1) It is difficult to program; most programmers have been trained to program with imperative languages (such as Pascal, Fortran, C). (2) The input and output are difficult; functions are not allowed to change data structures. Examples of functional programming languages include FP, Val, Id, Miranda, and Pure LISP [32]. Computer architectures for functional programming are described in Vegdahl [123].

LISP was developed by John McCarthy in the early 1960s [78]. Pure LISP is considered to be a functional programming language. Data structures (or symbol lists) are manipulated by functions. These functions allow recursion, which is largely used in LISP programs. Many LISP implementations have preserved the functional language characteristics. LISP has evolved since its introduction; LISP 1.5, MacLISP, InterLISP, Scheme, and Franz LISP are the most prominent stages in the evolution. The proliferation of many LISP versions has created a need for a LISP standard, which is Common LISP [108], as well as a set of benchmark programs [39].

Any LISP program is organized as a collection of functions that call each other. A function is allowed to call itself; thus, recursive approaches not only can be used, but also are frequently used. Function calls can be seen as function evaluation in the mathematical sense. Another feature of LISP is the data structures on which the functions operate; these structures are lists. LISP features, such as function calls, lists, binding, and data typing, are briefly described below.

Function Calls. LISP function evaluation takes place on a dynamically bound context; i.e., the most recent active value bound to a variable is used when this variable is referenced by a function. Due to recursive programming, there are a number of unfinished function calls. However, the most recent value of a variable is valid for only one of these functions (or a small number of functions). It is required, therefore, to keep track of a referencing context which is associated with each function. Every time a function is called, the arguments in the call are evaluated and then bound to the formal bound on the function. The environment (or active referencing context) must be modified to express the current conditions of the values of the variables. The function is then evaluated, and a value is returned to the calling function. Once a function call is completed, the control is returned to the caller and the reference context of the caller must be restored.

Lists in LISP. LISP data objects are called *symbolic expressions* (s expressions) which have two types: atoms and lists. Atoms are names and numbers, whereas lists are collections of atoms or other lists. Figure 10.2 shows the representation of a list. Each list cell has two pointers (*car* and *cdr*) that point to the "head" and "tail" symbols or lists that are associated with this cell.

Primitive functions to manipulate lists include *car*, which returns the first element of the list; *cdr*, which returns everything that follows the first element of the list; *rplaca*, which replaces the first element of the list; and *rplacd*, which is used to replace the *cdr* pointer of the list. All data that a LISP program manipulates are stored in a list representation; consequently, to access data requires following several pointers at run time. A large portion of LISP execution time is spent chasing these pointers [93].

Late Binding. In LISP, binding occurs when a function is called. To achieve this late binding, several features are introduced: generic operators (operand types are not declared) and implicit storage reclamation.

Data Typing. In most LISP programs there are no type declarations. This implies that data types must be checked at run time. In languages such as Pascal or C, variable types are declared and checked at compilation time. Having run-time type checking favors rapid

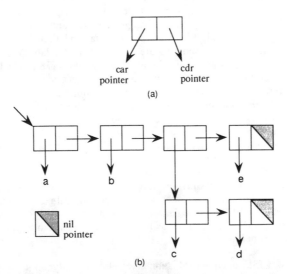

FIGURE 10.2 LISP representation of lists. *(a)* A list cell. *(b)* Representation of the list (a b (c d) e) using list cells.

program development but makes run-time operations more difficult. At run time, a function evaluation requires type checking on one or more of the following types: symbols, list cell, integer numbers, floating-point numbers, complex numbers, rational numbers, arrays, and lists.

Run-Time Memory. The number of list cells that would be required during the execution of a program is not known and difficult to predict. The dynamic creation of objects would require a large amount of memory at run time. LISP programmers tend to create many new data objects; programmers, however, do not reclaim these objects when they are no longer needed. Heap space would be a limiting factor if no memory reclamation mechanism were used; i.e., the machine would run out of heap space. When cells have no pointers that point to them, these cells are considered garbage. The heap space that these cells have should be recovered and made available for reuse.

10.2.2 Requirements for LISP Machines

To design and study LISP machines, it is necessary to review the requirements that must be met by such machines. Requirements for LISP machines include the following [46]:

Late binding: Many LISP operators are generic; their type and operand are not declared at compilation time and may not be known until run time.

Memory-access-intensive: Most LISP data structures use pointers that are stored in memory. Thus, a dedicated architecture must be able to process these pointers efficiently.

Frequent function invocation: Recursive calling of functions is not only a powerful feature of LISP but is also systematically used by programmers. In many instances, allocation of resources may be a problem, since there is no knowledge in advance of the number of recursive invocations.

Garbage collection: Due to late binding, memory resources are allocated dynamically. At run time LISP programs are "memory-hungry" and require a large amount of memory. The allocated memory must be reclaimed once it is not in use; this process is done by a garbage collection process. Garbage collection is frequently implemented in software, with hardware support. Without a garbage collection process, the amount of storage required to run AI programs would be unacceptably high.

Shared-memory model of data: Data objects created during execution time are considered to belong to the whole concurrent program.

10.2.3 Uniprocessor Machines for LISP

Single-processor architectures for LISP started to appear in the late 1970s. Most of these early processors were experimental architectures and limited by technology. However, important concepts were developed. Some of these processors as well as modern ones are listed here with their major contributions.

Scheme-79. This processor was developed and implemented at the Massachusetts Institute of Technology's Artificial Intelligence Laboratory [114]. Scheme-79 directly interprets typed-pointer Scheme, a LISP dialect. All compound data are built from list nodes which have two pointers (CAR and CDR). Each 32-bit pointer has three fields: a 24-bit data field, a 7-bit type field, and a 1-bit storage allocator bit. These two pointers allow the conversion of any expression into a list. The register file in Scheme-79 consists of a set of special-purpose registers with built-in operators. There are 10 specialized registers: the *EXP register* for the current expression, the *VAL register* that holds the value of the last expression, the *ARGS register* that points at the arguments of the current expression, the *STACK pointer,* the *DISPLAY register* which is a pointer to the CONS of the arguments, the *New CELL register* that has addresses for new cells, the *TEMP register* which stores intermediate arguments, the *MEMTOP register,* the *RETPC register* that stores the return program counter address, and the *MARKCOUNT register* which is used for garbage collection purposes. Static binding for LISP programs is used, and a marking garbage collection is implemented.

LISP Machine.   The LISP machine was developed and implemented at the Massachusetts Institute of Technology [8]. The LISP machine was designed as a single-task processor. A very unspecialized 32-bit microprogrammed CONS processor is employed. A large amount of specialized microcode to support LISP is stored in a microcode memory (16K of 68-bit words). LISP programs are dynamically bound. An incremental marking garbage collection is implemented in this architecture.

MIT CADR.   The CADR machine is the second generation of LISP machines at the Massachusetts Institute of Technology. The name comes from the way the second element of a list is extracted, e.g., (car (cdr *a-list*)). CADR is a 32-bit processor machine (24-bit data and 8-bit tag) and microcoded to check data types on all the operations. It is a stack machine (which seems natural for LISP processing). Incremental garbage collection was introduced in this machine.

Lambda Machine.   The Lambda Machine was based on the CADR architecture and developed by LISP Machines Inc. [22]. This machine combines the Lambda processor, 32 bit NuBu, ETHERNET-II, and Zeta LISP Operating environment. The processor is 32 bits wide (24-bit data and 8-bit data-type tags) with virtual memory and cache capabilities.

Symbolics 3600.   The Symbolics 3600 family models were designed by Symbolics based on the LISP machine [85, 86]. This machine uses a four-stage instruction pipeline under the control of a horizontal microcode. The pipeline stages are *instruction,* which has an instruction buffer that holds several instructions, providing fast access; *decode,* which finds addresses of the microcode functions and passes the arguments; the *execute stage,* which has a tag processor that allows it to check data types at run time; and the *write stage,* which stores the results. The Symbolics 3600 has a 36-bit processor: 32-bit data and 8-bit tag (4 bits are overlapped). The machine memory is tagged to allow garbage collection in hardware.

Alpha.   Alpha is a virtual stack machine that was developed by Fujitsu [49]. A value cache is introduced to search for current values of variables. When variables are not found in the value cache, frames on the stack are searched. Once the variable is found, it is put in the value stack for future references. The virtual stack architecture keeps a portion of some process stacks in the physical stack; therefore, there is no overhead when a process switch occurs. Garbage collection in this machine uses the virtual memory.

Table 10.1 summarizes the architectures presented here and provides information on some other machines. *Reduced instruction set computer* (RISC) approaches for LISP processing are increasing [109, 110].

TABLE 10.1 Uniprocessor Machines for LISP

LISP machine	Language	Features
Scheme-79 [114]	Scheme	Special-purpose registers Static binding Marking GC
LISP machine [8]	ZetaLISP	Microcoded processor Dynamic binding Incremental marking GC
Lambda machine [22]	ZetaLISP	NuBus multiprocessor 32-bit processor
Symbolics 3600 [85]	ZetaLISP, Flavors	Run-time type checking Hardware GC
Tektronix 4000	Franz LISP	Uses Motorola 68010/20
COLIBRI [45]	Common LISP	RISC coprocessor Generational dynamic GC
Alpha [49]	UtiLISP	Value cache Virtual stack Virtual memory GC
T1 Explorer	Common LISP	NuBus Tagged memory Microprogrammed

10.2.4 Multiprocessor Machines for LISP

Halstead [46] has identified the following as the major machine design challenges:

1. *Run-time typing*. Operand type is checked when a function is called.
2. *Function calling*. LISP programs are composed of many functions that could be called in a nested and recursive manner.
3. *Garbage collection*. Due to the large dynamic generation of data objects and structures (or lists), collection of unused memory space is required.
4. *Late binding*. Variable and function bindings occur at run time when the current value is required.
5. *Pointer chasing*. Lists are implemented with pointers (as shown in Fig. 10.2).
6. *Small data transfers*. Unanticipated small data transfers between processors (or processes) are frequent.
7. *Replication of data*. In multiprocessor machines, data replication is required in order to provide fast access to data structures. However, this may create a data consistency problem.

8. *Frequent process creation.* Recursive calls tend to create new processes at an extremely high rate.

9. *Frequent synchronization.* Synchronization between the processes is required to obtain deterministic computations.

These challenges lead to five major design decisions in the multiprocessor field [46]:

1. *Machine scale,* which deals with the number of processing elements in the machine
2. *Machine overall organization,* which deals with the processor synchronization, MIMD (multiple-instruction multiple-data) streams or SIMD (single-instruction multiple-data) architectures
3. *Addressing, caching, and replication,* which deal with data storage and access
4. *Run-time storage allocation and garbage collection,* which address the need for dynamic storage allocation and reclamation
5. *Latency avoidance and tolerance* (since there are always communication latencies the multiprocessor architecture should be able to tolerate some)

Most of the new architectures for LISP processing are multiprocessor architectures. A number of machines for LISP have been proposed, designed, and built. In this section, some architectures and their major contributions are described.

EM-3.   The ETL data-driven machine 3 (EM-3) was designed by the Electrotechnical Laboratory and Keio University [136, 137]. A novel control mechanism is implemented in order to provide eager evaluation, which is needed for data-driven computing. This mechanism generates pseudo- and partial results that are used when a function is called. Each of the homogeneous processing elements is based on the M68000 processor and has an I/O interface to the control processor and a packet memory control unit to interface with the other processing elements.

MASA.   The *MultiLISP architecture for symbolic applications* (MASA) is a communication-oriented architecture for parallel LISP programs. This architecture is being developed by the Massachusetts Institute of Technology and NEC Corporation [48]. Data values are tagged pointers with three fields: *data, type,* and *generation.* A MASA processor supports a four-stage pipeline. In stage 1, the instruction fetch unit determines the frame number of the task, reads the program counter, and fetches the instruction. In stage 2, two operands are fetched from the register file. In stage 3, tag checking and arithmetic and logic operations are executed. In stage 4, the results are stored. Incremental garbage collection is supported by an *old/new bit* that is associated with each memory location. MultiLISP, a dialect of LISP, is used to provide parallelism [47].

AHR Machine.   The AHR (Arquitecturas Heterarquicas Reconfigurables) machine for Pure LISP was developed and implemented at the National University of Mexico [44]. Argument evaluation is order-independent in Pure LISP, thus it is possible to evaluate them in parallel. The AHR machine has a high-speed bus to which each LISP processor is connected by means of a mailbox. There is a section of *active memory* that holds the programs being executed. A *fifo* has the pointer to LISP nodes ready to be executed. The distributor assigns a node to a LISP processor. The LISP processor has a Z-80A microprocessor with 16 kilobytes of private memory and mailbox petition latches.

SPUR.   The SPUR system (symbolic processing using RISCs) is an example of multiprocessor architectures for LISP [58, 117]. The architecture consists of 6 to 12 high-

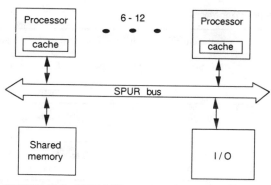

FIGURE 10.3 SPUR LISP machine.

performance homogeneous processors, a global shared memory, and a SPUR bus (see Fig. 10.3). To reduce traffic on the SPUR bus and improve system performance, each processor has a cache memory and virtual addressing is used. Virtual address needs no translation on any cache hit. The *central processing unit* (CPU) is based on the RISC II [92] design with hard-wired control and a large register file. The processing-element (PE) organization is shown in Fig. 10.4. Some implemented instructions in this CPU are tailored to process LISP programs; instructions include car, cdr, read-tag, write-tag, and load/store 40-bit word. The processor has a *floating-point unit* (FPU) that executes floating-point arithmetic operations; many symbolic computations require arithmetic operations as well.

Function call and return are implemented as basic instructions in the RISC CPU. This approach improves the machine performance, since these two instructions are frequently used. SPUR is a tagged architecture where the tags are used to identify the data type as well as for garbage collection purposes. Benchmarks have indicated that SPUR can be up to 10 times faster than existing computers. In Taylor [117], SPUR (with a clock of 6.67 MHz) is compared to Symbolics 3600 and DEC Vax 8600.

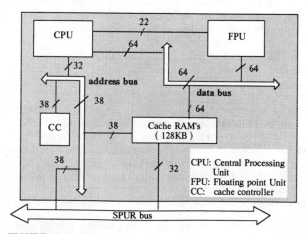

FIGURE 10.4 SPUR's processing element.

TABLE 10.2 Multiprocessor Machines for LISP

System	Language	Interconnection	Features
EM-3 [136]	EMLISP	Delta network	Data-driven 16 homogeneous PEs Incremental GC
MASA [48]	MultiLISP QLISP	N/A	Four-stage pipeline
AHR machine [44]	Pure LISP	High-speed bus	Mailbox communication Processors based on Z80
iPSC	Common LISP	Hypercube	256 Intel 80286 General-purpose multiprocessor
Connection Machine [59]	*LISP, CM-LISP	Hypercube	SIMD machine Bit-serial processors
Concurrent LISP machine [113]	C-LISP	Multibus	PEs based on MC68000 Hardware GC

Table 10.2 is a list of parallel architectures for LISP processing. Issues such as load balancing [16] and memory management [77] should be addressed in the design of a parallel architecture for LISP.

10.3 GARBAGE COLLECTION

Languages for AI applications tend to consume new storage locations at a much greater rate than do conventional programming languages. In conventional languages (such as Pascal, Fortran, C, and Ada), the variables that are stored in fixed locations are changed repeatedly. Thus, at compilation time these locations can be assigned. There is no need for run-time storage reallocation.

In languages for AI such as LISP and Prolog, most of the data structures are dynamically created; thus, no resource allocation can be done at compilation time. Therefore, any reuse of storage locations must be achieved by means of *garbage collection* (GC). Without a proper scheme to allow the reuse of storage locations, the amount of storage required to run AI programs would be unacceptably high. Large LISP programs spend 10 to 30 percent of the execution time in garbage collection [20, 96, 73].

In GC, a cell is defined as a number (1 or larger) of contiguous computer words; this is similar to a list. When cells are not required or needed, these cells become garbage. No pointer of reachable cells can access these unused cells.

Garbage collection is triggered automatically when there is no space in memory or shortly before this happens. When GC is performed, the program execution comes to a halt while the collector attempts to reclaim storage space. There are two basic GC phases:

- *Identification*. In this phase the collector identifies the storage space that may be reclaimed.

- *Incorporation*. Reclaimable space is incorporated into the memory area that is available to the user.

The identification phase can be performed by using counters or by marking cells. Counters keep track of the number of references to cells. Those cells with zero references are considered inaccessible. In the cell-marking method, all cells that can be accessed are marked; thus, inaccessible cells are not marked.

The incorporation phase can be accomplished by using a free-list method or a compaction method. The free-list method uses a list that has pointers to all available cells (or spaces); this list is updated every time that a cell is used or GC is executed. The compaction method moves all the cells that are in use to one side of the memory and the unused cells to the other side. There are three ways that compaction can be done: arbitrary, linearizing, and sliding. This classification is related to the relative position of cells after compaction; i.e., this tells how related cells are moved in memory. In arbitrary compaction, cells are put wherever they fit in memory. In linearizing compaction, all the cells are arranged in a linear manner; i.e., cells that have pointers to each other are put together. In sliding compaction, cells are moved without changing their relative position in memory, i.e., cells are slid to empty cells.

Collecting Single-Sized Cells. A LISP cell has two fields: left (car) and right (cdr). Each field has pointers to other cells or to atoms. An atom is a cell with no pointer; i.e., atoms are the leaves of a tree. Each cell has two boolean fields: atomic/nonatomic and marked. These fields help in the garbage collection process.

10.3.1 Garbage Collection Analysis

Let m be the total number of memory cells and n the number of marked cells. The collection time is defined as

$$\text{Collection time} = \alpha n + \beta(m - n)$$

where α is the average time to mark an unused cell and β is the average time to collect a free cell.

It is usually assumed that $\alpha > \beta$; that is, marking a cell takes longer than collection of a free cell. The term $m - n$ is the number of cells that will be collected. The cost per collected word is given as

$$\text{Cost per collected word} = \frac{\text{collection time}}{m - n}$$

$$= \frac{\alpha n + \beta(m - n)}{m - n}$$

$$= \frac{\alpha n}{m - n} + \beta$$

$$= \frac{\alpha \rho}{1 - \rho} + \beta$$

where $\rho = n/m$ represents the ratio between marked cells and total memory cells. When $\rho = \frac{1}{4}$, we have

$$\text{Cost per collected word} = \frac{\alpha}{3} + \beta$$

which shows how the cost is affected by the marking process.

Garbage Collection Analysis in the Entire Run.   The GC analysis for each collection was presented above. Here for the entire run the collection cost and performance are analyzed.

Let N be the total number of cells collected in the entire run and T the time spent in useful program execution. The execution time of the entire program is

$$\text{Total execution time} = N\left(\frac{\alpha\rho}{1 + \rho} + \beta\right) + T$$

The cost of collection should be proportional to the space (cells that can be in memory) and the time spent on computing. Thus, we have

$$\text{Cost} = m\left[N\left(\frac{\alpha\rho}{1 - \rho} + \beta\right) + T \right]$$

$$= mN\left(\frac{\alpha\rho}{1 - \rho} + \beta\right) + mT$$

$$= mN\left(\frac{\alpha\rho}{1 - \rho} + \beta + \gamma\right)$$

where γ is the useful computation time per word collected and is given by $\gamma = T/N$. The minimum cost with respect to m is when

$$\rho = \frac{1}{1 + \rho} \qquad \text{where} \qquad \rho = \left(\frac{\alpha}{\beta + \gamma}\right)^{1/2}$$

10.3.2 Garbage Collection Approaches

There are a number of GC approaches. The basic principle of these approaches is described below.

Compacting Collector.   In this GC approach, holes that are left by reclaimed data are put together; i.e., active data are compacted in memory. Figure 10.5 shows how this collector compresses the active data. This type of collection requires copying the active data as well as reallocating references, which may require considerable time. Advantages of this scheme include simple allocation of new data in the storage.

Incremental Collector.   This collector scans memory and copies few words at a time. With this approach it would seem that the user's program never stops, since no major garbage collection is done at a single step.

Generational Collector.   It has been observed that many of the data become garbage shortly after their creation while old data remain active most of the time. If data are grouped and stored by age, garbage collection could be done more efficiently. The

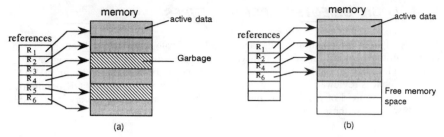

FIGURE 10.5 Compacting collector. *(a)* Memory before garbage collection. *(b)* Memory after garbage collection.

generational approach would attempt to collect the young cells more frequently and the old cells less frequently. In this approach references from old cells to young cells should be taken care of at collection time.

Reference Count. This approach requires an extra field to hold a count of the number of references. As functions finish computations, the data (or list) are abandoned, so the count must be decreased. However, when a new function is called and there is a pointer to the cell, the count is increased. When a cell has a count of zero (i.e., no cell is pointing to this cell), the cell space can be reclaimed by the GC. In cyclic structures (or lists), GC may not be easy since there will be always a pointer to the cells in the structure. For distributed systems this approach requires synchronization.

10.3.3 Hardware for Garbage Collection

Although most of the effort in GC algorithms and implementations has been in software approaches, there are new approaches that implement GC in hardware. Due to the demand for high performance required for AI machines, hardware solutions to GC may be attractive [82].

Table 10.3 shows the efforts that have been made to implement GC systems.

TABLE 10.3 Garbage Collection Systems

Scheme	GC approach	Features
Distributed GC [9]	Count	Distributed reference count Weighted references
Distributed GC [6]	Mark	Two-phase: marker and collector Synchronizer implemented
VLSI garbage collection [73]	Temporal	Compacting, incremental, generational GC Barrier traps trigger the GC Hardware modifications to MIPS R2000 proposed
Parallel machine GC [130]	Count	Graph reduction system Weighted reference counters

10.4 LOGIC-ORIENTED ARCHITECTURES

The use of logic programming languages (such as Prolog) for AI applications has increased in recent years. In this section we review the principles of logic programming. Most single-processor architectures are based on the *Warren abstract machine* (WAM) model, which is reviewed here along with some architectures. AND and OR parallelism are used in the field of parallel computer architectures for logic. In the last part of this section we review these architectures.

10.4.1 Predicate Calculus

Predicate calculus is a formal language that provides the bases for logic programming. Predicate calculus allows one to express a wide variety of statements. The legitimate expressions are called the *well-formed formulas* (wff's). The basic components of the predicate calculus language are *predicate symbols, variable symbols, function symbols,* and *constant symbols.* Predicate symbols are used to represent relations in a domain of discourse. Variable symbols are allowed to have indefinite assignments as well as set relationships that satisfy certain constraints. Function symbols denote functions within the domain of discourse. Constant symbols provide a means to specify facts that are not modifiable.

For example, the sentence "All elephants are gray" might be represented in predicate calculus as

$$\text{ELEPHANT } (x) \Rightarrow \text{COLOR}(x, \text{ GRAY})$$

where COLOR is a predicate symbol that denotes the relationship between an object (which is represented by a variable symbol x) and a color (that is represented by a constant symbol GRAY).

There are connectives that allow the combination of formulas to form complex wff's. These connectives include *and* ($\wedge$), *or* ($\vee$), and *implies* ($\Rightarrow$). The connective *and* is used to connect two wff's; the resulting formula is true only if the two formulas are true. The connective *or* is used to represent an "exclusive or" of two or more wff's. The connective *implies* is used for representing if-then statements.

Finding substitutions of terms for variables to make formulas (or expressions) identical is an important process in AI; this provides inference capabilities. This process of matching certain subexpressions is called *unification,* which involves substitution of variables (*substitution instance*) for another variable, a function, or a constant (*ground instance*).

Prolog is the most widely used among the logic programming languages. Many architectures for logic programming are designed to run Prolog or a Prolog-like language. Prolog consists mainly of a set of rules, facts, and variables. Within the rules there might be connectives (such as AND and OR). These connectives can be a source of parallelism (called *AND parallelism* and *OR parallelism*) since they are connecting two (or more) subgoals which may be processed in parallel.

For more information about predicate calculus, readers are referred to Nilsson [89, 90] and Winston [133].

10.4.2 Uniprocessor for Logic Programming

The majority of single-processor architectures for logic (or Prolog) are based on the WAM model. This model provides an abstract computer organization model for the execution of logic programs.

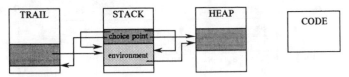

FIGURE 10.6 WAM storage model.

Warren Abstract Machine. David Warren developed a set of techniques for compiling Prolog that led to a very efficient implementation of unification [128]. The main data areas are the code area, which contains instructions and other program data, and three stack areas (the stack, the heap, and the trail). Procedure invocations make the stacks grow while backtracking contracts them. The heap contains all the structures and lists created by unification and procedure unification. The trail contains references to variables that have been bound during unification and which must be unbound when backtracking occurs. The WAM model defines a stack with two frames (*environments* and *choice points*) which are of variable length. The environment frame holds local variables and bookkeeping information, whereas the choice-point frame holds arguments passed to a procedure and backtracking information. The WAM model storage is shown in Fig. 10.6.

The WAM model has the following state and argument registers: E (a pointer to current environment), B (current choice point), H (heap pointer), HB (heap backtrack pointer), TR (trail pointer), P (current instruction pointer), CP (continuation instruction pointer), S (heap structure pointer), and X0, . . . , X15 (argument registers). The top of the stack has the most recent pointers for E and B. The backtracking information in a choice point has a pointer to the environment active when the choice point was created. The WAM model works as follows: A caller passes arguments (that are stored in dedicated argument registers) and control to the callee. When there are several clauses to try (i.e., more than one clause can potentially provide a match), a choice point is created and loaded with the arguments and backtracking information (E, B, H, CP, P, TR). Unification with the first clause is attempted; if the arguments match with the clause variables and constants, the goals of the clause are called sequentially. If there is no match, the machine state is restored to the current choice point. When no alternatives remain, the choice point is removed.

When a goal (or subgoal) is to be solved, there may be several different clauses that could unify with this goal. Some clauses may lead to failure while others may end successfully. In sequential logic only one clause can be analyzed at a time. Prolog implementations select the first unifying clause; if failure occurs, then the second clause is chosen after a backtracking process. This process continues until one clause leads to a satisfactory unification or until all the clauses have been tried.

Single-Processor Machines for Logic. The WAM model has influenced most of the uniprocessor architectures for logic programming (in particular Prolog). A brief description of some of these architectures and their contributions follows.

Pipelined Prolog Processor. This architecture is a single-user, single-pipeline Prolog processor [120]. The processor implements an instruction set with five types of instructions: *get, put, unify, procedural,* and *indexing*. The get instruction is responsible for getting and matching the head of a clause. The put instruction finds the arguments of a goal in the body of a clause and loads such arguments into the A registers. The unify instruction attempts unification of the arguments of a structure with existing structures; this instruction is responsible for creating new structures. The procedural instruction controls transfer and environment allocation. The indexing instruction links the different clauses that make up a procedure.

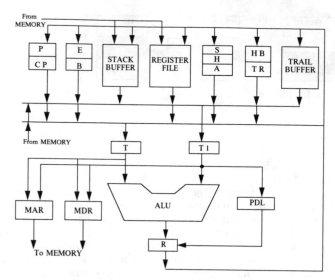

FIGURE 10.7 Pipelined Prolog processor data path.

The execution unit (shown in Fig. 10.7) of this architecture has a three-stage pipeline (called C, E, and P). During the C stage, the temporary registers (T and T1) are loaded with data from the stack buffer, register file, trail buffer, or control counters. In the E stage, the *arithmetic logic unit* (ALU) executes an instruction with arguments in T and T1 and stores the result in register R, memory address (MAR) and memory data (MDR) registers are set, and the push-down list (PDL) register (which is used during unification) may be modified. During the last stage, P, new values are put into the context arrays.

Prolog Processor. This 32-bit processor for compiled Prolog is based on the WAM model and a Harvard architecture structure [19]. The horizontal microprogrammed processor manages the data directly and uses an external unit to prefetch and align code, which is read from the program memory. In addition to the registers described for the WAM model, this processor has the following registers: Register file A, I (code address for register file A), M (frame address for A), NP (number of permanent variables used in the current count), and N (permanent variable displacement register). This processor has a prefetch structure that translates the opcode into a physical address of the macrocode and manages a buffer of instructions. This prefetch structure results in reduced memory bandwidth requirements. An architecture for a Prolog interpreter is proposed in Civera et al. [18].

PSI Machine. The *personal sequential inference* (PSI) machine was designed as part of the fifth-generation computer system project [115]. A modified version of Prolog called KL0 (kernel language version 0) is used as the machine language. The PSI CPU has a sequence control unit, a data processing address, and a memory. The data processing unit includes a *work file* (WF) which is a multipurpose register file (40-bit × 1K words). Of the WF 128 words are part of the directly addressable area; the other WF areas are accessed indirectly. There are two indirect accessing modes: The *indirect addressing mode using WFAR* uses two address registers, called WFAR1 and WFAR2, which point to a flexible boundary of words; this approach is used for push, pop, and limit checking operations. The *indirect addressing mode using PDR and CDR* uses registers PDR and

TABLE 10.4 Uniprocessor Machines for Logic Programming

Logic machine	Language	Features
Pipelined Prolog processor [120]	Prolog	Three-stage pipeline execution Interleaved memory Microprogrammed controller
Prolog processor [19]	Compiled Prolog	Harvard structure Horizontal microprogrammed controller Data memory organized in stacks
PSI machine [115]	KL0	Large work file Special addressing for WF Interpretive execution
IPP [1]	Prolog	Microprogrammed controller Dedicated tag processing hardware Address and data ALUs; write buffers
Data buffer for sequential Prolog [118,119]	Prolog	Local memories Smart cache (selective copyback)

CDR to point to the parent and current predicate call, respectively. The clause currently being processed is stored in a temporal *local frame buffer* (LFB).

Table 10.4 summarizes proposed or implemented uniprocessor architectures for logic programming. RISC approaches are being used in this application [124].

10.4.3 Parallelism in Logic Programming

A number of approaches for parallel execution of logic programming languages have been developed. The majority of approaches involve variations of two mechanisms: *OR parallelism* and *AND parallelism*. These mechanisms, as well as computer architectures for parallel execution logic programs, are described below.

OR Parallelism. When a subgoal can be solved by any of several independent clauses, then OR parallelism can be achieved. Although only one clause that leads to success is required, in OR parallelism several selected clauses may lead to success, thus several answers may be produced for a query. Variables can be assigned to different values in each of the subgoals. Assignments in one subgoal do not affect the assignments in another.

Backtracking is eliminated in this approach; there is no need to trace back on unification failures since the other clauses (in *choice points*) are being computed in parallel. This type of parallelism has an unlimited number of independent processes that should be controlled to avoid unnecessary computations. There is no need for communication and cooperation between the different activities.

Two issues need to be addressed in the design of a machine for this computing approach: *synchronization* and *merge*. In many cases, it is necessary to stop the computation of a subgoal when a solution is found. That is, unnecessary processes must be terminated. Once the processing has been stopped, the solution must be computed. This is done by tracing the solution path.

Bagof.   This architecture is based on the data flow concept [17]. There is a token pool where all the rules that can be executed are stored. The optimal number of *processing elements* (PEs) would depend on the OR parallelism level that would be accepted and the communication degradation between the pool of tokens and the PEs. Figure 10.8 shows the OR-parallel token machine model. This architecture has a static memory to store the program code and a dynamic memory block to deal with environment and storage management. Each PE takes a token from the pool, then reads the program to be executed (which is in the static allocation block). As a result of the program execution, new tokens are crated and the dynamic allocation block is modified. In the dynamic allocation block, the assignment of all the variables is stored.

AND Parallelism.   In this type of parallelism, only one of the clauses is attempted by processing two (or more) subgoals of this clause in parallel [21]. These subgoals may be processed separately. When a subgoal cannot be solved, backtracking to the previous (or parent) subgoal set must occur. All subgoals in a subgoal set in AND parallelism are working on the same problem; therefore, each must succeed if the subgoal set is to succeed. The subgoal set shares a common set of variables and data; any change to a variable may affect the computation of another subgoal. Special care should be taken when two (or more) subgoals attempt to assign values to variables; a variable must have the same value in all subgoals. This problem is called the *binding-conflict* problem. Therefore, a communication mechanism among leaves of the solution tree must be included in the design of machines for this type of parallelism. Such a communication mechanism may be accomplished by approaches in hardware, software, or a combination of both.

AND parallelism has the potential of producing a single solution more quickly than either sequential logic or OR-parallel logic; in producing a single solution all the different subgoals are solved in parallel. *Restricted AND parallelism* (RAP) has been proposed in order to deal with the binding-conflict problem and maintain Prolog side effects [24, 25, 56]. In RAP, only subgoals that have no common unsigned variables could be processed in parallel.

A description of some architectures for AND parallelism and AND/OR parallelism is provided below. In this description the main features of each system are pointed out.

MANIP-2.   MANIP-2 is a multiprocessor architecture for evaluating AND/OR logic trees [76]. This machine's search is based on heuristic information about the problem to be solved. A probabilistic model that helps to estimate a subgoal evaluation overhead is

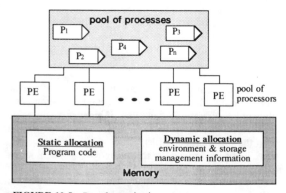

FIGURE 10.8   Bagof organization.

used to decide which part of the tree should be expanded. This approach reduces the searching process. MANIP consists of several subproblem memory controllers that have a number of processors; these controllers get a subgoal and compute it.

PIM-D. This architecture is a data flow approach to the *parallel inference machine* (PIM) [66, 67]. KL1 programs are compiled into data flow graphs for PIM-D execution. The PIM-D architecture is based on the tagged-token data flow architecture [5] and supports AND and OR parallelism. The configuration of the machine consists of PE modules and structure memory (SM) modules that are interconnected through a hierarchical bus structure. The PE structure includes the following modules: *packet queue unit* (PQU), which is a *first-in first-out* (FIFO) queue to store temporary results; *instruction control unit* (ICU), which checks the received data for instructions to be executed and readiness; several *atomic processing units* (APUs), which receive executable instruction packets; and a *network node* (NN), which sends and receives data from other PEs.

Table 10.5 lists a number of architectures for parallel processing of logic programs. The main features are listed as well as the interconnection network and the logic programming language.

To speed up logic computations, other hardware/software approaches may be used, including unification [134, 70], parallel matching [71], data flow computing [55], and concurrent logic programming [104].

10.5 KNOWLEDGE-ORIENTED ARCHITECTURES

Knowledge representation and manipulation are fundamental requirements for AI applications [105]. Knowledge representation has been studied intensively by the AI community for an extended time [63]. The objective in knowledge representation is to allow AI programs to behave as if they knew something about the problems they solve. Schemes for knowledge representation include logic programming, semantic networks, procedural interpretation, production systems, and frames [7, 116]. Knowledge representations are found in applications such as automated deduction systems, inference machines, expert systems, and knowledge bases. Processing a large body of knowledge tends to require considerable time due to the nondeterministic nature of the AI problems. Conventional uniprocessor architectures, which are designed mainly for sequential and deterministic computations, are not able to meet these performance requirements. As the domain and complexity of AI systems grow, the performance of existing computer systems tends to degrade drastically and these systems can no longer solve AI problems on acceptable time scales. Special-purpose computers are needed to manipulate large knowledge representations.

Rule-based systems and semantic networks are widely used for knowledge representation. In this section these approaches are presented as well as some architectures that compute them.

10.5.1 Rule-Based Systems

Rule-based systems (or production systems) have been extensively used in the field of cognitive science, in the study of problem-solving systems, and in the study of learning systems [43]. Rule-based programs have been developed for expert-systems applications which are used in a number of fields, such as computer-aided design, medicine, and computer operation and troubleshooting.

TABLE 10.5 Multiprocessor Machines for Logic Programming

Machine	Language	Interconnection	Features
Bagof [17]	Bagof	NA	OR parallelism Data flow approach Static and dynamic memory
Aquarius [33]	Prolog	Bus and crossbar	Special-purpose processor instructions for AND parallelism, OR parallelism, and backtracking Two memory modules: synchronization and main memory
MANIP-2 [125]		Global Broadcast bus	Heuristic guided AND/OR parallelism Message passing PE clusters with local memory
PIM-R [91]	KL1	Multistage network	Reduction computing approach Inference modules logically connected as a mesh
PIE [41]	An extension of Prolog (proof diagrams)	Switching network (two levels)	Goal-rewriting model for OR parallelism Large number of inference units that have unification processors and definition memory
PIM-D [67]	KL1	Hierarchical bus structure	Data flow computing approach Tagged-token architecture
PARK [80]	PARK-Prolog	Common and local busses	Four-processor (MC68000) shared memory AND/OR parallelism
Multitransputer [15, 68]	Prolog	Mesh	Inmos transputer processors

Rule-Based Systems Background.   Although there have been many different implementations of rule-based systems, all share some key properties [50]:

- Human knowledge is expressed in terms of conditional if-then rules.
- A rule-based system grows in skill as its collection of rules is increased.
- A wide range of possibly complex problems can be solved by selecting relevant rules and combining their results in appropriate ways.
- The best rule to be executed is determined dynamically.
- A rule-based system explains its conclusions by tracing back the rules that were applied to get a result.

Most of the rule-based systems are comprised of a set of if-then rules (which are called *productions* as well) stored in the rule memory, a database which is stored in a fact memory, and a working memory where assertions are stored. Each rule consists of a conjunction of condition elements corresponding to the if part of the rule and a set of actions that corresponds to the then part. Figure 10.9 shows the basic features of rule-based systems [50].

The cycle of a knowledge rule-based system consists of two phases:

1. *Match-and-select phase*. The system determines which rules can apply and chooses one in particular to execute. The if part of the rules is matched against the contents of the working memory (triggering data). The matching process yields a list of executable rules; one of these rules could be chosen for execution. If no rules are satisfied, then the interpreter halts.

2. *Execute (or act) phase*. The system interprets the selected rule and makes inferences that modify the system. Actions associated with each rule may add, delete, or modify elements in the working memory. At the end of this phase, the rule-based system goes back to the first phase again.

Parallelism in Rule-Based Systems. Gupta et al. [42, 43] have identified sources of parallelism within the rule-based system. These sources can potentially be exploited to improve the performance of computers for this application.

Rule-Level Parallelism. Triggering data are matched to each rule of the system in parallel, providing there are enough hardware resources (or a hardware scheme) to allow this level of parallelism. The rules that could process the data are then passed to the execution phase. Rule-level parallelism results in a small reduction of processing time. This is because of a small number of rules that are affected when there is a change in the working memory, sequential processing of the rules, and synchronization of parallel resources, memory contention, and scheduling.

Parallelism at rule level may be achieved by means of a *content-addressable memory* (CAM). Rules are stored in the CAM, and once the triggering data are available, they are matched with all the conditional parts of all the rules in memory [71].

Action Parallelism. When a rule fires, it makes a number of changes to the working memory. These changes, which are made to the right-hand side of the rule, could potentially be processed in parallel.

Architectures for Rule-Based Systems. Although the number of applications of rule-based systems is large, the number of computer architectures for these systems has remained small. As the complexity of the applications increases, new architectures are expected to be designed in order to achieve the performance demands.

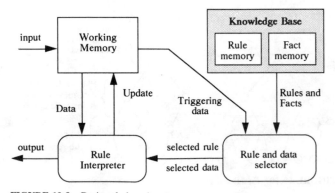

FIGURE 10.9 Basic rule-based system.

Production System Machine (PSM).   The PSM architecture is designed to process the rule-based systems which are based on a parallel rete algorithm [43]. The PSM is a shared-memory multiprocessor with 32 to 64 processing elements. For many large rule-based programs and shared-memory architecture, using more than 64 processors does not yield any additional speedup. There is hardware support for a task scheduler that helps to queue activation nodes and assess pending nodes. There is a processor that is in charge of performing conflict resolution and the right-hand evaluation. The remaining processors are used for evaluating node activations in the rete network. Each processing element is conceived to be a high-performance RISC processor.

DADO.   DADO is a fine-grained architecture based on a binary tree structure [111, 112]. The proposed machine consists of a large number (on the order of 100,000) of processing elements, each containing its own processor, a small amount of local memory, and a specialized I/O switch. Each PE is capable of executing instructions that are either broadcast by an ancestor or stored in the local memory; thus, this machine can operate in two modes: SIMD and MIMD.

In DADO, each processing element handles a single rule. MIMD mode execution allows it to match triggering data with the production memory (PM) in parallel. Thus, a conflict rule set could potentially be found at each machine cycle. The working memory is stored on the processing elements that are below the PM (see Fig. 10.10). The binary tree is used in the selection of a rule for execution. The actions that are required by the selected rule are broadcast to all the PEs at the PM level.

Non-Von.   The non-Von machine is a massively parallel tree-structured architecture [60]. The proposed machine consists of a large number of *small processing elements* (SPEs). Each SPE has an 8-bit processor, a small amount of local memory (a maximum of 256 bytes), and an I/O switch. This machine can be dynamically modified to support various communication schemes. The leaves can be interconnected to form a two-dimensional (2D) mesh. The non-Von architecture has a small number of *large processing elements* (LPEs). The LPEs, which are closer to the root of the tree, are 32-bit commercially available processors; each of these processors has a significant amount of memory. A large PE stores the programs that are to be executed by SPEs as well as broadcasts instructions to its offspring. This feature allows the non-Von machine to operate in a multiple-SIMD fashion.

Table 10.6 summarizes some architectures for rule-based systems applications.

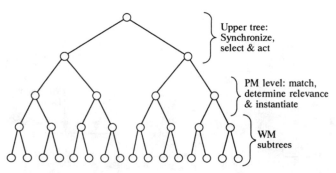

FIGURE 10.10   Functional divisions of the DADO tree.

TABLE 10.6 Computer Architectures for Rule-Based Systems

Machine	Interconnection	Features
PSM [43]	Shared busses	Shared memory Powerful processors Task scheduler in hardware
DADO [111]	Tree	Large number of processing elements Message passing SIMD and MIMD modes of operation
Non-Von [60]	Tree/mesh	Small processing elements in leaves Leaves connected in 2D mesh Large PEs at root levels
FAIM-1 [4]	Hexagonal mesh	Heterogeneous processors Shared memory

10.5.2 Semantic Networks

Semantic networks (SNs) have played a significant role in knowledge representation and manipulation research since their introduction [105, 107]. The SN approach provides a general capability for knowledge representation; it handles not only binary relations, but also unary and higher-order relations which make the SN an extremely powerful tool. An introduction to SN concepts and a description of some architectures for this application are presented below.

Semantic Network Background. R. M. Quillian introduced the idea of a semantic network [94]. Several proposals and changes have been made since. Brachman [13] provides an overview of these proposals. The basic principle of a semantic network is simple: Each node of the interpreted graph represents a concept, and the links between them represent relationships between concepts [135]. Figure 10.11 shows a semantic network. The more important issues of semantic networks are briefly described below.

Hierarchical Representation. Knowledge in a semantic network is represented in hierarchical form. The knowledge of whether an item belongs to a set is important for answering and retrieving facts [37]. A method of providing a hierarchical representation is to use the arcs (or links) to classify the concepts represented by various nodes [54, 105, 133]. An example of this method is shown in Fig. 10.11; the taxonomy is provided by means of arcs labeled is-a. For instance, in Fig. 10.11 the arc between ELEPHANT and MAMMAL represents the knowledge that ELEPHANT is a subset of MAMMAL.

Inheritance. As soon as human beings identify something, many assumptions are made, e.g., that birds fly, whales live in water, etc. A similar process can be done in semantic networks by means of inheritance. In a hierarchical representation, nodes at the lower levels inherit all the properties of nodes above them. The hierarchy determines the way that inheritance is passed; properties of a node do not affect the properties of nodes at higher levels. In Fig. 10.11, for example, Clyde is described as an elephant. However, there is no direct link that determines Clyde's color. By means of inheritance the color of Clyde can be obtained from the elephant description. Inheritance from another semantic network tree must be disallowed to avoid contradictions; e.g., any node below PLANT cannot inherit anything that is below ANIMAL.

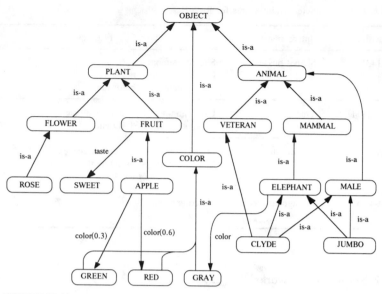

FIGURE 10.11   A semantic network.

Is-A Link.   Much representation of the world is concerned with the conceptual relations expressed in English sentences such as ''Peter is a bachelor'' and ''A dog is a domesticated mammal.'' The easiest way to get those statements into a semantic network scheme is to have a link that represents the ''is a'' part of such sentences [14]. Is-a connections form a hierarchy which makes semantic networks an efficient storage scheme. The link also allows the notion of inheritance of properties. There are a number of uses for an is-a link [14]. Among them are

- *Subset or superset:*   One node is a superset of another node. For example, the elephant set is a subset of mammals.

- *Generalization or specialization:*   Some properties of nodes may be true for a node below them. This is usually conditional to definitions on the higher-level node, providing there is no contradictory information.

- *Set membership:*   Nodes that represent individuals are set members of a higher-level node. For example, Clyde is a member of the elephant set.

Semantic Network Architectures.   Knowledge representations have been implemented on single-processor architectures. This approach, however, presents a serious drawback: Processing time is enormous due to large knowledge bases and no a priori search path. A simple query may lead to a search into many nodes in the knowledge tree. Some search-guiding heuristic algorithms may help to reduce the amount of searching. Such algorithms, however, are problem-domain-dependent and carefully handcrafted to handle each particular set of problems [36]. On a serial machine this process takes a time proportional to the number of nodes that have to be processed. With the advent of very large-scale integration (VLSI), the possibilities of *ultra-large-scale integration* (ULSI), and the possible advantages of *wafer-scale integration* (WSI), a cost-effective parallel architecture which can handle semantic networks may be achievable. Advantages of such an architecture include the following:

- Time is proportional to the number of nodes in the branch that provides the answer.
- Several alternatives are searched in parallel; if a query has more than one correct answer, all answers can be obtained with minimum extra effort.
- It is problem-domain-independent. The semantic network is processed in parallel; there is less need of problem-domain heuristic algorithms.
- Each node and link execute a small number of simple instructions.

Several systems for semantic networks have been developed in recent years; most of them have been implemented in hardware or simulated, although some are only proposals.

NETL. The NETL system was proposed by Fahlman [34, 36]. The NETL architecture consists of very simple hardware elements called *node units;* relationships among concepts are represented by hardware elements called *link units.* A serial controller is used to send simple instructions to node and link units by means of a shared bus. Each node has its own serial number, a few bits of information about the concept type that it represents and a few bits to mark the nodes. Links also have a few bits for information about relationship type. Two wires come out from the link unit, a wire is connected to the object being described, and a second wire goes to the node that represents the class where the object has been classified. Nodes and links are able to perform simple boolean operations. In a more recent version of NETL, a circuit-switching network called *hashnet* is used to establish communication between a node and a link. Hashnet is a permutation network that is able to establish one-to-one connections which can operate simultaneously. NETL can perform searches and inferences by means of a marker propagation scheme. The controller sets markers to nodes (which are part of a query), and then the markers are propagated; when they meet, the answer is found [34]. An example of the marker approach is shown in Fig. 10.12.

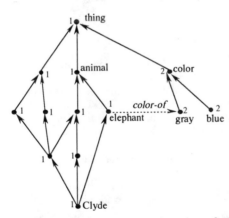

FIGURE 10.12 Marker propagation scheme for NETL. (All solid arcs are is-a links.)

The Connection Machine. The *Connection Machine* (CM) system was proposed by Hillis [59], and the prototype has been built at Thinking Machines Corporation (TMC). The TMC version of the full CM is intended to be a 1024 × 1024 PE array that is linked into a 14-cube. The system that has been built consists of 64K (256 × 256) synchronized-bit processors, each with a 4-kbit memory. The network of the CM was the prime effort of the machine design. The CM prototype has a 12-cube network with a packet-switching scheme. Each VLSI chip has 16 processing elements and a router processor, which is in charge of communicating between that PE cluster and the network. The CM is programmed in extensions of Common LISP and C. The original purpose of the CM design was to manipulate knowledge stored in semantic networks concurrently [59]. Each node and link are mapped onto a processing element; data are transferred by means of a message-passing scheme. The resulting architecture, however, turned out to be a general-purpose machine. This architecture executes data parallel algorithms: document retrieval from a large database, memory-based reasoning, and natural language processing.

Semantic Network Array Processor. The *semantic network array processor* (SNAP) architecture is currently under study at the University of Southern California [83]. The SNAP architecture consists of a square array of identical processing elements which are connected in a *nearest-neighbor interconnection* (NNI) scheme for local communication and in a column scheme for global communication. The SNAP architecture is operated by a single controller which also acts as an interface between the array and a host computer. Each cell can be microprogrammed if it is required; this feature allows cells to operate independently. Each cell (or processing element) has three units: a content-addressable memory, a processing unit (PU), and a communication unit (CU). The CAM has two modules: cell memory, which is the node local memory, and pointer memory, which is further subdivided to hold relation names and the addresses they relate to. The PU controls both processing in the CAM and the operation of the CU. The PU has a reduced set of primitive (micro-) instructions: AND, OR, NOT, SET, TEST, RESET, MASK, MATCH, CAR, and CDR. Data transfer between cells is executed by the communication unit. SNAP is capable of executing AI inference algorithms (i.e., deducing new facts from existing ones), since these algorithms are based on extensive searches and on a set of inference rules. The regularity of the SNAP array favors VLSI implementation.

Data Flow Approach. The use of data flow architectures for semantic network processing has been proposed by L. Bic [10]. In this approach, the semantic network is considered an interpreted data flow graph. Each node is able to accept, process, and emit value tokens which are transferred asynchronously in the network. The semantic network is represented as a data flow graph; any query must also be represented as a graph where at least one of the nodes or links corresponds to a constant while the others are variables. Processing a linear template is performed as follows: The template is sent, as a token, to all nodes in the semantic net that match the leftmost node. Data flow nodes which receive this token will replicate it along all edges that match the first template edge. These nodes then compare the second template, and the operation continues until the last template is compared. Then all the values of the variables can be obtained. All possible matches are found without the need for centralized control.

SNM. The *semantic network machine* (SNM) is based on a two-dimensional array [27]. SNM has a communication architecture that allows it to have local communication (this is with nearest neighbors) as well as global communication (with a host computer). A mapping algorithm is used to minimize long communication requirements as well as to achieve load balancing on the processing elements. Each PE has two sets of memories: CAM (where the semantic network is stored) and communication memory (where data are transferred to and from other processing elements). The PE handles all the pointers (which are required to represent a semantic network) in hardware. The CAM is used for parallel matching of symbols; thus, a symbol can be compared to the entire SN in parallel.

Table 10.7 lists the computer architectures that have been proposed for semantic network processing. A comprehensive discussion of the architectures for semantic networks can be found in Delgado-Frias and Moore [26]. Artificial intelligence processing features [83, 127] that influence the design of semantic network systems include these:

- Large problem size. The amount of information and the degree of parallelism are very large; therefore, a great deal of computational power is required.
- Intense memory access. To speed up computation and avoid bottlenecks, it is necessary to process data inside the memory.
- Frequent use of pattern retrieval operations. Parallel searches may be the most promising approach to this operation.
- Nondeterministic algorithms. There is no unique path from the initial state to the goal.

TABLE 10.7 Computer Architectures for Semantic Networks

Machine	Interconnection	Features
NETL [34]	Switching network	Marker-passing approach Processor handles up to 16 markers
THISTLE [35]	Switching network	Value-passing approach Simple PEs
Connection machine [59]	Hypercube	SIMD processing Bit-serial processors Message passing
SNAP [83, 84]	Mesh and global busses	2D array of processors CAM in each processor
Data flow [10]	NA	Data flow computing approach for semantic nets
SNM [27]	Mesh	2D array of processors Fault-tolerant architecture Static load balance CAM and memory in each processor
IX [38]	Pyramid	Pyramid structure with network processors

10.6 NEUROCOMPUTING ARCHITECTURES

The neurocomputing models are believed to have a potential for new architectures for computing systems; such systems may be able to achieve humanlike performance in some fields. In the literature, the artificial neural networks are also referred to as *connectionist models, parallel distributed processing models,* and *neuromorphic systems.* Regardless of the name, these networks are based on what is known about the biological nervous system. The potential benefits of these systems include fault tolerance, such that the malfunction of a few processing units does not significantly affect the overall performance. Learning is another benefit. A neural network modifies its internal connections and weights to satisfy the desired output with the present input sometime during a specific training stage. By building artificial neural networks, we may also generate a better understanding of the biological networks.

Interest in the field of neural networks (or neurocomputing) has greatly increased in recent years. Scientific publications, books, and new journals, as well as research and new developments, in this field have scaled up. In this section the main milestones in neurocomputing history are presented. This is followed by a description of the neural network computing requirements. Finally, some of the architectures for this application are described. This section's major concentration is on the architectural issues of neural networks; readers who are interested in fundamental issues of neurocomputing are referred to Chap. 18 of this book, Kohonen [72], Rumelhart [98, 99], Hecht-Nielsen [52], and Wasserman [129].

10.6.1 Historical Overview

Theories of modern neural computing probably started in 1943 with a paper by McCulloch and Pitts [79]. In this paper, the basic principle of neurocomputing used today was established. In 1949, Hebb proposed a learning law for the synapses of neurons [51]. Modifications of this learning algorithm are still in use.

The first functional neurocomputer, called *Mark I Perceptron,* was developed during 1957 and 1958 by Rosenblatt [97]. The Perceptron introduced the modern neural network computing concepts. Widrow and Hoff developed a neural network element called AD-ALINE (for *ada*ptive *line*ar *el*ement). This network was equipped with a new learning algorithm that introduced the concept of teacher, called *boss* in the paper [132].

In the late 1960s and early 1970s, serial processing (von Neumann style) dominated both psychology and artificial intelligence [98, 99]. In 1969, Minsky and Papert published the book *Perceptrons* which had devastating effects on neurocomputing research. *Perceptrons* discusses limitations of the neural networks that were investigated at that time based on a solid mathematical foundation.

It was not until 1982 that research on neurocomputing caught the attention of many researchers. This may be due to Hopfield's paper [61]. Hopfield, a well-established physicist, developed a model based on *energy landscapes* where neural networks are seeking minima in energy. In 1986, with the publication of the parallel distributed processing books [98, 99], the field received a tremendous amount of attention.

Readers interested in the history of neurocomputing are referred to Anderson and Rosenfeld [3]. Many of the historical papers that have contributed to the advance of neurocomputing have been reprinted in that book.

10.6.2 Neural Network Requirements

The computational task of a fully connected neural network is given by the following equation [98, 99]:

$$Y_i(t + 1) = F \left[\sum_{j=1}^{N} W_{ij} Y_j(t) - \phi \right] \qquad (10.1)$$

where N is the number of neurons in the network, W is the weight, Y is the output value of a neuron, ϕ is a threshold value (in many applications this value is set to zero), and F is the neuron activation function (usually a nonlinear one). This equation indicates that all Y_j's are involved in the computing of every neuron activation function. Every neuron is connected to every other neuron in the network through a connection weight W_{ij}. The following computational requirements can be drawn from the equation (for a fully connected network): N^2 multiplications, N product summations, N activation functions, and N-to-N neuron communications.

In order to achieve high performance for this type of neural network, two issues should be considered: *computation* and *communication*. The computation issue refers to the computing requirements (namely, multiplications, additions, and activation functions). The communication issue refers to the transfer of newly computed Y values to all neurons in the network. To achieve maximum computation performance would require N^2 multipliers, N summation units, and N activation function generators. When less hardware is involved, the resulting performance is degraded because not all the required computations can be done in parallel. Therefore, a degree of sequential processing is introduced. To achieve maximum communication performance would require an $N \times 1$–to–N communication scheme; each neuron has to communicate its output to the entire network. To achieve maximum performance, it is desired to execute computation and communication simultaneously. However, this is not possible due to the recursiveness of Eq. (10.1).

Although today's technology allows the integration of a large number of simple processors on a single chip, the high interconnectivity required by neural networks is one of the major challenges. In building a neural network circuit, a researcher faces many alternatives that are, in general, extremely difficult to evaluate. For example, decisions have to be made on the weight accuracy, storage devices, multiplication and addition circuits, communication scheme, and threshold function implementation as well as choosing whether to implement a high or a limited interconnectivity and whether to implement a learning algorithm on- or off-chip. A good design must take into account not only what is desired for a neural network system but also what is achievable with today's technology.

Another difficult choice is among digital, analog, or hybrid implementations. Each of these styles has advantages and drawbacks. A fully digital implementation of neural networks has some advantages: easier programmability, higher precision, freedom from noise, highly reliable storage devices, and technology-independent status. The main drawback is that arithmetic circuits are extremely large in comparison with analog devices; the size of the system will be dominated by these circuits. However, analog circuits for neurocomputing have some advantages: a smaller circuit size, higher speed, and possibly a lower power consumption. However, large integrated analog circuits may be difficult to design; problems such as weight storage, precision, and programmability must be addressed to implement analog networks.

10.6.3 Architectures for Neural Network Applications

Most of the research on neural networks has concentrated on theoretical studies and simulations on uniprocessor architectures. Simulations are, however, slow; therefore it is essential to have hardware implementations of such networks. A description of architectures for neurocomputing is provided here.

Ring Systolic Array. In the ring systolic array architecture [74], each processing element emulates a neuron. PEs are connected in a circular form, as shown in Fig. 10.13a. Weights are stored in a circular shifted order in the weight storage area. Figure 10.13b shows a simplified version of the processing element; the main hardware requirements would be a multiplier, an adder, and an accumulator.

At the initial step of a new update of the neural network values, all the accumulators of the ring systolic array are set to zero. The inputs to each processing element are the Y_j and W_{ij} values which are synchronized to arrive at the same time. All PEs multiply these two values and add the resulting value with the accumulator. Then the Y values are shifted by one; thus, Y_2 is an input to PE1, Y_3 is an input to PE2, and so on. At the same time the weights in all the weight storage areas are shifted: thus, W_{12} is an input to PE1, W_{23} is an input to PE2, and so on. After these two required shifts (which can be done at the same time), the PEs are used to multiply their inputs, add, and accumulate the result. This process continues until the Nth cycle, at which time the accumulators have the summations of all the products [see Eq. (10.1)]. New values for all the Y's are generated. Complex activation functions may increase the complexity of the PE. Kung and Hwang [74] describe how this architecture can deal with different learning algorithms in order to modify the weight strengths.

SPIN. The *s*equential *pi*pelined *n*eurocomputer (SPIN) processes completely one neuron at a time [122]. If Eq. (10.1) is expanded, the resulting set of equations shows that

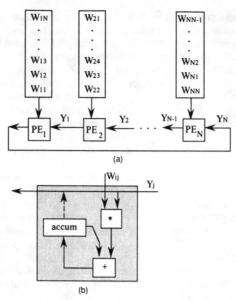

FIGURE 10.13 *(a)* Ring systolic array. *(b)* Simplified processing element.

each new Y value needs all the old Y values as well as a set of weights. Figure 10.14 shows this architecture. To obtain the maximum performance of this machine, it requires N multipliers, $\log_2 N$ binary adder stages, and an activation function generator.

The N products of a neuron are formed in parallel, these products are passed to the summation tree, and the resulting value is passed to the neuron activation function hardware. SPIN can use most of the hardware resources in a pipeline fashion: the multiplier stage might be computing the ith neuron, the summation tree might be computing the $(i - 1)$st neuron, and the activation function hardware might be working on the new value of the $(i - 2)$d neuron. If complex activation function hardware is required, this approach would need only one of these units.

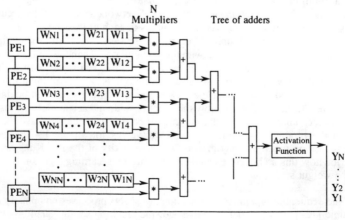

FIGURE 10.14 SPIN organization.

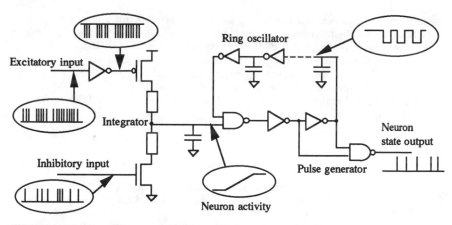

FIGURE 10.15 Circuit diagram of the pulse stream neuron.

Pulse Stream. A system that mimics biological neural networks is introduced in Murray et al. [88]. Each neuron circuit is fed with excitatory and inhibitory inputs which are pulse streams, shown in Fig. 10.15. These two pulses are integrated by using an *RC* circuit which provides the neuron activity (or state). To generate the output, an oscillator is used (as shown in the figure); if the neuron activity is low, the oscillator does not work. As the neuron is more *active*, the oscillation frequency increases. The output is another pulse

TABLE 10.8 Neurocomputer Architectures

Neurocomputer	Features
Ring systolic array [74]	Systolic approach Simple processing elements Complete connectivity
SPIN [122]	Bus communication Pipeline approach One activation function generator
Ring neurons [131]	Learning circuitry Simple processing elements
Neuromimetic [30]	Bus communication No multipliers required
Recurrent systolic array [12, 75]	Systolic approach 2D array of processing elements
Pulse stream [88, 87]	Analog/digital implementation Pulse stream arithmetic
Neuromorphic [2]	Analog implementation Digital weights

stream whose frequency is a function of the inputs. Two circuits are used to store the weights: one is a digital memory, and the other is an analog storage device. A comprehensive review of pulse stream neural networks is found in Murray [87].

In this section a small sample of the architectures for neural networks has been presented. Table 10.8 lists hardware approaches for neural network processing. Readers interested on this field are referred to Delgado-Frias and Moore [28, 29], Mead [81], Dayhoff [23], Eckmiller and Malsburg [31], IEEE [64, 65], and Ramacher and Rückert [95].

REFERENCES

1. S. Abe, T. Bandoh, S. Yamaguchi, K. Kurasawa, and K. Kiriyama, "High Performance Integrated Prolog Processor," *Proceedings of the 14th Annual International Symposium on Computer Architecture*, pp. 100–107, 1987.

2. J. Alspector and R. B. Allen, "A Neuromorphic VLSI Learning System," in P. Losleben, *Advanced Research in VLSI: Proceedings of the 1987 Stanford Conference*. Cambridge, Mass.: MIT Press, 1987.

3. J. A. Anderson and E. Rosenfeld (eds.), *Neurocomputing Foundations of Research*. Cambridge, Mass.: MIT Press, 1988.

4. J. M. Anderson, W. S. Coates, A. L. Davis, R. W. Hon, I. N. Robinson, S. V. Robinson, and K. S. Stevens, "The Architecture of FAIM-1," *Computer*, 20(1):55–65, January 1987.

5. Arvind and R. S. Nikhil, "Executing a Program on the MIT Tagged-Token Dataflow Architecture," *IEEE Transactions on Computers*, 39(3):300–318, March 1990.

6. L. Augusteijn, "Garbage Collection in a Distributed Environment," in J. W. Bakker, A. J. Nijman, and P. C. Treleaven (eds.), *PARLE Parallel Architectures and Languages Europe*, Lecture Notes in Computer Science, vols. 258, 259. New York: Springer-Verlag, 1987.

7. A. Barr and E. A. Feigenbaum, *The Handbook of Artificial Intelligence*, vols. 1, 2, and 3. Los Altos, Calif.: William Kaufmann, 1981.

8. A. Bawden, R. Greenblatt, J. Holloway, T. Knight, D. Moon, and D. Weinreb, "The LISP Machine," in P. H. Winston and R. H. Brown, *Artificial Intelligence: An MIT Perspective*. Cambridge, Mass.: MIT Press, 1979.

9. D. Bevan, "Distributed Garbage Collection Using Reference Counting," in J. W. Bakker, A. J. Nijman, and P. C. Treleaven (eds.), *PARLE Parallel Architectures and Languages Europe*, Lecture Notes in Computer Science, vols. 258, 259. New York: Springer-Verlag, 1987.

10. L. Bic, "Processing of Semantic Nets on Dataflow Architectures," *Artificial Intelligence*, 27:219–227, 1985.

11. P. Bishop, *Fifth Generation of Computers: Concepts, Implementations and Uses*. Chichester, England: Ellis Horwood Limited, 1986.

12. F. Blayo and P. Hurat, "A VLSI Systolic Array Dedicated to Hopfield Neural Networks," in J. G. Delgado-Frias and W. R. Moore (eds.), *VLSI for Artificial Intelligence*. Boston: Kluwer Academic, 1989.

13. R. J. Brachman, "On the Epistemological Status of Semantic Networks," in N. V. Findler (ed.), *Associative Networks*. New York: Academic Press, 1979, pp. 3–50.

14. R. J. Brachman, "What IS-A Is and Isn't: An Analysis of Taxonomic Links in Semantic Networks," *Computer*, 16(9):30–36, October 1983.

15. M. Cannataro, G. Spezzano, and D. Talia, "A Multi-Transputer Architecture for a Parallel Logic Machine," in J. G. Delgado-Frias and W. R. Moore (eds.), *VLSI for Artificial Intelligence and Neural Networks*. New York: Plenum, 1991.

16. R. Chowkwanyun and K. Hwang, "Multiprocessor Architectural Support for Balanced LISP Processing," in B. Wah and C. Ramammorthy (eds.), *Computer for Artificial Intelligence Processing*. New York: Wiley Interscience, 1990.

17. A. Ciepielewski and S. Haridi, "Execution of Bagof on the OR-Parallel Token Machine," *Proceedings of the International Conference on Fifth Generation Computer Systems,* pp. 551–560, 1984.

18. P. L. Civera, F. Maddaleno, G. L. Piccinini, and M. Zamboni, "An Experimental VLSI Prolog Interpreter: Preliminary Measurements and Results," *Proceedings of the 14th Annual International Symposium on Computer Architecture,* pp. 117–126, 1987.

19. P. Civera, D. Del Corso, G. Piccinini, and M. Zamboni, "A 32 Bit Processor for Compiled Prolog," in J. G. Delgado-Frias and W. R. Moore (eds.), *VLSI for Artificial Intelligence.* Boston: Kluwer Academic, 1989.

20. J. Cohen, "Garbage Collection of Linked Data Structures," *Computing Surveys,* 13(3):341–367, September 1981.

21. J. S. Conery and F. Kibler, "AND-Parallelism and Nondeterminism in Logic Programs," *New Generation Computing,* 3(2):43–70, 1985.

22. M. Creeger, "LISP Machines Come out of the Lab," *Computer Design,* 22(11):207–216, November 1983.

23. J. Dayhoff, *Neural Network Architectures: An Introduction.* New York: Van Nostrand Reinhold, 1990.

24. D. DeGroot, "Restricted AND-Parallelism and Side Effects in Logic Programming," in K. Hwang and D. DeGroot (eds.), *Parallel Processing for Supercomputers and Artificial Intelligence.* New York: McGraw-Hill, 1989.

25. D. DeGroot, "A Technique for Compiling Execution Graph Expressions for Restricted AND-Parallelism in Logic Programs," *Journal of Parallel and Distributed Computing,* 5(3):494–516, 1988.

26. J. G. Delgado-Frias and W. R. Moore, "Parallel Computer Architectures for AI Semantic Network Processing," *Knowledge-Based Systems,* 1(5):259–265, December 1988.

27. J. G. Delgado-Frias and W. R. Moore, "A Semantic Network Architecture for Knowledge Base Processing," *International Journal for Engineering Applications of Artificial Intelligence,* 3:4–10, March 1990.

28. J. G. Delgado-Frias and W. R. Moore (eds.), *VLSI for Artificial Intelligence.* Boston: Kluwer Academic, 1989.

29. J. G. Delgado-Frias and W. R. Moore (eds.), *VLSI for Artificial Intelligence and Neural Networks.* New York: Plenum, 1991.

30. M. Duranton, J. Gobert, and N. Mauduit, "A Digital VLSI Module for Neural Networks," in L. Personnaz and G. Dreyfus (eds.), *Neural Networks from Models to Applications.* Paris: I.D.S.E.T., 1989.

31. R. Eckmiller and C. Malsburg, *Neural Computers.* New York: Springer-Verlag, 1988.

32. S. Eisenbach (ed.), *Functional Programming: Languages, Tools and Architectures.* New York: Ellis Horwood Limited, 1987.

33. B. S. Fagin and A. M. Despain, "Performance Studies of a Parallel Prolog Architecture," *Proceedings of the 14th Annual International Symposium on Computer Architecture,* pp. 108–116, 1987.

34. S. E. Fahlman, *NETL: A System for Representing and Using Real-World Knowledge.* Cambridge, Mass.: MIT Press, 1979.

35. S. E. Fahlman and G. E. Hinton, "Connectionist Architectures for Artificial Intelligence," *Computer,* 20(1):100–109, January 1987.

36. S. E. Fahlman, G. E. Hinton, and T. J. Sejnowski, "Massively Parallel Architectures for AI: NETL, Thistle, and Boltzmann Machines," *AAAI Proceedings of the Annual Conference on Artificial Intelligence,* pp. 109–113, August 1983.

37. N. V. Findler (ed.), *Associative Networks.* New York: Academic Press, 1979.

38. T. Furuya, T. Higuchi, H. Kusumoto, K. Hanada, and A. Kokubu, "Architectural Evaluation of a Semantic Network Machine," in M. Kitsuregawa and H. Tanaka (eds.), *Database Machines and Knowledge Base Machines.* Boston: Kluwer Academic, 1988.

39. R. P. Gabriel, *Performance and Evaluation of LISP Systems*. Cambridge, Mass.: MIT Press, 1985.

40. M. R. Genesereth and N. J. Nilsson, *Logical Foundations of Artificial Intelligence*. Los Altos, Calif.: Morgan Kaufmann, 1987.

41. A. Goto, H. Tanaka, and T. Moto-oka, "Highly Parallel Inference Engine PIE—Goal Rewriting Model and Machine Architecture," *New Generation Computing*, 2:37–58, 1984.

42. A. Gupta, *Parallelism in Production Systems*. Los Altos, Calif.: Morgan Kaufmann, 1987.

43. A. Gupta, C. Forgy, and A. Newell, "High-Speed Implementations of Rule-Based Systems," *ACM Transactions on Computer Systems*, 7(2):119–146, May 1989.

44. A. Guzmán, "AHR: A Parallel Computer for Pure LISP," in J. S. Kowalik (ed.), *Parallel Computation and Computers for Artificial Intelligence*. Boston: Kluwer Academic, 1988.

45. C. Hafer, J. Planki, and F. J. Schmitt, "COLIBRI: A Coprocessor for LISP Based on RISC," in J. Delgado-Frias and W. R. Moore (eds.), *VLSI for Artificial Intelligence and Neural Networks*. New York: Plenum, 1991.

46. R. H. Halstead, "Design Requirements for Concurrent LISP Machines," in K. Hwang and D. DeGroot (eds.), *Parallel Processing for Supercomputers and Artificial Intelligence*. New York: McGraw-Hill, 1989.

47. R. H. Halstead, "Parallel Computation Using MultiLISP," in J. S. Kowalik (ed.), *Parallel Computation and Computers for Artificial Intelligence*. Boston: Kluwer Academic, 1988.

48. R. H. Halstead and T. Fujita, "MASA: A Multithreaded Processor Architecture for Parallel Symbolic Computing," *Proceedings of the 15th Annual Symposium on Computer Architecture*, pp. 443–451, 1988.

49. H. Hayashi, A. Hattori, and H. Akimoto, "ALPHA: A High-Performance LISP Machine Equipped with a New Stack Structure and Garbage Collection System," *Proceedings of the 10th Annual Symposium on Computer Architecture*, pp. 342–348, 1983.

50. F. Hayes-Roth, "Rule-Based Systems," in S. C. Shapiro (ed.), *Encyclopedia of Artificial Intelligence*. New York: Wiley, 1990.

51. D. O. Hebb, *The Organization of Behavior*. New York: Wiley, 1949. Reprinted in Anderson and Rosenfeld [3].

52. R. Hecht-Nielsen, *Neurocomputing*. Reading, Mass.: Addison-Wesley, 1990.

53. P. Henderson, *Functional Programming: Application and Implementation*. Englewood Cliffs, N.J.: Prentice-Hall, 1980.

54. G. G. Hendrix, "Encoding Knowledge in Partitioned Networks," in N. V. Findler (ed.), *Associative Networks*. New York: Academic Press, 1979, pp. 51–92.

55. J. Herath, Y. Yamaguchi, S. Herath, N. Saito, and T. Yuba, "Data-Flow Computing Models, Logic and Functional Languages, and Data-Flow Machines for Intelligence Computations," in B. Wah and C. Ramammorthy (eds.), *Computer for Artificial Intelligence Processing*. New York: Wiley Interscience, 1990.

56. M. V. Hermenegildo, *Restricted AND-Parallel Prolog and Its Architecture*. Boston: Kluwer Academic, 1988.

57. C. Hewitt and H. Lieberman, "Design Issues in Parallel Architectures for Artificial Intelligence," *IEEE Proceedings of COMPCON S'84*, pp. 418–423, 1984.

58. M. Hill et al., "Design Decisions in SPUR," *IEEE Computer*, 19(11):8–22, November 1986.

59. W. D. Hillis, *The Connection Machine*. Cambridge, Mass.: MIT Press, 1985.

60. B. K. Hillyer and D. E. Shaw, "Execution of OPS5 Production System on a Massively Parallel Architecture," *Journal of Parallel and Distributed Computing*, 3(2):236–268, 1986.

61. J. J. Hopfield, "Neural Networks and Physical Systems with Emergent Collective Computational Abilities," *Proceedings of the National Academy of Sciences*, 79:2554–2558, 1982. Reprinted in Anderson and Rosenfeld [3].

62. K. Hwang, R. Chowkwanyun, and J. Ghosh, "Parallel Architectures for Implementing Artificial Intelligence Systems," in K. Hwang and D. DeGroot (eds.), *Parallel Processing for Supercomputers and Artificial Intelligence*. New York: McGraw-Hill, 1989.

63. Special Issue on Knowledge Representation, *Proceedings of the IEEE,* 74(10), October 1986.

64. Special Issue on Neural Network Hardware, *IEEE Transactions on Neural Networks,* 2(2), March 1991.

65. Special Issue on Neural Network Hardware, *IEEE Transactions on Neural Networks,* 3(2), March 1992.

66. N. Ito, M. Sato, E. Kuno, and K. Rokusawa, "The Architecture and Preliminary Evaluation Results of the Experimental Parallel Inference Machine PIM-D," *Proceedings of the 13th Annual International Symposium on Computer Architecture,* pp. 149–156, 1986.

67. N. Ito, H. Shimizu, M. Kishi, G. Kuro, and K. Murakami, "Data-Flow Based Execution Mechanism of Parallel and Concurrent Prolog," *New Generation Computing,* 3(2):15–41, 1985.

68. P. Kacsuk and I. Futo, "Multi-Transputer Implementation of CS-Prolog," in M. Reeve and S. E. Zenith (eds.), *Parallel Processing and Artificial Intelligence*. Chichester, England: Wiley, 1989.

69. D. Kirsh, "Foundations of AI: The Big Issues," *Artificial Intelligence,* 47:3–30, 1991.

70. K. Knight, "Unification: A Multidisciplinary Survey," *ACM Computing Surveys,* 21(1):93–124, March 1989.

71. P. Kogge, J. Oldfield, M. Brule, and C. Stormon, "VLSI and Rule-Based Systems," in J. G. Delgado-Frias and W. R. Moore (eds.), *VLSI for Artificial Intelligence*. Boston: Kluwer Academic, 1989.

72. T. Kohonen, "An Introduction to Neural Computing," *Neural Networks,* 1(1):3–16, 1988.

73. S. Krueger, "VLSI-Appropriate Garbage Collection Support," in J. G. Delgado-Frias and W. R. Moore (eds.), *VLSI for Artificial Intelligence*. Boston: Kluwer Academic, 1989.

74. S. Y. Kung and J. N. Hwang, "A Unified Systolic Architecture for Artificial Neural Networks," *Journal of Parallel and Distributed Computing,* 6:358–387, 1989.

75. C. Lehmann and F. Blayo, "A VLSI Implementation of a Generic Systolic Synaptic Building Block for Neural Networks," in J. G. Delgado-Frias and W. R. Moore (eds.), *VLSI for Artificial Intelligence and Neural Networks*. New York: Plenum, 1991.

76. G. J. Li and B. W. Wah, "MANIP-2: A Multicomputer Architecture for Evaluating Logic Programs," *Proceedings of the International Conference on Parallel Processing,* pp. 123–130, 1985.

77. R. L. Llames and R. K. Iyer, "Memory Management and Usage in a LISP System: A Measurement-Based Study," in B. Wah and C. Ramammorthy (eds.), *Computer for Artificial Intelligence Processing*. New York: Wiley Interscience, 1990.

78. J. McCarthy, "History of LISP," *SIGPLAN Notices,* 13(8):217–222, August 1978.

79. W. S. McCulloch and W. A. Pitts, "A Logical Calculus of the Ideas Immanent in the Nervous Activity," *Bulletin of Mathematical Biophysics,* 5:115–133, 1943. Reprinted in Anderson and Rosenfeld [3].

80. H. Matsuda, M. Kohata, T. Masuo, Y. Kaneda, and S. Maekawa, "Implementing Parallel Prolog System on Multiprocessor System Park," in M. Kitsuregawa and H. Tanaka (eds.), *Database Machines and Knowledge Base Machines*. Boston: Kluwer Academic, 1988.

81. C. Mead, *Analog VLSI and Neural Systems*. Reading, Mass.: Addison-Wesley, 1989.

82. B. Meng, "AI Wars: Garbage Collection Gets Serious," *Digital Design,* 16(10):48–51, October 1986.

83. D. I. Moldovan and Y-W. Tung, "SNAP: A VLSI Architecture for Artificial Intelligence," *Journal of Parallel and Distributed Computing,* 2(2):109–131, 1985.

84. D. I. Moldovan and C. I. Wu, "Parallel Processing of a Knowledge-Based Vision System," *1986 Proceedings of the Fall Joint Computer Conference,* Dallas, pp. 269–276, November 2–3, 1986.

85. D. A. Moon, "Architecture of the Symbolic 3600," *Proceedings of the 12th Annual Symposium on Computer Architecture,* pp. 76–83, 1985.

86. D. A. Moon, "Symbolics Architecture," in B. W. Wah and C. V. Ramammorthy (eds.), *Computers for Artificial Intelligence Processing.* New York: Wiley, 1990.

87. A. Murray, D. Del Corso, and L. Tarassenko, "Pulse-Stream VLSI Neural Networks Mixing Analog and Digital Techniques," *IEEE Transactions on Neural Networks,* 2(2):193–204, March 1991.

88. A. Murray, A. Smith, and L. Tarassenko, "Fully-Programmable Analogue VLSI for the Implementation of Neural Networks," in J. Delgado-Frias and W. Moore (eds.), *VLSI for Artificial Intelligence.* Boston: Kluwer Academic, 1989.

89. N. J. Nilsson, "Logic and Artificial Intelligence," *Artificial Intelligence,* 47:31–56, 1991.

90. N. J. Nilsson, *Principles of Artificial Intelligence.* Palo Alto, Calif.: Tioga, 1980.

91. R. Onai et al., "Architecture of a Reduction-Based Parallel Inference Machine: PIM-R," *New Generation Computing,* 3(2):34–37, 1985.

92. D. A. Patterson, "Reduced Instruction Set Computers," *Communications of the ACM,* 28(1), January 1985.

93. A. R. Pleszkun and M. J. Thazhuthaveetil, "The Architecture of LISP Machines," *IEEE Computer,* 20(3):35–44, March 1987.

94. M. R. Quillian, "Semantic Memory," in M. Minsky (ed.), *Semantic Information Processing.* Cambridge, Mass.: MIT Press, 1968, pp. 216–270.

95. U. Ramacher and U. Rückert (eds.), *VLSI Design of Artificial Neural Networks.* Boston: Kluwer Academic, 1990.

96. O. Ridoux, "Deterministic and Stochastic Modeling of Parallel Garbage Collection—Towards Real-Time Criteria," *Proceedings of the 14th International Symposium on Computer Architecture,* pp. 128–136, 1987.

97. F. Rosenblatt, "The Perceptron: A Probabilistic Model for Information Storage and Organization of the Brain," *Psychological Reviews,* 65:386–408, 1958.

98. D. E. Rumelhart, G. E. Hinton, and J. L. McClelland, "A General Framework for Parallel Distributed Processor," in D. E. Rumelhart and J. L. McClelland (eds.), *Parallel Distributed Processing,* vol. 1: *Foundations.* Cambridge, Mass.: MIT Press, 1986.

99. D. E. Rumelhart, J. L. McClelland, and the PDP Research Group, *Parallel Distributed Processing, Explorations of the Microstructures of Cognition,* vol. 1. Cambridge, Mass.: MIT Press, 1986.

100. P. S. Sapaty, "A Wave Language for Parallel Processing of Semantic Networks," *Computers and Artificial Intelligence,* 5(4):289–314, 1986.

101. R. J. Schalkoff, *Artificial Intelligence: An Engineering Approach.* New York: McGraw-Hill, 1990.

102. R. C. Schank, "What Is AI, Anyway?" *AI Magazine,* 8(4):59–65, Winter 1987.

103. E. Shapiro, "The Family of Concurrent Logic Programming Languages," *ACM Computing Surveys,* 21(3):413–510, September 1989.

104. S. Shapiro (ed.), *The Encyclopedia of Artificial Intelligence.* New York: Wiley, 1987.

105. L. Shastri, *Semantic Networks: An Evidential Formalization and Its Connectionist Realization.* Los Altos, Calif.: Morgan Kaufmann, 1988.

106. H. E. Shrobe (ed.), *Exploring Artificial Intelligence: Survey Talks from the National Conference on Artificial Intelligence.* Los Altos, Calif.: Morgan Kaufmann, 1988.

107. J. F. Sowa (ed.), *Formal Aspects of Semantic Networks.* Los Altos, Calif.: Morgan Kaufmann, 1991.

108. G. L. Steele, *Common LISP Reference Manual*. Burlington, Mass.: Digital Press, 1984.

109. P. Steenkiste and J. Hennessy, "LISP on a Reduced-Instruction-Set Processor: Characterization and Optimization," *IEEE Computer*, 21(17):34–45, July 1988.

110. P. Steenkiste and J. Hennessy, "A Simple Interprocedural Register Allocation Algorithm and Its Effectiveness for LISP," *ACM Transactions on Programming and Systems*, 11(1):1–32, January 1989.

111. S. J. Stolfo, "Initial Performance of the DADO2 Prototype," *Computer*, 20(1):75–83, January 1987.

112. S. J. Stolfo and D. P. Miranker, "The DADO Production System Machine," *Journal of Parallel and Distributed Computing*, 3(2):269–296, 1986.

113. S. Sugimoto, K. Agusa, K. Tabata, and Y. Ohno, "A Multi-Microprocessor System for Concurrent LISP-Language Oriented System Architecture," *Proceedings of the International Conference on Parallel Processing*, pp. 443–452, 1983.

114. G. J. Sussman, J. Holloway, G. L. Steel, and A. Bell, "Scheme-79—LISP on a Chip," *Computer*, 14(7):10–21, July 1981.

115. K. Taki, M. Yokota, A. Yamamoto, H. Nishikawa, S. Uchida, and H. Nakashima, "Hardware Design and Implementation of the Personal Sequential Inference Machine," *Proceedings of the International Conference on Fifth Generation Computer Systems*, pp. 398–409, 1984.

116. L. Tanimoto, *The Elements of Artificial Intelligence*. New York: Computer Science Press, 1990.

117. G. S. Taylor, "Evaluation of the SPUR LISP Architecture," *The 13th Annual International Symposium on Computer Architecture*, Tokyo, June 2–5, 1986, pp. 444–452.

118. E. Tick, "Data Buffer Performance for Sequential Prolog Architectures," *Proceedings of the 15th Annual International Symposium on Computer Architecture*, pp. 434–442, 1988.

119. E. Tick, *Memory Performance of Prolog Architectures*. Boston: Kluwer Academic, 1988.

120. E. Tick and D. H. D. Warren, "Towards a Pipelined Prolog Processor," *New Generation Computing*, 2:323–345, 1984.

121. P. C. Treleaven, A. N. Refenes, K. J. Lees, and S. C. McCabe, "Computer Architectures for Artificial Intelligence," Department of Computer Science, University College London, Tech. Rep. 119 (UCL-CS-TR 119), March 1986.

122. S. Vassiliadis, G. G. Pechanek, and J. G. Delgado-Frias, "SPIN: A Sequential Pipelined Neurocomputer," *IEEE Third International Conference on Tools for Artificial Intelligence*, November 1991.

123. S. R. Vegdahl, "A Survey of Proposed Architectures for the Execution of Functional Languages," *IEEE Transactions on Computers*, 20(1):67–74, January 1987.

124. J. Vlahavas and C. Halatsis, "A RISC Prolog Machine Architecture," *Microprocessing and Microprogramming*, 21:259–266, 1987.

125. B. W. Wah and G-J. Li, *Computers for Artificial Intelligence Applications*. New York: IEEE Computer Society Press, 1986.

126. B. W. Wah and G-J. Li, "Design Issues of Multiprocessors for Artificial Intelligence," in K. Hwang and D. DeGroot (eds.), *Parallel Processing for Supercomputers and Artificial Intelligence*. New York: McGraw-Hill, 1989.

127. B. W. Wah and C. V. Ramammorthy (eds.), *Computer for Artificial Intelligence Processing*. New York: Wiley Interscience, 1990.

128. D. H. D. Warren, "An Abstract PROLOG Instruction Set," Tech. Rep. 309, Artificial Intelligence Center, SRI International, Stanford, Calif., 1983.

129. P. D. Wasserman, *Neural Computing: Theory and Practice*. New York: Van Nostrand Reinhold, 1989.

130. P. Watson and I. Watson, "An Efficient Garbage Collection Scheme for Parallel Computer Architectures," in J. W. Bakker, A. J. Nijman, and P. C. Treleaven (eds.), *PARLE Parallel*

Architectures and Languages Europe, Lecture Notes in Computer Science, vols. 258, 259. New York: Springer-Verlag, 1987.

131. M. Weinfeld, "A Fully Digital Integrated CMOS Hopfield Network Including the Learning Algorithm," in J. G. Delgado-Frias and W. R. Moore (eds.), *VLSI for Artificial Intelligence.* Boston: Kluwer Academic, 1989.

132. B. Widrow and M. E. Hoff, "Adaptive Switching Circuits," *1960 IRE WESCON Convention Record.* New York: IRE, 1960, pp. 96–104.

133. P. H. Winston, *Artificial Intelligence,* 2d ed. Reading, Mass.: Addison-Wesley, 1984.

134. N. M. Woo, "A Hardware Unification Unit: Design and Analysis," *Proceedings of the 12th Annual International Symposium on Computer Architecture,* pp. 198–205, 1985.

135. W. A. Woods, "What in a Link: Foundations for Semantic Networks," in R. J. Brachman and H. J. Levesque (eds.), *Knowledge Representation.* Los Altos, Calif.: Kaufmann, 1985.

136. Y. Yamaguchi, K. Toda, J. Herath, and T. Yuba, "EM-3: A LISP-Based Data-Driven Machine," *Proceedings of the International Conference on Fifth-Generation Computer Systems,* pp. 524–532, 1984.

137. Y. Yamaguchi, K. Toda, and T. Yuba, "A Performance Evaluation of a LISP-Based Data-Driven Machine," *Proceedings of the 10th Annual International Symposium on Computer Architecture,* pp. 363–369, 1983.

CHAPTER 11
COMPUTER VISION PRINCIPLES AND APPLICATIONS

Giovanni Garibotto and Stefano Masciangelo
Research and Development, Elsag Bailey spa

11.1 INTRODUCTION

This chapter provides an overview of computer vision techniques, highlighting the most recent advances of the research in this field. Actually such a scenario is extremely broad and complex, and any attempt to organize this subject in a unified comprehensive scheme may be questionable and necessarily reflects the viewpoint of the authors. However, this analysis comes from a direct experience of industrial vision systems ranging from the most challenging applications to real, practical problems which require reliable, robust solutions. Due to limited space, no algorithm details are provided here, but the proposed classification scheme is supported by many qualified references from the related literature.

The topic of computer vision has evolved a great deal in the last few years, covering a wide range of applications from very simple inspection tasks to very sophisticated intelligent behavior for autonomous robot control. A short summary of some major application domains is briefly given in Sec. 11.2. Section 11.3 describes the selected functional architecture of a generic computer vision system. Two different schemes are proposed, as representative of the main trends of the applied research in the field, namely, the reconstructive approach and the purposive, qualitative approach to artificial vision. Section 11.4 addresses some fundamental properties and constraints of the camera sensory system and their influence on the solutions of the vision task. Then the principal components of the system are described in more detail in Secs. 11.5, 11.6, 11.7, and 11.8, which are supported by a series of implementation results. The chapter concludes with a few comments on the present attitude to exploit an experimental approach for the design and realization of more robust and reliable computer vision systems.

First, it is necessary to distinguish between passive vision techniques, without any severe lighting control, and the use of structured projected light sources such as a laser beam or blade. Although the second approach is widely used and quite effective in many industrial machine vision applications, it is primarily a sensory system, specialized to three-dimensional (3D) data computation, and is not considered further here.

Furthermore, we cannot ignore the anthropomorphic visual model of perception, which has provided interesting cues for the solution of basic vision problems. This is not to say that machine vision should mimic completely the human visual system, but it may take advantage of some perceptual behavior concepts to simplify the current visual task. For instance, a well-known property is the space-variant behavior of the human retina where a central area, the *fovea*, has a higher density of photoreceptors which provide improved visual acuity and spatial resolution. By contrast, the peripheral area, with lower spatial resolution capabilities, exhibits very fast differential responses, in terms of both contrast and motion perception. Moreover, human visual perception is the best example of an *active vision* system, which is able to react to external events by dynamically driving the attention to the interesting area and keeping the foveal high-resolution sensor always oriented to it. A consequence of this target fixation capability is the use of an object-centered coordinate system as a basis for spatial memory. Such a model has been extensively investigated, by using a transformation from the (x, y) spatial coordinates into the (ρ, θ) polar domain, where invariant properties may be better exploited to simplify some operations, such as matching and tracking. This operation can be performed through either a software conversion module [81] or specially designed space-variant imaging sensors [76].

Finally, we mention the major debate of the last few years about the ultimate goals of computer vision and the way to achieve them [48]. This debate arose from a sense of disillusionment in the research community after the great expectations of success in applications in the early 1980s.

A primary philosophical problem is the following: Is the goal of computer vision (and artificial intelligence in general) to build creatures [14], trying to simulate human sensory and intellectual capabilities, or to solve real problems arising from fields of application?

Another basic issue involves achieving that goal: Is it better to first create a sound theoretical framework, possibly inspired by psychophysical research, and then implement modules, making a lot of unrealistic assumptions, or to try to solve a specific problem via an engineering approach?

Another dualism in the computer vision community is related to the original application field of the researchers: some are active in robotics; others, photogrammetry. Roboticists consider vision as the component of a possibly real-time closed loop (sense-plan-actuate) whereas photogrammetrists see vision as a self-contained measurement tool whose goal is to extract a precise representation of the real world.

11.1.1 The Reconstructive School

Historically this was the first successful paradigm in computer vision, and strongly influenced much subsequent research. The main goal of artificial vision is the reconstruction of physical parameters of the outside world. In robotics this means first to create an accurate geometric description and then to perform the visual task.

A number of criticisms are raised about this nonetheless successful paradigm:

- To reconstruct the world, a lot of specific assumptions, hypotheses, and models that are not valid in the real world must be accepted.

- Reconstructive algorithms are usually mathematically ill-posed problems,[†] and their solutions lack robustness and stability.[‡]

- The assumed models contain parameters which must be determined by solving the *calibration problem*.

[†]According to Hadamard's definition [42], a mathematical problem is well posed if and only if the solution exists, is unique, and is stable, that is, depends continuously on the initial data.

[‡]A computer vision application is stable (robust against noise) if a small amount of noise in the input data generates a bounded output error.

• Usually reconstructive algorithms are computationally intensive and difficult to implement in real time.

11.1.2 The Purposive School

This new paradigm, which originated at the University of Maryland [1], intends to answer previous criticisms by stating that the goal of computer vision is to recognize patterns or situations to accomplish a specific visual task.

Here the vision end-products are some units of behavior (or *competence*) such as decisions, alarms, or motor actions. The visual tasks are much less general (*simpler*) than before, but the solutions are effective.

Few assumptions, if any, are made about the real world. Moreover, the representations and metrics are not the usual engineering units such as seconds or millimeters but some ad hoc internal units strictly depending on the algorithm at hand. For example, *time to crash* can be a good measurement unit if the task is obstacle avoidance.

A few other new paradigms are based on the criticism of the reconstructive school and are strictly linked to the purposive approach. We mention the *active vision* or *exploratory vision* paradigm, which must not be confused with the techniques based on active sensors (such as structured lights, laser range finder, etc.). In this case *active* means that the observer is not a static sensor (in terms of position and optical parameters) but can control the geometric parameters of the sensing apparatus in order to turn ill-posed, nonlinear inverse problems into well-posed linear ones. In other words, if the camera can be moved to take another picture of the object from a slightly different point of view, there will be less ambiguity than by using just a single viewing position.

Another possible action is to change the optical parameters of the acquisition system. By changing the focal length it is possible to focus the system's attention on a relevant detail of the scene; by varying the focus setting and measuring the amount of blurring induced onto the image, the system can recover rough distance information.

The *qualitative vision* paradigm is again an extension of the purposive approach and is largely motivated by robotics applications.

Often in robotics precise information is unnecessary to accomplish a given task; humans themselves are not provided with accurate range finders but can navigate and grasp objects successfully. The basic idea is to consider not precisely computed values of physical attributes, which are often affected by noise and algorithmic instabilities, but some character or property of attributes representable by nonnumeric expressions. For instance, the sign of a value, the relative pose (left of . . ., right of . . ., closer than . . .), or the motion with respect to the viewer (toward . . ., away from . . ., faster than . . .) can be qualitative parameters that can be used to control an actuation loop.

In navigation tasks the use of *relative* information, such as the comparison of nonnumeric entities, can be enough to solve a large number of problems. A vision system making use of this information must be dynamic: Qualitative data are useful if they can be extracted continuously from the scene at a rate sufficient to support the control system with a frequent update of the perceived status of the world. This paradigm implies a change in the traditional robotic control, where first the perception module reconstructs the world and generates a target position (affected by noise) and then the planning and control modules try to reach the goal blindly, i.e., without any visual feedback. In the novel approach, perception and actuation have to be closely linked and always active in parallel during execution of a movement so that if wrong paths or dangerous situations are perceived, an immediate recovery action can be undertaken.

This chapter considers a generic vision system of the reconstructive school and a visual navigation module, as an example of the purposive school, in Sec. 11.8.

11.2 REFERENCE APPLICATIONS

Presently computer vision systems are used in many different domains, with such a large variety of application constraints that an exhaustive classification is hard to provide. Review papers [72] and market analysis of machine vision [12] already provide a thorough overview of the market evolution worldwide. In the following paragraphs, a taxonomy of computer vision applications is proposed based on the different visual tasks to be performed, rather than the various segments of the market. There are both well-established, consolidated examples of image processing and pattern recognition and new, challenging robotics problems which are still at an early stage of development.

11.2.1 Optical Measurements

In this case a machine vision system is supposed to provide quantitative data from the sensed scene, acting primarily as a special measuring device, with large autonomy but poor flexibility. The major requirements are high precision and processing speed. Yet the data acquisition phase is carried out in a very controlled environment, with light constraints and small volumes of analysis. For these reasons the calibration of the vision sensor is often an extremely important phase of the process. This class of applications includes image analysis for quality control, where early detection of defects in a production line is required. A quantitative analysis of such defects allows feedback control and correction to recover optimal conditions for the overall process. Such a problem is found in the paper and color printing industry, in packaging inspection, in clay articles and glass, in varnishing control of car body parts. Printed circuit board inspection is another important application of image processing techniques in which presence and position verification and component identification are required. Another promising area of application is the dimensional measurement machines in manufacturing, where optical systems are considered as a support to more traditional tactile sensors. One possibility is to achieve a fast, although not extremely precise, full object reconstruction, to simplify and improve human-machine interaction. Otherwise, vision tools themselves may become 3D sensors for surface and feature measurements, by reducing the field of view and using structured light techniques, or lasers. In this case computer vision and photogrammetry [75] become complementary disciplines with mutual support to solve the problem.

11.2.2 Character Segmentation and Recognition

This well-established problem has been addressed for many years in many applications. The key discipline is pattern recognition, but image processing techniques are essential too, mainly in preprocessing for image segmentation, character localization, and feature extraction. Mail sorting is probably the most relevant industrial application, with recent advances in automatic address block location for flats, parcels, and letters [78]. Another example is electronic archiving and retrieval of books and journals with the problem of page segmentation into heading lines, author, abstract, etc. Moreover, text has to be distinguished from graphics and stored accordingly [59] for multimedia systems, with integrated processing of text, sensor-derived imagery, graphics, and other data. There is an increasing interest also in handwriting in both mail sorting and automated document processing, as in form reading systems, where two-dimensional (2D) geometric feature analysis plays a more significant role. Finally we cite an emerging application field in the recognition of labels and identification numbers in transport systems, as in car-plate reading, container labels, etc. [50].

11.2.3 Model-Based Recognition in Industrial Robotics

The basic task here consists of ascertaining if a certain object is present in a static scene or in a continuous flow, to decide whether and how to perform some further robotic actions. For instance, bin picking, for flexible assembly operations, requires precise location of the piece for grasping, as investigated and experienced in many factory automation situations, especially for medium-size casting objects. Model matching is the basic tool required to solve this problem, and it may be used either on pictorial/iconic representations or on more symbolic high-level feature relationships, like relative position and orientation. A major requirement for such industrial applications of robotic vision is robustness against environmental changes, such as light variations, spatial positions, and viewing point and scale factors. Unfortunately most low-cost machine vision systems exhibit poor adaptability and require a tightly controlled environment, which may explain the limited success of this technology with respect to market expectations in the early 1980s. It seems that in the near future the mainstream of machine vision applications will change from assembly to inspection. Another interesting application is 3D parcel classification and sorting [36], where rolls have to be distinguished from packets of different sizes, bags, and irregular parcels.

11.2.4 Image Segmentation and Classification

This is the classical task of image processing, mostly discussed in textbooks, involving all levels of computer vision and dealing with still pictures and off-line classification. Examples of applications are satellite and aerial scene analysis in remote sensing for both civil land resource monitoring and military applications. For instance, stereo photogrammetry is used for the reconstruction of the digital terrain model of an area from a pair of stereo pictures [25]. Texture analysis is often used on satellite images, such as *synthetic aperture radar* (SAR) data, to detect and isolate certain regions in the scene. Infrared and multispectral image analysis is another powerful tool for classification [22] to detect and monitor pollution and fire fighting and as a support for meteorological forecasting.

11.2.5 Target Tracking

This is a typical dynamic application in which a computer vision system has to fix the attention on a selected target and keep track of it over time. Of course, there are well-known military applications using both visible images and infrared or radar data. Another example of industrial robotics is the control of the robot arm trajectory for special tasks, such as continuous arc welding operations, using lasers as position sensors.

11.2.6 Vision Support to Autonomous Navigation

A great interest in the vision system's capabilities comes from mobile robot builders: Vision is considered the most complete and powerful sensor for such vehicles. As soon as sufficient robustness and reliability are achieved, even through multisensory fusion, and costs are cut, vision will become the main sensorial technology to attain increased autonomy in different tasks.

Industrial AGVs. Industrial *autonomous guided vehicles* (AGVs) are an in-use technology, with known limits and problems. Vision is likely to provide the basis for the second-generation AGVs, the so-called "free-ranging" AGVs. Currently AGVs navigate by using the inductive guidance principle, which implies expensive and inflexible buried wires, or following reflective tape sealed on the floor, which does not stand up to the harsh conditions of the industrial environment.

Security is achieved by ultrasound belts, which limit the vehicle's maximum speed, IR proximity sensors, and mechanical bumpers, which create problems of encumbrance in cramped environments. Moreover, certain types of obstacles such as holes, steps, smooth surfaces, and thin metallic objects (chair legs) are not detected at all, emphasizing the limits of current technology.

Some new products no longer rely on buried wires for navigation but use triangulation laser systems with retroreflective targets or bar-code beacons spread all over the workspace [71]. There are at least two shortcomings in this approach: Laser systems are unsafe for the human eye and preclude the presence of human workers, and targets can be occluded by loads in stores and warehouses.

Finally, the process of docking and undocking at workstations is currently governed by fixed mechanical or optical devices, which require the design and realization of ad hoc solutions. On the other hand, vision is expected to do all the following:

- Widen the look-ahead distance and improve the overall reliability of the safety system
- Perform self-positioning in the environment with the help of landmarks
- Navigate freely by detecting free-space and unforeseen obstacles, including people
- Recover self-orientation with respect to a load or a docking point with incremental precision

Many of these points may have already been demonstrated by current vision technology. A careful engineering work and cost optimization is required to put this technology into use.

Outdoor Navigation. Vision and robotics communities are devoting their efforts to the realization of vehicles that autonomously follow roads and pathways in outdoor environments.

There are at least two fields of application requiring this technology: battlefield robotization and automotive industry. The U.S. Department of Defense sponsored the *autonomous land vehicle* (ALV) project which produced a few prototypes of land vehicles able to travel along country roads at considerable speeds (up to 15 km/h) [74]. In Europe attention focused on car automation and driver assistance during travel along well-structured environments such as highways [31].

In this context vision is the fundamental sensor; the overall task consists of finding the edges of the road, relying on a single TV camera, and sometimes making use of color images. Fast low-level processing with dedicated hardware, dynamic scene analysis, and strict coupling between perception and control theory are the crucial points.

11.2.7 Event Detection and Scene Understanding in Service Robotics

Service robotics refers to a novel concept and use of industrial robots in tasks that are not highly repetitive and constrained. Service robots therefore require much more intelligence, flexibility, and sensory capabilities than their industrial ancestors, and the application opportunities and potential markets of this emerging technology lie outside the domain of traditional industrial robots.

In traditional applications, robots are programmed to quickly accomplish well-defined actions without operator intervention, whereas service robots would be employed in delicate, nonrepetitive tasks in remote, hazardous, and unstructured environments, often under human supervision or telecontrol.

Automatic and semiautomatic surveillance of remote environments is another related field for potential industrial exploitation. The common technical motivation is the use of "intelligent sensors" and scene analysis capabilities. Passive artificial vision is the key technology and perhaps the only one which can guarantee the advanced performance and information completeness necessary to cope with the envisaged tasks.

In the following paragraphs, a few application fields where vision technology is most promising are surveyed. We distinguish three families of homogeneous applications:

- Mobile robotics in indoor environments
- Telerobotics in hazardous and remote environments
- Surveillance and inspection by mobile vehicles or fixed devices

Mobile robots with relatively simple locomotion can be used in indoor environments to automate routine transport activities. The main examples include hospitals where samples, specimens, medicines, and meals have to be carried around and large offices, banks, or post offices where mail, documents, and other items have to be transported through corridors, hallways, and other preassigned routes. Specifications for these mobile robots include free-ranging capabilities, flexibility in reconfiguring preplanned routes, safety even in peopled areas, and a simple human–machine interface.

Many operations in hazardous environments, such as nuclear power plants, chemical industries, and electrical power distribution substations, require remotely controlled machines and robots. However, current teleoperation technologies do not take advantage of any automated function; the human operator directly controls the robot at the servo level. This approach, common in nuclear power plants, is time-consuming and frequently very tiring and often suffers from poor *telepresence* due to poor sensory feedback from the robot to the teleoperator. In addition, it is prone to many problems and difficulties due to loss of communication links and transmission delays.

These and other considerations push toward an increased robot autonomy and machine intelligence, that is, to shift from teleoperation to *telerobotics* and teleguidance whenever mobile robots are involved. The paradigm of telerobotics as a new approach to teleoperation envisages the human operator no longer as a pilot but as a mission supervisor. Furthermore, the use of on-board sensors and processors would remove any need for high-bandwidth closed-loop communication between the robot at the remote site and the operator station. As a matter of fact, significant transmission delays may preclude a wide class of teleoperation tasks, with severe safety problems.

In addition, the role of the operator must change in order to meet industrial requirements for workforce cost reductions. In particular, in telerobotics the operator would control the robot at the *task level,* i.e., monitor the progress of the mission and every now and then reprogram the robot to perform a sequence of short, well-defined tasks in an autonomous way with the aid of sensors. The robot provides reflex actions in response to particular sensed events or stimuli while the reevaluation of task objectives, recovery from unforeseen situations, high-level decision making, etc. are left to the operator. Actually the intention is to decouple the reactive behavior from high-level interpretation. Again vision is the fundamental sensory channel to improve the autonomy of the remote side, and it could also be used to enhance the telepresence feedback for the operator.

Among the various application fields for telerobotics and vision systems is space, with its increasing need for automation in space station servicing, in order to avoid risky and costly staffed *extravehicular activity* (EVA) missions. Moreover, the space environment seems to be very suitable for vision system applications since it is highly structured and perfectly known and the illumination conditions are no worse than in the terrestrial outdoor environment.

Finally, surveillance tasks have similar specifications and problems: Guard service requires mobility on fixed routes (even if a certain degree of randomness and responsiveness to external events may be appropriate) and transportation capabilities of anti-intrusion devices. Currently the task is carried out by human workers who are affected by boredom and sometimes high risk. For such applications, an automatic vision-based system should be able to detect significant changes and anomalous situations in the scene and to alert the human supervisor located in a remote control room. Another application of a dynamic advanced vision system closely related to surveillance is the control of traffic on highways. Highway automation is considered a huge and unexplored market for vision systems able to cope with outdoor, all-weather conditions and dynamic event detection.

11.3 FUNCTIONAL ARCHITECTURES OF A VISION SYSTEM

In this section we provide a reference schema of a generic vision system as a basis for the following analysis. Our aim is to define a framework general enough to suit a great number of existing vision systems. An engineering approach is used to describe it and to give an idea of a possible implementation both in software and through special-purpose hardware.

The easiest way to describe this functional schema is to follow the datastream paths describing the intermediate representations and the transformations performed by the different algorithms.

Indeed, two different frameworks are discussed as representative of the classical reconstructive paradigm and the new purposive approach.

11.3.1 The Reconstructive Vision System

The general reconstructive vision system is modular, pyramidal, and data-driven. It is *modular* because it is constituted of specific algorithms which operate over data according to a fixed sequence. *Pyramidal* refers to the sequence of data transformations: each module generates a more synthetic output representation, thus reducing the datastream propagating through the computational chain. *Data-driven* means that at the early processing stages the output data depend only on the input data; a priori knowledge is explicitly used only by higher-level modules which operate on symbolic data.

Each module transforms the input data according to an embedded model by making a set of assumptions about the real world. Only if these assumptions are realistic will the algorithms perform well and successfully.

Typically such vision systems are intended to solve very general problems with the same flexible "general-purpose" architecture. This often leads to poor performance in real situations and an impractical computational burden.

Figure 11.1 depicts the breakdown of the general computer vision system. The schema includes both static and dynamic configurations. In a static or *snapshot* system, all the information is taken from a single image, while time-varying image sequence analysis is performed by dynamic systems. In the figure, dynamic systems are characterized by a feedback loop, since they usually combine new information extracted from the last image with a current, updatable representation of the status of the scene. This dynamic representation can be used to predict the expected position of some features prior to the elaboration of the subsequent image in a temporal sequence.

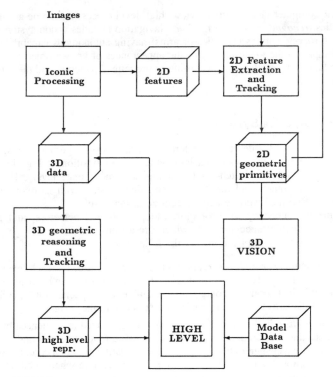

FIGURE 11.1 General architecture of a vision system: the main functional modules and the relative data flow.

The schema presents different classes of modules and typical representations:

- *Iconic processing* includes all the algorithms that operate on raw images or other matrix data representation; they can produce either iconic or symbolic output data, both 2D and 3D elaborating a stereo pair.

- *Feature extraction* is performed on data-driven 2D representations to find higher-level, geometrically meaningful primitives; *tracking* algorithms use these primitives to maintain a dynamic representation in the image reference system.

- The *3D vision* modules are used to infer 3D information from 2D representations coming from one or more images.

- *Three-dimensional geometric reasoning* is a collection of algorithms in which geometric and statistical rules are applied to raw 3D representations to extract high-level 3D primitives as well as to update and fuse dynamic 3D models of the world.

- The *high-level domain* includes the topmost part of the system, in charge of combining the obtained, data-driven information and the task-specific knowledge to attain the desired output or behavior.

The typology of high-level algorithms is very heterogeneous, depending on the application; the approach may range from artificial intelligence and expert systems to control theory algorithms in robotic systems.

From the computer vision point of view, high-level processing can be grouped in two large families: *recognition* and *navigation*. Navigation includes vision systems that support moving robotic entities (vehicles or arms) having autonomous capabilities. Recognition encompasses the identification of the appearances of known objects in the scene, the interpretation of visual events according to predefined patterns, and the building of a model of the scene.

11.3.2 The Purposive System

The diagram in Fig. 11.2 depicts the alternative framework of purposive vision.

We no longer have the functional hierarchical decomposition of Fig. 11.1, but the system is divided into competencies (or activities) which create layers. Each layer is independent of the others and forms a self-contained system with its own very narrow goal, depending on the resulting action required at that level.

Real time is defined by rates of closed-loop control of actuators, and perception modules must recognize special events which fire actions.

The most innovative implications are the following:

- There is no *central common representation* of the real world, but each level maintains the partial model it needs to perform its task. Even the metrics can be different from the usual natural units (meters, seconds) but can be based on special units (pixels, time to crash, stereo disparity) which are easier to extract from the images.

- There is *parallelism* in the modules which are not organized in sequences but are fully asynchronous and independent. That means improved robustness and fault tolerance of the system, since a change in the environment or a malfunction of a certain module does not affect the whole system (as opposed to the reconstructive schema) but inhibits only a single competence.

- Purposive vision modules do not usually require precise *calibration* or constraining assumptions, exact models, etc.

In the next sections we present visual modules following the classical reconstructive classification, which is much more common in practice, but we give examples from both paradigms according to our experience in practical vision systems.

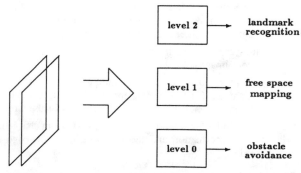

FIGURE 11.2 An example of *purposive* vision system dedicated to mobile robot navigation.

11.4 VISUAL SENSORY MODEL AND CAMERA CALIBRATION

Before we undertake a survey of computer vision modules, it is necessary to introduce the issue of modeling the acquisition subsystem. Actually, this is a fundamental assumption, which is implicitly or explicitly made by most vision algorithms.

The domain known as *camera calibration* can be related to the following problem: How can the relationship between the position of features in the image and the position of the objects in the scene be specified? To answer this question, we need a possibly simple model of the image formation process, including the lenses, the *charge-coupled device* (CCD) camera, and the *analog-to-digital* (A/D) conversion electronics, and a methodology to compute the parameters of the model [73]. More precisely, the camera calibration process consists of determining the relationship between each 3D observed point and the corresponding 2D position on the digitized image.

The relevance of the problem has been quite underestimated by the vision research community, which is much more interested in theoretical problems. Now the strong requirements of real applications are underlining its importance in many practical situations, since a wrong calibration can often destroy the results of the brightest algorithm. Actually, a good calibration is fundamental in measuring applications where it is necessary to model and compensate as much as possible for imaging errors and optical distortions, which are intrinsic in current TV camera technology.

Calibration can be described in terms of two sets of variables: the imaging (controllable) variables and the imaging model parameters. Controllable variables include

- Camera position and orientation
- Zoom (focal length)
- Focus
- Aperture

Control variables are *not* part of the *mathematical* imaging model which is embedded in the vision algorithms. Those quantities can be adjusted (manually or by means of automatic devices) and do not correspond to the values involved in the imaging equations.

11.4.1 The Image Formation Model

The image formation process can be divided into three steps:

1. A 3D-3D transformation from the world to the camera coordinates
2. A 3D-2D transformation expressing the projection of the scene onto the sensor plane
3. A 2D-2D transformation corresponding to the digitization process

The first transform is used to relate the position of the perspective center of the camera (a virtual 3D point that does not correspond to the controllable camera body position) with the world reference. The involved parameters are called *extrinsic* and can be expressed by a translation vector **t** and a rotation matrix **R**.

The 3D-2D transform is based on a simplified geometry of the optical system model in order to keep the computational complexity manageable. The most widely used model is the *pinhole model* depicted in Fig. 11.3, in which ideal lenses are considered as possessing an infinitesimally small aperture. This aperture is located at the center of

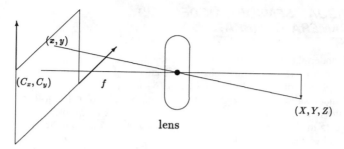

FIGURE 11.3 The pinhole camera model. The world point (X,Y,Z) projects onto the sensor plane in the point (x, y).

projection of the lenses, that is, the point used for calculating the principal rays from the scene to the sensor plane according to the laws of optics.

The transform associated with the pinhole model is the classical perspective projection. Thus the relation between a 3D point (X, Y, Z) and the corresponding 2D point (x, y) on the image plane is

$$x = \frac{Xf}{Z} \qquad y = \frac{Yf}{Z} \tag{11.1}$$

where f is the focal length of the lens.

Finally the digitization step can be modeled by the following linear relations, where (u, v) are the point coordinates in the stored image matrix:

$$u = k_u x + u_0 \qquad v = k_v y + v_0 \tag{11.2}$$

The values k_u and k_v are the conversion factors from pixels to millimeters in the horizontal and vertical directions, respectively, and their ratio is the *aspect ratio* of the acquisition system. In general, the aspect ratio is not unitary, causing a deformation in the digitized image and, as a consequence, a performance degradation of all algorithms for shape analysis. The estimation of the aspect ratio should take into account two different factors: the physical size of the sensor (l_x, l_y), which is rectangular, and the discrepancy between the camera clock and the resampling clock of the A/D converter. A heuristic formula which allows us to compute an approximated value for the aspect ratio is

$$\frac{k_u}{k_v} = \frac{l_x}{l_y} \frac{\text{clock}_{\text{sensor}}}{\text{clock}_{\text{sample}}} \tag{11.3}$$

The values u_0 and v_0 are the origin of the discretization of the intensity map and express the pixel coordinates of the intersection of the optical axis with the sensor plane.

The u_0, v_0, k_u, k_v, and f are the *intrinsic* camera parameters and have to be precomputed by means of the calibration procedure. These values are often used as inputs to vision algorithms, especially in the reconstructionist approach. However, on-line modifications of the controllable parameters of the imaging system may cause unpredictable changes in the intrinsic parameters. As such,

- It is not advisable to change the optical parameters (zoom, focus) while the vision system is working, but results are reliable and repeatable only if the acquisition setup is fixed.

- It is advisable to recalibrate the system every now and then since system performances may vary because of slight setup modifications.

The presented model does not take into consideration the effects of optical distortions of the lenses, which are not negligible if the focal length is below 30 mm. However, it is possible to include in Eq. 11.2 a polynomial term which models at least the radial distortion, which is caused by flawed radial curvatures of the lens elements [82].

11.4.2 Calibration Methods

Given a set of visible 3D noncoplanar points whose coordinates are known in the world reference system (usually ad hoc calibration patterns are used) and their corresponding pixel coordinates in the acquired image, we must identify the intrinsic and extrinsic parameters of the imaging model.

Now the calibration has been converted to an overconstrained equation system where the 3D points are the known input values, the 2D points are the observable outputs, and the model parameters are the unknowns, which can be computed by a least-squares minimization.

With respect to this general approach there are some differences in the algorithms mentioned in the literature. It is possible to distinguish two main classes:

- Closed-form solution methods
- Two-step iterative methods

In the former category a set of parameters is defined by using homogeneous coordinates, so that the problem turns out to be linear. Then model parameters are computed as a solution of a linear system in the least-squares sense [34]. In the latter category, intrinsic parameters are estimated separately from extrinsic parameters. Moreover, the focal length can be obtained through direct evaluation of the image center by means of a laser projector, and the aspect ratio can be computed by electronically measuring the clock ratio of the acquisition subsystem [52]. This approach is much more precise, since it avoids ill-conditioning problems which are typical of the closed-form approach where heterogeneous parameters with different metrics are estimated together.

In conclusion, a better comprehension of the calibration problem is vital to improve the performance of any vision system, even if off-the-shelf CCD cameras and commercial acquisition boards are used.

11.5 EARLY PROCESSING TOOLS

This section discusses those algorithms and techniques which perform image-to-feature transformations and provide geometric tools for 2D analysis at the level of the imaging plane.

11.5.1 2D Iconic Image Processing

This is the classical domain of low-level image processing tools, dealing with gray-level images (icons). It is possible to distinguish between static and dynamic algorithms according to the input datastream, being either a still picture or a temporal sequence of images.

Edge Feature Extraction.   The relevance of this phase of processing is due to the fact that most computer vision results are based on edge feature representations. Many different approaches have been proposed in the literature, with different levels of complexity and accuracy of the results [69, 77]. An efficient edge detection scheme should satisfy the following major requirements: robustness against noise (to avoid spurious edges) and accurate and stable localization in the spatial domain. Such a process is usually accomplished in the following steps:

- Filtering and preprocessing, to enhance edge points from the image
- Local analysis for edge map building
- Edge point linking to connected edge lists, in order to achieve a more synthetic description of the scene in terms of a few geometric entities

Quite often the first two steps are done together and are based on some threshold decision criterion. The most simple and common class of edge detection filters is given by local operators to perform matched filtering, according to all possible orientations of an edge. Such techniques as Sobel or Prewitt operators have been extensively used in the signal processing community as well as template matching for edge features. On the other hand, being a differentiation process, edge detection is by definition an ill-posed problem which needs a regularization process. At the beginning of the 1980s Marr [54] introduced the well-known edge detection scheme for artificial vision based on the use of the laplacian of a gaussian smoothing function $\nabla^2 G$ of standard deviation σ. In this approach the edge map is obtained by selecting the zero crossings of the filtered image. As such it always provides closed contours, but due to noise effects some are irregular and do not correspond to real edges in the scene.

Canny [18] proposed a theory for ''optimal'' linear shift-invariant filters to detect and localize edges, using three main criteria for the evaluation:

- Good detection capability, by maximizing the signal-to-noise ratio in the filter output
- Good localization when the spatial location of the maximum of the filter output has a small variance
- Minimization of multiple responses to a single edge feature in the scene

Following this optimal filter analysis, near-optimal performance has been obtained by using the first derivative of a gaussian G'_σ to detect step edges and the second derivative of a gaussian G''_σ to detect lines and roofs. Some major limitations are found in the incorrect localization of composite edges, like steps and roofs, as well as loss of junctions because of the poor orientation selectivity of the filters [9]. Anyway, this approach represents almost a standard in computer vision against which all new edge detection schemes are often compared [29]. After the computation of the smoothed gradient components, the edge location is obtained as the local maxima in the direction of the gradient vector, i.e., across the edge transition (nonmaxima suppression), as depicted in Fig. 11.4.

The final step is edge pixel linking, based on a local neighborhood analysis, using the so-called hysteresis thresholding, with two different values $T_1 < T_2$. Edge pixels with a gradient magnitude above threshold T_2 are selected as candidate starting points.

Contiguous edge pixels are then connected in a list, provided they exhibit a gradient value above T_1. In this way only significant edge contours are retained, with increased connectivity.

The straightforward implementation of the linking process would require random access to the filtered image to follow list propagation. On-line algorithms are also possible, by detecting local edge pixel configurations and then trying to fuse the created lists.

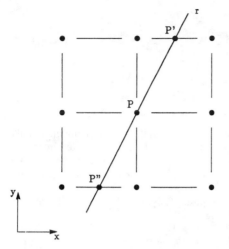

FIGURE 11.4 The Canny edge detection scheme: P is an edge point if its gradient absolute value is greater than the gradient absolute values in P' and P'', and r is the direction of the gradient in P.

Region Segmentation. This process is intended to select meaningful regions having a common property in the intensity value, texture, color composition, local gradients, etc. Generally speaking, it is a clustering process, performed by grouping a set of pixels in the image according to local properties of a feature vector. Region segmentation techniques can be classified in two main categories—region splitting and region growing—or a combination of them.

In the first case regions are split into smaller ones, according to some homogeneity criterion, and the process is repeated until an acceptable level of uniformity is achieved. An example is given in Ohlander et al. [62], where many different picture attributes are put in histograms for segmentation (color hue and saturation, intensity, etc.). Split-and-merge techniques have been also proposed [63] to come up with a picture tree describing relations between regions at different levels of resolution.

Region growing is another means of segmentation, by starting at a "seed" point and grouping all neighbor pixels, using either four or eight connectivity, until some similarity criterion is satisfied [64]. Again this uniformity test can be applied on raw intensity and color images or on filtered preprocessed data for feature or texture enhancement. The result of this segmentation is always an abstraction from an iconic representation to a more synthetic list of regions with attributes of shape, size, feature histograms, and mutual-adjacency relations.

Dynamic Modules: Optical Flow. We have already mentioned the increasing interest in dynamic computer vision, pushed also by the availability of much more powerful machines for real-time processing. The final goal is the understanding of 3D motion in the scene, but the first step is the computation of the projected 2D motion field on the image plane.

Typically, this is achieved by computation of the optical flow, which is a dense 2D vector field associated with the apparent motion of brightness patterns in the scene. Unfortunately, this does not always correspond to the actual 2D motion field. As a matter of fact, it has been demonstrated [79] that optical flow and the 2D motion field coincide only under certain assumptions, when there is sufficient contrast in the scene, i.e., at sharp edges. In the classical differential approach [46], the underlying hypothesis is that all intensity changes in the recorded irradiance function $I(x, y, t)$ are due to only the motion of objects in the scene, and such a motion is first-order approximated by small displacements, on a local basis. This corresponds to the well-known scalar motion equation which says that the global derivative of the image irradiance function, with respect to the time variable, is equal to zero.

$$\frac{dI(\mathbf{x},t)}{dt} = 0 \qquad \mathbf{x} = [x,y]^T \tag{11.4}$$

that is,

$$\frac{\partial I}{\partial x} v_x + \frac{\partial I}{\partial y} v_y = -\frac{\partial I}{\partial t} \tag{11.5}$$

or, in vector notation,

$$\nabla I \cdot \mathbf{v} = -\frac{\partial I}{\partial t} \qquad \mathbf{v} = [v_x, v_y]^T \tag{11.6}$$

From this equation only the normal component of the optical flow can be computed, in the direction of the spatial gradient function. As such, the problem is underdetermined, and the missing information about the tangential component of v (commonly known as the *aperture problem*) can be recovered by using additional assumptions like smoothness constraints.

An alternative vector equation has been proposed [58] with the assumption that the spatial gradient of the image pattern is stationary:

$$\frac{d\nabla I(\mathbf{x},t)}{dt} = 0 \tag{11.7}$$

In this way the vector components of the velocity field can be computed with no ambiguities, and it is proved to be appropriate for 3D motion analysis [38], based upon local computations around singular points. But since higher-order derivatives are required, a regularization smoothing filter is necessary (as derivative of gaussian functions) to minimize noise effects.

11.5.2 2D Geometric Reasoning

This section covers algorithms oriented to collect the extracted features organizing them into meaningful primitives. Again such techniques are divided into static and dynamic tools.

Static Modules: Primitive Extraction. Low-level iconic processing generates raw symbolic data which are a collection of pixel coordinates representing either gray-level discontinuities or uniform regions. The geometric meaning of the extracted data has to be made explicit by appropriate tools, producing a more synthetic representation in terms of simple geometric primitives or tokens. This kind of module, in the literature usually referred to as *intermediate vision,* is more model-driven than iconic algorithms. Assumptions about regularities in the image, geometric models and their properties, and perceptual heuristics such as the one suggested by the Gestalt laws are all used in different ways at this processing level.

The main points in favor of the inclusion of intermediate vision algorithms into the processing chain are

- *Robustness* with respect to the image formation process and low-level segmentation. In fact it is possible to recover lost structures by using model-based interpolation and fitting.
- *Reduction* of the amount of data and representation complexity.
- *Elimination* of isolated undesirable features.
- *Explicit* nature of shape, which provides relevant cues for 3D interpretation.

The following analysis is limited to the processing modules whose input representation is an edge point list, which seems to be more appropriate for 3D interpretation than a region-based image segmentation, much more used in 2D vision. At this level of representation, we have a list of edge contours described by their coordinates, with special local attributes such as gradient values, contrast, etc. Any attempt to fit these edge chains with predefined conics would be much too cumbersome computationally. An alternative, widely used approach consists of applying geometric reasoning to a more synthetic representation obtained by polygonal approximation of such edge chains.

Polygonal approximation can be implemented as a two-step process. Each chain is scanned, and breakpoints are selected when a change of curvature above a certain threshold occurs; then a linear regression algorithm is carried out, and the best least-squares segments approximating the curve between two breakpoints are created. The output is a list of chains of consecutive line segments described by initial and final coordinates and the direction cosines.

As we can see in Fig. 11.5*b,* the representation retains the pictorial content of the edge map but is more concise, and the geometric structure is more explicit.

Primitive extraction and perceptual grouping usually are performed over this representation, and the more commonly detected primitives are

- Long, straight-line segments
- Junctions as intersections of prolonged segments
- Regular arcs of curves such as ellipses and circles
- Parallelograms, that is, two pairs of symmetric segments
- Vanishing points that are intersections, on the image plane, of projected lines which are parallel in three dimensions

Heuristic rules, geometric laws, and least-squares best fit are the most common methods which are combined to extract such primitives. Gestaltlike perceptual heuristics include tests on the smoothness of the curves, collinearity of lines, local parallelism, etc. Geometric property rules are coded in specific routines aimed at verifying whether the image data are compatible with the model of the primitive which is the goal of the search. An example can be found in Masciangelo [55] where a specific property of the ellipse is exploited to search for elliptical arcs in the image (see Fig. 11.5*c*). Finally, best-fit procedures allow us to transform lists of coordinates to equations. Even if these procedures are quite standard, we must face a few caveats: Uniform sampling with respect to the curvature must be taken into account, and least-squares fitting is biased toward large-curvature solutions if only a portion of the curve is available [69].

2D Motion Analysis: Tracking of Features. Another tool for motion analysis is obtained by tracking a set of features of the moving objects in the scene. The result is a sparse set of vectors, as compared to the dense optical flow already discussed before. On the other hand, provided feature matching has been correctly performed, the obtained data correspond to the desired projected 2D motion field. The first step is to decide which are the most relevant features to track. A possible solution consists of tracking corners, whose position in the image plane is unique [45]. Otherwise, edge segments may be tracked, as mentioned in Deriche and Faugeras [30], although point-to-point correspondence is ambiguous, due to polygonal approximation, with the stable characteristics being line position and orientation. The tracking approach is always based on a combination of a prediction step and a matching process. A model of the system dynamics has to be established, from very complex situations to more manageable constant-velocity models for real-time implementation, as in De Paoli et al. [28]. Kalman filtering is then used to

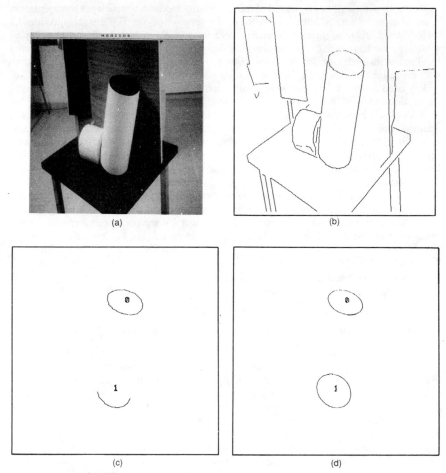

FIGURE 11.5 The ellipse detection process. *(a)* The original image. *(b)* The polygonal approximation of the contours. *(c)* Chains of segments recognized as elliptic arcs. *(d)* The fitted ellipses.

aid tracking, since it allows us to compute reasonable estimates of the region where the matching process searches for a possible match between tokens. In most token tracking implementations, a simplified separable version of Kalman filtering is used, for each of the descriptive parameters of the token (corner or edge segment), in the hypothesis that they are uncorrelated.

An alternative approach is based on tracking edge-connected chains as structured features by keeping connectivity information explicitly. Hildreth [45] has proposed a minimization process to include smoothness constraints on the second derivatives of the motion along the contours. A similar approach has been used by Garibotto [37] through a recursive computation of the normal component of the velocity along the edge chains to improve convergence of the process. Then this predicted position of the contours enables an easy matching with the new edge chains in the following image. This approach can track contours up to a fairly large displacement, provided no spurious edges appear in

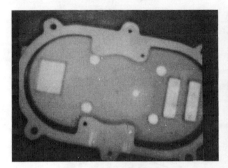 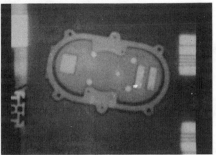

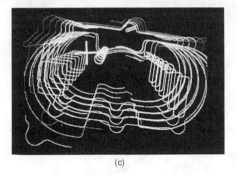

(c)

FIGURE 11.6   Tracking of contours of a zoom sequence. *(a)* First image of the sequence. *(b)* Last image of the sequence. *(c)* Result of motion prediction and matching.

between. The result is just a label propagation in the temporal sequence of images, as shown in Fig. 11.6. Explicit motion estimation can be performed afterward, at high-curvature pixels along the connected edge lists.

11.6 3D VISION

11.6.1 Passive Stereo Vision

Passive stereo vision represents the most general way of computing 3D range information, with close relationship to human stereopsis. To obtain stereo measures, it is necessary to solve two main problems, i.e., to find the pixel correspondence, typically from two camera views, and to compute the distance, by triangulation, once the cameras have been correctly calibrated (see Sec. 11.4).

Figure 11.7 describes the epipolar geometry of two arbitrarily oriented cameras and shows how the correspondence problem can be reduced to a one-dimensional (1D) search along the epipolar lines. In fact, the epipolar plane is defined as the plane passing through the two lens centers F_1 and F_2 and the target point P to be measured in 3D space. Hence, given a pixel P_1 as the projection of P onto the first image plane, the corresponding point

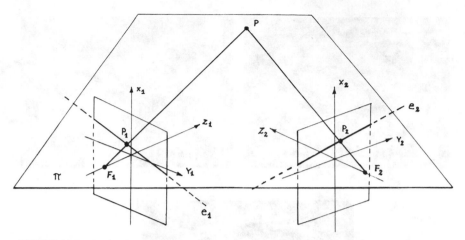

FIGURE 11.7 Epipolar geometry of a stereo setup. Here F_1 and F_2 are the centers of projection of the two cameras, P is a generic world point, π is the epipolar plane, and e_1 and e_2 are the two epipolar lines which contain the projections of P on the respective image planes.

P_2 in the other image must be found along the epipolar line e_2, which can be computed from the known spatial position of F_1, F_2, and P_1.

A first classification of stereo techniques may be related to the geometry of the stereo arrangement, so that we may have

- Binocular stereo with parallel axes. In this case the epipolar plane intersects the two image planes along parallel lines, which greatly simplifies the correspondence problem. But this is a mechanically fixed configuration, not optimal for short distance measurements.

- Binocular stereo with optical axes roughly convergent toward a common fixation volume, more appropriate for adaptive change of fixation point (animate vision). In this case image rectification is often performed to recover the parallelism of epipolar lines.

- Trinocular stereovision, to make the correspondence problem more robust and reliable, since one camera can be used for checking the matching hypothesis [3].

- Monocular stereo by translation or zoom; in the second case the direction of the camera motion is not necessarily that of the optical axis, provided the mutual orientations are known by calibration. Anyway, it is questionable whether to include this approach in stereovision techniques rather than in the computation of 3D structure from motion.

The choice of the most appropriate solution heavily depends on specific system requirements and constraints, such as the object distance and range, required precision, compactness of the sensor, adaptive properties, etc.

As far as the correspondence problem is concerned, stereo techniques can be further divided in two main classes: correlation and feature-based approaches.

In the first case, matching is performed on images, at the iconic level (as shown in Fig. 11.1), to obtain a dense range map by correlation of local neighborhoods (1D or 2D) in the hypothesis of sufficiently textured scenes. This is true in most natural scenes, as aerial or satellite pictures of the earth. Input data are gray-level images suitably filtered (high-frequency enhancement or histogram normalization) to achieve a more stable response from the image sensors. Very promising results have been reported [61] by using parallel computers, and the new advances in image processing architectures may further increase their application to many other domains.

The second class is feature-based matching, where 3D estimation is obtained only for a sparse set of selected features such as edge points, corners, segments, etc. This approach is more appropriate when one is dealing with quite untextured scenes, as in most manufactured objects and indoor environments (uniform walls, surfaces, etc.). The feature correspondence problem is almost the same as for token tracking, although the search is limited along epipolar lines, as mentioned above. Actually, it represents the most commonly used approach for stereovision in robotics applications [57, 65]. As a matter of fact, it provides an efficient data compression, from raw images to significant and descriptive 3D geometric entities, more appropriate for recognition and manipulation purposes.

11.6.2 3D Information from a Single View

In this section we present methods to interpret 3D scenes by means of a single view. This is a very challenging problem which has been tackled since the very beginning of the computer vision discipline by Brooks [13]. The intrinsic difficulty is the ill-posed nature of the problem: The shape of an object on an image depends on the viewpoint, and there are infinite 3D spatial attitudes which can generate the same image.

As a first step to recover 3D shape from a 2D projection, we need an explicit projection model. The two more widely accepted approaches are the

- *Perspective projection:* This is the pinhole model already presented in Sec. 11.4.

- *Orthographic projection:* Optic rays are parallel and perpendicular to the image plane [43].

The most correct model, according to both the human visual system and the CCD camera and optical setup, is the perspective model; but the orthographic hypothesis leads to simplified equations and good approximate results in some applications. On the other hand, the orthographic assumption holds whenever the focal length is adequate (zoom vision), the angle of view is small enough, and relevant objects are grouped in the same range of distances.

To better understand the different monocular approaches in vision, let us introduce the following broad classification of the main geometric properties according to their behavior under perspective projection:

- *Metric* properties such as length, orientation, and area are not invariant under projection.

- *Descriptive* properties such as collinearity and parallelism can be either variant or invariant; invariant properties are extremely important since they express unambiguous, global information about the scene.

Perspective Inversion.   To recover 3D *metric* properties of object attributes from 2D projections, we need to invert the perspective projection.

The problem is highly underconstrained. For example, an image point can be generated by any 3D point lying on the line joining it with the center of projection; a segment can come from any segment lying on the interpretation plane [6]. The *interpretation plane*

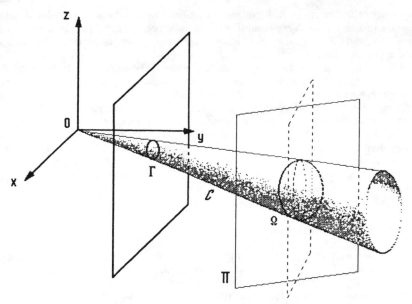

FIGURE 11.8   The two pencils of planes whose intersections with cone C over ellipse Γ and with vertex at the origin O are circles.

of an image segment is the plane containing both the segment and the origin of the camera reference system, i.e., the focal point. The analogy for image conics is the *interpretation cone* illustrated in Fig. 11.8.

Interpretation planes and cones help to represent the space of the solutions, but we need to impose *constraints* to solve the problem up to a finite ambiguity. Constraints may come from specific "metric" knowledge about the objects we are interested in as well as from general assumptions about the 3D configuration. In practice, the back projection process is limited to particular 3D geometric configurations and relative 2D projected primitives.

Typical 3D configurations, used as landmarks for self-positioning tasks in autonomous navigation, are planar circles, squares, triplets of orthogonal lines, etc. In any case the associated image primitives must be detectable by means of efficient and robust intermediate vision algorithms.

A few classical examples of such projective entities are the image of three mutually orthogonal segments, triangles, extremal boundaries of cylinders and cones, and ellipses projected by circles. In Mangili and Viano [53], the problem of inverting the perspective projection of an ellipse which is supposed to come from a 3D circle, is reduced to finding those planes whose intersections with the cone over the ellipse and with vertex in the origin are circles (see Fig. 11.8). The knowledge of the radius value allows us to choose, from an infinity of parallel planes, the correct position of the circle in 3D space.

As often happens in back projection problems, the given example does not lead to a unique solution: In this case there are two admissible circles in space. The ambiguity can be solved at a higher level by using more a priori information or data fusion techniques, as in Cassolino [20].

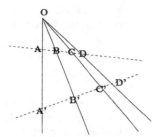

FIGURE 11.9 The cross ratio of four collinear points *(A, B, C, D)* is invariant under projective transformation.

The classical application of perspective inversion is model indexing in the hypothesis verification paradigm for object recognition (see Sec. 11.8). Some potentially interesting applications are related to landmark-based self-positioning in autonomous navigation.

Vanishing Points. A more qualitative approach is based on the extraction and analysis of the vanishing points in the image plane. Under perspective projection, those 2D segments in the image plane which correspond to parallel lines in the 3D space converge to a common point of intersection called the *vanishing point*.

By making a few assumptions on the structure of the scene, i.e., the number and relative position of the interesting vanishing points, it is possible to infer descriptive (usually not metric) information about the 3D world. A typical hypothesis for indoor or highly structured environments is the *Legoland assumption*, i.e., a block world in which physical edges have at most three mutually orthogonal directions. Therefore in Legoland there are, at most, three vanishing points [7].

An example of an application is as a support to navigation: Tracking vanishing points over an image sequence allows us to recover the heading direction for a robot in the presence of odometry uncertainty. Reasoning based on the line drawing of the scene, where each segment is labeled with the corresponding vanishing point, leads to a qualitative high-level interpretation in terms of semantic entities such as the floor, ceiling, walls, doors.

Another way to use the vanishing points can be found in monocular road following [24]. The problem is to extract the 3D orientation and position of the road with respect to the camera mounted on the vehicle, exploiting the vanishing point generated on the image by the projection of the two road boundaries.

Perspective Invariants. A recent approach to monocular 3D vision relies on the identification of shape descriptors which are unaffected by the perspective transformation. Measurements of these descriptors are representative of object properties regardless of the camera position.

Perspective invariants are currently used to infer quickly the appearance of an a priori known object belonging to a large-model database, without making Pose assumptions as in most 3D recognition systems.

Among the more popularly used perspective invariants are the joint scalar invariants of a pair of conics [83] and the *cross ratio* [56]. The cross ratio is an important projective geometry invariant, defined by the following property and illustrated in Fig. 11.9: Let A, B, C, D be four collinear points:

$$[A,B,C,D] = \frac{CA}{CB} : \frac{DA}{DB} = [A',B',C',D'] \qquad (11.8)$$

$$= \frac{C'A'}{C'B'} : \frac{D'A'}{D'B'}$$

This result is used as the basis for many back projection algorithms, since the defined proportionality holds both in 3D space and in the image. The difficulty is the recovery of the correspondence between 3D points and their 2D projections.

11.6.3 Structure from Motion

The goal of this approach is the recovery of the 3D structure of the scene, from the 2D motion field on the image plane, by using some basic assumptions on the sensed world. By considering the environment to be static, a reasonably good estimate of egomotion may be sufficient to obtain a 3D reconstruction of the objects in the scene. An example of this approach is found in 3D object modeling using a TV camera mounted on the wrist of an industrial robot whose motion has to be quite precise and controllable. Obstacle detection for mobile robotics can also be performed by motion analysis, through a prediction of the optical flow on the supposed planar surface of the pathway. Any irregular change of this flow field is a cue for the presence of an obstacle to be avoided [19]. In this case there is no need for an accurate knowledge of 3D motion which is, however, necessary for 3D object reconstruction.

Actually, there are many different approaches to compute 3D motion parameters from optical flow or feature correspondence. The basic problem can be formulated as the determination of the 6 degrees of freedom (3D rotation and translation) of rigid objects, from their images taken at different time instants. Through suitable algebraic techniques it has been proved that at least six features have to be correctly matched in the two consecutive views to obtain a unique solution.

Also 3D structure can be recovered via dynamic vision techniques, to obtain the relative position of the objects in the scene with respect to the fixation point of a moving camera [5].

11.6.4 Qualitative Motion Analysis: The Focus of Expansion

In some situations the main objective of an intelligent sensor is behavior control, such as for safe navigation in mobile robotics, rather than a precise reconstruction of the environment. Examples include time-to-crash analysis and trajectory control in a dynamic environment with multiple moving vehicles, to anticipate any trajectory interference.

A robust representative feature of the motion field is the *focus of expansion* (FOE) [or *focus of contraction* (FOC)], which provides the direction of a purely translational motion in the 3D scene. In the 2D image plane it is obtained as the intersection of all projected 3D motion vectors belonging to the same translational motion, as depicted in Fig. 11.10.

These vectors may come from token tracking, and the mathematical tools for the FOE computation are exactly the same as for vanishing-point estimation (see Sec. 11.6). Of course, since the local, short-time vectors are highly affected by measurement noise, the correct FOE position will be improved by integration in time.

From a dense optical flow of pure translation, as in Fig. 11.11, the FOE can also be estimated as the singular point where $v = 0$, and an estimate of *time to crash* is computed as the average

$$\frac{1}{N} \sum_{p \in w} \frac{v_p}{R_p} \tag{11.9}$$

where v_p is the magnitude of the motion field at a point p, R_p is the distance between p and the FOE, and p varies over a squared neighborhood w of the FOE including N samples

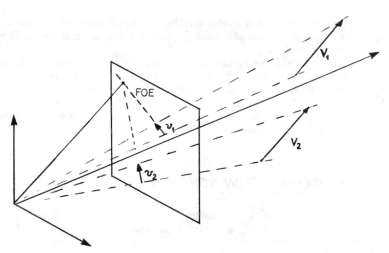

FIGURE 11.10 The focus of expansion. Here V_1 and V_2 are velocity vectors of a couple of 3D points; v_1 and v_2 are the corresponding velocity vectors projected onto the image plane, which converge into the FOE.

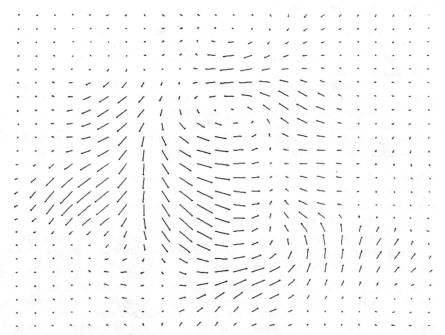

FIGURE 11.11 Flow fields from optical flow. *(Courtesy of Prof. Torre, University of Genoa, Italy.)*

of p [80]. This singular point may be also used for the identification and segmentation of moving objects in different directions, since they will generate different detectable FOEs in the image plane.

Moreover, this analysis is not limited to pure translation since any complex 3D motion can be approximated, on a short-time basis, by its local translational component using a first-order expansion. Hence, by tracking the instantaneous focus of expansion, it is possible in principle to follow the trajectory of a more complex motion. Of course, a key point for the success is the availability of a very robust and reliable FOE detector, which is not yet a fully solved problem.

11.7 3D REPRESENTATION SCHEMES

The choice of data representation depends heavily on the specific application constraints. Some general criteria can be stated, according to the fundamental requirement to keep just the essential information needed to accomplish the visual task at hand. For instance, edge points represent the primal sketch of the perceived scene and are the common basis for a more descriptive and synthetic representation. Corners are already significant features for scene understanding, especially when they correspond to robust and reliable geometric entities, such as 3D orthogonal joints [44]. Segments are again very useful representation features, as discussed in the previous examples of stereo reconstruction and token tracking.

11.7.1 Wire-Frame Representation

A 3D line segment representation of the world is the output of many successful vision systems, both monocular [7, 28] and stereo [57, 65]. Here we address the problem of the subsequent processing and utilization of such a representation, a relative example being shown in Fig. 11.12.

The wire-frame approach is applicable only to scenes which can be described by the principal surface discontinuities as a result of detectable intensity changes. Therefore, textured scenes and objects with smooth surfaces or curved physical boundaries are less manageable by such representation.

Three-dimensional processing is aimed at extracting the geometric structure of the reconstructed objects. Therefore the algorithms are supposed to do the following:

- Select the line segments which correspond to physical discontinuities, discarding outliers and pictorial evidences.
- Recover low-level segmentation errors by merging collinear or parallel segments which seem to belong to the same 3D boundary [17].
- Complete the wire-frame representation by inferring the existence of missing geometric elements: segments can be prolonged, junctions can be hypothesized, missing edges can be constructed by using heuristic reasoning.

A very advanced wire-frame completion system is under investigation at the University of Sheffield [67]. It combines geometry and statistics to test completion hypotheses, starting from real-time noisy data and the relative uncertainty estimates [68]. The systematic imposition of such constraints not only ensures the wire-frame geometric integrity

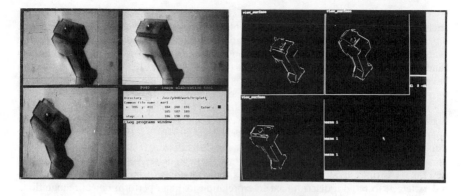

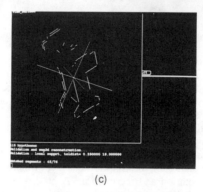

(c)

FIGURE 11.12 Stereo reconstruction of a mechanical piece. *(a)* A stereo triplet of a metallic object. *(b)* The line segments matched on the three images. *(c)* The 3D wire-frame reconstruction of the scene coming from the stereo process.

but also greatly improves accuracy, by compensating reconstruction errors through the assumption of object rigidity.

An alternative approach to 3D processing of line segments relies on the opposite initial hypothesis: Let us consider all the recovered segments, neglecting whether they come from physical discontinuities, but surely coming from a surface boundary. In this case we take advantage of textured scenes, where recovered data are dense. The idea is to extract surface primitives (planes, cylinders, cones) or regular patterns of lines, associated with semantic entities (tiles, windows, drawers), by grouping spatially adjacent segments on the basis of coplanarity or other geometric tests [40].

11.7.2 Surface Boundary Representation

A common approach for 3D scene representation involves the interpolation of the computed sparse 3D data, to obtain a boundary description of the perceived objects as they appear from a particular viewpoint.

With these methods, a 3D solid object is represented by segmenting its boundary (or enclosing surfaces) into a finite number of bounded subsets, usually called *faces* or *patches,* and describing the structural relationships between the segmented faces. An example of simple boundary representation is the triangle-faced polyhedron or boundary triangulation, which can be stored as a list of 3D triangles [10]. Also spline techniques have been proposed for surface interpolation, but in addition to computational problems they introduce an unsatisfactory smoothing effect at sharp discontinuities in the scene.

The main advantage of surface representations is the ready availability of representations for faces, edges, and the relations between them. Since surfaces are what is seen, the boundary representations are important for computer vision. In fact, when explicit surface information is required, a surface boundary representation is the natural choice to avoid unnecessary computations. Since boundary representations are verbose, a more synthetic description is often requested, in terms of simple quadratic primitives (like planes, cylinders, etc.), to build a discriminant interpretation tree and perform object recognition.

11.7.3 Volumetric Representation

Another approach for 3D data representation consists of a regular 3D cell decomposition of the scene according to a selected resolution. It has the advantage of a very simple description and ease of updating, but the fixed resolution sometimes is inadequate for the reproduction of certain details while it is redundant for big, uniform pieces. Such technique has received more attention especially for 3D graphical applications in medical applications [51], due to the availability of special architectures for voxel processing. It has been also proposed as a common reference domain for the integration of multiple stereo views and stereo-motion information [41]. Anyway a further processing step is required, to achieve some data compression into a subset of more descriptive volumetric primitives for scene segmentation and recognition. A promising solution has been proposed in Bajcsy and Solina [4] using superquadratics, where a careful selection of shape parameters allows a controllable deformation and composition of 3D model primitives.

11.7.4 The Delaunay Triangulation

An interesting representation scheme suitable for computer vision applications is the *Delaunay triangulation* (DT), whose 2D and 3D versions have been widely used in many different contexts, such as digital terrain modeling [26], cartography, and finite-element analysis [21]. In 3D versions, it provides a tessellation of the scene in terms of adjacent regular tetrahedra. Although it is based on 3D primitives (tetrahedra), it can also be used to achieve a linear interpolation of the scene surfaces, based on triangular patches [11].

Since in many applications it is useful to keep explicit the information about the relevant discontinuities, special versions of DT, referred to as *constrained Delaunay triangulations* (CDTs), have been developed, preserving the detected edge segments as sides of the triangles or of the boundary tetrahedra [27]. Due to its intrinsic discontinuity-preserving nature and updatability, CDT has been used successfully for representing stereo data in 3D scene reconstruction [33], obstacle avoidance, and trajectory planning [16]. A new technique for 3D surface reconstruction from stereo segments by using a two-dimensional CDT performed in the image plane has been recently proposed by Bruzzone et al. [15]. The novelty of the approach lies in the use of the most reliable data recorded in the image plane, the results of which are less affected by calibration and matching errors.

11.8 HIGH-LEVEL VISION

High-level vision can be defined as the functional layer which is more closely related to the final application of the sensory system. It is therefore difficult to classify high-level modules in a single framework, since approaches can be very different, even in terms of programming, ranging from real-time control to expert systems.

However, in a simplified scheme, it is possible to divide high-level vision modules in two broad categories: recognition and navigation. Recognition tasks are all kinds of image or sequence analysis oriented to identify a predefined object, event, or situation which can be relevant for the task of the sensory system. Navigation modules are supposed to acquire information about the environment which can support *collision-free* motion planning of any kind of autonomous moving agents, in both 2D (vehicles) and 3D (manipulating arms) situations.

In the following we present a few examples of recognition and navigation modules.

11.8.1 3D Model-Based Object Recognition

Object recognition can be considered a classical challenge for vision systems, and many keep it as their ultimate goal. The problem is academic in the sense that it represents a well-defined reference goal against which to compare the performance of a class of approaches. Nevertheless it has also application interests in the fields of robotic assembly, inspection, remote sensing, and surveillance.

The problem is defined as follows [8]: Given a collection of previously selected objects and digitized sensory data corresponding to one particular, but arbitrary, field of view of the real recorded scene, which objects appear in the digitized sensory data? For each occurrence, determine the 3D position and orientation.

A recognition process can be divided into two phases: the *off-line* model-building step and the *on-line* matching step, where sensory data are compared to the model database. The crucial issue is the choice of a common object representation framework for both models and data. Roughly all recognition systems may be characterized by three major elements:

- The 3D representation
- The model description and acquisition
- The matching paradigm

The Representation. The 3D representations related to vision algorithms are surveyed in Sec. 11.7. The selected geometric primitives are both the language for the description of the scene and the interface between low-level data-driven vision and high-level reasoning. They must be meaningful enough to disambiguate the recognition and, at the same time, suitable to be extracted from raw input data in a robust manner.

Model Database Building. There are two ways to acquire a full 3D model of an object: from a complete CAD representation, which is very rich but nonhomogeneous with vision-extracted data, or to build it by showing the object to the same vision system which is in charge of the recognition phase. In this latter case the extracted primitives are the same for both the model and the scene, but we are no more sure of the completeness and correctness of the model, which is prone to acquisition noise and reconstruction errors.

An alternative approach [47] suggests complicating the off-line phase by introducing as much a priori knowledge as possible about both the object and the sensory system models. In practice, a set of different recognition programs, each targeted to a specific model, are built off-line. They implement the best strategy to search for the most discriminant primitive first, in order to optimize on-line processing, where those programs are sequentially run until all the objects present in the scene are recognized. In this method the 3D models are subdivided into *characteristic views,* a set of 2D partial descriptions, each obtained from a particular point of view. The focus features which are detected by the low-level algorithms act as indexes to the correct view and the related recognition program.

Matching.   Generally speaking, the matching process consists of finding out which set of data features corresponds to a subset of the stored model. Methodological approaches often refer to consolidated problem-solving techniques such as graph matching, dynamic programming, and tree search.

The most successful matching paradigm, which avoids combinatorial explosion, is the *hypothesis verification* approach [39]. The idea is to search the interpretation tree, whose nodes are couples of matched data and model primitives, in a depth-first fashion in order to try all possible combinations. At the first level of the tree, an initial hypothesis is made, in terms of identification of the model sample and its spatial attitude. In the next processing step this initial guess is verified while looking for additional data model matchings supporting this hypothesis.

The matching criteria are geometric: When dealing with rigid objects, we have to find a transformation (translation and rotation) of the model into the sensed scene [32]. This transformation is estimated on the basis of the first matches and then confirmed or not by the other data primitives. The best interpretation, in terms of the number of matched primitives and geometric residual in the computation of the transformation, is the response of the system [20].

11.8.2 Navigation

Navigation, the second broad category of high-level vision applications, can be either in support to autonomous vehicles moving on the floor or to ascertain the safest trajectory for a robot arm gripper in the 3D space.

The visual tasks which are required, depending on the particular application and operative environment, as seen in Sec. 11.2, can be roughly classified according to the sensory range with respect to the vehicle:

- At short range, it is required to detect and avoid obstacles, providing safety conditions for the moving robot.
- At intermediate range, an estimation of the free *navigable* space in the vicinity of the robot is needed, in order to plan algorithms to choose the best safe route toward the goal.
- At long range, we need a way to orient the robot in an approximately known environment, by means of the recognition and positioning of prestored landmarks (self-location capability).

Short-range obstacle avoidance algorithms have to be very efficient in terms of real-time processing even if they are not required to be very "clever." In fact, they must provide quick alarms without any interpretation and do that at a high rate (at least 10 Hz) in order to guarantee the avoidance of an unforeseen, possibly moving obstacle, at robot speed of about 1 m/s. There exist quite a number of *ground plane obstacle detectors* (GPODs), both monocular and stereo. One is described here as an example of a purposive vision module.

Free-space map building provides the input for classical path-planning algorithms. In this case the real-time requirements are often relaxed since this step is usually performed at discrete intervals and the vehicle is stopped to allow 3D reconstruction of the environment. Typically 3D reconstruction is performed at first by means of stereo [16] or structure from motion [43]; then the attained 3D representation is projected onto the ground plane to obtain a 2D map containing free, occupied, and occluded space.

Global navigation encompasses the ability to recognize the environment and perform self-localization, to compensate for the accumulative errors of odometric sensors which are used in blind "navigation." In this case it is necessary not only to reconstruct the environment but also to solve a matching problem between the current reconstruction and a global map. Some other techniques are based on the recognition of a small number of predefined landmarks, which are accurately chosen as stable visual patterns in the scene.

A further interesting approach to visual navigation consists of continuous tracking of a given target by means of a dynamic vision system. A closed control loop makes it possible to guide the robot only on the basis of the sensory outcomes. The vision system can extract and maintain a 3D representation as in the stereo feedforward algorithm described in Pollard et al. [69] or track just 2D features and define the observable variables of the control system directly on the image plane. The control system is based on 4D discrete differential equations which provide the output commands to the actuators [31].

Purposive Visual Navigation. An example of a navigation module inspired by the purposive vision paradigm mentioned in Sec. 11.1 is as follows. The ground plane obstacle detector module provides not a reconstruction of the scene but a *visual competence,* i.e., the ability to detect unforeseen obstacles. This ability is strictly connected to the control system to achieve a reactive, almost *instinctive,* behavior of the mobile robot for obstacle avoidance.

The perceptual part of the layered control architecture which includes the GPOD is depicted in Fig. 11.13, which presents an ongoing research [2] aimed at building a vision-guided mobile robot.

The GPOD algorithm is based on a fast comparison between the current stereo disparity and a reference disparity map of the ground floor [35]. The principal constraint of the implemented approach is the necessity to work in an environment with a flat ground

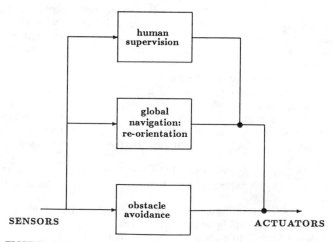

FIGURE 11.13 A layered mobile robot architecture based on visual modules.

floor. The definition of obstacle on which the algorithm is based is as follows: *Obstacle is everything higher than the ground floor*.

The first step is to produce a reference map of the ground floor. To this end a stereo algorithm based on a coarse-to-fine correlation procedure is used. This procedure is repeated iteratively, changing the image of the pattern of the ground floor through a displacement of the robot itself. A nice feature of this procedure is that the disparity map does not depend on the geometry of the camera, so that no calibration of the intrinsic parameters of the cameras is needed.

To check the presence of an obstacle inside the selected windows, a correlation procedure is used.

This algorithm illustrates the peculiarities of the qualitative vision approach:

- The algorithm is oriented to solve efficiently one particular visual task (obstacle detection) and nothing more.

- A simple motor action can be related directly to the module output as a qualitative command: no obstacles; obstacle on the right, on the left, or straight ahead.

- The module is robust and reliable and does not suffer from stability problems.

- The world is not represented metrically but relies upon a special representation, the disparity space, which is much more appropriate to solve the specific visual task. Furthermore, there is no need for intrinsic camera calibration, which is the main source of error for reconstructive algorithms.

11.9 CONCLUDING REMARKS: EXPERIMENTAL COMPUTER VISION

Computer vision is a young discipline with contributions from different branches of science and technology, and its final objective is still a controversial issue in the scientific community.

On one hand, industrialists consider it a technology to exploit in real applications, and they want to see robust, even if not elegant or general enough, algorithms able to deal with unconstrained environments and off-the-shelf hardware implementations. On the other hand, academic researchers are keen to solve challenging problems to better understand the human visual perception and to simulate intelligent behaviors with machines.

An appropriate solution seems to be a system engineering approach to pursue an experimental computer vision as opposed to the theoretical discipline that has prevailed so far.

That means that every reported work has to be supported by results obtained through a severe and controllable experimental methodology. Furthermore, experiments should be described in sufficient detail to make them repeatable, as in all "hard" sciences. Finally, algorithms have to be evaluated according to industrial criteria, taking into account practical problems such as the sensitivity to external illumination variations, the reflectance problems of real objects and environments, the performance stability of CCD cameras, etc.

Moreover, algorithm descriptions should be completed by an adequate error and stability analysis and by the explicit enumeration of the design parameters (thresholds) embedded in the algorithm.

The whole computer vision community would benefit from the adoption of an experimental methodology that would provide industrialists with a clear perspective on applicability and allow scientists to exchange ideas on a more solid basis.

REFERENCES

1. J. Aloimonos and D. Shulman, *Integration of Visual Modules.* San Diego: Academic Press, 1989.

2. S. Arrighetti, F. Ferrari, S. Masciangelo, and G. Sandini, "Implementation of a Subsumption Architecture for Mobile Robotics on the EMMA2 Multiprocessor," *Proceedings of BARNAIM-AGE 91,* Barcelona, Spain, 1991.

3. N. Ayache and L. Lustman, "Fast and Reliable Passive Stereovision Using Three Cameras," *Proceedings of the International Workshop on Industrial Application of Machine Vision and Machine Intelligence,* Tokyo, February 1987.

4. R. Bajcsy and F. Solina, "Three-Dimensional Object Representation Revisited," *Proceedings of the First International Conference on Computer Vision.* Tampa, Fla.: IEEE Computer Society Press, 1987, pp. 231–240.

5. D. H. Ballard and A. Ozcandarli, "Eye Fixation and Early Vision: Kinetic Depth," *Second International Conference on Computer Vision.* Tampa, Fla.: IEEE Computer Society Press, December 1988.

6. S. T. Barnard, "Interpreting Perspective Images," *Artificial Intelligence,* 21:435–462, 1983.

7. P. Bellutta, G. Collini, A. Verri, and V. Torre, "3D Visual Information from Vanishing Points," IEEE Workshop on Interpretation of 3D Scenes, Austin, Tex., 1989.

8. P. Besl and R. Jain, "Three-Dimensional Object Recognition," *Computing Survey,* 17(1), 1985.

9. D. J. Beymer, "Junctions: Their Detection and Use for Grouping in Images," master's thesis, Massachusetts Institute of Technology, Artificial Intelligence Laboratory, Cambridge, Mass., 1989.

10. J. D. Boissonnat, "Representation of Object Triangulating Points in 3-D Space," *Proceedings of International Conference on Pattern Recognition,* Munich, 1982.

11. J. D. Boissonnat, "Geometric Structures for Three-Dimensional Shape Representation," *ACM Transactions on Graphics,* 3(4), 1984.

12. D. Braggings and J. Hollingum, *The Machine Vision Sourcebook.* New York: IFS (publications) Ltd., Springer-Verlag, 1986.

13. R. A. Brooks, "Model Based Three-Dimensional Interpretation of Two-Dimensional Images," *IEEE Transactions on Pattern Analysis and Machine Intelligence,* 5(2), 1983.

14. R. A. Brooks, "Intelligence without Representation," *Artificial Intelligence.* Amsterdam: Elsevier, 1991, pp. 139–159.

15. E. Bruzzone, G. Garibotto, and F. Mangili, "Three-Dimensional Surface Reconstruction Using Delaunay Triangulation in the Image Plane," *Proceedings of International Workshop on Visual Form,* Capri, Italy, 1991.

16. M. Buffa, O. D. Faugeras, and Z. Zhang, "Obstacle Avoidance and Trajectory Planning for an Indoors Mobile Robot Using Stereo Vision and Delaunay Triangulation," *Proceedings of the Round-Table Discussion on Vision-Based Vehicle Guidance,* Tokyo, 1990.

17. M. Campani, C. Coelho, and M. Straforini, "A Fast and Accurate Method for Computing Vanishing Points," *Proceedings of ISPRS Symposium,* Zurich, Switzerland, 1990.

18. J. F. Canny, "Finding Edges and Lines in Images," AI Lab. Tech. Rep. 720, Massachusetts Institute of Technology, Cambridge, Mass., 1983.

19. S. Carlsson and J. O. Eklund, "Object Detection Using Model Based Prediction and Motion Parallax," *Proceedings of the First European Conference on Computer Vision,* 1990, pp. 297–306.

20. C. Cassolino, F. Mangili, and S. Masciangelo, "3-D Object Recognition: A Matching Paradigm Oriented to Data Fusion," *Proceedings of the International Conference on Intelligent Autonomous Systems,* vol. 2. Amsterdam, 1989.

21. J. C. Cavendish, "Automatic Triangulation of Arbitrary Planar Domains for the Finite Element Method," *International Journal of Numerical Methods in Engineering*, no. 8, 1978.

22. A. M. Cross, D. C. Mason, and S. J. Dury, "Segmentation of Remotely-Sensed Images by a Split-and-Merge Process," *International Journal of Remote Sensing*, 9(8):1329–1345, 1988.

23. J. L. Crowley and P. Stelmaszyk, "Measurement and Integration of 3-D Structures by Tracking Edge Lines," *Proceedings of the First European Conference on Computer Vision*, 1990, pp. 269–280.

24. L.S. Davis, D. DeMenthon, S. Dickinson, and P. Veatch, "Algorithms for Road Navigation," *Proceedings of Round-Table Discussion on Vision-Based Vehicle Guidance*, Tokyo, Japan, 1990.

25. T. Day and J. P. Muller, "Digital Elevation Model Production by Stereo-Matching SPOT Image Pairs: A Comparison of Algorithms," *Proceedings of the Fourth Alvey Vision Conference*, 1988, pp. 117–122.

26. L. De Floriani and E. Puppo, "Constrained Delaunay Triangulation for Multiresolution Surface Description," *Proceedings of Ninth International Conference on Pattern Recognition*, Rome, Italy, 1988.

27. L. De Floriani and E. Puppo, "A Survey of Constrained Delaunay Triangulation Algorithms for Surface Representation," in G. G. Pieroni (ed.), *Issues on Machine Vision*. New York: Springer-Verlag, 1988.

28. S. De Paoli, A. Chehikian, and P. Stelmaszyk, "Real Time Token Tracker," *Proceedings of EUSIPCO*, Barcelona, Spain, 1990.

29. R. Deriche, "Using Canny's Criteria to Derive a Recursively Implemented Optimal Edge Detector," *International Journal of Computer Vision*, 1(2):167–187, 1987.

30. R. Deriche and O. D. Faugeras, "Token Tracking," *First European Conference on Computer Vision*, Nice, France, 1990.

31. E. D. Dickmanns and V. Graefe, "Applications of Dynamic Monocular Machine Vision," *Machine Vision and Applications*, 1(4), 1988.

32. O. Faugeras and M. Hebert, "The Representation, Recognition, and Positioning of 3-D Shapes from Range Data," in A. Rosenfeld (ed.), *Techniques for 3-D Machine Perception*, 1986.

33. O. Faugeras, E. Le Bras-Mehlman, and J. D. Boissonat, "Representing Stereo Data with the Delaunay Triangulation," *Artificial Intelligence*, 44, 1990.

34. O. D. Faugeras and G. Toscani, "Camera Calibration for 3D Computer Vision," *Proceedings of International Workshop on Machine Vision and Machine Intelligence*, Tokyo, Japan, 1987.

35. F. Ferrari, E. Grosso, G. Sandini, and M. Magrassi, "A Stereo Vision System for Real Time Obstacle Avoidance in Unknown Environment," *Intelligent Robots and Systems 90*, Tsuchiura, Japan, 1990.

36. B. Frederick, R. M. Carrell, E. M. Alexander, and G. J. van Sant, "Handling of Irregular-Sized Mailpieces by Adaptive Robotics," *IEEE Control Systems Magazine*, 9(2):3–8, 1989.

37. G. Garibotto, "Motion Tracking of Connected Edge Contours," in V. Cappellini (ed.), *Time-Varying Image Processing and Moving Object Recognition*, vol. 2. Amsterdam: Elsevier, 1990, pp. 323–330.

38. F. Girosi, A. Verri, and V. Torre, "Constraints for the Computation of Optical Flow," *Workshop on Visual Motion*, March 20–22, 1989, Irvine, Calif., pp. 116–124.

39. E. Grimson and T. Lozano-Perez, "Search and Sensing Strategies for Recognition and Localization of Two- and Three-Dimensional Objects," *Proceedings of Third International Symposium of Robotics Research*, Gouvieux, France, 1985.

40. P. Grossmann, "COMPACT—A Surface Representation Scheme," *Proceedings of the Fourth Alvey Vision Conference*, Manchester, England, 1988.

41. E. Grosso, G. Sandini, and M. Tistarelli, "3-D Object Reconstruction Using Stereo and Motion," *IEEE Transactions on Systems, Man, and Cybernetics*, 18(6), 1989.

42. J. Hadamard, *Lectures on the Cauchy Problem in Linear Partial Differential Equations.* New Haven: Yale University Press, 1923.

43. C. G. Harris, "Structure from Motion under Orthographic Projection," *Proceedings of the European Conference on Computer Vision 90,* Antibes, France, 1990.

44. C. G. Harris and M. Stephens, "A Combined Corner and Edge Detector," *Proceedings of the Fourth Alvey Vision Conference,* Manchester, England, 1988.

45. E. C. Hildreth, "Computations Underlying the Measurement of Visual Motion," *Artificial Intelligence,* 23:309–354, 1984.

46. K. Horn, *Robot Vision.* M.I.T. Press and McGraw-Hill, 1986.

47. K. Ikeuchi and T. Kanade, "Towards Automatic Generation of Object Recognition Programs," Carnegie Mellon Tech. Rep. CMU-CS-88-138, Pittsburgh, 1988.

48. R. C. Jain and T. O. Binford, "Ignorance, Myopia and Naiveté in Computer Vision Systems," *CVGIP: Image Understanding,* 53(1), 1991.

49. R. A. Jarvis, "A Perspective of Range Finding Techniques for Computer Vision," *IEEE Transactions on Pattern Analysis and Machine Intelligence,* 5(2):122–139, 1983.

50. A. S. Johnson, and B. M. Bird, "Evaluation of an Automatic Number-Plate Recognition System for Real-Time Automatic Vehicle Identification," *Proceedings of ISATA Conference on Road Transport Informatics and Intelligent Vehicle-Highway Systems,* 1991.

51. A. Kaufman and R. Bakalash, "Memory and Processing Architecture for 3D Voxel Based Imagery," *IEEE Computer Graphics Applications,* November 1988, pp. 10–23.

52. R. K. Lenz and R. Y. Tsai, "Techniques for Calibration of the Scale Factor and Image Center for High Accuracy 3-D Machine Vision Metrology," *IEEE Transactions on Pattern Analysis and Machine Intelligence,* 10(5): 713–720, 1988.

53. F. Mangili and G. B. Viano, "Object Recognition and Positioning Methodologies in 3D Space from a Single View," *Proceedings of International Conference on Intelligent Autonomous Systems,* Amsterdam, 1986.

54. D. Marr, *Vision.* San Francisco: W. H. Freeman, 1982.

55. S. Masciangelo, "3D Cues from a Single View: Detection of Elliptical Arcs and Model-Based Perspective Backprojection," *Proceedings of British Machine Vision Conference '90,* Oxford, England, 1990.

56. R. Mohr and E. Arbogast, "It Can Be Done without Camera Calibration," *Pattern Recognition Letters,* 12, 1991.

57. G. Musso, "Depth and Motion Analysis: The ESPRIT Project P940," *Proceedings of ESPRIT Week, 89,* Brussels, Belgium, 1989.

58. H. H. Nagel, "Displacement Vectors Derived from Second-Order Intensity Variations in Image Sequences," *Computer Vision, Graphics, and Image Processing 21,* 1983, pp. 85–117.

59. G. Nagy, S. Seth, and S.D. Stoddard, "Document Analysis with an Expert System," in E.S. Gelsema and L. Kanal (eds.), *Pattern Recognition in Practice,* vol. 2. Amsterdam: Elsevier, 1986.

60. A. N. Netravali, T. S. Huang, A. S. Krishnakumar, and R. J. Holt, "Algebraic Methods in 3-D Motion Estimation from Two-Viewpoint Correspondences," Tech. Note ISP-901, University of Illinois, Coordinated Science Laboratory, February 1989.

61. H. K. Nishihara, "PRISM: A Practical Real Time Imaging Stereo Matcher," Memo 780, Massachusetts Institute of Technology, Artificial Intelligence Laboratory, Cambridge, Mass., 1984.

62. R. Ohlander, K. Price, and D. R. Reddy, "Picture Segmentation Using a Recursive Splitting Method," *Computer Graphics and Image Processing,* pp. 313–333, 1978.

63. T. Pavlidis, *Structural Pattern Recognition.* Berlin: Springer-Verlag, 1977.

64. T. Pavlidis, "A Critical Survey of Image Analysis Methods," *Proceedings of the International Conference on Pattern Recognition,* Paris, October 1986.

65. S. B. Pollard, J. E. W. Mayhew, and J. Frisby, "PMF: A Stereo Correspondence Algorithm Using a Disparity Gradient Limit," *Perception*, 14:449–470, 1985.

66. S. B. Pollard, J. Porril, and J. E. W. Mayhew, "Predictive Feed Forward Stereo Processing," *Proceedings of the Fifth Alvey Vision Conference*, Reading, United Kingdom, 1990.

67. S. B. Pollard, J. Porril, and J. E. W. Mayhew, "Recovering Partial 3D Wire Frame Descriptions from Stereo Data," *Proceedings of British Machine Vision Conference '90*, Oxford, England, 1990.

68. S. B. Pollard, T. P. Pridmore, J. Porril, J. E. W. Mayhew, and J. P. Frisby, "Geometrical Modeling from Multiple Stereo Views," *International Journal of Robotics Research*, 8(4), 1989.

69. J. Porril, "Fitting Ellipses and Predicting Confidence Envelopes Using a Bias Corrected Kalman Filter," *Proceedings of the Fifth Alvey Vision Conference*, Reading, United Kingdom, 1989.

70. W. Pratt, *Digital Image Processing*. New York: Wiley, 1978.

71. M. P. Robins, "Free-Ranging Automatic Guided Vehicle System," *GEC Review*, 2(2):129–132, 1986.

72. J. L. C. Sanz and A. K. Jain, "Machine Vision Techniques for Inspection of Printed Circuit Boards and Thick-Film Circuits," *Journal of the Optical Society of America*, 9:1465–1482, 1986.

73. S. A. Shafer, "Geometric Camera Calibration for Machine Vision Systems," *Manufacturing Engineering*, March 1989.

74. U. K. Sharma and D. Kuan, "Real-Time Model Based Geometric Reasoning for Vision-Guided Navigation," *Machine Vision and Applications*, 2:31–44, 1989.

75. SPIE, *ISPRS Fifth Symposium on Close-Range Photogrammetry Meets Machine Vision*, vol. 1395, Zurich, Switzerland, September 3–5, 1990.

76. M. Tistarelli and G. Sandini, "On the Estimation of Depth from Motion Using an Anthropomorphic Visual Sensor," *Proceedings of ECCV90*, Antibes, France, 1990.

77. V. Torre and T. Poggio, "On Edge Detection," *IEEE Transactions on Pattern Analysis and Machine Intelligence*, 8(2):147–163, 1986.

78. USPS, 4th Advanced Technology Conference, United States Postal Service, November 5–7, 1990.

79. A. Verri, F. Girosi, and V. Torre, "Mathematical Properties of the 2D Motion Field: From Singular Points to Motion Parameters," *Workshop on Visual Motion*, Irvine, Calif., 1989, pp. 116–124.

80. A. Verri and T. Poggio, "Against Quantitative Optical Flow," *First International Conference on Computer Vision*, London, 1987, pp. 171–180.

81. C.F.R. Weiman, "Exponential Sensor Array Geometry and Simulation," *Proceedings of SPIE Conference on Pattern Recognition and Signal Processing*, Orlando, Fla., 938:128–137, 1988.

82. J. Weng, P. Cohen, and M. Herniou, "Calibration of Stereo Cameras Using a Non-Linear Distortion Model," *Proceedings of Tenth International Conference on Pattern Recognition*, Atlantic City, 1990.

83. A. Zissermann, C. Marinos, D. A. Forsyth, J. Mundy, and C.A. Rothewell, "Relative Motion and Pose from Invariants," *Proceedings of British Machine Vision Conference '90*, Oxford, England, 1990.

CHAPTER 12

ARCHITECTURES FOR IMAGE PROCESSING AND COMPUTER VISION

Giovanni Garibotto

Research and Development,
Elsag Bailey spa, Genoa, Italy

12.1 INTRODUCTION

The main objective of this chapter is to provide a critical analysis of image processing architectures for computer vision with major emphasis on robotic applications.

As such, the wide range of powerful stand-alone image processing workstations, primarily designed for computer graphics and interactive operations, as well as video coding systems for telecommunications will not be considered here. This analysis focuses on hardware and software requirements and solutions of machine vision, as they appear in industrial robotics, service, and advanced robotics for unstructured environments. The more general methodologies and architectures of computer vision are examined and commented upon in the framework of practical machine vision applications.

Conventional computers are unable to fully meet these requirements, so that a number of special-purpose architectures have been developed for the analysis of static and time-varying images. So far no universal solution exists to cover all needs of computer vision. The ''optimal'' solutions may differ quite a lot, depending on specific constraints and the selected technology. The major drawback is the need to conceive and design new solutions for any new problem. However, a certain degree of flexibility is desirable, at least from the integration viewpoint, to avoid useless duplication of effort. As such, it is necessary to have an efficient hardware and software environment, with suitable tools, to include different modules as required by the application, without altering the basic architecture of the processing system. Some of these architectures for computer vision integration are discussed in Sec. 12.5, where high-level processing is considered.

This chapter begins with a short survey of some issues of image acquisition units and trends of the market. Then the rest is arranged according to the logical scheme of Chap. 11, pointing out the most promising architectural solutions corresponding to the three levels of computer vision system. This classification will be supported by references to commercial systems as well as to advanced prototypes, based on the direct experience of the author.

Sections 12.1, 12.2, and 12.3 will each include a quick analysis of major requirements and expected performance, which is used as reference evaluation criteria of the different possible solutions. Real-time constraints are considered as well as data size for local computation, to establish how much local or temporary storage a single processing unit must have and if independent processing may be performed on different subsets of the input data. Regular or random addressing requirements and data types involved are additional parameters considered in this analysis.

Of course, the most demanding level from the computational viewpoint is that of iconic processing where it is necessary also to deal with severe communication and memory addressing problems. Anyway, an increasing role in computer vision is played by more flexible processing on features and structured lists of elements (geometric reasoning and matching). Improved addressing capabilities, higher-level abstractions (linked lists and floating point), feedback and feedforward paths, and adaptive processing are just a few of the major requirements for intermediate-level processing and cannot be ignored in this architecture analysis. Other promising areas of development are symbolic processing and logic programming whose application is difficult to generalize since it is highly task-dependent.

To avoid the risk of making too generic an investigation of computer vision systems, a final section is devoted to briefly describe an example of an advanced front-end unit for real-time processing. It consists of a powerful and versatile architecture, for stereovision and motion tracking, suitable for a heterogeneous environment, which has been developed under a European ESPRIT project by a highly qualified research team. Some concluding remarks are made about the present efforts toward standardization and the foreseen major trends of the research.

12.2 IMAGE ACQUISITION UNITS

This is the first stage of the system to get all necessary pictorial information from the scene, and its relevance to the success of the full machine vision process is well known. The main components of an acquisition unit are summarized in the block diagram of Fig. 12.1.

There are *lookup tables* (LUTs) on the video input and output, where an input signal or byte configuration is used as an address into a stored array of values, so that it can approximate any function of one or more variables. The input LUT adjusts the signal range (normalization or equalization), and the output LUT is mostly used for pseudo-color display purposes.

The input signal from a TV camera is digitized and stored in a frame buffer. The most common image processing standards are RS-170, Committee on Colorimetry and Illumination Research (CCIR), and RS-343, all producing 2:1 interlaced images with different resolution [17]. Anyway, there are special applications (like optical character readers for mail sorting and document reading) where dedicated solutions are required to achieve higher speed and resolution. In these cases customized reading heads are realized, by using linear arrays of sensors and a special circuitry for preprocessing (enhancement, binarization) and sampling.

Conventional video digitization occurs in time to get a frame which is sampled in space (typical size is 512×512 pixels) and quantized in intensity (8 bits), to obtain a two-dimensional array of integer values representing image intensities in the memory. Depending on the buffer size or the availability of a fast communication link to powerful processing modules, time sampling can be performed at the maximum rate of 25 frames

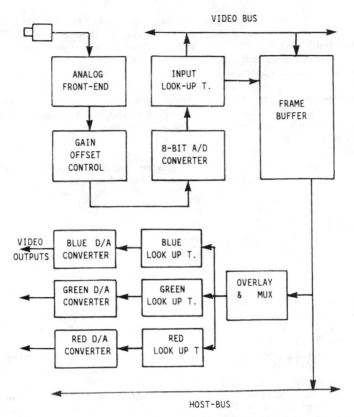

FIGURE 12.1   Block diagram of a general video frame grabber digitizer board; sometimes the frame grabber is located into another independent board, connected through the video bus.

per second in the European standard (30 frames, National Television System Committee (NTSC) standard) or 50 interlaced half-size fields each one every 20 ms.

Due to the spatial distribution of the sensory cells in the camera and the sampling frequency of the digitizer, the resulting image matrix has different spacings between horizontal and vertical pixels. This represents a strong limitation in some computer vision applications, especially in dimensional measuring, and alternative solutions are under development, although not yet widely used, for cost and nonstandard reasons. They use equally spaced camera sensors either with digital interface, to avoid the double step of D/A and A/D conversion, or connected to suitable digitization boards, using appropriate sampling frequencies. High-resolution sensors (for instance, 570 lines with 768 pixels) are already commercially available. They provide external synchronization to achieve a correct sampling of the square pixels (11 μm $\times$ 11 μm, CCIR version).

It is worthwhile to mention also the emerging new standards for high-definition TV. Another, fully nonstandard solution, which is tightly related to the computer vision task, is the design and realization of special space-variant "retinal" sensors [21], to mimic human perception.

There are different suppliers on the market for image acquisition modules (Data Translation, Matrox, Imaging Technology, Datacube, etc.), and the differences are mainly due to video bus characteristics for video data transfer to other processing modules. Most of these video busses provide three levels of synchronization (pixel timing, horizontal timing, and vertical timing) and sometimes a bus to support data transfer of arbitrarily sized windows or regions of interest in the image plane.

The existence of such different solutions to video bus communication actually prevents a wider interchange of modules for an integration, at least at the very low level of iconic video rate processing, although some standards are emerging de facto on the market. Additional problems come from the need for custom-designed optics and dedicated illumination systems for almost every application. Moreover, the speed of industrial processes is constantly increasing, which means that visual sensors are fast enough to supply the system with the required information.

In general, most technological efforts are now devoted to extend spatial resolution and increase the radiometric sensitivity and dynamic range of advanced visual sensors.

12.3 LOW-LEVEL IMAGE PROCESSING ARCHITECTURES

The main purpose of this stage of early processing is feature extraction and iconic-to-symbolic transformation to recover geometric parameters of shape, edges, physical and pictorial contours, textures, color blobs and regions, etc. The result is a strong compression of information to keep the most relevant description of the scene for the following processing steps of matching, representation, recognition, and understanding. The algorithms involved at the low-level stage are almost well defined and data-driven, and their flexibility is limited to the tuning and adaptation of parameters. A quite representative processing tool of this class is given by local neighborhood computation, as convolution, correlation, clustering or growing and the input data consist of one or more matrices of bytes or words. Many tasks require "real-time" computation, which means something in between video rate processing (25 or 30 Hz, according to video standards) and 1-s delay (1 Hz). General-purpose sequential processors are not adequate to provide the required computational power and data transfer rate.

In fact, in a video sequence the time interval between two consecutive pixels is about 100 ns. To perform a machine vision task of 100 or more operations per pixel, a sequential processor should have a cycle time of less than 1 ns, which is not affordable with present technology. This kind of performance may be achieved by dedicated hardware or parallel computing.

In particular, different kinds of parallelism are possible: parallelism of instructions [multiple-instruction single-data (MISD)], vector processing and parallelism of data [single-instruction multiple-data (SIMD)], and full multiprocessing [multiple-instruction multiple-data (MIMD)]. Some of these solutions are mentioned in the following with examples from existing vision machines.

12.3.1 Dedicated Hardware Boards and VLSI Technology

Advances in technology and the evolution of discrete logic into *very large-scale integrated circuits* (VLSI) have enabled cost-effective implementation of processing hardware chips and modules, particularly suited for intense computational tasks. These architectures are usually limited to the level of well-defined fixed-image operations, such as convolution or correlation, edge detection, and linear and nonlinear filtering.

In this case the approach is to map algorithms directly into silicon, to provide a set of chips as a building block for more specialized image processing boards [15].

This is the case of convolution chips from LSI logic for programmable one-dimensional finite impulse response (FIR) filtering, with coefficients up to 64 taps and video rate performance. A separable 2D convolution board may be easily designed and realized around this chip [14]. Recursive filtering chips are now becoming available to implement more general linear filtering, independent of the mask size. Another interesting class of VLSI chip is the programmable linear and nonlinear histogram filtering chip, which allows both median and min-max filtering [13]. Many vendors supply high-performance *digital signal processor* (DSP) boards as generic, programmable modules for intense computation; some now support IEEE floating-point standard operations (32 and 64 bits).

Sometimes VLSI technology is used to design a few different types of cells interconnected in a regular pattern where several datastreams flow synchronously through the network, interacting at the cells where they meet. A typical example of this approach is *systolic processing,* pioneered by H. T. Kung at Carnegie Mellon University [12]. The basic idea of this approach is to match the computation rate to the I/O bandwidth of the system, making extensive use of pipelining and parallel processing.

Systolic designs for two-dimensional convolution and template matching have been developed, using either a linear array or a two-dimensional mesh of connected cells. This solution is particularly suitable for those low-level functions where the operations to be performed are quite well defined and repetitive and their flow is independent of the data.

Sternberg [19] has proposed a serial array processor called the *cytocomputer,* based on neighborhood transformations. The heart of this structure is a *processing element* (PE) which performs a fixed function on a local neighborhood of the sample pixel. It is used as a basis for morphological filtering on binary images as well as gray-level erosion or dilation [20].

12.3.2 Parallelism of Instruction (Pipeline Implementation)

To achieve parallelism in instructions, it is possible to pipeline data. A *pipeline* is a stream of data that flow at a constant rate through a sequence of processors. Each processor in the pipeline may take as long as it needs to process the data, provided its input and output data rates are synchronous.

The final output is time-shifted from the input, but it flows at the same rate. In this way processing is expanded in space, to provide more computation time. This approach is the most widely used in commercial architectures for image processing. Examples are the Imaging Technology Inc. series 150 processors as well as the Datacube Maxvideo 20 product line. In both cases the integrator is provided with a set of boards, specialized to perform different tasks of image processing, for real-time convolution, linear and nonlinear filtering, histogram processing, morphology, etc. They can operate on subimages or region of interest, at a rate proportionately faster than the entire image size.

Third-party vendors offer other boards, interfaced to standard VME bus, to support high-speed disk control, a large variety of frame storage, and other general-purpose parallel or vector processing. Thus it is very easy to use these modules as building blocks for the realization of a *front-end image processing* (FIP) system, where each board, or a group of boards, can be seen as an element of the pipeline, with its own memory and processing capabilities. Moreover, this architecture can be easily expanded, by adding other boards according to specific requirements. However, pipeline processing is often limited in local storage, has poor flexibility in addressing capabilities, and has requirements to operate with a single data type (integer or fixed-point representation).

The host communication is usually performed through registers and mailbox protocols. On the host side a "manager" software accepts calls from a program and sends a message to the FIP system, which contains the function to be performed and its arguments. Typically the FIP system has a simple dispatcher or supervisor that interprets this message and initiates processing. Return values are sent back to the host manager and from there to the user's program. The host and the FIP system can operate asynchronously in a parallel concurrent way. To have an idea of the processing speed available in commercial systems, see Preston [16]. For instance, a 512×512 fast-Fourier transform (FFT) takes about 4 s or less depending on the computational power of special-purpose array processors. Geometric warping operations can be performed much faster, in less than 1 s. Unfortunately, more complex functions, such as image enhancement, edge detection, and linking or feature token tracking and stereo matching, cannot be implemented in a single step, and many boards have to be connected, with processing times of tens of seconds in the best case. Thus the real-time requirements of computer vision are not always satisfied by commercially available pipeline systems.

12.3.3 Parallelism of Data (SIMD)

An alternative for real-time implementation is provided by data parallel image processing hardware, where the same instruction is applied in parallel to a block of data. Most common examples of this class are the array processors, often used to efficiently execute a wide variety of DSP algorithms including one- and two-dimensional fast Fourier transforms, digital filters, vector and matrix operations, and other high-speed numeric processing. The local storage of array processors is limited by the number of processors available, and the addressing pattern is usually determined by how the array is loaded. Data types are fixed and may be integers or floating-point values.

Much research effort has been devoted to the development of 2D processing arrays with fixed interconnections, as in the cellular logic image processor (CLIP) program at University College [8] dealing with very simple processing units. In this approach, the structure and the operation of a two-dimensional array of PE modules are matched to the structure of the image data, and different interconnections are possible as in quad trees and pyramids. A pyramid machine [23] is realized by stacking progressively smaller two-dimensional arrays of processing elements, to allow a multiresolution analysis of an input image array. Image data are loaded into the base of the array, and results propagate up to the top of the pyramid. This approach enables efficient processing at different levels of abstraction and resolution, which, in principle, are important factors for both low-level and middle-level vision. Presently the fine-grained nature of these architectures restricts the controllability of each layer in an SIMD mode of operation. Of course, the increase in the number of connections is the key factor which limits the construction of large systems.

In Cantoni et al. [5] a bin pyramid is adopted, instead of the more common quad pyramid, with the resultant reduction in the total number of connections, at the expense of an increase in the number of planes and layers. A still controversial issue is the tradeoff between the number of processors and the computing power of each individual PE. Improved flexibility for middle- and high-level operations seems to suggest a different trend toward coarse-grained systems with increased computational capabilities.

Most SIMD machines have been used primarily for low-level processing or pixel-based transformations, although they are well suited also for certain middle- and high-level processing (consistent labeling and Hough transform). A well-known example of this potential application is given by the connection machine [11], briefly mentioned in Sec. 12.5.

12.3.4 Multiprocessing MIMD

These architectures consist of several processors applying different instruction sets to different datastreams. The individual processors may be quite powerful and programmable so that the granularity of the system is necessarily limited. Parallelism may be achieved by simple data partitioning or by concurrent processing. Such extreme versatility of the system may be excessive for low-level processing. But it represents an interesting alternative for a class of algorithms which are the bridge between iconic and symbolic processing. For instance, edge contour linking and pixel grouping and growing, as in region feature extraction, are typical functions where the input is represented by image data (on the video bus) and the output is a list of edge pixels or region features to be further analyzed and interpreted. Still real-time processing at the video rate is a heavy constraint of such implementations.

DSP technology now offers some interesting solutions in terms of integer processing of various word lengths (16 and 24 bits) [14], and suitable board architectures may be designed, by integrating multiple DSPs, to do these tasks in an efficient manner.

12.4 INTERMEDIATE LIST PROCESSING

This stage of processing is primarily oriented to perform feature clustering, matching, and ordering into higher-level structures. Examples are polygonal approximation of edge contour lists, token tracking, where tokens are already geometric features such as segments or corners, stereo matching, 3D computation and 3D geometric reasoning, and 3D interpolation.

The common property of this stage is the need for adaptive and parameterized processing, the unavailability of an established control flow, different data types and structures, and a large variety of addressing modes. The module architecture should be flexible enough to allow modification and different algorithm implementation and should deal with heterogeneous development environments.

According to the amount of computation needed, some general-purpose *reduced instruction set computer* (RISC) processors or DSP boards may be appropriate to perform geometric processing at a rate greater than 1 Hz. Some relatively simple algorithms such as segment token tracking may be performed at the rate of 10 Hz with a single DSP board [6]. Multiple DSP boards are necessary for more complex operations such as stereo matching or polygonal approximation at a fast rate (greater than 5 Hz) [9]. An alternative solution is provided by general-purpose powerful MIMD machines which may provide adequate computational power and a reasonable partitioning of data and code. An example of this approach is given by the transputer array which is used in many research laboratories, at both university sites and industrial groups [4], and as an alternative to DSPs and dedicated hardware for low-level processing. In this case the bottleneck is represented by image data transmission to the individual processors, and efficient video bus interfaces have to be provided.

12.5 HIGH-LEVEL PROCESSING AND SYSTEM SUPERVISION

This level of processing is most heavily conditioned by the application. It includes system coordination and task-oriented data processing, with scene interpretation and sensory feedback for actuators. At this level it is possible to identify different modules and functions requiring less computational power, but an intensive, though not always predictable, data exchange and interprocessor communications.

The driving criterion is the control architecture of the system. There are bottom-up strategies starting from low-level processing up to feature extraction, object recognition, and decision. Sometimes hierarchical schemes with feedback control are more appropriate to coordinate different machine vision operations. A distributed control system is probably the most flexible solution to address complex tasks, which may be split into a series of subtasks, to be performed independently in parallel. Unfortunately there is not yet a commonly agreed upon solution to process synchronization and activation which is solved in different ways for different machine architectures. Finally we may recall the subsumption architecture, arranged in layers of competencies [3], particularly attractive for robotics applications.

The most promising candidates for this task are MIMD machines. Among the various solutions currently proposed for computer vision applications, a few examples of different classes of control and integration systems have been selected. The discussion is based on the characteristics of the communication network system starting from an architecture based on a hierarchy of busses, another one with a ring bus topology, and a third one with a regular, fully connected mesh of high-level processing elements. We conclude with some comments on the fine-grain parallelism of the connection machine.

12.5.1 Hierarchical Distributed System

Both single-global-bus and multiple-bus structures have been used for connecting groups of processors and memory units. Information or message routing is very simple and is commonly accomplished through a memory-mapped scheme. An improved solution may be obtained by arranging a series of hierarchical levels of busses with reconfigurable clusters of processors, according to the application needs.

Figure 12.2 shows a block diagram for a hierarchical architecture, named EMMA2 [1], an MIMD, shared-memory parallel computer, which has been developed by Elsag to satisfy both intensive computation constraints and real-time requirements.

This machine is already in use in industrial applications, for mail sorting and document processing, including address localization and character recognition in real time, satellite image acquisition and reconstruction, speech understanding, artificial intelligence and expert systems, with integration of sequential and logic programming.

The efficiency of this hierarchical structure comes from partitioning the whole application into parallel independent subsystems, optimizing the large linear bus bandwidth at two levels of computation: the lower level, an array of processing elements called *families*, and the upper level, consisting of an array of such lower-level cooperant multiprocessor machines named *regions*, interconnected by point-to-point high-speed parallel links, as shown in Fig. 12.2.

The innermost level of this hierarchy is the processing element, an INTELiAPX 286/386 CPU, possibly coupled with an arithmetic standard coprocessor or a proprietary, application-oriented gate array custom chip (*arithmetic logical accelerator*, or ALA), for elementary vector processing operations.

The communication protocol is *message passing*, and the network topology is unconstrained and adaptable to application requirements. One of the "region" nodes may be replaced by a standard host computer of DEC VAX/micro VAX family, for software development and machine supervision.

The local busses support 32-bit-wide 10-Mbyte/s data transfer with fault tolerance, *interrupt program counter* (ipc), interrupt, and memory broadcasting mechanisms.

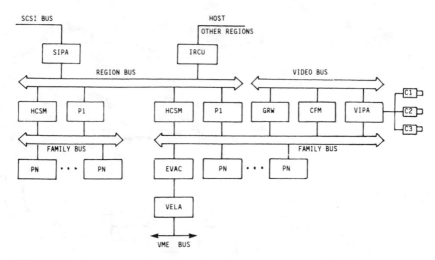

FIGURE 12.2 The structure of a region of multiprocessor architecture EMMA2; P1 is a single processor supervisor board in the "family"; PN is a three-processor board which may be equipped with a VLSI integer vector processor (low-level family) or a floating-point accelerator (high-level family); HCSM is a high-capacity system memory; VIPA is a video digitizer board; CFM is a real-time 2D FIR separable convolution filter (31 taps); GRW is a programmable pixel-grouping operator, based on a local (3 × 3) neighborhood. EVAc-VELA is a large-bandwidth communication channel to a standard VME environment.

This general-purpose multiprocessor architecture provides the necessary flexibility for realization of high-level computer vision tasks, by exploiting parallel processing. However, most image processing functions, at the iconic level, do not require such flexibility, being essentially data-driven, repetitive processes aimed to achieve data compression from images to features.

For that reason a front-end image processing subsystem has been integrated into a low-level family of processors, including an acquisition board, a 2D separable convolver, and a programmable pixel grouping module, on a dedicated video bus. There is also a large-bandwidth interface to standard VME environments, but an integrated solution is always more efficient than heterogeneous and distributed processing.

Another hierarchical architecture applied to computer vision is discussed by Dickmanns and Graefe [7] where real-time computation is deferred to different clusters of processors for robotics applications. Examples are shown in the precise position control for planar docking between 3D vehicles and in high-speed road vehicle guidance.

12.5.2 Pipeline Connection

We have already discussed the wide use of this interconnection of modules for image processing. Multiprocessors can be realized through many different fixed communication links arranged with various topology schemes.

An example of this architecture is shown in Fig. 12.3, corresponding to the CAPITAN machine from MS2i, which was first designed for space and military applications. It is an

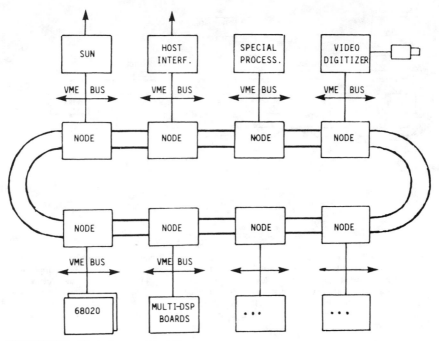

FIGURE 12.3 Block diagram of the MIMD processor CAPITAN, built around VME nodes connected through two ring busses, which may be split to create subring sections, each one with the original throughput.

MIMD distributed computer built around VME bus nodes, which may support a variety of general-purpose CPU boards, as well as DSP and multi-DSP boards, array processors, memory boards, etc. The interconnection network is composed of two ring busses which appear as a series of synchronously rotating slots, each one to convey elementary information.

To provide sufficient reliability of the implementation, a double ring bus is used [25], to be able to cope with almost any kind of failure of one element. This reconfiguration property is also useful to obtain a dedicated architecture according to traffic requirements, by splitting the ring bus into three or more subrings, with a smaller number of processing nodes. Again, the resulting architecture provides the necessary flexibility with individual nodes acting as specialized processors for low-level, intermediate-level, and high-level vision. The pipeline interconnection is quite appropriate for a bottom-up processing scheme, but the software reconfigurability of the machine allows also a promising environment for distributed processing. The selected standard environment allows an easy introduction of new advances in CPU and VLSI technology.

Yet the resulting configuration is not always the optimal compromise of cost versus performance for specific computer vision applications. The results of 3D vision experiments reported by Vaillant et al. [24] demonstrate that such flexible architecture is more appropriate for high-level processing than for low-level and middle-level image operations, such as gradient computation, edge detection, linking, and polygonal approximation.

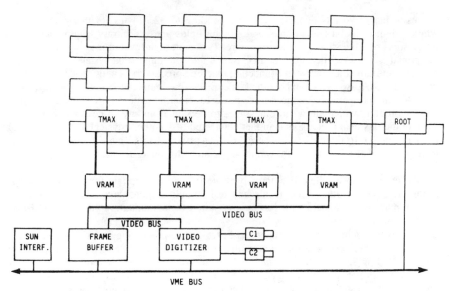

FIGURE 12.4   Block diagram of the MARVIN system architecture based on a regular mesh of transputer boards.

12.5.3 Regular Mesh of High-Level Processors

Another approach to multiprocessing is based on the use of a regular grid of processors connected together. An example of this scheme is given by the MARVIN multiprocessor [18] which has been designed and realized as a fully connected mesh of Transputers T800 and an extension to the root transputer, as shown in Fig. 12.4. One row of processors consists of specially developed transputer cards, named TMAX [4], to provide fast video bus communication, mainly for image data, minimizing data transit time. The adopted model of parallelism is based upon *communicating sequential processes* (CSPs), where the system comprises a number of sequential processes executing concurrently and communicating via channels.

The individual processors provide a varied repertoire of resources, as requested, in a client-server model. Vision processing is broken down into a number of tasks, each of which may itself be multithreaded, with dynamic changes of operation in the system. Due to the flexibility of high-level programming and the computational power of the TRAMs module, best performances are obtained for intermediate- and high-level vision tasks where feature parallelism may be exploited. Although video bus interconnection is provided by TMAX modules, low-level processing, heavily based on spatial data parallelism, is not optimally performed in this configuration. For instance, Canny edge detection takes about 5.5 s as opposed to 1.6 s for model matching [18].

12.5.4 Fine-Grain Parallel Machines

Different comments can be made about the connection machine which fully exploits the connectionist approach. It combines a very large number of physical processors (65,536) but may be configured for a much larger number of logical processors [11]. Each physical processor has 4096 bits of memory, corresponding to 32 Mbytes for the machine as a whole. Memory is bit-addressable, and all data fields are of arbitrary length. Individual processors are quite simple so they do not really permit high-level processing of data, and the primary characteristic of this architecture is the communication system. The simplest way of communication between connection machine processors is between nearest neighbors, to north, east, west, and south. General intercommunication and dynamic reconfiguration are performed by a much more powerful communication system, the connection machine router, which allows full messages to be sent from any processor to any other. Each of the physical processors is in fact connected to 16 other physical units in a special organization (a 16-dimensional hypercube) that provides large numbers of direct paths through the system. It takes a maximum of 12 steps to move from any chip to any other chip.

The connection machine is extremely powerful and appropriate for expensive simulation tasks where other experiments and tests would require days of computation on general-purpose computers. It is particularly suited for computer graphics 3D simulation by matching data topologies exactly.

Moreover, sophisticated new approaches for image processing and vision algorithms can be tested and verified on large amounts of data with a relatively small programming effort [22]. For instance, to compute depth maps from binocular stereo, a difference of gaussian filters is applied to both right and left images to detect edge points. Disparity is then computed by sliding one image over the other and producing a new image with incremental values for overlapping edge patterns. The same approach is used to efficiently compute the Hough transform for 2D recognition and labeling of objects in the scene.

From the practical viewpoint of an industrial cost-effective computer vision system for robotic applications, it is not yet an affordable solution.

12.6   A REFERENCE EXAMPLE: REAL-TIME 3D VISION SYSTEM

To avoid the vagueness of a chapter that summarizes computer vision technologies and architectures, an example of real-time implementation is now given. It is the result of development and integration of an ESPRIT program [14], aimed to realize a 3D vision system for robotic inspection and manipulation and mobile robot autonomous navigation. The adopted data representation is based on 2D edge segments, coming from minor modifications of Canny's edge detector, to obtain a strong data compression from input images. A trinocular stereo algorithm has been selected, including an accurate camera calibration and suitable epipolar transformation to simplify segment matching in the three images.

To support the implementation of these algorithms, a real-time vision system has been realized for low and intermediate levels of processing, up to 3D stereo reconstruction and token tracking.

This hardware front end, called *depth and motion analysis* (DMA), is an "open" architecture, which can be interfaced with different standard environments (VAX, SUN, PC) as well as integrated with additional boards from the market. Figure 12.5 shows the DMA chain for a reconfigurable pipeline structure, including one or more acquisition boards.

To solve communication problems, three different links have been selected:

- The VME for control and data transfer of features, such as edge chains or segments, for system start-up and monitoring

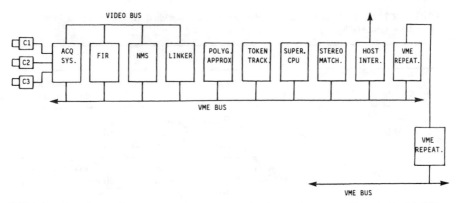

FIGURE 12.5   Block diagram of the 3D front-end DMA machine; the functions implemented by the different boards are explained in the text.

- The video bus MAXBUS (from Datacube) for TV-rate image transmission
- Some private interboard links for local communications

Besides standard modules for image acquisition and the supervisor CPU, the DMA machine has some dedicated hardware modules to perform well-defined operations with number crunching requirements, such as 2D separable filtering (up to 64 filter taps using the LSI Logic L64240 MFIR chip) and edge detection (non-maxima suppression). Other boards are based on fixed-point DSPs (ADSP2100) for edge linking and token tracking. General-purpose fixed-point multi-DSP boards (Motorola 56000) are available also for polygonal approximation and stereo matching, as well as a floating-point multi-DSP (Motorola 96000) for 3D reconstruction and uncertainty computation. Table 12.1 summarizes the performances of individual boards which have been integrated into the system.

The corresponding implementation may achieve a real-time processing rate at the expense of an overall input/output delay, related to the number of the stages in the pipeline. Particular attention has been paid, during the second phase of the project, to creating an efficient software environment for integration. A standard CPU supervisor on the VME bus has in charge the start-up initialization of all modules, their synchronization, and parameter modification. All DMA modules are VME slaves with interrupt capabilities, excluding FIR and *nonmaxima suppression* (NMS) boards. Communications among the CPU supervisor, the host computer, and the SUN graphic workstation are implemented by message exchange through mailboxes. A powerful software environment has been realized for human-machine interaction through a set of graphic facilities, on the SUN workstation, which allow

- Single-step commands for each individual module activation
- Global commands to run the whole chain or a subpart of it
- Different operating modes such as single shot, *n* times, or continuous
- Debugging facilities such as graphic and testing tools
- I/O files of off-line commands for each module
- Easy control and modification of parameters

TABLE 12.1 Main Characteristics and Performance of Individual Modules Integrated into Real-Time 3D Vision Machine DMA

	Hardware performance		
Module	Input	Output worst case	Hardware implementation
Finite impulse response (FIR) filtering	Gray-level image $512 \times 512 \times 8$	Gradient components G_x, G_y $2 \times (512 \times 512 \times 8)$	Dedicated hardware 40 ms
Nonmaxima suppression	Gradient components $2 \times (512 \times 512 \times 8)$	Gradient module + binary edge image 10% edge points	Dedicated hardware 40 ms
Edge linking	Gradient module + binary edge image + G_x + G_y	Linked chain lists 250 edge chains 10 kpixels	4 ADSP 2100 + coprocessor 120 ms[†]
Polygonal approximation	Linked edge chain lists	Segments less than 1000	4 Motorola DSP 56000D 200 ms[†]
Stereo matching	Segments + average gradient	Segment triples matched and validated hypothesis, worst case 1000, normal case 200	4 Motorola DSP 56000D 300 ms[†]
Token tracking	Segments + average gradient	Tracked segment list, max. 250 tokens	ADSP 2100 100 ms

[†]Expected computation time with typical configuration. Larger and faster configurations are allowed.

The higher levels of the system, such as symbolic processing or task-oriented control, are implemented on flexible and powerful general-purpose host environments, like the SUN workstation or parallel machines already available in the P940 consortium.

12.7 CONCLUSIONS

This chapter provides an overview of machine vision architectures, without any claim to cover the extremely challenging issue of advanced parallel processing systems. The only attempt has been directed to achieve a reference classification scheme for an integration engineer, to better understand the quickly evolving area of image processing for computer vision. The requirements of real-time processing and the need to match also control architectures more oriented to robotics represent strong limitations to possible solutions. As such the proposed scheme is somewhat different from classical reports, which are more oriented to general-purpose image processing machines.

The resulting architecture is actually a heterogeneous solution where a sufficiently powerful and flexible host processor (possibly an MIMD machine) is supposed to provide the integration environment to control and implement the high-level tasks. Different local architectures are possible, to implement low-level iconic processing and image-to-feature transformation (SIMD and pipeline solutions have been presented). Similar comments can be extended also to middle-level processing modules, where multi-DSP boards as well as SIMD or MIMD configurations are often proposed and have proved quite promising.

Standardization. In the last few years there has been a large effort toward standardization. In fact, it represents a key point to widen and consolidate the computer vision market and, as a consequence, to push greater investment in the realization of "standard" modules from a much larger number of vendors.

This subject of standardization is very relevant in telecommunications (video compression standards like CCITT M.261, JPEG, MPEG, and HDTV) but some initiatives have been recently reported also in the computer vision community [2]. Anyway, standardization is often contrary to optimization, because the increased generality, flexibility, and redundancy sometimes prevent the achievement of a specifically tailored solution to the current problem.

Hence, a full standardization of processing architectures for computer vision is unlikely to be achieved in the next few years. On the other hand, such standard solutions will definitely appear for the most established processing levels, such as histograms, convolution, mathematical morphology, edge and feature extraction, etc. Many hardware modules on the market are already quite similar, and there is some kind of consensus from the computer vision community on such low-level operations, so that standard solutions seem to be quite possible soon.

Actually, this could be extremely important for the evolution of vision research toward high-level application tasks, by minimizing the time spent to redesign quite well-established low-level functions.

Performance Evaluation. Any effort at classification has to be based on some criteria of evaluation, which should be general enough to cover most practical situations. Unfortunately this is not an easy task for computer vision. Actually some efforts have been reported in the literature to evaluate image processing computers, where conventional benchmarking techniques are not readily applicable.

A widely accepted tool for evaluation of image processing architectures is the Abingdon cross benchmark, where the task is to find the medial axis of a cross in a noisy background [16]. These results have been used to rate the quality factor against the price performance factor for many commercial systems, although they are limited to a set of very simple geometric functions and point or matrix computations. So far no similar tools are available for more complex machine vision systems belonging to different robotics applications. A possible solution consists of exploiting a systems engineering approach with a thorough evaluation of the full system as well as its individual components. Such an experimental method aims to stress the algorithms and the subsystems to ensure a sufficiently robust behavior. A robust machine vision technology should be almost invariant to sensing and illumination constraints. It needs adaptive mechanisms in the selection of the processing parameters (for instance, in image segmentation, classification, etc.) and should include geometric reasoning tools to deal with 3D scene transformations. Another essential component is an effective hardware and software environment for system control and integration. There are already promising display environments which permit iconic or "visual" programming and simplify the task of the operator, without the need to be expert at the image processing algorithms. Systems engineering criteria will remove the ad hoc nature of present solutions and provide the basis for the new generation of computer vision systems.

REFERENCES

1. E. Appiani, B. Conterno, V. Luperini, and L. Roncarolo, "EMMA2, a High-Performance Hierarchical Multiprocessor," *IEEE MICRO,* February 1989, pp. 42–56.

2. ARVISA, Advanced Real-Time Vision System Architecture, ESPRIT Project P5225, Technical Annex, February 1991.

3. R. A. Brooks, "A Robust, Layered Control System for a Mobile Robot," *IEEE Journal of Robotics and Automation,* 2:14, 1986.

4. C. Brown and M. Rygol, "MARVIN: Multiprocessor Architecture for Vision," *Proceedings of the 10th Occam User Group Technical Meeting,* 1989.

5. V. Cantoni, V. Di Gesu', M. Ferretti, S. Levialdi, R. Negrini, and R. Stefanelli, "The PAPIA System," *Journal of VLSI Signal Processing,* 2:195–217, 1991.

6. S. De Paoli, A. Chehikian, and P. Stelmaszyk, "Real Time Token Tracker," *Proceedings of EUSIPCO'90,* Barcelona, Spain, 1990.

7. E. D. Dickmanns and V. Graefe, "Applications of Dynamic Monocular Machine Vision," *Machine Vision and Applications,* 1988, pp. 241–261.

8. M. J. B. Duff, "Review of the CLIP Image Processing System," *Proceedings of the National Computer Conference,* 1978, pp. 1055–1060.

9. O. Faugeras, R. Deriche, N. Ayache, F. Lustman, and E. Giuliano, "Depth and Motion Analysis: The Machine Being Developed within ESPRIT Project P940," *IAPR Workshop on Computer Vision, Special Hardware and Industrial Applications,* October 12–14, 1988, Tokyo, Japan.

10. G. Gaillat, "Le calculateur parallele CAPITAN: 600 MIPS pour l'imagerie temps reel," *Revue Traitement du Signal,* 1(1):19–30, 1984.

11. D. Hillis, *The Connection Machine.* Cambridge, Mass.: M.I.T. Press, 1985.

12. H. T. Kung, "Let's Design Algorithms for VLSI Systems," *Proceedings of the Caltech Conference in VLSI,* California Institute of Technology, Pasadena, 1979, pp. 65–90.

13. LSI Logic Co., "L64220 Rank-Value Filter RVF," November 1987.

14. G. Musso, "Depth and Motion Analysis: The ESPRIT Project P940," *ESPRIT '89 Conference Proceedings,* pp. 10–30, November 1989.

15. G. R. Nudd, "Image Understanding Architectures," *Proceedings of the National Computer Conference,* 1980, pp. 377–390.

16. K. Preston, "The Abingdon Cross Benchmark Survey," *Computer,* July 1989, pp. 9–18.

17. J. M. Raynor and P. Seitz, "The Technology and Practical Problems of Pixel-Synchronous CCD Data Acquisition for Optical Metrology Applications," *Proceedings of SPIE,* vol. 1395, *Close-Range Photogrammetry Meets Machine Vision,* 1990.

18. M. Rygol, S. Pollard, and C. Brown, "A Multiprocessor 3D Vision System for Pick and Place," *Proceedings of the British Machine Conference,* Oxford, September 1990, pp. 169–174.

19. S. R. Sternberg, "Architecture for Neighborhood Processing," *Proceedings of Pattern Recognition and Image Processing Conference,* Dallas, 1981, pp. 374–380.

20. S. R. Sternberg, "Grayscale Morphology," *Computer Vision, Graphics and Image Processing,* 35:333–335, 1986.

21. M. Tistarelli and G. Sandini, "On the Estimation of Depth from Motion Using an Anthropomorphic Visual Sensor," *Proceedings of the European Conference on Computer Vision '90,* Antibes, France, 1990.

22. L. W. Tucker and G. G. Robertson, "Architecture and Applications of the Connection Machine," *Computer,* August 1988, pp. 26–38.

23. L. Uhr, "Pyramid Multi-computer Structures, and Augmented Pyramids," in M.J.B. Duff (ed.), *Computing Structures for Image Processing.* London: Academic Press, 1983.

24. R. Vaillant, R. Deriche, and O. Faugeras, "3D Vision on the Parallel Machine CAPITAN," *International Workshop on Industrial Applications of Machine Intelligence and Vision (MIV-89)*, Tokyo, April 10–12, 1989.

25. C. Weitzman, *Distributed Micro/minicomputer Systems*. Englewood Cliffs, N.J.: Prentice-Hall, 1980.

26. S. Yalamanchili, "Image Processing Architectures: A Taxonomy and Survey," in L. N. Kanal and A. Rosenfeld (eds.), *Progress in Pattern Recognition*, vol. 2. Amsterdam: Elsevier, 1985.

CHAPTER 13
VLSI SYSTEMS DESIGN

Donald W. Bouldin
Department of Electrical and Computer Engineering
University of Tennessee, Knoxville

13.1 INTRODUCTION

Very large-scale integration (VLSI) actually refers to the placing of 100,000 or more transistors on a single integrated circuit; yet the term is often misused by referring to any microelectronic circuit fabricated by using the latest monolithic technology. In this chapter an overview of microelectronic technology will be given with an emphasis on digital *complementary metal-oxide semiconductor* (CMOS) circuits that can economically achieve the density of VLSI levels. Following a brief explanation of the microelectronic fabrication process and a survey of the various technologies, the design methodology for VLSI systems will be described. Since microelectronic systems must be specified at every level of abstraction including the system, behavioral, register, logic, circuit, transistor, and process levels, the optimum design from an overall systems viewpoint may not require the designer to exploit a particular level to the maximum (e.g., compact the layout of an individual circuit to minimum size without regard for the routing of communication paths to other circuits). Often this means the designer (or team leader) need not be an expert in any one aspect of the design but instead is sufficiently knowledgeable about each level that tradeoffs can be made which result in an overall optimum design from the systems point of view.

13.2 MICROELECTRONIC FABRICATION

Integrated circuits are fabricated by a series of steps which involve the patterning of microelectronic devices on a substrate by using various layers of materials. A *field-effect transistor* (FET) is shown in Fig. 13.1. The material labeled *n* has been doped to permit conduction using negative charge carriers while that labeled *p* has been doped to permit conduction using positive charge carriers. A voltage applied to the gate material can be used to change the electric field between the gate and the substrate to either permit or not permit the flow of charge carriers between the two *n*-type materials. Thus, charge may be electronically steered through the device, which may also be constructed to amplify or attenuate the current.

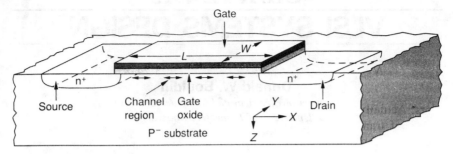

FIGURE 13.1   Simplified three-dimensional view of an FET. *(From R. Geiger, P. Allen, and N. Strader, VLSI Design Techniques for Analog and Digital Circuits, New York: McGraw-Hill, 1990)*

The fabrication process begins by growing a single crystal of material (usually silicon) into a cylinder that is perhaps 2 m long and 100 to 200 mm in diameter. The cylinder is then sliced into wafers that are typically 250 to 400 µm thick. A wafer is then doped with either *n*-type or *p*-type impurities so that the bottom layer, or substrate, not only provides the mechanical structure to support the other layers to be patterned but also becomes a part of the electric circuit itself.

Other layers of material can now be added as required on top of the substrate. First, a photosensitive material is applied to the entire wafer. Then a mask is used to prevent light from striking the photosensitive material in certain regions. The unexposed photosensitive material can be removed (or etched) by a wet chemical procedure or a dry plasma process. Thus, material for each layer can be added selectively in desired length and width and at specific locations. Each mask is made of glass covered with a thin film of opaque metal and typically costs about $2000. Processes may require from 10 to 20 of these masks to form the various layers [1].

Impurities to form positive and negative regions can be impregnated in a layer by using either diffusion or implantation techniques. In diffusion, a gas containing a high percentage of the type of carriers desired is heated in a chamber containing the wafer (see Fig. 13.2). Depending on the time and temperature, migration of the impurities occurs into the topmost layer. Implantation is an alternative method which involves accelerating impurities from an ion source to bombard the wafer such that the impurities remain lodged in the wafer very near the surface.

One very important factor in the fabrication process is the need to achieve a high level of contamination control. Processes in which the minimum feature size is less than 1 µm in width require that there be no more than one contaminant particle per cubic foot of space. If this level of cleanliness can be maintained, a 1-cm^2 region on a finished wafer will contain only one or two defects due to contaminants. An integrated circuit or die may have to be scrapped if the defect occurs in an area important to circuit operation.

A wafer is shown in Fig. 13.3 that contains two types of dies. One is the process control monitor that has been placed on the wafer 5 times. It consists of a known structure that is tested first to ensure that this wafer has been manufactured by using a process that was within acceptable limits. The other die is the circuit being produced for a particular application. Those dies marked with a dot of ink have been subjected to a quick and simple low-frequency test so that they will not be needlessly packaged. Other bad dies will be detected later after more thorough testing is performed to those that are packaged. Note that the yield (i.e., the number of good dies out of the number of sites) is dependent on the particular circuit designed since the circuit area on which contaminants land is dependent on the particular circuit designed.

FIGURE 13.2 Microelectronic fabrication facility. *(Courtesy of Texas Instruments)*

The yield is also dependent on the area of the die, since a larger die is more likely to be the recipient of contaminants than a smaller one. Also, as shown in Fig. 13.4, fewer of the larger dies can be patterned on a fixed-size wafer. Thus, increasing the area results in a dramatic increase in the cost per die. For example, consider a 127-mm wafer that has potentially 2500 sites for a 2×2 mm die. A process that has only two defects per square centimeter might yield 2250 good dies if the overall yield is 90 percent. Meanwhile, a 4×4 mm die on the same size wafer would have only 600 potential sites, with 450 of those being good for a yield of 75 percent. The area of the larger die is 4 times greater, but the cost per die is about 5 times higher. In general, the increase in area results in an exponential increase in the cost per die [1]. Consequently, a significant part of the design process concentrates on minimizing the size of the die required to meet the specifications of a particular application.

From the description above, it is obvious that the equipment and resources required to fabricate integrated circuits are complicated and expensive. The necessity to pattern fine lines of less than a micrometer in an environment that is nearly contaminant-free has driven costs of a state-of-the-art facility to over $100 million. The mechanism for amortizing these costs over just a few years of usefulness is to produce perhaps 2000 or more wafers per week. Thus, production facilities are generally geared to manufacturing

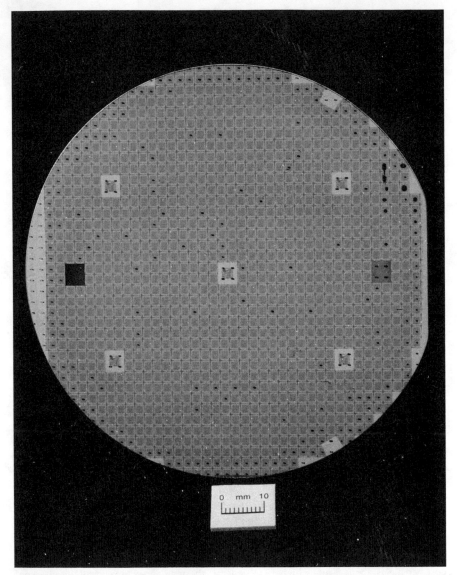

FIGURE 13.3 Tested wafer with process control monitor and application dies. *(Courtesy of Oak Ridge National Lab)*

batches of 1000 or even 1 million copies of the same design. There is usually a minimum charge of $50,000 for making masks and processing 10 wafers for a given design. Additional wafers may be produced for only $300 to $600 each, so the cost per die may be only a few dollars [1].

   This situation is very attractive economically for applications which require a quantity of tens of thousands. However, it discourages the use of the technology for applications

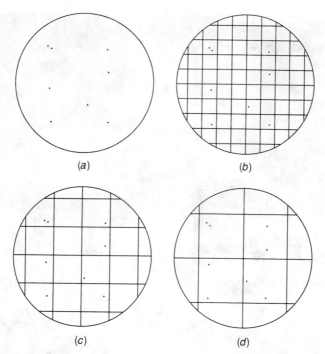

(a)   (b)

(c)   (d)

FIGURE 13.4 Effect of defects on yield. *(From R. Geiger, P. Allen, and N. Strader, VLSI Design Techniques for Analog and Digital Circuits, New York: McGraw-Hill, 1990)*

with less quantity or those which are being developed for the first time. To meet these needs, multiproject wafers, like that in Fig. 13.5, can be fabricated to permit the sharing of mask and wafer costs. A particular project is placed on the wafer in only a few sites, and a minimum lot of wafers is processed. Thus, the designer receives only a dozen or so copies of the integrated circuit but at a cost that divides the $50,000 among the number of users. Assuming 100 projects, the cost per project would be only $500.

In 1980 the Defense Advanced Research Projects Agency (DARPA) established *metal-oxide semiconductor implementation service* (MOSIS) to encourage this type of experimentation [2]. The National Science Foundation (NSF) supports the use of MOSIS by universities in the United States. Similar multiproject brokers support university and commercial users in the United States and other countries [3].

13.3 TECHNOLOGICAL CHOICES

Application-specific integrated circuits (ASICs) are those integrated circuits in which one or more of the internal layers are customized by the designer to perform special-purpose functions for a specific application. General-purpose or standard integrated circuits may be purchased as off-the-shelf items to be interconnected by the designer on a printed-circuit board. ASICs are increasingly being incorporated into electronics-based products to realize savings in production cost and space as well as to achieve more reliable and

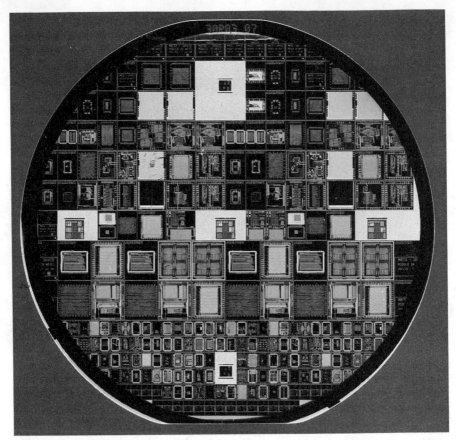

FIGURE 13.5 Multiproject wafer. *(Courtesy of MOSIS)*

higher-performing special-purpose systems. It has been forecast that this new technology will be included in half of all electronic products introduced in the 1990s [4].

In this section a description is given of the various technological choices available to a designer. These are outlined in Fig. 13.6.

13.3.1 Standard, Off-the-Shelf ICs

The one-time costs of designing standard integrated circuits can be amortized by potentially millions of users since these parts are general-purpose. These integrated circuits may be partitioned according to the number of devices available: *small-scale integration* (SSI) with tens of devices, *medium-scale integration* (MSI) with hundreds, *large-scale integration* (LSI) with thousands, and VLSI with hundreds of thousands of devices. Because of their price per performance of about 1¢ per gate, VLSI chips like microprocessors are the preferred choice for most applications if the required tasks can be accomplished within the allotted time. In fact, whenever the speed requirements cannot be met with one

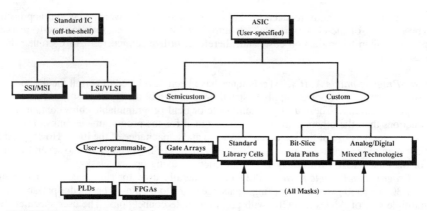

FIGURE 13.6 Technological choices.

microprocessor, the designer may choose to use multiples of these chips. Similarly, LSI chips such as video display controllers and network interface devices may be used for certain high-speed tasks to off-load these from the slower, more general-purpose microprocessors.

Whenever use of VLSI or LSI is impractical, or whenever only a few functions need to be implemented, the designer may choose to "glue" together the more cost-effective VLSI and LSI chips with SSI and MSI chips. However, since the price per performance of SSI and MSI is about 9¢ per gate, the designer is encouraged to minimize the use of these chips. Furthermore, the incentive is to minimize the number of packages used to implement the desired functions since each integrated circuit consumes board space, requires labor or production time for assembly, and decreases reliability because of mechanical connections and power consumption.

13.3.2 ASICs

ASICs are increasingly being incorporated into electronics-based products to realize savings in production cost and space as well as to achieve more reliable and higher-performing special-purpose systems. They are a means by which the designer adds value that cannot be provided by standard integrated circuits. The process of adding value to the integrated circuit consists of the designer or user specifying one or more of the internal layers. Thus, a variety of possibilities exist which differ primarily in the number of layers specified and the number of devices in the package.

Categories of ASICs are illustrated in Fig. 13.6, in which the initial distinction between custom and semicustom refers to the fact that custom designs permit (or force) the designer to specify every layer of the integrated circuit [5]. This flexibility enables the designer to implement only those functions needed for a special-purpose application so that essentially none of the physical space is wasted. Thus, the production cost per integrated circuit is kept to a minimum. In the semicustom approach, predefined library cells are interconnected by the designer's specifying one or more of the internal layers. Thus, some devices may be unused and/or some physical space wasted due to the routing of the interconnections. Consequently, generally fewer devices are available in the semicustom integrated circuits than in the custom ones. However, the time required for design is generally significantly reduced (perhaps by a factor of 10) over the custom approach. The majority of the electronic products introduced are more sensitive to time-to-market pressures than to production costs and, therefore, utilize semicustom ASICs rather than custom ones.

User-Programmable ASICs.   Techniques have been developed to permit the designer to use a programmable power supply to specify one or two of the layers in some semicustom integrated circuits. These user-programmable or field-programmable chips contain fewer functions than the others since space is consumed for the programmable links. They are also slower because of the increased resistance and capacitance of the links. However, the time required for customization is only a few minutes or hours compared to several weeks for the other ASICs whose layers are specified by using optical masks.

Programmable logic devices (PLDs) are generally used for simple designs requiring only 300 to 2000 gates within a single package of 20 to 84 pins. The vendor prefabricates multiple sets of ANDs and ORs with programmable connections. The user specifies the desired connections and electrically programs the chips. Some of these may be erased electrically or optically (by using ultraviolet light). A personal computer with software and an external programmable power supply can be used as a development system. The cost is generally between $3000 and $5000 but can be as high as $15,000 for a highly versatile system. The chips themselves cost only $3 to $20 each.

Field-programmable gate arrays (FPGAs) are presently used to implement logic functions requiring 2000 to 9000 gates with a production quantity of 1000 or less. As with PLDs, the vendor prefabricates the parts with programmable interconnect. However, instead of sets of ANDs and ORs, the current offerings include a collection of universal logic modules which can implement a variety of four- or five-function circuits. These may be erasable by using a memory-based architecture (e.g., Altera, Plus-Logic, and Xilinx) or may be one-time programmable if an antifuse technology is employed (e.g., Actel). Thus, the part appears to the designer as a collection of gates to be interconnected. Development systems for these integrated circuits generally cost $3000 to $15,000, whereas the parts cost $10 to $300 each.

Gate Arrays.   Gate arrays are used for designs requiring 10,000 to 50,000 (or more) gates and more than 1000 parts. In one style, the vendor prefabricates rows of gates with spaces or channels between the rows allocated for interconnections. In another style, the chip appears as a sea of gates in which some gates are used for processing and other gates for interconnections. The first style is used for less complex designs since the physical space is used less efficiently. Both styles have been adopted to make the task of performing automatic placement and routing straightforward.

User-specified gate arrays can be fabricated in only 3 to 5 weeks since the vendor stockpiles wafers and needs only to have the two interconnection masks made and to complete the wafer processing of these two layers. A development system for gate arrays generally uses an engineering workstation because of the power required for computation-intensive simulations. Hardware and software permitting schematic capture and timing simulation are frequently priced around $50,000. Placement and routing can also be accomplished on these workstations but are most commonly offered as a service by the gate array vendor. The *nonrecurring engineering* (NRE) charges from the vendor range from $20,000 to $50,000, whereas production parts cost $5 to $100 each.

Standard Library Cell ICs.   Standard library cell integrated circuits represent the top-of-the-line semicustom ASICs. Instead of prefabricating parts, the vendor provides the designer with a set of library disk files from which cells are selected and interconnected for a specific application. The cells may be primitive gates, or they may be significant functions such as central processing units, multipliers, RAM, etc. Thus, applications requiring 10,000 to 100,000 (or more) gates may be implemented by using this approach, which necessitates that masks be made for all layers. The turnaround time from completion of the design to receipt of parts is generally 8 to 12 weeks. The development system for standard library cell integrated circuits may be the same as that for gate arrays but often utilizes additional software to reduce design time further (e.g., RAM compilers). Thus, a configuration costing $100,000 is not unusual. NRE charges are generally $30,000 more than for a comparable gate array since additional masks must be made and more unique wafer processing steps are involved. However, the same functions can be implemented while using about one-third less space, so production parts will be correspondingly less expensive.

Custom ASICs. Custom ASICs may be divided into two types: one that uses bit-slice data paths and the other in which a variety of custom circuits and/or technologies are used. In bit-slice designs, cells are custom-crafted by the designer and then replicated many times to implement the desired function. Digital signal processing, systolic arrays, and other special-purpose processors can be partitioned into small, repeated modules whose input-output terminals are designed to abut one another. Thus, space for interconnection purposes is minimized (or, in some cases, eliminated). Price-per-performance improvements of 25 to 100 over standard, off-the-shelf microprocessors are frequently realized.

Custom ASICs which do not rely heavily on replicated modules are the most difficult and time-consuming to design but offer the greatest flexibility and the lowest production cost. Examples include analog operational amplifiers, analog-to-digital converters, digital-to-analog converters, analog neural networks, mixed analog and digital circuits, GaAs devices, etc. Development systems for custom integrated circuits generally cost at least $150,000 since a variety of software tools may be utilized. In addition to the capability to perform graphical editing in color, the system must check for design rule violations in which conductors may be spaced too closely, etc. Also there must be a means of extracting the physical layout information into a form that can be simulated at either the MOS switch or transistor level. The NRE charges from a vendor are the same as those for a standard library cell ASIC except there is no need to perform placement and routing. The production part price is generally another one-third lower for the same function due to the corresponding reduction in space. However, the time to market and expense of performing the design and detailed simulations are much higher (perhaps a factor of 10).

13.4 DESIGN METHODOLOGY

From the description of technological choices given in the previous section, clearly ASIC design involves making an economic tradeoff with performance, density, time to market, complexity management, and other factors. In 1980 the landmark text [6] by Carver Mead and Lynn Conway had the profound effect of introducing a design methodology that permitted many of the details of the manufacturing process to be hidden from the systems designer by a well-defined interface to the fabrication process. In essence, this design methodology espoused the use of abstraction to achieve an optimum design from an overall systems viewpoint.

Microelectronic systems must be specified at every level of abstraction including the system, behavioral, register, logic, circuit, transistor, and process levels. Some of these levels are shown in Fig. 13.7. Development of microelectronic systems involves mapping requirements into lower-level specifications that detail not only the internal functions but also the interactions among the components and the external world. This process often

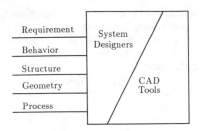

FIGURE 13.7 Levels of abstraction.

requires a symbiotic relationship between the system designer and the available *computer-aided design* (CAD) tools. In general, as a designer moves from a lower level of abstraction to a higher one, less design time is required since less information is being manipulated. However, control over the specific details at the lower level of abstraction is less, so there is a chance that maximum performance at that lower level will not be achieved. This tradeoff is generally welcomed because of the increasing pressures to reduce the time to market for products. For VLSI circuits, designing at the higher levels of abstraction has become a necessity since no individual designer (or even a team of designers) can wisely manage the myriad details [7].

Obviously custom ASICs are designed at the lowest level of abstraction since the premise is that performance and/or area is paramount. These circuits take longer to develop because the designer must specify every mask layer individually and verify the operation at a detailed level. Physical design layout tools are needed along with powerful circuit simulators and design rule checkers.

Standard library cell and gate array ASICs take less time to develop than custom ones because the designer manipulates library cells that have already been designed and verified. Only the interaction of this new, unique interconnection of cells needs to be verified to ensure that the system requirements are met. This interconnection is described by the designer at the structural (logic) level, and then CAD tools are used to perform automatically the physical placement and routing desired. For smaller designs of 20,000 gates or less, it is feasible to capture the design at the structural level by using a schematic. For designs larger than this, it is often desirable to capture the design at the behavioral level by using a text-based language. The text is then synthesized or mapped automatically into a structural description.

The design for a user-programmable ASIC generally is not as time-consuming as that for gate array and standard library cell ASICs since there are not as many gates available in these parts. The designer may use equations, a truth table, a schematic, or a text-based language to capture the intended behavior. In fact, CAD tools are now available that permit the designer to describe the application at the behavioral level and then select the appropriate ASIC technology for implementation. This approach permits the rapid prototyping of a design by using user-programmable ASICs and then cost-effective production of the design by using mask-based parts.

13.5 FUTURE DEVELOPMENTS

For more than 20 years, the performance and cost of microelectronic systems have improved primarily due to the availability of physically smaller devices with faster intrinsic speeds. During the next decade as limits on integrated-circuit technology are approached, further improvements in system-level performance and cost will require the designer to focus on timing issues and the interconnection of multiple chips. Hence, there will be an increasing need for computer scientists and engineers who are generalists. Tomorrow's microelectronic system builders must be equipped with a broad education in the fundamentals, a capacity to synthesize diverse information and viewpoints, and an ability to understand and manage extremely complex projects and processes. The trend will be to specify and optimize systems at a much higher level than in the past. This will require high-level software tools, integrated with existing synthesis tools, which will drive the design down through the synthesis hierarchy, to the level of technology and manufacturing processes. The building of higher-performing microelectronic systems will require consideration of interconnect technology, power and packaging, device and process simulation, optics and photonics, microassembly, and integration of multiple technologies in a single module or on a board. Teamwork skills and an interdisciplinary approach will be mandatory.

REFERENCES

1. R. Geiger, P. Allen, and N. Strader, *VLSI Design Techniques for Analog and Digital Circuits.* New York: McGraw-Hill, 1990.

2. C. Tomovich, "MOSIS—A Gateway to Silicon," *IEEE Circuits and Devices Magazine,* 4(2):22–23, March 1988.

3. D. Bouldin (ed.), "VLSI Designers' Interface Column," *IEEE Circuits and Devices Magazine,* 7(3):6, May 1991.

4. E. Waller (ed.), "Emerging Technologies Pioneer New Applications," *ASIC Technology and News Magazine,* 3(2):1, June 1991.

5. D. Bouldin, "VLSI Curriculum Development," *Proceedings of the 1990 Microelectronic System Education Conference,* San Jose, Calif. Menlo Park, Calif.: Conference Management Services, 1990, pp. 197–206.

6. C. Mead and L. Conway, *An Introduction to VLSI Systems.* Reading, Mass.: Addison-Wesley, 1980.

7. D. Bouldin (ed.), "Foreword for the First Special Issue on Microelectronic Systems," *IEEE Journal of Solid-State Circuits,* 26(5):690, May 1991.

CHAPTER 14

APPLICATION-SPECIFIC VLSI PROCESSORS

Earl E. Swartzlander, Jr.

Department of Electrical and Computer Engineering
University of Texas, Austin

In the last three decades, *integrated-circuit* (IC) technology has evolved from primitive devices with a few gates per package to the current level of *very large-scale integration* (VLSI). Although circuit capability has grown by several orders of magnitude since the first integrated circuits were introduced, significant further growth is expected.

VLSI circuits are, in fact, special-purpose or application-specific systems which differ greatly from earlier devices in how they are designed and used. Effective VLSI architecture development requires coordination of the technological constraints, internal functional structure, and external interfaces. The results are chip designs that are producible, efficient, and programmable so that they are useful for a variety of applications. References 1 and 2 are recommended sources for further detail on application-specific processors.

14.1 INTRODUCTION

Application-specific processing has become practical with the advent of VLSI. It is a major application of VLSI and provides much of the justification for continued VLSI technology development. One explanation for the emergence of ever-increasing requirements is that the historical growth in computing capability leads potential users to expect continually increasing levels of performance. Without the assumption of growth in capability, many potential users would concentrate on refinement of existing systems, and much of the impetus for technology development would be lost. Economic pressure would push the technology, but to a much lesser extent than is currently observed.

The challenge of VLSI in this context is to develop chip and system architectures that facilitate the implementation of special-purpose systems. In spite of the 5-order-of-magnitude improvement in circuit performance over the last two decades, chip architecture remains a problem area. To understand the constraints and limitations, it is necessary to be aware of the characteristics of VLSI circuit technology—these are examined (from an architectural perspective) in Sec. 14.2.

Section 14.3 examines the VLSI circuit architectures which have been developed in response to previous application-specific processing requirements. Examination of the design of a multiplier accumulator in Sec. 14.4 illustrates the VLSI architecture design process in detail. Section 14.5 examines the systems architecture of a high-performance signal processor.

Finally, Sec. 14.6 describes the development of VLSI components to implement an application-specific processor. Beyond the issues involved in developing a specialized processor, this example demonstrates the process of VLSI architecture development, including algorithm and technology selection.

14.2   CIRCUIT TECHNOLOGY

In this section, the evolution of circuit technology is examined. To provide the appropriate perspective, a brief history of IC technology is provided. Chip complexity metrics and current technology limitations are examined to provide the guidance necessary for chip and system architecture design.

14.2.1 History of Circuit Technology

Integrated-circuit technology has improved dramatically over the past three decades, as shown in Table 14.1. The initial integrated circuits were built by using what is now called *small-scale integration* (SSI). SSI circuits consist of a few unconnected gates or simple flip-flops. These functions duplicate vacuum tube (and transistor) logic modules that were proved by use in the large computers from 1940 to 1960. A significant characteristic of the SSI devices is that all logical variables are externalized (i.e., connected to package pins). There were two main reasons for this. (1) The circuit technology was so immature that complex functions (with many internal gates) were not producible, and (2) the chip designers wanted to develop ''universal'' circuits where the user could connect devices to meet a wide variety of application demands.

With the transition to *medium-scale integration* (MSI), more complex functions such as decimal, divide-by-12, and 4-bit binary counters and 1-, 2-, and 4-bit ripple carry adders were developed. A significant change between SSI and MSI was that the number of gates increased by an order of magnitude relative to SSI, but the number of externalized logic signals remained about the same. This requirement constrained the selection of functions for MSI implementation to those with a high degree of internal connectivity. A typical example is a 4-bit counter: it consists of four flip-flops arranged to permit division

TABLE 14.1   Circuit Technology Evolution

Technology	Dates	Gates per chip	Functions
SSI	1963–1967	1–30	Gates, flip-flops
MSI	1967–1971	10–300	Counters, multiplexers, adders
LSI	1971–1977	100–3000	Microprocessors, bit-slice ALUs
VLSI	1976–	1000–	Multipliers, A/D converters
WSI	1986–	10,000–	Signal processors, computers

by 2 and 8 with lines available to allow cascading to provide division by 16. This MSI circuit uses about one-third as many leads per flip-flop as SSI flip-flops.

Initially *large-scale integration* (LSI) devices were custom chips specially optimized for specific applications (as opposed to general-purpose functional building blocks suitable for a wide range of applications). The normal approach was to take an existing system design that had been implemented by using SSI and MSI and to create a unique custom LSI chip design which contained all the specialized interfaces required for compatibility with the earlier design. This approach was rationalized in two ways: (1) If the LSI chip was not producible, the "old" SSI/MSI design could be used; and (2) the LSI design would replace a maximum number of existing chips.

With the increasing cost and complexity of VLSI design, this highly customized approach has fallen into disfavor. Currently, generic designs are developed that stress generality and flexibility even though a few "extra" interface chips may be required. The resulting generic VLSI designs may then be used in a wide variety of systems.

At the higher levels of integration, the technique of duplicating existing modules is clearly unsatisfactory. The microprocessor is the critical architectural breakthrough! With the development of the microprocessor, a complete functional entity (i.e., central processor unit, register set, control sequencer, etc.) is implemented on a single chip, thus eliminating many package pins. As technology continues to advance, chips with hundreds of thousands of gates are becoming practical. At these levels of complexity, chips can be viewed as application-specific systems. Important architectural issues are the use of regular structures to simplify the design process and programmability to facilitate the reuse of a design for other potentially dissimilar applications, so that the high nonrecurring development cost can be shared by multiple projects.

14.2.2 Chip Complexity Metrics

As is becoming widely recognized, the utility of an integrated circuit depends on the product of speed and density. This is because most systems may be implemented with a simple but very fast processor or with a multiplicity of proportionately slower processors.

The attainable limits of chip complexity and gate performance for gallium arsenide (GaAs), silicon *emitter-coupled logic* (ECL), and *complementary metal-oxide semiconductor* (CMOS) technologies are shown in Fig. 14.1. These speeds and densities are indicative of devices that were commercially available in 1990. The speeds refer to the maximum clock rates of typical chips, and the densities to the number of equivalent two-input gates available on standard chips. This chart also shows a line corresponding to a "gate rate" (i.e., the product of the number of gates and the clock rate) of 10^{12}. The gate rate measure is equivalent to the *functional throughput rate* (FTR) used by various military programs to evaluate chip technology [3]. From the chart, it is clear that gate rate levels of approximately 10^{12} transitions per second are achievable over a wide range of speeds (that is, 10 MHz to 1 GHz) by selection of the proper technology.

14.2.3 Current Limitations

Currently packaging is a significant constraint to the development of high-complexity VLSI chips. Part of the explanation lies in the difficulty of constructing and using large packages, which are fragile and must be treated with considerable care to avoid breaking the package or damaging the pins. These constraints are expected to continue, posing a significant challenge in device and system architecture, as the exponentially increasing

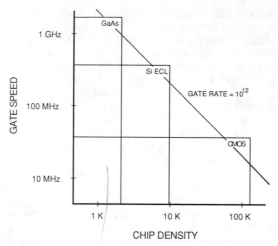

FIGURE 14.1   VLSI gate rate chart.

chip complexity must communicate through no more than about 300 package pins in the foreseeable future.

An obvious solution to the need for more gates per chip subject to the pin-out limitations is to employ architectures that reduce the number of chip outputs. Any reduction in the number and speed of outputs also reduces the chip power dissipation. Lithographic scaling of devices has reduced the power dissipation per device, but the number of devices per chip has increased at a faster rate, so that power management remains a significant VLSI problem. Power dissipation can be reduced by minimizing the number and speed of device output signals.

An intuitive relationship between the module pin count P and the number of logic blocks B in random logic was developed by E. F. Rent of IBM in 1960. The relation was based on analysis of the IBM 1400 series of computers and is referred to as *Rent's rule:*

$$P = aB^c$$

Here a and c are technology-dependent constants. For most examples $1 \leq a \leq 4$ and $0.5 \leq c \leq 1$. Subsequent analysis and examination of additional systems [4] have confirmed this relation with minor variation in the constants. Rent's rule fails to model pin requirements accurately at high levels of integration because when a complete function is implemented, many interconnections are eliminated. For example, for the ultimate case of a complete system on a single chip, a few pins are required for sensor inputs, all processing is done on chip, and a few pins are required for the output signals. Thus as the level of integration continues to increase, the pin requirements tend to decrease to levels far below that predicted with Rent's rule.

A final problem area is the large amount of time and effort required to design an advanced high-complexity custom chip [5]. Given advanced VLSI circuits (e.g., with 50,000 or more gates), hundreds of thousands of design decisions are required to optimize the design. At the very least, such large circuits must be partitioned into relatively independent functional entities so that several designers can be working concurrently. Although advanced *computer-aided design* (CAD) systems are beginning to simplify the design process, the high total complexity is still a serious problem. A second approach involves use of cellular logic structures where a small number of cell designs are replicated in one or two dimensions to realize a complex structure.

14.2.4 The Design Challenge

Thus, the challenge posed to application-specific processor designers is to design chips using highly structured logic design (to simplify design and test), clean functional partitioning (to simplify chip usage and minimize pin count), and minimum output pins (to reduce power and simplify packaging). At this point, it is appropriate to consider current VLSI architectural concepts.

14.3 VLSI ARCHITECTURE

In designing VLSI circuits, several constraints arise, as shown in Sec. 14.2. There is a real need to develop improved chip design approaches which will reduce the system design time and effort. Effective use of the new generation of IC technology demands careful attention to the chip-level functional partitioning. These VLSI architecture issues will be examined in this section, and examples of current VLSI chips will be presented to illustrate some of the compromises implicit in the development of real chips.

14.3.1 Hierarchical Chip Design and Layout

The importance of efficient VLSI design techniques is best understood by examining the design cost. For typical circuits, the design cost is a linear function of the number of gates unless advanced CAD techniques are used. The design problem cannot be isolated to a single horizontal level (i.e., logical, physical, fabrication, etc.) but instead requires a vertical view of the integrated circuit as a system. This approach was used and extended in the design of the Intel iAPX-432 microcomputer chip set [6]. The basic design approach is shown in Fig. 14.2. The design is viewed as hierarchical decomposition from the architecture through the logical, physical, and mask design.

The basic architectural requirements are clean functional partitioning, regular structures, and minimal chip output. Functional partitioning refers to the design of system-level building blocks. It is desirable to provide one or more complete functions (i.e., multiplier, adder, filter, memory, etc.) on a single chip. Functional design emphasizes the development and implementation of generic functions as opposed to absolute logic minimization. The intent is that the resulting chip will be useful in many applications even though it may include some features not required in each application.

Design simplification has become increasingly important with the growth in chip complexity. It is desirable to employ cellular chip structures where a carefully designed cell is replicated in one or two dimensions to produce the complete function. Cellular designs are generally somewhat less efficient than "custom-crafted circuits" in terms of silicon use, but the saving in design time is currently the overwhelming consideration. Cellular designs are directly applicable to arithmetic circuits because of the regularity of human pencil-and-paper arithmetic algorithms. Similarly, memory circuits are inherently highly regular. The main problem area in this regard is "random logic," as used to implement control units. As silicon compilers or alternative highly automated design procedures based on gate array chips become available, the need for regularity in chip structures may be mitigated.

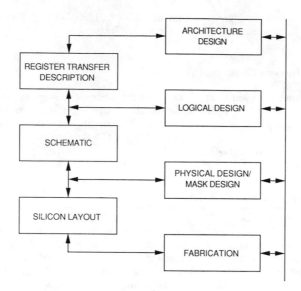

FIGURE 14.2 The VLSI design process.

The third architectural requirement is chip output minimization. The importance of this was discussed in Sec. 14.2 where the packaging issues were examined. Another consideration is the chip area required for output drivers and bonding pads, which can be as much as 30 percent of the total chip area for simple chips with high interface requirements.

14.3.2 Use of Metrics

The gate rate metric presented in Sec. 14.2 is useful in the initial partitioning of a system. When a technology is selected, the logic speed indicates the degree of parallelism required to implement the system. The system logic is partitioned into building blocks based on the attainable chip complexity.

14.3.3 Examples of VLSI Designs

A few examples of current VLSI circuit designs will illustrate the types of functions presently being implemented and will further clarify some of the architectural issues. The circuits are building blocks that are suitable for a variety of applications.

Multipliers.   One of the first commercial integrated circuits to achieve VLSI levels was the single-chip 16×16 parallel multiplier. The basic functional architecture is shown in Fig. 14.3. The two operands are loaded into input latches, the arithmetic function (in this case, multiplication) is performed asynchronously, and the result is loaded into an output register. Use of three-state drivers on the output simplifies interfacing in a variety of applications, as shown in Fig. 14.4. In single-port operation (typically used in general-purpose data processors), a single bus supplies operands to both data inputs of the

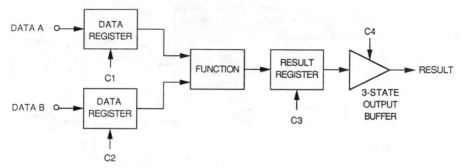

FIGURE 14.3   Generic arithmetic function architecture.

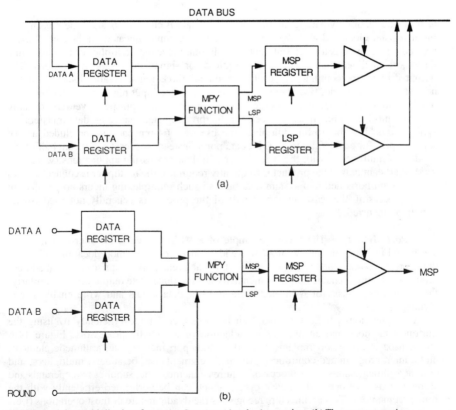

FIGURE 14.4   Multiplier interfaces. *(a)* One-port (data bus) operation. *(b)* Three-port operation.

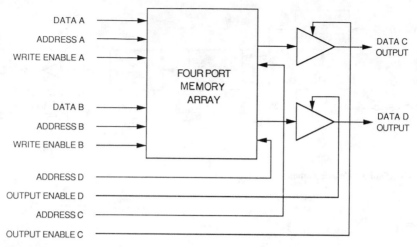

FIGURE 14.5 Four-port memory.

arithmetic function by paralleling the data A and data B chip inputs and time-phasing the input register clocks. Both halves of the product are communicated on the same bus, if desired, since there is a three-state output. Alternatively, the multiplier can be used in a three-port pipelined mode, as is often required for signal processing applications. The output drivers are continuously enabled, and all three registers are clocked simultaneously. On each cycle, two operands are loaded into the input register, and the previous result is clocked into the output register. This provides maximum speed, yet requires only simple control (a common signal clock for the three registers) since all data transfers are synchronous. For the 16-bit multiplier, the use of a 64-pin package precluded use of separate pins for each of the four 16-bit data ports; instead, the least significant half of the product is multiplexed with the B input port. In data processing applications (where the least significant half of the product is frequently required), the multiplier is connected with all three data ports tied to a system data bus, so such multiplexing incurs no penalty. In signal processing the least significant half of the product is generally not used, so no penalty is incurred.

Four-Port Memory.   The second example of a VLSI device is the four-port memory shown in Fig. 14.5. It consists of a K-bit-wide "slice" of 2^N memory locations with four data ports (two read ports and two write ports). Each read port comprises an N-bit address input and an output enable control which activates the three-state output driver. Similarly, the write ports consist of N-bit address and K-bit data inputs and write enable strobe signals.

An application-specific processor can be constructed quite efficiently by using the multiport memory and an appropriate selection of arithmetic processors. Figure 14.6 shows a basic processor implemented with a four-port memory, an arithmetic element, and a microprogrammed controller. Arithmetic elements can be adders, multipliers, and similar arithmetic units. This processor requires a memory that supplies two operands and stores at least one operand on each cycle, which can be performed efficiently with the four-port memory. This architecture recognizes the dyadic nature of most operations (i.e.,

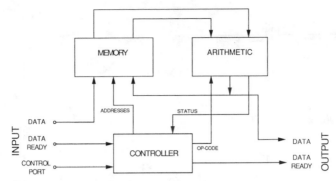

FIGURE 14.6   Processor implemented with four-port memory.

two operands are accessed, the computation is performed, and the result is returned to memory).

14.4 MULTIPLIER-ACCUMULATOR DESIGN EXAMPLE

To clarify the issues in chip-level architecture and approaches to their solution, the design of a multiterm multiplier-adder will be examined in detail. The multiplier-adder is used for the implementation of *finite impulse response* (FIR) filters for digital signal processing and for evaluation of inner products for image processing applications such as high-speed computed tomography; however, this analysis is directly applicable to many application-specific processors.

14.4.1 Performance Requirements

The basic circuit structure which will be implemented is a multiterm inner-product processor, as shown in Fig. 14.7. To form an inner product of two vectors of length M, the first K elements of the vectors are multiplied and summed; the next K elements are multiplied, summed, and added to the previous sum, etc. After this process is repeated M/K times, the inner product has been computed [7]. The obvious implementation uses K multipliers and an adder tree with $K - 1$ elements to multiply and sum K terms. An additional adder and latch accumulate the sums. At each stage in the adder tree, adders of sufficient width are used to avoid rounding or truncating the data. The accumulator width sets an upper limit on the number of vector elements which can be multiplied without the possibility of overflow; however, this width can easily be made large enough to satisfy practical requirements (i.e., with 10 growth bits, 1024 sums may be accumulated without overflow).

Three distinct arithmetic implementation approaches are considered: a modular array which serves as a building block for constructing multipliers and adders, a merged arithmetic multiterm multiplier-adder, and a commercial VLSI multiplier-accumulator. All three approaches use conventional 2's complement arithmetic, but because of different

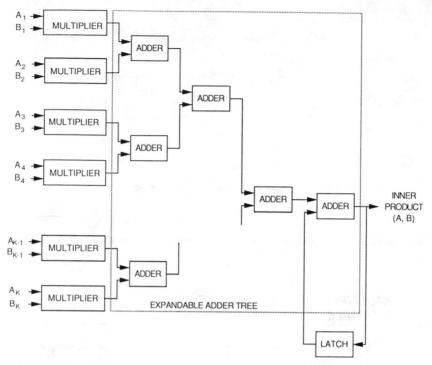

FIGURE 14.7 Inner-product processor.

assumptions about the available technology, markedly different designs have been developed.

14.4.2 Modular Array

The modular array is based on an ultra-high-speed 2's complement arithmetic circuit which is used for addition, subtraction, and multiplication. Such a device implemented with advanced silicon ECL, gallium arsenide, or Josephson junction technology can operate at clock rates well in excess of 500 MHz by pipelining, although the latency (the time from when the operands are entered until the result is available) may be many tens of clock cycles. In the multiterm inner-product processor (as well as many other signal processing applications), large blocks of data are processed without data-dependent branch instructions, so that achieving high processing rates is of greater utility than minimizing the latency.

The circuit is a carry-save implementation of Booth's multiplication algorithm [8], which has been widely accepted for both software and hardware multiplication applications. This algorithm is implemented for pipelining by using a carry-save approach for the addition or subtraction of the multiplicand to the partial product. For example, a 16×16 multiplier requires a 32-stage pipeline. The first 16 stages of the pipeline form two intermediate results (i.e., a sum word and a carry word) which sum to the product via the carry-save process; the final 16 stages add these two words. Since the pipeline clock interval need be only long enough to permit execution of a carry-save addition operation between successive clock cycles, pipeline rates in excess of 500 MHz can be attained with advanced oxide-isolated ECL process technology. Gallium arsenide technology should achieve clock rates of more than 1 GHz. Booth's algorithm was selected for possible implementation as a modular array because a single VLSI circuit design can be used to multiply (by using the complete multiplier configuration), or to add or subtract by using only the carry-save adder array.

In Booth's algorithm, adjacent bits in the multiplier operand are examined in overlapping pairs, and a decision is made either to add or subtract the multiplicand from the accumulated sum of partial products or to retain the previous sum. Two adjacent multiplier bits are inspected at a time; if both multiplier bits are the same (either 00 to 11), the partial product is shifted one position to the right. If the multiplier bit pattern is 10, the multiplicand is subtracted from the partial product; if the bit pattern is 01, the multiplicand is added to the partial product. This procedure is repeated N times for an N-bit multiplier. The requirement for physical realization of this algorithm is an array of full adders and a small amount of peripheral logic. Algebraic subtraction is performed, when required by adding the two's complement of the subtrahend, which is formed by adding a 1 bit at the least-significant bit position to the one's complement of the subtrahend.

The carry-save adder eliminates the usual requirement for horizontal carry propagation within a row of the full-adder matrix. This results in an array with maximum pipeline rate, since only a single full-add operation must be completed within each clock period. The integrated circuit implementing this modified form of Booth's algorithm consists of three sections: a triangular array of (multiplier) pipelining latches, a rectangular array of (multiplicand) pipelining latches, and an array of full adders supported by a small amount of ancillary logic. The two arrays of latches have all input and output leads externalized for independent use as delay elements. The triangular latch array appropriately delays the multiplier bits; this corresponds to the delay of the multiplicand and partial product in the carry-save adder circuit. Including pipeline latches at every level in the array ensures a 500-MHz operating speed.

The sizing of the modular array has been set at 8×4 which requires 56 signal pins and can be accommodated by a 64-pin package. Further increases in the array size (e.g., to 16 $\times$ 8 bits) would require packages with more than 100 pins.

The modular arithmetic array may be used to implement a variety of operations, which include addition, subtraction, and multiplication. The simplest designs generate the results on a "time-skewed" basis; i.e., the resulting bits are not all present simultaneously at the output, but emerge from the unit sequentially from the least significant to more significant bit positions as they are formed. For example, the least significant bit is available one clock period after the operands are presented to the device inputs. The next-most-significant bit is available one clock period later, and so on. If necessary, the skewed result can be deskewed by using the triangular latch arrays.

Table 14.2 summarizes the number of modular arrays required for the implementation of the various arithmetic circuits. The complexity level ranges from two devices for realization of an 8-bit adder to 30 devices for a 40-bit adder. All entries in this table include deskewing logic.

A pipelined adder with a 40-stage latency (e.g., the output is available 40 clock periods after the operands enter the adder) may appear unsuitable for use in computing inner products since the inner product requires serial accumulation. It is possible to achieve highly efficient operation by interleaving the computation for N (>40) distinct inner products and computing a new component for each of the inner products every N

TABLE 14.2 Modular Array Count to Implement Various Arithmetic Functions

Function	Number of 4 × 8 arrays
8-bit adder	2
16-bit adder	6
24-bit adder	12
32-bit adder	20
40-bit adder	30
8-bit multiplier	6
12-bit multiplier	12
16-bit multiplier	20

clock cycles. This process is shown for FIR filtering in Fig. 14.8. For each input data value H_i, N filter kernel values are accessed and multiplied to form N intermediate products, which become available after the multiplier latency time. These products are then summed in the accumulator, adding to each of the N partial results which are in progress. During each cycle, one of the FIR filter outputs will be completed and another initiated in its place.

To implement the inner-product processor, a multiplier and an accumulator are used. Assuming 16-bit operands and a 40-bit result, which allows summation of 256 full-precision products without overflow, a total of 50 modular arrays are required (20 for the multiplier and 30 for the adder). Allowing for control logic and clock buffers, the convolver implementation complexity increases to approximately 70 integrated circuits, with a computational capacity of at least 1 billion multiply-add operations per second. Dividing the throughput by the chip count gives a useful metric which is evaluated as 14 million multiply-add operations per second per integrated circuit for this approach. Note that the

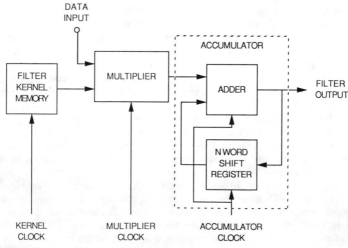

FIGURE 14.8 FIR filter architecture.

modular arithmetic array has not been developed, but its complexity is well within the current state of the art.

By adopting an unconventional approach to the development of a logical array which is realized via three separate (interacting) iterative functions on a single integrated circuit, a circuit design results that can be used efficiently as either an adder/subtractor or a multiplier. This circuit is well suited to those applications where its relatively long pipeline length and attendant latency are not a limitation. This level of latency would not be acceptable for general-purpose data processing applications (because of the frequent need to execute data-dependent branch instructions).

14.4.3 Merged Arithmetic Multiterm Multiplier-Adder

Merged arithmetic results from recognition that an optimal realization of a composite arithmetic function such as a multiterm inner product does not require distinct arithmetic operators (i.e., adders, subtractors, and multipliers), but instead may generate the output bits comprising the function directly from the operand bits [9]. To simplify the discussion, the algorithm will be described for sign/magnitude numbers. This design is easily modified to provide direct 2's complement operation by inclusion of correction terms as for two's complement multiplication [10]. The sequence of operations required to compute an inner product of two M-element (each of I bits) vectors via merged arithmetic involves three basic steps. First, the bit product matrix is generated with an array of I^2M AND gates. Second, the matrix is reduced by counting the 1 bits in each column and by performing carry processing to produce a two-row matrix. Third, the two rows are summed in a carry lookahead adder to generate the desired inner product.

The algorithm used for the second step, matrix height reduction, is the key to achieving an efficient design. Dadda's heuristic minimization procedure [11] which results in minimum complexity designs is based on use of full adders as three-input, two-output centers.

1. Let $d_1 = 2$ and $d_j = [3d_{j-1}/2]$, where $[x]$ denotes the largest integer that is less than or equal to x. Find the largest j such that at least one column of the bit matrix has more than d_j elements.

2. Use full or half adders as required to achieve a reduced matrix with no column containing more than d_j elements. Note that only columns with more than d_j elements (or those which will receive carries from less significant columns) are reduced.

3. Repeat step 2 with $j = j - 1$ until a matrix with only two rows is generated (that is, $j = 1$).

In implementing step 2, each full adder accepts three inputs from a given column and produces a sum bit which remains in that column and a carry bit which moves to the next significant column. Thus, each use of a full adder reduces the number of elements in the composite partial product matrix by 1. Similarly, half adders take in two elements from a column and produce two outputs: the sum in the original column and the carry in the next-more-significant column.

Figure 14.9 shows the computation of a two-term inner product (that is, $A \times B + C \times D$) for 8-bit operand precision. At the top, the two 8×8 trapezoidal bit product matrices are formed: one for $A \times B$ and one for $C \times D$. The highest column is that in the middle of the figure with a height of 16. Since the d_j sequence is 2, 3, 4, 6, 9, 13, 19, . . ., the first matrix reduction is to a matrix (matrix II) where each column has 13 or fewer elements. A total of six full adders are used to effect the reduction; these are shown by connecting the outputs of the adders with a line as they appear in matrix II. Thus, a full

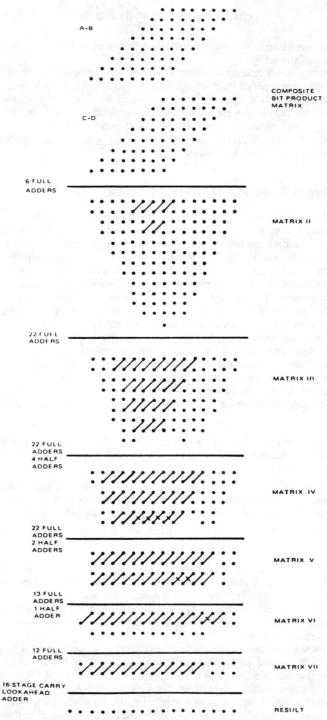

FIGURE 14.9 Two-term merged sum-of-products computation for 8-bit operands.

adder is used to reduce three of the entries in the seventh column from the right (which has a total of 14 entries) in the composite bit product (matrix) to a sum bit in column 7 of matrix II and a carry into column 8. The seventh column of matrix II now has 12 entries (the 11 "unreduced" entries and the sum bit) and satisfies the desired constraint. Columns 8 and 9 each require two full adders to satisfy the constraint, and column 10 requires a single full adder. Note that column 10 in the composite bit product matrix had only 12 entries, but that the two carries that resulted from reducing column 9 would have caused violation of the constraint. The reduction process continued with successive column height limits of 9 (matrix III), 6 (matrix IV), etc. Half adders are used in forming columns 7 to 10 of matrix IV. They are shown as two outputs connected by a line (like full adders) except that the connecting line is "crossed." Half adders are also used to form columns 5 and 6 of matrix V and column 3 of matrix VI. All the numbered matrices in the figure have been drawn with the dots pushed to the highest possible row of each matrix (with the sole exception of the third column of matrix V) to simplify checking each column's height.

In comparison to the direct methods exemplified by the modular array, the merged arithmetic implementation generates all the bit products and reduces them to a two-row result matrix by using a single (i.e., merged) reduction network. For the two-term 8-bit merged inner-product element example, the two bit product matrices are reduced through six stages of adders to produce a pair of intermediate operands which are summed with a single carry lookahead adder.

Comparison of the merged approach with conventional practice demonstrates that, for this example, merged arithmetic requires 20 more adder modules (i.e., full adders), but 2 fewer 15-bit carry lookahead adders. Since a 15-bit carry lookahead adder is significantly more complex than 20 adder modules, the merged approach is considerably simpler than the conventional implementation. In terms of timing, the merged approach incurs two additional levels of full-adder delays at a saving of one 15-bit carry lookahead delay. Examination of the gate-level timing indicates that the merged approach is slightly faster. From the viewpoint of VLSI technology implementation, the complexity reduction achieved through merged arithmetic is even greater than might be expected from gate count considerations. Since carry lookahead adders require interconnection topologies which are difficult to realize in VLSI circuits (because of the large number of signal crossovers), the saving of $2M - 2$ (M at the multiplier outputs and $M - 2$ in the adder tree) carry lookahead adders in an M-term convolver is quite significant. An expandable two-term convolver building block forms the sum of the three terms (the two products and the expansion input). The expansion input is used to convolve vectors of arbitrary length by repeatedly computing pairs of terms which are summed with other partial results.

Within current VLSI processing constraints, the implementation of a two-term convolution block is feasible as a single VLSI circuit. If implemented with a high-density technology, throughput of the merged arithmetic two-term multiplier-adder is estimated conservatively at 25 million operations per second. This is equivalent to 50 million multiply-add operations per second per integrated circuit.

The large number of package pins required for the signals is an apparent problem with this circuit. A total of 144 signals are required for the two-term convolver (two pairs of 16-bit inputs, a 40-bit expansion input, and a 40-bit result). In fact, in most applications that involve large inner products (i.e., FIR filters, convolution, etc.), the vectors are either elements of a time sequence or fixed kernels. In the first instance, a single input port is used with shift registers to propagate the data from one multiplier to the other. In the second, a similar shift register structure is used, but the kernel is loaded only at start-up or when a new kernel is required. This reduces the input pin count to 32 (excluding the expansion input). The expansion input and output still require 80 pins. A potential solution is to establish a communications protocol at the IC level which allows transfer of input data operands into the VLSI circuits in either a bit-serial or a byte-serial stream.

14.4.4 Commercial VLSI Multiplier-Accumulator

The third approach is to use a commercial multiplier-accumulator. This is exemplified by a 16 × 16 parallel multiplier-accumulator, which has been commercially available for about a decade. The basic structure is shown in Fig. 14.10. This multiplier-accumulator consists of input registers, a multiplier array, and an accumulator. Three-state output drivers allow reading and loading the accumulator. A variety of control signals are required: selection of 2's complement or unsigned arithmetic; accumulator commands (i.e., add/subtract, accumulator or pass-through, and load); three-state driver enables; and clocks for the registers.

This design shows the impact of package pin limitations. Since 67 signal pins would be required to accommodate the two 16-bit inputs and the 35-bit output word, compromise was required to use a standard 64-pin package. Specifically, the least significant 16 product bits are multiplexed with the Y_{IN} input on a bidirectional port. This reduces the number of data lines to 51, and a 64-pin package can be used.

The typical delay time for a commercial 16 × 16 multiplier-accumulator is 50 ns so that a multiply rate in excess of 20 million multiplies per second and an equivalent accumulation rate are achieved. This is comparable to the throughput or chip count of the modular array which assumed use of advanced bipolar technology.

14.4.5 Comparison of Implementations

Formal comparisons of the three implementations presented here for multiterm multiplication-addition must consider the state of the art of VLSI circuit technology, which affects both circuit speed and circuit density. Since the three implementations considered involve three technologies, the merit is best evaluated by comparing the performance and complexity. For this application, the performance is defined as the functional throughput (i.e., the number of multiply-add operations performed per second). A variety of complexity measures have been used for specific applications, but one of the most useful is the

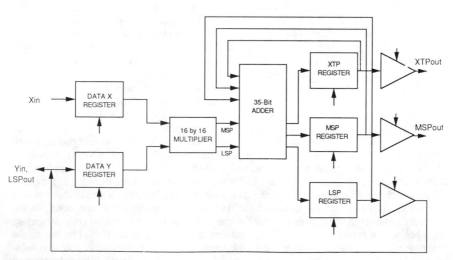

FIGURE 14.10   Commercial multiplier-accumulator.

TABLE 14.3 Comparison of FIR Filter Implementations

Approach	Terms per second	Complexity	Figure of merit
Modular array	500,000,000	70 chips	7
Merged arithmetic	80,000,000	1 chip	80
Commercial multiplier-accumulator	8,000,000	1 chip	8

number of integrated circuits required to implement the design. This measure corresponds well with more conventional criteria (e.g., cost, size, power, gate count, and LSI chip area), is easily computed, and is useful in preliminary feasibility assessments [12]. A large numerical value of the figure of merit implies increased computation per integrated circuit or, alternatively, fewer circuits to achieve equivalent computation rates.

As shown in Table 14.3, the merged arithmetic element achieves a figure of merit of 80 which is an order of magnitude greater than that of the modular array and the commercial multiplier-accumulator. The use of high-density moderate-speed VLSI technology is significantly more efficient than the ultra-high-speed ECL commercial bipolar technology. This finding corroborates one of the major motivations for the development of VLSI technology: Increases in circuit density greatly reduce partitioning problems by executing a complete function within a single-circuit package. This comparison may also be viewed as confirmation that, for this application, moderate performance technology provides higher utility than a technology which is at the leading edge of the current state of the art. The advantage of the merged arithmetic approach with respect to the commercial multiplier-accumulator is attributed in part to the growth in technological capability and in part to the advantages of a custom chip design.

A final consideration which relates to the high functional density of these mechanizations is the practical problem of packaging, given the limitations of present IC packages. A potential solution is to establish a communications protocol at the integrated-circuit level which allows transfer of input data operands into the VLSI circuits in either a bit-serial or a byte-serial stream.

14.5 PROCESSOR ARCHITECTURE

Over the four decades since the development of the first stored program computers, there has been much evolution in systems architecture, in part because of the increasing complexity of the requirements. In this section, processor architectures are surveyed to identify the basic approaches available to the systems architect. One of the major design decisions in developing an application-specific processor is the architecture selection.

14.5.1 Computer Architecture

The first computers, developed in the late 1940s and early 1950s, were designed with what has come to be called the von Neumann architecture, shown in Fig. 14.11. It uses a *central processing unit* (CPU) coupled to a read/write memory. The memory stores both the program instruction sequence and data values. During operation, the CPU reads the first word from memory and executes the appropriate instruction. Then the next word from memory is read and executed, and the process continues until the program is

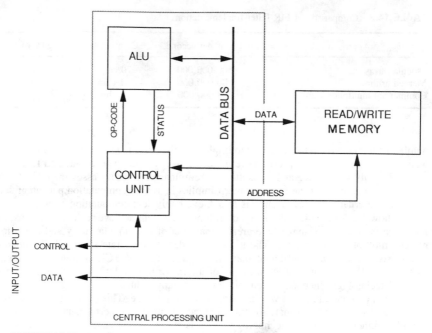

FIGURE 14.11   Von Neumann computer architecture.

completed. The significant aspect of this architecture is that a single memory is used for both the program and the data; accordingly, a program may access the memory and modify instructions to change the program. It is this stored-program concept which represents the attraction as well as the disadvantage of the von Neumann architecture: The attraction is the ease of program modification, while the disadvantage is that all operations performed within the machine—arithmetic, control, or input-output—require memory access. Therefore, the machine performance is directly constrained by the memory performance. Since three or more memory access operations are required to execute a single instruction, achieving high performance is very difficult. Part of the explanation for the preeminence of the von Neumann architecture is that it is relatively low in cost to implement: Only a single read/write memory is required to implement the entire storage for the system. This consideration was, of course, far more critical in the early days of computing, when the memory cost often dominated the cost of a computer.

Another major class of architectures is the Harvard architecture shown in Fig. 14.12. Here, two separate memories are used; one for data and another for the program. The data memory, like the memory used in the von Neumann architecture, is a read/write memory, while the program memory may be either a *read-only memory* (ROM) or a read/write memory. Generally, read/write memories are used early in the machine development cycle, and a ROM is used when the design is more mature (i.e., stable). This architecture achieves a degree of concurrency in its operation; in a single cycle, an operand is accessed from the data memory and used in a calculation by the *arithmetic logic unit* (ALU). Simultaneously, the program memory and control unit are accessing the next instruction and computing the addresses for the next data access. The processors built by using this architecture are generally tailored to reflect the requirements of the system, thus they are relatively inflexible and not suitable for other processing applications.

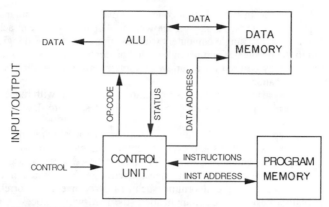

FIGURE 14.12 Harvard computer architecture.

In contrasting the von Neumann and Harvard architectures, the von Neumann architecture is clearly more flexible but offers lower performance. This is, in fact, a recurring theme in architecture design: Flexibility and generality are obtained only by sacrificing performance.

To achieve the performance required for many advanced applications, ultra-high-speed logic is required. Candidate technologies for this approach include ECL, CMOS, and gallium arsenide (GaAs). ECL and GaAs are currently in commercial production, but effort is required to increase the densities to levels necessary for signal processing systems. With CMOS, significant efforts are being devoted to achieve higher speeds. Severe problems currently exist in the areas of circuit density, thermal management, packaging, and propagation of ultra-high-speed logic signals between integrated circuits. It is appropriate to anticipate progress in all these areas, but in view of the level of improvement required to achieve practical systems, it appears that at least several years of additional development will be necessary.

When ultra-high-speed logic is used, a system is implemented with fewer integrated circuits, thereby improving the system reliability. This occurs because the reliability of a system is generally proportional to the number of individual components and particularly to the number of interconnects between these devices. Provided that proper design, fabrication, and test techniques are employed, the mean time to failure of a system is not significantly affected by increases in the system clock rate. Hence, a well-designed system which achieves a given throughput by an exploitation of high-speed device technology will demonstrate improved reliability in comparison to a system employing slower clock rates and a large number of integrated circuits to achieve the same throughput.

14.5.2 Array Processor Architecture

The second category of systems architecture is the array processor. These are general-purpose (host) computers with special-purpose adjunct processors that are used to provide high performance for restricted classes of processing. Since the host computers are conventional single computers, attention is focused here on the special-purpose adjuncts. The three primary types of array processors in common use are parallel processors, pipeline processors [13], and systolic processors [14–17].

Generally, parallel processors consist of a single specialized control unit that issues commands to an array of computational units which operate in parallel. Such processors often use a highly regular interconnection concept, allowing limited communication between the computational units. As is well known, parallel processors can achieve substantial speed increases over single computers while using moderate-speed logic, but they must be tailored to the problem. Commercial parallel processors are designed to be highly flexible so that they may be used for a variety of applications at a sacrifice of efficiency for any specific application.

Pipeline processors also achieve high computational throughput with moderate device speeds. Like the parallel processors, they pose significant software development problems.

The three main types of tailored array processors are the hard-wired processor, programmable signal processor, and multilevel processor. The early hard-wired array processors were direct digital emulations of previous analog processors that used fixed data routing and could not be modified without extensive redesign. Hard-wired processors are finely tuned to implement specific algorithms such as matrix inversion, correlation, etc. By creating a custom design for each application, the hard-wired processor achieves a higher level of efficiency than other array processors and minimizes the parts count to perform a given function.

In the last two decades, the concept of a *programmable signal processor* (PSP) has evolved. One to several specialized arithmetic units and an assortment of I/O channels are operated under stored-program control to provide an extremely flexible system. Although a single-PSP design can be used with different software to implement signal processors for a variety of applications, most PSP designs have special features to optimize their use within a single application area (e.g., radar signal processing, sonar beam forming, speech recognition, image enhancement, etc.). Programmability provides the flexibility to implement multiple operating modes within the single application area. Because of the desire to achieve efficiency with the PSP design, hardware is added to achieve a high level of data path flexibility. As a result, PSP hardware is much more complex than a hard-wired processor to do a given job. Also it is becoming well known that the wide-word microcode used by early PSP designs is quite expensive to design, code, debug, modify, and maintain. The PSP is an attractive approach where a high degree of flexibility is required, as, e.g., in the early phase of system development where the software flexibility of the PSP allows correction of design errors and optimization of the algorithms.

An alternate approach is the multilevel processor. Here a family of processing modules is interconnected as required to optimally implement the specific application. A typical multilevel processor architecture is shown in Fig. 14.13. A control microprocessor generates a stream of "high-level" commands to a number of specialized processing modules. The modules are customized to implement frequently used functions (e.g., fast Fourier transforms, digital filters, correlation, matrix inversion). In operation, the control microprocessor issues a command to one of the specialized processor modules which then begins processing; the control processor can now generate the command for another processor, etc. Since the first processor may require from 0.1 to 10 ms to perform the high-level task that it was commanded to do, and since there are seldom more than a dozen such processors in a system, the control microprocessor issues fewer than 100,000 commands per second. Typical rates range from 1000 to 10,000 commands per second. Software is used in this system at two different levels: High-level software in the control microprocessor is used to generate the stream of commands for the specialized processing modules, and wide-word microcode is used in the specialized processing modules to provide a limited degree of flexibility. The high-level microcode for the control microprocessor does not need to be as efficient as PSP software since it is not "in line" with the data processing [therefore, it is easier (and less expensive) to write and maintain]. However, the microcode for the processing modules is written only at design time as the modules are being developed. As a result, it is developed by the designer and can be optimized for the specific application.

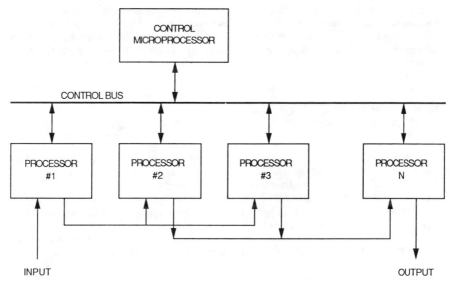

FIGURE 14.13   Multilevel processor architecture.

Each one of these tailored array processor architectures is optimal for specific types of applications. Generally, applications with well-established fixed algorithms are best suited for realization with the hard-wired processor. In contrast, the PSP approach is best where a high degree of flexibility is required, as in the early development stages where algorithms have not yet been finalized or where a processor must be reconfigured to accommodate greatly changing operational modes. The multilevel processor offers a compromise with more flexibility than hard-wired processors and better implementation efficiency than PSP-based systems. Part of the reason for the improvement in implementation efficiency is that the multilevel processor uses specialized interconnection between the processing modules as required by the specific problem. This specialization of the interconnection avoids much of the complexity of the PSP.

The hard-wired approach which was developed initially with SSI technology uses technology most efficiently in the sense that all gates are used. As greater levels of integration were achieved, the need to take full advantage of every gate on every chip became less important and the desire for flexibility led to the creation of the programmable signal processor. To develop optimized hard-wired processors with current (LSI or VLSI) technology means that new custom chips must be developed for every processor (and modified for every major modification to existing processors). At the other extreme, the PSP (because it achieves a high level of data path flexibility) does not use LSI or VLSI efficiently. This is because packaging constraints limit the interconnection flexibility. The middle ground is more attractive than either of these extremes at VLSI and higher levels of integration. For example, the specialized processing modules of the multilevel processor may be shared by many systems in much the same way as standard software subroutines are used for a variety of scientific applications with general-purpose computers. Thus, an investment in optimization can be amortized over a number of projects. Furthermore, because the specialized processing modules perform complete primitive operations, the input-output rates are relatively low and great interconnection flexibility is not required.

As the cost of software development has come to dominate most computational applications, array processors are recognized as useful for many (but not all) applications. All array processors are susceptible to failures in their centralized control units. Such failures may disable a complete system by disrupting the function of only a small portion of the system.

14.6 DEVELOPMENT OF AN APPLICATION-SPECIFIC PROCESSOR

This section describes recent progress in the implementation of a high-speed application-specific processor with commercial and semicustom VLSI circuits. The specific application is to develop fast Fourier transform (FFT) and inverse-FFT processors. The processors employ the radix 4 pipeline FFT algorithm to achieve data rates of up to 40 *million samples per second* (MSPS) with modest 10-MHz clock rates. The interstage reordering is performed by delay commutators realized with semicustom VLSI, while the arithmetic is performed by commercial floating-point adders and multipliers. This section describes the development process and explains the pipeline FFT implementation.

14.6.1 Application-Specific Processor Development Approach

The first step is determining the appropriate circuit technology. This is done by considering application environmental constraints (temperature, radiation, etc.), expected computational characteristics (throughput, arithmetic, etc.), and likely algorithm types (digital filtering, maximum entropy estimation, etc.). The characteristics of the selected circuit technology directly impact the algorithm design and determine appropriate architectures. For example, fast limited-complexity technologies, such as GaAs, are most effective in implementing simple serial architectures which perform recursive algorithms, while technologies that achieve higher complexity such as CMOS are most effective when implementing parallel or systolic architectures.

The next step is to perform an initial (high-level) design. This identifies areas where a better understanding is required, such as the arithmetic rounding characteristics. The initial design is simulated to resolve uncertainties about the operation of the algorithm.

Successive iterations of the technology selection, algorithm design, and processor architecture serve to refine the design at ever-increasing levels of detail. On completion of this process, a chip-level hardware design has been developed, software (if any) has been coded and debugged, and the algorithm execution has been extensively simulated (taking into account the arithmetic characteristics of the hardware design). When the system is constructed, the simulation serves as a reference for component checkout, debugging, and system integration.

14.6.2 FFT Processor Implementation

Although the Cooley-Tukey FFT algorithm developed in 1965 has made it possible to apply digital techniques to many signal processing applications, many others (described in other chapters of this book) require computational performance that exceeds the present state of the art. Current data acquisition technology generates input data streams at rates of 20 to 50 MSPS, which can only be processed with special-purpose signal processors. Signal processing systems require many diverse functions: transformation, time and frequency domain processing, and general-purpose computation. Work is underway to produce a growing family of building-block modules to facilitate the development of such systems on a semicustom basis. The result is the ability to quickly develop high-performance signal processing systems for a wide variety of algorithms. The use of predesigned and precharacterized modules reduces cost, development time, and most importantly risk.

The initial set of signal processing modules includes a data acquisition module, building-block elements that are replicated to realize pipeline FFT and inverse-FFT modules, a frequency-domain filter module, a power spectral density computational module, and an output interface module [18]. The modules all have separate data and control interfaces. The data interfaces satisfy a common interface protocol so that modules can be connected to form architectures to match the data flow of each specific application. Separation of the data and control is a contemporary realization of the Harvard architecture, described in the previous section, which uses separate data and instruction memories to eliminate the "von Neumann bottleneck." In this context the separation of data and control allows the (simple) data interfaces to operate at high speed while the more flexible (and complex) control interfaces operate at a slower rate.

The FFT processor implemented here uses the radix 4 pipeline algorithm developed at Lincoln Laboratory [19]. With this algorithm, four sets of complex data pass in parallel through a pipeline network comprising computational elements and delay commutators, as shown in Fig. 14.14. Data rates of 40 MSPS are achieved by using 10-MHz clock rates since the radix 4 architecture processes four data streams concurrently. An important feature of this algorithm and architecture is that only two types of elements are used: computational elements and delay commutators. Only minor changes are required to implement forward and inverse transforms of lengths that are powers of 4. The changes involve varying the number of stages connected in series, changing the length of the delays on the delay commutator, and changing the counter sequence and step size on the computational elements. The delay commutator reorders the data between computational stages as required for the FFT algorithm. The computational element performs a four-point discrete Fourier transform. In this realization 22-bit floating-point arithmetic is performed with single-chip adder-subtractors and multipliers.

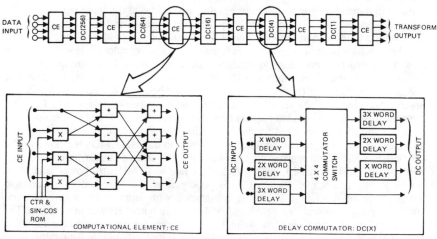

FIGURE 14.14 Radix 4 pipeline FFT processor.

TABLE 14.4 Comparison of Delay Commutator Implementations

Approach	Gates per chip	Width	Chips per stage	Relative development cost
Commercial	0	0	179	1
Gate array	10,000	1	44	2
Standard cell	40,000	4	11	3
Custom	100,000	10	5	10

Delay Commutator Circuit.   Careful examination of the FFT module design revealed that much of the complexity was due to the delay commutator element. Initial complexity estimates were 80 commercial integrated circuits for the computational element and 180 circuits for the delay commutator. Given the high complexity of the commercial implementation of the delay commutator, alternative approaches were examined. A B-bit-wide data slice of a delay commutator that can be programmed for $X = 1, 4, 16, 64$, and 256 requires approximately $400(B + 1)$ logic gates and $3072B$ shift register stages. Since a shift register stage is comparable in complexity to three random logic gates, this reduces to $400 + 9616B$ gates. Table 14.4 compares a commercial implementation with three VLSI versions (based on gate arrays, standard cells, and custom technology). For the VLSI implementations the maximum achievable bit-slice widths are currently limited to 1, 4, and 10, respectively. With such width limitations 44, 11, or 5 delay commutator circuits would be required for the complex pairs of 22-bit data. Given the desire to minimize system complexity and to avoid an expensive custom VLSI development activity, the standard cell approach was selected. The resulting delay commutator circuit is a 4-bit-wide slice that uses programmable-length shift registers and a 4×4 switch, as shown in Fig. 14.15. Data enter through shift registers with taps and multiplexers to set the delay at 1, 4, 16, 64, or 256 ($= X$) in the uppermost input register and multiples of $2X$ and $3X$ in the middle and lower registers, respectively. Four 4-to-1 multiplexers implement the commutator function under the control of the programmable rate counter. The final 2-bit counter-decoder that controls the multiplexers can be reset and held to disable the commutator switch function. Data from the 4-to-1 multiplexers are output through programmable-length shift registers that are similar to the input registers.

Operation of the delay commutator to reorder data is shown in Fig. 14.16, where the data flow for a 64-point transform is shown [20]. The input data (with a spacing of 16) are applied to a radix 4 butterfly computational element, producing output data with a spacing of 16. The reordering necessary to produce a data spacing of 4 is accomplished with delays of 0, 4, 8, and 12; commutation at a rate of one-fourth the data rate; and delays of 12, 8, 4, and 0. The data (with a spacing of 4) are applied to a second radix 4 butterfly computational element. The resulting data are reordered by use of delays of 0, 1, 2, and 3; commutation at a rate equal to the data rate; and delays of 3, 2, 1, and 0. The final data have a spacing of 1, as required for the final radix 4 butterfly computational element.

This circuit was designed and implemented with standard cell CMOS technology. The chip contains 12,288 shift register stages and about 2000 gates of random logic, for a total complexity of 108,000 transistors [21]. At a clock rate of 10 MHz, the power dissipation is under ½ W. The 9.5×10 mm chip is packaged in a 48-pin dual-in-line ceramic package. Each of the four bit slices is constructed with input registers in a column, switching logic in a second "random logic" column, and output register in a column. The four nearly identical slices are about 4 times as tall as they are wide, producing a roughly square chip when they are properly stacked. There is minor variation in the random logic of each bit slice to account for sharing of the counters, decoders, clock drivers, etc.

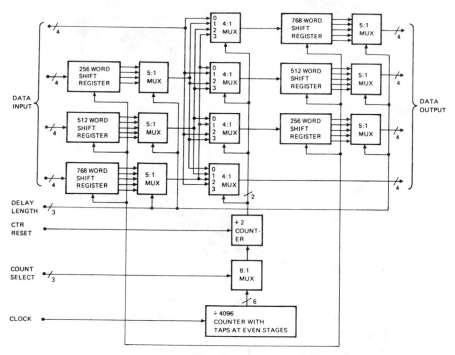

FIGURE 14.15 Delay commutator circuit.

Development of the delay commutator chip reduces the complexity of the 40-MHz 4096-point FFT from 1375 commercial integrated circuits to 546 circuits (of which 66 are delay commutator chips). This is a 60 percent complexity reduction achieved through the development of a single semicustom chip. Such a reduction greatly improves system reliability since connections between circuits represent the dominant failure mechanism in modern systems [22]. With 60 percent fewer circuits (and a corresponding reduction in the number of interconnections) the reliability is greatly improved.

Processing Element Realization. A critical design decision in signal processing concerns the arithmetic implementation of the radix 4 butterfly computational element shown in Fig. 14.17. There are three somewhat contradictory requirements: high speed, to accommodate high signal bandwidths; high precision, to minimize computational error; and wide dynamic range, to avoid overflow. A wide variety of techniques are employed in signal processing because of the differing relative importance of these requirements for specific applications. At the highest speeds, analog techniques are often employed. In audio and geophysical applications, where high accuracy is needed but speed is less critical, minicomputers can perform high-precision operations in firmware. In most digital signal processing applications, both accuracy and speed are important. Many users have compromised on 16-bit fixed-point arithmetic, although fast, fixed-point arithmetic can lead to overflow errors or loss of precision unless complex data-dependent scaling is provided. Floating-point arithmetic has not been used, because of size, cost, and speed limitations of available hardware. Recently single-chip adders and multipliers using the 22-bit floating-point format (16-bit fraction, 6-bit exponent) have been developed. This

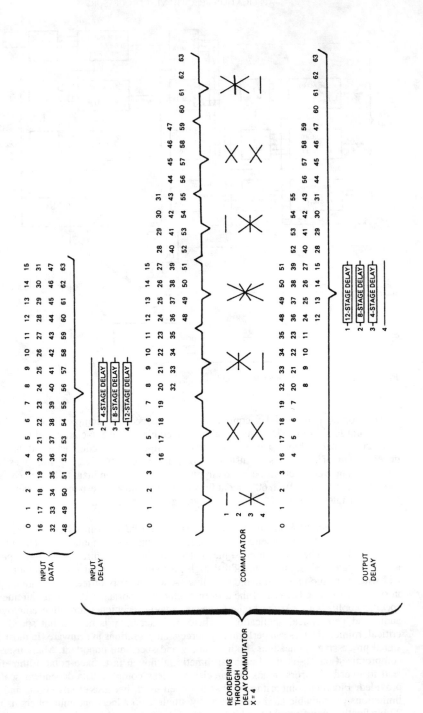

14.26

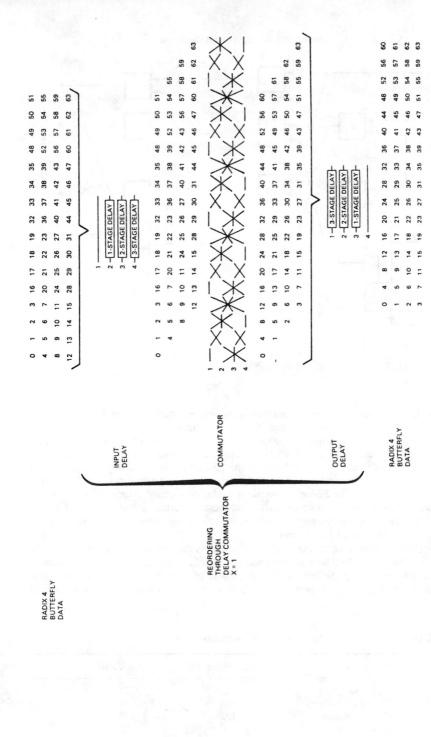

FIGURE 14.16 Operation of the delay commutator.

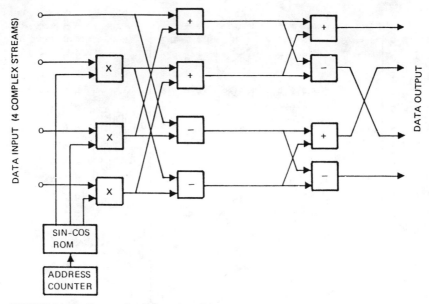

FIGURE 14.17 Computational element.

section describes the use of these components to perform the arithmetic required for the radix 4 butterfly computational element. The 22-bit format, with a 16-bit 2's complement fraction and a 6-bit 2's complement exponent, is a reasonable compromise among performance, speed, and size. Although single-chip 32-bit floating-point devices are commercially available, for a given technology the 22-bit format will always produce chips that are simpler and thus cheaper and faster, with adequate dynamic range and precision for most applications. The 32-bit arithmetic is useful in scientific computation for inverting matrices, evaluating eigenvectors, etc., but these operations are usually performed at much lower rates than those required for signal processing, where input data are often limited in precision to 14 bits or less.

The chief advantage of floating point arithmetic is the increased dynamic range. As shown in Table 14.5, the 22-bit floating-point arithmetic provides precision equivalent to 16-bit fixed-point arithmetic over a dynamic range of 476 dB. Although this dynamic range is less than the 1686 dB provided by 32-bit floating-point arithmetic, it is more than

TABLE 14.5 Comparison of Arithmetic Implementations

Approach	Dynamic range, dB	Precision, dB
12-bit fixed-point	72	72
16-bit fixed-point	96	96
22-bit fixed-point	132	132
22-bit floating-point	476	96
32-bit floating-point	1686	144

adequate for most signal processors. The 16-bit fixed-point format has a dynamic range of 96 dB; the 22-bit floating-point format provides a dynamic range of 476 dB.

Adder. Under user control, the 22-bit adder performs floating-point addition, accumulation, and conversions between fixed- and floating-point formats. Rounding and scaling (i.e., divide by 2) are also selectable if desired. For proper operation and maximum accuracy, nonzero floating-point operands are normalized.

The adder performs the three component operations of floating-point addition: denormalization (exponent alignment), addition, and renormalization. The first and last steps are hardware-intensive, involving shifting of the fraction and compensatory incrementing of the exponent. In the addition mode, the adder first selects the addend with the smaller exponent. It denormalizes this operand by shifting it rightward by the difference between the exponents of the two addends. The denormalized fraction is added to the other addend's unshifted fraction, and their sum passes to the renormalizing section, along with the larger addend's exponent. The sum is normalized by shifting its fraction leftward until the sign bit differs from the next bit, and the exponent is decremented by the number of bit positions of this shift.

Subtraction is identical to addition, except that the fraction of the subtrahend is complemented before the addition is performed. In standard 2's complement fashion, the bits are inverted and a 1 is introduced at the adder's least-significant-bit carry-in position. Fixed- to floating-point conversion and normalization of floating-point numbers are performed by left-shifting the fraction as necessary to eliminate redundant leading 0s or 1s while decrementing the exponent to compensate.

Multiplier. The floating-point multiplier is basically a 16-bit 2's complement fixed-point multiplier, a 6-bit adder, and a simple normalizer. The output conditioning requirements are minimal: If the input operands are normalized, then the product requires at most one shift for normalization. Hence, the 16-bit half-barrel shifter of the adder is replaced by a 16-bit wide, two-position multiplexer. The only interaction between fraction and exponent occurs in the final product normalization step, where the exponent must be decremented if the fraction requires a normalization shift. When the normalizer is bypassed, the chip performs 16-bit 2's complement fixed-point multiplication.

This section shows the high payoff of synergistic use of commercial and semicustom integrated circuits. Specifically, a 40-MHz pipeline FFT processor implementing 22-bit floating-point arithmetic has been developed. The processor complexity was decreased by 60 percent through the development of a standard cell VLSI delay commutator circuit. The arithmetic is performed with single-chip adders and multipliers that use a 22-bit floating-point format. The processor is simpler and correspondingly lower in power, size, and cost than designs using 32-bit floating-point arithmetic. Similar improvements can be achieved in a wide variety of signal processing systems by carefully tailoring the algorithms, processor architecture, arithmetic precision, and technology selection.

14.7 CONCLUSIONS

This chapter has addressed the major issues of VLSI technology in the context of application-specific processor development. The critical issues include basic technology constraints, VLSI design methodologies, and systems architecture. Examples to illustrate the concepts include current VLSI chip functional designs, a case study of a multiterm multiplier-accumulator, and a high-performance FFT processor development.

Although the growth in circuit technology has solved many system problems in the past, technology constraints in chip design, packaging, and interfacing remain serious issues. In the future, these issues will doubtless be solved through technological innovation, but other problems will arise. Through the use of advanced technology, systems costs will continue their historic decline.

Device architecture for VLSI requires striking a delicate balance between extremely efficient custom chips optimized for use in a single system and generic integrated functions designed for broad applicability to many systems. The design issues require development of cellular arrays to permit design of very complex chips with reasonable amounts of time and personnel. It is necessary to minimize the number of chip I/O signals (especially the number of outputs). Such I/O reduction minimizes the chip area required for bonding pads, reduces package size and cost, and decreases output driver power requirements. It requires great care, however, to ensure that the application flexibility of the chip is not compromised.

As the level of integration has grown, the distinction between chip architecture and system architecture has begun to dissolve. Crucial issues remain in the design of distributed systems, especially in the areas of control, fault detection or localization, and implementation. Examination of the development of an advanced FFT signal processing system illustrates the compromises implicit in systems optimization. Standard cell technology was used to design a delay commutator for FFT interstage data reordering. This approach is more expensive than gate arrays, but produces a greatly reduced processor chip count. Full custom design technology would have further reduced the chip count, but would have cost much more. A similar compromise led to the selection of 22-bit floating-point arithmetic instead of 16-bit fixed-point arithmetic (with dynamic range limitations) or 32-bit floating-point arithmetic (with greater precision than justified by the data).

REFERENCES

References 8, 10, and 11 are reprinted in Ref. 23

1. S.-Y. Kung, E. E. Swartzlander, Jr., J. A. B. Fortes, and K. W. Przytula (eds.), *Proceedings of the International Conference on Application Specific Array Processors*. Los Alamitos, Calif.: IEEE Computer Society Press, 1990.

2. M. Valero, S.-Y. Kung, T. Lang, and J. A. B. Fortes (eds.), *Proceedings of the International Conference on Application Specific Array Processors*. Los Alamitos, Calif.: IEEE Computer Society Press, 1991.

3. L. W. Sumney, "VLSI with a Vengeance," *IEEE Spectrum*, 17:24–27, April 1980.

4. B. S. Landman and R. L. Russo, "On a Pin versus Block Relationship for Partitions of Logic Graphs," *IEEE Transactions on Computers*, C-20:1469–1479, 1971.

5. A. L. Robinson, "Are VLSI Microcircuits Too Hard to Design?" *Science*, 209:258–262, 1980.

6. W. W. Lattin, J. A. Bayliss, D. L. Bodde, J. R. Rattner, and W. S. Richardson, "A Methodology for Chip Design," *LAMBDA*, 1:34–44, second quarter 1981.

7. E. E. Swartzlander, Jr., B. K. Gilbert, and I. S. Reed, "Inner Product Computers," *IEEE Transactions on Computers*, C-27:21–31, 1978.

8. A. D. Booth, "A Signed Binary Multiplication Technique." *Quarterly Journal of Mechanics and Applied Mathematics*, 4:236–240, 1951.

9. E. E. Swartzlander, Jr., "Merged Arithmetic," *IEEE Transactions on Computers*, C-29:946–950, 1980.

10. C. R. Baugh and B. A. Wooley, "A Two's Complement Parallel Array Multiplication Algorithm," *IEEE Transactions on Computers*, C-22:1045–1047, 1971.

11. L. Dadda, "Some Schemes for Parallel Multipliers," *Alta Frequenza*, 34:349–356, 1965.

12. E. E. Swartzlander, Jr., and B. K. Gilbert, "Arithmetic for Ultra-High-Speed Tomography," *IEEE Transactions on Computers,* C-29:341–353, 1980.

13. P. M. Kogge, *The Architecture of Pipelined Computers.* New York: McGraw-Hill, 1981.

14. W. Moore, A. McCabe, and R. Urquhart (eds.), *Systolic Arrays.* Boston: Adam Hilger, 1987.

15. E. E. Swartzlander, Jr. (ed.), *Systolic Signal Processing Systems.* New York: Marcel Dekker, 1987.

16. K. Bromley, S.-Y. Kung, and E. E. Swartzlander, Jr. (eds.), *Proceedings of the International Conference on Systolic Arrays.* Los Alamitos, Calif.: IEEE Computer Society Press, 1988.

17. J. McCanny, J. McWhirter, and E. E. Swartzlander, Jr. (eds.), *Systolic Array Processors.* Englewood Cliffs, N.J.: Prentice-Hall, 1989.

18. E. E. Swartzlander, Jr., L. S. Lome, and G. Hallnor, "Digital Signal Processing with VLSI Technology," *Proceedings of the IEEE International Conference on Acoustics, Speech, and Signal Processing.* New York: IEEE Press, 1983, pp. 951–954.

19. B. Gold and T. Bially, "Parallelism in Fast Fourier Transform Hardware," *IEEE Transactions on Audio and Electronics,* AU-21:5–16, 1973.

20. L. R. Rabiner and B. Gold, *Theory and Applications of Digital Signal Processing.* Englewood Cliffs, N.J.: Prentice-Hall, 1975, p. 611.

21. E. E. Swartzlander, Jr., W. K. W. Young, and S. J. Joseph, "A Radix 4 Delay Commutator for Fast Fourier Transform Processor Implementation," *IEEE Journal of Solid-State Circuits,* SC-19:702–709, 1984.

22. G. W. Preston, "The Very Large Scale Integrated Circuit," *American Scientist,* 71:466–472, 1983.

23. E. E. Swartzlander, Jr. (ed.), *Computer Arithmetic,* vol. 1. Los Alamitos, Calif.: IEEE Computer Society Press, 1990.

CHAPTER 15

ATTACHED VECTOR PROCESSORS IN SIGNAL PROCESSING

Richard C. Borgioli
CSPI Western Regional Office,
Newbury Park, California

The term *array processor* has been variously used to describe computing structures composed of arrays of parallel processing elements as well as processors which employ internal parallelism and pipelining to process arrays of numbers. The computational devices described in this chapter belong to the second category. Devices of this type have also been referred to as *peripheral array processors* because they require connection to a general-purpose computer and *vector processors* because of the data structures that they are designed to process. We deal with the terminology problem here by referring to this type of array processor by its more recent designation as an *attached vector processor* (AVP). Terminology problems aside, the architectural innovation and commercial significance of this class of computing devices continue to merit the attention of the signal processing systems engineer.

15.1 INTRODUCTION

Attached vector processors are specialized computational units that interface to general-purpose (host) computers to provide high computational speed and a high degree of programmability for numerical processing applications. Since their introduction as commercial products in the mid-1970s, AVPs have played an important role in signal processing and simulation [1–4], serving as the key computational component in high-speed workstations, network processing nodes, and dedicated processing systems. Throughout their history, AVPs have provided the signal processing community with a cost-effective tool for achieving the speed and throughput capability of a special-purpose hard-wired processor within the framework of a general-purpose computer.

AVPs take advantage of architectural innovations centered on parallelism and pipelining [5, 6] to deliver floating-point computation speeds for signal processing which are from 1 to 2 orders of magnitude greater than what can be achieved with present-day microcomputers based on *reduced instruction set computers* (RISCs). Advances in *very large-scale integration* (VLSI) chip technology have promoted the evolution of AVPs from yesterday's chassis-housed minicomputer attachments to today's single-card units which plug into microprocessor-based workstations and personal computers. Along with the size decrease has come an extraordinary increase in processing speed. As an example, a modern-day AVP, such as the CSPI SuperCard [7], provides a peak computational speed of 80 million floating-point operations per second (Mflops) to make possible signal processing tasks, such as spectrum analysis, at real-time rates in the megahertz range.

In terms of today's technology, an AVP offers the signal processing systems developer certain advantages over a *digital signal processing* (DSP) chip approach. An AVP is a much more highly integrated systems component. It incorporates a large self-contained memory system and a host computer interface along with a high-speed computation unit. In addition, AVPs may be optionally equipped with direct I/O interfaces to high-speed peripherals and auxiliary busses for interconnecting additional AVP units, I/O devices, and bulk memory [8]. An AVP is also equipped with an extensive amount of software to make possible the development of complete application programs in a high-level language. In utilizing an AVP, the systems developer can produce a highly programmable signal processing workstation or processing node at a fraction of the cost entailed in developing a comparable system utilizing DSP component chips.

In the sections that follow, the features and use of an AVP in signal processing are discussed. Section 15.2 begins by defining the functional aspects of an AVP as a programmable attachment to a general-purpose computer. Section 15.3 investigates the major architectural features that enable an AVP to achieve high speed in signal processing. The development of an application program on an AVP and the software tools involved are discussed in Sec. 15.4. Section 15.5 investigates the performance of an AVP-based system for real-time signal processing. We conclude with an assessment of the continuing role of AVPs in signal processing.

15.2 SYSTEM DESCRIPTION

An AVP is a numerical processing subsystem that attaches to a general-purpose computer for the purpose of obtaining high processing throughput. Data are passed from the general-purpose computer, termed the *host,* into the AVP, where they are processed at an extremely high rate of speed. As shown in Fig. 15.1, an AVP contains an interface to the host, a memory to hold data, and a high-speed calculation unit that runs the application program. Most AVPs also provide optional interfaces for directly exchanging data with peripherals in order to achieve faster I/O transfer speeds than are possible through the host.

We now focus on the major operational characteristics of an AVP: an attached processor, a vector processor, and a scaleable processor.

15.2.1 An Attached Processor

An AVP must be connected to and controlled by a host computer. A program must run in the host in conjunction with the application program that is to run in the AVP. Typically, the host must perform the following tasks:

1. Load the application program into the array processor.

2. Start the AVP program or make calls to subprograms in the AVP.

3. Transfer data to or from the AVP, if necessary.

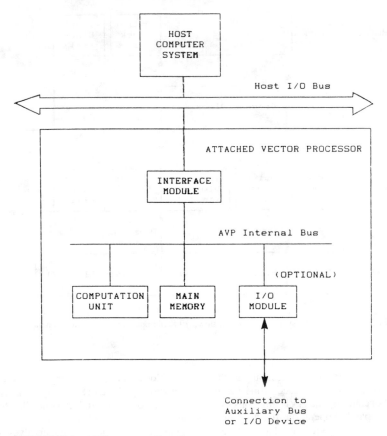

FIGURE 15.1 AVP system configuration.

Overall system control, including the passing of data between the system disk and the AVP, is maintained in the host, while numerical processing takes place in the AVP. Although some schemes make the required host program transparent to the user, a program must still run in the host to support the operation of the AVP. It is, therefore, essential that the AVP be compatible with both the hardware and the operating system of the host on which it is to run.

Operational Flow. The flow of operations through an AVP-based system is illustrated in Fig. 15.2. Two methods of operation are depicted.

In serial operation, the following sequence is repeated on each block of data to be processed:

1. The host inputs data from an input device or the system disk, passes them to the AVP, and sets a "ready" flag.
2. The AVP processes the data block and sets a "done" flag.
3. The host outputs the data block to an output device or the system disk.

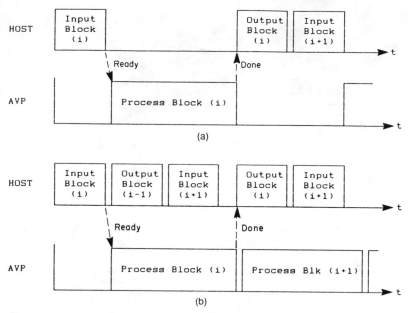

FIGURE 15.2   AVP system operational flow. *(a)* Serial operation. *(b)* Parallel operation.

In parallel operation, the host outputs the previous block processed and inputs data for the next block to be processed while the AVP is processing the current data block. In the serial operations, the AVP functions as a slave with its operation tightly controlled by the host. In parallel operation, the AVP functions as a coprocessor, where data transfers with the host are hidden behind processing operations. The second method involves more programming complexity, but leads to faster system throughput when the data transfer time is significant compared to the processing time.

Direct Memory Access versus Shared Memory.   Transfers between the host and the AVP may be made in either a *direct memory access* (DMA) or shared-memory mode of operation. When the transfer is by DMA, the transfer of a block of data must be explicitly initiated by the host, but the individual data samples in the block are transferred without loading the host CPU. Shared memory involves the allocation of a portion of host memory to a portion of the AVP memory. When the host performs transfers with its peripherals to or from this shared region of memory, individual data samples are also transferred by the host CPU to or from the memory system of the AVP.

15.2.2 A Vector Processor

AVPs derive their speed through the use of high-speed arithmetic components and specialized architectures which employ a high degree of parallelism. Unlike a general-purpose computer, an AVP does one thing extremely well: It performs repetitive floating-point calculations with great efficiency and speed. To take advantage of this specialized capability, data must be provided in blocks or arrays. Single-dimension arrays, called *vectors,* represent the fundamental unit of data input to an AVP. Indeed, the operation of an AVP is often referred to as *vector processing* and the mathematical routines that it executes as *vector functions.*

Vector Sources.   Data arrays and vectors occur naturally in digital signal processing, as illustrated in Fig. 15.3. The representation of a digital signal as a series of amplitude values in time or frequency fits precisely the definition of a vector as referred to in array processing. Multidimensional arrays found in image processing and scientific applications also fit the definition when one considers that each dimension can be treated as a vector. For example, a two-dimensional image array of 512 × 1024 picture elements (pixels) can be processed as a set of 512 row vectors each containing 1024 column elements or as 1024 column vectors of 512 row elements each.

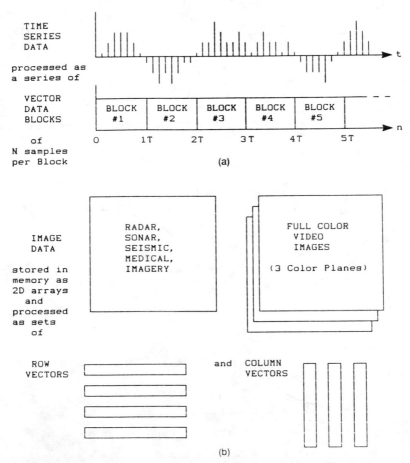

FIGURE 15.3   Data arrays in signal processing. *(a)* One-dimensional arrays (vectors). *(b)* Two-dimensional arrays (images).

Vector Performance.   The execution of a vector function on an AVP involves an initialization sequence, akin to starting a subroutine, followed by execution of a calculation loop, repeated an appropriate number of times to process all the samples in the array. The processing time for a vector function is given by

$$T_p = T_{oh} + Nt_p \tag{15.1}$$

where T_{oh} = overhead time (function initiation time)

     t_p = sample processing time (loop time)

     N = vector size, i.e., number of samples in vector array (number of loop iterations)

Processing speed can be expressed in terms of the number of samples processed per unit time or hertz. The actual function speed achieved S_a and the ideal loop speed S_p are given by

$$S_a = \frac{N}{T_p} \tag{15.2a}$$

$$S_p = \frac{1}{t_p} \tag{15.2b}$$

The ratio of the actual to ideal processing speed for a vector function is plotted in Fig. 15.4. The resulting "S curve" is a graphical representation of Amdahl's law that describes how the speed obtained from an AVP architecture relates to the size of the vector

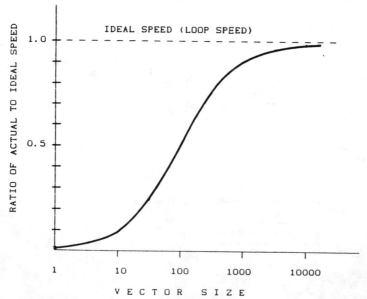

FIGURE 15.4   Vector processing performance. The plot is given for the case where the overhead time is equal to the loop processing time for 100 samples.

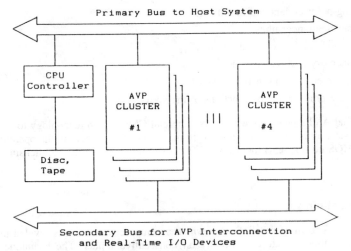

Primary Bus to Host System

Secondary Bus for AVP Interconnection
and Real-Time I/O Devices

FIGURE 15.5 Multiunit AVP system. This is based on a commercially available system from CSPI, the RTS-860. It can house up to 16 AVP units, each with 80 Mflops of peak processing speed, for a total of 1.28 Gflops of peak processing power. The system is contained in a 17.5 × 17 × 24 in chassis. *(CSPI product note, "SuperCard SC-2/VME," PNS-51.2, March 1991)*

array to be processed. The smaller, or more scalarlike, the array, the lower the achieved speed. As N gets larger, the overhead term becomes less important and the actual speed approaches the ideal loop speed.

15.2.3 A Scaleable Processor

AVPs commonly use a modular design approach to better fit the requirements of a specific application. Memory and arithmetic modules can often be added to increase the capabilities of a given unit. Generally, more than one AVP unit can be attached to a single host. Thus, the processing potential can be multiplied to provide additional speed in a dedicated application, or it may be spread among users in a multiuser host operating system environment.

Some AVPs offer a direct I/O connection and software support for peripheral devices such as analog-to-digital (A/D) converters and displays. These features enhance both throughput and ease of use in applications requiring high-speed I/O. Some manufacturers also provide an interface to an auxiliary bus, separate from the host bus, to enable multiple AVPs to communicate with one another, as well as other high-speed peripherals, without loading the host bus [8]. The interconnection scheme can be used to build processing systems with enormous processing power, as shown in Fig. 15.5.

15.3 ARCHITECTURE

AVPs achieve their advantages through the parallel deployment of commercial high-speed components. These components include

Floating-point adders and multipliers

Program sequencer units

Integer and address calculation units

Data memory and data caches

Program memory and instruction caches

Integrated chips with combinations of the above

Commercial AVPs generally employ commercial CMOS chip technology to keep down the cost, size, and power requirements. In many instances, a gain in the operating speed of the CMOS components themselves is achieved through internal parallelism and pipelining.

15.3.1 Pipelining

Pipelining is a form of parallelism in which a computer operation is divided into functional stages that operate concurrently on consecutive inputs. The technique may be illustrated by considering the operations required to perform a floating-point addition. Assume two numbers a and b are to be added in floating-point form, where

$$a = 34 = 3.4 \times 10^1 \quad \text{and} \quad b = 988 = 9.88 \times 10^2$$

In floating-point terminology, the part of the expression involving the decimal point is the *mantissa* and the part involving the power of the base is the *characteristic, or exponent.* When the decimal point is in standard position, shown here as one place to the right of the most significant digit, the number is said to be *normalized.* When the exponents are equal, the mantissas are said to be *aligned.*

The following steps are needed to perform the addition:

1. *Align* the exponents: 0.34×10^2, 9.88×10^2.
2. *Add* the mantissas: $0.34 + 9.88 = 10.22$.
3. *Normalize* the result: 1.022×10^3.

The benefit of pipelining the above stages of operation can be seen in the addition of two vectors:

$$Y(k) = U(k) + V(k) \quad \text{for } k = 1, N$$

The flow of operations for this vector calculation through a three-stage pipelined adder is as follows:

Cycle	Align	Add	Normalize	Result
1	$U(1), V(1)$			
2	$U(2), V(2)$	$U(1), V(1)$		
3	$U(3), V(3)$	$U(2), V(2)$	$U(1), V(1)$	
4	$U(4), V(4)$	$U(3), V(3)$	$U(2), V(2)$	$Y(1)$
5	$U(5), V(5)$	$U(4), V(4)$	$U(3), V(3)$	$Y(2)$
⋮	⋮	⋮	⋮	⋮
k	$U(k), V(k)$	$U(k-1), V(k-1)$	$U(k-2), V(k-2)$	$Y(k-3)$

A delay equal to the depth of the pipeline is incurred during start-up. This delay factor, or pipeline latency, contributes to the overhead in vector processing noted in Sec. 15.2.2. Once the pipeline has been primed, i.e., sufficient data have flowed to fill each stage, a new result is produced on each successive cycle.

15.3.2 Memory Partitioning

Memory speed is extremely important in an AVP, since memory transfers may limit the speed of critical vector processing algorithms, such as the FFT. *Memory partitioning* is an architectural technique that has long been utilized in the design of commercial AVP memory systems in order to achieve faster transfer rates without incurring the large expense of a full memory system based on a faster technology.

As a rule, AVPs employ a Harvard architecture in which program memory and data memory are physically separate units that run in parallel. Instructions are fetched out of program memory, which may take the form of an instruction cache, while associated operand and result transfers are made with the data memory. In addition, the data memory itself may be partitioned to provide faster operation. For example, a limited amount of higher-speed (and higher-cost) SRAM memory may be employed as a data cache or scratch pad, while less expensive DRAM is used for the main portion of data storage. In some systems, the effective transfer rate of DRAM memory is increased by providing for interleaved operation.

Memory Interleaving.   Interleaving is a form of parallelism in which data memory is partitioned into separately controlled regions, or banks, that run in parallel. Successive memory locations are physically located in separate banks, as shown in the four-way interleaving scheme of Fig. 15.6. Given that each memory bank requires 4 machine cycles per word transfer, the effective transfer rate can be increased to one transfer per cycle, by staging the operation of each bank on successive cycles, as shown. It should be evident that certain delays and inefficiencies will occur in this type of memory system when memory access patterns are irregular (random access) or adversely spaced to prevent concurrent memory operation. It is generally not difficult, however, to structure signal processing problems so that the data to be processed are placed into compact vector arrays, i.e., arrays of contiguously spaced locations in memory.

15.3.3 Parallel Computation

AVPs employ a wide instruction format in which the various component operations involved in a computational step can be carried out in parallel. These operations include

    Instruction fetches

    Data transfers

    Floating-point operations

    Integer operations

    Program control

Until recently, manufacturers of commercial AVPs designed and built their own computational units, using various commercial components and their own ideas on arithmetic architecture. Much of that has changed, however, with the introduction in 1989 of the Intel i860 microprocessor chip [9, 10] and its adoption by today's AVP manufacturers.

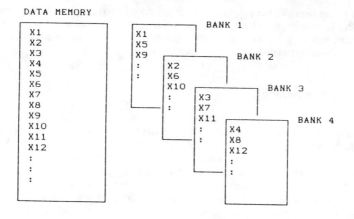

CYCLE	BANK 1 ACCESS	BANK 2 ACCESS	BANK 3 ACCESS	BANK 4 ACCESS	START	COMPLETE
1	X1	--	--	--	X1	--
2	:	X2	--	--	X2	--
3	:	:	X3	--	X3	--
4	X1	:	:	X4	X4	X1
5	X5	X2	:	:	X5	X2
6	:	X6	X3	:	X6	X3

FIGURE 15.6 A four-way memory interleaving scheme.

Although the memory system and I/O interfaces differ according to manufacturer, the processing unit is the same, the i860.

The Intel i860 in Array Processing. The i860 CPU is a single VLSI microprocessor chip which uses parallel instruction execution to achieve extremely high computational speed. Using 1-μm CHMOS technology, it is the first commercial 1,000,000-transistor microprocessor. Although CHMOS technology is slower than bipolar (TTL and ECL), the density and design of the i860 enable it to achieve extraordinary results by eliminating interchip communication overhead and utilizing parallel data and instruction paths. Although the details of the i860 are too numerous for this discussion, we will focus briefly on its parallel features as they relate to efficient signal and array processing. (See Refs. 11 and 12 for more complete information.)

A block diagram of the i860 is shown in Fig. 15.7. It uses a 64-bit-wide instruction path and a 128-bit data path to perform both integer and floating-point operations in parallel with data transfers. The *integer core unit* (ICU) fetches a 64-bit instruction from the instruction cache on every cycle. One 32-bit half of the instruction is taken into core while the other half is sent to the *floating-point unit* (FPU). The ICU fetches and stores data and performs loop control while the FPU performs pipelined arithmetic operations on data in either 32-bit or 64-bit format. Within the FPU, a pipelined add-and-multiply can be initiated on every cycle to perform 32-bit floating-point arithmetic (or 64-bit arithmetic on every 2 cycles). The 128-bit-wide data path between the FPU and the data cache makes it possible to initiate the transfer of two 64-bit operands or four 32-bit operands in a single cycle. The 64-bit path for external data allows for a 64-bit transfer on every 2 cycles for an average of one 32-bit transfer per cycle.

The flow of operations for an efficiently coded calculation loop takes the form of a pipeline. The ICU fetches operands to be processed while the FPU operates on previously

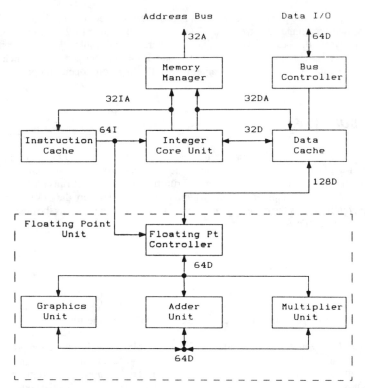

FIGURE 15.7 An AVP computation unit (Intel i860 microprocessor). I = instruction path; D = data path; IA = instruction address path; DA = data address path.

loaded values. The ICU also stores previously processed results during FPU operation. The operational flow for a vector processing problem can be illustrated by considering the following calculation:

$$Y(k) = A * X(k) + B \qquad \text{for } k = 1, N$$

where A and B are scalar constants and Y and X are vectors of length N. (Note: Data values are assumed to be in 32-bit floating-point format.)

Allowing for a three-deep pipeline within the adder and multiplier units of the FPU, the operational flow takes the following form:

	FPU		
ICU input	Multiply	Add	ICU output
$X(k)$	$AX(k-3)$	$AX(k-6) + B$	$Y(k-9)$
$X(k+1)$	$AX(k-2)$	$AX(k-5) + B$	$Y(k-8)$
$X(k+2)$	$AX(k-1)$	$AX(k-4) + B$	$Y(k-7)$
$X(k+3)$	$AX(k)$	$AX(k-3) + B$	$Y(k-6)$

Once the pipelines are primed, a new result is provided on every cycle, given that the data cache is used for temporary storage of data. A calculation rate of 2 floating-point operations per cycle, the peak rate of the i860, is thereby achievable. When external main memory is used, the transfer rate is limited to one 32-bit transfer per cycle, which in turn limits the calculation rate, for this problem, to 1 floating-point operation per cycle.

15.4   SOFTWARE

Modern AVPs are equipped with an extensive amount of software to facilitate the development of application programs. The software includes program development software that runs on a general-purpose computer and run-time software that runs on both the host and the AVP. The computer system which is used to develop the AVP application program, referred to as the *development system,* need not be the same as the host, or target system, that runs the AVP.

15.4.1 Development Software

The software provided for developing AVP application programs consists of a set of programs that run on the development system, as cross-development tools. These cross-development tools generally include, but are not limited to, the following:

Fortran and C Compilers.   Compilers make it possible to create application programs to run in the AVP from a high-level language. They generally include diagnostics and compile-time options that make it as convenient to create application programs for the AVP as it is for a general-purpose computer. The chief drawback is that the code produced is nowhere near as efficient as it could be if it were written in the assembly language of the AVP. Although work has been proceeding in the development of more optimal compilers for complex computational architectures, such as the i860, the user still needs to incorporate specific calls to mathematical library routines, coded in AVP assembly language, in order to achieve full speed.

Utility Software.   Linkers, assemblers, and debuggers are provided for building and testing AVP application programs. The assembler converts AVP source code, produced by either a compiler or an assembly language programmer, to a relocatable AVP object module. The linker is used to combine specified object modules, which will generally include the AVP mathematics library, into an executable program that runs on the AVP. Debugging tools are provided for enabling the user to test AVP programs at both the compiler source language level (symbolic debuggers) and AVP assembly language levels. Symbolic debuggers for multiple-AVP unit systems are also becoming available [13].

15.4.2 Run-Time Software

Support software is required to run in both the host and the AVP during the execution of an application program. This software consists of the following:

Host Drivers.   Since an AVP is a peripheral to the host, driver software must run in the host to support the operation of the AVP. The driver package operates within the framework of the host operating system and must include routines to access, or open, the AVP, load programs into it, call programs and subroutines which run in the AVP, and transfer data to the memory of the AVP, when necessary. Other operations may need to be supported, such as interrupt handling, DMA transfers, and memory mapping, depending upon the specifics of the host-AVP interface.

AVP Control Program.   A supervisory program or operating system must run in the AVP which fields commands from the host driver package and directs appropriate action within the AVP. This program is also responsible for reporting status and error conditions back to the host.

AVP Mathematics Library.   A library of mathematical subroutines is provided for convenience in writing application programs and to make the full speed of the AVP accessible to the user via high-level language calls. These library routines are generally written for optimized speed in the assembly language of the AVP. They perform a variety of mathematical and signal processing operations on vector arrays. The following categories of functions are generally included:

Real and complex vector arithmetic

Fast Fourier transforms

Correlation and convolution

FIR and IIR digital filters

Data format conversions

Trigonometric and transcendental functions

AVP I/O Functions.   A set of functions to control transfers with external devices may also be provided. These functions may be used to initiate DMA transfers, handle interrupts, or make *remote procedure calls* (RPCs) to devices on the host I/O bus or on a separate auxiliary bus used for interfacing peripherals directly to the AVP.

15.5   PERFORMANCE IN SIGNAL PROCESSING

AVPs were developed, in large part, to solve real-time signal processing problems [14]. Signal processing systems for radar, sonar, speech, oil exploration, mechanical vibration, and image processing must often process data as they are being acquired from some transducer or signal reception device. To meet the critical real-time requirement, the data must be processed at a rate at least as fast as they are being collected. In determining the potential effectiveness of an AVP-based signal processing system to meet real-time requirements, the following must be considered:

1. The rate at which data can be transferred between the host and the AVP. Often the data transfer speed through the host may be the chief bottleneck that limits the throughput capability of the system. The ability to perform high-speed data transfers directly between the memory of the AVP and real-time I/O devices may be essential.

2. The availability and speed of the algorithms needed to run the application efficiently on the AVP. In most instances, it is possible to make a reasonable estimate of the processing rate, given the execution times of the algorithms to be used. The overhead

factors involved in calling vector functions must also be considered, as noted in Sec. 15.2.2.

3. The amount of memory provided in the AVP. This factor is particularly important in image processing and multidimensional signal processing applications. The desire is to fit as much of the database as possible inside the memory of the AVP, to avoid slowdowns associated with excess data transfers between the host system and the AVP.

4. The ability to increase system throughput by incorporating multiple AVP units. The availability of an AVP interconnection bus to add AVP units without loading the host bus becomes important.

15.5.1 I/O Considerations

When a real-time processing problem is to be implemented on a host-AVP system, the real-time data path must be carefully considered as well as the speed of processing. There are two alternatives for implementing the system, as indicated in Fig. 15.8. The first configuration is the conventional host-directed scheme. Here I/O transfers with the AVP are directed by and passed through the host, with peak obtainable rates in the range of a few megabytes per second, at best. The second configuration involves the connection of real-time peripherals directly to the AVP. This local connection eliminates the host-AVP data path as a possible performance bottleneck and provides for an order-of-magnitude increase in the I/O rate [7].

15.5.2 Algorithm Speed

A reasonable estimate of the time it takes to run a signal processing problem on an AVP can generally be made by summing the execution times of the various functions used in

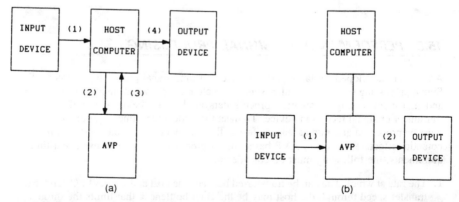

FIGURE 15.8 Implementation alternatives on a host-AVP system. *(a)* Host-directed I/O: The host receives data from the input device (1), passes the data to the AVP (2), receives the results from the AVP (3), and then passes the data to the output device (4). *(b)* AVP-directed I/O: The AVP receives data directly from the input device (1), processes them, and then passes the results directly to the output device (2). The host may perform support tasks but is not involved in the transfer of data.

TABLE 15.1 Performance Evaluation Chart for a SuperCard-2 in a Power Spectral Density Calculation

	Arithmetic execution time	
Function	128-Sample data block, μs	1024-Sample data block, μs
1. Format conversion (8 + 0.098N)	21	108
2. Weighting multiply (9 + 0.085N)	20	96
3. Real FFT (tabulated)	72	520
4. Average power (9 + 0.136N)	26	148
Processing time T_p, μs	139	872
Processing speed S_p, kHz	920	1174

the processing sequence. The function execution time for each function can be determined from a knowledge of the loop execution time of the function and the size of the vector, or data block, to be processed. The estimate should include the start-up overhead, as given in Eq. (15.1). As an example, Table 15.1 shows a performance estimate for a CSPI SuperCard-2 on a spectral analysis problem. The estimated throughput speed is calculated by dividing the block size by the calculated processing time, as given in Eq. (15.2a). A higher speed is generally obtained for larger data blocks, since the percentage of overhead is less. The processing throughput figure should be compared to the I/O rate obtainable through the host to determine if a faster direct I/O connection to the AVP is needed.

15.5.3 Multiple-AVP Configurations

Multiple-AVP units may be employed to realize higher throughput requirements. Real-time data may be passed directly through the AVP units, while system control and status operations are maintained by the host. As an example, say that the real-time spectrum analysis problem illustrated in the previous section needed to be performed at a 4-times-faster throughput rate. Figure 15.9 shows how such a problem may be solved by using a configuration of four AVP units.

Successive input data blocks are distributed to the AVP units in a round-robin fashion, where the first AVP unit processes the first block, the second AVP unit processes the second block, etc. The time to process a data block in a given AVP is essentially the same as given previously, neglecting some small amount of additional control overhead for synchronization. However, with four AVPs operating in parallel, 4 times as many data are processed per unit time, for a fourfold improvement in throughput. Multi-AVP schemes of this type prove quite effective for implementing multichannel signal processors and image processing systems, where simple parallel operation can be exploited. More complex schemes requiring communication and data passing between AVPs are also possible.

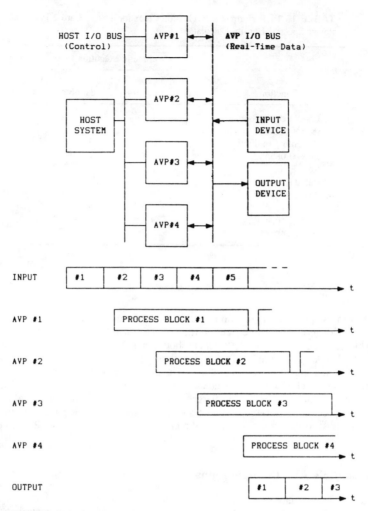

FIGURE 15.9 Multiunit AVP operation for real-time processing.

15.6 CONCLUSION

The array processors designated here as attached vector processors have proved their value in signal processing applications for over 15 years. Now, with the incorporation of their innovative architectural concepts into standard VLSI chips, they are providing a breakthrough in the level of performance and integration offered to the signal processing systems builder. A standardized chip for the processing unit means standardized high-level language compilers and symbolic debuggers, to facilitate applications program development. Reduced chip area means that large memory systems and direct I/O interfaces can be included on a single plug-in board, to make practical the delivery of multiunit

AVP systems which rival supercomputers in programmability and performance while approaching the compact size of a DSP chip implementation.

REFERENCES

1. W. J. Karplus (ed.), *Peripheral Array Processors,* Simulation Series, vol. 11, no. 1, Simulation Councils, 1982.

2. W. J. Karplus (ed.), *Peripheral Array Processors,* Simulation Series, vol. 14, no. 1, Simulation Councils, 1984.

3. W. J. Karplus (ed.), *Multiprocessors and Array Processors,* Simulation Series, vol. 18, no. 2, Simulation Councils, 1987.

4. W. J. Karplus (ed.), *Multiprocessors and Array Processors,* Simulation Series, vol. 21, no. 1, Simulation Councils, 1989.

5. E. U. Cohler and J. E. Storer, "Functionally Parallel Architecture for Array Processors," *IEEE Computer,* 14:28–35, September 1981.

6. A. E. Charlesworth, "An Approach to Scientific Array Processing. The Architectural Design of the AP-120B/FPS-164 Family," *IEEE Computer,* 14:18–27, September 1981.

7. CSPI product note, "SuperCard SC-2/VME," PNS-51.2, Billerica, Mass., March 1991.

8. CSPI product note, "Introduction to the RTS-860 Multiprocessor," PNS-60.0, April 1991.

9. R. Wilson, "80860 Blends Vector Processing into RISC-Like Architecture," *Computer Design,* April 1, 1989.

10. E. Henning, "Intel's RISC Revolution for the '90s," *PC User,* April 24, 1989.

11. N. Margulus, *i860 Microcomputer Architecture,* New York: McGraw-Hill, 1990.

12. Intel Corp., *i860 64-bit Microprocessor Programmer's Reference Manual,* 1990.

13. K. Rowe, "Remedy: A Real-Time Heterogeneous Multiprocessor System Level Debugger for ORKID," *Proceedings of BUSCON-West,* 1990.

14. R. C. Borgioli, "Real Time Performance Considerations in Array Processing," *Simulation Series,* 11(1):49–60, 1982.

CHAPTER 16
PARALLEL COMPUTING SYSTEMS

Tse-yun Feng and A. R. Hurson
Department of Electrical and Computer Engineering
Pennsylvania State University, University Park

Chuan-lin Wu
Department of Electrical and Computer Engineering
University of Texas, Austin

16.1 INTRODUCTION

A typical uniprocessor system consists of four interrelated functional units: the main memory, the *control unit* (CU), the *arithmetic logic unit* (ALU), and input-output subsystems (I/O). Usually the CU and ALU are combined and known as the *central processing unit* (CPU). Central to such organization is the concept of the stored program— the principle that instructions and data are to be stored intermixed in a single and uniform storage medium. A uniprocessor system, based on the concept of the stored program, is known as the *von Neumann machine*. During the past four decades, the von Neumann concept has proved itself in practical applications. However, it has been shown that many real-time applications demand a computational power beyond the extended computational capability of the von Neumann design. Such a computation gap has motivated the concept of parallelism and parallel processing as a generic term to cope with the ever-increasing demands for faster operations and higher performance. For the sake of clarity, before any further discussion, the following terms are defined:

- *Parallelism:* A generic term to define the capability of simultaneous execution of many actions at any instant.

- *Parallel processing:* An efficient form of information processing that emphasizes the exploitation of concurrent events in the computing process. Concurrency implies parallelism, simultaneity, and pipelining. Parallel events may occur in multiple resources during the same time interval, simultaneous events may occur at the same time instant, and pipelined events may occur in overlapped time spans. Parallel processing demands concurrent execution of many programs in the computer, in contrast to sequential processing. It is a cost-effective means to improve system performance through concurrent activities in the computer [1].

- *Parallel computing systems:* The systems that emphasize parallel processing.

This chapter is divided in four sections (16.2 through 16.5). Section 16.2 discusses the classification of parallel computer system organizations, which are based on the von

Neumann principle. Section 16.3 addresses the architectural classification. Section 16.4 provides an overview of some contemporary parallel computer systems. Section 16.5 offers comments on the general utilization and shortcomings of the conventional parallel computer systems.

16.2 ORGANIZATIONS AND CLASSIFICATIONS

Figure 16.1 illustrates four approaches to processing. In the early processors, the ALU was designed to perform operations only on a bit or a bit pair (serial ALU; point A in Fig. 16.1). Therefore, an operation on an M-bit operand or operand pair must be repeated bit serially M times. To speed up the processing, a parallel ALU (point B) is usually used, so that all bits of an operand or operand pair can be operated on simultaneously. This discussion can be extended to the cases in which either (1) all the ith bits of N operands or operand pairs (i.e., bit slice, or bis) may be operated on simultaneously (point C) or (2) the operation is performed on N M-bit operands or operand pairs (point D).

This discussion represents Feng's classification [2], where the concurrent space is identified as a two-dimensional space based on the bit and word multiplicities. Figure 16.1 shows the allocation of some of the systems in Feng's concurrent space.

Flynn [3] has classified the concurrent space according to the multiplicity of instruction and data streams, where computer systems are partitioned into four groups:

1. SISD (single-instruction single-data): The classical von Neumann architecture (with serial or parallel ALU).
2. SIMD (single-instruction multiple-data): The multiple-ALU-type architectures (e.g., array processor).
3. MISD (multiple-instruction single-data): Not as practical as the other classes. A database machine-search processor [4] represents a model in this class.
4. MIMD (multiple-instruction multiple-data): The multiprocessor system (loosely or tightly coupled).

As a general rule, one could conclude that SISD and SIMD machines are single-CU systems, whereas MIMD machines are multiple-CU systems. Flynn's classification does not address the interactions among the processing modules and the methods by which processing modules in concurrent systems are controlled. As a result, one can classify a pipeline computer and a uniprocessor computer as SISD machines, because both instructions and data are provided sequentially.

Händler [5] has extended Feng's concurrent space by a third dimension, namely, the number of control units. Händler's space is defined as $t = (k, d, w)$, in which k is the number of CUs interpreting a program, d is the number of ALUs controlled by a CU, and w is the word length or number of bits handled in one of the ALUs. According to this classification, a von Neumann machine with serial/parallel ALUs is represented as $(1, 1, 1)/(1, 1, M)$, respectively. Figure 16.2 depicts the position of some of the computer systems in the Händler space. To represent pipelining at different levels (e.g., macropipeline, instruction pipeline, and arithmetic pipeline) and illustrate the diversity, sequentiality, and flexibility and adaptability of an organization, the above triplet has been extended by three variables (k', d', w') and three operators $(+, *, v)$, where k' represents the macropipeline (the number of CUs interpreting tasks of a program, where the data flow through them is sequential); d' represents the instruction pipeline (the number of functional units managed by one CU and working on one data stream); w' represents the

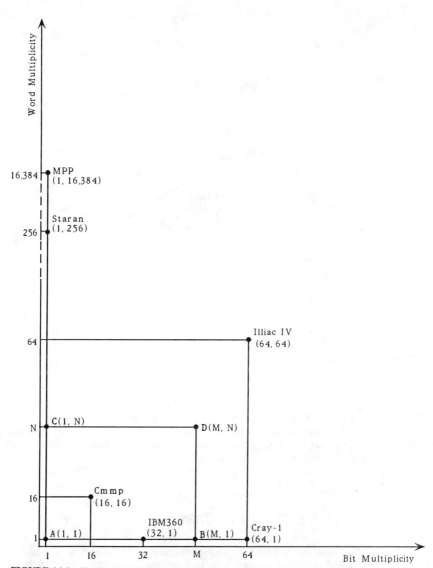

FIGURE 16.1 Feng's classification.

arithmetic pipeline (the number of stages); + represents diversity (existence of more than one structure); ∗ represents sequentiality (for sequentially ordered structures); and v represents flexibility and adaptability (for reconfigurable organization). According to this extension to Händler's notation, CDC 7600 [1] and DAP [6, 7] are represented as (15∗1, 1∗1, 12∗1)∗(1∗1, 1∗9, 60∗1) and (1∗1, 1∗1, 32∗1)∗[(1∗1, 128∗1, 32∗1) v (1∗1, 4096∗1, 1∗1)], respectively.

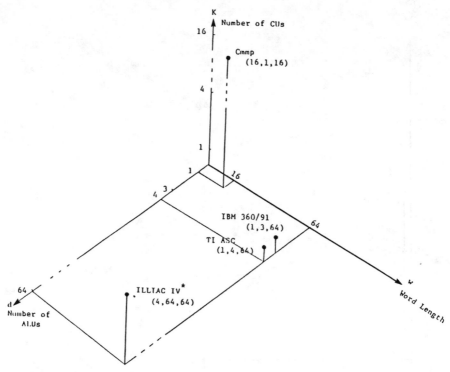

FIGURE 16.2 Händler's space.

These classifications suffer from the fact that either they do not uniquely identify a specific organization or they cannot thoroughly determine the interrelationships among different modules in an organization. In the following section, we classify parallel computer systems in terms of architectural interaction.

16.3 ARCHITECTURE CLASSIFICATION

Parallel computer systems can be broadly classified as control flow, data flow, reduction, actor, logic, and neural networks, according to architectural features.

These six classes of computers have their own styles of programming: conventional, single-assignment, applicative, object-oriented, predicate logic, and learning, respectively. While current supercomputing simply falls into the conventional control flow class, other classes may still be promising for future applications. The VLSI architectural developments presented here render their execution model into one or more of those decentralized architectures in one way or another. We discuss each in terms of execution sequence control.

16.3.1 Control Flow

The simplest control flow employs single-instruction stream and single-data stream (SISD). Instruction execution is implicitly sequential from instruction to instruction unless changed by branch conditions. The instructions share data by placing the data in memories which are accessed, using reference addresses. The SISD has been implemented in the traditional uniprocessor system [8]. The VLSI processors described in Sec. 16.4 employ this strategy, with various features for improving execution speed.

In the parallel execution with multiple processors, a simple extension from SISD is to connect a number of functional units to form a pipeline [9]. From a system function point of view, the architecture known as a pipelined processor remains to be SISD. Another approach is to execute a number of processors under a centralized control known as single-instruction stream multiple-data stream (SIMD) or array processors [10]. A third approach is to execute multiple-instruction streams in different processors concurrently. Explicit control operators are needed to fork and join parallel execution sequences for synchronization. This parallel execution model is known to be multiple-instruction stream multiple-data stream or multiprocessor [11].

16.3.2 Data Flow

In the data flow model [12], the availability of all operands of an instruction causes its execution. The result of an instruction execution is sent as a data token to each consuming instruction waiting for the availability of this operand. An example of a data flow program is shown in Fig. 16.3. In Fig. 16.3, black dots on the arcs are used to indicate the availability of a data token. When the instruction generates a result, the result is packed in a data token template and sent to every waiting instruction argument position such as i1/1 or i2/1, where i1 (i2) indicates the destination of a data token, and /1 indicates the first operand of the destination instruction.

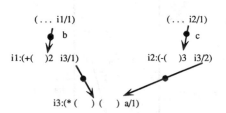

FIGURE 16.3 Data flow program for $a = (b + 2) * (c - 3)$.

Explicit procedure call operators such as CALL and RETURN are required. The data flow model can be very effective for simple expression. Conditional alternatives can be executed in parallel with alternative branches until the conditions for choice become known.

16.3.3 Reduction Model

In the reduction model [13, 14], an instruction is executed when the result it produces is required by an instruction which is actively being executed. Two types of reduction are invented: string reduction and graph reduction. String reduction takes a separate copy of a shared data, while the graph reduction just updates the shared data in place without making a separate copy. Figure 16.4 shows an example of a reduction program for both types. As illustrated by Fig. 16.4*a*, in string reduction, some instruction containing the reference "a" demands the value associated with the definition, (*i1 i2), to be loaded into the instruction, overwriting the reference "a." The references i1 and i2 then cause the copy of their definitions to be loaded.

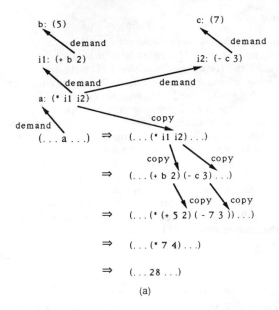

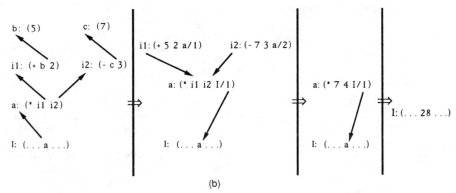

FIGURE 16.4   Reduction program for $a = (b + 2) * (c - 3)$. *(a)* String reduction. *(b)* Graph reduction.

The graph reduction, as illustrated in Fig. 16.4*b*, demands the value associated with "a" by traversing the reference to return with the actual value. An embedded reference, such as I/1 and a/1, is used to return the demanded value.

16.3.4 Actor Model

In the actor model [15], the arrival of a message for an instruction causes the instruction to be executed. Execution of actor instructions may be control-driven, data-driven, or demand-driven. The main features of actor models include these: (1) Instructions are object-oriented, changing state as the message arrives. (2) Data are passed directly be-

b: (5 i1/1 ...)	b : (5)	b : (5)	b : (5)
c: (7 i2/1 ...)	c : (7)	c : (7)	c : (7)
i1: (+ ( ) 2 a/1)	i1 : (+ (5) 2 a/1)	i1 : (+ ( ) 2 7 a/1)	i1 : (+ ( ) 2 a/1)
i2: (- ( ) 3 a/2)	i2 : (- (7) 3 a/2)	i2 : (- ( ) 3 4 a/2)	i2 : (- ( ) 3 a/2)
a: (* ( ) ( ) ...)	a : (* ( ) ( ) ...)	a : (* ( ) ( ) ...)	a : (* (7) (4) ...)
(i) execution 1	(ii) execution 2	(iii) execution 3	(iv) execution 4

(a)

b : (5)	b : (5)	b : (5, i1/1)	b : (5)	b : (5)
c : (7)	c : (7)	c : (7, i2/1)	c : (7)	c : (7)
i1 : (+ b 2)	i1 : (+ b 2 a/1)	i1: (+ ( ) 2 a/1)	i1 : (+ 5 2 a/1)	i1: (+ b 2 7 a/1)
i2 : (- c 3)	i2 : (- c 3 a/2)	i2: (- ( ) 3 a/2)	i2 : (- 7 3 a/2)	i2: (- c 3 4 a/1)
a : * (i1 i2) ...)	a: (* ( ) ( ) ...)	a: (* ( ) ( ) ...)	a: (* ( ) ( ) ...)	a: (* ( ) ( ) ...)

(b)

FIGURE 16.5 Actor program for $a = (b + 2) * (c - 3)$. *(a)* Data-driven. *(b)* Demand-driven.

tween instructions through the use of messages. (3) Messages may contain literals, references, or code. The object-oriented execution is illustrated in Fig. 16.5.

In Fig. 16.5a, instruction executions of i1 and i2 are driven with objects "b" and "c" sending messages containing the values 5 and 7. These values are stored in i1 and i2, respectively. Instruction i1 executes, sends its results to instruction "a," and returns to its original state to await the arrival of further messages. Instruction i2 executes and accomplishes the similar.

In Fig. 16.5b, the instruction execution is demand-driven with instruction a sending the message demanding the values of i1 and i2. The return addresses are appended in i1 and i2. Execution of i1 and i2 causes further messages to be sent to "b" and "c." Following these demand-driven messages and executions, results will be returned to the demanding object.

16.3.5 Logic

Logic programming, in the broad sense, uses (extended Horn clause) logic to represent programs and uses deduction to perform computation [16, 17]. The principal component of a logic programming language is a *Horn clause*, which consists of a set of literals in the following form:

$$p_0(arg_0): p_1(arg_1), p_2(arg_2), \ldots, p_n(arg_n)$$

The above clause can be read declaratively as

$p_0(arg_0)$ is true if $p_1(arg_1)$ and $p_2(arg_2)$ and $\ldots p_n(arg_n)$ are true procedurally as

to solve $p_0(arg_0)$ first solve $p_1(arg_1)$ and $p_2(arg_2)$ and . . . , $p_n(arg_n)$ or in set

relationship as

the solution of $(p_1(arg_1), . . . , p_n(arg_n))$ is a subset of the solution of $p_0(arg_0)$.

From the above broad-sense definition and three different ways of reading, logic programming can be regarded as combining the characteristics of functional programming and database query.

In the solution of logic programs, clauses with the same predicate and arity comprise a procedure. A procedure thus defines the solution domain of literals with the same predicate and arity. Clauses in a procedure have OR relationship, since each clause results in a subset of the solution domain. Procedures can be used to solve various queries that contain sets of literals (called *goals*). A query is solved by matching its goals with the clauses.

Since Horn clauses do not specify the execution sequences, logic programming enables users to concentrate more easily on the logic of problem solving without understanding the executional behavior of a program, while providing system designers a great flexibility on directing the behavior. To visualize the flexibility of execution, one can represent a query and its associated clauses as an AND/OR tree (see the example below). The solution of a query is then the traversal of the tree. Since the traversal can be performed either forward or backward and either sequentially or concurrently, all kinds of execution models can be constructed for the solution of logic programs. The concurrent traversal constitutes a large amount of AND and OR parallelism.

An example is illustrated in Fig. 16.6, in which [query 1] asks who the grandfathers of jack are, [query 2] asks who the grandchildren of tom are, [gf1] and [gf2] define the grandfather relation, and fathers and mothers provide the facts.

The program for solving [query 1] (or [query 2]) can be expressed as a two-level AND/OR tree, as shown in Fig. 16.7, where gf, f, and m stand for grandfather, father, and mother, respectively.

For simplicity, consider the solution of the two queries with [gf1] only. The execution sequences for solving the two queries in three types of interpreters are as follows:

- In a demand-driven interpreter, father(jack,Z) will be solved before father(Z,Y) when [query 1] is solved, and father(Z,tom) will be solved before father(X,Z) when [query 2] is solved.

- In a brute-force parallel-exploitation interpreter, both father literals will be solved simultaneously, regardless of the bindings of the queries.

- In a sequential Prolog interpreter, the first father literal, e.g., father(jack,Z) and father(X,Z) for [query 1] and [query 2], respectively, will be solved first.

```
[query 1]    ?-  grandfather(jack,Y),
[query 2]    ?-  grandfather(X,tom),
[gf1]        grandfather ( X,Y):-  father(X,Z),  father(Z,Y),
[gf2]        grandfather(X,Y):-  mother(X,Z),  father(Z,Y),
             father(jack,paul),   . . .
             mother(jack,mary),   . . .
```

FIGURE 16.6 Logic programs.

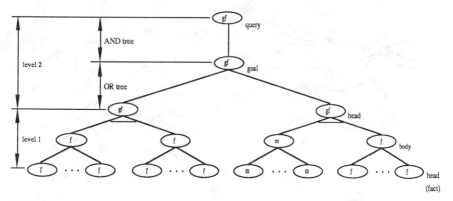

FIGURE 16.7 Tree representation of a logic program.

Based on the consideration of the ease of implementation, potential applications, efficiency, and generalization, many languages and execution models have been proposed as foundations of logic programming environments [18]. The conventional (sequential) Prolog implants a top-down and left-to-right traversal strategy into its semantics. Models exploiting only OR parallelism emphasize database applications and the reduction of overhead in parallel processing. For higher efficiency, languages such as Parlog and Concurrent Prolog are developed. However, they associate themselves more tightly with functional languages than with pure logic programming languages, and they require users to be more sophisticated programmers. As a remedy, models based on the demand-driven concept have been proposed. However, these models either result in a large overhead or exploit only AND parallelism. To generalize the application of logic programming, a few models are proposed for concurrent exploitation of AND and OR parallelism. The effective exploitation of AND and OR parallelism poses a task for both system designs and advances in VLSI technologies.

16.3.6 Neural Networks

A neural network is a computational structure modeled on biological processes [19]. Figure 16.8 illustrates the sort of a biological neuron which has influenced the development of "artificial," or computational, neural networks. It shows two neurons in synaptic contact:

The *soma,* or nerve cell, which is the large round central body of the neuron, is anywhere from 5 to 100 μm in diameter.

The *axon* is attached to the soma and is electrically active, producing the pulse which is emitted by the neuron.

The electrically passive *dendrites* receive inputs from other neurons by means of a specialized contact—this is the *synapse,* which occurs where the dendrites of two different nerve cells meet.

The synapse is the tissue connecting neurons, and it is capable of changing a dendrite's local potential in a positive or negative direction, depending on the pulse it transmits. Note that these transmissions occur in very large numbers, but since they are chemical, they occur fairly slowly.

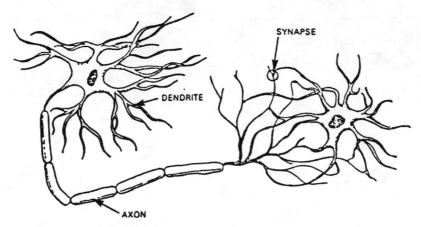

FIGURE 16.8   Biological neurons.

Artificial neurons, as illustrated in Fig. 16.9, are analogous to their biological inspirers. Figure 16.9 presents the simplest artificial neuron configuration. Here neurons become *processing elements* (PEs), the axons and dendrites become wires, and the synapses become variable resistors carrying *weighted* inputs that represent data or the sums of weights of still other processing elements.

Processing elements can interact in many ways by virtue of the manner in which they are *interconnected*. Prosaic as it is, Fig. 16.9 actually suggests a variety of possibilities:

processing elements which *feed forward* only

processing elements which have a *feedback* loop

processing elements that are *fully connected* to all other processing elements

processing elements that are *sparsely connected,* linked only to a few others

The nature and number of these feedback loops and connections depend on the model or architecture used to construct the neural network. The design of a neural network's feedback loops has implications for the nature of its adaptivity and trainability, while the design of a network's interconnections has implications for its parallelism.

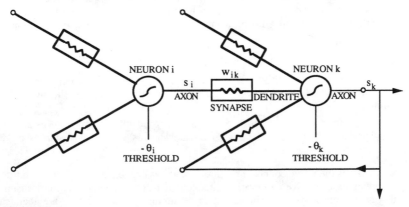

FIGURE 16.9   Artificial neurons.

Neural networks with sparse local connections are most suitable for VLSI implementations.

The following two key features illustrate the nature of the neural networks.

- *Neural networks are adaptive or trainable.* Neural networks are not so much programmed as they are *trained with data.* Thus many believe that the use of neural networks can relieve today's computer programmers of a significant portion of their present programming load. Moreover, neural networks are said to improve with experience—the more data they are fed, the more accurate or complete their response.

- *Neural networks are naturally massively parallel.* This suggests they should be able to make decisions at high speed and be fault-tolerant.

There are many techniques, generally articulated as algorithms, used to train neural networks; they fall into three basic categories [20]:

1. *Supervised training* requires the presence of an external teacher and labeling of the data used to train the network. The teacher knows the correct response wanted from the network and inputs an error signal when the network produces an incorrect response. The error signal "teaches" the network the correct response in a process that is explained below, and after a succession of learning trials the network consistently produces the correct response.

2. *Unsupervised training* uses unlabeled training data and requires no external teacher. Data are presented to the network, which forms internal clusters that compress the input data into classification categories.

3. *Self-supervised training* is used by certain kinds of neural networks. The networks monitor performance internally, requiring no external teacher; an error signal is generated by the system and fed back to itself, and the correct response is produced after a number of iterations.

16.4 SPECIFIC PARALLEL COMPUTING SYSTEMS

Contemporary parallel computing systems exemplify the classification spaces. We discuss specifics in four categories: parallel SIMD systems, multiprocessor systems, pipeline systems, and special-purpose systems.

16.4.1 Parallel SIMD Systems

Parallel SIMD systems are the natural extension of parallel ALU systems. Point D in Feng's concurrent space represents parallel SIMD systems, where concurrency is exploited through the replication of the processing modules under the management of a unique control unit. As a result, arithmetic and logic operations can be performed on a collection of operands (operand pairs) simultaneously. In this study we distinguish three groups of parallel SIMD systems: ensemble processors, array processors, and associative processors.

Ensemble Processors. An ensemble system is an extension of the conventional uniprocessor systems. It is a collection of N PEs (a PE consists of an ALU, a set of local registers, and very limited local control capability) and N memories, under the control of a single CU. Such a simple organization does not provide any direct communication paths among PEs. Moreover, it does not allow flexible interconnections between PEs and memories. Such communications are done through the CU. As a result, the system is able to execute up to N identical jobs simultaneously. However, due to the lack of direct interprocessor communications, this organization has very limited applications.

Array Processors.   The schematic diagram of an array processor is shown in Fig. 16.10. The system is composed of N identical PEs under the control of a single CU and a number of memory units [6, 7, 21–24]. The PEs and memory units communicate with each other through an interconnection network (the simplest interconnection network is a unibus). This network usually provides a uniform interconnection among PEs on one hand and PEs and memory modules on the other hand. In ILLIAC IV [10, 24], the complexity of the interconnection networks among the memory modules and PEs has been reduced by distribution of memory modules among the PEs. As a result, the system is a collection of N identical PEs with their own local memory modules. Different array processor organizations might use different interconnection networks among the processing elements. ILLIAC IV uses a mesh-structured network, whereas the Burroughs Scientific Processor (BSP) [25] uses a cross-bar network.

The CU is usually a computer with its own high-speed registers, local memory, and arithmetic unit. As in conventional machines, the instructions are stored in a main memory, together with data. However, in ILLIAC IV design, programs are distributed among the local memories of the PEs. Hence, the instructions are fetched from the processors' memory modules into an instruction buffer in the CU. Each instruction is either a local-type instruction, where it is executed entirely within the CU, or it is a vector instruction and is executed in the processing array. The primary function of the CU is to examine each instruction as it is to be executed and to determine where the execution should take place.

An array processor is a synchronous parallel computer. PEs are synchronized to perform in parallel the same function at the same time. The problem of data structuring and detecting parallelism in a program can create a major bottleneck, although the design

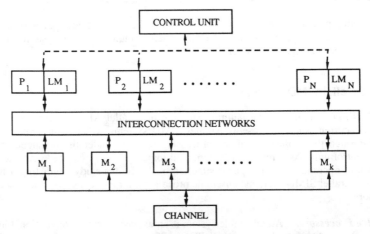

FIGURE 16.10   Array processor system: Processor (P), local memory (LM), memory module (M).

of the CU is simple and is almost like the one in sequential systems. In array processors an operation such as

$$x(i) = A(i) * B(i) \qquad i = 1, 2, \ldots, N \tag{16.1}$$

could be executed in one step, if the elements of the A and B arrays are distributed properly among the N processors; as a result, the ith processor is assigned the task of computing $x(i)$. However, if we have to compute

$$y = \sum_{i=1}^{T} A(i) * B(i) \tag{16.2}$$

while the product terms are generated in one step as discussed before, the summations will be performed in $\log_2 N$ steps, assuming that the intermediate operands are properly aligned and only a subset of processors that handle these operands becomes active at successive steps. Thus, the speedup ratio becomes

$$S = \frac{2N - 1}{1 + \log_2 N} \approx O\left(\frac{N}{\log_2 N}\right) \tag{16.3}$$

Note that in an algorithm as discussed above, such a speedup factor is at the expense of poor resource utilization.

Associative Processor. Associative memories have been generally defined as a collection or assemblage of data storage elements that are accessed in parallel on the basis of data content rather than by specific address or location [26–30]. As a result, each associative cell should have hardware capability to store and search its contents against the data that are broadcast by the CU. With such a definition in mind, one could conclude that although read and write are the basic operations in the conventional *random-access memory* (RAM), search and read and write are the basic operations for associative memory. The typical components of an associative memory are depicted in Fig. 16.11. The memory array provides storage space for the data; the comparand register holds the data to be compared against the contents of the memory array. However, by proper setting of

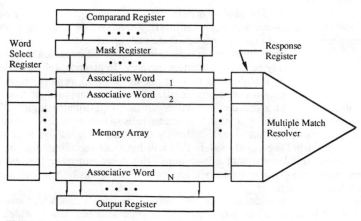

FIGURE 16.11 A word parallel associative memory.

the bit pattern in the mask register, one can mask off portions of the data words from comparison and other operations; a response bit indicates the success or failure of a search against the content of the corresponding associative word; and finally a multiple match resolver is used to narrow the result of a search to a specific word in case of multiple responses (e.g., matches). An *associative processor* is defined as an associative memory capable of performing arithmetic and logic operations. Usually, in such an organization, arithmetic and logic operations are performed in *bit-slice* (bis) fashion. This implies the extension of each associative word by a serial ALU. An *associative computer* then is defined as a system that uses an associative processor as an essential component for storage and processing. An obvious advantage of associative processing can be found in its application in nonnumeric processing, radar signal tracking and processing, image processing, and arithmetic and logarithmic operations on large sets of data. The main motivation for the study of associative systems centers on its capability in (1) reducing the semantic gap (i.e., a measure of the difference between the concepts in high-level languages and the concepts in the underlying computer architectures [31]) in the conventional systems and (2) increasing the performance due to the parallel operations at the storage level and elimination of address computation.

The concept of electronic associative memory was first introduced by Slade and McMahon [26], who described the design of a cryogenic memory system. Since then, associative memories have been implemented by using techniques such as tunnel diodes, evaporated organic diode arrays, magnetic cores, plated wires, semiconductors, bubble memory, integrated circuits [29], and recently optical technology. Moreover, the literature has addressed several modifications to the basic associative operations (e.g., hybrid associative memory, read-only associative memory [30]). However, up to the last decade, a widespread application of associative memory had not been fully explored. This was due to the hardware complexity of associative cells in comparison with RAM cells, conservatism, and lack of suitable associative algorithms. However, since the mid-1970s there is growing evidence that the above trend has changed. This is due to the advances in technology and their effect on the cost and size of the hardware components as well as the strong applications of associative processing in nonnumeric operations, image processing, and pattern recognition.

Associative memories have been classified into four categories: fully parallel, bit-serial, word-serial, and block-oriented [26, 29]. This classification is in accordance with the basic unit of data to which the search operation is applied and reflects the tradeoff between speed and cost.

Fully Parallel. In a fully parallel organization, the search capability is associated with the basic unit of information (e.g., bit level). Therefore, the associative operation can be performed along two dimensions simultaneously. Such a direction implies larger cell size and more expensive modules, in comparison with a bit in the RAM. Point D in Fig. 16.1 represents a fully parallel associative memory. In practice, fully parallel associative memories have been realized as two- or one-dimensional memory arrays. In the two-dimensional organization (word-organized), memory is composed of fixed-length entities called *words*. In a one-dimensional organization (distributed logic) [32, 33], memory is arranged as a string of search character cells, where each cell communicates with its neighbor and the control unit. Naturally fixed-length record size is an obvious shortcoming of a word-organized model. This will limit and complicate the implementation of the variable-length word applications. However, remember that associative operations in a word-organized memory are handled more easily than the ones in a distributed logic organization.

Bit-Serial. This organization represents point C in Feng's concurrent space (Fig. 16.1). Memory is organized as a collection of circular shift registers in which search capability is associated with a designated bit within each word (e.g., bit slice). To achieve efficiency at a reasonable cost, a variation of this organization (i.e., byte-serial associative memory) has also been proposed in the literature. In a byte-serial model, byte search capability is associated with each associative word.

Word-Serial. In this class, search capability is associated with a word. This will represent point B in Fig. 16.1. As can be seen, this class of associative memory is very similar to the parallel ALU systems. However, one should recognize that the hardware realization of word-serial organization is totally different from the one in the parallel ALU systems. This organization represents a hardware realization of a simple program loop in linear search.

Block-Oriented. In this class, associative capability is provided at the mass storage level (e.g., secondary storage). This concept is an extension of fixed-head rotating secondary storage technology. However, the fixed read/write heads are extended as a small processor (i.e., logic per track). As the data pass under the read/write heads, they will be investigated and marked for the later accesses. During the 1970s, the concept of logic per track, originally proposed by Slotnick [34], was used as a guideline in the design of many database machines.

16.4.2 Multiprocessor Systems

The multiprocessor organization (Fig. 16.12) is the practical extension of array processing [1, 11, 35–38]. Originally, multiprocessors were designed as a model to improve the fault-tolerance capability of the conventional systems. Two types of multiprocessor systems exist: shared-memory multiprocessor systems [39–42] and distributed-memory multiprocessor systems [43, 44]. The argument that justifies such an approach is the existence of a large class of problems, which can be split up into a number of tasks. Each task can be simultaneously run on a different processor in a multiprocessor system. This will reduce the execution time and hence increase the system's throughput. Reliability is a major advantage of multiprocessor systems, because failure in any of the redundant components can be tolerated due to the reconfigurability of the system. However, in multiprocessor systems, one has to find practical solutions for problems such as task partitioning, processor coordination and communication, and resource allocation and contention; otherwise, lack of such sophisticated algorithms will drastically degrade the performance and resource utilization. These problems have enforced a limitation on a number of processors, as will be discussed later.

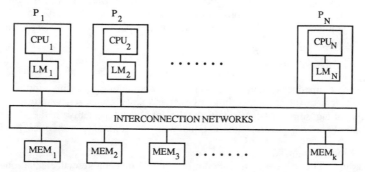

FIGURE 16.12 Multiprocessor system: Processor (P), memory module (MEM), central processing unit (CPU), local memory (LM).

In general, a multiprocessor system can be defined as follows:

- There are two or more CPUs. The processors could be homogeneous or nonhomogeneous. However, they should be general enough to be able to perform general-purpose operations.
- In shared-memory multiprocessor systems, main memory is shared among the processors. However, we do not rule out the possibility of private memory for each processor. As a matter of fact, recently there has been a surge to study the so-called coherence problem in a multiprocessor environment with private memory [45–49]. In distributed-memory multiprocessor systems, each processor has its private memory, and no global shared memory is available.
- The resources are sharable among the processors.
- The whole system is under control of a single integrated operating system.
- There should be a means of interaction at different levels (i.e., hardware/software) among the system's modules.

By a close observation, one can realize the natural trend in the evolution of the multiprocessor systems. Practically multiprocessing, like parallel processing, achieves concurrency as the result of hardware replication (e.g., redundancy). However, in a multiprocessor system, the degree of freedom associated with the processors is much higher than that in parallel systems. Therefore, processors are more independent with respect to each other and the central CU. This independence and resource-sharing capability of multiprocessor systems will introduce a degree of complexity on the dynamic communication capability among the processors and among the processors and the global memory. In addition, in contrast to the parallel systems, the CU and software supports should be much more complex in order to map application programs into the hardware features. Shared-memory multiprocessor systems are referred to as *tightly coupled systems,* and distributed-memory multiprocessors systems are referred as *loosely coupled systems*. This distinction is based on the degree of communication among the system's modules. Although it is not within the scope of this chapter, the aforementioned freedom can be traced in the evolution of distributed systems.

The performance of a multiprocessor system depends on a mix of jobs. With N processors, the throughput is certainly less than the sum of the throughput of N independent processors. For $N = 2$ and $N = 4$, typical values of throughput are 1.5 and 2.5, respectively. Note that, in practice, the number of the PEs in an array processor can be relatively much larger than the number of processors in a multiprocessor system. For example, the design of the *Massively Parallel Processor* (MPP) was based on 16,384 PEs, whereas Cmmp utilized 16 processors in its organization. This difference is due to the overall complexity of MIMD organizations in comparison to SIMD organizations.

16.4.3 Pipeline Systems

The idea of a pipeline system is similar to an automobile assembly line. The term *pipelining* refers to the design techniques that introduce concurrency into a computer system by taking some basic functions to be involved repeatedly in the system and partitioning them into several subfunctions with the following properties [1, 9, 38, 48, 49]:

- Evaluation of the basic function is equivalent to some sequential evaluation of the subfunctions.

- Other than the exchange of inputs and outputs, there are no interrelationships between subfunctions.

- Hardware may be developed to execute each subfunction.

- The time required for these hardware units to perform their individual evaluations is usually approximately equal.

Therefore, in a pipeline system a process is decomposed into a series of sequential subprocesses. Each subprocess is executed on a dedicated module called a *segment, stage,* or *station*. In addition, because the logic that actually performs the subprocesses at each stage is without memory, the presentation of data to each stage usually demands some kind of buffer to be included at either the beginning or the end of each stage. This will help to synchronize the overall flow of data throughout the pipe. The concept of pipelining has been implemented in systems such as Amdahl 470 V/8 [50], Cray [51, 52], TI ASC [53], CDC Star-100 [54], CDC 7600-6600 [55], and IBM 360/91 [56, 57].

Figure 16.13 depicts a schematic diagram of a pipeline processor where k different stages correspond to the distinct hardware steps. Thus, several partial operations can be

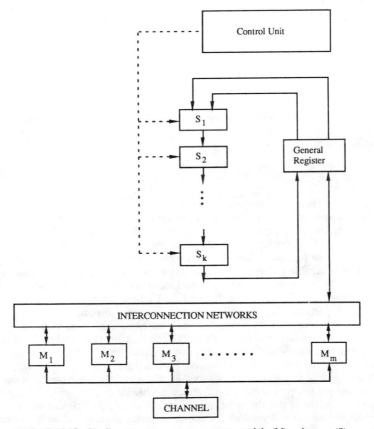

FIGURE 16.13 Pipeline processor system: memory module (M) and stages (S).

in progress concurrently within a pipeline, which will result in an increase in throughput. Interconnection networks [58] are needed to supply data.

Suppose we want to compute the elements $x(i)$ defined as

$$x(i) = A(i) * B(i) \qquad i = 1, 2, \ldots, N \qquad (16.4)$$

Assuming that the multiplier unit is a pipeline of five stages, the overall execution time will be $[(N - 1) + 5] \Delta t$ (where Δt is the delay time due to operation in a stage) provided that a constant flow of data is always available to the pipeline and the system can store $x(i)$ as rapidly as it is generated. Now, suppose one has to calculate

$$y = \sum_{i=1}^{T} x(i) \qquad (16.5)$$

using the same pipe for addition. The formation of products will take $N + 4$ stage delays. Then the pipeline is drained out and set for addition operations. Due to the data dependence, additions are performed in several passes. After the first pass, the pipeline yields $N/2$ results; in the second pass, it yields approximately $N/4$ results, etc. Hence, the total execution time would be

$$5 + \left(\frac{N}{2} - 1\right) + 5 + \left(\frac{N}{4} - 1\right) + \cdots + 5 + (1 - 1)$$

$$= 4 \log_2 N + \frac{N}{2} + \frac{N}{4} + \cdots$$

$$\leq 4 \log_2 N + N \qquad (16.6)$$

stage delays. Hence, the total execution time is $\leq 2N + 4 \log_2 N + 4$ stage delays. A serial process would have taken $5(2N - 1) = 10N - 5$ stage delays. As a result, the speedup ratio is equal to

$$S = \frac{10N - 5}{2N + 4 \log_2 N + 4} \qquad (16.7)$$

However, experiences on Cray have shown that vector operations for small vectors demonstrate a performance degradation over scalar operations [51]. This is due to the fact that performance of the pipeline operations is heavily dependent on the number of operands and uniformity of operations. Pipelines can be classified according to their capabilities. A *unifunction* pipeline is capable of only one basic kind of operation. A *multifunction* pipeline is capable of handling several different kinds of functional evaluation. A multifunctional pipeline can be further grouped into *statically configured* and *dynamically configured* pipelines. This classification is based on the frequency of changes in the functions they perform. A concept known as *hazard* is a major concern in a pipeline architecture. A hazard prevents the pipeline from accepting data at the maximum rate that the staging clock might support. Hazard is the result of the structural and data dependence. A structural hazard is the one where two different pieces of data attempt to use the same stage at the same time (e.g., collisions). Data-dependent hazards occur when a pass through a stage is a function of the data value. For statically configured pipelines, the designers can predict precisely when a structural hazard might occur and hence can schedule the pipeline so that the collisions do not occur. The data-dependent hazards are clearly system- and usage-dependent and not as amenable to analytical study as structural hazards.

16.4.4 Special-Purpose Architectures

In this section, two examples of special-purpose architectures—one for nonnumeric applications and the other for numeric applications—influenced by application areas and advances in technology, will be described. Although these architectures utilize the concept of parallelism as discussed earlier, they are not based on the von Neumann philosophy conceptually.

Database Machines. Since the early 1970s, the complexity of the conventional database management systems has been gradually increased by the number and size of databases, the number and type of application programs, and the number and type of on-line users. For example, among the estimated 20,000 U.S. government databases, the Patent Office has a database of 65 billion characters and a query retrieval of one item every 24 s. As another example, the Ballistic Missile Defense Systems require a distributed and dynamic database that can maintain and upgrade itself in a complex and rapidly evolving battleground. The system should be able to perform about 60 to 120 million operations per second to verify, track, classify, and eliminate a threat. It is projected that by 1995 the Defense Mapping Agency will have a database of 10^{19} bits supporting 1000 on-line users needing 10^{14} bits each.

Conventional systems using typical software approaches fail to meet the requirements of the aforementioned applications. A software implementation of direct search on an IBM 370/158 can process approximately 100,000 characters per second. But even if this speed could be increased 10-fold, it would take 18 h to search the 65 billion characters in the U.S. Patent Office's data file system.

To avoid the need for an exhaustive search, most existing software systems are based on an indexing mechanism. An indexed system improves performance by means of a sophisticated software system and additional redundancy of data. Nevertheless, this has created some more problems. The indexed structures require extra space for the indices. It has been estimated that in a fully inverted file, the space needed to store the index ranges from 50 to 300 percent of the size of the database itself [59]. In addition, the use of a directory creates complexity in the search, update, and delete algorithms. In fact, indexing merely shifts the processing burden, and so it offers only a partial solution in terms of the efficiency of database operations.

The inefficiency of conventional systems in handling large databases can be associated with the existing semantic gap, computation gap, and size gap. These gaps stem from the fact that (1) conventional systems by their very nature are sequential machines, (2) a conventional ALU is structured for numeric computations (e.g., the Cray-1 is able to perform 250 million floating-point operations per second, although it cannot handle more than 15 million characters per second), and (3) the memory hierarchy has a passive role in the organization, hence there is a massive amount of data movement between processing elements and storage units. Therefore, there is a great need to design and develop new architectures specialized to the demand of a database environment.

Since the mid-1970s, a great deal of effort has been directed toward the design of special-purpose architectures for efficient handling of large database systems [60–70]. In addition, recent advances in technology have forced drastic changes in the architectural aspects of these machines.

A viable database machine suitable for current and future database environments should satisfy

1. The constraints imposed by technology that will be available in the foreseeable future
2. The throughput and functionality demanded by the database environment

3. The reliability, fault tolerance, reconfigurability, and survivability demanded by the database environment
4. Issues related to integrity, recovery, security, and privacy in a multiple-user environment

Conditions 1 through 3 could be satisfied through the design of an inherently parallel special-purpose database machine that satisfies the constraints imposed by the technology. Conditions 3 and 4 will be fulfilled by consideration of the aforementioned issues during the design phase. The next section presents an overview of different classifications of the database machines, as proposed in the literature. In addition, a set of criteria will be discussed for evaluation of the database machines.

Classification of Database Machines.   Databases fall into two general categories, *formatted* and *unformatted* structures. Formatted databases are mainly time-variant entities and are subject to extensive alteration as well as search operations. Unformatted databases (bibliographic or full text) are archival in nature and are processed by searching for a pattern or a combination of patterns. As a result, operations on the formatted databases are based on the contents of the attribute values of the records, whereas the patterns are unpredictable combinations of terms and words in the unformatted databases. The discussion in this section is centered on formatted databases. Unformatted database systems are the subject of the next section. Several classifications of database machines have been addressed in the literature [60–63, 66–69]. In the following, we concentrate on three classifications. Table 16.1 summarizes different classifications and their comparisons to the Bray and Freeman classification.

Bray and Freeman [63] have classified database machines into five categories: *single-processor indirect-search* (SPIS), *single-processor direct-search* (SPDS), *multiple-processor direct-search* (MPDS), *multiple-processor indirect-search* (MPIS), and *multiple-processor combined-search* (MPCS). Direct-search processing implies the ability to search a database at the secondary storage level, whereas indirect search represents the fact that data need to be transferred to an intermediate storage medium before the search can be conducted.

An SPIS machine represents the conventional von Neumann type of architecture with no degree of parallelism. Naturally, such an architecture bears all the aforementioned deficiencies in handling large databases. An SPDS machine represents a conventional system enhanced by searching capability at the secondary storage. As a result, only the desired records or their specified parts are sent to the host. MPDS and MPIS machines represent parallel versions of SPDS and SPIS organizations. MPCS is a combination of the MPDS and MPIS organizations, where the search is performed on the data loaded into intermediate storage, whereas multiple processing units are assigned to the blocks of intermediate storage.

Song [68] has defined database machines as computer systems enhanced by special-purpose logic for handling database operations. With such a view, he has classified these machines according to three parameters:

1. The place where hardware logic is applied. This could be at (close to) either secondary storage or primary memory.
2. Allocation of logic to the storage unit. This could be static or dynamic. Naturally, a dynamic allocation offers better resource utilization.
3. Degree of logic distribution, which defines the number of storage elements associated with each processing unit. This parameter represents the degree of parallelism and hence directly affects the performance.

TABLE 16.1 Relationships among Different Classifications of Database Machines

Bray and Freeman [63]	Rosenthal [60]	Berra [61]	Champine [62]	Su [66]	Hsiao [67]	Song [68]	Qadah [69]
SPDS	Smart peripheral system		Intelligent peripheral CU			Logic at secondary storage with static allocation (sequential operation)	SOSD with relation indexing on the disk search
SPIS	Large back-end	Back-end system	Back-end processor			Logic at primary storage with static allocation (sequential operation)	SOSD with relation or page indexing off-disk search
MPDS	Smart peripheral system	Logic in memory	Intelligent peripheral CU	Cellular logic	Cellular logic	Logic at secondary storage with static/dynamic allocation (parallel operation)	MOMD/SOMD with relation indexing on-disk search
MPIS	Large back-end processor	Back-end system/ large associative processor	Back-end processor	High-speed associative system/back-end system	Associate array	Logic at primary memory with static/dynamic (parallel operation)	MOMD/SOMD with relation or page indexing off-disk search
MPCS	Distributed network data node		Network node	Integrated database machine	Functionally specialized system	Logic at primary/ secondary memory with static/dynamic allocation; medium to high level of parallelism	MOMD/SOMD with relation or page indexing on/off hybrid search

Qadah [69] has extended Bray and Freeman's database space by a third dimension, namely, the indexing level. The coordinates of this database space are the indexing level, query processing place, and processing multiplicity. The indexing coordinate represents the smallest addressable unit of data. Along this coordinate, database machines can be grouped into database indexing level, relation indexing level, and page indexing level. The query processing place determines the location where data are searched. This could be away from the secondary storage, on the secondary storage, or a hybrid of both. The third coordinate represents the degree of parallelism. Along this coordinate, we can group database machines into single-operation single-data (SOSD) stream, single-operation multiple-data (SOMD) stream, and multiple-operation multiple-data (MOMD) stream.

A New Classification.   Similar to Flynn's classification of computer systems [3], some of the proposed classifications suffer from the fact that there is some overlap between the categories. For example, there is no clear way of determining when a smart peripheral system becomes a back-end computer as functions are moved from the host to the peripheral system. In addition, these classifications do not address the effect of the advances in technology on the architecture and adaptability of a specific architecture for the current and foreseeable technology. We believe such a parameter should be used as a coordinate of the database space. Recent developments in technology have influenced the architecture of these systems in two directions:

1. Reconfiguration and reevaluation of the previously designed database architectures according to the constraints imposed by the technology (The evolution of RAP [71] demonstrates the validity of this discussion.)

2. The design of new architectures based on the constraints imposed by the technology [72–74]

Qadah's database space can be extended by a fourth dimension, namely, technological adaptability. Therefore, one can define a database space of four coordinates: technological adaptability, degree of parallelism, query processing place, and indexing level. According to these parameters, one can characterize an architecture based on its ability to handle computational gap, semantic gap, size gap, data communication problem, and name-mapping resolution.

The indexing level determines the smallest accessible unit of data. Such a coordinate determines name-mapping resolution and the proper protocol that one should take to enforce the security and guarantee the system's integrity. Along the technological adaptability coordinate, database architectures are characterized as fully, semi-, or low adaptable designs. The query-processing coordinate characterizes four classes: searching at the secondary storage, close to the secondary storage, indirect, or a combination of different approaches.

Systolic Organizations.   Recent advances in technology have made it economically possible to implant systems with gate complexity of the order of 10^5 on a single chip. Nevertheless, with the exception of memory organization, the great potential of such a development has not yet been exploited fully. Such a gap between theory and practice is partially due to the lack of suitable architectures for hardware implementation. A suitable architecture should bear a set of constraints in order to be suitable for hardware implementation. A suitable architecture should reduce communications as well as computation, based on the replication of a few basic building blocks in space or time. This simply implies modularity, regularity, and simplicity.

The systolic architecture [75, 76], originally proposed for VLSI implementation of some matrix operations, is a general methodology for mapping high-level computations into hardware structure with respect to the technological constraints. Systolic organization is a collection of few basic blocks (e.g., processing elements) replicated in a one- or two-dimensional space, with simple and regular communication paths among the processing elements. Moreover, the flow of data from memory to the PEs is rhythmic, and each set of data passes through many PEs before it returns to the memory, much as blood circulates in the human body. This allows multiple computations for each memory access in a computer bound operation without increasing I/O requirements. Figure 16.14 shows a systolic model proposed for text retrieval operation [77]. Each cell (e.g., PE) performs two separate functions; hence, the cell is composed of two separate basic cells, namely, the comparator and the accumulator. The operations within the comparator and accumulator cells are defined as in Fig. 16.14, where λ and x are the end-of-pattern and don't-care markers, respectively. According to this discussion, systolic organization is similar to the pipelining discussed in Sec. 16.4.3. However, remember that the pipeline systems are linear organization, whereas systolic systems can be organized in a two-dimensional space. Moreover, the basic elements can be rectangular, triangular, or hexagonal [75] to achieve a higher degree of parallelism in the operations. In addition, data flow in a systolic organization can be at multiple speeds in multiple directions, i.e., both inputs and partial results, whereas in classical pipelined organizations only partial results are flowing among stages in one direction.

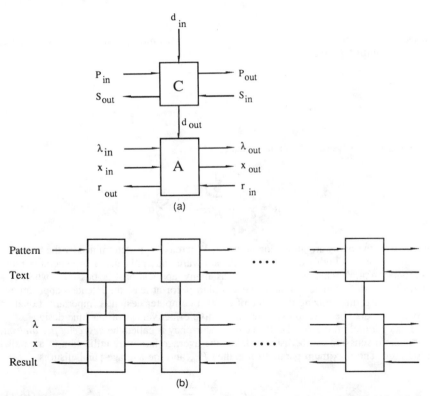

FIGURE 16.14 A systolic model for pattern-matching operation. *(a)* Structure of a cell. *(b)* Systolic array.

The basic philosophy of the systolic model has been used as a model to design many special-purpose units to enhance the performance of the conventional, as well as unconventional, parallel systems [73, 77, 78]. The ability to use each input data item in a number of computations, modular expandability, simple and uniform interconnection and communication paths among the PE, and finally fast response time are among the many advantages of systolic models.

16.5 UTILIZATION AND SHORTCOMINGS

16.5.1 System Utilization

As discussed previously, for any computer there is a maximum number of bits or bit pairs that can be processed concurrently, whether it is under single-instruction or multiple-instruction control [2, 79]. This maximum degree of concurrency, or *maximum concurrency* C_m, is an indication of the computer processing capability. The actual utilization of this capability is indicated by the average concurrency, defined to be

$$C_a = \frac{\Sigma c_i \, \Delta t_i}{\Sigma \Delta t_i} \tag{16.8}$$

where c_i is the concurrency at Δt_i. If Δt_i is set to 1 time unit, then the average concurrency over a period of T time units is

$$C_a = \frac{\displaystyle\sum_{i=1}^{T} c_i}{T} \tag{16.9}$$

The average hardware utilization is then

$$\mu = \frac{C_a}{C_m} = \frac{\displaystyle\sum_{i=1}^{T} c_i}{T C_m} = \frac{1}{T} \sum_{i=1}^{T} \sigma_i \tag{16.10}$$

where σ_i is the hardware utilization at time i. Whereas C_m is determined by the hardware design, C_a or μ is highly dependent on the software and applications. A general-purpose computer should achieve a high μ for as many applications as possible, whereas a special-purpose computer would achieve a high μ for at least the intended applications. In either case, maximizing the value of μ for a computer design is important. Equation (16.10) can also be used to evaluate the relative effectiveness of machine designs.

For a parallel processor, the degree of concurrency is called the *degree of parallelism*. A similar discussion can be used to define the average hardware utilization of a parallel processor. The maximum parallelism is then P_m, and the average parallelism is

$$P_a = \frac{\Sigma p_i \, \Delta t_i}{\Sigma \Delta t_i} \tag{16.11}$$

or

$$P_a = \frac{\sum_{i=1}^{T} p_i}{T} \qquad (16.12)$$

for T time units. The average hardware utilization becomes

$$v = \frac{P_a}{P_m} = \frac{\sum_{i=1}^{T} p_i}{TP_m} = \frac{1}{T} \sum_{i=1}^{T} \rho_i \qquad (16.13)$$

where ρ_i is the hardware utilization for parallel processors at time i. With appropriate instrumentation, the average hardware utilization of a system can be determined.

In practice, however, it is not always true that every bit or bit pair that is being processed would be productive. Some of the bits produce only repetitious (superfluous) or even meaningless results. This happens more often and more severely in a parallel processor than in a word sequential processor. Consider, e.g., performing a maximum search operation in a mesh-connected parallel processor (such as ILLIAC IV). For N operands, it takes $(N/2) \log_2 N$ comparisons ($N/2$ comparisons for each $\log_2 N$ iterations) instead of the usual $N - 1$ comparisons in word sequential machines. Thus, in effect there are

$$\left(\frac{N}{2} \log_2 N \right) - (N - 1) = \frac{N}{2} (\log_2 N - 2) + 1 \qquad (16.14)$$

comparisons that are nonproductive. If we let $\hat{P}_a$ be the effective parallelism over a period of T time units and $\hat{v}$, $\hat{p}_i$, and $\hat{\rho}_i$ be the corresponding effective values, the effective hardware utilization is then

$$\hat{v} = \frac{\hat{P}_a}{P_m} = \frac{\sum_{i=1}^{T} \hat{p}_i}{TP_m} = \frac{1}{T} \sum_{i=1}^{T} \hat{\rho}_i \qquad (6.15)$$

A successful parallel processor design should yield a high $\hat{v}$ as well as the required throughput for at least the intended applications. This involves not only a proper hardware and software design but also the development of efficient parallel algorithms for these applications.

Suppose T_u is the execution time of an application program using a conventional von Neumann machine and T_c is the execution time of the same program using a concurrent system; the *speedup ratio* is then defined as

$$S = \frac{T_u}{T_c} \qquad (6.16)$$

Naturally, for a specific parallel organization, the speedup ratio determines how well an application program can utilize the hardware resources. Supporting softwares have a direct effect on the speedup ratio.

16.5.2 Shortcomings of Conventional Parallel Systems

The parallel system and its successors have shown their effectiveness in many real-time applications. By their very nature, these computers are more complex than their predecessor architectures. This complexity is mainly due to the simultaneous competition and cooperation of several modules over common resources, which leads to more complexity and sophistication at (1) the control structure, to manage the flow of data and operations within the system's modules; (2) the interconnection network, to allow simultaneous interactions among the system's modules.

Although the growth in complexity could result in higher cost, lower resource utilization, and performance degradation, the major disadvantage of these systems is associated with two interrelated factors, namely, *specialization* and *semantic gap*.

In contrast to the conventional von Neumann architectures, parallel systems are specialized architectures. For example, parallel systems are superior in handling computation-bound applications; however, they offer low performance in I/O-bound applications such as database systems. In addition, these machines demand specific domain(s) to guarantee the performance improvement. Studies on ILLIAC IV–type architecture have shown that the allocation of data within the memory modules has a drastic effect on the performance [80]. Experiences on Cray have shown that vector operations for small vectors demonstrate a performance degradation over scalar operations [51]. These examples reflect the fact that the conventional concurrent systems require specialized and sometimes different programming skills for efficient resource utilization. As a result, in a multifunctional unit system (i.e., an extension of the conventional systems consists of a single CU and a processor unit composed of several independent functional units), a mixed sequence of instructions increases the performance, whereas in a pipeline system a uniform sequence of instructions increases the performance. Therefore, we can conclude that conventional parallel systems introduce a wider semantic gap than the conventional uniprocessor systems in handling general-purpose applications. Therefore, they require an extensive software support to express and determine the inherent parallelism in an application programs.

The performance improvement of parallel systems is greatly dependent on the proper utilization of hardware resources. However, it has been shown in practice that in many applications such goals are usually not achieved. This problem is attributed to (1) the inherent sequential nature of many algorithms; (2) overhead time required for data alignment, process coordination, etc., in a parallel system; (3) lack of suitable parallel algorithms for various application areas; (4) lack of suitable parallel high-level language, which enables the programmer to express the inherent parallelism explicitly in the problem being encoded; and (5) lack of suitable compilation techniques to detect embedded parallelism in sequential program.

High-level languages rooted in the 1950s have been developed as programming tools to increase the machine's independence and productivity. Naturally, these languages reflect the structure of the conventional uniprocessor systems, i.e., the existence of a primitive set of arithmetic operations, which are carried out sequentially on data stored in some form of memory device. However, for a parallel system there is a need to express the parallelism in an algorithm for parallel execution. This goal can be achieved through either the definition of new parallel languages or the addition of parallel constructs in the definition of the conventional sequential high-level languages.

Since the introduction of parallelism and parallel computers, there has been a surge to design and develop parallel languages to facilitate the utilization and performance of parallel systems [81–84]. The so-called Parallel Fortran (P-FOR) proposed for PEPE architecture [81], TRANQUIL for ILLIAC IV [82], and APPLE for STARAN [83] are among the pioneer efforts in this area.

Generation of parallelism from sequential constructs (e.g., vectorization) requires an extensive analysis of the sequential programs. This analysis must check that the ordering is, in fact, arbitrary and that there are no sequential dependencies in the process. This approach is a means of increasing the adaptability of the parallel systems and protecting the previous investments of the users. Naturally, this direction requires the development of sophisticated compilers (e.g., vectorizing compilers) to generate parallel machine instructions from sequences of operations without violating the program semantics. This means more sophisticated compilation techniques, more complex operating systems, and more advanced program development tools.

REFERENCES

1. K. Hwang and F. A. Briggs, *Computer Architecture and Parallel Processing*. New York: McGraw-Hill, 1984.

2. T. Y. Feng, "An Overview of Parallel Processing Systems," *1972 WESCON Technical Papers*, Session 1: Parallel Processing Systems, September 1972, pp. 1–2.

3. M. J. Flynn, "Very High Speed Computing Systems," *Proceedings of the IEEE*, 54(12): 1901–1909, December 1966.

4. H. O. Leilich, G. Stiege, and H. C. Zeidler, "A Search Processor for Database Management Systems," technical reports, University of Braunschwieg, Germany, 1978.

5. W. Händler, "Innovative Computer Architecture—How to Increase Parallelism but Not Complexity," in D. J. Evans (ed.), *Parallel Processing Systems*. London: Cambridge University Press, 1982, pp. 1–41.

6. S. F. Reddaway, "DAP—A Distributed Array Processor," *Proceedings of First Symposium on Computer Architecture*, University of Florida, Gainesville, December 1973. Los Alamitos, Calif.: IEEE Computer Society, 1973. Pp. 61–65.

7. T. Fountain, *Processor Arrays: Architectures and Applications*. London: Academic Press, 1987.

8. J. von Neumann, "Probabilistic Logics and the Synthesis of Reliable Organisms from Unreliable Components," in C. E. Shannon and J. McCarthy (eds.), *Automata Studies*. Princeton, N.J.: Princeton University Press, 1956. Pp. 43–98.

9. C. V. Ramamoorthy and H. F. Li, "Pipeline Architecture," *ACM Computing Survey*, 9(1): 61–102, March 1977.

10. G. H. Barnes, R. M. Brown, M. Kato, D. J. Kuck, D. L. Slotnick, and R. A. Stokes, "The ILLIAC IV Computer," *IEEE Transactions on Computers*, C-7:746–757, 1968.

11. P. H. Enslow, Jr., "Multiprocessor Organization—A Survey," *ACM Computing Survey*, 9(1): 103–129, 1977.

12. J. B. Dennis, "Data-Flow Supercomputer," *Computer*, 13:48–56, 1980.

13. G. A. Magó, "A Cellular Computer Architecture for Functional Programming," *Proceedings of the IEEE COMPCON 80*, 1980, pp. 179–187.

14. R. M. Keller, S. S. Patil, and G. Lindstrom, "A Loosely-Coupled Applicative Multiprocessing System," *Proceedings of the National Computer Conference*. Reston, Va.: American Federation of Information Processing Societies, 1978. Pp. 861–870.

15. *Byte* magazine, special issue on the smalltalk programming language, 1981.

16. R. A. Kowalski, "Predicate Logic as a Programming Language," *Proceedings of the International Federation of Information Processing*, 1974.

17. R. A. Kowalski, *Logic for Problem Solving*. Amsterdam: North-Holland, 1979.

18. A. C. Chen and C.-L. Wu, "A Parallel Execution Model of Logic Programs," *IEEE Transactions on Parallel and Distributed Systems,* 2:79–92, 1991.

19. W. S. M. Culloch and W. Pitts, "A Logical Calculus of the Ideas Imminent in Nervous Activity," *Bulletin of Mathematical Biophysics,* 5:115–133, 1943.

20. DARPA, *Neural Network Study,* AFCEA, 1988.

21. K. J. Thurber, *Large Scale Computer Architecture.* Rochelle Park, N.J.: Hayden Book Company, 1976.

22. "Array Processor Architecture," *Computer,* Special Issue on Array Processors, 14(9), September 1981.

23. K. Hwang, S. P. Su, and L. M. Ni, "Vector Computer Architecture and Processing Techniques," *Advances in Computers,* 20:115–197, 1981.

24. R. M. Hold, *The ILLIAC IV.* Rockville, Md.: Computer Science Press, 1982.

25. D. J. Kuck and R. A. Stokes, "The Borroughs Scientific Processor (BSP)," *IEEE Transactions on Computers,* C-31(5):363–376, May 1982.

26. B. Parhami, "Associative Memories and Processors: An Overview and Selected Bibliography," *Proceedings of the IEEE,* 61(6):772–730, 1973.

27. T. Y. Feng, "Search Algorithms for Associative Memories," in *Proceedings of Fourth Annual Princeton Conference on Information Science and Systems.* Princeton, N.J.: Princeton University Press, 1970. Pp. 442–446.

28. C. R. Petrie and A. R. Hurson, "A VLSI Join Module," *VLSI System Design,* 9(10):48–58, 1988.

29. S. S. Yau and H. S. Fung, "Associative Processor Architecture—A Survey," *ACM Computing Survey,* 9(1):3–28, 1977.

30. T. Kohonen, *Content Addressable Memories.* Berlin: Springer-Verlag, 1980.

31. G. J. Myers, *Advances in Computer Architecture,* 2d ed. New York: Wiley, 1982.

32. C. Y. Lee and M. C. Paull, "A Content Addressable Distributed Logic Memory with Applications to Information Retrieval," *Proceedings of the IEEE,* 51(7):924–932, 1963.

33. R. S. Gaines and C. Y. Lee, "An Improved Cell Memory," *IEEE Transactions on Electronic Computers,* 14(2):72–75, 1965.

34. D. L. Slotnick, "Logic per Track Devices," in *Advances in Computers,* 10:291–296, 1970.

35. M. Satyanarayan, *Multiprocessors—A Comparative Study.* Englewood Cliffs, N.J.: Prentice-Hall, 1980.

36. M. Satyanarayan, "Multiprocessing: An Annotated Bibliography," *Computer,* 5:101–116, May 1980.

37. W. A. Wulf, R. Levin, and S. P. Harbison, *HYDRA/Cmmp: An Experimental Computer System.* New York: McGraw-Hill, 1981.

38. H. S. Stone, *High-Performance Computer Architecture.* Reading, Mass.: Addison-Wesley, 1987.

39. BBN Advanced Computers Inc., *Butterfly GP 1000 Overview,* 1988.

40. G. F. Pfister, W. C. Brantly, D. A. George, S. L. Harvey, W. J. Kleinfelder, K. P. McAnliffe, E. A. Melton, V. A. Norton, and J. Weiss, "The IBM Research Parallel Processor Prototype (RP3): Introduction and Architecture," *Proceedings of 1985 International Conference on Parallel Processing.* Los Alamitos, Calif.: IEEE Computer Society, 1985. Pp. 764–771.

41. FLEX/32 Multicomputer System Overview, Flexible Computer Corporation, Dallas, Tex., 1981.

42. J. Konicek, "The Organization of the Cedar System," *Proceedings of 1991 International Conference on Parallel Processing,* August 1991, pp. I-49–I-58.

43. Intel iPSC manuals, Beaverton, Ore., 1986.

44. R. A. Olson, "Parallel Processing in a Message-Based Operating System," *IEEE Software,* 2(4), July 1985.

45. M. Dubois and F. A. Briggs, "Effects of Cache Coherency in Multiprocessors," *IEEE Transactions on Computers,* C-31(11):1083–1099, November 1982.

46. F. A. Briggs and M. Dubois, "Effectiveness of Private Caches in Multiprocessor Systems with Parallel Pipelined Memories," *IEEE Transactions on Computers,* C-32(1):48–59, January 1983.

47. M. S. Papamarcos and J. H. Patel, "A Low-Overhead Coherence Solution for Multiprocessors with Private Cache Memories," in *International Symposium on Computer Architecture.* Silver Spring, Md.: IEEE Computer Society Press, 1984, pp. 1–7.

48. P. M. Kogge, *The Architecture of Pipelined Computers.* New York: McGraw-Hill, 1981.

49. R. W. Hockney and C. R. Jesshope, *Parallel Computers.* Bristol, England: Adam Hilger Ltd., 1981.

50. R. W. Doran, "The Amdahl 470V/8 and the IBM 3033: A Comparison of Processor Designs," *Computer,* 15(4): 28–36, April 1982.

51. R. M. Russell, "The CRAY-1 Computer System," *Communications of the ACM,* 21(2):63–72, January 1978.

52. J. S. Koladzey, "CRAY-1 Computer Technology," *IEEE Transactions on Components, Hybrids, and Manufacturing Technology,* 4(2):181–186, 1981.

53. W. J. Watson, "The TI ASC—A Highly Modular and Flexible Super Computer Architecture," *AFIPS,* 41:221–228, 1972.

54. R. G. Hintz and D. P. Tate, "Control Data STAR-100 Processor Design," in *Proceedings of ComCon 72.* Silver Spring, Md.: IEEE Computer Society Press, 1972, pp. 1–4.

55. J. E. Thornton, *Design of a Computer, The Control Data 6600.* New York: Scott, Foresman, 1970.

56. R. M. Tomasulo, "An Efficient Algorithm for Exploiting Multiple Arithmetic Unit," *IBM Journal,* 11:25–33, January 1967.

57. S. F. Anderson, J. G. Earle, R. E. Goldschmidt, and D. M. Powers, "The IBM System/360 Model 91: Floating Point Execution Unit," *IBM Journal,* 11:34–53, January 1967.

58. T. Y. Feng and C.-L. Wu, *Interconnection Networks for Parallel and Distributed Processing.* Los Alamitos, Calif.: Computer Society Press, 1984.

59. R. Haskin, "Hardware for Searching Very Large Text Databases," in *Proceedings of Fifth Workshop on Computer Architecture for Non-Numeric Processing.* New York: Association for Computing Machinery, 1979, pp. 49–56.

60. R. S. Rosenthal, "The Data Management Machine, A Classification," in *Third Computer Architecture for Non-Numeric Processing.* New York: Association for Computing Machinery, 1977, pp. 35–39.

61. B. P. Berra, "Database Machines," *ACM Special Interest Group Information Retrieval Forum,* 13(3):4–23, 1977.

62. G. A. Champine, "Four Approaches to a Data Base Computer," *Datamation,* 24(12):101–106, December 1978.

63. H. O. Bray and H. A. Freeman, *Database Computers,* Lexington, Mass.: Lexington Books, 1979.

64. W. Kim, "Relational Database Systems," *ACM Computing Survey,* 11:185–211, 1979.

65. F. J. Maryanski, "Backend Database Systems," *ACM Computing Survey,* 12:3–26, 1980.

66. S. Y. W. Su, *Database Computers: Principles, Architectures, and Techniques.* New York: McGraw-Hill, 1988.

67. D. K. Hsiao, "Data Base Computers," in *Advances in Computers.* New York: Academic Press, 1980, pp. 1–64.

68. S. W. Song, "A Survey and Taxonomy of Database Machines," *Database Engineering,* 1: 5–15, 1983.

69. G. Z. Qadah, "Database Machines: A Survey," *American Federation of Information Processing Societies,* 54:211–223, 1985.

70. E. Ozkarahan, *Database Machines and Database Management.* Englewood Cliffs, N.J.: Prentice-Hall, 1986.

71. K. Oflazer, "A Reconfigurable VLSI Architecture for a Database Processor," *American Federation of Information Processing Societies,* 52:271–281, 1983.

72. S. W. Song, "A Highly Concurrent Tree Machine for Database Applications," *Proceedings of the International Conference on Parallel Processing.* Los Alamitos, Calif.: IEEE Computer Society, 1980. Pp. 259–268.

73. P. L. Lehman, "A Systolic (VLSI) Array for Processing Simple Relational Queries," in H. T. Kung, B. Sprouli, and G. Steele (eds.), *VLSI Systems and Computations.* Rockville, Md.: Computer Science Press, 1981, pp. 285–295.

74. A. R. Hurson, "VLSI Time/Space Complexities of an Associative Join Module," *Proceedings of the International Conference on Parallel Processing.* Silver Spring, Md.: IEEE Computer Society Press, 1986, pp. 379–386.

75. H. T. Kung, "The Structure of Parallel Algorithms," *Advances in Computers,* 19:65–112, 1980.

76. H. T. Kung, "Why Systolic Architectures?" *Computer,* 15(1):37–46, 1982.

77. M. J. Foster and H. T. Kung, "The Design of Special Purpose VLSI Chips," *Computer,* 13(1): 26–40, 1980.

78. A. R. Hurson and B. Shirazi, "A Systolic Multiplier Unit and Its VLSI Design," *Proceedings of the 12th Annual International Symposium on Computer Architecture.* Silver Spring, Md.: IEEE Computer Society Press, 1985, pp. 302–309.

79. T. Feng, *Parallel Processing Characteristics and Implementation of Data Manipulating Functions,* Tech. Rep. TR-73-189, Rome Air Development Center, U.S. Air Force, Rome, N.Y., July 1973.

80. D. J. Kuck, "A Survey of Parallel Machine Organization and Programming," *ACM Computing Survey,* 9(1):29–59, March 1977.

81. R. O. Berg, G. H. Schmitz, and S. J. Nuspl, "PEPE—An Overview of Architecture, Operations, and Implementation," *Proceedings of the National Electronics Conference,* Chicago, Ill., 1972. Oak Brook, Ill.: National Electronic Conference, 1972. Pp. 312–317.

82. D. J. Kuck, "ILLIAC IV Software and Application Programming," *IEEE Transactions on Computers,* C-17(8):758–770, August 1968.

83. E. W. Davis, "STARAN/RADCAP System Software," *Proceedings of the 1973 Sagamore Computer Conference on Parallel Processing,* Syracuse University, 1973, pp. 153–159.

84. *Computer,* special issue on parallel programming languages, 19(8), August 1986.

CHAPTER 17

PARALLEL SUPERCOMPUTERS

Geoffrey C. Fox

Northeast Parallel Architecture Centers
Syracuse University, New York

Supercomputers with teraflop and greater performance will be available in the next 5 years. We survey some of the research of the last 10 years, which has shown that these machines require no technical breakthroughs and can be expected to have wide applicability.

17.1 INTRODUCTION AND GOALS

The federal high-performance computing and communication initiative is centered on the importance of parallel computing as the necessary and sufficient methodology to produce machines of staggering performance. We will discuss some of the application, hardware, and software issues that suggest that this project will succeed and produce a parallel supercomputer of very high performance on a wide variety of applications. The main limiting problem will be the parallel software environment, and the development of this will pace the project. Further, until we understand better the appropriate software support for parallel machines, we cannot speculate on the final hardware architecture.

In this chapter the focus is on the teraflop machine—one capable of sustaining a performance of 10^{12} floating-point operations per second. Several companies have announced their intention to produce such machines in the next 5 years, and these machines would be about a factor of 100 more powerful than the most powerful computers currently deployed. This computer would demonstrate clearly the capability of a parallel architecture to give the highest performance in a cost-effective fashion. If such a machine were available to the scientific community, it would not only lead to major computational breakthroughs but also provide an impetus to system software and application development that could have a crucial effect on the parallel processing field. In this chapter, the emphasis is on scientific computation with which we have the greatest experience, although such large parallel machines have much wider applicability. The need for such powerful computers is not addressed here, as this has been documented in many places, including the brochure and plans defining the federal high-performance initiative and the list of grand challenge applications [62, 63].

This work was based on a collaboration with Sandy Frey at IBM, whom I thank for many conversations.

A wealth of research into parallel processing has led to great successes. Machines of several architectures have shown good performance in a wide variety of fields. However, computers of conventional (sequential or von Neumann) architectures still dominate the commercial market. A limited amount of parallelism (2 to 16 processors), possibly with vector units attached, is used sometimes for the most demanding applications. But highly parallel machines with over 100 processors are largely confined to university and industry research organizations.

There are several reasons for this, which can be identified at different levels. The bottom line is that current parallel machines with their current software do not offer either a peak performance or cost-effectiveness advantage that is sufficient to compete with the best sequential machines. At a deeper level is the belief that software is the fundamental stumbling block for the development of parallel computers as a significant component of mainline computing. Most parallel computers, especially those with very many nodes, require novel software, and it is not easy to modify existing code—the notorious "dusty deck" problem.

The "software crisis" is nontrivial to solve; it can be naturally addressed only when powerful parallel machines are freely available to application programmers. These machines need to be powerful enough for major production computations. It is not sufficient to produce small software development systems. However, it has already been argued that parallel hardware will have a large market only when the software base is established. This chicken-and-egg problem is not insoluble, but it will certainly slow down the development of parallel processing. The current research has demonstrated that a broad range of problems can be expected to get high performance on parallel machines, but current implementations tend to be of model problems and not of fully functional commercial or even university applications.

Section 17.2 reviews a basic architecture classification and sets the approach on the context of existing parallel computing research. In Secs. 17.3, 17.4, and 17.5, respectively, are detailed application, software, and hardware issues for the particular *multiple-instruction multiple-data* (MIMD) coarse-grain architectures considered here. Section 17.6 presents details of a possible teraflop computer, and Sec. 17.7 summarizes the conclusions to be drawn.

17.2 ARCHITECTURE ISSUES IN CONCURRENT SUPERCOMPUTING

Current supercomputing is dominated by the vector supercomputing. As illustrated in Fig. 17.1, the performance of sequential machines of this type is only increasing slowly; indeed, such systems are only increasing their performance by parallelism, using up to 16 processors and/or several "pipes" (pipelined vector floating-point units). However, the rapid evolution of VLSI technology suggests that the most cost-effective supercomputer in the future will be very many microprocessors linked together rather than the smaller number of very fast central processing units (CPUs) that one sees today. There are, in fact, many ways to reach teraflop performance in a supercomputer:

About 1000 very fast CPUs each capable of over a gigaflop

About 16K tightly coupled nodes, each capable of around 100 megaflops (the natural implementation if the basic unit is a *reduced instruction set computer* (RISC) microprocessor)

A high-speed network of workstations

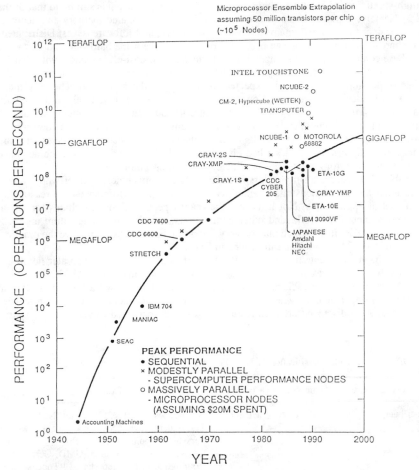

FIGURE 17.1 Supercomputer performance.

A *single-instruction multiple-data* (SIMD) (synchronous) architecture of very many 1-bit (CM-1, 2, DAP) or $\geqq$ 4-bit processors (Maspar)

A tightly or loosely coupled network of components with disparate architectures, e.g., a vector supercomputer sharing memory with an MIMD or SIMD parallel unit

Here the discussion is general, although MIMD machines are specifically discussed. Parallel machines of a somewhat conservative nature are considered. These are the coarse-grain distributed- or shared-memory machines, such as the hypercube developed at the California Institute of Technology, CEDAR at Illinois, the many systems built around the Inmos Transputer, the Butterfly by BBN, and the RP3 by IBM Yorktown. The only real distinction made here between the distributed- and shared-memory machines is that the distributed machines have access to each other's memory only through message passing, whereas the shared-memory machines have common access to memory directly through a high-speed queued communication network. The approach taken is similar to that of the RP3. Namely, it makes sense to consider distributed- and shared-memory architectures together since they share so many application, hardware, and software issues. Distributed- and shared-memory systems can make use of much of the same hardware and software, but these components are optimized for performance and cost-effectiveness with distributed memory and optimized for programmability with shared memory. In either case, the range of possible applications is expected to be very similar and broad. The very interesting SIMD designs such as the Connection Machine are considered only in the general discussions. The latter may be important in current and future supercomputers, but it is not convenient to discuss the detailed issues for them at the same time as the coarse-grain machines. The fine grain size and synchronous nodes introduce new issues that are considered only briefly. As described elsewhere [80], SIMD and MIMD machines have many similarities for applications dominated by floating-point arithmetic.

Table 17.1 records a simple classification of parallel machines, each of whose architecture has already demonstrated the ability to obtain high performance on a reasonably broad set of applications. Not listed are the many special-purpose machines for signal processing, neural network, and other applications, nor the promising future architectures, such as data flow, which may be very important but have yet to receive the practical testing of the architectures and machines in Table 17.1.

This chapter concentrates on the MIMD architectures, which offer greater flexibility but possibly lower peak performance than the SIMD machines. Here MIMD is used to denote machines where each node can perform independent tasks asynchronously and SIMD, lockstep machines where on each clock cycle each node operates identical instructions. Also discussed are architectures that can be extended to very large systems.

TABLE 17.1   Simple Classification of High-Performance Concurrent Computers

Memory structure	Grain size	Control	Examples
Distributed	Coarse	MIMD	Hypercubes (Ametek, FPS, Intel, NCUBE) Transputer arrays (CSA, Inmos, Levco, Meiko Parsytec, Topologix, Transtech) Crossed busses: Suprenum (GMD, Germany) Routing mesh: Intel i860-based "Touchstone," Intel iWARP, Symult Large high-speed network of workstations
Distributed	Coarse	SIMD	IBM GF11 Columbia QCD machine APE (Rome)
Distributed	Small	SIMD	AMT DAP 510 Connection Machine CM-1, CM-2 Goodyear MPP, ICL DAP, Maspar
Shared—many processors	Coarse	MIMD	BBN Butterfly, CEDAR IBM RP3, NYU Ultracomputer
Shared—modest number of processors	Coarse	MIMD	Alliant, Cray X-MP, Cray Y-MP, Cray 2, Convex, ELXSI, Encore, ETA-10, Flex, IBM 3090VF, SSI, Sequent, Silicon Graphics

This requires a complex network to connect nodes to memory in the shared-memory case or nodes to other nodes in the distributed-memory case. Currently, such machines have a number of nodes, in the range of 64 to 1024, and we base our analysis on extrapolating experience with machines in this size range. Much larger systems can be expected in the future, and later we speculate on a relatively near-term possibility of a 16K to 64K node teraflop machine.

In Fig. 17.2 are four architectures that are discussed in Sec. 17.5. These are obtained by dividing the shared- and distributed-memory classes into two subclasses each, based on the nature of the memory design. Homogeneous, hierarchical multicomputers, homogeneous shared-memory, and hierarchical shared-memory machines are considered. Here, the term *multicomputer* denotes any distributed-memory machine communicating by message passing with a reasonably rich topology. The term *homogeneous* describes any design where, to the user and probably also the compiler, the memory is "flat" (uniform) and is not structured into a hierarchy of decreasing access time and smaller size. We have recently presented a unified treatment of memory hierarchy and distributed systems [74]. As will be shown in Secs. 17.3 and 17.4 and Table 17.4, these four subclasses trade off in different ways—programmability, peak performance, average performance, and ability—to use existing codes.

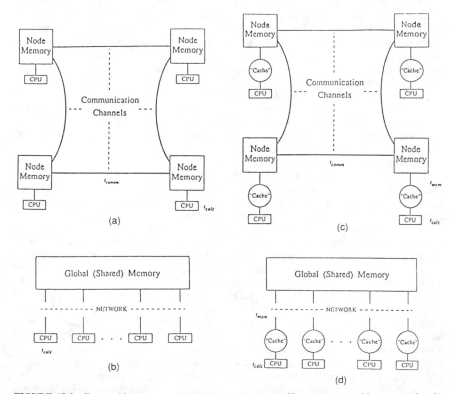

FIGURE 17.2 Four architectures considered in this chapter. *(a)* Homogeneous multicomputer ($d = 2$). *(b)* Shared-memory computer with homogeneous memory. *(c)* Hierarchical memory multicomputer ($d = 2$). *(d)* Shared-memory computer with hierarchical memory. "Cache" may be a true cache or user-controlled memory.

It is not a major purpose of this chapter to choose between different architectures or even to advocate that, as suggested above, one develop hardware building blocks that are usable in several architectures. Rather, there is a broad class of "correct" or "acceptable" architectures. It is more important at this time to produce powerful, cost-effective machines and to develop the application and system software base rather than to choose the "optimal" architectures.

17.3 APPLICATION ISSUES

Our current experience with highly parallel medium-grain computers of shared or distributed memory can be conservatively summarized as follows:

Currently all interesting, large, loosely synchronous computations have run well, and we can expect them to perform well on future machines with many more nodes.

There are three important technical terms in the above—*large, interesting,* and *loosely synchronous*—which are defined below.

The set of all problems that have been and should be expected to be "solved" or "simulated" on any computer is a small subset (surely of measure zero) of all conceivable problems. Typical computations simulate structures coming from nature or humans. Many of these have an intrinsic parallelism or modularity which gives good performance when mapped onto a concurrent computer. So with the restriction of *interesting* or more reasonably *currently interesting,* we are restricting ourselves to those problems currently run on large-scale computers. This expresses one crucial fact: One cannot make statements about the "general problem" but must input "reality"; however, this makes it clear that we cannot exclude the possibility that future important applications may run poorly on general or particular machines of the type discussed. However, we have intuitive faith that there are good general reasons (nature's parallelism, humans' modularity) not to expect drastic changes in the structure of interesting problems.

The term *large* will be made quantitative in Sec. 17.5, but the basic idea is described here. For given hardware parameters, the performance (expressed as the ratio ϵ, the *efficiency,* of speedup to the number of nodes) depends on the *grain size,* i.e., the average number n of fundamental entities stored in each node of the concurrent machine. The value n could be the number of grid points in a finite difference solution to a seismic simulation or the number of galaxies in a study of the evolution of the universe. In every case, the total problem has Nn entities, where the parallel computer has a total of N processing nodes. For given hardware (given node features and internode communication parameters), there is a problem-dependent minimum grain size n_{min} such that one will get good performance as long as the problem has at least Nn_{min} fundamental entities. For the initial California Institute of Technology Cosmic Cube and Mark II hypercubes, two- and three-dimensional finite element problems need $n_{min} = 100$ and 1000 nodal points, respectively. Thus, the requirement of *large* problem size translates to a minimum problem size for each set of *local* hardware and problem parameters. One achieves a linear (in N) performance speedup as long as the problem size also increases linearly with the number of nodes. This constraint is not disturbing. Supercomputers should be used to supercompute while small problems are best suited to small computers.

The third term, *loosely synchronous,* is the least well understood and is further a sufficient and not a necessary condition to be able to use efficiently a large number N of nodes. Operationally, this specialization ensures that there is no significant overhead in synchronizing the different nodes of the concurrent computer [86]. As discussed above, we have typically decomposed our problem with a certain number n of entities in each node of the processor. The value n would be the number of galaxies in a subdomain of the universe or the number of matrix elements in a submatrix for a distributed equation-solving application. Each node performs the part of the overall calculation associated with ''its'' entities. This will not be purely local but will involve communication with other nodes or access to a shared memory. This external access is not the point here because the constraint on problem size, quantified in Sec. 17.5, ensures that its overhead is small. Rather, in *loosely synchronous* problems, there is some natural parameter or label of the computation which provides a local macroscopic synchronization. This label is time in any physical ''time-driven'' synchronization. It is, e.g., the row number currently being eliminated in a matrix *LU* decomposition. The condition could also be called *temporal regularity*, since it corresponds to time synchronization in physical simulations. However, the same term is used for other problems where it is a more abstract iteration count that synchronizes. For these problems, the temporal variable is discretized, and problems are divided into ''compute'' cycles and ''communication'' cycles by iterating on this label. Temporal regularity ensures that there is little overhead in synchronizing the nodes, and one can naturally scale the implementations to a very large number of nodes N.

The loose synchronization implies that the nodes synchronize every now and then and are not running lockstep. The term *synchronous* was introduced [80] to describe the subset of loosely synchronous problems that exhibit microscopic synchronization, i.e., can run in lockstep. It was shown how synchronous applications are suitable for SIMD architectures and how the full MIMD capabilities of multicomputers or shared-memory machines are exploited by those truly loosely synchronous problems which are not synchronous. We call the latter *properly loosely synchronous,* and we can illustrate this type of problem with a circuit simulation with many different types of fundamental components and irregular interconnects. The start of each time cycle provides macroscopic synchronization, but microscopically each node will be simulating distinct components and so is not in lockstep.

An obvious class of problems not obeying the temporal regularity constraint is discrete event simulations, where the representation of reality as events irregularly occurring in space and time creates issues in available and realizable concurrency which are still unresolved [123, 197, 199]. We term such applications *asynchronous* [80]. However, simulations of turbulent flow with irregular and dynamic refinement are properly loosely synchronous as we define it. These are spatially irregular but locally regular in a time variable which can still provide the necessary synchronization. The majority of large-scale scientific problems fall into the loosely synchronous class.

There is one other important class of problems that have performed well on concurrent machines. These are covered by this assertion:

Large, asynchronous, irregular but spatially disconnected problems perform well on large concurrent machines.

We have used, in the above statement and in this section, a physical language that we should define better. Problems are typically associated with an underlying data domain containing the fundamental entities mentioned above. We refer to this data domain (whether it contains particles, grid points, matrix elements, or chess moves) as the underlying space and label the properties of this domain *spatial*. The computation involves calculations on the elements of the space, and as described earlier, we refer to the label of this calculation as *temporal*. For a physical simulation, this definition of space and time reduces to the natural one. In general, our terminology maps the computation of a general system into a space-time system. Returning to the above assertion, one example is the use of distributed-memory computers as ''Fortran farms.'' A typical example comes from high-energy physics, when one needs the independent analysis of very many (up to 10^7) accelerator-induced particle interactions. These separate interactions are analyzed as separate job streams on each node [97]. Essentially no node-to-node communication is needed, and very high efficiency is obtained even though the job streams are temporally irregular due to the wide variation in processing time of individual interactions. A more sophisticated example of the above assertion is in artificial intelligence applications such as branch and bound search algorithms [57, 167] and other tree topology problems typified by computer chess [60, 61]. Now the temporal variable labels the depth of the tree and the spatial dimension individual branches. We can contrast the above examples which currently run on concurrent processors with more complex artificial intelligence problems and the discrete event simulations where the concurrent issues are unclear. These have similar temporal irregularities, but their concurrent implementation is difficult due to significant and unpredictable spatial couplings between the entities.

Table 17.2 lists some general references on applications for different parallel machines.

In a basic paper [80], we analyzed 84 separate applications, each on one or more of these machines. The wealth of current practical parallel applications is illustrated by Table 17.3a to 17.3l. Note the predominance of loosely synchronous algorithms. Additional information will be found in [11, 81, 86]. This analysis has not been updated since the end of 1988, but the qualitative picture is believed to be correct for current applications.

Tables 17.3a to 17.3i are adapted and updated [11, 80]. The originals give more detail and also further parallel applications. Some excellent applications [11] are omitted because we could not easily explain them in a simple sentence, as required in the table. The tables below are biased to hypercube work, but an unbiased survey of all parallel machines available in 1988—the hypercube, BBN Butterfly, transputer arrays, Goodyear MPP, Thinking Machines, CM-1, CM-2, and ICL DAP—can be found elsewhere [80].

TABLE 17.2 Successful Applications of Large ($N \geq 64$) Parallel Machines and References on Their Uses

---

Distributed-memory MIMD (multicomputer)
   Hypercubes (California Institute of Technology inhouse, FPS, Intel, NCUBE, Symult) [72, 73, 77, 80, 81, 86, 87, 105, 106, 110, 111, 146, 184].
   Suprenum [180].
   Transputer arrays (Meiko, Inmos, Southampton) [28, 112, 113, 159, 160, 163, 186–188].
   Fortran farms (Stanford linear accelerator, Fermilab) for analysis of high-energy physics data [92, 93, 97, 132].

SIMD coarse-grain machines
   GF11 (IBM Yorktown) [24].
   Columbia QCD [40].
   APE (Rome) [140].

MIMD shared memory
   BBN Butterfly [22, 23, 38, 129].
   CEDAR [131].
   RP3 [32, 33, 49].

SIMD small-grain distributed memory
   ICL DAP [28, 29, 185, 186].
   Connection Machine CM-1, CM-2 [26, 66, 114, 116, 122, 147, 172, 189].
   Goodyear MPP [56, 67, 122, 147].
   AMT DAP, Maspar. See AMT, Maspar Corporation literature.

TABLE 17.3a Parallel Applications in Biology and Machine Vision

Label	Field	Algorithm	Synchronism[a]	Fox [86]	Angus [11]	Application[c] presented at hypercube conference [81]	Further reading[d]
Bi1	Simulation of biological neural networks	Circuit simulation	LS	Sec. 22-4	Sec. 9-7	X	[91]
Bi2	Back-propagation neural networks	Circuit simulation (complete interconnect)	S	Chap. 9 (alg. only[b])	Sec. 8-6	X	[5] [119]
Bi3	(Early) Vision	Local iteration Higher vision is unknown complex algorithm	S	Chaps. 5, 7 (alg. only[b])	Sec. 9-7	X	[21] [91] [96] [125] [191]
Bi4	Ecological simulation (WATOR)	Irregular time simulation	PLS	Chap. 17	Sec. 8-11	—	—
Bi5	Medical imaging	Detection of surfaces	A	—	—	—	[150]
Bi6	Map of human genome	Database and/or neural network (see A7)	S	—	—	—	[12] [20]

[a]S = synchronous (lockstep); PLS = loosely synchronous but not synchronous; LS = typically synchronous if regular geometry but irregularities in system can make properly loosely synchronous; A = asynchronous; A(E-P) = asynchronous but "embarrassingly parallel"—different components are executed independently as spatially disconnected.

[b]Similar algorithms are discussed in quoted section.

[c]This application was covered in the Third Hypercube Conference, held in Pasadena, Calif., January 19–20, 1988 [81].

[d]Suggestions for follow-up references are found in Table 17.2.

17.9

TABLE 17.3b Parallel Applications in Chemistry and Chemical Engineering[a]

Label	Field	Algorithm	Synchronism[b]	Fox [86]	Angus [11]	Application[d] presented at hypercube conference [81]	Further reading[e]
Ch1	Three- and four-body chemical reactions	Multichannel Schrödinger equation (matrix inversion and finite elements)	S	Matrix: Sec. 21-5 FEM: Chap. 8 Chap. 12	Matrix: Similar to Sec. 8-14 FEM: Sec. 8-5, Sec. 9-4	X	[117, 118, 202]
Ch2	Protein mechanics	Long-range Monte Carlo	S	Chap. 12	—	X	[51]
Ch3	High T_c superconductivity	Monte Carlo	S	Chap. 12	Similar to Sec. 9-2	—	[54, 95] [95]
Ch4	Chemical engineering simulations (processes and distribution)	Circuit simulation	PLS	Chap. 22 (alg. only[c])	—	X	[173–175] [173, 174]

[a]See also topics Ph3 and Ph4.
[b]S = synchronous (lockstep); PLS = loosely synchronous but not synchronous; LS = typically synchronous if regular geometry but irregularities in system can make properly loosely synchronous; A = asynchronous; A (E-P) = asynchronous but "embarrassingly parallel"—different components are executed independently as spatially disconnected.
[c]Similar algorithms are discussed in quoted section.
[d]This application was covered in the Third Hypercube Conference, held in Pasadena, Calif., January 19–20, 1988 [81].
[e]Suggestions for follow-up references are found in Table 17.2.

17.10

TABLE 17.3c Parallel Applications in Engineering

Label	Field	Algorithm	Synchronism[a]	Fox [86]	Angus [11]	Application[c] presented at hypercube conference [81]	Further reading[d]
E1	Computational fluid dynamics (CFD) Navier-Stokes	Local partial differential equation (PDE)	LS	Chap. 8 (alg. only[b])	Secs. 8-4, 8-5	X	[3, 34, 194]
E2	CFD—vortex methods	Long-range force between vortices; Clustering method possible for $O(N \log N)$	LS; LS	Chap. 9	Secs. 8-6, 9-5	X	[14, 164, 193]
E3	CFD—cellular automata	Local movement of simple (1-bit) automata	S	—	—	—	[27, 104, 201]
E4	Flux-corrected transport	Finite difference evolution	S	Chap. 7 (alg. only[b])	Sec. 8-4	X	
E5	Plasma physics	Particle in cell with PDE and particle evolution	LS	—	Sec. 9-6	X	[135, 136]
E6	Electromagnetic fields (antennas)	Finite difference evolution	LS	Chap. 7 (alg. only[b])	Sec. 8-4	X	[35]
E7	Electric power distribution	Circuit simulation	PLS	Chap. 22 (alg. only[b])	—	—	[63] —
E8	Structural analysis	Finite element approach to PDE	LS	Chap. 8	Sec. 8-5	X	[106]
E9	Robotics	See vision (Bi3), structures (E8), and control (M1)	PLS	—	—	X	[19, 127]
E10	Convolutional decoding	Similar to binary FFT for Viterbi algorithm	S	Chap. 11, Sec. 23-4 (alg. only[b])	—	—	[158]

[a] S = synchronous (lockstep); PLS = loosely synchronous but synchronous; LS = loosely synchronous = typically synchronous if regular geometry but irregularities in system can make properly loosely synchronous; A = asynchronous; A(E-P) = asynchronous but "embarrassingly parallel"—different components are executed independently as spatially disconnected.
[b] Similar algorithms are discussed in quoted section.
[c] This application was covered in the Third Hypercube Conference, held in Pasadena, Calif., January 19–20, 1988 [81].
[d] Suggestions for follow-up references are found in Table 17.2.

TABLE 17.3d Parallel Applications in Geology, Earth, and Space Sciences

Label	Field	Algorithm	Synchronism[a]	Fox [86]	Angus [11]	Application[c] presented at hypercube conference [81]	Further reading[d]
G1	Seismic modeling	Finite difference or ray tracing	S	Chap. 7	Secs. 8-3, 8-4	X	[18, 42, 43, 162, 176]
G2	Simulation of earth's mantle	Finite element approach to PDE	LS	Chap. 8	Sec. 8-5	X	[104]
G3	Reservoir simulation	Finite element approach to PDE	LS	Chap. 8 (alg. only[b])	Sec. 8-5	—	[144]
G4	Seismic data analysis	Finite difference approximation to velocity field	PLS	—	—	X	[2, 139]
G5	Meteorology climate modeling	Finite difference, spectral method	LS	Chap. 7 (alg. only[b])	Sec. 8-4	—	[130]
G6	Large-scale oceanography	Finite difference	LS	Chap. 7 (alg. only[b])	Sec. 8-4	—	[72, 77]
G7	Wave motion on offshore structures	Integral equation linking all nodal points of finite element grid	S	Chap. 9 (alg. only[b])	Sec. 8-6	—	[149]
G8	Image processing	Local and nonlocal (FFT) convolutions	S	Chaps. 3, 11 (FFT alg. only[b])	Sec. 8-8	X	[103]
G9	Synthetic aperture radar data analysis	FFT	S	Chap. 11	Sec. 8-8	X	[8]

[a]S = synchronous (lockstep); PLS = loosely synchronous but not synchronous; LS = typically synchronous if regular geometry but irregularities in system can make properly loosely synchronous; A = asynchronous; A(E-P) = asynchronous but "embarrassingly parallel" —different components are executed independently as spatially disconnected.
[b]Similar algorithms are discussed in quoted section.
[c]This application was covered in the Third Hypercube Conference, held in Pasadena, Calif., January 19–20, 1988 [88].
[d]Suggestions for follow-up references are found in Table 17.2.

TABLE 17.3e Parallel Applications in Physics

Label	Field	Algorithm	Synchronism[a]	Fox [86]	Angus [11]	Application[c] presented at hypercube conference [81]	Further reading[d]
Ph1	Lattice gauge theory	Monte Carlo on a regular 4D lattice	S	Chap. 13	Sec. 9-2	X	[31, 52, 53, 69, 186]
Ph2	Liquid/solid phase transitions	Monte Carlo in an irregular 2D or 3D system	PLS	Chap. 13	—	—	[126]
Ph3	Liquid molecular dynamics	Time evolution of an irregular system of particles	PLS	Chap. 16	Sec. 8-10	X	[68, 153, 154]
Ph4	Solid molecular dynamics	Time evolution of a regular lattice of particles	S	Chap. 16	Sec. 8-10	—	[155]
Ph5	Ising models	Monte Carlo on 1-bit variables in regular 2D or 3D lattice	S	Chap. 13 (alg. only[b])	—	X	[15, 16, 113]
Ph6	High-energy physics data analysis	Independent analysis of events on individual nodes of parallel computers	A(E-P)	—	—	X	[97, 113]
Ph7	Granular physics	Evolution of (sand) grains under wind, gravity, and contact with other grains	PLS	Chap. 16 (alg. only[b])	—	X	[107, 195, 196]

[a]S = synchronous (lockstep); PLS = loosely synchronous but not synchronous; LS = typically synchronous if regular geometry but irregularities in system can make properly loosely synchronous; A = asynchronous; A(E-P) = asynchronous but "embarrassingly parallel"—different components are executed independently as spatially disconnected.
[b]Similar algorithms are discussed in quoted section.
[c]This application was covered in the Third Hypercube Conference, held in Pasadena, Calif., January 19–20, 1988 [81].
[d]Suggestions for follow-up references are found in Table 17.2.

TABLE 17.3f Parallel Applications in Astronomy and Astrophysics

Label	Field	Algorithm	Synchronism[a]	Fox [86]	Angus [11]	Application[b] presented at hypercube conference [81]	Further reading[c]
A1	Stellar and stellar medium structure	Finite difference with possibly plasma effects	LS	Chap. 7	Sec. 8-4	—	—
A2	Evolution of the universe	Particle dynamics solved by FFT or $O(N \log N)$ clustering	LS	Chap. 11, Sec. 9-5	Sec. 8-8	X	[115, 164, 166, 193]
A3	Initial astronomical data analysis	Multiple binary FFT	S	Chap. 11	Sec. 8-8	X	[99, 100]
A4	Image deconvolution of astronomical data	Pattern recognition —perhaps neural networks	PLS	—	Sec. 9-7	—	—

[a]S = synchronous (lockstep); PLS = loosely synchronous but not synchronous; LS = typically synchronous if regular geometry but irregularities in system can make properly loosely synchronous; A = synchronous; A(E-P) = asynchronous but "embarrassingly parallel" —different components are executed independently as spatially disconnected.
[b]This application was covered in the Third Hypercube Conference, held in Pasadena, Calif., January 19—20, 1988 [81].
[c]Suggestions for follow-up references are found in Table 17.2.

TABLE 17.3g Parallel Applications in Computer Science

Label	Field	Algorithm	Synchronism[a]	Fox [86]	Angus [11]	Application[b] presented at hypercube conference [81]	Further reading[c]
CS1	Graphical rendering —ray tracing	Independent rays traverse distributed database	A(E-P)	—	—	X	[98, 124]
CS2	Computer circuit simulation	Circuit simulation	LS	Sec. 22-3	—	X	[142, 143, 151]
CS3	Optimizing circuit layout	Simulated annealing (parallel Monte Carlo as in A8)	LS	Chap. 13	—	—	[37, 66]
CS4	Computer chess	Search of $\alpha - \beta$ pruned tree	A	—	—	X	[60, 61]
CS5	Artificial intelligence	Communicating agents, expert systems	A	—	—	X	[94, 133]
CS6	Database and transition analysis	Concurrent access to disks	A	—	—	X	[157, 190]

[a] S = synchronous (lockstep); PLS = loosely synchronous but not synchronous; LS = loosely synchronous; A = synchronous; A(E-P) = asynchronous but "embarrassingly parallel"; —different components are executed independently as spatially disconnected. LS = typically synchronous if regular geometry but irregularities in system can make properly loosely synchronous.

[b] This application was covered in the Third Hypercube Conference, held in Pasadena, Calif., January 19–20, 1988 [81].

[c] Suggestions for follow-up references are found in Table 17.2.

TABLE 17.3h Parallel Applications in Military and Commercial Areas

Label	Field	Algorithm	Synchronism[a]	Fox [86]	Angus [11]	Application[c] presented at hypercube conference [81]	Further reading[d]
M1	Situation (battle) management	Expert system	A	—	—	X	[145, 192]
M2	Battle simulations	Event-driven simulation	A	—	—	X	[108, 123, 198, 199]
M3	Multitarget Kalman filter	Almost independent tracking of targets in different nodes	PLS	Sec. 22-2	Sec. 9-3	X	[101, 102]
M4	Assignment (weapons to targets)	Neural networks or other optimization algorithms	LS	Chap. 13 (alg. only[b])	—	X	[36]
M5	Air traffic simulation	Event-driven simulation	A	—	—	X	[17, 55]

[a] S = synchronous (lockstep); PLS = loosely synchronous but not synchronous; LS = typically synchronous if regular geometry but irregularities in system can make properly loosely synchronous; A = asynchronous; A(E-P) = asynchronous but "embarrassingly parallel"—different components are executed independently as spatially disconnected.
[b] Similar algorithms are discussed in quoted section.
[c] This application was covered in the Third Hypercube Conference, held in Pasadena, Calif., January 19–20, 1988 [81].
[d] Suggestions for follow-up references are found in Table 17.2.

17.16

Label	Field	Synchronism[a]	Fox [86]	Angus [11]	Application[b] presented at hypercube conference [81]	Further reading[c]
A1a	Full matrix algorithms —multiplication	S	Chap. 10	Sec. 8-7	—	[84]
A1b	Full matrix algorithms —LU decomposition	S	Chap. 20	Sec. 8-14	X	[4, 169]
A1c	Full matrix algorithms —inversion	S	Sec. 21-5	—	X	[118]
A1d	Full matrix algorithms —eigenvalue/functions	S	Sec. 21-5	—	X	[89]
A2	Banded matrix algorithms (band size $\geq \sqrt{\text{number of nodes } N}$)	S	Chap. 20	Sec. 8-14	X	[4]
A3	Tridiagonal matrices—QR	S	Sec. 21-5	—	X	[121, 148]
A4a	Sparse matrices —multigrid	LS	Sec. 8-7	—	X	[88, 181, 182]
A4b	Sparse matrices —conjugate gradient	LS	Chap. 8	Sec. 8-5	X	[13, 141]
A4c	Sparse matrices —domain decomposition	LS	—	—	—	[44]
A5	Linear programming	S	—	—	X	[177, 178]
A6	Optimization —branch and bound	A	—	—	X	[1, 57, 138, 152, 168]
A7	Optimization —neural networks	S	—	Sec. 9-7	X	[83, 179]
A8	Optimization —simulated annealing	LS	Chap. 13	—	X	[30, 58, 70]
A9	Sorting	A, S, or LS	Chap. 18	Sec. 8-12	X	[134, 170]
A10	Fast Fourier transform —binary	S	Chap. 11	Sec. 8-8	X	[41, 128, 137]
A11	Fast Fourier transform —nonbinary	PLS	Sec. 22-3	—	X	[6, 7, 9]

[a] S = synchronous (lockstep); PLS = loosely synchronous but not synchronous; LS = typically synchronous if regular geometry but irregularities in system can make properly loosely synchronous; A = synchronous; A(E-P) = asynchronous but "embarrassingly parallel" —different components are executed independently as spatially disconnected.

[b] This application was covered in the Third Hypercube Conference, held in Pasadena, Calif., January 19–20, 1988 [81].

[c] Suggestions for follow-up references are found in Table 17.2.

17.17

17.4 SOFTWARE ISSUES

17.4.1 Overview

We do not want to describe in detail the software issues for coarse-grain MIMD machines, just the broad concepts that affect the architectural choices [75]. The differences between the four architectural subclasses introduced in Sec. 17.2 and Fig. 17.2 are seen mainly in the different tradeoffs among construction, software, and performance issues. This tradeoff includes not only peak performance but the "convenient" performance which can be obtained with modest programming effort. We have presented [74] a unified decomposition and performance analysis for loosely synchronous problems, and this has been extended [75, 78]. This suggests all four architectures in Fig. 17.2 will perform well in this problem class, but there are still the tradeoffs listed below, such as the ease in realizing that possible performance does depend on the architecture.

In the following, we consider first applications and then systems software for MIMD machines.

17.4.2 Applications Software Environment

Perhaps the most important, and indeed controversial, issue is the programming methodology with which the user can exploit the *parallelism* of the problem and the machine. We have a spectrum of possibilities [76], illustrated in Fig. 17.3.

User Prepares Whole Program.   Here we distinguish two possible choices, which differ according to the language used.

Use of Traditional Languages.   Here the user prepares sequential code in Fortran, C, or a similar language. Indeed, sometimes an old dusty deck is used, and the compiler decomposes the code over the nodes of the parallel machine. There are variants of this approach where the user helps the compiler by identifying areas in which parallelization will be successful and by modifying his or her code to avoid unnecessary sequential bottlenecks. This approach typically finds the natural parallelism available by concurrent execution of code for different values of a DO loop index. This approach is successful in some cases and has the obvious advantage of allowing one to tap the huge reservoir of existing codes. The approach is currently limited to shared-memory machines because, at present, automated parallelizing compilers decompose only the processing and not the data. Kennedy and Fox have proposed additions to Fortran which help the compiler to identify arrays to be decomposed and how they are to be distributed, but we have no practical experience with this and related approaches. It is also clear that some applications and some languages are harder to decompose, because the expression of a problem in a particular programming language may well disguise natural parallelism. For instance, the extensive use of pointers in C renders automatic decomposition difficult. Further, these approaches may not find it easy to exploit a memory hierarchy since this typically implies that parts of the data should be stored locally and not globally accessible. This issue would also be manifested in an environment requiring cache coherency. However, we emphasize that these automated parallel compiler techniques exploit the "same" intrinsic parallelism of the more direct but user-intensive methods to be discussed later.

Use of Data Parallel Languages.   Several of the SIMD machines have successfully used array-extended Fortran, typified by CM Fortran or Fortran 90, with straightforward parallelism generated by the compiler. We have proposed that Fortran 90 be viewed as a language for synchronous problems (in classification of Sec. 17.3) and not as a language for synchronous (SIMD) machines [71, 75, 78, 130]. From this point of view, Fortran 90

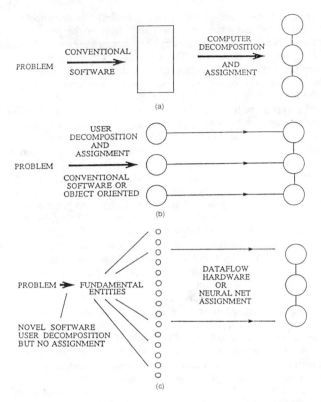

FIGURE 17.3 Three programming styles. *(a)* Whole program. *(b)* Large-grain objects. *(c)* Small-grain objects.

can be used for a limited problem set—the synchronous applications—but mapped to any of the architectures considered in Sec. 17.2. It is not clear yet what fraction of applications can be expressed in such data parallel languages. A survey [78, 80] suggests that 50 percent of applications can be expressed in Fortran 90 with modest extensions [75, 85]. It is possible that this fraction can be extended with appropriate extensions to Fortran 90 [25].

User Prepares Large-Grain Objects. We now consider the methods in which the parallelism is found before the software is generated and expressed by the relationship between several large objects or threads of execution. By *large,* we mean that typically the number of objects is between 1 and $10N$, where N is the number of nodes in the computer. One can use this programming methodology for both shared- and distributed-memory machines. The architecture will determine if, say, monitors or message passing is the natural synchronization and communication mechanism between the objects. In the following, we concentrate on the distributed-memory issues with which we are most familiar.

As discussed in Sec. 17.3, parallelism in the processing is typically associated with decomposition of a data domain (space) and simultaneous processing of the different grains formed in the decomposition. The automatic parallelizing Fortran 77 compiler techniques discussed above are presently unable to find this decomposition of the data, even though it is implied by the DO loop parallelism of the processing that they can detect. For this reason, distributed-memory architectures are currently usable only with some form of domain decomposition. The latter has not been found very hard, at least in reasonably regular problems, but it does require substantial amounts of new software for most applications. In terms of Fig. 17.3, the large-grain objects simulate the subdomains formed by the decomposition. At the California Institute of Technology, essentially all software for the hypercube has been written from scratch, although it is worth noting that this new software can usually be run on either parallel or sequential machines. In a typical problem, the concurrent code can be thought of as the software for a subdomain rather than the full domain needed for a sequential machine. The full domain and subdomain code differ in boundary value and geometry modules but are clearly quite similar.

We can remark that we have found powerful ways to aid the user in choosing subdomains, i.e., decomposing the algorithm—this is an optimization problem that is relatively easy to automate [79, 83]—but we currently have no good tools to help the user generate the software corresponding to this decomposition. Typically, the approach is to supplement a traditional high-level language, such as C or Fortran, with subroutine calls to communicate either between nodes or within a shared memory. One can build communication and synchronization aspects of parallelism into a new language, such as OCCAM or Ada, although these suffer from supporting particular models of interprocess communication and synchronization. More promising is the development of a modern object-oriented approach using perhaps an evolution of SMALLTALK or C++ [46, 89]. This style of programming, whether naive decomposition into Fortran-coded subdomains or a concurrent SMALLTALK, has implications for the underlying computer architecture. One would like to insulate the user from the details of the underlying hardware and let the user decompose and program for a virtual machine that is mapped transparently onto the particular hardware. The virtual machine is an abstract general target machine implementing the message-passing programming methodology [86, 183]. One finds a similar constraint from our goal to build common systems for shared- and distributed-memory machines. Dynamic load balancing while a time-dependent application runs on the machine is possible but only if the virtual machine, described above, has at least an order of magnitude more nodes than the hardware. This allows movement of processes, or objects, or nodes of the virtual machine between nodes of the real hardware to balance the load. These considerations lead to systems software issues described in Sec. 17.4.3.

We note that even if high-level data parallel languages are used, they will "compile down" into large-grain objects communicating with messages. Thus, it is essential to have good support for this programming methodology.

Fine-Grain Objects.   The use of large-grain objects, as described above, dominates the current use of multicomputers. However, it is in many ways artificial and can require significant effort implementing the appropriate geometry and boundary-value codes to reflect the (arbitrary but necessary) object boundaries. It is attractive to consider a fine-grain programming style where the user implements the code to address the fundamental entities in the problem. This fits trends in VLSI [45]. This approach is taken by data flow, but we believe it should be possible to use similar ideas on general-purpose hardware but with the restriction that the user, and not expensive hardware, will control communication between fine-grain objects. At the California Institute of Technology, Otto and Felten have built such a system, CPC (Coherent Parallel C), for the commercial NCUBE hypercube [62]. Here, the *loosely synchronous* constraint allows efficient scheduling of the objects, and this language is a natural MIMD generalization of C* built for the SIMD Connection Machine [161]. Both loosely synchronous and more general applications may well be helped by the neural network load balancers discussed above. It is interesting to compare the whole program approach which needs decomposing compilers to the fine-grain style for which "gluing compilers" are more appropriate! This style is still in its infancy, but if successful, it will require the same low message-passing latency and fast interprocess switching needed by the conventional approaches.

17.4.3 Systems Software

The above considerations of the application environment suggest that the hardware and systems software should be designed for very fast interprocess switching and communication. The latter is needed both intranode and internode, and common hardware support would be natural. The transputer T414,800 chips, produced by Inmos and used as the node of some commercial distributed-memory computers, were designed with these issues in mind. It may also be that more radical programming methodologies such as data flow languages like LUCID, VAL, or ID not only will be attractive but also will be able to run efficiently on the coarse-grain MIMD architectures considered here. Support of such languages will certainly be helped by the fast process switching and communication discussed above. Data flow has analogs to the fine-grain limit (process, not necessarily the hardware) of the object-oriented approach.

The systems software area must respect the process switching and communication speed constraints as discussed above, and now we discuss other general features needed. We note that most present large parallel machines are incomplete in that they lack appropriate parallel input and output subsystems. These need to provide back-end disk storage, graphics, and the necessary user interface. Future large systems should be designed with careful attention to the hardware and software issues of such integrated machines that are themselves integrated in a networked user environment. This will be tentative as one currently does not have any accepted standard for how the interface to the parallel mass storage and graphics should look to the user. This largely reflects our lack of experience because current hardware has not encouraged applications with intensive use of input or output subsystems. It seems possible that some overall operating system, like the MACH Unix or POSIX, will be adopted for large shared-memory machines, but the choice of operating system for a distributed-memory computer is even less clear. Should Unix run on the parallel computer itself or only on the subsystem ("host") seen by the user? Much more research is needed in this area, where we expect that the dominant issue will be the number of nodes, and not the memory architecture. If we run a synchronous or loosely synchronous problem on a multicomputer, then the processes assigned to a single job cannot be treated with the freedom normally allowed in Unix. Thus, if a job assigned to part of a data parallel domain is swapped out on one node, then all other nodes will soon grind to a halt, waiting for messages sent to the swapped node. It seems quite likely that a common approach for the overall systems software for distributed and shared memories will emerge from this research.

We also note that debugging has been, and will be, a key problem, and future hardware should have excellent support for this. This is particularly important for the more challenging irregular problems. At the California Institute of Technology, we found the debugging of asynchronous problems, such as parallel computer chess, extremely hard [59, 61]. Debugging was similarly found to be very hard during development of new operating systems for the hypercube [165]. We did find that the natural synchronization in synchronous or loosely synchronous problems made debugging much easier in these cases. We developed *ndb*, which was a natural generalization of sequential debuggers. This has been improved and is now marketed by ParaSoft [11].

We close this section by noting that one can use the same decomposition methodology to treat both hierarchical and distributed memories and one can establish ground rules to

TABLE 17.4 Coarse-Grain Concurrent Architectures

Architecture[†]	Construction	Programmability	Performance
(a) Homogeneous multicomputer	Straightforward simple node may not match (c), (d) in performance	Needs user decomposition but of simple type	Best architecture for getting peak performance at modest software cost
(b) Homogeneous shared memory	Network performance crucial. See also node comment in (a). Difficult if node powerful	Allows compiler decomposition. Easiest of four architectures	Limited by network
(c) Hierarchical multicomputer	Easiest way to get peak node performance and cost-effective machine	Decomposition methodology harder than (a) but exists	Optimal performance possible at more user effort than for (a)
(d) Hierarchical shared memory	Harder than (c) but allows easier programming	Can be programmed for peak performance as in (c) but allows compiler-generated concurrency	Can be as good as (c) but this requires comparable programming techniques. Lower but good performance with compiler-generated concurrency

[†]See Fig. 17.2.

obtain good performance from either memory construct. We show [74] that the decompositions needed for homogeneous memories are easier to find than those for hierarchical memories. However, the degradation in performance coming from not using a decomposition to exploit memory hierarchy, i.e., to make good use of a cache, is typically at worst a factor of 10. But one would pay a performance penalty which is a factor of N and hence potentially much larger if forced to run a nondecomposed (sequential) code on a single node of a distributed-memory machine with N nodes. We see that the architectural tradeoffs are very different for peak versus "reasonable" performance. A simplified summary of this has been given in Table 17.4.

17.5 HARDWARE AND CONCURRENT COMPUTER PERFORMANCE ISSUES

17.5.1 Introduction

We have introduced the basic computer architectures in Sec. 17.2 and Fig. 17.2. Their numerical performance is broadly controlled by the three parameters t_{comm}, t_{mem}, and t_{calc}. These can be used in a simplified model of the performance of coarse-grain MIMD machines [74, 86]. These three parameters are illustrated in Fig. 17.2 and defined as

$$t_{comm} = \text{typical time to send one word between two nodes of distributed-memory machine}$$

t_{mem} = typical time to read and write one word between two
levels of a memory hierarchy

t_{calc} = typical time to perform single floating-point
operation within single node

In most hardware, peak performance for communication or calculation is only obtained for block operations. One finds poor performance for small-size messages or calculations that do not involve vectors or blocks of data. We describe this by Hockney's startup lengths $l_{1/2comm}$, $l_{1/2mem}$, and $l_{1/2calc}$ [120]. In each case, one needs $l_{1/2}$ words to obtain 50 percent of the peak communication or calculation performance. Our discussion will not be accurate to factors of order $1/2$ to 2, and in particular one would typically get such a factor from the difference between 32- and 64-bit arithmetic. The value t_{calc} may depend on the word length by up to a factor of 2, and $l_{1/2comm,mem}$ is likely to be expressed naturally in bytes with, therefore, a factor-of-2 difference when converted to 32- or 64-bit words. We restrict our discussion to 64-bit arithmetic here, as we expect this to become more important on the large problems appropriate for the large supercomputers we contemplate. Further 32-bit addressing will definitely be inadequate for the large total memories on machines in the very near future. Thus, we may expect 64-bit words to be basic in future large parallel supercomputers. Larger-size words than this may be useful for fault tolerance considerations [200].

To illustrate Hockney's parameters, we assume that the only overhead in communication is a nonzero start-up time present for zero-length messages. Then the time to send a message of l words between two nodes adjacent in the hardware is

$$T_{comm}(l) - (l + l_{1/2comm}) \, t_{comm} \tag{17.1}$$

The communication time per word for a message of length $l_{1/2comm}$ is $T_{comm}(l_{1/2comm})/l_{1/2comm} = 1/2 t_{comm}$, or one-half the peak rate.

In terms of the above parameters, the fraction of time used in communication can be written as

$$f_C \sim \frac{\text{constant}}{n^{1/d}} \frac{t_{comm}}{t_{calc}} \tag{17.2}$$

for node-to-node communication and

$$f_H \sim \frac{\text{constant}}{n^{1/d}} \frac{t_{mem}}{t_{calc}} \tag{17.3}$$

for transfers between different levels of the memory hierarchy. Here n was introduced in Sec. 17.3 as the number of entities within each grain. In Eqs. (17.2) and (17.3), d is the *system dimension* of the problem. It can be defined quite generally and is equal to the *topological dimension* for geometric systems [86].

17.5.2 Node Properties

Consider the node of a hypercube (distributed memory) or a hierarchical shared-memory machine. In the latter case, each node will have its own memory either configured as a cache or a genuine local memory. The analysis [74] only applies directly to local memories but can be used for a cache where the write-through is under user control. Let us make some remarks about Eq. (17.3). It can be applied between any two levels of a memory with many levels of hierarchy. In each case, one uses the appropriate value of t_{mem}, and n is the number of entities that can be simultaneously resident in the lower level of the memory hierarchy. We illustrate the different concepts with four examples from the initial parallel MIMD machines.

1. The NCUBE-1 hypercube is homogeneous, and t_{mem} and f_H are not relevant. Each node has 0.5 Mbyte of memory. In this respect, the architectures of the Transputer arrays from MEIKO and other vendors are similar, and this general design is shown in Fig. 17.2a.

2. The Mark IIIfp hypercube built at the Jet Propulsion Laboratory (JPL), Pasadena, California, has t_{comm} controlling communication between 4-Mbyte main memories of hypercube nodes. Each node has a two-level hierarchy with a 64K cache between the main memory and a pipelined 10-megaflop floating-point unit. Both t_{comm} and t_{mem} are relevant. For f_C one should use the n value appropriate for the large 4-Mbyte memory; for f_H a smaller value of n corresponding to the 64K cache size is used. This architecture is shown in Fig. 17.2c.

3. For the BBN Butterfly, the memory hierarchy is not local to the node but represents transfers between a 1-Mbyte local memory and a large shared memory, which is the sum of all the local memories. Apart from this feature, we have the situation of Fig. 17.2d. In its earliest design, the BBN Butterfly has rather slow performance nodes based on either the Motorola 68000 or 68020. Thus, t_{calc} is large, and both f_C and f_H are relatively small. If one added a high-performance floating-point unit, one might again see a situation like that in (2) with a significant hierarchy within the node. The performance of new models of the Butterfly, based on the Motorola 88000, is better.

4. In the case of IBM's RP3, each node has a true 32K cache and a user-definable division of the remaining memory into local and shared memory. This is the situation contemplated above with a three-level hierarchy with two levels within each node. Considering just the cache and the remaining memory as shared, one finds Fig. 17.2d again.

We see a natural analogy between the memory hierarchy connecting the node of a shared-memory machine to a global memory with the communication channels connecting the node of a hypercube with the other nodes of the array. This is explored in the next subsection, and here we concentrate on the issues internal to the node. These are, of course, not that different from those for individual sequential computers.

One interesting point discussed in Sec. 17.4 is the prejudice toward an object-oriented multiprocessing environment with a virtual machine that is at least an order of magnitude larger (in terms of number of nodes) than the real machine. We need to choose the performance and sizing of the memory so that

- At least two of the fundamental objects fit into each level of the hierarchy. This assumes that we double-buffer any cache so that we can be loading one process while processing another.
- Ten or more objects or processes fit into each node.
- The hardware supports rapid intranode switching between processes and the communication between them.

We also need memory management on each node so as to be able to build robust operating systems with protection from inadvertent but potentially disastrous user errors. Further, we need to be able to move objects between nodes.

The constraints on f_H depend on the application—which determines the values of *constant d* in Eq. (17.3)—and on possible concurrency between calculation and communication (between processes or between memory levels). The least-demanding constraints come when memory transfers and calculation are overlapped. For the problems surveyed in Table 17.3a to i, one would typically find

$$f_H \sim 0.12 \, \frac{t_{\text{mem}}}{t_{\text{calc}}} \tag{17.4}$$

for $n \sim 100$ to 1000 and $d \sim 2$ to 3. This corresponds to object sizes up to about 1 Mbyte.

Using overlapped memory transfer in Eq. (17.4) would require $t_{\text{mem}}/t_{\text{calc}} \lesssim 10$ for $f_H \lesssim 1.25$ and if memory transfer is sequential with calculation, $t_{\text{mem}}/t_{\text{calc}} \lesssim 2$ to achieve $f_H \lesssim 0.25$. The f_H values would lead to an acceptable 20 percent overhead in each case. Smaller object sizes corresponding to smaller caches would need $t_{\text{mem}}/t_{\text{calc}} \lesssim 5$ for object sizes of about 128K and overlapped transfer.

We see that total node memory sizes on the order of 4 to 16 Mbytes are appropriate to allow many objects each of reasonable size. This size is quite consistent with the memories available on a modem ($\sim$1991) low-end workstation. Such memory sizes also allow code space for reasonably sophisticated operating systems. In general, larger node memories than this may not be cost-effective. It may be more effective to spend one's silicon on more processors than on more memory.

17.5.3 Node Communications

Here we review some of the issues in the design and performance of the communication channels between nodes in a distributed-memory system. These issues are similar to those for the switches needed for shared-memory machines, but the local memory of the hypercube-class machines means that hypercubes have less stringent design criteria.

The essential requirement on the communication capability of a distributed-memory machine is contained in Eq. (17.2) with the analogous result to Eq. (17.4), namely,

$$f_C \sim 0.08 \, \frac{t_{\text{comm}}}{t_{\text{calc}}} \tag{17.5}$$

for total node memories of order 4 Mbytes. Note that f_H is controlled by the individual object size, but f_C is controlled by the sum of the sizes of the objects contained in a node.

For a design in which communication and calculation are nonoverlapped, $f_C \lesssim 0.25$ corresponds to an efficiency $\epsilon \gtrsim 0.8$; here the speedup S is a factor ϵ times the number of nodes N. This constraint implies for nodes of the 4-Mbyte size quoted above.

$$\frac{t_{\text{comm}}}{t_{\text{calc}}} \lesssim 3 \qquad \text{nonoverlapped} \tag{17.6}$$

For the case of fully overlapped communication and calculation, an 80 percent efficiency corresponds to $f_C \lesssim 1.25$ and

$$\frac{t_{\text{comm}}}{t_{\text{calc}}} \lesssim 15 \qquad \text{overlapped} \tag{17.7}$$

Larger memories require less stringent constraints on $t_{\text{comm}}/t_{\text{calc}}$. Thus, for typical dimension $d \sim 2$ to 3 values, 16-Mbyte nodes would increase the limits in Eqs. (17.6) and (17.7) by a factor of about 1.8.

We have found that most algorithms allow overlapped communication, but it is certainly easier to program applications corresponding to nonoverlapped communication. In this case, one "asks for data" when needed, and the user is not responsible for putting the communication requests before information is to be used.

Suppose multitasking is provided by the operating system and one can switch processes in a time

$$T_{\text{switch}} \lesssim T_{\text{comm}}(l_{\text{typical}}) \tag{17.8}$$

Then the "ask-for-data-and-wait" programming methodology may be used with the efficiency of overlapped communication. One treats process-to-process communication like most I/O requests on modern fast computers; the process requesting I/O is suspended, and another process resumes execution. In many cases, one finds that $l_{\text{typical}} \sim 10$, the typical number of words in a message, is quite small, and hence Eq. (17.8) is hard to satisfy. Thus, we do not expect this method of treating communication to be generally used. One could expect a hybrid model. For closely coupled synchronous or loosely synchronous applications, the compiler (or user) will optimize communication to allow overlap; the regularity of these applications aids this process. For coarse-grain asynchronous applications, larger and less frequent messages are common, and the strategy of suspending processes awaiting I/O seems effective.

The above discussion leads into a discussion of latency or the nonzero value of $l_{1/2\text{comm}}$ in Eq. (17.1). Several of the initial hypercubes have been handicapped by rather long communication start-up times corresponding to values of $l_{1/2\text{comm}} \gtrsim 100$. As indicated above, we have found that short messages are quite common, and generally good results require $l_{1/2\text{comm}} \sim 10$.

In the above, we have discussed the communication latency and bandwidth between nodes. If these nodes are directly linked in the hardware, this translates into a direct statement about the parameters of a single hardware channel. It is our experience that for a hypercube topology and scientific computations, the majority of the communication is along the hard-wired links. Thus, the values of t_{comm} and $l_{1/2\text{comm}}$ given above are the appropriate values for the node-to-node interconnects for a hypercube topology. The hypercube is a very rich interconnection topology, including within it mesh connections and the binary fast Fourier transform (FFT) connections. Further, the maximum routing distance between any two nodes only grows as $\log_2 N$.

However, other topologies can also be expected to give good results, and the binary hypercube is not essential. If the topologies are "rich" as described above for the hypercube, one can expect that the results [Eqs. (17.6) and (17.7)] would apply to the hardware links. The AOSP (large DOD project centered at Raytheon Corporation) space-based processor and Suprenum, under construction at GMD (laboratory in St. Augustin, Germany), both use crossed busses and multiple busses or rings (network links) as a feasible, if poorly explored, alternative to the direct node-to-node connections of the hypercube. There has been a lot of interest in lower-dimensional topologies. Clearly, interconnect topologies such as the three- and four-dimensional torus, with a fixed branching factor at each node, have a broad range of applicability. Simulations of physical phenomena (typically three- and sometimes four-dimensional in the relativistic limit) and matrix algorithms can naturally use these topologies. Moreover, Seitz and Dally [45, 47, 171] have pointed out the advantages of high-bandwidth two-dimensional mesh-related topologies which fit naturally with VLSI locality constraints. There is as yet little experience on the large systems which would probe differences between low- and high-dimension topologies. A large i860-based multicomputer (the Intel Touchstone Delta Prototype) with 528 nodes was installed in May 1991 at the California Institute of Technology. This has a modem routing network based on the ideas of Dally and Seitz, and we will be able to compare it with the earlier hypercube-connected Touchstone machines with up to 128 nodes based on the same i860 chip. Unfortunately, no very large transputer systems (or modern machines built around the similar iWARP chip) with a mesh inter-connect have been used to study the effectiveness of this topology. Transputer and iWARP systems are built with reconfigurable switches or on chip routing, and one should be able to evaluate the utility of this. The transputer systems allow overlap between the transmission on the different channels of the node. This is a useful feature which should be present in future designs.

Another interesting development has been routing switches for the hypercube, which have been subject to extensive research at JPL [39, 156]. A JPL group has designed routing chips that dynamically select the optimal circuits between nodes to improve performance. These chips also support overlap between the different node channels and have a communication bandwidth that grows as $N \log N$, and not N. We believe that such dynamic routing chips should probably be used in future hypercubelike designs. Many scientific applications do not need it, but applications, such as real-time control and transaction analysis, clearly benefit from dynamic routing.

An alternative approach to distributed-memory systems uses a large $N \rightarrow N$ switch to connect the N nodes of a processor. This is typified by the BBN Butterfly, the IBM RP3 and GF11, and the new TF-1 proposal from Denneau at IBM Yorktown [50]. The TF-1 proposal has evolved into the Vulcan project, based on Intel i860 or IBM RS6000 nodes, and a prototype should be available early in 1992. There is a tentative plan to build and obtain a feasibility analysis of a 32K-node Vulcan, which will realize a teraflop perfor-mance. Such a machine can be considered as either a shared-memory design or a dis-tributed-memory system with a full interconnect between nodes. The shared-memory view is appropriate with a high-performance switch as in the RP3 or Butterfly. We are not aware of comparisons of switches versus node connections for practical applications. The tradeoffs between the two approaches involve bandwidth and latency. One can also consider hybrid designs. For instance, the crossed bus or ring designs mentioned above could be considered as using two $\sqrt{N} \times \sqrt{N}$ switches or equivalently as a two-dimensional hypercube to base $\sqrt{N}$. Yet another hybrid cube-switch design would lead to k^d nodes connected as a hypercube of base k and dimension d [45, 47, 48]. Such a system would be built from $k \rightarrow k$ switches. Clearly, this is a more complex building block than the simple node connections used in the current binary hypercube. However, the additional complexity of the $k \rightarrow k$ switch is offset by the reduced wiring needed. For instance, for a system with $65,536 = 2^{16} = 16^4$ nodes, 32,768 (serial full duplex) communication channels will cross the bisection of a binary hypercube design. A factor-of-8 fewer wires are needed for the base-16 hypercube. We note that when k is a power of 2, the base-k hypercube topology is a superset of the binary hypercube. So all problems running well on the current hypercubes will certainly perform satisfactorily on the more general topology.

Communication speeds on current hypercubes are limited by the processing times for the messages at the source and destination nodes. The transputer has fast but limited (to the OCCAM model) hardware support which leads to factors of 10 to 100 lower start-up times on such systems compared to the current hypercubes [$t_{1/2\text{comm}}$ (transputer) ~ 1]. We believe that more research is needed here, and good hardware support of the complete message-passing task is essential in future high-performance systems.

The most sophisticated shared-memory designs such as CEDAR and RP3 feature combining switches for instructions like "fetch and add." It is interesting that some of the best matrix algorithms for the hypercube require essentially the same function on the node for a distributed-memory communication system. This application requires floating-point as well as integer combination; conventional shared-memory designs usually only support integer fetch-and-add. This combining is, of course, possible on the hypercube by using the node itself as the engine to combine (add, merge) messages. This only works well on those hypercubes, like the original California Institute of Technology Cosmic Cube, Mark II, and the NCUBE, where the CPU and communication are highly integrated. There are large overheads in (floating-point) combining on machines like the Mark III and the Intel Touchstone with very distinct calculation and communication modules on each node. We believe that more research on the common properties of shared-memory and distributed-memory networks will be very fruitful.

17.5.4 I/O Subsystems

Many of the current distributed-memory machines are weak in the I/O interface area. This affects three aspects:

- User interface
- Real-time graphics
- Mass storage (disk, tape, etc.)

Hypercubes and the other similar machines have potentially good I/O bandwidth, and the current difficulties in this area reflect the immaturity of the field. The rush to get out the initial machines put the consideration of I/O to one of secondary importance. More fundamentally, the structure of the I/O hardware is unclear because, as discussed in Sec. 17.3, there is as yet no agreement on the right user or software model for I/O in a distributed environment. This is an interesting contrast to the shared-memory machines like the Butterfly, Sequent, and Encore where the I/O-user interface is reasonably satisfactory. These machines, unlike the hypercubes, run an integrated operating system—typically a version of distributed UNIX—and so there is a much more natural software model, and there are reasonably clear hardware design criteria. It should be emphasized that the successful I/O model here reflects the use of a largely sequential design; the difficulties with the hypercube come from the immediate confrontation with the parallel I/O.

We believe that the I/O subsystem should be thought through carefully in any future high-performance machine whether of shared or distributed memory. In either case, the I/O subsystem will itself be a concurrent system; e.g., it will interface with a "back-end" hypercube through many parallel channels. Thus, one can talk about the concurrent architecture of the I/O system. One simple possibility is to configure it as a shared-memory computer optimized for I/O.

The SIMD Connection Machine, as well as the Intel and NCUBE multicomputers, have offered reasonable parallel disk I/O subsystems during the last three years, but we have little practical experience with them. As an example of the early difficulties, the California Institute of Technology used the parallel I/O subsystem on the 512-node NCUBE-1 hypercube to analyze radio astronomy data and search for pulsars [10]. This work was astoundingly successful, but the messaging overhead between the hypercube and parallel I/O subsystem limited the I/O rates to less than that attainable on a modest workstation. One interesting development is the availability (1991) of the standard database system Oracle on specially configured NCUBE-2's with large node memory (16 Mbytes) and a large parallel disk system. Several grand challenges contemplated in the federal high-performance computing initiative will need major I/O subsystems. As an example, we can mention the "mission to planet earth" where both the analysis of satellite data and theoretical climate modeling will necessitate some 100 Tbytes of storage.

17.6 A TERACUBE DESIGN

17.6.1 Node

Here we speculate on a particular relatively near-term realization of these ideas in a concurrent supercomputer of teraflop performance [82].

Assuming that the research and technology developments, already made public, are incorporated into the supercomputer, a natural node, designed within the next year, would have 20- to 40-megaflop performance or

$$t_{calc} \sim 0.025 \text{ to } 0.05 \text{ } \mu s \tag{17.9}$$

This estimate can be compared with the Intel i860 chip, which can realize 5 to 20 megaflops at present, or the IBM RS6000 workstation, which achieves 30 megaflops on Linpack when the chip is run at its highest clock rate.

A RISC architecture is characteristic of many of the new microprocessors designed for workstations. If vector coprocessor units are added to these, one can expect over 150-megaflop performance per node. The difference between the cost performance of the 20- to 40-megaflop node and the 150-megaflop node is not expected to be a factor sufficient to dictate which design should be used. Nor are other factors, such as power per megaflop or volume per megaflop. However, ease of programming, particularly ease of writing efficient compilers, will probably make the RISC architecture without a vector coprocessor the node of choice.

Thus, in the remainder of this section we make the conservative assumption that the next-generation processor node will have a 20-megaflop performance. Given this, if a parallel processor is to have a total usable performance of a teraflop, then it will need to have 2^{16} nodes.

These arguments are not accurate to factors of 2. Maybe the node will get a 40-megaflop performance, but maybe the parallel efficiency is 50 percent due to either load imbalance or communication overheads. Our choice of 2^{16} nodes is typical of an analysis that would be needed for any machine within a factor of 2 of this size. The formal number of nodes, in the distributed-memory sense, may well also be reduced if one chooses to use it as a building block, a small shared-memory machine with perhaps four nodes. These will soon be available from many vendors in low-end workstations.

17.6.2 Communication

If we consider the communication subsystem for such a machine, the criteria of Eq. (17.7) would require

$$t_{comm} \lesssim 0.5 \text{ } \mu s \tag{17.10}$$

for overlapped calculation and communication. For 32-bit words, this implies a channel bandwidth of 64 Mbits. This could be realized with 100 Mbit/s optical links which could exploit technology developed for the new computer networking standard, FDDI. The wiring difficulties for 2^{16} nodes suggest, as discussed in Sec. 17.3, that a five-dimensional cube of radix 8 or a four-dimensional cube of radix 16 could be used for such a large array. In this case, the radix in any dimension of the cube could be lowered without adversely affecting performance or node architecture to provide modularity to smaller versions. The performance estimated in Eq. (17.10) assumed concurrent communication and I/O processing, which does not interfere with the computational processor in each node. New parallel processors should be designed to include concurrent I/O. The concurrent I/O should include independent I/O buffers because node memory bandwidth is likely to become the next resource bottleneck. Use of dual-ported memory is another technique that should be considered to minimize this potential bottleneck.

17.6.3 Reliability and Fault Tolerance

One issue that has received relatively little attention is the need for higher reliability and fault tolerance. As long as the number of nodes in the parallel processor is fairly small, the difference between the needs in uniprocessors and such parallel arrays is small. But when we try to scale the parallel approach to massive parallelism, the problem becomes much bigger. For example, suppose the mean time between failures (MTBF) for a single node were 50 years (a not unreasonable number for next-generation technology). If we had a system with 2^{16} nodes, then the MTBF of that system would be only 6.5 h. If peripherals, power, and cabling were added, this already intolerable number would become much worse.

The potential of applying redundant processors for fault detection and recovery is clearly available, but appropriate techniques have not been implemented. It is likely that a combination of hardware and software techniques is necessary. Frequent check pointing to a dedicated back end will probably be necessary. Once errors are detected and the data set integrity is restored, one can route around "bad nodes," using hardware routing chips [39] and the automatic decomposers [79, 83] based on neural networks. No breakthroughs appear to be needed to find a reasonable solution to the reliability problem.

17.6.4 Power

The initial parallel processors available from Intel and NCUBE did not provide more than 50,000 flops of sustained performance per watt of power. In fact, this may be an optimistic estimate. Also, this power consumption does not include the requirements for peripherals, power supplies, and cooling systems. If all these factors were included and that technology were scaled to teraflop performance, the resulting power consumption for such a teraflop processor would exceed 100 MW. This would not constitute a practical or even feasible design. External I/O subsystems for parallel machines are still in their infancy, but surely this will change, as discussed in Sec. 17.5.4. Historically, the power for peripherals has been in the range of 4 to 6 times the power required for the CPU. One might expect this ratio to be somewhat smaller for such a teraflop processor, but without more standardization, more engineering, and more examination of very large applications one cannot be sure.

However, various technological improvements already announced or on the horizon can be projected to provide almost a factor-of-100 improvement in performance measured by flops per watt. We can see this as the difference between the 0.2-megaflop performance of scalar floating-point units like the Motorola 68882 and the 20-megaflop performance of the node used in Sec. 17.6.1, which is almost the performance of the 1990–1991 i860-based Touchstone machines from Intel.

Improvements in lithography should provide at least a factor of 10 of this improvement. Architecture enhancements including pipelining in RISC machines, concurrent I/O, and faster context switching will provide the remaining order of magnitude. New compilers to automate vectorization, pipeline optimization, and process decomposition will be necessary to exploit these architectural improvements. But even with all these improvements, a teraflop processor will still need over 1 MW of power, perhaps as much as 5 MW including cooling requirements and inefficiencies of power supplies.

Such a system might use an independent power generator, but again this would not exceed the present state-of-the-art capability. The power requirements of a teraflop processing configuration depend on only predictable engineering development, not any technological breakthroughs.

17.7 CONCLUSION

We have reviewed some of the hardware, software, and application issues which strongly suggest that a teraflop parallel supercomputer is a realistic possibility in the next 5 years. We are confident that a broad range of applications will run well on these machines, which are the spearhead of the federal high-performance computing and communication initiative. However, it will take some time to both develop the parallel code and learn how to perform meaningful simulations—technology is perhaps advancing more rapidly than the computational scientist's ability to exploit it. Such machines will require breakthroughs in the human-computer interface to allow meaningful interpretation of the factor of 100 to 1000 more information produced by our teraflop behemoth. Fledgling technologies, such as virtual reality, may be critical here.

The future of computational science is bright as it is driven by the inexorable progress of technology. Hopefully, more young scientists will be attracted to this field, which will grow in stature compared to the traditional experimental and theoretical methodologies.

REFERENCES

1. T. S. Abdelraham and T. N. Mudge, "Parallel Branch and Bound Algorithms on Hypercube Multiprocessors," in G. C. Fox (ed.), *Proceedings of the Third Conference on Hypercube Concurrent Computers and Applications,* vol. 2, pp. 1492–1499. New York: ACM Press, 1988.

2. C. A. Addison, J. M. Cook, and L. R. Hagen, "An Interactive System for Seismic Velocity Analysis," in G. C. Fox (ed.), *Proceedings of the Third Conference on Hypercube Concurrent Computers and Applications,* vol. 2, pp. 1138–1145. New York: ACM Press, 1988.

3. R. K. Agarwal, "Development of a Navier-Stokes Code on a Connection Machine," in H. D. Simon (ed.), *Proceedings of the Conference on Scientific Applications of the Connection Machine,* p. 27. Teaneck, N.J.: World Scientific Publishing Co., 1989.

4. T. Aldcroft, A. Cisneros, G. C. Fox, W. Furmanski, and D. W. Walker, "LU Decomposition of Banded Matrices and the Solution of Linear Systems on Hypercubes," in G. C. Fox (ed.), *The Third Conference on Hypercube Concurrent Computers and Applications,* vol. 2, pp. 1635–1655. Caltech Report C3P-348b. New York: ACM Press, 1988.

5. W. Allen and A. Saha, "Parallel Neural-Network Simulation Using Back-Propagation for the ES-Kit Environment," in J. L. Gustafson (ed.), *Proceedings of the Fourth Conference on Hypercubes, Concurrent Computers and Applications,* pp. 1097–1102, Los Altos, Calif.: Golden Gate Enterprises, 1989.

6. G. Aloisio, G. C. Fox, J. S. Kim, and N. Veneziani, "A Concurrent Implementation of the Prime Factor Algorithm on a Hypercube," Caltech Report C3P-468b, *IEEE Transactions on ASSP,* 39(1):160–170, January 1991.

7. G. Aloisio, E. Lopinto, N. Veneziani, G. C. Fox, and J. S. Kim, "Two Approaches for a Concurrent Implementation of the Prime Factor Algorithm on a Hypercube," *Concurrency: Practice and Experience,* 1991. Caltech Report C3P-874.

8. G. Aloisio, N. Veneziani, G. Fox, and G. Milillo, "Computational Load Evaluation for the Real-Time Compression of X-SAR Raw Data," Caltech Report C3P-740b, *Space Technology,* 10(4):189–199, November 1990.

9. G. Aloisio, N. Veneziani, J. S. Kim, and G. C. Fox, "The Prime Factor Non-binary Discrete Fourier Transform and Use of Crystal-Router as a General Purpose Communication Routine,"

in G. C. Fox (ed.), *The Third Conference on Hypercube Concurrent Computers and Applications*, vol. 2, pp. 1322–1327. Caltech Report C3P-523. New York: ACM Press, 1988.

10. S. B. Anderson, G.P.W., S. R. Kulkarni, T. A. Prince, and A. Wolszczan, "Discovery of Two Radio Pulsars in the Globular Cluster M15," Technical Report C3P-864, California Institute of Technology, February 1990, *Nature*, 346:42, 1990.

11. I. G. Angus, G. C. Fox, J. S. Kim, and D. W. Walker, *Solving Problems on Concurrent Processors: Software for Concurrent Processors*, vol. 2. Englewood Cliffs, N.J.: Prentice-Hall, 1990.

12. M. J. Atallah and S. McFaddin, "Sequence Comparison on the Connection Machine," *Concurrency: Practice and Experience*, 3(2):89–107, 1991.

13. C. Aykanat, F. Ozguner, and D. S. Scott, "Implementation of the Conjugate Gradient Algorithm on a Vector Hypercube Multiprocessor," in G. C. Fox (ed.), *Proceedings of the Third Conference on Hypercube Concurrent Computers and Applications*, vol. 2, pp. 1687–1697. New York: ACM Press, 1988.

14. S. B. Baden, "Run-Time Partitioning of Scientific Continuum Calculations Running on Multiprocessors," PhD thesis, University of California, Berkeley, 1987.

15. C. F. Baillie, "Lattice Spin Models and New Algorithms—A Review of Monte Carlo Computer Simulations," *International Journal of Modern Physics C*, Caltech Report C3P-854, 1(1):92–117, 1990.

16. C. F. Baillie and P. D. Coddington, "Cluster Identification Algorithms for Spin Models," *Concurrency: Practice and Experience*, Caltech Report C3P-855, 3(2):129–144, April 1991.

17. W. L. Bain, "Air Traffic Simulation: An Object Oriented, Discrete Event Simulation on the Intel iPSC/2 Parallel System," in D. W. Walker and Q. F. Stout (eds.), *The Fifth Distributed Memory Computing Conference*, April 9–12, Charleston, South Carolina, pp. 95–100, Los Alamitos: IEEE Computer Society Press, 1990.

18. L. J. Baker, "Hypercube Performance for 2-D Seismic Finite-Difference Modeling," in G. C. Fox (ed.), *Proceedings of the Third Conference on Hypercube Concurrent Computers and Applications, Volume 2*, pp. 1146–1156. New York: ACM Press, 1988.

19. J. Barhen, J. R. Einstein, and C. C. Jorgensen, "Advances in Concurrent Computation for Machine Intelligence and Robotics," Caltech Report C3P-418, *Proceedings of the Second International Conference on Supercomputing*, St. Petersberg, Florida, May 1987. International Supercomputing Institute, Inc.

20. C. Barnes, R. Farber, and A. Lapedes, "Applications of New Neural Net Methods to Genetic Database Analysis," Technical report, Los Alamos National Laboratory, 1988.

21. R. Battiti, "Real-Time Multiscale Vision on Multicomputers," Caltech Report C3P-932b, *Concurrency: Practice and Experience*, 3(2):55–87, 1991.

22. BBN Advanced Computers, Inc., "Butterfly Parallel Processing—Mathematical Techniques and Physical Applications," Cambridge, Mass., 1987.

23. BBN Advanced Computers, Inc., "Butterfly University Applications." Cambridge, Mass., 1987.

24. J. Beetem, M. Denneau, and D. Weingarten, "GF 11," in J. E. Gubernatis (ed.), *Proceedings of the Conference on Frontiers of Quantum Monte Carlo*, September 3–6, 1985, Los Alamos, *Journal of Statistical Physics*, 43(5/6), June 1986.

25. H. Berryman, J. Saltz, and J. Scroggs, "Execution Time Support for Adaptive Scientific Algorithms on Distributed Memory Machines," *Concurrency: Practice and Experience*, 3(3), 1991.

26. G. E. Blelloch, "Applications and Algorithms on the Connection Machine," MIT Report TR87-1, September 1987.

27. B. M. Boghosian, "Computational Physics on the Connection Machine: Massive Parallelism—A New Paradigm," *Computers in Physics*, pp. 14–33, January 1990.

28. K. C. Bowler, A. D. Bruce, R. D. Kenway, G. S. Pawley, and D. J. Wallace, "Exploiting Highly Concurrent Computers for Physics," *Physics Today,* October 1987.

29. K. C. Bowler, A. D. Bruce, R. D. Kenway, G. S. Pawley, D. J. Wallace, and A. McKendrick, "Scientific Computation on the Edinburgh DAPs: NG15908," Technical report, Edinburgh University, 1987.

30. B. Braschi, "Solving the Traveling Salesman Problem Using the Simulated Annealing on a Hypercube," in J. L. Gustafson (ed.), *Proceedings of the Fourth Conference on Hypercubes, Concurrent Computers and Applications.* Los Altos, Calif.: Golden Gate Enterprises, March 1989. Pp. 765–768.

31. R. G. Brickner and C. F. Baillie, "Pure Gauge QCD on the Connection Machine," *International Journal of High Speed Computing,* Caltech Report C3P-710, 1(2):303–320, June 1989.

32. L. Brochard and A. Freau, "Computation and Data Movement on RP3," *Concurrency: Practice and Experience,* 4:57, 1992.

33. L. Brochard and A. Freau, "Designing Algorithms on RP3," *Concurrency: Practice and Experience,* 4:79, 1992.

34. J. Bruno and P. R. Cappello, "Implementing the Beam and Warming Method on the Hypercube," in G. C. Fox (ed.), *Proceedings of the Third Conference on Hypercube Concurrent Computers and Applications.* New York: ACM Press, 1988. Vol. 2, pp. 1073–1087.

35. R. H. Calalo, J. R. Lyons, and W. A. Imbriale, "Finite Difference Time Domain Solution of Electromagnetic Scattering on the Hypercube," Caltech Report C3P-596, in G. C. Fox, ed., *The Third Conference on Hypercube Concurrent Computers and Applications.* New York: ACM Press, January 1988.

36. B. A. Carpenter and N. J. Davis, "Implementation and Performance Analysis of Parallel Assignment Algorithms on a Hypercube Computer," in G. C. Fox (ed.), *Proceedings of the Third Conference on Hypercube Concurrent Computers and Applications.* New York: ACM Press, 1988. Vol. 2, pp. 1231–1235.

37. A. Casotto and A. Sangiovanni-Vincintelli, "Placement of Standard Cells Using Simulated Annealing on the Connection Machine," Technical report, University of California at Berkeley, 1986.

38. W. Celmaster, "Parallelization of Physical Systems on the BBN Butterfly: Some Examples," *Proceedings of the IMA Workshop,* 1986. Springer-Verlag, 1986.

39. E. Chow, H. Maden, J. Peterson, D. Grunwald, and D. Reed, "Hyperswitch Network for the Hypercube Computer," Caltech Report C3P-484, in H. J. Siegel (ed.), *Proceedings of the 15th Annual International Symposium on Computer Architecture, Computer Architecture News,* 16, no. 2, May 1987.

40. N. H. Christ, "Lattice Gauge Theory with a Fast Highly Parallel Computer," in J. E. Gubernatis (ed.), *Proceedings of the Conference on Frontiers of Quantum Monte Carlo,* September 3–6, 1985, Los Alamos, *Journal of Statistical Physics,* 43(5/6), June 1986.

41. C. Y. Chu, "Comparison of Two-Dimensional FFT Methods on the Hypercube," in G. C. Fox (ed.), *Proceedings of the Third Conference on Hypercube Concurrent Computers and Applications.* New York: ACM Press, 1988. Vol. 2, pp. 1430–1437.

42. R. W. Clayton and R. W. Graves, "Acoustic Wavefield Propagation Using Paraxial Extrapolators," Caltech Report C3P-613, in G. C. Fox (ed.), *The Third Conference on Hypercube Concurrent Computers and Applications.* New York: ACM Press, January 1988. Vol. 2, pp. 1157–1175.

43. R. Clayton, B. Hager, and T. Tanimoto, "Applications of Concurrent Processors in Geophysics," Caltech Report C3P-408, *Proceedings of the Second International Conference on Supercomputing,* St. Petersburg, Florida, May 1987.

44. C. C. Christara and E. N. Houstis, "A Domain Decomposition Spline Collocation Method for Elliptic Partial Differential Equations," in J. L. Gustafson (ed.), *Proceedings of the Fourth Conference on Hypercubes, Concurrent Computers and Applications.* Los Altos, Calif., March 1989. Pp. 1267–1274.

45. W. J. Dally, "Fine-Grain Message-Passing Concurrent Computers," in G. C. Fox (ed.), *Proceedings of the Third Conference on Hypercube Concurrent Computers and Applications.* New York: ACM Press, 1988. Vol. 1, pp. 2–12.

46. W. J. Dally and A. A. Chien, "Object-Oriented Concurrent Programming in CST," in G. C. Fox (ed.), *Proceedings of the Third Conference on Hypercube Concurrent Computers and Applications.* New York: ACM Press, 1988. Vol. 1, pp. 434–439.

47. W. J. Dally and C. Seitz, "The Torus Routing Chip," *Journal of Distributed Systems,* 1:187, 1986.

48. W. Dally and C. Seitz, "A VLSI Architecture for Concurrent Data Structures," *Journal of Distributed Systems,* 1:187, 1986.

49. F. Darema, "Applications Environment for the IBM Research Parallel Processor Prototype, RP3," in C. Polychronoupolos (ed.), *ICS 87, International Conference on Supercomputing,* Athens, N.Y., 1987. New York: Springer-Verlag.

50. M. Denneau, "TF-1," Seminar at NASA Ames and presentation at VAPP-2, Rome, September 21–23, 1987. TF-1 has evolved to the Vulcan machine under construction (1991) at IBM Yorktown.

51. H.-Q. Ding, "Polymer Simulation on the Hypercube," Caltech Report C3P-574, in G. C. Fox (ed.), *The Third Conference on Hypercube Concurrent Computers and Applications.* New York: ACM Press, January 1988. Vol. 2, pp. 1044–1050.

52. H.-Q. Ding, "The 600 Megaflops Performance of the QCD code on the Mark IIIfp Hypercube," Caltech Report C3P-799b, in D. W. Walker and Q. F. Stout (eds.), *The Fifth Distributed Memory Computing Conference* (Charleston, S.C.). Los Alamitos, Calif.: IEEE Computer Society Press, 1990. Vol. 2, pp. 1295–1301.

53. H.-Q. Ding, C. F. Baillie, and G. C. Fox, "Calculation of the Heavy Quark Potential at Large Separation on a Hypercube Parallel Computer," Caltech Report C3P-779b, *Physical Review D,* 41(9):2912–2916, May 1990.

54. H.-Q. Ding and M. Makivic, "Spin Correlations of 2d Quantum Antiferromagnet at Low Temperatures and a Direct Comparison with Neutron Scattering Experiments," Caltech Report C3P-844, *Physics Review Letters,* 64:1449, 1990.

55. D. J. Doorly and S. Pesmajoglou, "Application of Transputers to Aircraft Simulation and Control," in D. W. Walker and Q. F. Stout (eds.), *The Fifth Distributed Memory Computing Conference* (Charleston, S.C.). Los Alamitos, Calif.: IEEE Computer Society Press, 1990. Vol. 1, pp. 101–106.

56. R. O. Faiss, "The Goodyear SIMD Processors: Insights Gained from 20 Years of Usage," in W. J. Karplus (ed.), *Proceedings of the Third Conference on Multiprocessors and Array Processors, Simulation Series.* San Diego, Calif.: Society for Computer Simulation, 1987. Vol. 18/2, p. 157.

57. E. W. Felten, "Best-First Branch-and-Bound on a Hypercube," Caltech Report C3P-590, in G. C. Fox (ed.), *The Third Conference on Hypercube Concurrent Computers and Applications.* New York: ACM Press, January 1988. Vol. 2, pp. 1500–1504.

58. E. Felten, S. Karlin, and S. Otto, "The Traveling Salesman Problem on a Hypercube, MIMD Computer," Caltech Report C3P-093b (St. Charles, Ill.). *Proceedings of 1985 International Conference on Parallel Processing,* pp. 6–10, 1985.

59. E. Felten, R. Morison, S. Otto, K. Barish, R. Fätland, and F. Ho, "Chess on a Hypercube," Caltech Report C3P-383, in M. T. Heath (ed.), *Hypercube Multiprocessors.* Philadelphia: SIAM, 1987. Pp. 327–332.

60. E. W. Felten and S. W. Otto, "A Highly Parallel Chess Program," Caltech Report C3P-579c, *Proceedings of International Conference on Fifth Generation Computer Systems 1988* (Tokyo), Tokyo, Japan: ICOT, November 1988. Pp. 1001–1009.

61. E. W. Felten and S. W. Otto, "Chess on a Hypercube," Caltech Report C3P-579, in G. C. Fox (ed.), *The Third Conference on Hypercube Concurrent Computers and Applications.* New York: ACM Press, January 1988. Vol. 2, pp. 1329–1381.

62. E. W. Felten and S. W. Otto, "Coherent Parallel C," Caltech Report C3P-527, in G. C. Fox (ed.), *The Third Conference on Hypercube Concurrent Computers and Applications*. New York: ACM Press, January 1988. Vol. 1, pp. 440–450.

63. R. D. Ferraro, N. Jacobi, P. C. Liewer, T. G. Lockhart, G. A. Lyzenga, J. Parker, and J. E. Patterson, "Parallel Finite Elements Applied to the Electromagnetic Scattering Problem," Caltech Report C3P-903, in D. W. Walker and Q. F. Stout (eds.), *The Fifth Distributed Memory Computing Conference* (Charleston, S.C.). Los Alamitos, Calif.: IEEE Computer Society Press, 1990. Vol. 1, pp. 417–420.

64. "Grand Challenges: High Performance Computing and Communications." A Report by the Committee on Physical, Mathematical and Engineering Sciences, 1991, FY 1992 U.S. Research and Development Program, to supplement the President's Fiscal Year 1992 Budget.

65. "The Federal High Performance Computing Program," Executive Office of the President, Office of Science and Technology Policy, September 1989.

66. R. D. Fiebrich, "Data Parallel Algorithms for Engineering Applications," in *Proceedings of the Second International Conference on Supercomputing, St. Petersburg, Fla.*, International Supercomputing Institute, 1987. Vol. 2, p. 17.

67. J. R. Fischer, "Frontiers of Massively Parallel Scientific Computation," in J. R. Fischer (ed.), *Proceedings of Goddard Space Flight Center Symposium* (September 24–25, 1986), NASA Conference Publication 2478, 1987.

68. P. A. Flinn, "Molecular Dynamics Simulation on an iPSC of Defects in Crystals," in G. C. Fox (ed.), *Proceedings of the Third Conference on Hypercube Concurrent Computers and Applications*. New York: ACM Press, 1988. Vol. 2, pp. 1303–1312.

69. J. Flower, J. Apostolakis, C. Baillie, and H.-Q. Ding, "Lattice Gauge Theory on the Hypercube," Caltech Report C3P-605, in G. C. Fox (ed.), *The Third Conference on Hypercube Concurrent Computers and Applications*. New York: ACM Press, January 1988. Vol. 2, pp. 1278–1287.

70. J. Flower, S. Otto, and M. Salama, "Optimal Mapping of Irregular Finite Element Domains to Parallel Processors," Technical Report C3P-292b, California Institute of Technology, August 1987, *Proceedings, Symposium on Parallel Computations and Their Impact on Mechanics*, ASME Winter Meeting, December 14–16, Boston, Mass.

71. G. C. Fox, "Achievements and Prospects for Parallel Computing," in *Proceedings of the International Conference on Parallel Computing: Achievements, Problems and Prospects*, Anacapri, Italy, June 3–9, 1990, *Concurrency: Practice and Experience*, 3:725, 1991.

72. G. C. Fox, "Applications of Parallel Supercomputers: Scientific Results and Computer Science Lessons," Caltech Report C3P-806b, in M. A. Arbib and J. A. Robinson (eds.), *Natural and Artificial Parallel Computation*. Cambridge, Mass.: MIT Press, 1990. SCCS-23. Pp. 47–90.

73. G. Fox, "The Caltech Concurrent Computation Program," Caltech Report C3P-290b, in M. T. Heath (ed.), *Hypercube Multiprocessors*. Philadelphia: SIAM, 1987. Pp. 353–381.

74. G. Fox, "Domain Decomposition in Distributed and Shared Memory Environments: I. A Uniform Decomposition and Performance Analysis for the NCUBE and JPL Mark IIIfp Hypercubes," Caltech Report C3P-392, *Lecture Notes in Computer Science*. New York: Springer-Verlag, 1987. E. N. Houstis, T. S. Papatheodorou, and C. D. Polychronopoulos (eds.), *Supercomputing*, Vol. 297 of *Lecture Notes in Computer Science*. Pp. 1092–1073.

75. G. C. Fox, "FortranD as a Portable Software System for Parallel Computers," Technical Report SCCS-91, Syracuse University, June 1991, *Proceedings of Supercomputing USA/Pacific 91*, Santa Clara, Calif., CRPC-TR91128.

76. G. C. Fox, "Issues in Software Development for Concurrent Computers," Caltech Report C3P-640, in G. J. Knaff (ed.), *Proceedings of the Twelfth Annual International Computer Software and Applications Conference*. Washington, D.C.: Computer Society Press of the IEEE, October 1988. Pp. 382–405.

77. G. C. Fox, "Parallel Computing Comes of Age: Supercomputer Level Parallel Computations at Caltech," Caltech Report C3P-795, *Concurrency: Practice and Experience*, 1(1):63–103, September 1989.

78. G. C. Fox, "Parallel Problem Architectures and Their Implications for Portable Parallel Software Systems," Technical report C3P-967, Northeast Parallel Architectures Center, May 1991. CRPC-TR91120, SCCS-78, Presentation at DARPA Workshop, Providence, R.I., February 28, 1991.

79. G. C. Fox, "A Review of Automatic Load Balancing and Decomposition Methods for the Hypercube," Caltech Report C3P-385, in M. Schultz (ed.), *Numerical Algorithms for Modern Parallel Computer Architectures*. New York: Springer-Verlag, 1988. Pp. 63–76.

80. G. C. Fox, "What Have We Learnt from Using Real Parallel Machines to Solve Real Problems?," Caltech Report C3P-552, in G. C. Fox (ed.), *The Third Conference on Hypercube Concurrent Computers and Applications*. New York: ACM Press, January 1988. Vol. 2, pp. 897–955.

81. G. C. Fox (ed.), *The Third Conference on Hypercube Concurrent Computers and Applications*, Jet Propulsion Laboratory of the California Institute of Technology. New York: ACM Press, January 1988. Vol. 1. *Architecture, Software, Computer Systems and General Issues;* vol. 2. *Applications*.

82. G. C. Fox and A. Frey, "Problems and Approaches for a Teraflop Processor," Caltech Report C3P-606, in G. C. Fox (ed.), *The Third Conference on Hypercube Concurrent Computers and Applications*. New York: ACM Press, January 1988. Vol. 1, pp. 21–25.

83. G. C. Fox and W. Furmanski, "Load Balancing Loosely Synchronous Problems with a Neural Network," Caltech Report C3P-363b, in G. C. Fox (ed.), *The Third Conference on Hypercube Concurrent Computers and Applications*. New York: ACM Press, January 1988. Vol. 1, pp. 241–278.

84. G. Fox, A. J. G. Hey, and S. Otto, "Matrix Algorithms on the Hypercube I: Matrix Multiplication," Caltech Report C3P-206, *Parallel Computing,* 4:17, 1987.

85. G. C. Fox, S. Hiranandani, K. Kennedy, C. Koelbel, U. Kremer, C.-W. Tseng, and M.-Y. Wu, "Fortran D Language Specification," Technical Report SCCS-42c, Rice Center for Research in Parallel Computation, CRPC-TR90079, April 1991.

86. G. C. Fox, M. A. Johnson, G. A. Lyzenga, S. W. Otto, J. K. Salmon, and D. W. Walker, *Solving Problems on Concurrent Processors,* vol. 1: Englewood Cliffs, N.J.: Prentice-Hall, 1988.

87. G. C. Fox and P. Messina, "The Caltech Concurrent Computation Program Annual Report 1986–1987," Annual Report C3P-487, California Institute of Technology, November 1987.

88. P. O. Frederickson, "Totally Parallel Multilevel Algorithms," in H. D. Simon (ed.), *Proceedings of the Conference on Scientific Applications of the Connection Machine,* September 12–14, 1988. World Scientific Publishing Co., 1989.

89. W. Furmanski, "MOVIE and Map Separates," Technical Report SCCS-82, JTF Semiannual Coordination Meeting, Syracuse University, April 1991.

90. W. Furmanski, J. M. Bower, M. E. Nelson, M. A. Wilson, and G. Fox, "Piriform (Olfactory) Cortex Model on the Hypercube," Caltech Report C3P-404b, in G. C. Fox (ed.), *The Third Conference on Hypercube Concurrent Computers and Applications*. New York: ACM Press, January 1988. Vol. 2, pp. 977–999.

91. W. Furmanski, G. C. Fox, and D. Walker, "Optimal Matrix Algorithms on Homogeneous Hypercubes," Caltech Report C3P-386b, in G. C. Fox (ed.), *The Third Conference on Hypercube Concurrent Computers and Applications*. New York: ACM Press, January 1988. Vol. 2, pp. 1656–1673.

92. I. Gaines, H. Areti, R. Atac, J. Biel, A. Cook, M. Fischler, R. Hance, D. Husby, T. Nash, and T. Zmuda, "The ACP Multiprocessor System at Fermilab," *Computer Physics Communication,* 45:323, 1987.

93. I. Gaines and T. Nash, "Use of New Computer Technologies in Elementary Particle Physics," in J. D. Jackson (ed.), *Annual Reviews in Nuclear Particle Science,* vol. 37, 1987.

94. L. Gasser, "Large-Scale Concurrent Computing in Artificial Intelligence Research," in G. C. Fox (ed.), *Proceedings of the Third Conference on Hypercube Concurrent Computers and Applications*. New York: ACM Press, 1988. Vol. 2, pp. 1342–1351.

95. G. A. Geist, B. W. Peyton, W. A. Shelton, and G. M. Stocks, "Metallic Alloys on the Intel iPSC/860," in D. W. Walker and Q. F. Stout (eds.), *The Fifth Distributed Memory Computing Conference,* April 9–12, Charleston, S.C. Los Alamitos, Calif.: IEEE Computer Society Press, 1990. Vol. 1, pp. 504–512.

96. D. C. Gerogiannis, S. C. Orphanoudakis, and S. Johnsson, "Histogram Computation on Distributed Memory Architectures," *Concurrency: Practice and Experience,* 1(2):219–237, December 1989.

97. I. Glendinning and A. J. G. Hey, "Transputer Arrays as Fortran Farms for Particle Physics," *Computer Physics Communications,* 45:367–371, 1987.

98. J. Goldsmith and J. Salmon, "A Hypercube Ray-Tracer," Caltech Report C3P-592, in G. C. Fox (ed.), *The Third Conference on Hypercube Concurrent Computers and Applications.* New York: ACM Press, January 1988. Vol. 2, pp. 1194–1206.

99. P. W. Gorham, "Computational Aspects of Bispectral Analysis in Interferometric Imaging," Caltech Report C3P-637, in F. Merkle (ed.), *Proceedings of the NOAO-ESO Conference on High Resolution Imaging by Interferometry.* Garching: ESO, 1988. Vol. 1, p. 191.

100. P. W. Gorham, T. A. Prince, and S. Anderson, "Hypercube Data Analysis in Astronomy: Optical Interferometry and Millisecond Pulsar Searches," Caltech Report C3P-571, in G. C. Fox (ed.), *The Third Conference on Hypercube Concurrent Computers and Applications.* New York: ACM Press, January 1988. Vol. 2, pp. 957–962.

101. T. D. Gottschalk, "Concurrent Multiple Target Tracking," Caltech Report C3P-567, in G. C. Fox (ed.), *The Third Conference on Hypercube Concurrent Computers and Applications.* New York: ACM Press, January 1988. Vol. 2, pp. 1247–1268.

102. T. D. Gottschalk, "Concurrent Multi-Target Tracking," Caltech Report C3P-908, in D. W. Walker and Q. F. Stout (eds.), *The Fifth Distributed Memory Computing Conference.* April 9–12, Charleston, S.C. Los Alamitos, Calif.: IEEE Computer Society Press, 1990. Vol. 1, pp. 85–88.

103. S. L. Groom, M. Lee, A. S. Mazer, and W. I. Williams, "Design and Implementation of a Concurrent Image Processing Workstation Based on the Mark III Hypercube," Caltech Report C3P-599, in G. C. Fox (ed.), *The Third Conference on Hypercube Concurrent Computers and Applications.* New York: ACM Press, January 1988. Vol. 2, pp. 1320–1321.

104. M. Gurnis, A. Raefsky, G. A. Lyzenga, and B. H. Hager, "Finite Element Solution of Thermal Convection on a Hypercube Concurrent Computer," Caltech Report C3P-595, in G. C. Fox (ed.), *The Third Conference on Hypercube Concurrent Computers and Applications.* New York: ACM Press, January 1988. Vol. 2, pp. 1176–1179.

105. J. L. Gustafson (ed.,) *The Fourth Conference on Hypercubes, Concurrent Computers, and Applications.* Los Altos, Calif., Golden Gate Enterprises, March 1989.

106. J. L. Gustafson, G. R. Montry, and R. E. Benner, "Development of Parallel Methods for a 1024-Processor Hypercube," *SIAM Journal of Science and Statistical Computation,* 9(4):609–638, July 1988.

107. G. M. Gutt, "An Automata Model of Granular Materials," Caltech Report C3P-890, in D. W. Walker and Q. F. Stout (eds.), *The Fifth Distributed Memory Computing Conference,* April 9–12, Charleston, S.C. Los Alamitos, Calif.: IEEE Computer Society Press, 1990. Vol. 1, pp. 522–529.

108. T. C. Hartrum and B. J. Donlan, "Hypersim: Distributed Discrete-Event Simulation on an iPSC," in G. C. Fox (ed.), *Proceedings of the Third Conference on Hypercube Concurrent Computers and Applications.* New York: ACM Press, 1988. Vol. 1, pp. 745–747.

109. F. Hayot, M. Mandal, and P. Sadayappan, "Implementation and Performance of a Binary Lattice Gas Algorithm on Parallel Processor Systems," Technical report, Ohio State University, 1987.

110. M. T. Heath (ed.), *Proceedings of the First Hypercube Conference, Hypercube Multiprocessors,* August 26–27, 1985, Knoxville, Tenn. Philadelphia: SIAM, 1986.

111. M. T. Heath (ed.), *Proceedings of the Second Hypercube Conference, Hypercube Multiprocessors,* Knoxville, Tenn., September 29–October 1, 1986. Philadelphia: SIAM, 1987.

112. A. J. G. Hey, "Concurrent Supercomputing in Europe," in D. W. Walker and Q. F. Stout (eds.), *The Fifth Distributed Memory Computing Conference,* April 9–12, Charleston, S.C. Los Alamitos, Calif.: IEEE Computer Society Press, 1990. Vol. 2, pp. 630–646.

113. A. J. G. Hey, "Practical Parallel Processing with Transputers," in G. C. Fox (ed.), *Proceedings of the Third Conference on Hypercube Concurrent Computers and Applications.* New York: ACM Press, 1988. Vol. 1, pp. 115–121.

114. D. Hillis, "The Connection Machine," *Scientific American,* page 108, June 1987.

115. D. Hillis and J. Barnes, "Programming a Highly Parallel Computer," *Nature,* 326:27, 1987.

116. D. Hillis and G. Steele, "Data Parallel Algorithms," *Communications of ACM,* 29:1170, 1986.

117. P. G. Hipes and A. Kuppermann, "Gauss-Jordan Inversion with Pivoting on the Caltech Mark II Hypercube," Caltech Report C3P-578, in G. C. Fox (ed.), *The Third Conference on Hypercube Concurrent Computers and Applications.* New York: ACM Press, January 1988. Vol. 2, pp. 1621–1634.

118. P. Hipes, T. Mattson, M. Wu, and A. Kuppermann, "Chemical Reaction Dynamics: Integration of Coupled Sets of Ordinary Differential Equations on the Caltech Hypercube," Caltech Report C3P-570, in G. C. Fox (ed.), *The Third Conference on Hypercube Concurrent Computers and Applications.* New York: ACM Press, January 1988. Vol. 2, pp. 1051–1061.

119. A. Ho and W. Furmanski, "Pattern Recognition by Neural Network Model on Hypercubes," Caltech Report C3P-528, in G. C. Fox (ed.), *The Third Conference on Hypercube Concurrent Computers and Applications.* New York: ACM Press, January 1988. Vol. 2, pp. 1011–1021.

120. R. Hockney, "The $n_{1/2}$ Method of Algorithm Analysis," in B. Engquist and T. Smedsaas (eds.), *PDE Software: Modules, Interfaces, and Systems.* Elsevier, 1984. P. 429.

121. I. C. F. Ipsen and E. R. Jessup, "Two Methods for Solving the Symmetric Tridiagonal Eigenvalue Problem on the Hypercube," in M. T. Heath (ed.), *Hypercube Multiprocessors.* Philadelphia: SIAM 1987. Pp. 627–638.

122. J. Jaja (ed.), *The Third Symposium on the Frontiers of Massively Parallel Computation,* Proceedings of Frontiers '90, University of Maryland, College Park, Md. IEEE Computer Society Press, October 1990.

123. D. Jefferson, B. Beckman, L. Blume, M. Diloreto, P. Hontalas, P. Reiher, K. Sturdevant, J. Tupman, J. Wedel, F. Wieland, and H. Younger, "The Status of the Time Warp Operating System," Caltech Report C3P-627, in G. C. Fox (ed.), *The Third Conference on Hypercube Concurrent Computers and Applications.* New York: ACM Press, January 1988. Vol. 1, pp. 738–744.

124. D. W. Jensen and D. A. Reed, "A Performance Analysis Exemplar: Parallel Ray Tracing," *Concurrency: Practice and Experience,* 1992.

125. K. Joe, Y. Mori, and S. Miyake, "Construction of a Large-Scale Neural Network," *Concurrency: Practice and Experience,* 2(2):79–107, June 1990.

126. M. A. Johnson, "Concurrent Computation and Its Application to the Study of Melting in Two Dimensions," Caltech Report C3P-268, PhD thesis, California Institute of Technology, 1986.

127. J. P. Jones, "A Concurrent On-Board Vision System for a Mobile Robot," in G. C. Fox (ed.), *Proceedings of the Third Conference on Hypercube Concurrent Computers and Applications.* New York: ACM Press, 1988. Vol. 2, pp. 1022–1032.

128. R. A. Kamin and G. B. Adams, "Fast Fourier Transform Algorithm Design and Tradeoffs on the CM-2," in H. D. Simon (ed.), *Proceedings of the Conference on Scientific Applications of the Connection Machine,* September 12–14, 1988. Teaneck, N.J. World Scientific Publishing, 1989. P. 134.

129. W. J. Karplus (ed.), *The BBN Advanced Computer Butterfly Parallel Processor: A MIMD Computer for Simulation of Complex Systems,* Proceedings of the Third Conference on Multiprocessors and Array Processors, Simulation Series. San Diego: Society for Computer Simulation, 1987. Vol. 18, no. 2.

130. L. Keppenne, M. Ghil, G. C. Fox, J. W. Flower, A. Kolawa, P. N. Papaccio, J. J. Rosati, J. F. Shepanski, F. G. Spadaro, and J. O. Dickey, "Parallel Processing Applied to Climate Modeling," Technical Report SCCS-22, Syracuse University, November 1990.

131. D. J. Kuck, E. S. Davidson, D. H. Lawrie, and A. H. Sameh, "Parallel Supercomputing Today and the Cedar Approach," *Science*, 231:967, 1986.

132. P. Kunz, "Use of Emulating Processors in High Energy Physics," *Physical Science*, 23:492, 1981.

133. G. B. Lamont and D. J. Shakley, "Parallel Expert System Search Techniques for a Real-Time Application," in G. C. Fox (ed.), *Proceedings of the Third Conference on Hypercube Concurrent Computers and Applications*. New York: ACM Press, 1988. Vol. 2, pp. 1352–1359.

134. P. Li and Y.-W. Tung, "Parallel Sorting on Symult 2010," in D. W. Walker and Q. F. Stout (eds.), *The Fifth Distributed Memory Computing Conference*, April 9–12, Charleston, S.C., Caltech Report C3P-901. Los Alamitos, Calif.: IEEE Computer Society Press, 1990. Vol. 1, pp. 224–229.

135. P. C. Liewer, V. K. Decyk, J. D. Dawson, and G. C. Fox, "A Universal Concurrent Algorithm for Plasma Particle-in-Cell Simulation Codes," Caltech Report C3P-562, in G. C. Fox (ed.), *The Third Conference on Hypercube Concurrent Computers and Applications*. New York: ACM Press, January 1988. Vol. 2, pp. 1101–1107.

136. P. C. Liewer, V. K. Decyk, J. M. Dawson, and Lembège, "Numerical Studies of Electron Dynamics in Oblique Quasi-Perpendicular Collisionless Shock Waves," Technical Report C3P-964, Jet Propulsion Laboratory/California Institute of Technology, 1991, *Journal of Geophysical Research*, A6:9455–9465, 1991.

137. X. Lin, T. F. Chan, and W. J. Karplus, "The Fast Hartley Transform on the Hypercube Multiprocessors," in G. C. Fox (ed.), *Proceedings of the Third Conference on Hypercube Concurrent Computers and Applications*, New York: ACM Press, 1988. Vol. 2, pp. 1451–1454.

138. R. P. Ma, F. S. Tsung, and M. M-H., "A Dynamic Load Balancer for a Parallel Branch and Bound Algorithm," in G. C. Fox (ed.), *Proceedings of the Third Conference on Hypercube Concurrent Computers and Applications*. New York: ACM Press, 1988. Vol. 2, pp. 1505–1513.

139. V. K. Madisetti and D. G. Messerschmitt, "Seismic Migration Algorithms on Parallel Computers," in G. C. Fox (ed.), *Proceedings of the Third Conference on Hypercube Concurrent Computers and Applications*. New York: ACM Press, 1988. Vol. 2, pp. 1180–1186.

140. E. Marinari, "The APE Computer and Lattice Gauge Theory," in R. Burk, K. H. Mutter, and K. Schilling (eds.), *Proceedings of the Wuppertal Workshop on Lattice Gauge Theory*. New York: Plenum Press, 1986.

141. K. K. Mathur and S. L. Johnsson, "The Finite Element Method on a Data Parallel Computing System," *International Journal of High-Speed Computing*, 1(1):29–44, May 1989.

142. S. Mattisson, "CONCISE, A Concurrent Circuit Simulation Program," PhD thesis, Department of Applied Electronics, Lund Institute of Technology, Sweden, 1986.

143. S. Mattisson, L. Peterson, A. Skjellum, and C. L. Seitz, "Circuit Simulation on a Hypercube," in J. L. Gustafson (ed.), *The Proceedings of the Fourth Conference on Hypercubes, Concurrent Computers and Applications*. Los Altos, Calif.: Golden Gate Enterprises, March 1989. Pp. 1297–1302.

144. O. A. McBryan, "Connection Machine Application Performance," in H. D. Simon (ed.), *Proceedings of the Conference on Scientific Applications of the Connection Machine*, September 12–14, 1988. Teaneck, N.J.: World Scientific Publishing, 1989.

145. D. L. Meier, K. L. Cloud, J. C. Horvath, L. D. Allan, W. H. Hammond, and H. A. Maxfield, "A General Framework for Complex Time-Driven Simulations on Hypercubes," Caltech Report C3P-960, in D. W. Walker and Q. F. Stout (eds.), *The Fifth Distributed Memory Computing Conference*, I, April 9–12, Charleston, S.C. Los Alamitos, Calif.: IEEE Computer Society Press, 1990. Vol. 1, pp. 117–121.

146. P. Messina, C. F. Baillie, E. W. Felten, P. G. Hipes, D. W. Walker, R. D. Williams, W. Pfeiffer, A. Alagar, A. Kamrath, R. H. Leary, and J. Rogers, "Benchmarking Advanced Architecture Computers," Caltech Report C3P-712b, *Concurrency: Practice and Experience,* 2(3):195–256, 1990.

147. R. Mills (ed.), *The Second Symposium on the Frontiers of Massively Parallel Computation.* Fairfax, Va.: IEEE Computer Society Press, October 1988.

148. S. M. Müller, "A Method to Parallelize Tridiagonal Solvers," in D. W. Walker and Q. F. Stout (eds.), *The Fifth Distributed Memory Computing Conference,* April 9–12, Charleston, S.C. Los Alamitos, Calif.: IEEE Computer Society Press, 1990. Vol. 1, pp. 340–345.

149. J. N. Newman and P. D. Sclavounos, "The Computation of Wave Loads on Large Offshore Structures," paper given at Conference on the Behavior of Offshore Structures, June 1988, Trondheim.

150. M. G. Norman, "A Three-Dimensional Image Processing Program for a Parallel Computer," Master of Science thesis, Department of Artificial Intelligence, University of Edinburgh, 1987.

151. F. Ozguner, C. Aykanat, and O. Khalid, "Logic Fault Simulation on a Vector Hypercube Multiprocessor," in G. C. Fox (ed.), *Proceedings of the Third Conference on Hypercube Concurrent Computers and Applications.* New York: ACM Press, 1988. Vol. 2, pp. 1108–1113.

152. R. P. Pargas and D. E. Wooster, "Branch-and-Bound Algorithms on a Hypercube," in G. C. Fox (ed.), *Proceedings of the Third Conference on Hypercube Concurrent Computers and Applications.* New York: ACM Press, 1988. Vol. 2, pp. 1514–1519.

153. G. S. Pawley, C. F. Baillie, E. Tenenbaum, and W. Celmaster, "The BBN Butterfly Used to Simulate a Molecular Liquid," Caltech Report C3P-529, *Parallel Computing,* 11:321–329, 1989.

154. G. S. Pawley and M. T. Dove, "A Molecular Dynamics Simulation Study of the Orientationally Disordered Phase of Sulphur Hexafluoride," *Journal of Physics,* 17:6851, 1984.

155. G. S. Pawley and G. W. Thomas, "Computer Simulation of the Plastic-to-Crystalline Phase Transition in SF_6," *Physical Review Letters,* 48:410, 1982.

156. J. Peterson, E. Chow, and H. Madan, "A High-Speed Message-Driven Communication Architecture," Caltech Report C3P-628, in *The International Conference on Supercomputing,* July 4–8, St. Malo, France. New York: Association for Computing Machinery, July 1988, pp. 355–366.

157. J. L. Pfaltz, S. H. Son, and J. C. French, "ADAMS Interface Language," in G. C. Fox (ed.), *Proceedings of the Third Conference on Hypercube Concurrent Computers and Applications.* New York: ACM Press, 1988. Vol. 2, pp. 1382–1389.

158. F. Pollara, "Concurrent Viterbi Algorithm with Trace-Back," Caltech Report C3P-462, *Advanced Algorithms and Architectures for Signal Processing,* 696:204, 1986.

159. D. J. Pritchard, C. R. Askew, D. B. Carpenter, I. Glendinning, A. J. G. Hey, and D. A. Nicole, "Practical Parallelism Using Transputer Arrays," in J. W. de Bakker, A. J. Nijman, and P. C. Treleaven (eds.), *Lecture Notes in Computer Science.* New York: Springer-Verlag, 1987. Pp. 278–294.

160. D. J. Pritchard and C. J. Scott (eds.), *Applications of Transputers 2.* IOS Press, July 1990.

161. M. J. Quinn and P. J. Hatcher, "Data-Parallel Programming on Multicomputers," *IEEE Software,* pages 69–76, September 1990.

162. R. Renault and J. Petersen, "Evaluation of a Vector Hypercube for Seismic Modelling," in G. C. Fox (ed.), *Proceedings of the Third Conference on Hypercube Concurrent Computers and Applications.* New York: ACM Press, 1988. Vol. 2, pp. 1187–1192.

163. P. Van Renterghem, "Transputers for Industrial Applications," *Concurrency: Practice and Experience,* 1(2):135–169, December 1989.

164. J. Salmon, "Parallel Hierarchical N-Body Methods," Caltech Report C3P-966, PhD thesis, California Institute of Technology, December 1990.

165. J. Salmon, S. Callahan, J. Flower, and A. Kolawa, "MOOSE: A Multi-Tasking Operating System for Hypercubes," Caltech Report C3P-586, in G. C. Fox (ed.), *The Third Conference on Hypercube Concurrent Computers and Applications.* New York: ACM Press, January 1988. Vol. 1, pp. 391–396.

166. J. Salmon, P. Quinn, and M. Warren, "Using Parallel Computers for Very Large N-Body Simulations: Shell Formation Using 180K Particles," Caltech Report C3P-780b, in A. Toomre and R. Wielen (eds.), *Proceedings of the Heidelberg Conference on the Dynamics and Interactions of Galaxies.* New York: Springer-Verlag, 1989.

167. K. Schwan, W. Bo, B. Blake, and J. Gawkowski, "OS Primitives for the Implementation of Distributed Objects in Multicomputers: Experimentation with a Parallel Branch-and-Bound Algorithm," *Concurrency: Practice and Experience,* 1(2):191–218, December 1989.

168. K. Schwan, J. Gawkowski, and B. Blake, "Process and Work-Load Migration for a Parallel Branch-and-Bound Algorithm on a Hypercube Multiprocessor," in G. C. Fox (ed.), *Proceedings of the Third Conference on Hypercube Concurrent Computers and Applications.* New York: ACM Press, 1988. Vol. 2, pp. 1520–1530.

169. D. S. Scott, E. Castro-Leon, and E. J. Kushner, "Solving Very Large Dense Systems of Linear Equations on the iPSC/860," in D. W. Walker and Q. F. Stout (eds.), *The Fifth Distributed Memory Computing Conference,* April 9–12, Charleston, S.C. Los Alamitos, Calif.: IEEE Computer Society Press, 1990. Vol. 1, pp. 288–290.

170. S. R. Seidel and W. L. George, "Binsorting on Hypercubes with d-Port Communication," in G. C. Fox (ed.), *Proceedings of the Third Conference on Hypercube Concurrent Computers and Applications.* New York: ACM Press, 1988. Vol. 2, pp. 1455–1461.

171. C. L. Seitz, W. C. Athas, C. M. Flaig, A. J. Martin, J. Seizovic, C. S. Steele, and W.-K. Su, "The Architecture and Programming of the Ametek Series 2010 Multicomputer," in G. C. Fox (ed.), *Proceedings of the Third Conference on Hypercube Concurrent Computers and Applications.* New York: ACM Press, 1988. Vol. 1, pp. 33–36.

172. H. D. Simon (ed.), *Proceedings of the 1988 International Conference on Scientific Applications of the Connection Machine,* Teaneck, N.J.: World Scientific Publishing Co., September 1989.

173. A. Skjellum, "Concurrent Dynamic Simulation: Multicomputer Algorithms Research Applied to Ordinary Differential-Algebraic Process Systems in Chemical Engineering," Caltech Report C3P-940, PhD thesis, California Institute of Technology, July 1990.

174. A. Skjellum and M. Morari, "Concurrent DASSL: Applied to Dynamic Distillation Column Simulation," Caltech Report C3P-892, in D. W. Walker and Q. F. Stout (eds.), *The Fifth Distributed Memory Computing Conference,* April 9–12, Charleston, S.C. Los Alamitos, Calif.: IEEE Computer Society Press, 1990. Vol. 1, pp. 595–604.

175. A. Skjellum, M. Morari, and S. Mattisson, "Waveform Relaxation for Concurrent Dynamic Simulation of Distillation Columns," Caltech Report C3P-588, in G. C. Fox (ed.), *The Third Conference on Hypercube Concurrent Computers and Applications.* New York: ACM Press, January 1988. Vol. 2, pp. 1062–1071.

176. J. Sochacki, P. O'Leary, C. Bennett, R. E. Ewing, and R. C. Sharpley, "Seismic Modeling and Inversion on the NCUBE," in D. W. Walker and Q. F. Stout (eds.), *The Fifth Distributed Memory Computing Conference,* April 9–12, Charleston, S.C. Los Alamitos, Calif.: IEEE Computer Society Press, 1990. Vol. 1, pp. 530–535.

177. C. B. Stunkel, W. K. Fuchs, D. C. Rudolph, and D. A. Reed, "Linear Optimization: A Case Study in Performance Analysis," in J. L. Gustafson (ed.), *The Proceedings of the Fourth Conference on Hypercubes, Concurrent Computers and Applications.* Los Altos, Calif.: Golden Gate Enterprises, March 1989. Pp. 265–268.

178. C. B. Stunkel and D. A. Reed, "Hypercube Implementation of the Simplex Algorithm," in G. C. Fox (ed.), *Proceedings of the Third Conference on Hypercube Concurrent Computers and Applications.* New York: ACM Press, 1988. Vol. 2, pp. 1473–1482.

179. N. Toomarian, "A Concurrent Neural Network Algorithm for the Traveling Salesman Problem," in G. C. Fox (ed.), *Proceedings of the Third Conference on Hypercube Concurrent Computers and Applications.* New York: ACM Press, 1988. Vol. 2, pp. 1483–1490.

180. U. Trottenberg, "On the SUPRENUM Machine," in C. Polychronoupolos (ed.), *ICS 87 International Conference on Supercomputing*. New York: Springer-Verlag, 1987.

181. E. F. Van de Velde and H. B. Keller, "The Design of a Parallel Multigrid Algorithm," Caltech Report C3P-406, in L. Kartashev and S. Kartashev (eds.), *Proceedings of the Second International Conference on Supercomputing at Santa Clara*. St. Petersburg, Fla.: International Supercomputing Institute, 1987.

182. E. F. Van de Velde and H. B. Keller, "The Parallel Solution of Nonlinear Elliptic Equations," Caltech Report C3P-447, in A. K. Noor (ed.), *Parallel Computations and Their Impact on Mechanics*, ASME, 1987. Pp. 127–153.

183. D. W. Walker and G. C. Fox, "A Portable Programming Environment for Multiprocessors," Caltech Report C3P-496, in R. Vichnevetsky, P. Borne, and J. Vignes (eds.), *12th IMACS World Congress*. Paris, France: IMACS, July 1988. Pp. 475–478.

184. D. W. Walker and Q. F. Stout (eds.), *The Fifth Distributed Memory Computing Conference*. Los Alamitos, Calif.: IEEE Computer Society Press, 1990.

185. D. J. Wallace, "Numerical Simulation on the ICL Distributed Array Processor," *Physical Rep.*, 103:191, 1984.

186. D. J. Wallace, "Scientific Computation on SIMD and MIMD Machines," *Philosophical Transactions of the Royal Society of London*, 326, 1988.

187. D. Wallace, K. Bowler, and R. Kenway, "The Edinburgh Concurrent Supercomputer: Project and Applications," in L. P. Kartashev and S. I. Kartashev (eds.), *Proceedings of the Third International Conference on Supercomputing*, May 15–20, Boston, Massachusetts. St. Petersburg, Fla.: International Supercomputing Institute, 1988.

188. D. J. Wallace and M. G. Norman, "Theory, Application and Technology Transfer in the Edinburgh Parallel Computing Center," in *Proceedings of the International Conference on Parallel Computing: Achievements, Problems and Prospects*, Anacapri, Italy, June 3–9, 1990; to be published in the special issue of *Concurrency: Practice and Experience*.

189. D. L. Waltz, "Applications of the Connection Machine," *IEEE Computer*, 85, 1987.

190. D. Waltz, C. Stanfill, S. Smith, and R. Thau, "Very Large Database Applications of the Connection Machine Systems," Technical Report, Cambridge, Mass.: Thinking Machines Corporation, 1987.

191. H. Wang, P. W. Dew, and J. A. Webb, "Implementation of Apply on a Transputer Array," *Concurrency: Practice and Experience*, 3(1):43–54, February 1991.

192. L. V. Warren, "Graphics Techniques in Concurrent Simulation," in G. C. Fox (ed.), *The Third Conference on Hypercube Concurrent Computers and Applications*, Caltech Report C3P-600. New York: ACM Press, January 1988. Vol. 1, pp. 772–785.

193. M. Warren and J. Salmon, "An O(N Log N) Hypercube N-Body Integrator," Caltech Report C3P-593. in G. C. Fox (ed.), *The Third Conference on Hypercube Concurrent Computers and Applications*. New York: ACM Press, January 1988. Vol. 2, pp. 971–975.

194. D. A. Weissbein, J. F. Mangus, and M. W. George, "Solution of the 3-D Euler Equations for the Flow about a Fighter Aircraft Configuration Using a Hypercube Parallel Processor," in G. C. Fox (ed.), *Proceedings of the Third Conference on Hypercube Concurrent Computers and Applications*. New York: ACM Press, 1988. Vol. 2, pp. 1127–1136.

195. B. T. Werner, "A Steady-State Model of Wind-Blown Sand Transport," Caltech Report C3P-971, *Journal of Geology*, 98:1–17, 1990.

196. B. T. Werner and P. K. Haff, "Dynamical Simulations of Granular Materials Using the Caltech Hypercube," Caltech Report C3P-612, in G. C. Fox (ed.), *The Third Conference on Hypercube Concurrent Computers and Applications*. New York: ACM Press, January 1988. Vol. 2, pp. 1313–1318.

197. F. Wieland, L. Hawley, and L. Blume, "An Empirical Study of Data Partitioning and Replication in Parallel Simulation," Caltech Report C3P-907, in D. W. Walker and Q. F. Stout (eds.), *The Fifth Distributed Memory Computing Conference*, April 9–12, Charleston, S.C. Los Alamitos, Calif.: IEEE Computer Society Press, 1990. Vol. 2, pp. 915–921.

198. F. Wieland, L. Hawley, and A. Feinberg, "Implementing a Distributed Combat Simulation on the Time Warp Operating System," Caltech Report C3P-601, in G. C. Fox (ed.), *The Third Conference on Hypercube Concurrent Computers and Applications.* New York: ACM Press, January 1988. Vol. 2, pp. 1269–1276.

199. F. Wieland, L. Hawley, A. Feinberg, M. DiLoreto, L. Blume, J. Ruffles, P. Reiher, B. Beckman, P. Hontalas, S. Bellenot, and D. Jefferson, "The Performance of a Distributed Combat Simulation with the Time Warp Operating System," Caltech Report C3P-798, *Concurrency: Practice and Experience,* 1(1):35–50, 1989.

200. D. Wiener, Private communication, 1987.

201. S. Wolfram, *Theory and Applications of Cellular Automata.* World Scientific Publishing, 1986.

202. Y.-S. M. Wu, S. A. Cuccaro, P. G. Hipes, and A. Kuppermann, "Quantum Mechanical Reactive Scattering Using a High-Performance Distributed-Memory Parallel Computer," Technical Report C3P-860, California Institute of Technology, January 1990. Accepted for publication in *Chemical Physics Letters.*

CHAPTER 18
NEURAL NETWORK COMPUTING

Pietro G. Morasso

Dipartimento di Informatica, Sistemistica, e Telematica
Università di Genova, Italy

18.1 INTRODUCTION

Neurocomputing is an information processing technology which has been inspired by the neural and cognitive sciences; it aims at reproducing the microstructure of human cognition as a parallel process performed by a distributed architecture, still preserving the sequential macrostructure. While in a conventional computing environment, problems are represented and solved by intricate algorithms that operate on complex data structures, in a neurocomputing system relaxation and adaptation are the relevant paradigms. In other words, neurocomputers can be considered as adaptable dynamic systems that operate in a highly parallel way on distributed representations. They are best at doing some of the things that biological systems are good at, such as pattern classification and functional synthesis in an adaptive way.

The key point is indeed learning, i.e., the ability to exploit some kind of measurement of similarity or dissimilarity for changing the behavior of the network. Learning is close to impossible for traditional algorithmic computation because it is very difficult in general to assign the credits for the performance to the different instructions of an algorithm in order to change them. Neural network architecture, on the contrary, is sufficiently simple computationally for formulating general credit assignment methods, the heart of neurocomputing.

On the other hand, there are very well-defined problems for which algorithmic or logic solutions are well established, even if very complex, and in those cases it is really worthless, at least from an engineering point of view, to relearn them, with approximations and after a long training procedure. This necessarily will lead to techniques for integrating neural with traditional computing modules, as regards both the hardware and software aspects. The available tools are still primitive, and this is a significant obstacle for the dissemination of engineering applications. But a greater obstacle, perhaps, is of a cultural nature, because engineering problem solving cannot help relying on a consistent degree of creative thinking, and this is constrained by the qualitative paradigms that are culturally dominant. There is no question that the conventional wisdom in the field is strongly biased in favor of traditional algorithmic reasoning. Therefore, the purpose of this chapter is to stimulate the imagination of creative engineers who are new to the concepts of neurocomputing. The presentation is sufficiently mathematical, in order to transmit the feeling of how things work, without going into too much detail in any specific model. The collection of models presented in the following is certainly not complete because the field is growing so rapidly, but the major computational ideas, potentially useful for engineering application, are presented. The reader may refer, for reviews from different viewpoints, to the works of Lippmann [62], Hecht-Nielsen [30], Hinton [32], Carpenter [10], and Simpson [96] among others.

The basic components of neural network models are initially presented (processing elements, patterns of connections, learning, memorization); then the basic computational paradigms are analyzed: association (multilayer networks with back propagation), relaxation (Hopfield networks and simulated annealing), and self-organization (with different versions of the competitive learning idea). Finally, some applications in the robotic and control area are examined.

18.2 THE BASIC COMPONENTS OF NEURAL NETWORK MODELS

Neural networks are collections of a (large) number of interconnected *processing elements* (PEs) that transform patterns; processing is articulated in two main neurodynamic phases: *learning* and *recall*.

18.2.1 Processing Elements

PEs are intended to play the role, in a neural network, of the neurons in the brain. Different types of PEs are used, with continuous-time as well as discrete-time models:

Continuous model $\quad\quad dy/dt = f(y(t), \mathbf{x}(t), I(t); \mathbf{w}, \theta)$

Discrete model $\quad\quad y(k + 1) = y(k) + g(y(k), \mathbf{x}(k), I(k); \mathbf{w}, \theta)$

These are characterized by variables ($\mathbf{x}, I, y$), adaptable parameters ($\mathbf{w}, \theta$), and an activation function (f or g). Here y is the output variable (the *firing rate* of the unit), $\mathbf{x}$ is the array of input variables coming from the other units, I is an external input, $\mathbf{w}$ is a set of adaptable *weight* parameters that play the role of synapses in the biological neurons, and θ is an adaptable threshold parameter (Fig. 18.1). The exact functional structure of the activation (or transfer) functions f or g is not critical for most architectures. However, the following qualitative requirements are satisfied in most network models:

- *Selectivity.* This means that the unit must perform some kind of pattern matching between the input vector $\mathbf{x}$ and the stored parameter vector $\mathbf{w}$. This is achieved by means of an *input operator* which in most cases is linear and produces an internal or net *activation level* $a(t) = \mathbf{w}^T\mathbf{x}(t)$, where $a(t)$ is analogous to the membrane potential of biological neurons resulting from the superimposition of the different synaptic currents. In some models, the input operator is meant to perform a measurement of distance between $\mathbf{x}$ and $\mathbf{w}$, such as the euclidean distance, the Hamming distance, or the cosine of the angle between the two vectors (the scalar product of the normalized vectors).

- *Monotonicity.* This means that the influence of each input signal on the output of the PE must be uniformly excitatory or inhibitory, irrespective of the values of the other inputs.

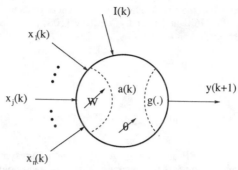

FIGURE 18.1 Generic processing element of a neural network: x's are the internal inputs, I is the external input, y is the output, a is the activity level, W and θ are adaptable parameters, and g is the discrimination function.

- *Bounded activity.* This implies a nonlinearity of the transfer function that is analogous to the saturation of the firing rate of biological neurons as a function of the membrane potential and is useful for the representational power of the network and for the dynamic stability. In accordance with this requirement, as well as the previous one, several types of discriminators (also called *squashing* or *quenching* functions) have been used in practice:

1. Binary threshold or unit step function: $y = U(x)$
2. Linear ramp with saturation or hard limit: $y = R(x)$
3. Sigmoid: $y = \sigma(x) = 1/(1 + e^{-x})$
4. Hyperbolic tangent: $y = h(x) = (e^x - e^{-x})/(e^x + e^{-x})$
5. Gaussian: $y = G(x)$

The asymptotes, determined by the squashing function, can be either balanced $(-1, +1)$ or unbalanced $(0, +1)$; in any case, the state of a network is constrained inside a hypercube.

Different types of PEs are defined by a combination of an *input operator* with a *discriminant operator,* in the context of a differential or difference equation (continuous versus discrete models). The following list is a representative sample of models:

- *Linear units*

$$y(k + 1) = \sum_j w_j x_j(k)$$

These units have been used particularly in associative networks.

- *Linear threshold units*

$$y(k + 1) = U(a(k))$$

$$a(k) = \sum_j w_j x_j(k) - \theta + I$$

where $a(k)$ is the current *activation level* of the unit. These units were originally studied by McCulloch and Pitts [68] and later by Widrow [108], who called them *adalines* (adaptive linear elements).

- *Semilinear units*

$$\frac{dy}{dt} = a((t) - \gamma(y(t)))$$

$$a(t) = \sum_j w_j x_j(t) - \theta + I$$

This model considers the PE as a leaky integrator of the presynaptic signals with a nonlinear "loss term" where γ is the inverse function of a sigmoid. At steady state or assuming that the activation $a(t)$ changes much more slowly than the internal dynamics, the differential equation is reduced to the following difference equation:

$$y(k + 1) = \sigma(a(k))$$

$$a(k) = \sum_j w_j x_j(k) - \theta + I$$

The term θ loses the meaning of threshold and is usually referred to as *bias*.

- *Shunting units*

$$\frac{dy}{dt} = a(t) - \alpha y(t)$$

$$a(t) = [y_{\text{high}} - y(t)]\sum_j w_j^e x_j(t) + [y(t) - y_{\text{low}}]\sum_k w_k^h x_k(t)$$

In this model [25] a leaky integration of the input signals is performed as in the previous case, but the nonlinear term (that quenches the output in the $<y_{\text{low}}, y_{\text{high}}>$ range) is a shunting (or blocking) action on the input signal, with different asymptotes for the excitatory (w_j^e) and inhibitory (w_k^h) synapses. The model is equivalent to the Hodgkin-Huxley equations of the electrical activity of the neuronal membrane.

- *Sigma-pi units*

$$y(k + 1) = \sigma(a(k))$$

$$a(k) = \sum_i w_i \prod_k x_{ik}$$

These units provide multiplicative connections that allow, e.g., one unit to *gate* another, a phenomenon that occurs in neurobiology as presynaptic inhibition.

- *Cognitron units*

$$y(k + 1) = R(a(k))$$

$$a(k) = \frac{1 + e}{1 + h} - 1$$

where the activation level $a(k)$ is computed by balancing the total excitation $e = \sum_j w_j^e x_j$ (the connection weights are only positive) with the total inhibition

$h = \theta\sum_j x_j^2$. In these units, which have been proposed by Fukushima [18] for pattern recognition applications, the output measures the degree of similarity between the input pattern and the weight pattern, normalized with respect to the energy of the input pattern.

- *Winner-takes-all units*

$$y_i = \begin{cases} 1 \\ 0 \end{cases} \quad i = i_{\text{res}}$$

otherwise

$$a_i(k) = \sum_j w_{ij} x_j(k)$$

$$i_{\text{res}} = \max_i a_i(k)$$

where i_{res} identifies the *resonant* unit. A variant of this behavior is given by the *bubble* function, where the winning set is extended to a neighborhood of i_{res}.

- *Radial-basis function units*

$$y(k + 1) = e^{-a(k)}$$

$$a(k) = \sum_i \frac{(x_i - \theta)^2}{2\sigma^2}$$

This is a recent model [71, 85] that uses a gaussian transfer function with a quadratic input operator. Since the discriminator has two parameters (the bias and the variance) instead of one parameter, as in the case of the sigmoid, mappings that require two hidden layers of sigmoid PEs can sometimes be accomplished by a single layer of PEs of this kind.

The continuous-time models are reduced to a discrete form if we assume that the network is sampled in some sense and the transients die out between one sample and the next. Discrete-time models can have a binary or graded response, depending on the type of transfer function: In binary models the state vector of a network can only jump from one vertex of the hypercube to another one, whereas in graded models the state vector can move continuously inside the hypercube. Another classification, as regards the dynamics of PEs, can be made between deterministic and probabilistic (or thermodynamic) models. In the latter case, the linear input operator can be followed by a stochastic discriminator, or alternatively a probabilistic term is added to the input operator before a deterministic discrimination. In both cases, the noise factor is usually modulated by a *temperature* parameter that is adapted during the learning process.

18.2.2 Connection Topology and Network Dynamics

A neural network is a collection of processing elements (or units or neurons) with an assigned pattern of connectivity. The state of the network is identified by the set of values of the output variables, which can be represented by means of a vector **Y**. The input variables of each unit may come from three sources: the output value of some unit, external input values, and threshold or bias signals. A collective vector **X** can be formed, and the corresponding connection topology can be represented by means of a connectivity

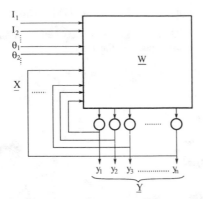

y_1 y_2 y_3 .... y_h
$\underbrace{}$
Y

FIGURE 18.2 Generic neural network. Here **W** is the matrix of connection from input set (external input vector **I**, bias parameter vector θ, and internal input vector **X**) to the output vector **Y**.

matrix **W** that stores the connection weights from each of the x's to each processing element (Fig. 18.2). The dynamics of the whole network, e.g., in the case of a discrete model with semilinear units, can be represented synthetically by the following equations:

$$A(k) = WX(k)$$

$$Y(k + 1) = \sigma(A(k))$$

where **A** is the array of internal activation levels of the PEs. The connectivity of the network is reflected in the structure of **W**.

The *short-term memory* (STM) of a network is stored in the y's, while the *long-term memory* (LTM) is stored in the w's. The PEs of a network are usually divided into three sets: input PEs, output PEs, and hidden PEs. In particular, the following models have been investigated in depth:

- Multilayer, feedforward networks
- Single-layer networks with symmetric recurrent connections
- Single-layer networks, topologically arranged
- Bilayer networks with feedforward/feedback connections
- Multilayer cooperative/competitive networks

Moreover, complex applications may be solved by means of composite architectures, i.e., networks of networks that can be formed in two ways: (1) direct interconnection of different networks and (2) recursive interconnection, in the sense that the PEs of a network are networks themselves (e.g., a relaxation network of multilayer networks). The dynamics of a network are determined by the pattern of connections. In a multilayer network, e.g., the input pattern is immediately propagated to the output layer through the hidden layer; in networks with symmetric connections, the behavior is a settling in an energy landscape, i.e., convergent dynamics. More complex dynamic behaviors have also been studied (oscillatory networks and chaotic networks), but the mathematical and heuristic tools for their analysis are still limited [35].

18.2.3 Learning

Learning is the process of adapting the connection weights **W** and the other adaptable parameters via experience, in order to optimize some performance criterion. Adaptive methods are not restricted to neural networks; indeed, several adaptive paradigms have been developed in signal processing, system identification, and optimal control, but most require computations to be performed in a highly centralized way, with an intricate program control flow. In contrast, parameter adaptation in neural networks is rather straightforward and can be carried out in a largely local way.

Early work on learning was done by Hebb [28], Rosenblatt [90, 91], Widrow and Hoff [109], Caianiello [9], Steinbuch [99], and Amari [2] among others. Two basic types of learning methods in neural networks can be distinguished: *associative* (or correlation type) learning and *reinforcement* learning (or feedback type). A typical example of the first method is *Hebb's rule,* which follows the studies by Hebb on brain plasticity and can be formulated qualitatively as follows: If a neuron N_i repeatedly and persistently participates in firing neuron N_j, then the synapse w_{ij} between N_i and N_j will be potentiated. A frequently adopted learning formula uses the instantaneous correlation between the input signal $x_i(t)$ and the output signal $y(t)$ as a reinforcement signal:

$$\Delta w_{ij} = \eta x_i y_j$$

where η is a learning rate coefficient. Grossberg [24] suggested to add a *forgetting term* $dw_{ij}/dt = \eta x_i y_j - w_{ij}$ to allow the weight to compute the long-term correlation of synaptic input and output. Different modifications of this scheme also have been studied. For example, a model proposed by Sutton and Barto [108] is based on the notion of eligibility of synaptic adaptation, i.e., the distinction between a process that opens temporal windows of possible synaptic adaptation, following a sustained activity of the presynaptic activity x_i, and another process that actually carries out the adaptation.

True reinforcement rules require some kind of performance measure of the neuron's behavior, i.e., some kind of feedback. For example, a typical example of a reinforcement paradigm is the *delta rule,* devised by Widrow and Hoff [109], or the equivalent perceptron convergence procedure [90, 91]

$$\Delta w_{ij} = \eta x_i \delta_j$$

where δ_j is the output error associated with a given input pattern.[†] In the simplest case (e.g., single-layer perceptrons), the error value is computed as the explicit difference between a target output value (provided by a supervising teacher) and the actual output value (guessed by the neuron); in more general cases (e.g., multilayer networks with hidden units), the error vector is estimated by propagation of the output error. It has been shown that applying the delta rule to a complex network implies the minimization of the output mean square error

$$E_{mse} = \sum_i (\hat{y}_i - y_i)^2$$

where $\hat{y}_i$ is the target value of the ith output PE. Other error functions have been investigated for reinforcement learning, such as the Kullback divergence [17, 34], a well-known measure in information theory:

$$E_{kd} = \sum_i \hat{y}_i \ln (\hat{y}_i/y_i)$$

Another example of reinforcement learning is provided by Klopf [50], who hypothesizes a goal-seeking behavior for all the neurons of a network. The goal, according to Klopf, is to maximize the total excitation of the neuron while minimizing the total inhibition, and this can be achieved by opening a time window after the generation of each action potential during which synapses can be potentiated.

Associative and reinforcement learning can be put in relation with two classical approaches studied by psychologists in the field of conditioning: *classical conditioning,* studied by Pavlov and Bekhterev, which is based on the correlation between conditioned and unconditioned stimuli, and *operant conditioning,* studied by Thorndike and Skinner, which is based on the explicit use of reward and punishment, i.e., a direct measure of performance.

[†]The difference is that in Widrow's adaline the error signal δ is computed before the output threshold, whereas in Rosenblatt's perceptron it is computed afterward.

An associative learning rule, which is used in self-organizing networks and is somehow midway between correlation and reinforcement learning, is the following one:

$$\Delta w_{ij} = \eta(x_i - w_{ij})y_j$$

This rule allows a processing element PE_j to become a sort of adaptive filter which gives a maximum response when the input vector $\mathbf{x}$ matches the vector of weight coefficients $\mathbf{w}_j$.

Since learning is described by difference or differential equations, it may be possible to think of it as a dynamic process: *adaptation dynamics,* to be distinguished from the dynamics of the network state vector, i.e., *activation dynamics.* Usually, to avoid very complex dynamic behavior, the two types of dynamics are kept separate in the sense that only one is operant at any time. However, there is debate about the usefulness of a combined dynamics, particularly for the recognition of nonstationary patterns [6].

18.3 COMPUTATIONAL PARADIGMS OF NEURAL NETWORKS

The collective behavior of neural networks allows us to store and recall data in a way which is fundamentally different from the traditional technique in von Neumann machines. We can distinguish three computational paradigms

- Association
- Relaxation
- Self-organization

from which most types of computational architectures can be developed. Several application domains naturally derive from the above-mentioned computational paradigms, considered singularly or in composite configurations: prediction, classification, data conceptualization, data filtering and/or compression, and optimization.

18.4 MEMORIZATION: CAM VERSUS RAM

In a conventional digital computer, memory is segregated from processing and data items are segregated from one another in a *random access memory* (RAM) that works as a lookup table: memory locations can store only one datum at a time and are accessed via unique numeric keys (their addresses). RAMs are fast, storage-efficient, and secure. But they also have serious drawbacks; they are passive devices and require complex and large data structures to be broken down into small pieces, losing intrinsic links. Moreover, RAMs lack the key feature of human memory, a basic ingredient of human intelligence, i.e., the ability to form *associations* among memory items of different complexity with some noise resistance. This implies, among other things, the ability of an associative memory to actively go from one internal representation to another, according to some measure of similarity, or to recover a complex representation from a portion of it.

Content-addressable memories (CAMs) are various formalizations of the associative memory concept. CAM models differ as regards the activation function, the learning methods, and other aspects but share a *holographic* representation. This means that in a CAM the different data are represented by the collective state of the same set of units, determined by the same set of parameters. The output of the CAM can be represented as an n-dimensional vector $\mathbf{y}$, and the purpose of the network is to store and recall a number of data items $(\mathbf{y}_1, \mathbf{y}_2, \ldots, \mathbf{y}_p)$ which may or may not be associated with keys $(\mathbf{x}_1, \mathbf{x}_2, \ldots, \mathbf{x}_p)$. Moreover, a feedback path from the output units to the CAM may or may not be present. If there is no feedback, the CAM is static, i.e., the key vector is immediately mapped into the output vector. If the feedback is present, the CAM is dynamic and its output vector follows a path before settling into a stable state, if existent; in other words, for dynamic CAMs stored data must be equilibrium patterns. In particular, if there is no key, the CAM can be defined as an autoassociative network that performs pattern completion. For example, if $\mathbf{y}$ represents images, then the recall of a stored image can be triggered by specifying a portion of it, setting the corresponding elements of $\mathbf{y}$ as initial conditions of the CAM, and allowing the dynamics of the network to fill in the gaps.

18.4.1 Linear Static CAMs

Early models of CAMs were linear and static [3, 51, 52, 78]. This means that each element of the output vector is simply computed as $y_j = \sum_i w_{ji} x_i$, or $\mathbf{y} = \mathbf{W}\mathbf{x}$ in vector form. The problem is to determine a set of connection weights, stored in the matrix $\mathbf{W}$, that allow us to recall a set of p output vectors from a corresponding set of keys. This is a problem of linear algebra that can also be solved by using Hebb's rule. Let us assume that the gain factor is 1; then the modification of the weight matrix with Hebb's rule, after presentation of the pattern $(\mathbf{x}_p, \mathbf{y}_p)$, is the correlation matrix $\Delta\mathbf{W}_p = \mathbf{y}_p \mathbf{x}_p^T$. If we add the contributions of all the associated pairs, we get the following weight matrix:

$$\mathbf{W} = \sum_p \mathbf{y}_p \mathbf{x}_p^T = \mathbf{Y}\mathbf{X}^T$$

where $\mathbf{X}$ and $\mathbf{Y}$ are two matrices whose columns are the input and output vectors of the training set. It is easy to see that this network enables a perfect recall of all the vectors of the training set if and only if the keys are orthonormal. Suppose, indeed, that we provide a key $\mathbf{x}_k$; then the extracted vector $\hat{\mathbf{y}}$ is equal to

$$\hat{\mathbf{y}} = \mathbf{W}\mathbf{x}_k = \mathbf{y}_k(\mathbf{x}_k^T \mathbf{x}_k) + \sum_{p \neq k} \mathbf{y}_p(\mathbf{x}_p^T \mathbf{x}_k)$$

The second part vanishes if the keys are orthogonal (i.e., the mutual scalar products are null), and the first part recovers the stored vector if each key is normal.

The orthonormality is not required if we use the delta rule while storing the same set of patterns. In this case, it is possible to see that we end up with the following weight matrix:

$$\mathbf{W} = \mathbf{Y}\mathbf{X}^+$$

where $\mathbf{X}^+$ is the pseudo-inverse matrix of $\mathbf{X}$ [75]. This guarantees perfect recall if the input keys are simply linearly independent and provides a minimum error solution if the keys are linearly dependent.

18.4.2 Relaxation CAMs

Relaxation CAMs are dynamic neural networks that are multistable, i.e., admit several equilibrium configurations; these can be used as distributed storage elements in association with a relaxation technique [13, 37, 38]. Relaxation CAMs admit a Lyapunov function (an energy landscape) which guarantees global stability, and their dynamics can be described as a descent in the energy landscape. Hopfield, in particular, noted an analogy with the behavior of spin glasses [98], a material which consists of atoms with an amorphous distribution of Ising spins and which can display pattern formation properties.

A *Hopfield network* (HN) has a single-layer architecture of PEs (Fig. 18.3) which can be either linear-threshold units (binary model) or semilinear units (graded model). In either case, a sufficient condition for the network dynamics to admit point attractors (convergent flow to stable states) is that the connections be symmetric and there be no autoconnections. In this hypothesis, it is indeed possible to verify that the following function of the state of the network (for the discrete model)

$$E = E(\mathbf{y}) = -\frac{1}{2}\sum_i\sum_j w_{ij}y_iy_j - \sum_i I_iy_i + \sum_i \theta_iy_i$$

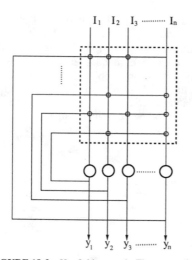

behaves as a potential-energy function; i.e., it can only decrease during relaxation, and this guarantees that the relaxation search will indeed terminate. Relaxation proceeds in an asynchronous way, according to a random sampling scheme, and the network jumps from one vertex to another of an n-dimensional hypercube, decreasing its energy E until it settles in a stable state.[†] In the continuous model, which can be implemented by a set of interconnected analog amplifiers, relaxation is equivalent to analog simulation and the state trajectory follows a continuous path contained in the same hypercube. These kinds of networks, when operated as CAMs, are usually trained by means of Hebb's rule, similarly to what we said for linear CAMs. Relaxation CAMs are more insensitive to noise in the recall phase because the stored patterns are point attractors. Moreover, orthogonality of the stored patterns is not strictly necessary, although there must be a sufficient Hamming distance. The storage capacity, which requires the energy landscape to have distinct wells for each stored pattern without spurious wells, is of the order of $N/\log N$ [69].

FIGURE 18.3 Hopfield network. The connection matrix is symmetric, and there are no recurrent connections.

Other examples of autoassociative networks are the *Hamming network* [62] and the *brain-state-in-a-box network* [3]. A heteroassociative network architecture that shares with HNs the relaxation dynamics and the symmetry of connections is the *bidirectional associative memory* (BAM) [55]. In this network, the purpose is to associate input patterns (**x**'s) applied to input PEs with output patterns (**y**'s) applied to output PEs. This is achieved by means of a connection matrix **M** from **x** to **y** and a symmetric set of connections $\mathbf{M}^T$ in the opposite direction. Hebb training is adopted in the usual way

---

[†]Considering the generic element of an HN, PE_j, the gradient of E with respect to y_j, that is, the *local field*, is $g_j = \partial E/\partial y_j = -\sum_i w_{ij}y_i - I_j + \theta_j$, and it is the opposite of the activity level of the PE: $g_j = -a_j$. Since $dE/dt = \sum_j dy_j/dt$, it follows that during relaxation $dE/dt = \leq 0$.

achieved by means of a connection matrix $\mathbf{M}$ from $\mathbf{x}$ to $\mathbf{y}$ and a symmetric set of connections $\mathbf{M}^T$ in the opposite direction. Hebb training is adopted in the usual way

$$\mathbf{M} = \sum_i \mathbf{x}_i^T \mathbf{y}_i$$

with regard to a set of input-output patterns. During recall, an interrogating input pattern $\mathbf{x}$ is set on the input PEs, and the BAM, following the Hopfield dynamics, will bounce it back and forth until equilibrium is reached (which is called *resonance*). At that point, the state of the output PEs gives the output pattern which is associated in the best way with the interrogating input pattern. New input-output associations can be added or deleted by adding or subtracting the corresponding correlation matrix to $\mathbf{M}$.

18.4.3 Representation of I/O Variables

The input-output variables of a neural network, which are directly linked with the problem we attempt to solve by their use, can be represented in either a localized or a distributed way. In the first case, there is a one-to-one correspondence between a variable and the activity of a PE. This is also called *rate coding* in neurophysiology, i.e., the idea that the modulation of the firing rate of neurons has a direct connection with some variable or parameter directly affecting behavior. For example, in the classic exclusive-or problem, the two input PEs and the output PE directly code the input/output binary variables; in many signal classification problems, a specific output PE is used for each class, and an input PE is associated with each sample of the signal (after appropriate preprocessing).

In a distributed representation, a population of PEs is used for coding a variable. In a typical scheme, sometimes called *value-unit coding* or *population coding,* the PEs are characterized by *tuning functions* that peak at a specific value of the variable and then die off more or less quickly (broad versus narrow tuning). According to this scheme, a variable is coded by the population activity and can be decoded by a weighted summation of the activities. The variable can either be monodimensional or multidimensional. A variation of this coding scheme, more easily adopted for scalar variables, is based on the idea of *recruitment,* which implies a distribution of thresholds to cover the range of the variable. Similar techniques have been conceived for representing integer numbers [102] by means of binary PEs.

18.5 ASSOCIATION: MULTILAYER FEEDFORWARD NETWORKS

Multilayer feedforward networks (MLNs) are general-purpose processing modules in neurocomputing architectures for performing associations of patterns. MLNs can approximate a very large class of functions, and effective learning procedures have been identified for training them. In an MLN the connections run only from one layer to the next, without loops or intralayer links, and this determines a specific structure of the connectivity matrix. With regard to the network equation

$$\mathbf{Y}(k + 1) = \sigma(\mathbf{W}\mathbf{X}(k))$$

let us suppose that $\mathbf{Y} = [y_1, y_2, \ldots, y_n]$ stores the set of the PE output variables, ordered from the first layer on, and $\mathbf{X} = [y_1, y_2, \ldots, y_n, b_1, b_2, \ldots, b_n, I_1, I_2, \ldots, I_m]$ stores the set of input variables, i.e., the same set of y's together with the threshold or bias values of each unit (b_i's) and the external input variables (I_k's). Then the $n \times (n + n + m)$ connectivity matrix $\mathbf{W}$ has the structure shown in Fig. 18.4.

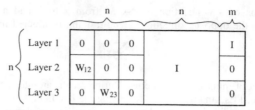

FIGURE 18.4   Connectivity matrix of a three-layer feedforward network. Here $\mathbf{W}_{12}$ and $\mathbf{W}_{23}$ are the connection submatrices from level 1 to level 2 and from level 2 to level 3, respectively; $\mathbf{I}$ is an identity submatrix.

18.5.1 Perceptrons

Classical perceptrons [90, 91] apply the early work with adalines to pattern recognition. A basic form of perceptron is a network with two layers of linear threshold units (an input layer and an output layer), and it can represent boolean functions or, more generally, classification functions if the threshold operator is taken away from the input PEs. For this kind of network it has been shown that if a function is representable at all with an appropriate number of units, then by the previously mentioned delta rule it can be found (perceptron convergence theorem). However, Minsky and Papert [70] demonstrated that two-layer perceptrons are incapable of representing simple functions such as the exclusive OR, and Fig. 18.5a shows why: The output PE operates as a linear discriminator in the input feature space (I_1, I_2), and the exclusive OR function must discriminate the (0, 0) and (1, 1) patterns from the (0, 1) and (1, 0) patterns, a clearly impossible task regardless of the choice of the free parameters (w_1, w_2, b). This objective, however, can be achieved by the conjunction of two discriminations (Fig. 18.5b), requiring an additional level of PEs.

In general, two-layer networks cannot classify concave sets, and additional layers are necessary [62]. The PEs in the first intermediate layer of a perceptron compute a linear discriminant function $y = U(\mathbf{w}^T \mathbf{x} - b)$ that divides the n-dimensional input vector space (feature space) into two half-spaces by means of a hyperplane whose normal is the weight vector $\mathbf{w}$ and whose position is determined by the bias b. It has been shown that the perceptron learning rule is equivalent to a gaussian classifier, in the sense that it finds the same decision hyperplane [62]. Many interesting classification problems, however, imply nonconvex regions for possibly disjoint sets (this includes arbitrary boolean functions). Multilayer perceptrons have the required discriminating power. The four-layer perceptron depicted in Fig. 18.5c shows how a general classification example could be solved:

- Suppose that the classification sets can be approximated by means of polygons (polyhedra, in general). The PEs of the first hidden layer are tuned in order to identify the lines of the polygon.

- The units of the second hidden layer are meant to identify suitable convex regions and therefore are activated by the logical AND of subsets of units of the first hidden layer. These regions must be chosen so as to represent a tessellation of the concave decision regions.

- The units of the output layer (one per class) are meant to identify the composite concave decision regions and therefore are activated by the logical OR of a suitable subset of units of the previous layer.

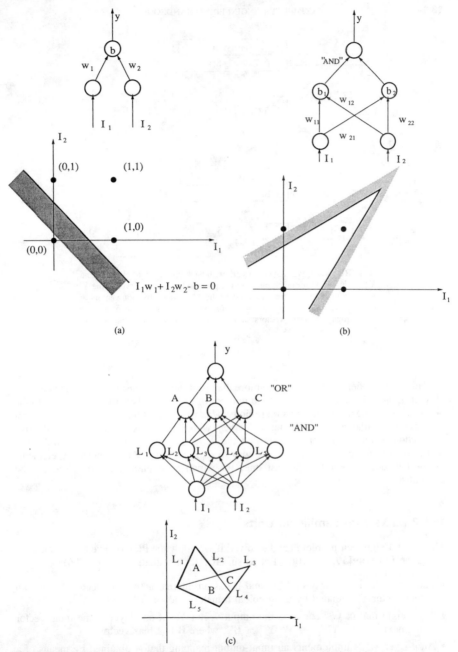

FIGURE 18.5 Classification with single and multilayer perceptrons; I_1, I_2: input features; y: output classification variable. *(a)* A single-layer perceptron cannot compute the EX-OR function (the decision line is determined by the weights w_1 and w_2 and by the bias b). *(b)* A two-layer perceptron can compute the EX-OR function (the output neuron computes the logical AND of the two intermediate neurons, i.e., it responds to the intersection of the two half planes). *(c)* A four-layer perceptron can approximate concave decision territories (the first hidden layer encodes the lines of the five polygon sides; the second hidden layer computes a logical AND function and responds to the three convex regions *a, b,* and *c;* the output neuron computes a logical OR function and responds to the global concave region).

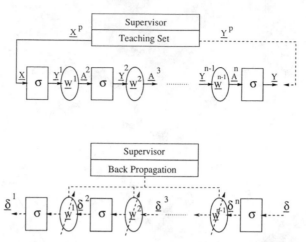

FIGURE 18.6 Multilayer network with back propagation. Here $\mathbf{X}_p$ and $\mathbf{Y}_p$ are input-output teaching patterns, provided by the supervisor; the $\mathbf{Y}^i$ are the output vectors from each layer; the $\mathbf{A}^i$ are the activation vectors of each layer; the $\mathbf{W}^i$ are the connection weight matrices; the δ^i are the back-propagated error vectors; and σ is the sigmoid discrimination function.

This example demonstrates that no more than four layers are necessary to carry out any classification task, and it shows that the number of required PEs is directly related to the geometric complexity of the decision regions. *Madalines* (multiple adalines) were the first example of multilayer predictive networks [82], with partially fixed and partially adaptive connection weights. The problem is that the delta rule is not applicable to multilayer perceptrons because there is no simple way to *assign credits* to the processing elements of the network, except for the last one, for which an explicit error measure can be computed.

18.5.2 MLNs with Semilinear Units

The credit assignment problem can be solved if we allow the PEs to have a differentiable activation function [59, 92, 106]. Let us summarize the equations (Fig. 18.6):

- Each layer L_m is an array of PEs, and it has an internal activation vector $\mathbf{A}^m$ and an output vector $\mathbf{Y}^m$, related by a sigmoidal transfer function $\mathbf{Y}^m = \sigma(\mathbf{A}^m)$.

- The weight matrix $\mathbf{W}^m$ connects the output vector $\mathbf{Y}^m$ of one layer to the input vector of the next layer: $\mathbf{A}^{m+1} = \mathbf{W}^m\mathbf{Y}^m + \mathbf{B}^m$, where $\mathbf{B}$ is a bias vector.

- An n-layer MLN implements an input-output mapping that is obtained by means of a forward propagation of an input pattern $\mathbf{X}$ through the input layer (which usually has a linear transfer function), one or more intermediate (hidden) layers, and then an output layer: $\mathbf{Y} = \text{MLN}(\mathbf{X};\mathbf{W},\mathbf{B})$.

An MLN can be trained by a supervisor on the basis of a teaching set $[(\mathbf{X}^p, \mathbf{Y}^p), p = 1, 2, \ldots]$ and a learning technique, known as *back propagation* (BP) [59, 92, 106]. BP adapts the weights via gradient descent of the norm E of the output error vector $\delta = \Sigma(\mathbf{Y}^p - \mathbf{Y})$:

$$E = E\,(\mathbf{W}) = \sum_{p,i}(y_i^p - y_i)^2$$

$$\mathbf{W}(k + 1) = \mathbf{W}(k) - \eta\,\frac{\partial E}{\partial \mathbf{W}}$$

The name of the technique, which is also called the *generalized delta rule,* comes from the fact that the output error vector δ is propagated backward to the input of the different layers $(\delta \to \delta^n \to \delta^{n-1} \cdots \to \delta^1)$, according to the recurrent equations

$$\delta_i = y_i^p - y_i$$

$$\delta_i^n = \sigma'(a_i^n)\delta_i$$

$$\delta_i^m = \sigma'(a_i^m)\sum_j w_{ij}^m\delta_j^{m+1} \qquad m = n-1,\ n-2,\ \ldots,\ 1$$

where $\sigma'(a_i^m)$ is the slope of the sigmoid function for the current internal activation level a_i^m of unit i at level m and w_{ij}^m is the connection weight between unit i at level m and unit j at level $m + 1$. The adaptation rule is then[†]

$$\Delta w_{ij}^m = -\eta\nabla_{ij}^m = -\eta y_i^m\delta_j^{m+1}$$

In comparing this rule with the standard delta rule of the previous section, we can observe the similarity: The rate of change of a connection weight is proportional to the correlation between the input signal and the output error of the connection. The rule can be applied also to the bias parameters, by simply interpreting the bias coefficient of each PE as the weight of an additional connection with a virtual PE that is permanently on ($y = 1$). The parameter η modulates the speed of descent, and a value in the range $(0.1, 1.0)$ is usually appropriate. Good results are usually found by adopting a higher value in the hidden layers than in the output layer.

The speed of descent can be increased without triggering instability if the variations of the weights are smoothed out by low-pass filtering. This is frequently implemented with the *momentum term* which subtracts a portion of the weight variation in the previous adaptation step:

$$\Delta w_{ij}^m(k) = -\eta y_i^m\delta_j^{m+1} + \alpha\,\Delta w_{ij}^m(k - 1)$$

[†]The generalized delta rule can be derived by assuming the following definition of the error vectors at the input of each layer ($\delta^m = \partial E/\partial \mathbf{A}^m$) and then applying the chain rule for the computation of these vectors

$$\delta_i^m = \frac{\partial E}{\partial a_i^m} = \sum_j \frac{\partial E}{\partial a_j^{m+1}}\frac{\partial a_j^{m+1}}{\partial y_i^m}\frac{\partial y_i^m}{\partial a_i^m} = \sum_j \delta_j^{m+1}\sigma'(a_i^m)w_{ij}^m$$

as well as for the computation of the gradient of E:

$$\frac{\partial E}{\partial w_{ij}^m} = \frac{\partial E}{\partial a_j^{m+1}}\frac{\partial a_j^{m+1}}{\partial w_{ij}^m} = \delta_j^{m+1}y_i^m$$

It is interesting to note that for the logistic function $y = \sigma(x)$ it holds that $y' = y(1 - y)$. This derivative reaches its maximum at midrange ($y = 0.5$) and goes to zero at either limit of the range. Since the rate of weight change is proportional to the slope, it follows that "uncommitted" PEs (i.e., units close to midrange) tend to change their weights more quickly than PEs that are committed already.

(a value of α around 0.9 is usually appropriate). Back propagation, as a gradient descent technique, can only reach local minima and can remain trapped in pathological conditions for specific choices of the initial values of the weighting parameters. Experimentally, it has been found that randomly chosen values of small amplitudes are usually appropriate. The computational process can be organized in two ways: batch adaptation (the weights are changed only when the whole training set has been presented to the network) or immediate adaptation, after each pattern presentation. In both cases, the presentation of the whole training set is called an *epoch,* and a condition of stationarity for the error function E is achieved, signaling the termination of learning, after a large number of epochs (typically thousands). The gain parameter is usually decreased during learning in order to stabilize the learned connections. Batch adaptation is particularly useful when the network must process noisy data. In summary, BP implies two operational phases: a forward propagation of input (which allows us to compute the output error) and a backward propagation of error, which may (or may not) be accompanied by weight changes. The back propagation without weight change is used for computing the input increment $\delta\mathbf{x}$ which is necessary to produce a desired output increment $\delta\mathbf{y}.$

18.5.3 Speed

BP implements steepest descent in $E(\mathbf{W})$; that is, the weights are updated in the direction that yields the maximum error reduction. It is well known from optimization theory that steepest descent is frequently very inefficient due to the shape of the error surface, particularly as regards the presence of steep and narrow ravines, and in fact various extensions of the basic delta rule have been proposed [12, 42, 95]. The distributed and parallel nature of neural networks limits the learning algorithms to local ones, and a basic idea is to let each synapse adapt its own learning parameter. In other words, there is no longer a single learning rate coefficient η but a whole set η_{ij}^m. The adaptive strategy suggested by Silva and Almeida [95] is the following:

$$w_{ij}^m(k) = w_{ij}^m(k-1) - \eta_{ij}^m(k)\ \nabla_{ij}^m(k)$$

$$\eta_{ij}^m(k) = \begin{cases} (1 + \epsilon)\eta_{ij}^m(k-1) & \text{if } \nabla_{ij}^m(k)\nabla_{ij}^m(k-1) > 0 \\ (1 - \epsilon)\eta_{ij}^m(k-1) & \text{if } \nabla_{ij}^m(k)\nabla_{ij}^m(k-1) < 0 \end{cases}$$

where $\nabla_{ij}^m = \partial E/\partial w_{ij}^m = y_i^m\delta_j^{m+1}$ and ϵ is a small positive constant. This strategy, which operates in the batch mode, has two effects:

- It tends to increase the gain for the directions where the gradient keeps its sign in successive steps (a likely symptom of a long and gentle slope); this generally has a speeding effect that accelerates the convergence along a long and narrow valley.
- It tends to depress the gain in the directions where the gradient changes its sign, a clear indication of oscillation across a ravine.

Simulation results have shown a very consistent reduction in the total training time.

18.5.4 Representational Power

MLNs have been shown to be a class of universal approximators [7, 14, 21, 40] in the sense that nonlinear functions mapping a compact set to its image can be approximated to any degree of accuracy by an MLN with at least three layers and with a sufficient number of hidden units. Moreover, this property does not strictly require the activation function to be continuous and sigmoidal, but simply measurable [40]. However, for the application of BP, it is necessary that the squashing function be differentiable, and the attractive feature of this algorithm is the possibility of implementing it in a parallel and distributed way. Teaching a network to memorize a set of input-output associations is sometimes called a problem of *loading* the data onto the architecture. This problem has been studied from the point of view of computational complexity [46], and it has been found that, in the general case, the loading problem is *hard,* i.e., it is *NP-complete.* It is a fact, however, that in most useful applications simple heuristics have been found that do the job.

18.5.5 Generalization

The above-mentioned computational properties of MLNs are the basis for their "generalization" capabilities, i.e., their ability to interpolate a mapping after a teaching based on a limited set of samples or to correctly classify test patterns not present during training. Two significant problems must be faced in the development of applications: *overtraining* and *overfitting.* They have to do with the interplay among several factors: the number of iterations of the BP algorithm, the number of examples in the training set, the number of connections, and the number of independent parameters in the network architecture. Overtraining is the phenomenon for which the *generalization performance,* i.e., the error rate on the test set, may not be monotonically decreasing with the number of epochs of learning the training set, but may worsen after having reached a minimum value. This happens, particularly when the network gives a poor approximation anyway. Overfitting is a typical problem in regression and approximation: When the number of free parameters becomes too large with respect to the size of the data and/or the order of the unknown function, learning tends to approximate the measurement noise rather than the underlying structure in the data. To overcome this problem, it is necessary to minimize the number of free parameters, somehow trimming the default choice of full connection between one layer and the next. Among the different techniques that can be used for this purpose [60], two are mentioned here:

- *Local versus full connections.* This is a technique similar to the receptive field concept of biological brain structures. For example, if the input layer represents some kind of image, then PEs in the first hidden layer might perform some kind of local processing by only being connected to small regions of the input layer.

- *Weight sharing.* The general concept is that having many connections is good because it gives more flexibility to the approximation power of the network, but the connections need not be independent. In particular, groups of connections can share the same set of weights. For example, in pattern recognition applications, it may be useful to have *feature maps,* i.e., collections of PEs whose receptive fields cover the PEs of the previous layer, with a set of connection weights that is the same for all the PEs of the map (Fig. 18.7). BP can be applied to weight-sharing MLNs with a minor modification: Error vectors are back-propagated in the usual way, and the potential connection weight changes are estimated accordingly. The actual updates, however, are computed by averaging the estimated changes for the shared weights.

The topic of the generalization capability of MLNs as a function of network size has been investigated by Baum [7]. A significant result is that a network with N nodes and W weights can correctly classify at least a fraction $1 - \epsilon/2$ of test samples, drawn from the same statistical population of the training set, provided that the size of the latter is

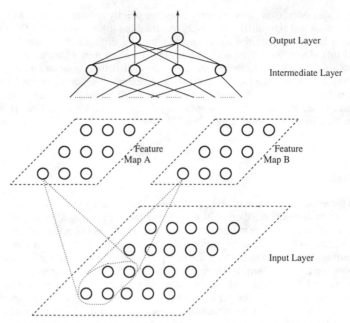

FIGURE 18.7 Feature maps in a multilayer network. The PEs in the first hidden layer are organized into two feature maps, which means that they have a reduced connectivity with the input layer and all the PEs in the same map share the same set of weights.

$O(W/\epsilon \log (V/\epsilon))$. A good rule of thumb is that the size of the teaching set must be at least an order of magnitude larger than the number of weights.

18.5.6 Ill-Posed Mappings—Identity Mappings

Suppose that we wish to teach an MLN an ill-posed mapping, i.e., a function that admits infinite equivalent output patterns **Y** for a given input pattern **X**. An example is the inverse kinematics of redundant robots: **X** is the pose of the end-effector (six variables), and **Y** is the set of joint angles (n variables, $n > 6$). We can still apply BP with a suitable training set, but there is room for an additional task, e.g., the minimization of a given criterion or additional constraints. Let us suppose that the criterion can be expressed as the norm of a cost vector $\mathbf{v}_{cost}$; then it is possible to compute a composite error vector $\delta_{comp} = \alpha\delta_{out} + \beta\mathbf{v}_{cost}$ and apply it in the standard BP procedure. However, it is difficult to obtain directly a training set for an ill-posed mapping, and an elegant solution of this problem involves the idea of joining the network that models the ill-posed (inverse) mapping with a network that models the well-posed (direct) mapping, i.e., the *forward modeling* idea [5, 43–45], depicted in Fig. 18.8a. According to this idea, two phases are required. In the first phase, the forward model is trained separately in the standard way; in the second phase, the output errors are back-propagated through the forward model without adapting the weights (with the sole purpose of estimating the error vector at the output of the ill-posed network), a composite error vector is formed at the interface of the two net-

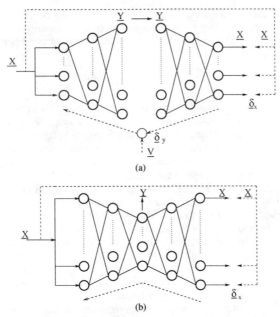

FIGURE 18.8 Neural models that compute an identity mapping. *(a)* Ill-posed mapping (from input pattern **X** to output pattern **Y**) cascaded with a well-posed forward model (the output error δ_x is back-propagated through the forward model in order to estimate δ_y and then back-propagated to the composite error). *(b)* Compression-decompression network (the input pattern **X** is compressed to a lower-dimension representation **Y** and then decompressed again).

works, and it is back-propagated through the ill-posed network with weight adaptation. All together, this kind of network computes an *identity mapping* from **X** to **Y** to **X** again, a mapping which is characterized by an expansion and a compression and is an effective way to deal with redundancy. As noted by Jordan, the forward model operates as a *distant teacher:* It emulates the system by propagating activation forward, and it estimates the derivative of the output error with respect to the network input by back-propagating the error, which means differentiating the model.

A complementary architecture for the computation of identity mappings also can be conceived; it is a network in which the input pattern, which is assumed to be somehow redundant, is compressed and then expanded again in an attempt to reproduce the original pattern (Fig. 18.8*b*). Suppose, e.g., that the training set is an ensemble of (somehow similar) images, and the purpose is to find a compressed representation that exploits the intrinsic structure of the images. In this case, the two networks (compression and expansion nets) are trained together with the same patterns presented at the input and at the output, and the minimum number of intermediate units is searched that guarantees a desired reproduction error. When this is found, the network architecture can be used as a device for compressing and expanding an image database or for codebook design in signal processing.

This kind of network architecture can be used for filtering because the input data are smoothed by compressing and reconstructing them. The network acts as a nonlinear low-pass filter whose transition frequency is controlled by the number of hidden units.

18.5.7 Representation of Time

MLNs are basically mechanisms for transforming patterns, without any relation to time. However, a representation of time can be added in many ways. The simplest way, adopted sometimes in pattern recognition, is to consider an input spatiotemporal pattern, say a sonar spectrogram [23], as a static pattern. This allows us to use MLN and BP directly. But the problem, in general, is that this network is not at all time-shift-invariant, in the sense that recognition is very sensitive to small time shifts.

Shift invariance can be achieved with special architectures. Fukushima's neocognitron, considered in greater detail in a subsequent section, shows a possibility which is based on the idea of splitting the recognition process in feature extraction layers followed by layers of shift-invariant operators. Another approach to shift invariance is provided by the *time-delay neural network* (TDNN) model [28, 105] which is, in principle, an MLN complemented with time-delay links. This means that the activity in the first hidden layer depends on the current input pattern plus as many previous patterns as the number of delay elements in each link; in the second layer, that may have a different number of delays than in the first layer, the time horizon is larger because it compounds the delays of elements in the first two layers; the final recognition layer must obviously have a time horizon which covers the whole time span, in order to achieve a good degree of time-shift-invariant recognition. In other words, the architecture has a bipyramidal scaling: Each layer has a coarser time representation than the preceding layer, and this is compensated by an increase in the number of features. The use of time-delay links means a multiplication of connection weights with respect to a standard MLN, but this number is much smaller than in the direct application of MLNs to spatiotemporal patterns. In practical implementation, TDNNs *unroll* spatiotemporal patterns (Fig. 18.9a) which are treated as static patterns similar to the direct approach mentioned above; the difference is that the same set of weights for a given PE must apply for all the observation time, and this is accomplished by a mechanism of *weight sharing* that is similar to the concept of *feature maps* used by le Cun [60] for an MLN and by Fukushima [18, 19] for the cognitron and neocognitron. Learning occurs by averaging for the shared weights the changes estimated with the standard BP.

Apart from applications in signal processing, time is relevant in control applications which may require MLNs with feedback, i.e., recurrent MLNs. A simple technique for training these kinds of networks is *back propagation through time* (BTT) [92, 107] which consists of unfolding in time the network and therefore multiplying the number of layers (Fig. 18.9b). In the unfolded system, there are many copies of the same network (denoted as *N*) and many copies of the system (denoted as *S*), which in the limit might simply consist of an identity mapping. Again, as in TDNNs, there is a weight-sharing problem, and so back propagation must be applied in this case with the provision of averaging the changes estimated in the different time slots. An additional modification is necessary if the system's model is not an identity mapping; in this case, the back propagation of the error vector, from the output lines to the input lines of *S*, can be performed either in an analytic way if the Jacobian of *S* is known or in a neural way through a "forward" model of the system, trained separately. Alternatively, it is possible to use more complex variations of BP for real-time learning in recurrent networks [1, 112].

A particular type of recurrent MLN has been studied by Jordan [43–45] which has the standard input, hidden, and output layers of the regular MLN, plus a layer of *state units*

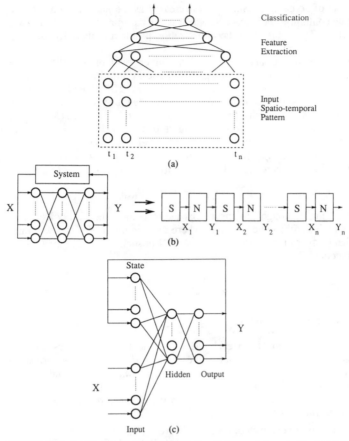

FIGURE 18.9 MLNs and time. *(a)* TDNN (time-delay neural network). *(b)* BTT (back propagation through time). *(c)* Jordan model.

that receive their inputs from the output units (with fixed weights) and send their outputs to the hidden units (with adaptable weights); see Fig. 18.9c. In this case, the input layer can be used for representing the plan of an action, from which an output trajectory is generated over time.

18.6 RELAXATION

In relaxation CAMs, like HNs, the existence of a computational potential energy E is somehow incidental, although it guarantees the stability of the memorized patterns and drives the overall neurodynamics. However, it is possible to exploit this computational feature in an explicit way, by designing network architectures whose energy function E coincides with an intended cost function in an optimization problem, possibly subjected to a number of constraints. Since E is decreased as the network computes, eventually a stable state configuration is reached which is a local minimum of E and therefore of the cost function. The solution of the optimization problem is then decoded from the equilibrium configuration.

An example of this approach has been given by Hopfield [36, 39], who used a relaxation neural network and its associated energy minimization principle to devise a solution to the classic *traveling salesperson problem* (TSP): The cost function is the total path P of the tour, subjected to the constraint that the tour visits each city once and returns to the starting city. The n-city TSP can be mapped into a discrete HN architecture with n^2 PEs, logically arranged into an $n \times n$ square matrix, with the convention that columns identify the n cities and rows identify the n travel steps. The idea is to use the classic penalty function method of constrained optimization with a penalty function C_{pen} that is zero for valid tours [there are $n!/(2n)$ of them] and is strongly positive for invalid tours[†]

$$C_{\text{TSP}} = P + \alpha C_{\text{pen}}$$

where α is "large enough" to ensure that the relaxation stays away from invalid configurations and therefore settles in states where the minimum of C is also a minimum of P. The design problem is then to configure an HN in such a way that the previously defined energy function E_{HN} coincides with C_{TSP}:

$$E_{\text{HN}} = -\frac{1}{2}\sum_i\sum_j w_{ij}y_iy_j - \sum_i I_iy_i = C_{\text{TSP}}$$

A simple solution is the following:

- There is a connection from each PE to all the PEs in the previous and following columns, with the weight equal to the distance d_{ij} between the corresponding cities: $w_{ij} = w_{ji} = -d_{ij}$ (Fig. 18.10a). The minus sign is necessary, to take into account that the generic connection weight w_{ij} contributes a term $-\frac{1}{2}(w_{ij} + w_{ji})y_iy_j$ to E. Therefore, if both PEs are active ($y_i = y_j = 1$), then the distance d_{ij} between the corresponding cities contributes to E.

- There is a strong negative connection $-\alpha$ from each PE to all the PEs in the same row (any city can be visited at one step only) and all the PEs in the same column (at any step only one city can be visited); see Fig. 18.10b. Therefore, illegal tours imply energy terms $-\frac{1}{2}(w_{ij} + w_{ji})y_iy_j = \alpha$ which are very big, and since the relaxation tends to local minima, illegal tours are likely to be avoided.

- Each PE must receive an external excitatory input in order to avoid the trivial equilibrium state in which all the PEs are inactive. In practice, a positive constant $x_i = \beta n$ proportional to the network size is sufficient (Fig. 18.10c), but its effect on the energy function must be balanced. At equilibrium, indeed, these inputs contribute a term $-\sum_i\beta ny_i = -\beta n^2$ to E because the strong α inhibitions tend to force the state to valid tour representations for which only a subset n of the n^2 PEs is active. This spurious energy term can be counterbalanced by means of additional connection weights $w_{ij} =$

[†]A penalty function must be zero if the constraints are satisfied, and it should become very big when the search process enters the forbidden area. This function is combined with the main cost function, producing a composite cost function that can be minimized according to an unconstrained relaxation scheme. Valid tours are characterized as follows: one and only one PE must be active for each row, and one and only one PE must be active for each column.

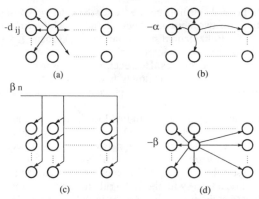

FIGURE 18.10 Patterns of connections for the Hopfield network that solves the traveling salesperson problem. *(a)* Inhibitory connections for expressing the distance cost. *(b)* Strong inhibitory connections for forcing consistent solutions. *(c)* Common excitatory input for avoiding the trivial null state. *(d)* Full connection mutual inhibition for counterbalancing the effect of the external inputs.

$-\beta$ between all the PEs (Fig. 18.10*d*) because the corresponding energy term is $-\frac{1}{2}\sum_{ij}(-\beta y_i y_j) = \beta n^2$.

In summary, the energy function has the following form:

$$E = \frac{1}{2} \sum_{ij}(d_{ij} + \alpha v_{ij} + \beta)y_i y_j - \sum_i \beta n y_i$$

(v_{ij} simply selects rows and columns of the n^2 PEs). Equilibrium states are local minima of the total distance on a legal tour. In general, HNs can be applied to all the engineering applications in which it is necessary to minimize a cost function and the function can be reduced to the form of the energy function for an HN. The technique is to use a PE for each variable of the cost function and to turn the coefficients into connection weights.

Simulated Annealing   HNs follow gradient descent and therefore get stuck in local as opposed to global minima. This is not a problem when an HN is used as a CAM, because multistability is functional in that case, but optimization problems require global minima and HNs can offer only suboptimal solutions.

The suboptimal trapping of gradient descent can be overcome with the aid of a thermodynamic concept: simulated annealing [48]. This technique is akin to the annealing of a metal, i.e., the process of determining a very low-energy state of a metal by melting and then slowly freezing it. Thermic noise causes a random exploration of the state space, and low-energy states turn out to be more probable; then freezing after a sufficient shake-out probably leads to the global minimum.

Simulated annealing can be applied to HNs by allowing the transfer function to operate in a stochastic way, e.g., by adding a zero-mean noise term n to the input operator of the PEs: $y_i = U(a_i + n_i)$. The noise power is proportional to the "temperature," and its effect is that the state change of a generic PE at a given time instant (Δy_i) does not necessarily decrease the total network energy because Δy_i and a_i may have different signs due to the effect of noise, the more likely the greater the temperature, and so $\Delta E_i = -a_i \Delta y_i$ and Δy_i

may be positive. At thermal equilibrium, i.e., after the dynamic transients have died out, the relative probability of two network states S_1 and S_2 with energy values E_1 and E_2, respectively, follows the Boltzmann distribution: $\text{Prob}(S_1)/\text{Prob}(S_2) = e^{-(E_1 - E_2)/T}$. Therefore, low-energy states are always more probable than higher-energy states, the ratio being greater for smaller temperatures. However, at low T it may take a long time before settling to the global minimum, and so slowly freezing is the compromise that speeds up the exploration of the state space in the initial phase and then firmly stabilizes the network in the final phase.

The idea of using simulated annealing to find low-energy states in relaxation networks has been investigated by several people [22, 34, 97]. Hinton and Sejnowski [34], in particular, proposed a technique for teaching networks that relax according to the Boltzmann distribution, i.e., *Boltzmann machines* (BMs). A typical application is *pattern completion,* which is somehow a generalization of the associative recall performed by an HN. The HN, indeed, is trained with the Hebb rule to store a discrete set of patterns and is supposed to reconstruct them exactly from an initial fragment. The BM, on the other hand, is taught to learn the underlying statistics of the training set of patterns, and this knowledge is exploited, in the recall phase, to complete an input fragment pattern in a way which is maximally consistent with the whole training data set. For this reason, the BM cannot content itself with local minima and therefore uses simulated annealing. The training set does not imply a direct storage but is simply supposed to represent a significant sample drawn from a probabilistically distributed population of patterns.

Although the topology of a BM is identical to that of an HN, in the latter case there is no way to have *hidden* units, capable of learning some kind of *internal representation.* This is possible with BMs whose PEs can be logically grouped into two different sets. Some of the PEs are designated as *visible,* in the sense that they can interact with the outside world, while the other PEs are *hidden* and are supposed to develop, as a result of training, internal representations of the data structures. The BM learning technique aims at the absolute minimization of an information-theoretic measure G of the distance between the *free-running* probability distribution $\text{Prob}^-(S_\alpha)$ ($\alpha = 1, 2, \ldots$) and the *forced* probability distribution $\text{Prob}^+(S_\alpha)$ ($\alpha = 1, 2, \ldots$) of the state vector of the visible units, at thermal equilibrium. In the latter case, the visible units are connected to the external environment and simply reflect its probabilistic structure, whereas in the former case the visible units are free to evolve on the basis of the network internal structure. In other words, BM is supposed to learn by making an internal representation of its environment. Hinton and Sejnowski [34] demonstrated that, by using the following form of G

$$G = \sum_\alpha \text{Prob}^+(S_\alpha) \ln \frac{\text{Prob}^+(S_\alpha)}{\text{Prob}^-(S_\alpha)}$$

and expressing learning as a gradient descent in $G(\mathbf{w})$, the gradient can be estimated locally, irrespective of whether the weight w_{ij} is connected to a visible unit:

$$\Delta w_{ij} = -\eta \, \frac{\partial G}{\partial w_{ij}} = \eta(p_{ij}^+ - p_{ij}^-)$$

Here p_{ij}^- is the probability that two processing elements PE_i and PE_j are both active in the free-running phase, and p_{ij}^+ is the probability that the same elements are both active in the forced phase. The two statistics are computed in the two computational phases at thermal equilibrium, after annealing. The connection weights among visible PEs learn first-order correlations in the input data, whereas the hidden units learn to capture higher-order correlations.

The dependence on simulated annealing makes the BM slow. Among the techniques which have been developed to speed it up, a model uses *mean field theory* (MFT), an approximation that aims at replacing the stochastic process due to thermal noise with a set of deterministic equations that capture the notion of noise [84]. The idea is to consider the *local field* of each PE ($\phi_i = \partial E/\partial y_i$) and to approximate its stochastic fluctuations with a thermal average. It can be shown that the stochastic relaxation with the binary network $y_i = U[\sum_j w_{ij} y_j + n_i(T)]$ can be substituted by a deterministic relaxation with a graded network, whose PEs have a sigmoidal discrimination function $\hat{y}_i = \sigma(\sum_j w_{ij}\hat{y}_j/T)$. Another model for speeding up the BM, developed by Szu and Hartley [101], is called *Cauchy machine* and uses both "random walks" and "flights" to generate new states.

18.7 SELF-ORGANIZATION

Competitive learning is a technique for allowing a neural network, exposed to a structured population of signals, to discover statistically salient features of the population without any supervision or a priori specification of categories. The basic idea is to establish patterns of mutual inhibition in a collection of PEs that are stimulated by the same input pattern. The consequent neural dynamics are usually characterized by the fact that each input pattern determines a population of *winners*, i.e., a set of maximally activated PEs that depress the activity of all the others.[†] In the extreme case, there is only one winner and the corresponding neurodynamics is named *winner takes all*. This kind of connectivity and behavior is clearly inspired by neurobiology because the brain structure is rich of examples of such an arrangement. In any case, a learning strategy is associated with the dynamic behavior of the network and it rewards the winning PEs by tuning their input synapses with respect to the input pattern. The recurrent inhibitory connections remain fixed, while the input connections of each PE are plastically changed by experience: the distribution of these connection vectors is the key internal representation learned by the network whereas the recurrent inhibition is just a "neutral" technique to allow the network to absorb knowledge a piece at a time.

Many variants of competitive learning exist and many composite architectures have been studied [18, 26, 52, 61, 91, 93, 104].

18.7.1 Distribution of Weights to the Winner

The winner-takes-all dynamics can be achieved by a set of m linear threshold PEs where each one is connected with a strong negative weight to all the others. Let us also suppose that each PE is connected to an n-dimensional input vector ($\mathbf{X}: x_1, x_2, \ldots, x_m$) by means

---

[†]In particular, let us consider a model of shunting competitive networks [25]

$$\frac{dy_j}{dt} = -y_j + (A - y_j)[I_j + f(y_j)] - y_j \sum_k f(y_k)$$

Depending upon the shape of the discrimination function f, different behaviors can be obtained. For example, the winner-takes-all strategy requires a faster-than-linear characteristic whereas a sigmoid characteristic suppresses the noise in the input pattern $\mathbf{I}$ and contrast enhances it.

of a set of weights ($\mathbf{W}_j$: $w_{1j}, w_{2j}, \ldots, w_{ij}, \ldots, w_{mj}$). A learning strategy proposed by von der Malsburg [104] consists of having a set of weights for each PE with an invariant total quantity ($\sum_i w_{ij} = 1$) and changing the weights of the winning PE by a strategy that takes away a portion of weight from all the connections (ηw_{ij}) and redistributes it equally to the connections which correspond to active input lines ($x_i = 1$):

$$\Delta w_{ij} = -\eta w_{ij} + \frac{\eta x_i}{\sum_i x_i}$$

The weights of the losing PEs are left unchanged. The functional characteristics of this computational architecture is feature discovery by competitive learning (Fig. 18.11) in the sense that if the input signal is indeed characterized by well-identified clusters of values, then competitive learning will converge to a distribution of connection weights centered in the corresponding clusters. This kind of behavior, that in fact characterizes all competitive learning paradigms, is consistent with results in experimental psychology according to which prototypical patterns are better recognized than the actual examples [86].

18.7.2 The Cognitron and Neocognitron

In the case of the cognitron [18] and the neocognitron [19, 20], the winner-takes-all strategy is paired with hebbian learning and with the use of feature maps; the purpose is to specialize the PEs to become feature extractors, useful in pattern recognition tasks. In particular, the computational architecture of the neocognitron is organized in a number of layers, which somehow mirror the processing stages in the human visual system, and it can be characterized as follows:

- An image activates an input layer which is followed by a number of double layers, a layer of feature extraction cells (S cells), and a layer of categorization cells (C cells); see

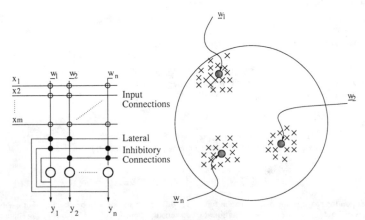

FIGURE 18.11 Feature discovery by competitive learning: weight vectors $\mathbf{w}_i$ are attracted by clusters of input samples.

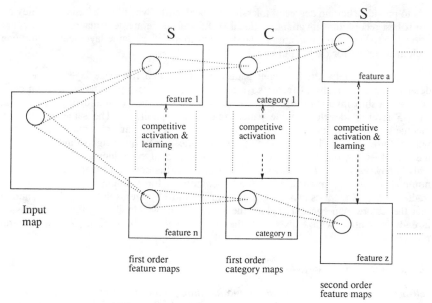

FIGURE 18.12   Neocognitron.

Fig. 18.12. For example, in an application of the recognition of numerals [20], four double layers are used (S_1, C_1, S_2, C_2, S_3, C_3, S_4, C_4), the last of which has one PE for each numeral.

- At each layer, the PEs are arranged in a number of *feature maps* (S layers) or *category maps* (C layers), respectively. This means that the PEs in any map have a direct correspondence with the two-dimensional (2D) arrangement of the input stimuli.

- The connections run only forward, from one layer to the next, if we exclude the intralayer connections that would be necessary to implement the winner-takes-all strategy. These connections are limited to small receptive fields that are *retinotopically* organized (a PE of a map receives its inputs from those PEs in the previous layer that correspond to a small neighborhood in the input space). The connections from a C layer (or the input layer) to the next S layer are adapted during learning in order to develop feature extraction capabilities. The connections from an S layer to the next C layer are fixed.

- The S cells are characterized by the transfer function described in Sec. 18.2 that allows a cell to estimate the presence of a feature in its domain of competence. The PEs in the same map all share the same set of weights; this means that all the PEs of an S map perform the same kind of feature extraction in different parts of the input space. Competition dictates the interaction among the different maps in the same layer; for each input coordinate, the winning PE denotes the *resonant feature*. Learning affects resonant cells, which are tuned to the input pattern. Therefore, the different feature maps during training become more and more specialized in a self-organized way.

- The C cells are simply activated by an "OR-like" invariant rule: They detect the presence of a feature in any point of their receptive field. The purpose of this mechanism is to provide a certain degree of tolerance to local shifts, which is the basis for achieving a robust recognition invariant to global shifts and moderate deformations (differential local shifts). Competition among the different maps of the same layer leaves only one element active for each input coordinate.

In a trained network, the input pattern is propagated from one layer to the next, determining a hierarchy of features (from low-level features up to the recognition categories, via shift invariance operators). Learning is concerned with allowing the maps at each S layer to develop unique pattern-matching capabilities. The same competition mechanism used in the recognition phase is also operant during training and gives a winner for each input location. The winner modifies her or his weights (and those of all the PEs of its map) in the hebbian way, i.e., proportional to the input-output correlation. This is how each map becomes specialized in the extraction of a unique feature. In the numeral recognition application of the neocognitron, for example, 12 features are extracted in S_1, 38 features in S_2, 35 features in S_3, and 11 features in S_4. It is worth noting that the feature map concept exploits the same idea of weight sharing that we discussed already in relation with TDNNs and the MLN developed by le Cun [60] for numeral recognition.

18.7.3 Self-Organizing Maps

Self-organizing map (SOM) networks and *learning vector quantization* (LVQ) networks use a similar neurodynamics and learning strategy [54]. The networks have a single-layer architecture of PEs that are connected to a common input vector $\mathbf{x}$ by means of adaptable connection weight vectors $\mathbf{w}_i$. The network dynamics are characterized by a variant of the winner-takes-all activation function, a *bubble* function. This function has a value 1 for a set of PEs that stay in a given neighborhood $N_{i-\text{res}}$ of the *resonant* PE and has a value 0 otherwise:

$$y_i = \begin{cases} 1 & \text{if } i \in N_{i-\text{res}} \\ 0 \end{cases}$$

otherwise

$$i - \text{res} = \max_i \mathbf{x}^T \mathbf{w}_i$$

The bubble function implies that the set of PEs is arranged in a map—monodimensional, two-dimensional, or m-dimensional—in accordance with the structure of the resonant neighborhood $N_{i-\text{res}}$ (the bubble); 2D maps are used in most applications, with the PEs on a grid, either rectangular or hexagonal (Fig. 18.13).

A possible mechanism for implementing the bubble function in a neural way [54] is to use a recurrent pattern of connections that combines inhibition with excitation (i.e., competition with cooperation) differently from the purely competitive mechanisms previously considered. The result is that the winner does not take all, but shares the activity with its clan ($N_{i-\text{res}}$). In particular, the right balance between excitation and inhibition is given by a pattern of recurrent connections that follow a *Mexican hat* profile, an arrangement which is well known in brain physiology, particularly as regards the visual system. The overall network, which includes the input connections as well as the recurrent connections, has been shown to have convergent dynamics, which settles in a state characterized by a bubble centered around the resonant PE. At the simulation level, however, the bubble function can be implemented directly by the explicit search of the resonant PE and the selection of the corresponding neighborhood.

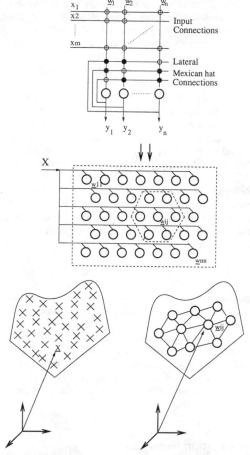

FIGURE 18.13 Self-organizing feature map. The weight vectors of the PEs **w** are distributed in the feature space, preserving the topology of the input distribution.

As regards learning, a variant of the unsupervised hebbian learning rule is adopted by SOM models, similar to the rule used in competitive learning. During training, which has the purpose of adapting the input connection weights, the network is exposed to examples of an input vector $\mathbf{x}(k) \in \mathbf{R}^n$ drawn from $\mathbf{R}^n$ in accordance with a fixed probability density function. The learning rule states that

$$\Delta\mathbf{w}_j = \eta(\mathbf{x} - \mathbf{w}_j)y_j$$

Thus for each input vector **x,** the connection weight vectors of those PEs that stay in the winning bubble are updated by moving them to a new position that is closer to **x.** This rule tends to improve the *order* of the network, which means that, during training, the distribution of weight vectors across the map "unfolds" from an initial disorder to a better and better approximation of the input function. At the end of training, neighboring PEs in the map correspond to closest neighbors in the weight vector space, a concept that is described as a *topology-preserving representation*. Moreover, the weight vectors arrange themselves in $\mathbf{R}^n$ so as to become approximately equiprobable in the nearest-neighbor sense with respect to the input probability distribution function.

The size of an SOM that is necessary for a given application depends on the complexity of the domain of the input feature vector $\mathbf{x}$; we can estimate the minimum size by looking, after training, at the degree of uniformity of the selection of the different PEs or, alternatively, at the reconstruction errors of input patterns. The size of the training set also depends on the complexity of the input domain. It is different from MLNs, however; the necessary number of epochs is in the tens, not in the hundreds or thousands. The learning protocol usually adopted for trading speed of convergence for stability of the map consists of using a large bubble size (of the order of one-third of the network size) and a large gain factor η (close to 1) for the initial epoch and then decrease these values down to a bubble size of 1 and a gain factor close to 0.1.

The main difference with respect to competitive learning is the construction of an ordered map which comes from the fact that the bubble function does not kill cooperation among PEs, as is the case with the winner-takes-all strategy.

SOMs are a very general-purpose neurocomputing paradigm that can be exploited usefully in a large number of applications; in particular, SOMs are naturally suited for data compression which can be used for codebook design in signal processing and for the identification of phonemes in speech processing [54] or graphemes in cursive handwriting [72, 74]. In the latter case, e.g., the input vector is 10-dimensional and is derived after preprocessing the data generated by a digitizing tablet during handwriting and segmenting the continuous signals in appropriate chunks (called *strokes*). Figure 18.14 shows the parameter vectors (i.e., the strokes) learned by the PEs after training. Since a trained SOM is a sort of lookup table, it also can be used for representing the same kind of input-output associations for which MLNs are used. In this case, the input vector $\mathbf{x}$ is logically divided into an input and an output component, and recall is equivalent to a partial match as regards the input component and a readout of the corresponding output component, with or without interpolation.

18.7.4 Counterpropagation Networks

Counterpropagation networks are a family of architectures that combine an SOM with the outstar structure [24]. In the simplest configuration, in which the network is intended to learn a mapping from $\mathbf{x} \in \mathbf{R}^n$ to $\mathbf{y} \in \mathbf{R}^m$, training is broken down into two parts:

- First, the SOM is trained in an unsupervised way, allowing the weight vectors of each PE ($\mathbf{m}_i$ in Fig. 18.15) to self-adjust in such a way that they become approximately equiprobable in a nearest-neighbor sense with respect to $\mathbf{x}$ samples drawn from $\mathbf{R}^n$ in accordance with the input probability density function.

- Second, the connection weights of the SOM are frozen, and the SOM units are activated by the input patterns with the winner-takes-all function. Their activity is passed to the output units (which use a linear activation function), and the connection weights are adapted in a supervised way by using the delta rule: $\Delta w_{ij} = \eta(y_j - w_{ij})z_i$. Here z_i is 1 or 0 according to the competition in the SOM layer, and y_j is the teacher-defined output value. As a consequence, each connection weight w_{ij} is updated only for those samples for which the SOM unit wins the competition and the weight values tend to become approximately equal to the average of the subpopulation of the corresponding output vectors.

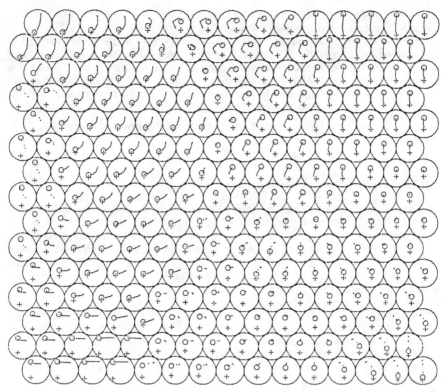

FIGURE 18.14 Self-organizing feature map for cursive handwriting (each PE learns a stroke descriptor).

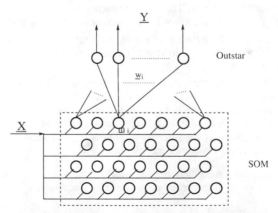

FIGURE 18.15 Counterpropagation network. First the SOM is trained with the Hebb rule in order to tessellate the input domain; then the outstar is trained with the delta rule to learn the input-output mapping.

At the end of training, the network looks like a lookup table: The SOM layer quantizes the input space, and the weight vectors emanating from these PEs ($\mathbf{w}_i$ in Fig. 18.15) represent the corresponding output vectors. The accuracy of the input-output mapping can be improved by allowing the network, during normal operation, to function in an *interpolation mode*. To this end, the winner-takes-all activation function of the SOM units is relaxed somehow, e.g., by allowing more than one winner and by setting their activation levels z_i to values proportional to the euclidean distance from the input pattern, with the normalization constraint that $\sum_i z_i = 1$. The result is that the output vectors are approximated by the linear interpolation (with interpolation coefficients z_i) of the winning SOM vectors.

18.7.5 Adaptive Resonance Theory

The heart of the *adaptive resonance theory* (ART) family of network models [11] consists of two bilaterally interconnected layers of PEs, F1 and F2, that *resonate* in a way somehow similar to the *bidirectional associative memory* (BAM) model. ART-1 deals with binary patterns whereas ART-2 recognizes analog patterns. The difference between BAM and ART is that in the latter case resonance is a much more sophisticated process that requires an additional control circuitry (an *orienting subsystem*) to guide the resonance of the two layers of PEs (the *attentional subsystem*):

- An input pattern $\mathbf{x}$ leads to activity in the feature detection PEs of F1 (the *bottom layer*, in a neurophysiological sense). The other set of PEs in F2 (the *top layer*) is meant to categorize the input patterns in a self-adaptive way. Different from other networks, however, categories are formed and explored in a sequential way, in the sense that initially all the PEs in F2 are *uncommitted* and gradually, during training, new PEs are committed to new categories until eventually the category space in F2 is exhausted.

- The PEs in F1 have a local memory in the sense that they store the initial input activity level as well as the subsequent levels during the resonance process. The activity in this layer passes through connections to the PEs in F2. The input activity a_i of F2 neurons is computed as the scalar product of $\mathbf{x}$ and a weight vector $\mathbf{w}_i$ (bottom-up adaptive filtering of the input): $a_i = \mathbf{w}_i^T \mathbf{x}$. The transfer function of these PEs is the winner-takes-all type, where the winner identifies the tentatively selected category.

- The winner PE_j sends to F1 a pattern of activity $\mathbf{y}_j$ (a top-down expectancy), determined by the weight vector $\mathbf{m}_j$ of the downgoing connections, and $\mathbf{y}_j$ is matched with the original input pattern $\mathbf{x}$.

- Resonance is detected by the orienting subsystem, according to a scalar *vigilance* parameter, a threshold against which the difference between $\mathbf{x}$ and $\mathbf{y}_j$ is measured. The same subsystem initiates a new iteration in the interaction between F1 and F2 if the network is out of resonance, inhibiting the previous winner in F2 from taking part in the competition. If an erroneous classification is contradicted by subsequent environmental evidence, then the system becomes more vigilant.

A complex dynamic interaction between the attentional and orienting subsystems determines a search through the set of categories in F2 until one of three events occurs:

1. A resonant state is reached. This means that the category has been found. In this case, the ascending and descending weight vectors of the winning category neuron are updated according to a rule similar to the SOM model, in order to refine the discrimination of the category filters.

2. All the committed PEs in F2 have been exhausted without a match. This means that the memory capacity has been reached, and the current input pattern cannot be categorized.

3. An uncommitted PE is still available for instantiating a new category which is initialized with the appropriate weight vectors. This is the first step in learning the new category.

Perhaps the most significant idea in the ART architectures is the attempt to trade *plasticity* for *stability* of learning. Most neural models, indeed, rigidly separate a learning phase from a normal operational phase, and the stability of the learned patterns is ensured by a carefully crafted learning protocol. On the contrary, ART models are ready, at any moment, for either learning and/or recognizing, and they learn while recognizing. However, this is not achieved without a price, which is the complexity of the global dynamics.

18.7.6 RCE

Reduced connectivity Coulomb energy (RCE) neural networks [88, 89] are models intended specifically for category learning; the networks are characterized by a reduced connectivity and by an analogy with the electrostatic or Coulomb energy. The electrostatic analogy comes from the fact that, given a set of electric charges Q_i positioned in points $\mathbf{r}_i$, the electrostatic energy

$$E(\mathbf{r}) = -\frac{1}{2} \sum_j \frac{Q_i}{|\mathbf{r} - \mathbf{r}_i|}$$

has minima only at the charge sites and the corresponding relaxation cannot risk, in contrast with Hopfield networks, to settle in spurious minima. However, RCE networks take the electrostatic analogy only as an inspiration, because they do not depend on any kind of relaxation dynamics. The metaphor of the charged particles is used for approximating, in the feature space, the territory of each category with the spheres of influence of a number of virtual particles. In the model, the electrostatic potential function of each particle (that ideally has an infinite support) is reduced to a binary function which has a value 1 inside a sphere and a value 0 outside. The location of the sphere, in the feature space, identifies a categorized feature vector, and the radius, which is analogous to the magnitude of the charge, is adapted during training. The purpose of learning is to *fill* the territory of each category with a sufficient number of (overlapping) spheres, while avoiding the interference among the spheres of different categories.

In practice, RCE models use feedforward networks with three layers (Fig. 18.16):

- An input layer of PEs that code a set of features **x**, relevant for the categorization problem

- An output layer with one PE for each category

- An intermediate layer (the heart of the network) of simulated charged particles

The size of the input layer is fixed, because it depends on the dimensionality of the feature vector, whereas the size of the other two layers is expanded during learning, a procedure called *commitment*. This is a point of contact with ART and a marked difference from all the other major model classes that always operate with a fixed number of PEs.

The intermediate PEs are connected to all the inputs **x**; each PE_i computes the euclidean distance between **x** and the weight vector $\mathbf{w}_i$ and then clamps it, with an adaptable

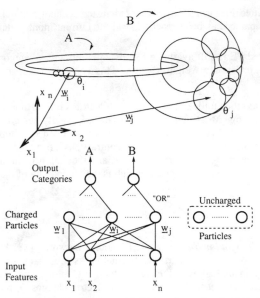

FIGURE 18.16   RCE network. The territory of each category (*A* and *B*) is approximated by clusters of spherical attraction basins of "charged particles." Each particle is identified by a feature vector $\mathbf{w}_i$ and a size parameter θ_i. The output PEs are activated by a logical OR function.

threshold θ_i. As a consequence, the activation basin of each PE in the intermediate layer is a hypersphere in the feature space, characterized by a position $\mathbf{w}_i$ and a radius θ_i. Each PE in the intermediate layer is connected with only one output PE; i.e., it supports only one category.

The output PEs are connected to several intermediate PEs, and their transfer function is simply a logical OR. As a consequence, the activation basin of the output PEs is the union of the hyperspheres of the incoming intermediate PEs. Arbitrary feature sets or category territories in feature space can be approximated by "grapes of bubbles." In comparison, as we explained earlier, MLNs attempt to approximate category territories by intersecting a number of half planes, i.e., a polyhedral approximation instead of the bubblelike approximation of RCEs. Although the number of primitives for both approximations is probably of the same order of magnitude, the advantage of RCEs is that the reduced connectivity allows us to create PEs dynamically, in a self-adapting way during training.

Learning is of the supervised type and consists of presenting a number of feature patterns with the corresponding categorization. Learning is concerned with two aspects, committing new PEs and adapting the thresholds:

- A new PE is committed when, during training, an input pattern fails to activate the specified category unit. The new PE is assigned a weight vector equal to the input vector and an appropriate large threshold.

- Thresholds are reduced, during training, in the case of false positives, i.e., when a category unit is erroneously activated.

New category units can be created in advanced stages of learning, and special provisions are made for dealing with overlapping categories, i.e., confusion zones. Multiple-RCE systems have also been developed in which a high-level control algorithm coordinates partial categorizations performed by a number of RCEs. The weight vectors of the committed PEs are not adapted during learning, but are assigned only once. Therefore, the order of presentation of the input data during training may be relevant. This is an unpleasant side effect that could be overcome by somehow allowing a dynamic displacement of the PEs, similar to the SOMs. As categorization devices, RCEs are conceptually simple and very efficient. Outside categorization, however, their use seems to be limited.

18.7.7 Neural Darwinism

Darwin networks are a family of composite neuronal architectures [16, 87] that attempt to model with biological fidelity various parts of the brain in order to generate experimentally testable hypotheses. In particular, selective recognition automata have been developed that have visual and tactile sensors as well as two robotic arms. The different subnetworks are trained to reach out, touch, and feel the border of objects by using self-organized competitive learning. Although their complexity keeps them from direct engineering applications, there is significant potential as regards self-organization in sensory-motor systems that could be fully developed in advanced robotic applications.

18.8 CONTROL AND ROBOTIC APPLICATIONS

Control and robotic applications are particularly well suited for understanding the problems that arise when neural computing modules are integrated with other types of mechanisms, resulting in global hybrid systems [51, 79, 80]. Many of the key ideas in neurocomputing, such as learning, were already investigated in adaptive control and adaptive signal processing, but were mostly limited to linear models. The adaptive linear combiner, e.g., which is the input operator of the transfer function of most PEs, is the building block of adaptive filters, where the input to the combiner is a tapped delay line [111] and the output is the filtered signal. Figure 18.17 summarizes common functions in a control system that can be carried out by neural modules (e.g., MLNs) trained in a supervisory way by means of signals derived from the processes:

- *Imitation of an existing nonlinear regulator*. In Fig. 18.17a the regulator maps the process output variables **y** into a set of control variables **u**; the neural regulator can read these variables during the actual performance of the control system, use them as a training set, and learn to reproduce the mapping. Imitation is a useful technique of "reverse engineering" when the regulator is effective but unknown, e.g., a human being.

- *System identification*. In Fig. 18.17b the unknown system's input is applied to a nonlinear adaptive filter (i.e., a neural network with a tapped delay line connected to the input PEs). The unknown system's output is used as the teaching signal of the network. The technique is useful for quasi-time-invariant nonlinear systems. In some cases, for discrete-time systems, what is being sought is the next-state function, i.e., the function that maps the current state and input vectors into the state vector for the next time step. The network model is directly trainable from historic readings of the system's state and input signals.

- *Prediction (C)*. It consists of estimating future samples of time-correlated signals from present and past samples, a problem for which optimal Wiener filters were de-

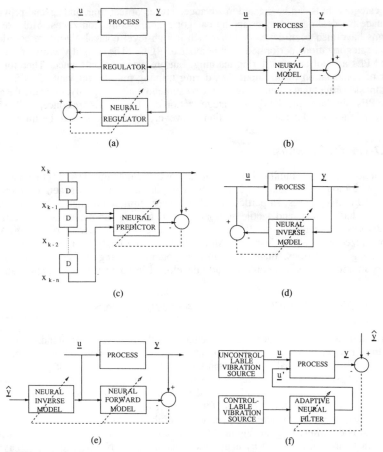

FIGURE 18.17 Typical control applications of neural modules. *(a)* Training a neural regulator by imitation. *(b)* Training a neural process model. *(c)* Training a neural predictor with a tapped delay line; training a neural inverse model in the direct way *(d)* or through a forward model *(e)*. *(f)* Noise/vibration canceling through a controllable vibration source and an adaptive filter.

veloped, based on the autocorrelation function (Fig. 18.17c). Neural models can be used for a nonlinear prediction by employing, as a training set, pairs of <current value, delayed value> of the unknown signal; the current value is the teaching signal, and the delayed value is the input value to a tapped delay line.

- *Identification of a system's inverse model.* Here the purpose of the neural module is to learn the inverse dynamics of the plant, i.e., a method of inferring from the process output the necessary control signals. If the inverse mapping is well posed, the problem is simple and can be solved in the direct way (Fig. 18.17d). If the inverse mapping is ill posed, the problem is hard and require, a more sophisticated approach, such as the use of the forward model (Fig. 18.17e described in a previous section.

- *Noise/vibration canceling* (Fig. 18.17*f*).   Noise suppression in signal processing and vibration suppression in a physical environment traditionally are conceived in terms of killing the noise or vibration by some kind of optimal filtering or damping. Neurocomputing offers an alternative approach which has an additive instead of a subtractive character. The idea is to cancel the undesirable effects, due to some uncontrollable source of noise or vibration, with an additional source of noise or vibration whose transfer function can be modulated by an adaptive neural filter.

One reason for which neural models are interesting is the possibility of setting up robust nonlinear adaptive control schemes because, in classic control, a well-established theory of adaptive strategies exists only for linear time-invariant systems with unknown parameters. The choice of the specific neural network model is wide and is not limited to MLNs. In many cases, a self-organizing paradigm can be better suited to capture the specific nature of the application. In any case, if we restrict our attention to MLNs, an alternative to the standard BP teaching technique has been investigated, called *reinforcement learning* [4]; this technique does not require target values for some designated output variables but only some global performance index and uses an *adaptive critic* network to predict future values of the performance index, distributing reward or punishment signals to the controller.

As regards robotic applications, many problems can be usefully approached with neural models [52], particularly in the area of inverse perceptual computations, sensory-motor integration, task planning, and control. In the following sections we consider a few examples.

18.8.1 Stereo Matching

Stereo matching is one of the many inverse problems that must be solved in robotic perception when an attempt is made to reconstruct the shape of objects from a set of sensory data. Frequently, inverse problems are ill posed, in the sense that the same set of data can give rise to many different reconstructions. A popular approach is to force the reconstruction system to choose the correct or, at least, a feasible solution by means of constraints directly linked to the physics of the sensing system. In stereo vision, the purpose is to estimate the depth (i.e., the distance) of the visible points of an object from a pair of slightly different images. It can be shown [67] that the depth of a point is inversely proportional to the disparity of its images, i.e., the difference of their coordinates in the two image planes. In summary, for each pixel p_{ij} of one of the two images (chosen as a master) it is necessary to estimate a disparity measure, i.e., to match that pixel with one and only one pixel of the other image (p'_{ij}). False matches give wrong depth estimates, and purely local matching algorithms tend to give very noisy estimates that contrast with the continuity of natural objects. Therefore, stereo matching can be formulated as an optimization problem in which we attempt to estimate a disparity map d_{ij} which is maximally consistent with the two images and, at the same time, is maximally smooth. This can be solved in neural terms by a Boltzmann or Hopfield network [113] of the binary type by turning the disparity map into a 3D array δ_{ijk} of binary values, where the first two indices identify the pixel coordinates (for $N \times N$ images) and the third one, which can range in a small interval of integers (say, 0 to M), identifies the disparity of the given pixel, quantized to M values. The array has $N \times N \times M$ binary elements, and estimating the depth map is equivalent to turning on a subset of the array elements and turning off all the others, according to appropriate criteria. The neural implementation (Fig. 18.18) uses one PE for each element of the array, and the connection weights are

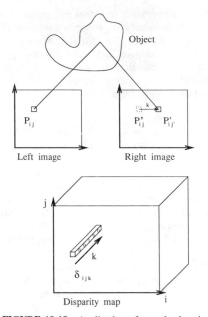

FIGURE 18.18 Application of neural relaxation to stereo matching. Given a pair of cameras looking at the same object (left image P_{ij} and right image P'_{ij}), the purpose is to find a disparity map. The relaxation is applied to a binary Hopfield network that has one PE for each combination of input coordinates (i, j) and disparity value k.

derived (according to the method described in the relaxation section) from a cost function which consists of three elements:

- A measure of the similarity between a pixel p_{ij} and the matched pixel from the other image $p'_{ij'}$ (where $j' = j + k$),[†] summed all over the image: $C_1 = \sum_{ijk}(p_{ij} - p'_{ij'})^2 \delta_{ijk}$.

- A measure of the smoothness of the disparity map, which can be expressed by summing all over the image the changes of disparity of neighboring pixels: $C_2 = \sum_{ij}[\sum_{i'j'k}(\delta_{ijk} - \delta_{i'j'k})^2]$, where (i', j') vary in a small neighborhood of (i, j).

- A uniqueness constraint, i.e., the fact that at each image position (i, j) there must be one and only one disparity value $\sum_{k}\delta_{ijk} = 1$. This constraint can be treated as a penalty function $C_3 = \alpha\sum_{ij}(\sum_{k}\delta_{ijk} - 1)^2$, where α is a large positive constant.

The optimization problem is mapped into the HN or BM architecture by sorting out, in the combined cost function, the linear terms in δ_{ijk}, which are assigned to the external inputs or the bias coefficients, and the quadratic terms in δ_{ijk}, which determine the symmetric cross connections of the network. Relaxation or simulated annealing generates, in a parallel distributed way, the pattern of activations in δ_{ijk} that gives the disparity map.

18.8.2 Visual-Motor Coordination

The visual guidance of a robotic manipulator needs to represent the complex association between the images of an object and the joint motions that are necessary for reaching and then grasping it. A simple example of how this problem can be solved by neural networks is given by INFANT [57], a neural motor controller that learns to use visual information, coming from a pair of TV cameras, for grasping objects. Learning is totally unsupervised in the sense that the teaching set is autonomously generated in a "babbling phase" and the neural controller is designed to learn self-consistency between sensory and motor signals. The structure and the function of INFANT can be summarized as follows (see Fig. 18.19):

[†]For simplicity, we assume that the two cameras have been arranged in such a way that the possible match pairs are restricted to the same scan line.

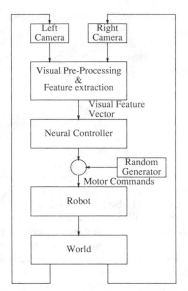

FIGURE 18.19 The visual-motor INFANT system. The neural controller, trained with the delta rule, has one layer of input units (one PE for each visual feature) and one layer of output units (one PE for each robot actuator). Teaching patterns are self-generated during the training phase by a random generator of movements.

- The robot manipulator is controlled in joint coordinates by a motor command vector **MC** which is generated either by the output of the visually guided neural controller or, during training, by a pseudo-random generator.

- A stereo pair of TV cameras looks at the scene which contains a cylindrical object and the manipulator. It is assumed that the visual preprocessing system is able to separate the object from the background and to extract the essential features for the motor controller. The features are measured by 18 numbers: the image coordinates of the centroid of the object and values of their disparity plus measures of normalized orientations of the object obtained by convolution of the images with kernels oriented in four different directions, 45° apart. The 18 scalar features are transformed to 18 monodimensional maps by a spatial coding scheme, according to which scanning a map is equivalent to addressing the range of values of the corresponding feature. The feature maps are activated with a bell-shaped distribution of activity, centered on the unit that codes the current value of the feature.

- A two-layer neural network maps the ensemble of feature maps (logically, a single, long array of units) into an array of motor commands **MC'**. It is very similar to a classical perceptron, except that the neurons have linear activation functions. The network is trained to generate a visually induced motor command **MC'** which matches as closely as possible the actual training command **MC**.

- After training, the babbling generator is disconnected, and the presentation of an object of roughly similar shape to the teaching object will trigger a "reaching reflex" that tends to superimpose the hand on the object. Conventional methods are then used to provide the grasping commands.

Although limited to a very controlled environment, INFANT is a very good example of how complex sensory-motor coordination can be achieved by a rather simple method of self-teaching, where the essential link is played by the feedback through the real world, a self-organizing principle which is shared, in more general terms, by neural darwinistic networks.

18.8.3 Path Planning and Robot Control

Visual-motor coordination, i.e., the association between visual and motor variables, as represented in INFANT, leaves open the problem of coordinating the multiple degrees of freedom of a robot or of a robotic system with multiple manipulators while reaching a target. This is an ill-posed problem in many respects: as regards the path of the end-effector, the motion of the joints (in the case of redundant manipulators), and the timing. Inverse kinematics are a limiting case of this problem, when the path of the end-effector is already chosen, and we discussed previously how to solve it by means of MLNs. Path planning is much more general, and we consider two different approaches.

A Cascaded Neural Network with Minimum Torque-Change Criterion. A cascaded neural network with minimum torque-change criterion (CN-MT) is a composite network architecture [47] that combines the paradigm of association (a set of MLNs for representing direct kinematics or dynamics) with the paradigm of relaxation, for representing motor optimization. The optimization task is instrumental for guiding the planner to produce *smooth* trajectories while reaching the target. The input to the neural architecture is the predefined duration T_f of the movement, the target (i.e., the endpoint position to be reached at the final time) and intermediate via points and obstacles, if necessary. The network is supposed to produce a pattern of torques (for all the joints and the total time span) that is compatible with the task constraints and, at the same time, minimizes the integral of the squared torque derivatives, computed for the total movement duration and summed over all the joints. To solve the problem, the model is unfolded in time, as in the previously considered BTT model; i.e., a spatial representation of time is set up where system variables and system transformations are replicated for each time instant. The inner skeleton of the network (Fig. 18.20) is a cascaded network where FD and FK are two MLNs that were previously trained to implement forward dynamic and forward

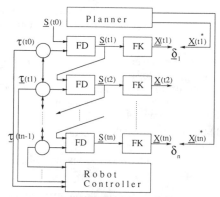

FIGURE 18.20 The cascaded neural network with minimum torque-change criterion. The planner only specifies the endpoint coordinates at the initial and final instants of time $\mathbf{X}(t_i)^*$ and $\mathbf{X}(t_n)^*$. FD is an MLN trained to compute the forward dynamic mapping (next-state function, where $\mathbf{S}$ is the state vector) and FK is an MLN trained to compute the forward kinematic mapping. The robot movement plan is unfolded in time, from t_1 to t_n, and the time course of the actuator torques $\tau\,(t_i)\,(i = 1, \ldots, n)$ is computed by a relaxation network coupled with the time-unfolded FD and FK networks. At equilibrium, the robot controller receives the time-delayed torque vectors.

kinematic transformations, respectively. FD, in particular, receives in input the current torque vector and the current state vector (joint angles and joint rotation speeds) and produces in output the next state vector which is the input both to FK, for predicting the endpoint movement, and to another copy of FD, in order to propagate the computation to the next time step.

All together, the time-unfolded network maps the global spatiotemporal torque pattern into the predicted trajectory of the end-effector. To make this pattern consistent with the above-mentioned plan constraints, relaxation is combined with association by having the torque pattern generated by a continuous HN, which has one PE for each element of the torque vector. The torque units are cross-connected by means of symmetric synapses of constant weight that link each unit (identified by a joint and a time instant) with the two units that correspond to the same joint, one time step before and one step after. This set of connections [47] corresponds to a minimization of the desired minimum torque-change criterion.

The optimal torque patterns are constrained by the task errors that are back-propagated through the recurrent MLNs, similar to the previously described forward modeling technique. In other words, the errors detected at some of the units of the output layer are back-propagated in order to estimate the corresponding torque input errors; and these errors, in turn, are spread throughout the torque units via relaxation. The resulting torque variations are then propagated forward for updating the samples of the endpoint trajectory, and the three processes (forward and back propagation as well as relaxation) proceed until an equilibrium configuration is reached. In that situation, the whole torque pattern, localized on the torque units, can be transmitted through a delay line to the motor system which carries out the actual movement.

M-Net—A Muscle-Oriented Synergy Formation Model. M-Net (motor relaxation network) is a neural mechanism of synergy formation and path planning that is based on an analogy with the motion of a kinematic chain in a force field [73, 75, 76], an idea that also has been used in robot navigation [49]. The force field is determined by modeling the actuators as tunable elastic elements, and path planning is intended to generate a sequence of arm configurations, at equilibrium in the force field, that can be found by means of relaxation. The problem is then to find a way to modulate the force field during trajectory formation in accordance with the kinematic constraints (such as the joint limits, expressed in the joint space) and the task constraints (such as the target point as well as via points and/or obstacles, usually expressed in the environment space). A solution to this problem is given by the *passive motion paradigm* (PMP) [77], according to which the continuous modification of equilibrium points can be produced via a neural mechanism that simulates *passive movements,* i.e., movements driven by *virtual force impulses* that correspond to the intended movement direction. The PMP can be viewed as a conceptual mechanism for establishing a well-defined mapping between a high-dimensional neural activation pattern (for highly redundant robots) and a lower-dimensional kinematic representation. M-Net is a relaxation network that has been proposed as an implementation of the simulation mechanism discussed above. The model is constructed as a network of PEs that correspond to the different constituent parts of the robotic manipulator: S units (skeletal segments), M units (elastic actuators), and L units (elastic ligaments).

These units are defined by the local computations they perform: M units and S units behave as impedances; i.e., they receive positional information and react, feeding back force information. The S units, however, behave as admittances; i.e., they receive force information and react, modifying positional parameters. The S units model the different skeletal linkages, considered as rigid bodies to which complex sets of forces are applied: *internal forces,* applied by M and L units for taking into account the kinematic constraints, and *external forces,* applied as sequences of impulses from outside the M-Net for ex-

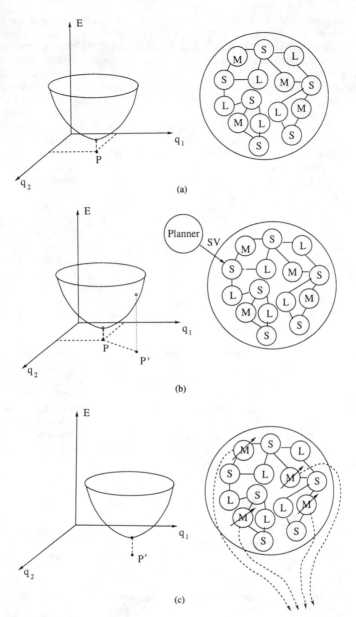

FIGURE 18.21 The motor relaxation network (M-Net). *S:* Skeletal units; *M:* muscle units; *L:* ligament units. *(a)* The network is initially in an equilibrium state (point *P* in the potential-energy landscape *E*). *(b)* The planner fires a synergy vector (SV) that displaces the equilibrium point of the net from *P* to *P'* (passive phase). *(c)* The *M* units are updated to regain equilibrium (active phase).

pressing intended directions of movement. With these units it is possible to build networks that can relax in a similar way to the passive movements of the human musculoskeletal system. The inputs to an M-Net are sequences of virtual force impulses, called *synergy vectors*, that express the intended direction of motion. These vectors displace the equilibrium state of the network, and the ensuing dynamics provide two streams of output data at the same time, a stream of *motor commands* and a stream of *kinematic expectations*. From the network modeling point of view, M-Nets are dynamic systems with a well-defined Lyapunov function that behave similarly to HNs (Fig. 18.21).

- The role of neurons in HNs is played by S units; the difference is that inputs and outputs in M-Nets are vectors, not scalars, and the activation function is more complex.
- The role of connections (which are linear functions in Hopfield nets) is played by M units and L units, which are nonlinear functions.
- The role of input signals is played by the synergy vectors.

In spite of significant differences, in both cases we have a similar relaxation behavior which is driven by a potential-energy function. The multistability of HNs has no meaning for M-Nets because they have only one significant equilibrium configuration (the current posture) and this is changed during the simulation process in accordance with the passive-motion principle. Therefore, the pseudo connection weights represented by M units must be adaptively changed during relaxation, and this can be achieved by interleaving a *passive phase* and an *active phase*. In the passive phase, an M-Net reacts to the application of a synergy vector by relaxing to a new equilibrium state in an isoelectric way, i.e., without changing the control variables of M units; at equilibrium, these variables are changed in order to shift the minimum point of the energy landscape onto the current configuration: this is the active phase. In other words, the neural relaxation process operates in such a way that the minimum point in the potential field *tracks* the sequence of equilibrium configurations determined by the sequence of synergy vectors. Symmetrically, the mechanical relaxation induced by the neural relaxation evolves the other way round: The potential field *leads* the current posture and attracts it. The PEs in an M-Net are multi-input multi-output units with a complex input-output transfer function, i.e., a mapping that can be represented and learned by means of simple neural networks such as MLNs or SOMs. These networks can be trained in a self-organized way during a babbling phase, similar to the one previously explained for INFANT. In this sense, M-Nets are networks of networks, with an outer relaxation shell and inner nonlinear associations.

REFERENCES

1. L. B. Almeida, "A Learning Rule for Asynchronous Perceptrons with Feedback in a Combinatorial Environment," in M. Caudill and C. Butler (eds.), *Proceedings of the First Annual Conference on Neural Networks*. San Diego: SOS Printing, 1987, pp. 609–618.

2. S. Amari, "A Theory of Adaptive Pattern Classification," *IEEE Transactions on Electronic Computers,* EC-16:299–307, 1967.

3. J. A. Anderson, "A Simple Neural Network Generating Interactive Memory," *Mathematical Biosciences,* 14:197–220, 1972.

4. A. G. Barto, "Connectionist Learning for Control," in W. T. Miller, R. S. Sutton, and P. Werbos (eds.), *Neural Networks for Control*. Cambridge, Mass.: M.I.T. Press, 1990, pp. 5–58.

5. A. G. Barto and M. Jordan, "Gradient Following without Back-Propagation in Layered Networks," in M. Caudill and C. Butler (eds.), *Proceedings of the First Annual Conference on Neural Networks*. San Diego: SOS Printing, 1987, pp. 629–636.

6. G. F. Basti and A. Perrone, "Time-Dependent Short-Term Memories in Neural Networks," in E. R. Caianiello (ed.), *Neural Networks*. Singapore: World Scientific Publishing Co., 1990, pp. 69–74.

7. E. B. Baum, "On the Capabilities of Multilayer Perceptrons," *Journal of Complexity*, 4:193–215, 1988.

8. E. B. Baum and D. Haussler, "What Size Net Gives Valid Generalization?" *Neural Computation*, 1:151–160, 1988.

9. E. R. Caianiello, "Outline of a Theory of Thought Processes and Thinking Machines," *Journal of Theoretical Biology*, 2:204–235, 1961.

10. G. Carpenter, "Neural Network Models for Pattern Recognition and Associative Memory," *Neural Networks*, 2:243–257, 1989.

11. G. Carpenter and S. Grossberg, "The ART of Adaptive Pattern Recognition," *IEEE Computer Magazine*, 1988, pp. 77–78.

12. L. W. Chan and F. Fallside, "An Adaptive Training Algorithm for Back Propagation Networks," *Computer Speech and Language*, 2:205–218, 1987.

13. M. A. Cohen and S. Grossberg, "Absolute Stability of Global Pattern Formation and Parallel Memory Storage by Competitive Neural Networks," *IEEE Transactions on Systems, Man, and Cybernetics*, SMC-13:815–826, 1983.

14. G. Cybenko, "Complexity Theory of Neural Networks and Classification Problems," in L. B. Almeida and C. J. Wellekens (eds.), *Neural Networks*. Berlin: Springer-Verlag, 1990, pp. 26–44.

15. R. Eckmiller, "Neural Computers for Motor Control," in R. Eckmiller (ed.), *Advanced Neural Computers*. Amsterdam: North-Holland/Elsevier, 1990, pp. 357–364.

16. G. M. Edelman, *Neural Darwinism*. New York: Basic Books, 1987.

17. T. Ejima, "A Comparison between Learning Algorithms for Layered Neural Networks," *IEEE Proceedings of the International Symposium on Signal Processing and Its Applications*, 1:299–302, 1990.

18. K. Fukushima, "Cognitron: A Self-organizing Multilayered Neural Network," *Biological Cybernetics*, 20:121–136, 1975.

19. K. Fukushima, "Neocognitron: A Self-organizing Neural Network Model for a Mechanism of Pattern Recognition Unaffected by Shift in Position," *Biological Cybernetics*, 36:193–202, 1980.

20. K. Fukushima, "Neocognitron: A Hierarchical Neural Network Capable of Visual Pattern Recognition," *Neural Networks*, 1:119–130, 1988.

21. K. I. Funahashi, "On the Approximate Realization of Continuous Mappings by Neural Networks," *Neural Networks*, 2:183–192, 1989.

22. S. Geman and D. Geman, "Stochastic Relaxation, Gibbs Distributions, and the Bayesian Restoration of Images," *IEEE Transactions on Pattern Analysis and Machine Intelligence*, PAMI-6:721–741, 1984.

23. R. P. Gorman and T. J. Sejnowski, "Analysis of Hidden Units in a Layered Network Trained to Classify Sonar Targets," *Neural Networks*, 1:75, 91, 1988.

24. S. Grossberg, "Some Networks that Can Learn, Remember, and Reproduce Any Number of Complicated Space-Time Patterns," *International Journal of Mathematics and Mechanics*, 19:53–91, 1969.

25. S. Grossberg, "Contour Enhancement, Short Term Memory, and Constancies in Reverberating Neural Networks," *Studies in Applied Mathematics*, 52:217–257, 1973.

26. S. Grossberg, "Adaptive Pattern Classification and Universal Recoding: Part I. Parallel Development and Coding of Neural Feature Detectors," *Biological Cybernetics*, 23:121–134, 1976.

27. S. Grossberg, "Competitive Learning: From Interactive Activation to Adaptive Resonance," *Cognitive Science,* 11:23–63, 1987.

28. J. B. Hampshire and A. H. Waibel, "A Novel Objective Function for Improved Phoneme Recognition Using Time-Delay Neural Networks," *IEEE Transactions on Neural Networks,* 1:216–228, 1990.

29. D. O. Hebb, *The Organization of Behaviour: A Neurophysiological Study.* New York: Wiley, 1949.

30. R. Hecht-Nielsen, "Counterpropagation Networks," *Applied Optics,* 26:4979–4984, 1987.

31. R. Hecht-Nielsen, "Neurocomputing: Picking the Human Brain," *IEEE Spectrum,* March 1987, pp. 36–41.

32. G. E. Hinton, *Artificial Intelligence,* 40:185–234, 1989.

33. G. E. Hinton and J. A. Anderson (eds.), *Parallel Models of Associative Memory.* Hillsdale, N.J.: Erlbaum, 1981.

34. G. E. Hinton and T. J. Sejnowski, "Learning and Relearning in Boltzmann Machines," in D. E. Rumelhart and J. L. McClelland (eds.), *Parallel Distributed Processing,* vol. 1. Cambridge, Mass.: M.I.T. Press, 1986, pp. 282–317.

35. M. W. Hirsch, "Convergent Activation Dynamics in Continuous Time Networks," *Neural Networks,* 2:331–350, 1989.

36. J. J. Hopfield, "Computing with Neural Circuits: A Model," *Science,* 233:625–633, 1986.

37. J. J. Hopfield, "Neural Networks and Physical Systems with Emergent Collective Computational Abilities," *Proceedings of the National Academy of Sciences (USA),* vol. 79, 1982, pp. 2554–2558.

38. J. J. Hopfield, "Neurons with Graded Response Have Collective Computational Properties like Those of Two State Neurons," *Proceedings of the National Academy of Sciences (USA),* vol. 81, 1984, pp. 3088–3092.

39. J. J. Hopfield and D. Tank, "Neural Computation of Decisions in Optimization Problems," *Biological Cybernetics,* 52:141–152, 1985.

40. K. Hornik, M. Stinchombe, and H. White, "Multilayer Feedforward Networks Are Universal Approximators," *Neural Networks,* 2:359–366, 1989.

41. J. C. Houk, S. P. Singh, C. Fisher, and A. G. Barto, "An Adaptive Sensorimotor Network Inspired by the Anatomy and Physiology of the Cerebellum," in W. T. Miller, R. S. Sutton, and P. J. Werbos (eds.), *Neural Networks for Control.* Cambridge, Mass.: M.I.T. Press, 1990, Chap. 14.

42. R. Jacobs, "Increased Rates of Convergence through Learning Rate Adaptation," *Neural Networks,* 1:4, 1988.

43. M. Jordan, "Supervised Learning and Systems with Excess Degrees of Freedom," Technical Report, COINS 88-27, University of Massachusetts, Amherst, Computer and Information Science Department, 1988.

44. M. I. Jordan, "Indeterminate Motor Skill Learning Problems," in H. Jeannerod (ed.), *Attention and Performance,* vol. 13. Cambridge, Mass.: M.I.T. Press, 1989.

45. M. I. Jordan, "Serial Order: A Parallel, Distributed Processing Approach," in J. L. Elman and D. E. Rumelhart (eds.), *Advances in Connectionist Theory: Speech.* Hillsdale, N.J.: Lawrence Erlbaum, 1989, pp. 44–93.

46. S. Judd, "Learning in Networks Is Hard," *Proceedings of the IEEE First International Conference on Neural Networks,* San Diego, Calif., June 21–24, 1987, pp. 685–692.

47. M. Kawato, Y. Maeda, Y. Uno, and R. Suzuki, "Trajectory Formation of Arm Movement by Cascade Neural Network Model Based on Minimum Torque-Change Criterion," *Biological Cybernetics,* 62:275–288, 1990.

48. S. Kirkpatrick, C. D. Gelatt, and M. P. Vecchi, "Optimization by Simulated Annealing," *Science,* 220:671–680, 1983.

49. O. Khatib, "Real Time Obstacle Avoidance for Manipulators and Mobile Robots," *The International Journal of Robotics Research,* 5:90–99, 1986.

50. A. H. Klopf, *The Edonistic Neuron: A Theory of Memory, Learning, and Intelligence*. Washington, D.C.: Hemisphere, 1982.

51. T. Kohonen, "Correlation Matrix Memories," *IEEE Transactions on Computers*, C-21:353–359, 1972.

52. T. Kohonen, *Associative Memory: A System Theoretic Approach*. Berlin: Springer-Verlag, 1977.

53. T. Kohonen, *Self-Organisation and Associative Memory*. Berlin: Springer-Verlag Series in Information Sciences, 1984.

54. T. Kohonen, "The Neural Phonetic Typewriter," *IEEE Computer Magazine*, March 1988, pp. 11–22.

55. B. Kosko, "Bidirectional Associative Memories," *IEEE Transactions on Systems, Man, and Cybernetics*, SMC-18:49–60, 1988.

56. S. Kung and J. Hwang, "Neural Network Architectures for Robotic Applications," *IEEE Transactions on Robotics and Automation*, 5:641, 1989.

57. M. Kuperstein and J. Rubinstein, "Implementation of an Adaptive Neural Controller for Sensory-Motor Coordination," in R. Pfeifer, Z. Schreter, F. Fogelman-Soulie, and L. Steels (eds.), *Connectionism in Perspective*. Amsterdam: Elsevier, 1989, pp. 49–61.

58. K. J. Lang, A. H. Waibel, and G. E. Hinton, "A Time-Delay Neural Network Architecture for Isolated Word Recognition," *Neural Networks*, 3:23–43, 1990.

59. Y. le Cun, "A Learning Scheme for Asymmetric Threshold Networks," *Proceedings of Cognitiva 85*, Paris, 1985.

60. Y. le Cun, "Generalization and Network Design Strategies," in R. Pfeifer, Z. Schreter, F. Fogelman-Soulie, and L. Steels (eds.), *Connectionism in Perspective*. Amsterdam: North-Holland, 1989, pp. 143–155.

61. R. Linsker, "From Basic Network Principles to Neural Architectures," *Proceedings of the National Academy of Sciences (USA)*, I: Emergence of Spatial Opponent Cells; II: Emergence of Orientation Selective Cells, 83:7508–7512, 8390–8394, 1986.

62. R. P. Lippmann, "An Introduction to Computing with Neural Nets," *IEEE ASSP Magazine*, 3:4–22, 1987.

63. R. P. Lippmann, "Review of Neural Networks for Speech Recognition," *Neural Computation*, 1:1–38, 1988.

64. W. A. Little and G. L. Shaw, "A Statistical Theory of Short and Long Term Memory," *Behavioral Biology*, 14:115–133, 1975.

65. A. J. Maren, "Neural Networks for Spatio-Temporal Pattern Recognition," in A. Maren, C. Harston, and R. Pap (eds.), *Handbook of Neural Computing Applications*. New York: Academic Press, 1990, pp. 295–308.

66. D. Marr, "A Theory of Cerebellar Cortex," *Journal of Physiology*, 202:437–470, 1969.

67. D. Marr and T. Poggio, "A Computational Theory of Stereo Vision," *Proceedings of the Royal Society (London)*, 204:301–328, 1979.

68. W. S. McCulloch and W. Pitts, "A Logical Calculus of the Ideas Immanent in the Nervous Activity," *Bulletin of Mathematics and Biophysics*, 5:115–143, 1943.

69. R. J. McEliece, E. C. Posner, E. R. Rodemich, and S. S. Venkatesh, "The Capacity of the Hopfield Associative Memory," *IEEE Transactions on Information Theory*, 33:461–482, 1987.

70. M. Minsky and S. Papert, *Perceptrons*. Cambridge, Mass.: M.I.T. Press, 1969.

71. J. Moody and C. J. Darken, "Fast-Learning in Networks of Locally-Tuned Processing Units," *Neural Computation*, 1:281–294, 1989.

72. P. Morasso, "Neural Models of Cursive Script Handwriting," *Proceedings of the International Joint Conference on Neural Networks*, Washington, vol. 2. San Diego: IEEE TAB, 1989, pp. 539–542.

73. P. Morasso, "Neural Representation of Motor Synergies," in R. Eckmiller (ed.), *Advanced Neural Computers*. Amsterdam: North-Holland, 1990, pp. 51–59.

74. P. Morasso, J. Kennedy, E. Antonj, S. Di Marco, and M. Dordoni, "Self-organisation of an Allograph Lexicon," *Proceedings of the International Neural Network Conference (Paris)*. Dordrecht: Kluwer Academic Publishers, 1990, pp. 141–144.

75. P. Morasso, F. A. Mussa Ivaldi, G. Vercelli, and R. Zaccaria, "A Connectionist Formulation of Motor Planning," in R. Pfeifer, Z. Schreter, F. Fogelman-Soulie, and L. Steels (eds.), *Connectionism in Perspective*. Amsterdam: Elsevier, 1989, pp. 413–420.

76. P. Morasso and V. Sanguinetti, "Neurocomputing Concepts in Motor Control," in J. Paillard (ed.), *Brain and Space*. Oxford: Oxford University Press, 1991, pp. 404–432.

77. F. A. Mussa Ivaldi, P. Morasso, and R. Zaccaria, "Kinematic Networks—A Distributed Model for Representing and Regularizing Motor Redundancy," *Biological Cybernetics*, 60:1–16, 1988.

78. N. Nakano, "Associatron: A Model of Associative Memory," *IEEE Transactions on Systems, Man, and Cybernetics*, SMC-2:381–388, 1972.

79. K. Narendra and K. Parthasarathy, "Identification and Control of Dynamical Systems Using Neural Networks," *IEEE Transactions on Neural Networks*, March 1990, pp. 4–27.

80. D. Nguyen and B. Widrow, "Neural Networks for Self-learning Control Systems," *IEEE Control Systems Magazine*, 10:18, 1990.

81. D. Nguyen and B. Widrow, "The Truck Backer-Upper," in R. Eckmiller (ed.), *Advanced Neural Computers*. Amsterdam: North-Holland, 1990, pp. 11–17.

82. N. Nilsson, *Learning Machines*. New York: McGraw-Hill, 1965.

83. R. Penrose, "A Generalized Inverse for Matrices," *Proceedings of the Philosophical Society (London)*, vol. 51, 1955, pp. 406–413.

84. C. Peterson and J. R. Anderson, "A Mean Field Theory Learning Algorithm for Neural Networks," *Complex Systems*, 1:995–1019, 1987.

85. T. Poggio and F. Girosi, "Regularization Algorithms for Learning that Are Equivalent to Multilayer Networks," *Science*, 247:978–982, 1990.

86. M. I. Posner, *Chronometric Explorations of Mind*. Hillsdale, N.J.: Erlbaum, 1978.

87. G. N. Reeke, L. H. Finkel, and G. M. Edelman, "Selective Recognition Automata," in S. F. Zornetzer, J. L. Davis, and C. Lau (eds.), *An Introduction to Neural and Electronic Networks*. San Diego: Academic Press, 1990, pp. 203–226.

88. D. L. Reilly, L. N. Cooper, and C. Elbaum, "A Neural Model for Category Learning," *Biological Cybernetics*, 45:35–41, 1982.

89. D. L. Reilly, C. Scofield, C. Elbaum, and L. N. Cooper, "Learning Systems Architectures Composed of Multiple Learning Modules," *IEEE International Conference on Neural Networks*, 2:495–503, 1987.

90. F. Rosenblatt, "The Perceptron: A Probabilistic Model for Information Storage and Organization in the Brain," *Psychological Review*, 65:386–408, 1958.

91. F. Rosenblatt, *Principles of Neurodynamics: Perceptrons and the Theory of Brain Mechanisms*. Washington, D.C.: Spartan Books, 1961.

92. D. E. Rumelhart, G. E. Hinton, and R. J. Williams, "Learning Internal Representations by Error Propagation," in D. E. Rumelhart and J. L. McClelland (eds.), *Parallel Distributed Processing*, vol. 1. Cambridge, Mass.: M.I.T. Press, 1986, pp. 318–363.

93. D. E. Rumelhart and D. Zipser, "Feature Discovery by Competitive Learning," in D. E. Rumelhart and J. L. McClelland (eds.), *Parallel Distributed Processing*, vol. 1. Cambridge, Mass.: M.I.T. Press, 1986, pp. 151–193.

94. E. Saund, "Dimensionality Reduction Using Connectionist Networks," *IEEE Transactions on Pattern Analysis and Machine Intelligence*, PAMI-11:304–313, 1989.

95. F. M. Silva and L. B. Almeida, "Acceleration Techniques for the Backpropagation Algorithm," in L. B. Almeida and C. J. Wellekens (eds.), *Neural Networks*. Berlin: Springer-Verlag, 1990, pp. 110–119.

96. P. K. Simpson, *Artificial Neural Systems: Foundations, Paradigms, Applications, and Implementations*. New York: Pergamon Press, 1990.

97. P. Smolensky, "Information Processing in Dynamical Systems: Foundations of Harmony Theory," in D. E. Rumelhart and J. L. McClelland (eds.), *Parallel Distributed Processing*, vol. 1. Cambridge, Mass.: M.I.T. Press, 1986, pp. 194–281.

98. D. L. Stein, "Spin Glasses," *Scientific American*, 261:36–42, 1989.

99. K. Steinbuch, "Die lernmatrix," *Kybernetik*, 1:36–45, 1961.

100. R. Sutton and A. Barto, "Toward a Modern Theory of Adaptive Networks: Expectation and Prediction," *Psychological Review*, 88:135–170, 1981.

101. H. Szu and R. Hartley, "Nonconvex Optimization by Fast Simulated Annealing," *Proceedings of the IEEE*, 75:1538–1540, 1987.

102. M. Takeda and J. W. Goodman, "Neural Networks for Computation: Number Representations and Programming Complexity," *Applied Optics*, 25:3033–3046, 1986.

103. Y. Uno, M. Kawato, and R. Suzuki, "Formation and Control of Optimal Trajectory in Human Multijoint Arm Movement, Minimum Torque-Change Model," *Biological Cybernetics*, 61:89–101, 1989.

104. C. von der Malsburg, "Self-organizing of Orientation Sensitive Cells in the Striate Cortex," *Kybernetik*, 14:85–100, 1973.

105. A. Waibel, T. Hanazawa, G. E. Hinton, K. Shikano, and K. Lang, "Phoneme Recognition Using Time Delay Neural Networks," *IEEE Transactions on Acoustics, Speech and Signal Processing*, 37:3, 1989.

106. P. J. Werbos, "Generalization of Back Propagation with Application to a Recurrent Gas Market Model," *Neural Networks*, 1:339–356, 1988.

107. P. J. Werbos, "Backpropagation through Time: What It Is and How to Do It," *Proceedings of the IEEE*, August 1990.

108. B. Widrow, "Generalization and Information Storage in Networks of Adaline Neurons," in M. C. Yovitz, G. T. Jacobi, and G. D. Goldstein (eds.), *Self-Organizing Systems*. Washington: Spartan, 1962, pp. 435–461.

109. B. Widrow and M. E. Hoff, "Adaptive Switching Circuits," WESCON-1960 Convention Record Part IV, 96–104, 1960.

110. B. Widrow and S. D. Stearns, *Adaptive Signal Processing*. Englewood Cliffs, N.J.: Prentice-Hall, 1985.

111. B. Widrow and R. Winter, "Neural Nets for Adaptive Filtering and Adaptive Pattern Recognition," in S. F. Zornetzer, J. L. Davis, and C. Lau (eds.), *An Introduction to Neural and Electronic Networks*. New York: Academic Press, 1990.

112. R. J. Williams and D. Zipser, "A Learning Algorithm for Continually Running Fully Recurrent Neural Networks," *Neural Computation*, 1:270–280, 1989.

113. Y. T. Zhou and R. Chellappa, "Stereo Matching Using a Neural Network," *Proceedings of IEEE ICASSP'88*, New York, 1988, pp. 940–943.

CHAPTER 19
OPTICS IN COMPUTERS

Henri H. Arsenault and Yunlong Sheng
Department of Physics, Université Laval, Quebec, Canada

19.1 INTRODUCTION

In the past few years optics has made rapid inroads into the field of computers. This has involved both the introduction of optics into electronic computers and proposals to carry out by optical means computer operations normally done with electronics. It still is uncertain whether an all-optical computer will ever see the light of day, but clearly all supercomputers of the future will have some optics.

To keep this chapter to a manageable size, we restricted our coverage to what we consider the most advanced or the most promising avenues. For an unripe field such as optical computing, this requires some arbitrary decisions and probably mistaken judgments, so we apologize to any researchers whose work is not covered.

In particular, we forgo a description of optical neural networks, which on a long-time basis may turn out to be the most important application for optical computing, although we are not likely to see practical optical neural networks in the near future. Optical neural networks, as well as more detailed discussions of some items in this chapter, are covered in our book on optical computing [2]. Most of the information presented here was gathered in the course of a contract for the Communications Research Center of Canada [3].

19.1.1 What Is Optical Computing?

Within the past few years, the field of optical computing has grown considerably and has become one of the major areas of optics. Optics has made its way into digital computers, the parallelism of optics has been exploited to implement optical neural nets, and the development of technology promises optical components that can surpass the performance of electronic components found in digital computers. Some laboratories have promised all-optical computers in the near future.

The technologies for optics in computers and the technologies for optical communications are closely related, but one should be careful about too easily transposing optical communications technology into optical computing, because the needs are quite different. For example, optical communications systems typically deal with the propagation over long distances and switching of a large number of signals, each with a relatively narrow bandwidth, which must not be switched very often and which can tolerate error rates on the order of 10^{-9} or less. Digital computer applications, however, typically require the high-speed switching of accurately synchronized digital signals with very high bandwidths over small distances, with bit-error rates of 10^{-12}. Moreover, the transmission of digital signals from computer chips requires that groups of signals (all the signal lines from one chip, typically 64 lines) be switched together. These requirements apply to optical interconnects between electronic chips, but more advanced optical architectures have requirements that do not exist in communications systems (such as the accuracy of holograms or switching speeds of two-dimensional spatial light modulators).

One might expect that analog optical computing, which deals mostly with one-dimensional signal processing and Fourier optical correlators, should be excluded from the field of optical computing. However, it turns out that some of the main families of optical computers, especially of neural network architectures and of knowledge-based systems, are based on a correlator architecture. With the advent of rapid spatial light modulators, such correlators have the potential to come into their own as useful information processing systems. In addition, this is an area of optics that is relatively well developed and ready to exploit new technology.

Digital optical computing components and architectures have been proposed and demonstrated, but the practicality of such systems is largely undemonstrated, and it is still not possible to say if optics can displace electronics for this kind of application, although it seems probable that at least special-purpose optical computers will eventually be built.

Optical interconnects comprise the area of optical computing that is most developed. Optical interconnects are already used in computers, and more sophisticated components and systems are on the way. This is clearly the area of optical computing that is the closest to industrial application, indeed that is already being used in computer systems.

Because of the intrinsic parallelism of optics, many researchers are working toward implementing neural nets by optical means. The area of neural nets itself is highly volatile and controversial, so the field of optical neural nets is doubly so. Although a few optical neural nets have been built and demonstrated, no really practical system has been demonstrated yet.

An important factor in both the development and the limitations of optical computing is the state of technology and the status of devices and components for optical computing. The costs of certain devices such as spatial light modulators are still too high, materials for real-time holography are still too slow, and so on. But this is changing very rapidly, and it is difficult to predict what will be available in the near future.

Any computer must have an input and an output, a memory for temporary or long-term storage, a processor or processor array to carry out its operations, and interconnections to tie all the parts together. Optics is most developed at the interconnection level and least developed at the processor level. At the input and output levels, some devices are more developed than others; e.g., detector arrays are more developed than spatial light modulators, many of which are still in the research stage.

19.1.2 Optics versus Electronics

We now consider the comparative limitations of optics versus electronics. The main properties of optics that give it an advantage over electronics are related to speed, parallelism, and energy requirements. The storage capacity of optics versus electronics is obvious from the amount of data that can be stored on compact disks, which are read out by means of optics. However, new magnetic storage techniques promise to surpass the storage densities of present optical disks. But newer optical technologies may enable optics to increase storage densities by orders of magnitude.

Speed. The propagation speed of light is sometimes quoted as a major advantage of optics over electronics. It is true that light propagates more rapidly than electrons, but this is not a major advantage of optics. A major advantage lies instead in the fact that electrons need conductors and give off heat, while photons do not. (However, some optical architectures require waveguides.)

The very high frequency of near-infrared and of visible light (about 10^{14} Hz) gives light a major advantage over electronics. *Field-effect transistor* (FET) technology, which provides the fastest technology with devices such as the metal-semiconductor (MESFET), promises devices with cutoff frequencies of several hundred gigahertz, but is near physical limits for semiconductor technology.

Because of the lack of sources, the physical limitations of devices, and the attenuation of very high-frequency signals transmitted by wire, it is unlikely that all-electronic devices will reach speeds as short as 1 ps. Hybrid systems using optics may reach speeds 1 order or 2 of magnitude higher (100 fs). All-optical systems have the potential for speeds up to 1 fs with visible or near-infrared light, but such systems will not be seen in the near future, and it is more likely that hybrid optoelectronic systems will become the order of the day.

Parallelism. One area where optics has a natural advantage over electronics is in its natural parallelism. This is particularly true when free-space propagation can be exploited. The space-bandwidth product (SW) of a linear optical system, which is the maximum number of spatial degrees of freedom, is equal to

$$SW = \frac{aA}{(\lambda f)^2} \tag{19.1}$$

where λ is the wavelength of the light, f is the focal length of the system, a is the area of the input plane, and A is the area of the spatial frequency plane. For wavelengths near the visible end, this is approximately equal to 100 spatial degrees of freedom per square micrometer, which is about the same as the limit for a single electronic device. If we consider the time degrees of freedom, the theoretical limit is about 10^{14} Hz, so the total number of optical degrees of freedom for visible light is about 10^{24} per square centimeter. However, the fastest modulation speeds available now are about 10^{10} Hz, so the practical limit is below 10^{20} per square centimeter. Much progress has been made in recent years in approaching these numbers.

Shamir and Caulfield [105] have estimated that systems using available light modulators are capable of storing 10^{10} bits of information and of forming 10^{11} interconnections. A general architecture using a holographic array and a spatial light modulator could form up to 10^{12} interconnections by using free-space propagation, but this would require two holographic arrays, each 1 m^2, and it is questionable whether this could be built. (However, Caulfield has estimated that such a system will be available soon [5].)

Researchers at Bellcore [63] have recently developed a *surface-emitting microlaser diode array* (SELDA) that contains more than 1 million lasers on a 1-cm^2 surface, with each laser having a diameter of about 1.5 μm (see Sec. 19.3.8). Each laser can be modulated independently (at present there is some correlation between close lasers), with modulation speeds of 100 ps having been demonstrated. The contrast is 1, and each laser has a power of about 1 mW, which is plenty to illuminate a hologram or a spatial light modulator. Such a laser array therefore has about 10^{16} degrees of freedom per second. It remains to be seen whether the array can be run continuously at such speeds.

A 128 × 128 Litton-Semetex spatial light modulator has been operated at frame rates of 2000 frames per second by researchers at Litton Industries, and Semetex has announced a device with 256×256 pixels. Such a device would have $2000 \times 256^2 = 1.31 \times 10^8$ degrees of freedom per second, which is 8 orders of magnitude below that of the SELDA. A spatial light modulator with 1000×1000 pixels running at 1000 frames per second would have 10^9 degrees of freedom per second. The SELDA could replace the holographic array in some systems, and with the new announced 256×256 spatial light modulator announced by Semetex, 4×10^{10} interconnections could be achieved. But not all these interconnections are independent, because only rank 1 interconnection matrices are possible [22] with this configuration.

Energy. Caulfield [21] has shown that both electronic and optical computing systems presently require an energy e of about $10^4 kT$ per binary decision, where k is Boltzmann's constant and T is the temperature. This is close to the theoretical limit for electronics, whereas for optics the theoretical lower energy limit is $10MkT$, where M is the number of events per decision. For analog operations, according to Caulfield, there is no lower theoretical limit for the energy per operation.

A detailed study of the limitations of optics and electronics for interconnects has been carried out by Goodman [38]. He concluded that for cases where the electrical interconnect solution requires a terminated transmission line, the optical interconnect solution can have a distinct advantage.

From the point of view of power, optics can have a distinct advantage at the board-to-board and the chip-to-chip levels, whereas electronics has the advantage at the gate-to-gate level. This means that for classical computers, optics will probably not be competitive in making chips that mimic the operations of electronic chips, but will eventually replace electronics in routing the signals from such chips, between boards, and between computers, and perhaps become more effective in new computer architectures of the future.

Accuracy. One of the most critical problems of electronic computers running at high speeds is the synchronization of the signals. When the clock signals are delayed too long, the resulting synchronization problem is known as *clock skew*. In very fast computers such as the Cray 2 and 3, this is solved by standardizing the propagation lengths of the electric signals by using a geometry in the form of a doughnut. Optical signals can be synchronized much more easily because the imaging conditions for optics also equalize the path lengths. This may turn out to be the main advantage of optical computers.

Optical signals can also be used to synchronize electronic signals by placing a master optical source above electronic circuits [24] that have detectors near the places where clock signals are required.

The above considerations show that optics clearly has the potential to surpass electronics for computing, but to what extent the potential can be fully realized remains to be seen.

We further discuss the capabilities and limitations of optics in Secs. 19.4.1 and 19.5.

19.1.3 Optical Systems and Components

Optical system architectures and components are discussed in Secs. 19.2 and 19.3, respectively. But we touch briefly here on the question in the context of the capabilities of optics.

Input and output devices suitable for optical computing applications are in different stages of development. Light sources of the future clearly will be laser diodes and laser diode arrays, which are evolving rapidly and which will no doubt reach a stage of development where they will no longer limit the performance of optical computing systems. Compact solid-state lasers will eventually have clock frequencies in the range of 10 to 1000 GHz. Detector arrays have also reached a high degree of development and should not be a limiting factor either. Bandwidths as high as 110 GHz have been attained in experimental Schottky diode structures.

Holograms are to be key elements in some types of systems. The development of holography has been hampered by the lack of suitable materials for real-time recording and erasing. In addition, the recording of high-density holograms has required very expensive electron-beam writers or integrated-circuit facilities that are not widely available. The advent of high-density postscript-driven laser printers has given everyone with a personal computer the capability of printing low-cost holograms with a resolution of up to 100 dots per millimeter, using commercial Linotronics printers. Thus, holograms with up to 10^6 dots per square centimeter may be cheaply produced, in practical sizes up to 100 cm^2, thus storing up to 10^8 binary data. But since holograms use only about 10 percent of their capacity for effective storage, the effective storage capacity is about an order of magnitude less. Improvements in holographic recording techniques and in materials, discussed in Sec. 19.3.3, may enable holograms to become useful elements in optical computing systems. For systems that do not need erasable holograms, such as some interconnection systems, present techniques are already suitable.

One of the key components of most optical computing and processing architectures is the light modulator. There are three kinds of modulators: modulators that change the intensity of a beam (e.g., on/off switches), modulators that change the direction of a beam (e.g., acoustooptics modulators), and spatial light modulators that modify the spatial distribution of light in space.

Optical switches are under intense development, and switching speeds as fast as 100 GHz are feasible for optical pulses as short as 100 fs. However, high switching rates, switching speeds, and pulse lengths tend to be mutually exclusive. Optical switches can be combined in sophisticated devices such as crossbars, which are discussed under interconnections.

Acoustooptics light modulators can also modulate light intensity, but are widely used in applications in the mode where a beam of light containing a signal is deflected by an angle that depends on the signal frequency. Typical switching frequencies of signals with frequencies up to 200 GHz are of the order of 1 to 10 ms, and about 5000 resolvable spots are achievable. A review of beam-steering devices was given by Henshaw and Haskel [47] at a recent optical computing meeting.

Spatial light modulators, which modify the spatial distribution of a light field, are the single most important optical device holding up the development of optical computers and particularly of optical neural nets. Spatial light modulators can be either optically or electronically addressed, and both kinds are commercially available. Optically addressed spatial light modulators, although potentially faster than electronically addressed ones, are at present slower by several orders of magnitude, but there are indications that this may soon change.

For example, the Hughes *liquid-crystal light valve* (LCLV), because it uses a phosphor to generate the output optical signal, has a decay time of about 30 ms, so it cannot be switched at speeds higher than this. However, it has a resolution of about 30 mm^{-1} over an area of about 400 mm^2, which gives it about 10^6 degrees of freedom per second. The light valve recently announced by Nippon Telephone and Telegraph (NTT) is 1000 times faster and has twice the resolution, and so it has about 10^{11} degrees of freedom per second.

The electronically addressed Semetex Light-Mod (Litton iron garnet H-triggered magnetooptics device) has 128 × 128 individually addressed pixels that can be individually switched in 10^{-4} s, and it has been reported to run at 2000 frames per second by researchers at Litton Industries. A modulator running at this rate would have more than 10^7 degrees of freedom per second.

Other electrically addressed spatial light modulators such as the Texas Instruments deformable-mirror modulator or the ferroelectric modulator being developed by the University of Colorado have the promise to surpass these numbers, but they are not yet commercially available. Spatial light modulators are discussed in Sec. 19.3.1.

A number of optical component designs have been proposed at the gate level for optical computers. For example, Murdocca et al. [93] have proposed designs for optical two-dimensional (2D) *programmable logic arrays* (PLAs), and Goutzoulis et al. [41] have built a 7×7 laser-diode-based position-coded lookup-table (LUT) processor for doing fundamental operations that has run at clock speeds of 500 MHz. They claim that such systems can have a multiplication efficiency 2 to 3 orders of magnitude greater than that of GaAs multipliers. The latter would have a system-volume advantage of about 10, but the system efficiency of the optical LUT would be at least 100 times greater. Such devices are discussed in Secs. 2.13, 2.14, and 3.7.

Hybrid Systems. The early computing systems using optics will definitely be hybrid systems that employ optics for some operations and electronics for others. We have already pointed out that optical interconnections are being used in electronic computers and that their use will increase.

A typical example of a hybrid optical digital system is an optical inspection system marketed by Global Holonetics [23] which uses a wedge-ring detector to sample an optical Fourier transform, together with an electronic neural net. The neural net uses the measurements from the detector for rotation and scale-invariant classification of patterns. The system has been used to classify defects in such things as TV dinners and bottles. This system has also been used for applications such as fingerprint recognition.

19.1.4 Optical Computers

Analog Optical Computing. The oldest optical computers are analog systems. The 2D optical correlator has existed since the 1950s. This kind of system, whose main application is in accomplishing optical Fourier transforms or recognizing objects by means of matched filtering, has seen a renaissance because of the availability of new input devices, especially spatial light modulators. The Fourier-transforming part of the correlator has also found practical use in systems such as the Global Holonetics system discussed in Sec. 19.1.3. The architecture for a typical system is shown in Fig. 19.1.

A spatial light modulator can be used in the input plane to rapidly input objects; a second spatial light modulator can be used in the Fourier plane to rapidly change spatial filters. A detector array at the output plane can be used with a small computer for detecting correlation peaks. A compact version of this correlator suitable to be put in a missile with a diameter of 6 in was built by Perkin-Elmer for Jet Propulsion Laboratories, and preliminary tests were carried out on it [42]. The correlator used had a fixed filter on film, and the ground scenes were input by means of a liquid-crystal light valve used as an incoherent-to-coherent light converter. At present no performance numbers are available. During a panel discussion at the International Society for Optical Engineering (SPIE) symposium held in San Diego in July 1990, a representative of Litton Data Systems stated that they had successfully used an optical correlator in military field tests, but he gave no details. Litton has also built a prototype of a compact optical correlator, but as far as we know, it has not yet been published. More information on this architecture and on how it can be used is given in the section on architectures.

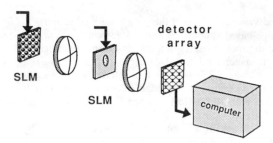

FIGURE 19.1   Optical correlator for real-time pattern recognition.

The recent development of improved matched filters by us [1] and by others promises to make this type of system practical for real-time pattern recognition. Such systems have been demonstrated in the field at frame rates of 30 frames per second, using LCLV light modulators with resolutions of 30 mm^{-1}. This corresponds to a respectable 10^6 operations per second, a speed that can be increased by orders of magnitude given available technology.

Integrated optics has the capacity to integrate optical devices such as couplers, prisms, gratings, acoustooptic deflectors, and modulators on planar substrates. An integrated optic device for matrix-matrix multiplication was recently demonstrated [77]. Bandpass responses of up to 8 GHz have been demonstrated by using Y-fed directional couplers [13]. Researchers at Bell Laboratories are working on the integration of such devices into bulk modules.

Digital Optical Computing.   It is uncertain at present whether an all-optical general-purpose computer will ever be built. But optics is definitely finding a place in computers, and it is certain that many computers will use optical interconnects at the chip-to-chip and the board-to-board levels. It is likely that the first all-optical computers, if they ever appear, will be special-purpose computers. However, general-purpose architectures for optical computers have been proposed. The optical computer architectures and devices are discussed in Sec. 19.2.

A simple prototype built by Bell Laboratories using S-SEEDs is described in the section on architectures. Harold Szu of Naval Research Laboratories (NRL) claimed that he would build a computer capable of 10^{15} operations per second, using optics and superconducting technology, but so far he has not come forward with a prototype.

In the above discussion of the capabilities of optics versus electronics, it was established that optics may not be competitive with electronics at the gate level because of the interconnections. However, the fact remains that optical switches have the potential to be faster than electronic switches, so researchers have not given up on the question of optical chips. Optical switches with switching times of 100 fs have been demonstrated in the laboratory, and switches that have bandwidths in excess of 100 GHz should be feasible.

Optical computing architectures as well as the future potential of components and architectures are discussed in Sec. 19.2. Switching technology is discussed in Sec. 19.4. Digital computing by means of optical systems is still in the early research stages, and there are as yet no practical implementations, although Guilfoyle [43] has built a prototype using optical gates, and is presently building a computer that can be characterized as all-optical.

Knowledge-Based Systems.   One of the promising application areas for optical computing is in knowledge-based systems. A *knowledge-based system* (KBS) manipulates symbolic information to produce useful outputs for given input queries. Typical applications include database managers, relational database systems, and expert systems. A fundamental operation of most KBSs is deductive inference. Optics research in this area has dealt mainly with representing knowledge by using matrixlike formalisms, designing system architectures based on optical inner-product processors, the use of optical substitution, and neural network ideas.

Conventional KBSs are implemented in electronic computers by using languages like LISP or PROLOG. A connectionist approach has recently been applied that uses neural networks [36] to achieve a trainable system. Typical optical KBSs use holograms and spatial light modulators [119] to achieve simplified PROLOG-type operations. Casasent and Botha [18] have used KBS techniques to recognize, identify, and classify objects. Derstine and Guha [27] have proposed an architecture called *SPARO* (symbolic processing architecture in optics) to implement PROLOG-type operations.

Symbolic computing systems such as those described in Sec. 19.2 could also be considered as knowledge-based systems.

Optical knowledge-based systems are still in the research stage, and no practical systems have yet been built. This is partially due to the novelty of the field for optics researchers and partially to the limitations of available optical components, notably spatial light modulators, most of which are still too slow. The availability of faster and larger spatial light modulators could make this an important applications area. A discussion of the various aspects of optical knowledge-based systems was published by Berra et al. [11]. More recently, Berra [9] has shown the advantages of optical database machines for applications such as relational database management.

19.2   OPTICAL COMPUTER ARCHITECTURES

19.2.1 Introduction

Although specific optical architectures have been proposed, it is not possible at present to present a classification of optical computer architectures because, on one hand, the field is still too new and fluid and, on the other hand, many optical architectures are total or partial implementations of architectures mentioned above in Sec. 19.1.4. In general, purely optical architectures, since they are designed to exploit the inherent parallelism of optics, fall within the *single-instruction multiple-data* (SIMD) or *multiple-instruction multiple-data* (MIMD) categories.

Many optical computing systems use a vector-matrix architecture or a correlator architecture as part of the computer, in order to carry out inner products. Although we consider optical neural net systems separately from digital computing architectures, this division is somewhat artificial, because the massively parallel nature of many optical computers makes the boundary between optical computers and optical neural networks rather ill defined.

In the near term, the impact of optics is to be felt mostly at the interconnection level. This includes using optical interconnections in classical digital computer architectures, although it does not preclude interconnection architectures specifically designed to exploit optics.

More than half of the optical computing architectures proposed employ either a vector-matrix architecture or a correlator architecture.

Many purely optical architectures have been proposed to accomplish computing operations such as symbolic substitution or, at the component level, parallel inputs and outputs, switching, logic and gate arrays, and so on. However, no general-purpose all-optical computer has yet been built, and it is likely that the first ones built will not be competitive with computers using electronics to carry out logic operations. This section emphasizes what we see as the main ideas driving the development of optical computing architectures, in order to give more space to areas of optical computing that are more mature. See McAulay [88] for a more detailed study of digital optical computer architectures.

19.2.2 General Architectures

Optics can be used in various manners in computers. Different architectures can result whether optics is used primarily for memory, for interconnections, for processing, or for all three. Berra et al. [10] have considered architectures for using optics in conjunction with digital supercomputers. In the first, optics is used for memory. Both disk-based optical memories and page-oriented holograms are considered. Disk-based architectures are described later in Sec. 19.2.6. The detected optical signals are then fed into an electronic supercomputer.

In a more complex system, the optical signals from disks or page-oriented holographic memories are broadcast to multiple supercomputer processors to be processed in parallel.

In a still more sophisticated system, some optical processing is carried out before the data are fed into the digital computers. Note that the optical part of this last system can itself be a supercomputer, and it is possible to imagine that the supercomputers at the end of the line themselves are at least partially optical.

19.2.3 The Bell Laboratories Architecture

In March 1990, the optical computing research department at Bell Laboratories announced an optical computer using new electrooptical devices. The computer consisted of only four modules that did a modest amount of computing. The demonstration showed the computer counting. The computer showed can function at speeds of a few hundred megahertz, but it is claimed that the device can be scaled to operate at rates in excess of 1 GHz with a much larger array of modules. In this device, the input and output beams were 4 × 8 arrays of data, but the chips used are capable of having 2048 symmetric *self-electrooptic-effect devices* (SEEDs) on each chip. The SEED is a bistable device that changes its state when a packet of light strikes it, and in this computer, it is used as a NOR gate.

Each module has its own laser diode source, which illuminates the SEED array through a beam splitter and a grating that broadcasts the beam to the SEED. An input beam from the previous module is reflected off a mask that determines the operation to be accomplished and is also incident on the SEED array. The SEED array redirects its output through the mask and a mirror to the output, where it goes to the next module. The modules are assembled in a loop, as shown in Fig. 19.2.

It is difficult at this time to determine the capabilities of this system or what class of computer architecture it fits into. Since the SEED array is capable of containing at least 2048 devices functioning at rates of over 1 GHz, it is likely that architectures based on this device will play a major role in the development of future optical computers. SEED arrays are discussed in Sec. 19.3.2.

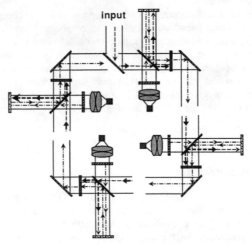

FIGURE 19.2 Bell Laboratories optical computer. *(Adapted from N. C. Craft and M. E. Prise, "Processor Does Light Logic," Laser Focus World, May 1990, pp. 191–200)*

19.2.4 Correlation-Based Architectures

Developments in input and output devices have improved the capabilities of analog optical systems such as Fourier processors or correlators, which can be used for real-time pattern recognition.

Optical correlator architectures not only are important for analog optical processing, but also are used for other operations, including neural networks, which are not covered here.

Optical correlator architectures are useful for two reasons: their ability to carry out correlations or inner products in parallel and their properties of shift invariance.

When the input to an optical correlator is $f(x, y)$, the output is $f(x, y) * h(x, y)$, where $h(x, y)$, is the impulse response of the system. At the origin $(0, 0)$, the output is

$$g(0,0) = \int\int f(x, y)h(x, y)\, dx\, dy \qquad (19.2)$$

which is the inner product between the two-dimensional arrays $f(x, y)$ and $h(x, y)$.

The number of spatial degrees of freedom of an optical correlator can be in excess of 10^{12}, and if appropriate *spatial light modulators* (SLMs) with, say, 2000 frames per second were available, such systems could have a capacity in excess of 10^{14} bits/s. Because of the limitations of present SLMs, the data rates achievable in practice today are about 10^7 bits/s.

Correlator-based architectures also play an important role in symbolic substitution and in neural net optical architectures.

19.2.5 Vector-Matrix-Based Systems

Many computing operations can be cast in the form of products of vectors and matrices. One of the first optical systems capable of carrying out calculations with discrete data was

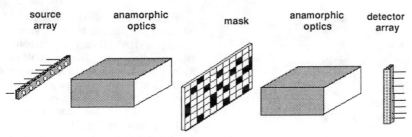

FIGURE 19.3   Optical vector-matrix multiplier.

an optical configuration known as the *vector-matrix*, or *Stanford, processor*. Such a system is shown in Fig. 19.3.

Each source of the source array (or spatial light modulator) is spread out by means of anamorphic optics to one column of the matrix mask, which may be a fixed mask or a 2D spatial light modulator. The second set of anamorphic optics focuses the output from one row of the mask on one detector at the output. It is easy to see that if the sources are incoherent with respect to each other, this operation will yield on the output detector array the product of the input vector with the matrix containing the transparencies of the mask

$$\mathbf{y} = \mathbf{Mx} \tag{19.3}$$

where $\mathbf{x}$ is a vector containing the intensities of the input source array, $\mathbf{M}$ is a matrix (usually binary) containing the transparency values of the mask, and $\mathbf{y}$ is a vector containing the set of intensities arriving on each detector of the array at the output.

All the calculations are carried out in parallel, so this system allows very rapid calculations. Such systems are useful, because discrete data are often formatted into vectors or matrices, and the operations to be carried out on the data can often be cast as products of matrices and vectors. Examples of applications where such systems have been used, besides calculating matrix products, include spectrum analysis, discrete Fourier transforms, and optical neural networks.

By adding feedback from the output to the input and/or systolic functioning, many more operations can be carried out. For example, the similarity transform, a triple matrix product operation, has been demonstrated [4] by using a time-integrating architecture.

Because of its capability for carrying out inner products, the vector-matrix architecture is popular both in digital optical computer architectures and in optical neural net architectures.

19.2.6 Optical-Disk-Based Architectures

One of the areas in which optics has surpassed electronics is optical disk storage. Whereas current magnetic disks can store about 6.7 Mbits/cm^2, optical disks can store hundreds of megabits per square centimeter. At present optical disks have slower input and output rates than magnetic disks, but they are rapidly catching up. The most advanced technology for optical disks is a magnetooptic method based on the Kerr effect, where the recording medium is a thin layer of vertically oriented magnetic material. The material is written by heating it above its Curie point with a laser and changing the magnetic orientation with a magnetic field. The material can be written and erased millions of times, because the process is nondestructive.

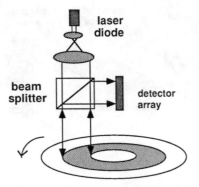

FIGURE 19.4 Parallel readout of multiple tracks. *(After D. Psaltis, A. A. Yamamura, M. A. Neifeld, and S. Kobayashi, "Parallel Readout of Optical Disks," in Proceedings of Optical Society of America Topical Meeting on Optical Computing, vol. 9, pp. 58–61, February 1989)*

With magnetic disks, data rates of 3 Mbytes/s are possible by using sequential reading, and 50 Mbytes/s is attainable by using parallel reading from multiple disks. By reading multiple tracks from such optical disks simultaneously, data rates of the order of 500 Mbytes/s are possible [10]. One architecture for reading multiple tracks is shown in Fig. 19.4.

This configuration is not suitable for writing, since each of the beams cannot be modulated independently. For this, one possible solution is to use multiple reading and writing heads [101]. Instead of detecting the output optical beams, the latter may be input directly into an optical processor. So the system shown can be considered as a parallel memory for an optical or a digital computer. Given that the data rate coming out of the disk can be as high as 500 Mbytes/s, the computers using this datastream will need a high degree of parallelism to be able to process this amount of data. In particular, this kind of memory can be used as the front end of some of the architectures discussed above.

Magnetic disks are expected to overtake optical disks with respect to storage density in the near future, although it seems improbable that magnetic disks can be read out with the degree of parallelism that is possible with optics.

19.2.7 Optical Cellular Processors

Optical cellular processors include cellular automata and symbolic substitution systems. Both are easy to implement in optics. The concepts underlying optical cellular automata are very similar to those underlying symbolic substitution, which are discussed in Sec. 19.2.8. An optical cellular processor is an array in which the state of one cell is determined by its prior state as well as the states of its neighbors. Such processors can be implemented by holographic interconnects [108]. As opposed to symbolic substitution, cellular automata do not need to have a pattern recognition step to recognize the data. Among the operations that can be carried out by cellular automata are pattern recognition and logic operations. The most advanced types of optical cellular processors are symbolic substitution systems.

19.2.8 Optical Symbolic Substitution

Symbolic substitution is the operation whereby a given input bit pattern is replaced by an output bit pattern according to a set of rules. Such operations can simulate a Turing machine, which means that symbolic substitution can do all the operations that a digital computer can do, including boolean logic, binary arithmetic, and so on. Some systems use repeated applications of rules, but single-substitution rule systems may be used to implement general-purpose systems. Such systems have been the object of considerable

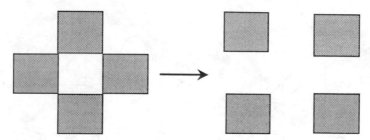

FIGURE 19.5   A transition rule for symbolic substitution.

study, and optics is well suited for such operations because of its ability to carry out operations in parallel on two-dimensional patterns. A mathematical formulation of symbolic substitution algebras has been worked out [53].

An example of a simple transition rule is shown in Fig. 19.5. Murdocca [92] has shown that this rule and its inverse are enough to create a general-purpose computer.

The basic idea of symbolic substitution derived from cellular automata, where locally interconnected cells interact according to certain transition rules (but some symbolic substitution ideas are not implemented in cellular automata). Every occurrence of one pattern is replaced by another pattern. Certain bits in the pattern are called *control* bits, and they play the role of the algorithm. The system must first recognize the pattern, then carry out the substitution. This involves replicating, shifting, and combining images, which are easy to implement by optics and for which two approaches have been proposed [16, 86]. One is based on geometric optics and uses conventional optical components such as prisms and beam splitters; the other is based on diffractive optics and uses holograms. The geometric optics approach usually suffers from light losses, whereas the holographic approach suffers from clock skew problems associated with different phase delays caused by different optical paths.

Brenner et al. [16] have used a correlator architecture to implement optical logic by symbolic substitution, using spatial filtering. With this technique, the logic operation itself does not require an active device; only the coding of the data requires an active device. The logic states (1 and 0) are coded by changing the direction of the light rather than by changing the intensity, using theta modulation coding, random carrier coding, directional random carrier coding, prism deflection coding, and deflection by polarization coding. Three basic recognition setups were described to accomplish the recognition steps: the cyclic recognizer, the linear recognizer, and the folded recognizer. All these techniques require passing the signals more than once through the optical correlator. The substitution operation can be accomplished by means of an optical pattern substituter, whose input is the spatial-frequency-encoded output of a pattern recognizer. Such a substituter is shown in Fig. 19.6. The input signal is the spatial-frequency-coded output of a pattern recognizer; F marks the filter planes, and the M are spatial frequency masks whose job it is to mask out those patterns that do not correspond to the searched patterns.

In the final pattern, only those pixels where the search pattern was found will be bright. The above system is capable of doing any possible logic operation between the pixels of one pattern [83].

Experiments have been carried out by the authors for proof-of-principle purposes, but the important features, such as fan-in, fan-out, storage, etc., have not yet been addressed.

A harsh criticism of symbolic substitution optical computing approaches has been published by Kamiliev et al. [68]. The authors claim that the high clock rate of symbolic

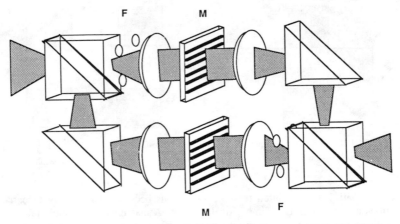

FIGURE 19.6 Pattern substituter *(After K. H. Brenner, A. Huang, and N. Streibl, "Digital Optical Computing with Symbolic Substitution," Applied Optics, 25:3054, 1986)*

substitution systems precludes the use of holographic elements and forces the use of refractive optics, which reduces symbolic substitution to the equivalent of a 2D mesh-connected architecture, which they claim is known to be inefficient for many computing problems. However, newer symbolic substitution architectures have incorporated global interconnections and may overcome some of the problems of the locally connected architectures, in architectures such as programmable logic arrays (PLAs) [93], although Kamiliev et al. do not think so. In addition, other types of architectures not based on interconnections are possible. See, e.g., the correlator-based architectures discussed in Sec. 19.2.4.

We think that although symbolic substitution systems are contested by many optical researchers, the jury is still out on whether such optical systems can be made practical.

19.2.9 Symbolic Computing

Symbolic computing is not necessarily equivalent to symbolic substitution. Neff [95] has described symbolic computing as fine-grained, tightly coupled multiprocessor systems, applied to problems in speech recognition, image understanding, natural language understanding, and expert systems. Thus symbolic computing can be understood as a subset of artificial intelligence, with the purpose of emulating human intelligence, whereas symbolic substitution is usually (but not always) associated with logic operations. He has proposed a few general architectures for parallel processing, but he did not show how they could be used for symbolic computing.

19.2.10 Programmable Optoelectronic Multiprocessors

The *programmable optoelectronic multiprocessor* (POEM) approach is an architecture proposed by researchers at the University of California in San Diego [68] to achieve general-purpose parallel computing by combining the advantages of silicon technology and of programmable global communications provided by optical interconnects. The system is based on wafer-scale integration of optoelectronic processing elements and on reconfigurable free-space interconnects. The *processing element* (PE) arrays can be realized with silicon/PLZT, and the interconnects can be implemented with dichromated gelatin as the volume holographic medium. The local communication within a PE is done with electrical interconnects, and holographic optical interconnects connect the PEs among themselves. In principle, the interconnects between PEs can be made reconfigurable by using a real-time holographic medium (but currently available media tend to be slow or to require high power).

The POEM architecture uses light modulators as optical transmitters because they mitigate heat dissipation problems and are easier to integrate with silicon, but recent developments in microlaser arrays could make such sources competitive for this application. The architecture can support any class of computers.

Figure 19.7 illustrates a fine-grained system containing a very large number of one-bit silicon processors.

The instructions and master clock are broadcast through a computer-generated hologram on top of the processing elements, each of which has its own memory and electrical wires for its internal interconnections. The global interconnection between PEs is optical and is activated by illuminating different holograms in the high-capacity volume holographic array, by means of a random code on a spatial light modulator. According to the authors, the topology of this system can be adapted to the algorithms required for a given set of problems by using reconfigurable global interconnections. They claim that 0.5 million PEs can be implemented on two highly interconnected wafers, that the system is more energy-efficient than symbolic substitution systems, and that the architecture is more amenable to reconfigurable interconnections.

However, those allegations are not yet supported by experimental results. This architecture does, however, address the contention that optics is not competitive with electronics at the gate-to-gate level, since this level of interconnection in a POEM architecture is electronic. It is still too early to draw definitive conclusions about the ultimate value of this approach, but it is certainly worth following.

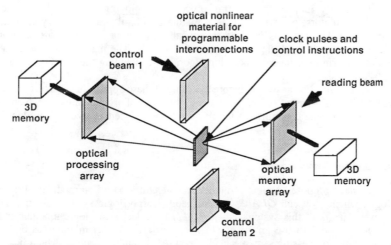

FIGURE 19.7 POEM architecture. *(After F. Kamilev and S. C. Esener, "Implementation of NETL Knowledge-Base System with Programmable Opto-electronic Multiprocessor Architecture," Optical Society of America Topical Meeting on Optical Computing, Technical Digest, 9:303–306, 1989)*

19.2.11 DOC-II

Guilfoyle et al. [44] are building an all-optical 32-bit general-purpose computer using 64-channel acoustooptics spatial light modulators, eight-element index guided laser diode bars, and a 128-element high-speed avalanche photodiode array. The authors claim that the system will be capable of processing speeds in excess of 10^9 bits/s. The system uses some electronics for GaAs discrete logic and for programmable array logic arrays, and for the inputs to the acoustooptics cells and for amplifying the signals at the detector array, so this system must be considered as a hybrid optodigital system.

SMOEC Computer.   Researchers at the Aerospace Corporation and at the University of Southern California are building a *shared-memory optical/electronic computer* (SMOEC), which integrates an integration of electronic processing elements and memories with a reconfigurable optical interconnection network [120]. The authors claim that this is the first application of a general-purpose *multiple-instruction multiple-data* (MIMD) shared-memory paradigm to optical computing. The authors did not say what the performance of the machine is expected to be.

19.2.12 Optical Bit-Serial Architectures

A bit-serial computer using $LiNbO_3$ directional couplers as logic elements and fiber-optic delay lines as memory elements has been designed and is being built by the University of Colorado [66]. The couplers are used as five-terminal optical devices that can do a variety of digital operations including AND, AND-NOT, NOT, Buffer, out MUX, DEMUX, and SPLITTER. The optical delay line can store 1024 16-bit words in a fiber-optic loop having a length of 3.3 m, at a clock frequency of 1 THz, but it is not clear if the device has been run at this rate. These units can be used in a variety of roles including an optical ALU [19].

Researchers at Herriott-Watt University have designed a demonstrator programmable optical 16 × 16 array processor [118], using their *cellular logic image processor* (CLIP) [121], which uses a looped optical array processor employing lasers, beam splitters, spatial light modulators, polarization optics, gratings, and holograms to carry out digital logic operations. The CLIP is used as an optical coprocessor inside a host electronic computer which provides all the necessary control signals. The machine will be capable of a number of primitive image processing algorithms, including the fast Fourier transform.

Questions that must be answered before the value of these approaches can be estimated involve the practical speeds that can be attained, the types of architectures for which they are best suited, and the capability of the devices to be reduced in size and produced in large arrays.

19.2.13 Optical Array Logic

Tanida et al. have proposed optical computing architectures based on modules of optical array logic, which they call *OPALS* (optical parallel array logic system). In the more recent developments of this system, called *OALMA* (optical array logic modular architecture), they propose to use arrays of *OAL* (optical array logic) modules as building blocks for a large processing system [112]. The OAL modules, each of which has two parallel inputs and one output port, are connected in cascade. They have simulated a system for multiplication of 27 pairs of 16-bit integers on a SUN workstation, but the optical system has not yet been built.

19.2.14 Optical Lookup Tables

Systems based on *lookup tables* (LUTs) are generally arithmetic logic units and do not constitute a complete architecture. Tables contain all possible outputs to be read out when the appropriate inputs are present, and such architectures are appropriate for pipelined processing. Some systems combine lookup tables with other architectures (see Sec. 19.2.15). Such systems often use residue arithmetic, which requires no carry bit but which requires conversion from the residue form to the arithmetic form and vice versa. Because optical systems can be inherently parallel and because lookup tables are strongly interconnected systems, optics is well suited to implement LUTs.

One such system using laser diodes and fiber interconnections has been operated at data rates exceeding 250 MHz, the speed being limited by the pulse generator. By using GaAs technology, rates close to 3 GHz could be attainable [40].

Optical LUTs can have power requirements 2 orders of magnitude lower than electronic ones, but they require a larger volume. Although this approach has some promising aspects, the development is not sufficiently advanced to draw conclusions about its practicality; but it seems likely that at least some specialized systems in the future will use optical lookup tables.

19.2.15 Arithmetic Logic Unit Based on Optical Crossbar

General-purpose computers based on classical architectures will require arithmetic logic units (ALUs). Falk et al. [31] have built a prototype ALU based on an optical crossbar architecture. The concept, which is similar to a previous system using electronic interconnects [7], consists of combining residue number theory and a one-of-many representation with a lookup-table approach. One input serves as the column label and another as the row label to a modulo 3 addition table. The prototype built used fiber-optic interconnects and commercially available light-emitting diodes. Detector-threshold circuits performed the decision logic. The test circuitry limited the speed of the device to 50×10^6 arithmetic operations per second, and the error rate was less than 10^{-12}. It is claimed that by using integrated optics, much higher rates are achievable.

19.3 COMPONENTS AND TECHNOLOGIES

Whether optics will be an alternative or a complement to electronics for computing depends to a large extent on the technological advances in optical devices and materials. Architectural considerations for optical computing also depend on novel devices and materials. Optical computing requires light sources, detectors, switches, and optical refractive, reflective, and diffractive components. These devices should have distinct characteristics and should also be compatible with electronic VLSI technologies.

Optoelectronic and photonic technologies are a fast-growing area in the industries related to optical fiber communications, optical disk memories, optoelectronic displays, laser printers, fax machines, and photocopiers. There have also been significant advances in particular devices and materials for optical analog, digital, parallel, and neural computing. A remarkable technological advance is the applications of electronic VLSI fabrication technologies to optics and optoelectronics, resulting in new devices and new technologies, such as multiple quantum well effect devices, binary optics, micro-optic components, etc. We now examine some of the major optical and optoelectronic devices and materials for optical computing.

19.3.1 Spatial Light Modulators

Spatial light modulators (SLMs) represent a key element in a wide variety of optical systems. They are a fundamental component in parallel optical and neural computing architectures. Optics offers inherent parallelism for computing. To exploit the parallelism, two-dimensional spatial information patterns have to be imposed on optical beams by the SLMs. The SLMs are in fact 2D arrays of photonic switches modulating the intensities, phases, or polarizations of the passing light beams. Various physical mechanisms can be used in SLMs such as the linear electrooptic (Pockel) effect, quadratic electrooptic (Kerr) effect, acoustooptic Bragg cells (1D), magnetooptical (Faraday) effect, and electromechanical effects. Some SLMs are addressed optically, and others are addressed electrically [111, 35, 29, 30]. A diagram of an electrically addressed SLM is shown in Fig. 19.8.

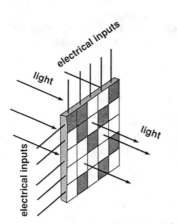

FIGURE 19.8   Electrically addressed spatial light modulator.

The SLM technologies have seen significant progress in the last years and have been used in practical applications for optical coherent correlators. To satisfy the needs of optical analog, digital, neural computing, and optical interconnection applications, SLMs should have characteristics such as high spatial resolution (>100 line pairs per millimeter), large size (>1000 × 1000 pixels), high speed (megahertz frame rates), a high extinction ratio (>1000:1), gray levels (>100), low power dissipation, and low cost. Input sensitivity and spectral response are also important for optically addressed SLMs.

NTT has recently announced a ferroelectric liquid-crystal light valve with twice the resolution of the existing commercial LCLVs and 100 times faster, with a time resolution of 70 μs. Assuming the size is about the same (about 25 cm²) and assuming each pixel can be individually addressed, the capacity of this device comes to about 10^{11} operations per second.

Although the full specifications of this new device are not yet available, new devices such as this one, along with Bell Laboratories' microlaser arrays with millions of lasers on a square centimeter and Bellcore's new arrays of SEEDs whose technology will allow many optical microswitches on a single chip, should enable the practical realization of parallel optical architectures that were not possible before, with speeds from 10^{10} to 10^{12} bits/s.

One area where optics will temporarily lose its advantage is in disk storage. New magnetic technologies soon to be available will allow storage densities higher than those of optical disks, and magnetic disks are usually faster. Does this mean that optical disk storage is dead? Not at all. One exciting and promising recent development is the parallel readout of optical disks. With present technologies, data rates of 600 Mbits/s are feasible. Magnetic disks will always be difficult to read out in parallel, whereas multiple tracks of optical disks can be read out just by shining light on them. In addition, new optical technologies such as spectral hole burning promise optical resolutions 100 times smaller than the spatial resolution limit, but this is still some time in the future.

If nothing else, the past year has shown that the technology allowing higher speeds is evolving very fast for both optics and electronics, and it is probably too early for any definitive evaluation of their respective capabilities.

We now briefly review recent developments of the most widely used SLMs.

Magnetooptic SLMs. Sight-Mod magnetooptic SLMs were developed by Litton Data Systems and are marketed by Semetex. When a linearly polarized light beam traverses the magnetooptic element, its polarization direction changes due to the Faraday effect. The polarization modulation of the light beam is transformed to a light intensity modulation or to a phase modulation by a polarizer-analyzer combination placed on the two sides of the SLM.

The switching time may be less than 1 μs [103]. A 128 × 128 Sight-Mod magnetooptic SLM has been successfully run at a continuous speed of 351 frames per second for 35 days. An array speed of 1000 frames per second will be possible [104]. In 1991, Semetex announced a 256 × 256 device.

The Sight-Mod SLMs are mostly used in coherent optical correlators to introduce input images and binary-phase-only filters for real-time pattern recognition. If the images are input at TV rates (30 frames per second), the SLMs will allow 10 to 30 filters per input. This speed can be exploited for digital optical computers, optical neural nets, 2D distortion-invariant pattern recognition, or 3D target recognition.

Liquid-Crystal Light Valve. The LCLV was developed by Hughes and is commercially available. The device consists of a sandwich of thin films, a cadmium sulfide photosensor layer, a liquid-crystal layer, and several other thin films, as shown in Fig. 19.9.

The modulation of the polarization in the readout light beam is a function of the writing beam intensity and may be converted to an intensity modulation or to a phase modulation in the readout beam by using a polarizer and analyzer placed in the incident and reflected readout beams.

The LCLV has a resolution of approximately 30 lines per millimeter and medium contrast which makes it unsuitable for applications requiring high contrast such as some optical neural net applications. The LCLVs are mostly used as an incoherent-to-coherent input image converter for real-time optical coherent processors and are now used in some optical and neural computing systems [12].

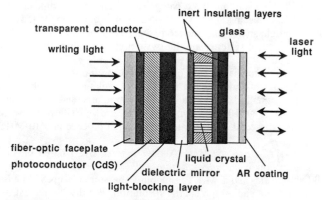

FIGURE 19.9 Hughes liquid-crystal light valve construction.

NTT of Japan has recently announced an optically addressed ferroelectric LCLV that has a much improved performance [50], with a speed 2 orders of magnitude faster than conventional liquid crystals. They claim that it has a frame speed of 2000 frames per second, a 70-μs response time, an input sensitivity of 20 nJ/cm^2, and a resolution of more than 60 lines per millimeter. Assuming that it is 5 cm $\times$ 5 cm, this corresponds to a potential rate of over 10^{11} operations per second, although it remains to be seen if it can process data at that rate. NTT scientists affirm that two such devices can carry out operations such as subtraction on two randomly selected images in 50 ms, which corresponds to a data rate of 4×10^8 operations per second. The device does not have to be refreshed and can hold an image for more than a week.

Electrically Addressed Ferroelectric Liquid-Crystal SLMs.   Liquid-crystal modulators that can be addressed electrically have also been developed. The advantages of the *ferroelectric liquid-crystal* (FLC) modulators are the small pixel size and the high switching speed. The potential resolution of a ferroelectric liquid-crystal SLM is of the order of 333 pixels per millimeter. A 32 $\times$ 32 FLC spatial modulator with 17 $\times$ 17 μm pixels and 5-μm spacing between pixels has been fabricated. This pixel size is smaller than the SLMs using other materials such as that described above. The switching time ranges from 20 μs to 20 ns. This speed is limited by the power dissipation of the device. Energy dissipation in FLCs is inversely proportional to the switching time. Slower speeds dissipate less energy [65].

PLZT Spatial Light Modulators.   PLZT is a ceramic material composed of lead, lanthanum, zirconium, and titanium. The basis of the use of PLZT as an optical switch is the quadratic electrooptic effect. If a sufficient voltage is applied to the PLZT through the electrodes, the electrooptic effect will introduce birefringence in the PLZT and the PLZT element will act as a half-wave plate; an input polarization at 45° to the axes will be rotated by 90° upon exit from the material. PLZT is one of the materials with the highest electrooptic coefficient and is available in large-area wafers. PLZT SLMs have high power efficiency of about 20 percent for the on state. The switching time is about 25 μs, and a high voltage (200 V) should be applied for half-wave modulation. This voltage could be reduced in transverse modulators. An Si/PLZT light modulator was proposed for an integrated optoelectronic multiple-processor array [80].

Deformable Mirror SLMs.   *Deformable mirror device* (DMD) SLMs were developed by Texas Instruments [51]. There are three categories of DMD: elastometers, membranes, and cantilever or torsion beams. The DMDs operate in a binary mode [55]. The mirrors are illuminated with light so that undeflected pixels reflect the light at an angle outside the entrance pupil of an optical system, and the twisted mirrors reflect the illuminating light into the entrance pupil.

A DMD light modulator has a high contrast and low noise and works at all wavelengths. It is light-efficient and does not require high voltages; only about 5 to 10 V is required. DMDs have small pixels about 15 $\times$ 15 μm in area and can be scaled to large formats. Arrays as large as 1024 $\times$ 1024 could be grown. The response time of the mirrors is several microseconds, and the addressing can proceed at a 10-MHz rate [25].

Multiple-Quantum-Well-Based SLMs.   A new type of SLM based on the enhanced exitonic electroabsorption in *multiple-quantum-well* (MQW) structures is being developed in AT&T Bell Laboratories and at M.I.T. Lincoln Laboratories. This SLM has a potential for a very fast frame rate and a high spatial resolution. We discuss the MQW device in the next section.

There are many other types of SLMs such as nonlinear Fabry-Perot microarray [64], *microchannel SLMs* (MSLMs) developed by M.I.T. and Hamamatsu [45], oil-film light valves developed by GE, etc.

MQW Light Modulators.   The incorporation of a mirror between the MQW layer structure and the substrate gives an MQW light modulator operating in reflection [15]. Based on the *quantum-confined Stark effect* (QCSE), there are two distinct modes of operation: off, in which the increasing voltage gives increasing reflection, or on, in which the decreasing voltage results in reduced reflection. The normal on/off contrast ratio of the modulator is defined as the ratio between the reflection with a specified voltage to that at 0 V. This ratio can be about 5 at 853 nm with a voltage of 5 V. The advantage of the QCSE modulators compared with other types of SLMs is their high speed of operation. Their speed is essentially limited by the time taken to apply the electric field on them. The microscopic physics suggests fundamental limits <1 ps. The best high-speed performance is in the range of 20 GHz in a real device. There have been successful attempts in making quantum well modulators on silicon substrates [87].

Acoustooptical Cells.   An acoustooptical cell consists of a photoelastic interaction material, such as water, glass, or an exotic crystal, to which a piezoelectric transducer is bonded. The device is driven by an electric signal that creates changes in the density and in the index of refraction within the interaction medium. The light passing through the acoustooptic cell is then modulated in phase according to changes in the optical path length. When the interaction length between the light and the medium is long enough, the acoustooptic cell is operating in the Bragg mode with more than 95 percent of the diffracted light in a single order. Otherwise the cells operate in the Raman-Nath mode as a phase grating [78].

The acoustooptic cell is a one-dimensional traveling-wave spatial light modulator [72]. This is one of the most successful SLM techniques used to perform intensive signal processing operations. In the past decade an enormous amount of progress has been made. The high level of development for acoustooptic cells, laser diodes, and high-speed high-dynamic-range photodetector arrays has resulted in analog acoustooptic processors with high signal throughput, small and compact volume, and low power consumption. Acoustooptic materials, devices, and techniques now enable systems having up to 2-GHz bandwidths, storage times up to 80 μs of signal history, and the time-bandwidth products from 1000 to 2000. Acoustooptic cells have a high light modulation efficiency, good phase response, and high optical quality.

Acoustooptic cells and processors have been used for spectrum analysis [115], interferometric spectrum analysis, correlations [17], heterodyne transform in radar signal processing, synthetic aperture radar data processing [97], and other computing systems.

19.3.2 Symmetric Self-Electrooptic-Effect Devices

A *self-electrooptic-effect device* (SEED) generally consists of a diode containing multiple quantum wells (MQWs), an electric load, and a reverse bias voltage supply. The MQW diode functions simultaneously as an absorption modulator and a detector. The wavelength of the input beam is chosen so that the absorption of the MQW layers increases with decreasing reverse bias voltage on the diode. That is at 853 nm. Hence increasing incident light gives increasing photocurrent which in turn results in reduced voltage applied on the MQW diode because of the voltage drop across the resistor. Consequently, the absorption and photocurrent increase, giving a positive feedback that leads to switch-

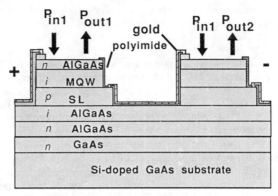

FIGURE 19.10 S-SEED. *(After D. A. B. Miller et al., "Integrated Quantum Well Self-Electro-Optic Effect Device: 2 × 2 Array of Optically Bistable Switches," Applied Physics Letters, 49:821–823, 1986)*

ing to a high-absorption state of the SEED diode. At a lower light power, the positive feedback operates in reverse, and the device switches back to a low-absorption (high-voltage) state [91].

A symmetric SEED (S-SEED) is a complete bistable logic device (Fig. 19.10). Instead of having a resistor load for the MQW diode as described above, it uses another MQW diode.

This diode behaves as a resistor whose value is determined by the state of the diode and by the power of the light beam illuminating this diode. The S-SEED uses a pair of beams as the input and output. It will be bistable only when the two optical input power levels for the two S-SEED diodes are comparable. The device will be in a single state when the light power for one diode significantly exceeds the power in the other. In this case, this diode has a high absorption and a low voltage, and the other diode has a low absorption and a high voltage. The bistable S-SEED can be set into one of the two states by a pair of unequal-power signal beams, and the state can be read by another pair of equal-power clock beams.

The clock beam powers may be many times greater than the input signal powers that were used to set the state of the device. In this way, we obtain a "time-sequential gain," the weaker signal beams control the stronger clock beams. This power gain is necessary to compensate for the power loss in the operation such as the loss of the quantum well device by 67 percent power absorption in the on state and the loss in the optical interconnection [81].

Using the quantum well bistable S-SEEDs as basic logic gates, the AT&T Bell Laboratories in Holmdel, New Jersey, on January 29, 1990, built an optical computing prototype that we briefly described above.

The switching time of the bistable S-SEEDs depends on the input light power. The fastest switching time measured was 40 ns with the signal modulation frequency of 1 MHz and the laser power below 100 μw. There is also a time delay between the input signals to set the state of the S-SEED diodes and the clock beams to read the state of the devices and to output the signals. In the demonstration system, the S-SEED works at 1 MHz, which is slower than most personal computers, though AT&T researchers said an optical computing operation at several hundred megahertz is possible in the near future. The

S-SEEDs have a potential speed of 1 GHz and a switching energy of 1 pJ. The speed of the processor is actually limited by the input laser power (10 μW).

The S-SEEDs in an array have been made with 10×10 μm sizes with 5×10 μm optical windows on 20-μm centers. A 64×32 array of S-SEEDs is 1.3 mm square. The S-SEED optical logic arrays require a uniform light spot array as power supplies. This illuminating spot array may be generated by the Dammann-type binary phase grating [26]. By using multiple binary phase gratings, an 81×81 spot array was obtained from a single laser beam [89].

19.3.3 Holograms

Holograms are one of the most important components for optical computing. In what follows, we discuss recent developments in *computer-generated holograms* (CGHs) and holographic materials.

In some applications, holograms are used to store data on spatial light modulators, e.g., in optical correlator systems used for pattern recognition. In other applications, the holograms are used to store data such as page-oriented data, in which case the storage capacities of volume holograms can be exploited.

In the first case, the main limitation is the resolution of spatial light modulators that must contain the hologram. In the second case, the main practical limitation is the slow speed of writing data on the volume hologram, which is usually a photorefractive crystal.

Computer-Generated Holograms. A hologram may be optically recorded or generated by computer. A *computer-generated hologram* (CGH) is a binary transmittance, reflectance, or phase pattern representing a sampled complex field which yields a desired optical wavefront by diffraction. CGHs offer advantages over conventional refractive elements in terms of size, weight, and cost. Most importantly, CGHs can generate any desired wavefront [79].

Computer-generated holograms have seen considerable progress in recent times, partly due to the advent of more powerful computers. A new technique for coding CGHs [8] allows such holograms to have a much improved storage capacity and improved signal-to-noise ratio.

CGHs may be fabricated with the same technology used in the manufacture of VLSI circuits using computer-controlled writing devices such as an *e*-beam lithography machine or realized by writing the pattern on a spatial light modulator for real-time holography.

Photorefractive Nonlinear Optics. Photorefractive materials such as $LiNbO_3$, $BaTiO_3$, SBN, BSO, and BGO are the most efficient media for nonlinear optical phenomena with relatively low light intensity levels (about 1 W/cm^2). The photorefractive effect arises when the crystal is exposed to an illumination pattern with photons having sufficient energy, and migration of the charge carrier optically generated gives rise to a strong space-charge field, which induces a refractive index change via the Pockel effect. When two coherent beams interfere inside a photorefractive medium, they create a volume index grating. This is a real-time hologram and can also be erased by uniform light illumination [48]. When two beams propagate through the self-induced grating, they undergo Bragg scattering. In a so-called two-mixing process, there is a nonreciprocal steady-state transfer of energy between the beams. In the four-wave mixing process using the photorefractive medium and two counterpropagating beams, the device behaves as a phase conjugate mirror. An incident beam will be reflected backward by the photorefractive device.

The photorefractive materials can be used for optical image amplification, image subtraction, exclusive-OR logic, matrix calculation, and, more interesting, for dynamic holograms for optical reconfigurable interconnects and optical implementations of neural networks [123].

Recently, photorefractive fibers of strontium barium niobate (SBN) have been developed. Multiple holograms stored in photorefractive fibers have a much higher angular sensitivity.

The main limitation of holograms recorded in photorefractive fibers is the relatively slow speed of reading and writing (milliseconds).

Photopolymers and Biopolymers.   More research interest has been paid to photopolymers as holographic recording materials and as materials for optical waveguides [82]. High-quality photopolymer holographic films fabricated by DuPont are now commercially available. This material is not sensitive to humidity or temperature and is environmentally stable. The processing consists of recording, ultraviolet processing, and heating, and it requires neither a dark room nor wet processing. The films have a resolution of 1000 line pairs per millimeter and a diffraction efficiency of 99 percent. They may be made sensitive to a wide range of wavelengths. DuPont has been successful in increasing the index modulation of the material up from 0.003 to 0.07 [112]. Other U.S. industries are developing polymers for fast recording, which should be announced soon.

Researchers in the U.S.S.R. are at the forefront of developing biopolymers for holographic recording [6]. Such materials have wide flexibility for the fabrication of various recording materials; they allow processing times down to 10^{-11} s and switching times down to 10 ps; they have very high resolution (10^9 bits/cm^2), are sensitive in the visible and infrared regions, have useful polarization properties, and can be controlled by electrical fields, temperature, and so on.

19.3.4 Binary or Diffractive Optics

Advances in the semiconductor microlithography industry, such as computer-controlled *e*-beam mask exposure systems, mask aligners, and various wet or dry etching machines, have recently been applied in optics to create new kinds of holographic optical elements. They are not conventional computer-generated holograms but have a microscopic relief profile on the surfaces of a substrate glass or a semiconductor material. The techniques are also called *binary optics* because they are based on (1) a binary electronic masking; (2) a binary mask design coding, 2^N phase steps for N binary masks; and (3) a two-level ion etching process [116]. In fact the term *binary optics* was coined to avoid using terms that would pigeonhole the technology into existing niches, and many people agree that the term *diffractive optics* is better and more descriptive.

Binary optics elements such as thin lenses, prisms, gratings, holograms, or phase plates may be used in infrared imagers, cameras, telescopes; in optical communications; and in optical disk systems [90]. Because of their quality, fabrication precision, and integratability with electronic VLSI technology, binary optics elements will be useful in optical computing systems.

Researchers at the Institute of Automation and Electrometry in the U.S.S.R. have developed advanced techniques and applications for diffractive optical elements [71]. They state that such elements enable the performance of a wider class of transforms of wavefronts, can be made of thin substrate, and are light; their weight and cost are independent of the aperture; they can work in a wide spectral range; they can make elements that are difficult or impossible to fabricate; several elements can be combined into a single one, they do not require special glasses, they are relatively cheap and easy to duplicate, and their efficiency approaches 100 percent. A number of optical elements have been fabricated by the authors, including kinoform axicons, lenses with a ring impulse response, wavefront correctors, diffraction lenses with mirrors, microlenses, a bifocus microscope, and an optical string.

19.3.5 Planar Optics

The optical computing group at AT&T Bell Laboratories is developing the idea of *optical modules,* which could be grouped like electronic modules [52]. Part of this concept is *planar optics,* which consists of planar optical elements on a flat bulk surface [59], as shown in Fig. 19.11. Such modules would need no adjustment and could be coupled together accurately by using grooves. Individual elements of this kind can be made by using diffractive optics or other planar etching techniques.

Successful experiments have been carried out with such modules. Other standard modules being developed by Bell Laboratories include microlaser arrays, optical logic gates, and optical computing modules.

19.3.6 Microoptics

Microoptical components are microrefractive, diffractive, and gradient index optical elements, such as lenslets, beam splitters, waveplates, mirrors, and prisms, with sizes ranging from several microns to a few millimeters. They are fabricated by nontraditional manufacturing techniques such as microlithography ion exchange, electromigration, or diffusion, which modulate the index of refraction in the substrate, and photo-assisted etching, photoelectrochemical etching, etc. Microoptical elements mounted on the substrate surfaces are called *planar optical elements.* The same processes that are used in the semiconductor industry may be used for patterning the substrate before the optical elements are formed. Two-dimensional arrays of optical components which are precisely aligned can be stacked to form three-dimensional stacked planar optical elements using masks with markers, as is done in *large-scale integration* (LSI) production for alignment [58].

Microoptics was developed to ease the interconnection problem in optical fibers and planar optical waveguides in optical fiber communications, optical disk systems, lightwave sensing, and laser printers. It will play an essential role for optical computing [61], optoelectronic processors, and optical interconnection systems [59].

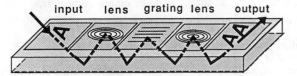

FIGURE 19.11 Planar optical module. *(After J. Jahns and A. Huang, "Planar Integration of Free-Space Optical Components," Applied Optics, 28:1602–1605, 1989)*

19.3.7 Integrated Optoelectronic Processor Arrays

An integrated optoelectronic processor array is a hybrid system which utilizes the massively parallel interconnection potential of optics while performing logic functions in electronics [56]. The system combines the advantages of the efficient processing ability of electronics and the global communications provided by optical interconnects and could be used for cellular image processing [102, 109], pattern recognition [54], knowledge-based processing [67], neural networks [94], and general-purpose computers. The research is underway at the University of California at San Diego, University of Southern California at Los Angeles, Institut d'Optique in Paris, AT&T, Honeywell, DuPont, etc.

Each cell of the array consists of an electronic processing element together with optoelectronic sources and detectors which perform the input-output functions. Surface-emitting diode lasers or LEDs could be used as light sources. Progress in the surface-emitting microlasers by AT&T Bell Laboratories is described in the next section. Diode lasers have high power efficiency (0.5), a narrow spectral width for holographic interconnects, and high speed (>1 GHz). LEDs are easier to fabricate, but have low power efficiency (0.001). Another approach uses SLMs as passive light sources in the PEs to reduce the power dissipation. The SLMs could be the MQW SLMs or PLZT SLMs described in the SLM section. PIN photodiodes can be used for high-speed computing, and photoconductors provide a relatively high current output but a low speed.

A great technical challenge in the development of optoelectronic processor arrays is the monolithic integration of optical devices such as lasers and detectors with materials having high electrooptic coefficients, such as GaAs, LiNbO$_3$, PLZT, and KH$_2$PO$_4$ (KDP), on a common semiconductor Si chip. The Si-PLZT integration currently under investigation at the University of California at San Diego is the laser recrystallization of *low-pressure chemical vapor deposition* (LPCVD)–deposited Si on SiO$_2$ on a polycrystalline PLZT substrate. Honeywell has been successful in the fabrication of a LED structure on a semi-insulating substrate, maintaining the planarity of the wafer surface. This LED structure is then integratable with the standard E/D MESFET process for integrated circuits [49]. Another approach uses GaAs electronics. GaAs electronics has advantages with respect to speed and resistance to radiation. Monolithic GaAs chips have been produced by Honeywell and IBM.

I. Hayashi of Japan has proposed the concept of the *optoelectronic integrated circuit* (OEIC), to effectively exploit the capabilities of both optics and electronics [46]. An OEIC device is an integrated circuit that contains both electronic devices, such as transistors, and optoelectronic devices, such as lasers and photodetectors. Hayashi expects much technology involving such devices to develop toward the end of the century. Experiments in Japan on using OEICs for communications systems reached the conclusion that the key to OEIC fabrication was in materials technology.

According to Kogelnik [70], so far the only practical commercial applications of integrated optics are distributed feedback lasers and guided-wave LiNbO$_3$ modulators, which have been demonstrated at speeds up to 20 GHz; but more practical applications should be expected in the near future. It would therefore be premature to predict with any confidence the role of this technology in future optical computers.

19.3.8 Microlaser Array

Surface-emitting semiconductor laser diodes have been investigated in many laboratories. AT&T Bell Laboratories has been successful in the development of vertical-cavity, surface-emitting cylindrical microlaser arrays with 1-, 1.5-, 2-, 3-, 4-, and 5-μm diameters, as shown in Fig. 19.12.

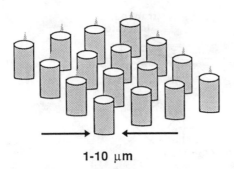

1-10 μm

FIGURE 19.12 Surface-emitting laser diode array.

The chip contains over 1 million microlasers. The wavelength was 983 nm. The threshold voltage was about 8 V at 2 mA and 1.5 mA and 5.0 V (cw) for the 5-μm lasers with 28 percent quantum efficiency [98].

They first grew a Fabry-Perot resonator with GaAs/AlAs, using *molecular beam epitaxy* (MBE) on an Si-doped $n+$-GaAs substrate. The interference mirrors were alternating layers of AlAs and GaAs. One of the mirrors used Be as the dopant. The active layer was an undoped, 10-nm layer of $In_{0.2}Ga_{0.8}As$. Above the Be-doped mirror, an AlAs layer was grown with approximately a 0.2 optical wave thickness. On the top of this was grown a 30-nm GaAs cap. There were 600 of these epitaxial layers deposited. The lasers were carved into the entire surface by using chemically assisted ion-beam etching [60].

In one experiment [62], an array of lasers was modulated by a pseudo-random bit generator at 1 Gbit/s with an error rate less than 10^{-10}.

These lasers will have a substantial impact on the laser diode market. Their applications could be for optical chip-to-chip interconnections, signal processing, neural networks, and pattern recognition.

19.3.9 Optoelectronic VLSI Chips

It has been proposed to integrate photodiodes into VLSI chips to provide optically controlled weights [14] while maintaining electronic gates, in a matrix-vector multiplier architecture. Photodiodes are compatible with CMOS technology, and back-to-back photodiodes would be used as synapses.

19.3.10 GaAs/AlGaAs Optical Neuron

Researchers at Mitsubishi Electric Corporation have reported an optical synaptic interconnection device for neural networks which consists of an LED array, an interconnection matrix, and a photodiode array integrated into a hybrid-layered structure on a GaAs substrate [96]. This architecture had also been proposed by MacDonald [85] for a switching matrix which has bandwidths up to 500 MHz. The optical synaptic chip is diagramed in Fig. 19.13. This device has been built for an optical neural network, but since it does a vector-matrix multiplication, it can be used for other kinds of optical computing as well.

The 7.6 × 7.6 mm chip, mounted on a flat package with 128 pins, has three layers. Line-shaped LEDs and photodetectors in a crossbar configuration grown on n-type GaAs wafers have the interconnection matrix sandwiched between them. The device had 32 neurons and therefore required a 32 × 32 matrix. The cycle time of the synaptic chip was 1 μs, limited by the response times of the LEDs, assuming that the responses of the electronic circuits associated with the chip are much faster. The system was used as a Hopfield associative memory with 32 neurons, which means that it was not very efficient in associating nonorthogonal patterns. Better classification rates than the 70 percent achieved could be obtained by using other neural models that can be done with this chip.

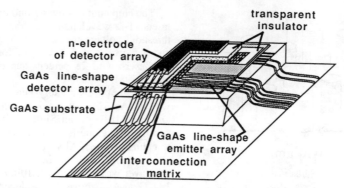

FIGURE 19.13   Optical synaptic chip. *(After K. Kyuma, Y. Nitta, J. Ohta, S. Tai, and M. Takahashi, "The First Demonstration of an Optical Learning Chip," Topical Meeting on Optical Computing, Technical Digest (Optical Society of America), 6:291–294, 1991)*

The cycle time is independent of the number of neurons, so with larger matrices, the effective data rate could be increased considerably.

A modified version of this chip where the static interconnection mask was replaced with a dynamic mask by using a variable-sensitivity photodiode has recently been used for learning and pattern classification [76].

19.3.11 SRS Inverter

Petrov and Kuzin [99] have used nonlinear effects in optical fibers for computer applications; in one system, they used *stimulated Raman scattering* (SRS) in fibers for logic operations, as shown in Fig. 19.14.

One of the input pulses is a Stokes signal pulse, and the other is a pump pulse. When the input signal pulse is present, the pump pulse, which is used as an output signal pulse, disappears. This system may be used for any boolean logic operation.

The same authors used stimulated Mandelstam-Brillouin scattering to build a fiber-optic switch where a nonlinear interaction causes a hypersonic wave in the fiber, and a

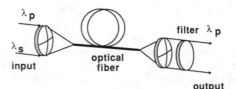

FIGURE 19.14   An SRS inverter for logic functions. *(After M. P. Petrov and Y. A. Kuzin, "Nonlinear Phenomena in Optical Fibers and the Feasibility of Their Application in Optical Computers," in H. H. Arsenault, T. Szoplik, and B. Macukow (eds.), Optical Processing and Computing, New York: Academic Press, 1989)*

complete transfer of energy from the signal wave to the counterstreaming driving beam can occur.

These systems are interesting in that they show that optical logic operations based on optical switching are possible. The question remains as to whether such systems can be sufficiently miniaturized and built in arrays. At this time it is unclear whether this is possible, because of the lengths of fibers required.

19.4 OPTICAL INTERCONNECTS

Computer optics is most advanced in the implementation of interconnections [39]. A thorough discussion of optical interconnects would be too lengthy for this chapter, but it is important to have at least a general idea of the impact that optical interconnects are already having on computer technology. Although no competitive all-optical computers are on the horizon, hybrid computers in which electronics does nonlinear and logic operations and optics does massively parallel interconnections have been proposed [57]. An all-optical computer would use optical gates and optical interconnects and would require no conversion of electronic signals.

An optical interconnection system requires sources, interconnects, and receivers. In an electronic computer, the light sources are transmitters which can be directly modulated: diode lasers and light-emitting diodes or electrically addressed spatial light modulators illuminated by an external light source. In an all-optical computer, the source can illuminate optically addressed SLMs, and the optical interconnects can be implemented by using guided optics and free-space optics. The receivers are generally photodetectors or photoconductors or an optically addressed SLM that combines photodetectors and switching elements, such as a SEED.

Optical interconnects may be fixed or dynamic. They may be used for regular or irregular interconnections. Many optical interconnection systems have been implemented for network topologies such as the crossover, perfect shuffle, hypercube, and Clos networks and for crossbar and *multistage interconnection networks* (MINs), etc.

Optical interconnects can offer large bandwidths and a high spatial density. Photons can propagate without interacting with other photons. Optical interconnects also offer potentially lower power dissipation, flexibility for routing, and dynamic reconfigurable interconnections.

Optical interconnects have been of interest at all levels in digital computers including

Machine to machine

Device to device

Board to board

Chip to chip

Gate to gate

For machine-to-machine, device-to-device, and board-to-board communications, the distances involved vary from many kilometers to several meters. For these levels, optical links can be built with commercially available optical sources, detectors, fibers, and waveguides. Existing technologies developed for telecommunications, such as time-division and frequency-division multiplexing and demultiplexing, couplers, switches, and microoptic elements, can be used. Computer-to-computer interconnects are in the realm of fiber-optic communications; but the accuracy requirements, tolerable error rates, multiplexing needs, and bandwidths required are different enough that communications technology cannot be transferred directly to computers. For example, the bit error rates for computer communications are orders of magnitude more severe than those required for normal data communications.

Optical interconnects have large bandwidths and large fan-outs and consume less power. They are immune to interference and crosstalk and can be compact and light-weight. These advantages over the conventional system using electric wires are obvious at these levels of computer architecture.

Board-to-board communications usually use optical fibers and optical waveguides. Free-space optics can also be used for board-to-board interconnects by using laser diodes, as shown in Fig. 19.15. Tsang has built for such interconnects, which are aligned by insertion into the board [114].

Fiber optics and waveguides require devices and are difficult to reconfigure, so for reconfigurable and high-density massively parallel interconnects, free-space interconnects have the edge, at least in principle. Many new components and architectures for optical interconnects have been developed recently.

Tsang has demonstrated 1-Gbit/s free-space chip-to-chip interconnections [114]. A 1.3-μm GaInAs laser was connected directly to a GaAs code generator. The light was collimated by an aspheric compact-disk lens with an F number of 0.55 and a diameter of 5 mm. The signal traveled 24 cm and was focused by an identical lens onto a GaInAs photodiode having a diameter of 100 μm. The output of the photodiode was connected directly to another gate. The laser threshold was 5 mA, which allowed the interconnect to be driven directly by logic gates. The external differential quantum efficiency of the diode laser was 35 percent, and the nominal quantum efficiency of the photodiode was 70 percent, allowing the signal generated by the photodiode to be connected directly to other gates without preamplification. The overall efficiency for the link exceeded 18 percent, which is high for optical interconnects.

For chip-to-chip and intrachip interconnections, electric microstrips and strip lines occupy strong positions and can handle signals with bandwidths of many gigahertz. The present-day electrical interconnections also have flexibility so that any two of the 30,000 logic terminals on a single substrate can be connected.

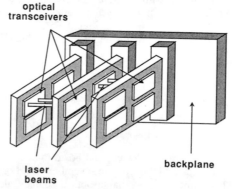

optical
transceivers

laser
beams

backplane

FIGURE 19.15 Free-space board-to-board intercon-nects. (*After D. Z. Tsang, "Techniques for Implementation of High-Speed Free-Space Optical Interconnections," Optical Society of America 1991 Topical Meeting on Optical Computing Technical Digest, 6:132–135, 1991*)

In chip-to-chip and intrachip levels, the distances involved range from a few tens of centimeters to a few micrometers. For these levels, optical interconnections can be implemented mainly by free-space optical systems. Optical fibers and waveguides can also be used for chip-to-chip interconnections, as shown in Fig. 19.16. A number of companies including IBM and Texas Instruments are developing transducers for optical chip-to-chip interconnections.

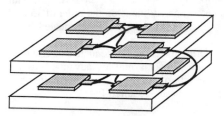

FIGURE 19.16 Optical interconnects between chips using guided optics.

The strength of optical interconnects in this domain lies in their capability for high density and in their flexibility. The geometries of VLSI chips are growing smaller and denser. The strength of mutual coupling associated with electrical interconnects is proportional to the frequency of the signals. An electric strip line interconnect requires at least 100 μm^2 at 1 GHz. They have to be spaced at no less than 20 to 50 μm to minimize crosstalk. They cannot cross and therefore must be routed over or under one another through multiple interconnect layers. A VLSI chip including as many as 100,000 gates would require 1000 or more input-output pins per chip, which would be impossible with electrical connections. Optical interconnections potentially offer freedom from mutual coupling effects. Optical interconnects can be routed in a flexible manner through three-dimensional space. They can even propagate through the same space without interaction.

Other challenges for optical chip-to-chip interconnections are the packaging issue: Optical alignment, the presence of both GaAs (for optoelectronic components) and Si (for electronic components) in the same package, and the very limited space available above the chip plane (several centimeters) to accommodate an optical interconnection system all are difficult problems.

It is still debatable whether optical gate-to-gate interconnects will be competitive with electrical interconnects. At present both technologies have about the same limiting sizes, and according to Goodman [38], electronics is faster when the lines do not have to be terminated. The answer to this question is so highly dependent on many factors that a definite answer cannot be agreed on by specialists now.

19.4.1 Optical versus Electrical Interconnections

Numerous studies have compared optical and electrical interconnect technologies in terms of interconnect density, distances, data rate, and power consumption.

With increasing component density and data rates, electrical interconnects reach the limit imposed by interline crosstalk and by transmission line attenuation. Optical interconnects allow a much higher density. Free-space interconnections are limited by diffraction. The data rate of optical interconnects is limited by the speed of the optoelectronic transceiver, modulator, and interface.

For low speeds and short distances, simple wire interconnections will predominate. Goodman has made an estimate showing that for gate-to-gate interconnections where the length of the link is about 1 mm, optical interconnects require more power than electrical interconnects because of the low power efficiency in the optic-electric conversion of the light source and detector. For chip-to-chip interconnections, electrical links could require more power because of the large capacitance of bonding pads used in the connections.

When some degree of fan-out is needed, the power required for electrical interconnects grows much faster than that required for optical interconnects.

An electrical interconnect line must be terminated to eliminate the reflection of the signal from the end. The terminating resistor dramatically increases the drive power for electrical connections. To avoid this, the length of an unterminated line must not be longer than the travel distance of the signal in a bit period. For a standard 50-Ω coaxial line with 1 Gbit/s data rate, the maximum length of an unterminated line is on the order of 15 cm. Beyond this length optical interconnects have a distinct advantage over terminated transmission lines with respect to drive power.

Feldman et al. gave an estimation also considering the energy dependence on rise time and fan-out. Such studies suggest that optical interconnects may be advantageous for intrachip communication for large-area VLSI circuits or for wafer-scale integrated circuits, especially when high data rate and large fan-out are required [34].

19.4.2 Free-Space Interconnects

Free-space interconnects are used mainly in low levels of computer architectures for intrachip, chip-to-chip, and board-to-board interconnections, such as clock signal distribution, processor-to-processor and processor-to-memory interconnections, and gate-to-gate interconnections in all-optical digital computers. Free-space interconnections can be regular and fixed or dynamically reconfigurable.

In a free-space optical architecture, optical interconnects use the third dimension perpendicular to the 2D chip plane. This architecture could allow more on-chip real estate for electronic logic, reduce VLSI chip layout complexity, reduce pin-outs, increase on-chip speed, and allow new VLSI chip architectures. Since propagating photons do not interfere with each other, optical free-space interconnects will offer freedom from mutual coupling between electronic signals and promise high spatial density and flexibility in VLSI design. This architecture takes full advantage of the parallelism of optical computing for the implementation of massively parallel global interconnections such as those required in neural networks.

Another type of computer architecture such as the connection machine uses integrated optoelectronic cellular arrays. Each cell consists of an electronic processing element (PE) together with optoelectronic devices for input and output functions. It is projected that a PE array consisting of as many as 1 million PEs (1000 × 1000 array), each of which consists of as many as 1000 active devices, could be fabricated in an area as small as 100 mm on a side. Global communication among PEs would be implemented by free-space optical interconnects. These fine-grained machines could be useful for parallel image processing, knowledge processing, and neural networks [94].

Clock Distribution to VLSI Chips.   Optics can be used to transmit a clock signal to all parts of a chip. The optical clock signal can be generated by an off-chip laser diode. The optical beam is then mapped through a holographic element to various photodetector sites on the chip surface, as shown in Fig. 19.17.

The electronic signals from the detectors are then sent to nearby clocked devices. Optical clock distribution has the potential to avoid the major problems associated with signal distribution on VLSI chips via conductors, such as clock skew, broadening of the clock pulses caused by large capacitive loads, and very large loading of the clock drive. All these factors slow the overall operation of the chip. The optical interconnects can support large fan-outs. The communication time-delay differences from the laser to the various detector sites are negligible. The prime source of clock skew is variations in the response time of the photodetectors and amplifiers. It is predicted that with a 2-μm

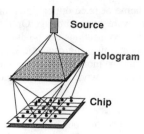

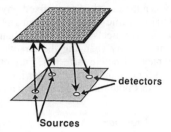

FIGURE 19.17 Optical clock distribution. *(After J. W. Goodman, "Optics as an Interconnect Technology," in H. H. Arsenault, T. Szoplik, and B. Macukow (eds.), Optical Processing and Computing. New York: Academic Press, 1989)*

FIGURE 19.18 Holographic free-space interconnects. *(After R. Kostuk, J. W. Goodman, and L. Hesselink, "Design Considerations for Holographic Optical Interconnects," Applied Optics, 26:3947–3957, 1987)*

CMOS process and free-running digital ring oscillators and a photodetector within a phase-locked loop circuit to force locking of each ring oscillator, the skew between individual frequency-locked ring oscillators could be on the order of 50 ps at clock frequencies up to 150 MHz.

Holographic Multiple Imaging. The basic functions of an interconnection network are to split (fan-out), shift, and combine (fan-in) the signals [37]. These functions may be implemented by an optical multiple-imaging system which images a light source into multiple image spots and then shifts the spots onto destinations. Multiple imaging may be obtained by multifacet holograms, as shown in Fig. 19.18. Light emitted by a laser diode forms an elliptical spot illuminating the hologram. The hologram then focuses the light onto multiple detectors. The multifacet hologram is, in fact, a set of overlapping Fresnel zone plates, one facet hologram for each detector.

The advantage of holographic multiple imaging resides in the ability to multiplex many optical elements in a thin medium. Decentered faceted Fresnel zone plate elements provide off-axis images, and the holograms can be easily replicated.

Because of the lack of holographic recording materials compatible with laser diode wavelengths (0.78 to 1.6 mm), the holograms used for interconnections were not optically recorded [75], but were computer-generated *holographic elements* (HEs) [74]. The HEs allow arbitrary interconnect patterns and low F numbers (about F/1). The theoretical total diffraction efficiency for multiple-image spots is 24 percent for Fresnel zone plates sampled at the Nyquist rate [32]. Higher diffraction efficiencies can be obtained by relief-surface diffractive elements, discussed in Sec. 19.3.4. An HE was fabricated by electron-beam lithography at the University of California at San Diego for replacing the row address lines in a RAM chip [33]. The HE had dimensions of 10×10 mm, separated from the chip by 20 mm for interconnection distances of 3 to 6 mm. The image spots obtained had dimensions of 15×15 μm.

19.4.3 Dynamic Interconnects

Parallel algorithms are faster and more efficient when dynamic or irregular interconnects are used [84]. Many algorithms require the interconnections to be reconfigurable. In most neural networks, the interconnection weights must be dynamically changed during the learning process.

When the circuits have a fixed physical wiring scheme or fixed optical interconnects, general dynamic connections can be achieved by software programming. Optical free-space interconnects require no mechanical contacts. The connections can be dynamically reconfigured by changing the directions of optical beams by using dynamic holograms with photorefractive materials. Furthermore, optics could be more competitive than electronics for dynamic and irregular interconnections. But much work remains to be done to realize this potential of optical interconnects.

Optical Crossbar.   A crossbar can dynamically interconnect any one of N input nodes to any one of N output nodes by using an $N \times N$ switch array. The interconnection is reconfigurable by changing the states of the switches and should be nonblocking: an interconnect path can be changed without disturbing the other existing interconnects.

One architecture for an optical crossbar is based on the optical matrix-vector multiplier. The light from each input node is shaped to illuminate one column of a two-dimensional photonic switch array (SLM), by using an optical spherocylindrical lens system or using optical fiber splitters. Similar optics is used on the output side of the SLM for collecting the light from each row of the SLM to a detector. This system has a switch complexity of N^2 and a minimum power loss of $(N - 1)/N$.

One such crossbar [28] with 4×4 capability with a reconfiguration time of 20 ms that can handle data rates in excess of 1 Gbit/s is available commercially from Opticomp. Its principle of construction is shown in Fig. 19.19. According to the authors, their approach is capable of achieving a 16×16 switch at 1 Gbit/s and a 32×32 switch at greater than 100 Mbits/s. The system uses PLZT switches.

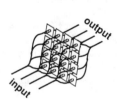

FIGURE 19.19 Optical crossbar based on the vector-matrix multiplier. *(After A. R. Dias, R. F. Kalman, J. W. Goodman, and A. A. Sawchuk, "Fiber-Optic Crossbar with Broadcast Capability," Optical Engineering, 27:955–960, 1988)*

Optoelectronic crossbars with dimensions of 16×16 and 32×32 having a 50-ns reconfiguration time and running at 2 Gbits/s have been developed by Photel, Inc., and are now commercially available. These systems use electronic crossbar switching with optoelectronic converters for optical input and output signals [69].

Another optical crossbar developed by Hughes uses $1 \times N$ optical fiber splitters for each input and a linear array of N detectors. This is a vector-matrix multiplication architecture. Switching and summing of the signals are implemented electronically in the detector arrays. The detector arrays have very high bandwidth (>5 GHz), and the whole system was operated at 100 and 200 MHz. The on/off ratio was >35 dB [110].

Because of the N^2 switch complexity, a large electrical crossbar is very difficult to fabricate; an optical crossbar using a vector-matrix architecture is also difficult to implement for large sizes because of the high power loss.

Optical MINs.   Reconfigurable interconnects can also be achieved using optical multistage interconnection networks (MINs) such as omega/shuffle-exchange networks, Clos/Benes networks, and other architectures that have been mostly developed for communications and used for parallel computing.

These approaches require fewer switches and have less power loss than the crossbar does. The optical MINs are cascaded stages. Each consists of an optical interconnection network and an optical logic array or SLMs as exchange switches. Some optical implementations such as a 2D perfect shuffle for the omega network have been demonstrated. Much attention is paid to research on photonic switches for this application.

19.4.4 Massively Parallel Dynamic Holographic Interconnections

Optical artificial neural networks require full interconnections between $N \times N$ input nodes and $N \times N$ output nodes with dynamic interconnection weights. This can be implemented by exploiting the huge storage capacity of holograms. Several methods using page-oriented holograms and photorefractive crystal volume holograms have been proposed, but more research has to be done for a real implementation of such networks.

N^4 *Weighted Interconnections.* This architecture utilizes an $N \times N$ page-oriented hologram array with hologram element i, j containing an $N \times N$ weight matrix T_{ijkl}. The hologram array is illuminated by an $N \times N$ laser diode array. A hologram element i, j is illuminated by an element source a_{ij}. All the reconstructed images from the $N \times N$ holograms fall onto an $N \times N$ output detector array. The power detected by the detector kl is

$$b_{kl} = \sum_{ij} T_{ijkl} a_{ij} \tag{19.4}$$

If the a_{ij} are the input nodes, we have N^4 interconnections between two $N \times N$ input and output arrays [20].

This is a space-variant multiple-imaging architecture discussed previously. Several modified architectures have been proposed using spatial light modulators [105]. Because of the large size of the projected hologram array, the holograms should be recorded optically. Design considerations have shown that such a system having 256×256 channels should be feasible. This corresponds to a storage capacity of 10^{11} interconnections.

A pinhole imaging hologram has been suggested [122] for holographic interconnections. The pinhole imaging hologram records an image of the object, a mask of interconnection patterns, formed through a pinhole. The interconnection pattern is reconstructed with the pinhole from the hologram, which allows one to process or program the reconstructed interconnections by manipulations in the plane of the reconstructed pinholes. These holograms could also be integrated into N^4 networks to achieve massively parallel, programmable interconnections.

Dynamic Volume Holographic Interconnections. Volume photorefractive crystals have been proposed for holographic interconnections in neural networks. The light beams emitted by an input neuron i and by a neuron j in the training plane form an interference grating in the photorefractive crystal. The hologram recorded in the crystal will couple the light from the ith input neuron to the jth output neuron, which is the image of the jth training neuron in the output plane. Thus the connection strength between the ith input neuron and the jth output neuron increases [100]. The density of interconnections which can be recorded in a crystal is limited by physical and geometric constraints. It has been shown that in a 1-cm^3 crystal up to 10^{10} interconnections can be recorded. The gratings recorded in a photorefractive crystal can be erased. Incoherent erasure, selective erasure using a phase-shifted reference, and repetitive phase-shift writing and erasure have been demonstrated. This interconnection architecture has been proposed for implementation of the back propagation learning procedure in optical neural networks [117].

Alignment.   An important challenge for the practical application of free-space optical interconnects is the alignment of components. Free-space interconnections are intended for high-density VLSIs. Optical signal spots must fall onto the detectors with a typical precision of several micrometers. Each component in an optical system has to be individually aligned in three spatial and three angular coordinates with very narrow tolerances. This requires pushing the possibilities of mechanical alignment tools to or beyond their limits. Furthermore, the complex mechanical system must remain stable with time despite varying environmental influences, and this mechanical system is usually incompatible with VLSI electronic components [59]. Several researchers have considered the alignment problem [73, 106, 61]. One solution is to use reflecting microprisms, as shown in Fig. 19.20, which self-corrects for minor misalignments of the system. One beam from a source on the processor array board is broadcast to multiple detectors on the same board by specially designed prisms; such interconnects have been demonstrated for fixed-mesh and hypercube interconnection schemes, which play an important role in parallel supercomputers [107].

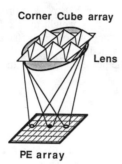

FIGURE 19.20   Corner-cube array for optical interconnects. *(After Y. Sheng and H. H. Arsenault, "Corner-Cube Array for Integrated Optoelectronic Cellular Array Interconnections," Proceedings of the SPIE, 1215:123–130, 1990)*

Some solutions will involve integration of microoptical interconnection elements: lenses, holograms, mirrors, prisms, etc. with optical sources, modulators, and detectors into a monolithic substrate of glass or semiconductor material. This issue is discussed in Secs. 19.3.4 and 19.3.5 on microoptics and diffractive optical elements.

19.5   THE FUTURE OF OPTICAL COMPUTING

In the hybrid electrooptical supercomputers of the near future, there are no applications specific to optics; the applications will be those that are made possible by faster computers and that can exploit parallel systems. As the optical computing technology develops, more massive parallelism will become possible, and new kinds of computers will appear, which will enable new kinds of operations, and new applications previously impossible to do should be made possible by optics.

In the present state of things, optics is faster for carrying information, and electronics is faster for processing it. This fact makes it reasonable to think that in the near future the most efficient computers will be hybrid optoelectronic systems that will exploit the capabilities of both optics and electronics. There are people who think that optics will one day be faster than electronics for processing data, and there are people who believe the opposite. Because both camps contain individuals who are intelligent and capable, it must be concluded that the issue is still undecided. If the first group is right, an all-optical computer is probably possible; but if the second group is right, an all-optical computer will never be built. No one contests that optics will play a major role in computers of the future.

It is in the area of neural nets that applications specific to optics should appear first, since this area is so highly dependent on high-density interconnects, where the capacity of optics for speed and the massive parallelism of optics give it a clear advantage. Because the development of electronic neural chips is progressing very rapidly (chips with up to 10^9 interconnections per second have been unofficially reported), early applications of optics in neural systems will probably be in the area of loading interconnection patterns onto electronic neural chips, which can take up to 10 min or more for a major interconnect modification. The advent of faster spatial light modulators, better storage materials, improved optoelectronic LSI technology, and improvement of miniaturization should soon bring about hybrid optoelectronic neural systems and perhaps all-optical neural networks.

Before optical computers can become a reality, certain breakthroughs will be required, some of which are on the horizon. One is an integrated large-scale integrated optical chip. Optoelectronic LSI technology can bridge the gap between optical device technology and electronic established LSI technology. Many of the most interesting optical architectures are large and bulky; some research has shown that such systems can be made much more compact. Examples are the compact optical correlators developed by Perkin-Elmer, Jet Propulsion Laboratories, and Litton Data Systems; the Mitsubishi compact optical neural network, which collapses the vector-matrix architecture onto a wafer; IBM's GaAs transducer for transforming digital signals from VLSI chips into optical signals; Bell Laboratories' microlaser array; and Bellcore's SEED arrays. To exploit the new technologies becoming available, more research is required in exploring parallelism and time-division multiplexing.

19.6 CONCLUSION

Optics has the potential for massive computing and processing that surpasses that of electronics by orders of magnitude. Except for a few areas, this potential has not been realized because of technological limitations, especially of devices. However, the advent of new devices such as the SELDA, SEEDs, and faster and larger spatial light modulators promises to push the capabilities of optics at least to those of electronics.

Except for storage applications such as compact disks and high-capacity optical hard disks for computers, acoustooptics-based signal processing systems, and optical interconnections between electronic devices, optical computing is still mostly at the research laboratory level. Some systems such as optical correlators for real-time pattern recognition have reached the prototype stage and have been field-tested, as well as some interconnection devices and a few small prototypes of systems capable of carrying out digital operations such as multiplications.

Although some researchers are speaking of optical computers within a few years, it may take as much as 10 years or more for practical systems, assuming that sufficient resources are put into the field.

Because optical computing is more advanced in optical interconnects, it is certain that this technology will be widely used in supercomputers to facilitate board-to-board and chip-to-chip communications, and indeed optics is already being used for this purpose. Although optical interconnects play a key role in optical neural computers, this field is still in its infancy, and much development will be necessary before optical neural computers become a practical reality.

As for the all-optical computer, the fact that optical gate-to-gate interconnects are not competitive with electronics except when the connections must be terminated leads to the conclusion that competitive optical computers should use architectures that are totally different from the electronic architectures that we know today.

These conclusions should be modulated by the knowledge that scientists are notoriously incompetent at predicting the future and that we are probably no better at reading the future than most.

REFERENCES

1. H. H. Arsenault, L. Leclerc, and Y. Sheng, "Similarity and Invariance in Pattern Recognition," in B. Javidi (ed.), *Real-Time Signal Processing for Industrial Applications: Critical Reviews of Optical Science and Technology, Proceedings of the SPIE,* 960:2–17, 1989.

2. H. H. Arsenault and Y. Sheng, *An Introduction to Optics in Computers, SPIE Tutorial Texts Series,* vol. TT8, 1992.

3. H. H. Arsenault and Y. Sheng, "Optical and Neural Computing Architectures," final report, Contract number 36001-9-3519/01-SS, Communications Research Center of Canada, Ottawa, August 31, 1990.

4. R. A. Athale and J. N. Lee, "Optical Systems for Efficient Triple-Matrix-Product Processing," *Optics Letters,* 8:590, 1983.

5. P. Batacan, "Can Physics Make Optics Compute?" *Computers in Physics,* 2:14, 1988.

6. V. Yu. Bazhenov, M. S. Soskin, V. B. Taranenko, and M. V. Vasnetsov, "Biopolymers for Real-Time Optical Processing," in H. H. Arsenault et al. (eds.), *Optical Processing and Computing.* New York: Academic Press, 1989.

7. P. R. Beaudet, A. P. Goutzoulis, E. C. Malarkey, and J. C. Bradley, "Residue Arithmetic Techniques for Optical Processing of Adaptive Phased Array Radars," *Applied Optics,* 25:3097, 1986.

8. A. Bergeron, G. April, and H. H. Arsenault, "Improved 2 × 2 Computer-Generated Holographic Matched Filters for Spatial Light Modulators," in I. Cindrich (ed.), *Computer and Optically Formed Holographic Optics,* O-E Lase '90, Los Angeles, January 17–19, 1990. *Proceedings of SPIE,* vol. 1211, paper 23.

9. P. B. Berra, "Optical Database Machines," Optical Society of America Topical Meeting on Optical Computing, March 4–6, 1991, Salt Lake City, 1991 Technical Digest Series, vol. 6.

10. P. B. Berra, et al., "Optical and Supercomputing," *Proceedings of the IEEE,* 77, 1797–1815, 1989.

11. P. B. Berra et al., "Optical Database/Knowledgebase Machines," *Applied Optics,* 29:195–205, 1990.

12. W. P. Bleha et al., "Application of the Liquid Crystal Valve to Real-Time Optical Data Processing," *Optical Engineering,* 17(4):371–384, 1978.

13. Y. Bourbin et al., "High Frequency Intrinsic Resonance in Traveling Wave Y-Fed Directional Couplers," Paper WD6, IGWO '88, Sante Fe, 1988.

14. G. D. Boyd, "Optically Excited Synapse for Neural Network," *Applied Optics,* 26:2712–2719, 1987.

15. G. D. Boyd et al., "Multiple Quantum Well Reflection Modulator," *Applied Physics Letters,* 50(17):1119–1121, 1987.

16. K. H. Brenner, A. Huang, and N. Streibl, "Digital Optical Computing with Symbolic Substitution," *Applied Optics,* 25:3054, 1986.

17. D. Casasent, "Acoustooptic Linear Algebra Processors: Architectures, Algorithms and Applications," *Proceedings of the IEEE,* 52:631, 1984.

18. D. Casasent and D. C. Botha, "Knowledge in Optical Symbolic Pattern Recognition Processors," *Optical Engineering,* 26:34, 1987.

19. W. T. Cathey, K. Wagner, and W. J. Miceli, "Digital Computing with Optics," *Proceedings of the IEEE,* 77:1558–1572, 1989.

20. H. J. Caulfield, "Parallel N^4 Weighted Optical Interconnections," *Applied Optics,* 26(19):4039–4040, 1987.

21. H. J. Caulfield, "Energetic Advantage of Analog over Digital Computing," *Optical Computing 1989 Technical Digest Series,* vol. 9. Washington: Optical Society of America, 1989, p. 180.

22. H. J. Caulfield, "Variable and Fixed Rank 1 n^4 Interconnections," *Proceedings of the 1989 IEEE International Conference on Systems, Man, and Cybernetics*, Boston, Mass., November 14–17, 1989, p. II-405.

23. D. Clark, "An Optical Feature Extractor for Machine Vision Inspection," *Vision 87 Conference Proceedings*. Dearborn, Mich.: Society of Manufacturing Engineers, 1987.

24. B. D. Clymer and J. W. Goodman, "Optical Clock Distribution to Silicon Chips," *Optical Engineering*, 25:1103, 1986.

25. D. R. Collins et al., "Deformable Mirror Device Spatial Light Modulators and Their Applicability to Optical Neural Networks," *Applied Optics*, 28(22):4900–4907, 1989.

26. H. Dammann and K. Gortler, "High-Efficiency In-line Multiple Imaging by Means of Multiple Phase Holograms," *Optical Communications* 3(5):312–315, 1971.

27. M. W. Derstine and A. Guha, "Design Considerations for an Optical Symbolic Processing Architecture," *Optical Engineering*, 28:434, 1989.

28. A. R. Dias, R. F. Kalman, J. W. Goodman, and A. A. Sawchuk, "Fiber-Optic Crossbar with Broadcast Capability," *Optical Engineering*, 27:955–960, 1988.

29. U. Efron (ed.), *Spatial Light Modulators and Applications, Proceedings of the SPIE*, 465, 1984.

30. U. Efron et al. (eds.), "Special Issue on the Technology and Application of SLMs," *Applied Optics*, 28:4739, 1989.

31. R. A. Falk, D. Capps, and T. L. Houk, "Arithmetic/Logic Unit Based on Optical Crossbar Architecture," *Applied Optics*, 27:1634–1635, 1988.

32. M. R. Feldman and C. C. Guest, "Computer Generated Holographic Optical Elements for Optical Interconnection of Very Large Scale Integrated Circuits," *Applied Optics*, 26(20): 4377–4384, 1987.

33. M. R. Feldman and C. C. Guest, "Holograms for Optical Interconnects for Very Large Scale Integrated Circuits Fabricated by Electron-Beam Lithography," *Optical Engineering*, 28(8): 915–921, 1989.

34. M. R. Feldman et al., "Comparison between Optical and Electrical Interconnects Based on Power and Speed Considerations," *Applied Optics*, 27(9):1742–1751, 1988.

35. A. D. Fisher, "A Review of Spatial Light Modulators," Optical Society of America, Topical Meeting on Optical Computing, Washington, 1985, Technical Digest Series, paper Tuc1.

36. S. I. Gallant, "Connectionist Expert Systems," *Communications of the Association of Computer Manufacturers*, 31:152, 1988.

37. J. W. Goodman, "Fan-in and Fan-out with Optical Interconnections," *Optica Acta*, 32(12): 1489–1496, 1985.

38. J. W. Goodman, "Optics as an Interconnect Technology," in H. H. Arsenault, T. Szoplik, and B. Macukow (eds.), *Optical Processing and Computing*. New York: Academic Press, 1989.

39. J. W. Goodman et al., "Optical Interconnections for VLSI Systems," *Proceedings of the IEEE*, 72(7):850–865, 1984.

40. A. P. Goutzoulis, D. K. Davies, and E. C. Malarkey, "Prototype Position-Coded Residue Look-up Table Using Laser Diodes," *Optical Communications*, 61:302, 1987.

41. A. P. Goutzoulis, E. C. Malarkey, D. K. Davies, J. C. Bradley, and P. R. Beaudet, "Optical Processing with Residue LED/LD Lookup Tables," *Applied Optics*, 27:1674, 1988.

42. D. A. Gregory, J. C. Kirsch, and W. M. Crowe, "Optical Correlator Guidance and Tracking Field Tests," *Proceedings of the 1989 IEEE International Conference on Systems, Man, and Cybernetics*, November 14–17, Boston, Mass., 2:645, 1989.

43. P. S. Guilfoyle, "Systolic Acousto-Optic Binary Convolver," *Optical Engineering*, 23:20, 1984.

44. P. S. Guilfoyle, R. S. Rudokas, R. V. Stone, and E. V. Roos, "Digital Optical Computer II (DOC-II): Performance Specifications," Optical Society of America Topical Meeting on Optical Computing, Salt Lake City, 1991 Technical Digest Series, 6:203–206, 1991.

45. T. Haya et al., "Transfer Characteristics of the Microchannel Spatial Light Modulator," *Applied Optics,* 28(22):4781–4786, 1989.

46. I. Hayashi, "Optoelectronic Integrated Circuit—The Key to Optical Computing," *Science and Technology in Japan,* 9:8–10, 1990.

47. P. D. Henshaw and H. M. Haskel, "Applicability of Laser Beamsteering Devices for Rapid Access in 2D, 3D, and 4D Optical Memories," in J. W. Goodman, P. Chavel, and G. Roblin (eds.), *Optical Computing 88, Proceedings of the SPIE,* 963:200, 1989.

48. L. Hesselink and S. Redfield, "Photorefractive Holographic Recording in Strontium Barium Niobate Fibers," *Optics Letters,* 13:877, 1988.

49. M. Hibbs-Brenner, et al., "Integrated Optoelectronic Cellular Array for Fine-Grained Parallel Processing Systems," Optical Society of America Topical Meeting on Optical Computing, Salt Lake City, Topical Digest Series, 9:223–226, 1989.

50. "High-Speed Image Processor Works in Optical Domain," *Laser Focus World,* June 1990, p. 56.

51. L. J. Horneck, "128 × 128 Deformable Mirror Device," *IEEE Transactions on Electron Devices,* ED-30:539–545, 1983.

52. A. Huang, "Towards a Digital Optics Platform," in F. Lanzl, H. J. Preuss, and G. Weigelt (eds.), *Optics in Complex Systems, Proceedings of the SPIE,* 1319:156–160, 1990.

53. K. S. Huang, B. K. Jenkins, and A. A. Sawchuk, "Optical Symbolic Substitution and Pattern Recognition Algorithms Based on Binary Image Algebra," *Optical Computing 88,* in *Proceedings of the SPIE,* J. W. Goodman, P. Chavel, and G. Roblin (eds.), Toulon, France, August 29–September 2, 1988, 963:711–719, 1989.

54. K. S. Huang et al., "A Prototype Digital Optical Cellular Image Processor (DOCIP)," *Proceedings of the SPIE,* 963:687–694, 1988.

55. T. D. Hudson et al., "Real Time Optical Correlator Architectures Using a Deformable Mirror Spatial Light Modulator," *Applied Optics,* 28(22):4853–4860, 1989.

56. L. D. Hutcheson (ed.), *Integrated Optical Circuits and Components.* New York: Marcel Dekker, 1987.

57. L. D. Hutcheson et al., "Optical Interconnects Replace Hardwire," *IEEE Spectrum,* March 1987, pp. 30–35.

58. K. Iga et al., "Stacked Planar Optics: An Application of the Planar Microlens," *Applied Optics* 21(19):3456–3460, 1982.

59. J. Jahns and A. Huang, "Planar Integration of Free-Space Optical Components," *Applied Optics,* 28:1602–1605, 1989.

60. Jack Jewell, "Nonlinear FP and Microresonator Devices," *Proceedings of the SPIE,* OE LASE 90, 1214, 1990.

61. J. L. Jewell and S. L. McCall, "Microoptic Systems: Essential for Optical Computing," Optical Society of America Topical Meeting on Optical Computing, Salt Lake City, Technical Digest Series, 9:136–139, 1989.

62. J. L. Jewell et al., "Surface-Emitting Microlasers for Photonic Switching and Interchip Connections," *Optical Engineering,* 29:210–214, 1990.

63. J. Jewell, A. Scherer, S. L. McCall, Y. H. Lee, J. P. Harbison, and L. T. Florez, *Electronics Letters,* 25:123, 1989.

64. R. Jin et al., "All-Optical Switching in a GaAs/AlGaAs Strip-Loaded Nonlinear Directional Coupler," Optical Society of America Annual Meeting, Technical Digest Series, p. 83, 1988.

65. K. M. Johnson and G. Moddel, "Motivations for Using Ferroelectric Liquid Crystal Spatial Light Modulators in Neurocomputing," *Applied Optics,* 28(22):4888–4899, 1989.

66. H. F. Jordan, "Digital Optical Computing with Fibers and Directional Couplers," Optical Society of America Topical Meeting on Optical Computing, Salt Lake City, February 27–March 1, 1989, Technical Digest Series, 9:352–355, 1989.

67. F. Kamilev et al., "Implementation of NETL Knowledge-Base System with Programmable Opto-Electronic Multiprocessor Architecture," Optical Society of America Topical Meeting on Optical Computing, Salt Lake City, Topical Digest Series, vol. 9, 1989.

68. F. Kamiliev et al., "Programmable Optoelectronic Multiprocessors and Their Comparison with Symbolic Substitution for Digital Optical Computing," *Optical Engineering*, 28:396–409, 1989.

69. M. K. Kilcoyne, "Gigabit Optoelectronic Crossbar Switching Networks—State of the Art," *Proceedings of the SPIE*, 1215, 1990.

70. H. Kogelnik, "Integrated Optics, OEICs or PIC's?" in J. W. Goodman (ed.), *International Trends in Optics*. New York: Academic Press, 1991.

71. V. P. Koronkevich, "Computer Synthesis of Diffraction Optical Elements," in H. H. Arsenault et al. (eds.), *Optical Processing and Computing*. New York: Academic Press, 1989.

72. A. Korpel, "Acousto-optics—A Review of Fundamentals," *Proceedings of the IEEE*, 69:41, 1981.

73. R. K. Kostuk, "Reducing Alignment with Chromatic Sensitivity of Holographic Optical Interconnects with Substrate-Mode Holograms," *Applied Optics*, 28(22):4939–4944, 1989.

74. K. Kostuk et al., "Optical Imaging Applied to Microelectronic Chip-to-Chip Interconnections," *Applied Optics*, 24(17):2851–2858, 1985.

75. R. Kostuk et al., "Design Considerations for Holographic Optical Interconnects," *Applied Optics*, 26(18):3947–3957, 1987.

76. K. Kyuma, Y. Nitta, J. Ohta, S. Tai, and M. Takahashi, "The First Demonstration of an Optical Learning Chip," Optical Society of America Topical Meeting on Optical Computing, Salt Lake City, 1991, Technical Digest Series, 6:291–294, 1991.

77. P. Le, D. Y. Zand, and C. S. Tsai, "Integrated Electrooptic Bragg Modulator Modules for Matrix-Vector and Matrix-Matrix Multiplications," *Applied Optics*, 27:1780, 1988.

78. J. N. Lee and A. VanderLugt, "Acoustooptic Signal Processing and Computing," *Proceedings IEEE*, 77(10):1528–1557, 1989.

79. S. H. Lee (ed.), "Computer-Generated Holography II," *Proceedings of the SPIE*, 884, 1988.

80. S. H. Lee et al., "Two-Dimensional Silicon/PLZT Spatial Light Modulators: Design Considerations and Technology," *Optical Engineering*, 25(2):250–260, 1986.

81. A. L. Lentine et al., "Symmetric Self-electrooptic Effect Device: Optical Set-Reset Latch, Differential Logic Gate and Differential Modulator/Detector," *IEEE Journal of Quantum Electronics*, 25(8):1928–1936, 1989.

82. R. Lessard (ed.), "Photopolymer Device Physics, Chemistry and Applications," *Proceedings of the SPIE*, 1213, 1990.

83. A. W. Lohmann, "Polarization and Optical Logic," *Applied Optics*, 25:1594, 1986.

84. D. T. Lu et al., "Parallel Algorithms with Irregular Interconnections and Optical Technology," Optical Society of America Annual Meeting, October 15–20, 1989, Orlando, Fla., Technical Digest, p. 60.

85. R. I. MacDonald, "Optoelectronic Matrix Switching," *Canadian Journal of Physics*, 67:389–393, 1989.

86. J. M. Mait and K. H. Brenner, "Optical Symbolic Substitution: System Design Using Phase-only Holograms," *Applied Optics*, 27:1692, 1988.

87. J. Maserjian et al., "Optically Addressed Spatial Light Modulators by MBE-Grown Nipi MQW Structures," *Applied Optics*, 28(22):4801–4807, 1989.

88. Alistair D. McAulay, *Optical Computer Architectures*. New York: Wiley, 1991.

89. F. B. McCormick, "Generation of Large Spot Arrays from a Single Laser Beam by Multiple Imaging with Binary Phase Gratings," *Optical Engineering*, 28(4):299–304, 1989.

90. T. J. McHugh and H. A. Levenstein, "An Overview of Binary Optics at the Perkin-Elmer Corporation," *Proceedings of the SPIE*, 884:100–104, 1988.

91. D. A. B. Miller et al., "Integrated Quantum Well Self-electro-optic Effect Device: 2 × 2 Array of Optically Bistable Switches," *Applied Physics Letters,* 49(13):821–823, 1986.

92. M. J. Murdocca, "Digital Optical Computing with One-Rule Cellular Automata," *Applied Optics,* 26:682, 1987.

93. M. J. Murdocca, A. Huang, J. Jahns, and N. Streibl, "Optical Design of Programmable Logic Arrays," *Applied Optics,* 27:1651, 1988.

94. J. A. Neff, "Optical Computing at DuPont," *Proceedings of the SPIE,* 1397:496–508, 1990.

95. J. A. Neff, "Optics and Symbolic Computing," in Harold S. Szu (ed.), *Optical and Hybrid Computing, Proceedings of the SPIE,* 634:24, 1987.

96. J. Ohta et al., "GaAs/AlGaAs Optical Synaptic Interconnection Device for Neural Networks," *Optical Letters,* 14:844–846, 1989.

97. D. Osaltis and M. Haney, "Acoustooptic Synthetic Aperture Radar Processors," in J. Horner (ed.), *Optical Signal Processing.* San Diego: Academic Press, 1987.

98. C. Y. Ozberkmen, "New Micro-Lasers Make Debut," *Optics News,* October 1989, p. 30.

99. M. P. Petrov and Y. A. Kuzin, "Nonlinear Phenomena in Optical Fibers and the Feasibility of Their Application in Optical Computers," in H. H. Arsenault et al. (eds.), *Optical Computing and Processing.* New York: Academic Press, 1989.

100. D. Psaltis et al., "Adaptive Optical Networks Using Photorefractive Crystals," *Applied Optics,* 27(9):1752–1759, 1988.

101. D. Psaltis, A. A. Yamamura, M. A. Neifeld, and S. Kobayashi, "Parallel Readout of Optical Disks," *Proceedings of Optical Society of America Topical Meeting on Optical Computing,* Salt Lake City, vol. 9. February 1989, pp. 58–61.

102. A. Rosenfeld, "Parallel Image Processing Using Cellular Arrays," *IEEE Computer,* January 14–20, 1983.

103. W. E. Ross et al., "Fundamental Characteristics of the Litton Iron Garnet Magneto-optic Spatial Light Modulator," *Proceedings of the SPIE,* 388:55–64, 1983.

104. Semetex Corporation internal communication, Torrance, Calif., 1989.

105. J. Shamir, H. J. Caulfield, and R. B. Johnson, "Massive Holographic Interconnection Networks and Their Limitations," *Applied Optics,* 28:311–324, 1989.

106. Y. Sheng and H. H. Arsenault, "Corner-Cube Array for Integrated Optoelectronic Cellular Array Interconnections," *Proceedings of the SPIE,* 1215:123–130, 1990.

107. Y. Sheng, "Corner-Cube Retroreflectors for Optical Chip-to-Chip Interconnections," *Optics Letters,* 15(13):755–757, 1990.

108. J. Taboury, J. M. Wang, P. Chavel, F. Devos, and P. Garda, "Optical Cellular Processor Architecture. 1: Principles," *Applied Optics,* 27:1643–1650, 1988.

109. J. Taboury et al., "Optical Cellular Processor Architecture. 2: Illustration and System Considerations," *Applied Optics,* 28(15):3138–3147, 1989.

110. G. L. Tangonan et al., "8 × 8 Optoelectronic Crossbar Switch," Optical Fiber Conference '88, Optical Society of America, paper WF4, 1988.

111. A. R. Tanguay (ed.), "Special Issue on SLMs: Critical Issues," *Optical Engineering,* 22:663, 1983.

112. T. J. Trout, "A New Generation of Holographic Photopolymers," Gerdon Research Conference on Holography, Plymouth, Mass., 1989.

113. Tanida, Y. Nishimura, and Y. Ichioka, "A Design of an Optical Parallel Multiprocessor Based on Optical Array Logic Modular Architecture," Optical Society of America Topical Meeting on Optical Computing, Salt Lake City, 1991, Technical Digest, Series, post-deadline paper PdP1-1.

114. D. Z. Tsang, "Techniques for Implementation of High-Speed Free-Space Optical Interconnections," Optical Society of America Topical Meeting on Optical Computing, Salt Lake City, 1991 Technical Digest Series, 6:132–135, 1991.

115. A. VanderLugt, "Interferometric Spectrum Analyzer," *Applied Optics,* 20:2771, 1981.

116. W. B. Veldkamp and G. J. Swanson, "Developments in Fabrication of Binary Optical Elements," *Proceedings of the SPIE,* 437:54–59, 1983.

117. K. Wagner and D. Psaltis, "Multilayer Optical Learning Networks," *Applied Optics,* 26(23): 5061–5076, 1987.

118. A. C. Walker et al., "Design and Construction of a Programmable Optical 16 × 16 Array Processor," Optical Society of America Topical Meeting on Optical Computing, Salt Lake City, 1991 Technical Digest Series, 6:199–202, 1991.

119. C. A. Warde and T. Kottas, "Hybrid Optical Inference Machines: Architectural Considerations," *Applied Optics,* 25:940, 1986.

120. C. Waterson and K. Jenkins, "Shared Memory Optical/Electronic Computer: Architecture Design," Optical Society of America Topical Meeting on Optical Computing, Salt Lake City, 1991, Technical Digest Series, 6:195–197, 1991.

121. B. S. Wherrett et al., *Proceedings of the SPIE* 1215:264–273, 1990.

122. S. Xu et al., "Pinhole Imaging Holograms for Optical Interconnects," *Proceedings of the SPIE,* 963: 288–295, 1988.

123. P. Yeh et al., "Photorefractive Nonlinear Optics and Optical Computing," *Optical Engineering,* 28(2):328–343, 1989.

CHAPTER 20

COMPUTER NETWORKS (LAN, MAN, AND WAN): AN OVERVIEW

Gurdeep S. Hura

Department of Computer Science and Engineering
Wright State University, Dayton, Ohio

20.1 INTRODUCTION

20.1.1 Network Goals

Computers have become an integral part of many organizations, businesses, and universities. They perform many different functions. For example, universities use computers for student registration, course offerings, graduate and undergraduate enrollment, employee records, payroll, research on funded projects, etc. Each computer works in a different environment without interacting with the others. If computers can be connected and managed properly, much of the overlap of tasks can be avoided and a useful strategy can be developed for the universities. Similarly, for organizations or businesses sharing resources, databases or programs, costs, and communication, utilization for short- and long-term benefits may determine whether these computers, terminals, or peripheral devices should be connected. If the computers are connected by a network, then information can be extracted from each of them and shared globally or locally. By integrating data communication and computer technologies, it is possible to provide access to remote locations, databases, programs, files, etc. [7, 14].

The main goal of a network is to enable its users to share resources and to access these resources (hard disks, high-quality expensive laser printers, modems, peripheral devices, electronic mail, licensed software, etc.), regardless of their physical locations. Physical locations may be a few feet or even thousands of miles apart, but users exchange data programs in the same way. In other words, distance should not be a problem in the network because the network creates a "global environment" for its users and computers.

A variety of applications based on the concept of integration have been developed and implemented, such as the automated teller machine, communication between a user's computer and a bank's computer system, electronic mail, file transfer, as well as voice, video, and data communications.

Thanks are due to Jim Geier for supplying me with a lot of reports on wireless LANs. Special thanks go to my son Devendra Singh, who not only helped me in typing but also did a lot of proofreading.

20.1.2 Network Structure

The general network structure includes hosts (computer, terminal, telephone, or any other communication device) and communication subnets, also referred to as *network nodes, subnets,* or *transport systems.* Each host is connected to communication subnets. The set of subnets defines the boundary of networks and transfers the data from source host to destination host via a transmission medium (e.g., cable system, satellite, or leased telephone system) across the network. The host provides various services to its users while subnets provide the communication environment for the transfer of data. In most *wide-area networks* (WANs), the communication subnet consists of switching systems and communication links. Communication links (also known as *circuits,* or *channels*) carry the bits from one computer to another through networks. The system, however, is responsible for forwarding the data to the destination over transmission media. The switching system receives the data from one transmission medium and sends the data to another switching system over another transmission medium. Different names have been used for switching systems, such as *interface message processors* (IMPs), *packet switch mode, intermediate system,* and *data exchange system* [9, 14]. The switching system provides interface to the host and establishes a logic connection between hosts over the communication links. The various operations within communication systems are performed by dedicated and specialized computers [7, 14].

Each host is connected to one or sometimes more than one IMP. All the data originated from the host first arrive at one of the IMPs from where they are delivered to the destination host on the other side. The IMPs of the network are connected by communication links (cables, twisted pair, satellite link, leased telephone lines, etc.) and define the topology of the network.

For transmitting the text (in telegraphy), a public telex network was defined. Similarly, for voice (in telephony), a public switched telephone network has been defined. The common carriers help in establishing the connection between two customers. Bell Operating Companies usually provides the exchange-access carrier (inter-LATA), while interexchange carriers (such as AT&T, MCI, and Sprint) and carriers such as Telenet provide interexchange and other special types of customer services. The main aim of public switched telephone networks (voice communication networks) is to provide voice services, although data can also be transmitted via this network by using a modem (*mo*dulator-*dem*odulator) on both sides of the link. The modem converts the data to an acoustic signal which is easily accommodated in a standard telephone channel (4 kHz). Modems provide required translation and interface between digital equipment and analog communication links and transform the data to acoustic signals. The customer-premises equipment accepts the user's voice, data, or video signals and encodes them. It provides a digital-domain to voice-domain conversion. It is used in voiceband network. This type of transmission of data on public switched networks is also known as *voiceband communication.* The common carriers (AT&T, MCI, Sprint) support the public networks. Various components in voice networks include the telephone set, key telephone equipment, *private branch* exchanges (PBXs), recording, answering, internal wiring, etc. [2, 4, 5, 11].

20.1.3 Communication System

The communication system offers three types of links to the users: point-to-point, multicasting, and broadcasting.

Point-to-Point Communication. In this communication, data from one host are transmitted over either direct link or indirect link between IMPs (to which these hosts are connected). In direct link, IMPs are directly connected via links during the transfer of data. In indirect link, the data are transferred over a number of intermediate IMPs until the data are delivered to the destination host. Here the data coming from the incoming link arrive at the IMP, which stores them, waiting for a free link between IMPs. If it finds a free link, the data are transmitted over it; otherwise the IMP sends the data over to the intermediate IMPs. At each intermediate IMP, data are stored on disk and forwarded to the next available link or IMP, and this process is repeated until the data are received by the destination host. In the case of indirect link, the main aim is always to minimize the number of hops between hosts. (A *hop* is defined as a simple path of length 1.) The number of hops is determined by all possible paths of different lengths.

A communication system supporting point-to-point communication is also known as *store-and-forward* or *packet-switched subnets*. Some of the topologies for point-to-point communication are star, ring, tree, etc. These topologies are discussed in detail in Sec. 20.4.6.

Multicasting Communication. In multicasting communication, the data can be sent to a selected group of users. The usual way of implementing this type of communication is that a high-order bit in the address field of the data is set to logic 1. Thus, the data will be delivered to all those addresses whose high-order bit is set to 1. There exists only one channel or circuit which is shared by all connected hosts or IMPs. This communication suffers from the problem of "contention." This problem can be solved either by using a centralized dedicated processor (deciding which host can send the data next) or by using the distributed method (where each IMP resolves the problem independently).

Broadcasting Communication. This is a more general form of multicasting communication. Here data are delivered to all hosts or IMPs which are connected to the network. This type of communication uses a shared communication link which defines the topology of communication subnets, e.g., bus or ring. A special code in the address field of the data is used to distinguish it from point-to-point or multicasting communication. The data are sent on the circuit which is checked by every host or IMP connected to it. If its address matches the address contained in the data, it copies the data into its buffer [3, 4, 8, 12, 14].

20.1.4 Data Communication Networks

A data communication network can be viewed as an ensemble of sender-transmitter, transmission link/communication channel, and receiver. Each of these components may be further divided into a number of subcomponents. Networks can be either public or private. The main difference between the two lies in accessing the network; i.e., the public networks can be used by the public while the private networks can be used only by an organization or by a group of organizations. Both networks have the same functionality and capabilities [8, 11].

A data communication network is different from voice communication networks, and it includes components such as printers, computers, *local-area networks* (LANs), private and public networks, remote peripherals, modems, multiplexers, etc. A *data communication equipment* system is defined as *data terminal equipment* (DTE), *data circuit* (terminating) *equipment* (DCE), and *transmission circuits* (link, channel, trunk, etc.). The DTE includes devices such as mainframes, minicomputers, microcomputers, terminals, etc., while DTE provides various end-user applications such as data entry, database management, etc. The DCE provides interface between the user's customer-premises equipment (CPE) and communication networks. The physical layer of the data communication network can be point-to-point link (e.g., voice-grade, digital data service), point-to-point microwave link, satellite link, infrared link, etc.

20.1.5 Advantages of Data Communication Networks

Data communication networks offer many advantages such as simplified and reduced wiring, high reliability, reduction in operational costs, and expansion of life of obsolete and old equipment in universities and various government and private organizations. This old equipment would otherwise be wasted, but thanks to network technology we can use them for a few more years. Further, this equipment can be slowly replaced by standby inexpensive computers (minicomputers, microcomputers); files and programs can be copied on more than one file-server computer, so in the event of failure of one, another can be used as a backup system.

Data communication networks can be classified as a *local-area network* (LAN) and *wide-area network* (WAN) or *long-haul network* (LHN). All classes of network provide the same services, such as resource sharing and access to remote programs, databases, information (voice, video, and data), etc. LAN is used for a limited distance (typically a 2-km range) such as a university campus, the premises of organizations, etc. WAN is used for a longer range because this is an interconnection between LANs and MANs which provides interconnectivity over wide geographic areas. The internet is a prime example of WAN. In general, WANs are based on 56K bits/s or T1 link speed [3, 4, 6, 10].

20.1.6 Applications of Data Communication Networks

One of the main applications of data communication networks is electronic mail, where we can send messages or mail from our terminal, personal computer (PC), or even workstation to any one of our colleagues anywhere within the country or anywhere in the world. This service will be available to everybody (not only computer professionals) in the future just like postal services, telephone services, etc. Other new technologies, such as digitization of voice, television pictures, video image patterns, etc., can also be used in electronic mail to provide various services to users. These services together provide a variety of applications, e.g., accessing of an encyclopedia, language interpretation and learning at distant locations, pattern recognition and construction of patterns with different symbols and meanings at various locations, labeling the patterns/drawings, etc. A closely related application of electronic mail service is the electronic bulletin board system, which gained popularity especially in the universities and research and development division of organizations, where faculty members, graduate students, researchers, and others can access information about locations and dates of conferences, new products, employment, news about different countries, etc. New products and advances in various areas of computer networks like LANs, WANs, *integrated service digital networks* (ISDNs), MANs, broadband ISDN, frame relay, and others can also be accessed separately.

It is hoped that once these facilities and services become available at national and international levels, they can be accessed by not only computer-oriented technical users but also nontechnical users around the world if they have access to WANs. The applications of networks can be time-constrained or non-time-constrained. In the former category, an acknowledgment or indication control signal is required from the remote host before connection can be established (e.g., airline reservation system, bank automated teller system, automation of equipment, customized software, control and guidance system for engines, etc.) while the latter category includes applications such as electronic mail, office automation, resource sharing, etc. Although time (time of transfer or transmission of data and control) is not a critical issue, still a high reliability and accurate transmission of data are important [2, 13].

20.1.7 Network Evolution

The Advanced Research Projects Agency (ARPA) research and development program, part of the Department of Defense (DoD), designed ARPANET in 1969, the start of network technology. This network was the pioneer of packet-switching networks and provided communication between heterogeneous computers. The main aim of this program was to design an experimental network which connected a few universities and organizations in the United States and allowed them to access and use the computer resource-sharing projects. As ARPANET became successful, more functionality, applications, expansion, and complexities were added to it. This technology was handed over to the Defense Communication Agency (DCA) to develop and improve it. As a result, in 1983 the *defense data network* (DDN) based on ARPANET technology was defined. DDN is a packet-switching network with dynamic routing capabilities and is able to adjust itself in the event of crash or failure without affecting services to users. These networks have been defined and designed so as to provide survivability, security, and privacy [2, 7, 8].

20.2 STANDARDS ORGANIZATION

Today a large number of network products are available, and it is difficult (if not impossible) to connect even heterogeneous systems (defined by different vendors) for the transfer of data from one system to another. In some cases these systems are incompatible, and hence there can be no communication between them. A serious problem involves the architecture of the networks. Vendor-customized network architecture may have different layers and interfaces with common functions. Here the computer vendor defines a network architecture that encompasses all the vendor's communication products. Other vendors can access the network if they meet its specifications. IBM's *systems network architecture* (SNA) falls into this category.

To encourage the use of communication and computer products from different vendors to minimize burdens on users, customers were required to develop "protocol conversion software" on their computers to communicate with different vendor computer systems. This was achieved by defining several standards organizations so that differences between two communities (communication equipment and computer products) could be reduced and customers could avail themselves of services offered by the network just by using these standards. Some of the advantages of using standards in the networks are as follows [2, 6, 7, 9, 13, 14]:

- Standards help vendors to produce a large quantity of the products (conforming to the standard defined by the appropriate organization) in the market. Both hardware and software communities will be encouraged to mass-produce, thus lowering their costs.
- Different vendor products can exchange data, thus offering greater flexibility to customers in the selection and use of products.
- Customers are not stuck with only one vendor's products.
- Use of standards will enhance the competition among vendors, which will help improve the quality of network products and reduce the costs.

The only major disadvantage or drawback with standardization is that it tends to standardize obsolete technology. Usually it takes a very long time to review, approve, and adopt a standard. Considering the fast pace of emerging technologies, new technologies are likely to be overlooked in the standardization process. In spite of this drawback and the extra cost, standards are slowly being accepted. Customers are willing to pay more because they want to use their equipment or resources, before they become obsolete [3, 4, 9].

The standards organization is a hierarchical structure based on the bottom-up technique for reviewing and approving standards. We can classify the standards organization into two main groups [6]: international standards organization and national standards organization.

20.2.1 International Standards Organizations

This group comprises three different and distinct international standards organizations, with each performing specific tasks.

International Telecommunication Union (ITU). This is an agency of the United Nations that coordinates the development of standards for various governments. It is a treaty organization formed within the United Nations in 1965. ITU now has become a special body in the United Nations. The other organizations which either are part of ITU or interact with ITU are the International Radio Consultative Committee (IRCC) and International Telegraph and Telephone Consultative Committee (CCITT). The former organization includes two subgroups; one deals with international radio broadcasting and the other with telephone and data communication.

International Telegraph and Telephone Consultative Committee. It is a member of ITU, and its goal (as mentioned in its charter) is "to study and issue recommendations on technical, operating and tariff questions related to telegraphy and telephony." It submits recommendations to ITU on data communications, networks, telephone switching standards, digital system terminals, etc. Since CCITT comes under ITU, various governments (voting members) are the members of CCITT. The U.S. Department of State is a government representative in this organization. Several other categories (nonvoting members) of membership at different levels have also been included; e.g., recognized private operating agencies (RPOAs) are nonvoting members of CCITT.

The primary objective of CCITT is to define standards, techniques, and operations in telecommunications to provide end-to-end service on international telecommunication connections regardless of the origin, destination, or culture of the countries. This organization is dedicated to establishing effective and compatible telecommunications among members of the United Nations. It has five classes of members:

Class A (national telecommunication administrations): This class includes the government agencies and representatives of the nationalized company (duly approved by the government of that country). These agencies or representatives of nationalized companies, in general, are known as the postal, telegraph, and telephone (PTT) administration. In the United States, there is no PTT, so the Federal Communications Commission (FCC) under the Department of State represents the United States under this class, while many European and third world countries are represented by their respective PTT administrations. Only class A members have voting powers.

Class B: This includes private organization administrations which are duly recognized by their respective governments. For example, a private company, American

Telegraph and Telephone (AT&T), is a representative of the United States in this class of membership in CCITT.

Class C: This includes scientific and industrial organizations.

Class D: This class includes other international organizations engaged in data communication standards for telegraph and telephones.

Class E: This group includes miscellaneous organizations which are not directly involved in, but have interests in, CCITT's work.

Standard X.25, which defines three layers of *open-system interconnection* (OSI) model (physical, data link, and network layers), is very popular and is being used in all public-switched networks around the world. The public networks are packet-switched networks, and Standard X.25 provides interface between a public network and computers. Another standard defined by CCITT that is also widely accepted is V.24. This connector provides interface between terminals and networks. In the United States, there is a similar although incompatible, set of standards which is usually referred to as the Bell standards. The AT&T Bell Laboratories and the Electrical Industries Association (EIA) have jointly developed the Bell standards defined as modems. That is why the modems are always regarded as industry standards. The CCITT has also defined a set of standards in the form of recommendations in Europe as the V series (voice series). The best example of the CCITT V-standard is V.24, which is adopted in the United States and is equivalent to Bell or EIA RS-232C, also known as the physical layer DTE/DCE interface.

International Standards Organization (ISO).   The ISO is a nontreaty voluntary organization which has over 90 members, who are members of the national standards organization of their respective countries. This organization was founded in 1946 and has defined more than 5050 standards in different areas. Although it is a nontreaty (nongovernment) organization, a majority of its members are either from government standards agencies or from standards organizations duly recognized by public law. The main objective of this organization is to define and issue various standards and other products to provide an exchange of services and other items at the international level and to provide a framework for the interaction among various technical, economic, and scientific activities.

Various *technical committees* (TCs) have been formed to define standards in specific areas. The ISO currently has almost 200 TCs, each dealing with a specific area or subject. Further, TCs are broken into subcommittees and subgroups that actually develop the standards for specific tasks. For example, TC-97 is concerned with the standardization of computers and information processing systems. TC-97 has two subcommittees; SC-6 deals with telecommunication and information exchange between computers, in particular, various layers of architecture and interfaces between the layers, while SC-21 deals with data access, data transfer, and management of the network.

There are over 100,000 volunteers worldwide working in different subcommittees and subgroups. These volunteers include employees of the organization whose products are under consideration for standards and government representatives proposing ways of implementing technologies as standards in their respective countries while academicians offer their knowledge and expertise.

Although both CCITT and ISO are separate international organizations, they do cooperate in some areas, such as telecommunication standards (ISO is a D class of CCITT), but in the areas of communication and information processing, they have defined a boundary between them. Per this agreement, ISO is mainly concerned with layers 4 through 7 (defining the host part in the OSI reference model) which cover computer communication and distributed processing issues. The lower three layers (1 through 3) of the OSI model, which deal with data communication and communication networks (defining the communication subnetworks part in the OSI model) (Fig. 20.8), will be the responsibility of CCITT.

With the integration of various technologies such as data communications, information and data processing, and distributed processing, there can be an overlap between standards, but due to their mutual cooperation, so far they have not defined different standards for the same service or function.

As indicated earlier, ISO has members from various national standards organizations or organizations duly recognized by public law. Here are some representative members of different countries: The United States is represented by the *American National Standards Institute* (ANSI), which is a private, nonprofit, nongovernment national organization. The members of ANSI are from manufacturing institutions, common carriers (AT&T, Sprint, MCI), and other interested organizations. Many of the standards recommended by ANSI have been defined or accepted as international standards. Great Britain is represented by the British Standards Institute (BSI), France by AFNOR, West Germany (now a United Germany) by DIN, Japan by the Japanese Industrial Standards Committee, while other countries are represented by their government agencies.

20.2.2 National Standards Organizations

For data and computer communication networks, there are two international standards organizations, CCITT and ISO (as discussed above). There are other standards organizations which are also involved in defining standards for data communication networks. Some of these organizations are in the United States while others are in European countries. Following is a brief description of these organizations and their role in the standardization process.

American National Standards Institute (ANSI). It is a nongovernment, nonprofit, and voluntary organization. It includes members from manufacturing institutions, communication carriers, customers, and other interested organizations. Due to its nature, it is also known as the national clearinghouse (NCH) and coordinating agency for standards defined or implemented in the United States on a voluntary basis. ANSI is a member of ISO, and its main objective is to define and coordinate standards in data communication (office systems, encryption) for ISO. ANSI formed committee X.3 (in 1960) to define standards for data communications, programming, magnetic storage media, and the OSI reference model. It is a voting member in ISO and has the same interests as the ISO's TC-97.

National Bureau of Standards (NBS). This organization is governed by the U.S. Department of Commerce, and is very active in international standards organizations. Its main objective is to define *federal information processing standards* (FIPSs) used for the equipment bought by federal agencies, publish *government open system interconnection protocols* (GOSIPs), and define protocols for upper layers of the OSI reference model. GOSIP is mainly concerned with the protocols used only by U.S. government agencies. The Department of Defense (DoD) does not have to comply with FIPS or any other standards defined by NBS. NBS provides services to both CCITT and ISO.

U.S. National Committee. This committee is the coordinating group for the United States in CCITT, while the State Department is the principal member of CCITT. There are four CCITT study groups in the United States which give their input to advisory committees which in turn coordinate with the CCITT study group at an international level. The *National Communication System* (NCS) is a consortium of various federal agencies which have telecommunication interests and capabilities. The main objective of NCS is to coordinate with other organizations such as the Electronics Industries Association, ISO, and CCITT. NCS provides inputs to international standards organizations from federal agencies, and the majority of these inputs or recommendations are based on the OSI reference model.

Electronics Industries Association (EIA). This is a national trade association of a vast number of electronic firms. It is mainly concerned with the physical layer of the OSI reference model. Its main job is to define hardware-oriented standards, and it is a member of ANSI. It has defined best-known standard RS-232, which is a DTE/DCE interface. The first standard EIA-232 was defined in 1962 and subsequently modified as RS-232-C, which was renamed as EIA-232-D in 1987. Some of the limitations of RS-232 were overcome in RS-449 (RS-422-A and RS-423-A) in 1975.

Defense Communication Agency (DCA). This organization mainly deals with communication-related military standards (Mil-Std).

Federal Telecommunication Standards Committee (FTSC). The FTSC is a federal government agency and defines interoperability between government-owned networks and equipments. It adopts existing standards of CCITT and EIA. Both the FTSC and NBS try to work together. The lower layers of the OSI reference model are being handled by FTCS while higher layers are handled by NBS.

Institute of Electrical and Electronics Engineers (IEEE). This is a number one professional society with various sections and chapters throughout the world. It is a member of ANSI. The IEEE is mainly concerned with *local-area networks* (LANs) and many other standards. The IEEE 802 committee has defined a number of local-area networks and is primarily concerned with the lower two layers (physical and data of OSI model) of standards:

IEEE 802.1   Higher Layer Interface (HLI) Standards

IEEE 802.2   Logical Link Control (LLC) Standards

IEEE 802.3   Carrier Sense Multiple Access with Collision Detection (CSMA/CD) LAN

IEEE 802.4   Token-Passing Bus LAN

IEEE 802.5   IBM's Token Ring LAN

IEEE 802.6   Metropolitan-Area Network (MAN)

IEEE 802.7   Broadband Technical Advisory Group

IEEE 802.8   Fiber-Optics Technical Advisory Group

IEEE 802.9   Integrated Voice and Data LAN Working Group

IEEE 802.10 LAN Security Working Group

IEEE 802.11 Wireless LAN Working Group

IEEE 802.7 and IEEE 802.8 basically are working on broadband cable systems and optical fiber as transmission media which may be used in different LANs for higher data rates and bandwidth. IEEE 802.9 was set up in 1986, and its main objective is to define an architecture and interface between desktop devices and LANs and ISDNs [12].

British Standards Institute (BSI). It is a recognized United Kingdom organization for the formulation of national standards. It participates in ISO meetings through membership of various technical subcommittees.

Deutsche Institut für Normung (DIN). This is a West German national standards body analogous to BSI. DIN standards are well recognized in areas of everyday use.

Association Française de Normalisation (AFNOR). This is the French national standards body. It is very active within ISO.

International Electrotechnical Commission (IEC). This is an independent international agency which specializes in the formulation of international standards in the area referred to by its name.

International Federation for Information Processing (IFIP). This is an international federation of technical groups with interests in promoting information science and technology and assessing research development and education.

The European Computer Manufacturers Association (ECMA). The ECMA was founded in 1961 as a noncommercial organization to define standards for data processing and communication systems. It includes all European computer manufacturers, European divisions of some U.S. companies (IBM World Trade Europe Corporation International Computers and Tabulators Limited). It is a nonvoting member of CCITT and ISO and works closely with many technical committees of ISO and CCITT. Members include AEG-Telefunken, Buroughs, Honeywell, IBM Europe, Siemens, Olivetti, Ferranti, ICL, Nixdorf, and NCR.

These standards organizations (international and national) define standards for data communication networks. On the basis of these standards, vendors and customers have to accept products which must comply with the standards. Due to widespread standardization throughout the world, many organizations have been formed during recent years. The main objective of these organizations is to foster acceptance between the vendors (supplying the products) and the customers (buying the products).

20.3 ANALOG AND DIGITAL TRANSMISSION SYSTEM BASICS

A communication system is made up of three subsystems: the transmitter, transmission medium, and receiver. The transmitter at the source station transmits the voltage signal (corresponding to the information or message to be sent) on transmission media. Depending on the type of transmission, the signal may be either baseband or broadband. The difference between baseband and broadband from the point of transmission is that broadband signals require modulation before transmission through media while baseband signals do not require modulation. The voltage signal may be represented as either continuous information (analog transmission) or discrete information (digital transmission). Based on these two types of information, two categories of transmission have been defined—analog and digital.

20.3.1 Analog Transmission

An analog signal is a sinusoidal waveform where amplitude is varying continuously over time (Fig. 20.1a). In this type of transmission, user information is represented by continuous variation of the amplitude frequency and phase of the carrier signal with respect to the information signal. The transmitted signal from the transmitter is known as the *modulated signal*. On the receiving side this modulated signal is demodulated to retrieve

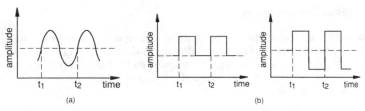

FIGURE 20.1   *(a)* Analog waveform. *(b)* Digital waveform.

the original user information. The analog signal corresponding to user information is modulated over a carrier signal of high frequency which carries the signal to the receiving side. There are three types of modulation.

In *amplitude modulation* (AM), the amplitude of the sinusoidal carrier signal is varied in accordance with the instantaneous value of the user information signal amplitude. The frequency and phase of the "modulated" signal remain the same as those of the user signal. This type of modulation has been used in various applications such as medium- and shortwave radio broadcasting systems, and it provides a reasonable bandwidth. AM is very sensitive to atmospheric noise, which affects the quality of reproduction (signal-to-noise) of the user signal at the receiving side.

In *frequency modulation* (FM), the frequency of the carrier signal is varied in accordance with the instantaneous value of the frequency of the user signal, keeping the amplitude and phase of the carrier signal constant. FM is immune to atmospheric noises and thus finds applications in satellite communication, microwave communication, and high-radio-frequency communications.

In *phase modulation* (PM), the phase of the carrier signal is varied in accordance with the phase of the carrier signal, keeping both the amplitude and the frequency of the modulated signal the same as those of the user signal. Due to a few similarities between FM and PM, with appropriate small changes in the demodulating or detection circuit, it is possible to demodulate FM from PM or vice versa.

If we consider the carrier signal as a series of periodic pulses, different types of pulse modulation are defined. Accordingly, if the amplitude of the carrier signal is varied in accordance with the user information, a *pulse amplitude modulation* (PAM) is defined. *Pulse frequency modulation* (PFM) and *pulse phase modulation* (PPM) are defined similarly. These modulations are used to transmit different types of signals, e.g., audio, video, optical, telemetric, etc.

Instead of considering the carrier signal as a series of pulses, if we consider the sampled user information signal, we get three types of modulations: *amplitude-shift keying* (ASK), *frequency-shift keying* (FSK), and *phase-shift keying* (PSK). In these modulation techniques, the carrier signal is considered as a sinusoidal signal. ASK modulates the carrier with a binary signal to produce the AM signal. Logic 0 is represented by no amplitude, and logic 1 is represented by a full amplitude carrier. ASK is very sensitive to noise and external interference. FSK modulates the carrier to switch between the two frequencies. These modulation techniques find application in transmitting data and text transmission on analog channel or link, digital data transmission on wireless transmission media, and optical communication on fiber media. (They are of high bandwidth, thin, lightweight, and immune to electromagnetic interference.)

It is important to note that all the modulation techniques discussed above transmit an analog signal, which is a continuous signal. The input signal and carrier signal can be in any form, i.e., sinusoid or a series of periodic pulses [2, 3, 6, 9, 11].

20.3.2 Digital Transmission

Here the signals are transmitted in digital form. The input could be in any form; at the transmitter it is converted to digital form after the modulation process. Various modulation techniques used in digital transmission are *pulse code modulation* (PCM), *differential PCM* (DPCM), *delta modulation* (DM), and *adaptive delta modulation* (ADM). Digital transmission has the following advantages:

1. It allows the data and voice to be integrated and thus defines the main concept used in integrated services digital networks (ISDNs).
2. It allows the digital signal to be regenerated in the presence of noise and thus provides a very good quality of service.
3. It provides ease in encrypting data.
4. With inexpensive integrated chips, we can multiplex different types of information (analog or digital) which improves the utilization of the communication media. The carrier signal is defined by a clock signal which provides the bit rate for digital transmission. The conversion of an analog signal to digital form is called *sampling,* while compressing the infinite analog signals to a finite number is called *quantizing*.

However, this system possesses the following disadvantages:

1. There is a bandwidth requirement. For digital transmission, a minimum rate of 64K bits/s is required for each channel while the analog system requires 4 kHz of voice-grade data.
2. Since we are dealing with digital signals, we need to provide synchronization between source and destination nodes.
3. The noises due to the sampling of user signals, phase jitter, high alteration, etc., restrict the use of high-speed transmission media with digital transmission.

The waveform for a digital signal shown in Fig. 20.1b is a square wave represented in binary signal form. Here a pulse (or positive side of the wave) is defined by logic 1 (higher voltage or positive voltage), while no pulse (or negative side of the wave, or zero voltage) is defined by logic 0 (lower voltage or negative voltage).

A cycle of waveforms (Fig. 20.1a and b) defines complete oscillation between t_1 and t_2. The frequency is given in cycles per second, or hertz (Hz). The duration of one cycle $(t_2 - t_1)$ is defined by the time period of one cycle. During this time, the signal travels one complete oscillation or wavelength. The frequency of the waveform is the reciprocal of the time period of 1 cycle, and vice versa.

$$\text{Frequency} = \frac{1}{\text{time period of one cycle } (t_2 - t_1)}$$

The bandwidth of an analog signal is defined as the difference between the highest and lowest frequency values and is expressed in hertz.

20.3.3 Baseband and Broadband Signals

Based on the nature of transmission, signals can be classified as baseband or broadband. The baseband signal is a digital signal and does not use modulation. The bandwidth of this signal is limited, and it uses *time-division multiplexing* (TDM) to provide better utilization of transmission media. The broadband signal is an analog signal and uses modulation. It offers a larger bandwidth than baseband, and it uses *frequency-division multiplexing* (FDM) for better utilization of transmission media.

20.3.4 Transmission Circuits

The communication system can operate in different transmission circuits: simplex, half duplex, and full duplex.

In a simplex transmission circuit, signals flow in one direction only. No acknowledgment is required since the sender is concerned only with sending while the receiver is concerned only with receiving. This type of transmission circuit finds application in radio and TV broadcasting systems and teleconferencing.

In the half duplex circuit, the signal flows in one direction at a time. Both stations can send signals to each other on the same medium at the same time. This circuit finds application in telephone systems, walkie-talkie systems, and wireless communication.

In the full duplex circuit, both stations can send data to each other at the same time. It uses two pairs of wires.

20.3.5 Modes of Transmission

The data can be transmitted on transmission media in two modes: serial and parallel.

Serial Transmission.   In this mode, data are transmitted bit by bit, packet by packet (Fig. 20.2a). This mode can transmit the data over a larger distance but suffers from low speed of transmission. The signaling speed of the transmission circuit is usually defined as the baud rate and data rate.

The *baud rate (B)* is a measure of the signaling speed of a line, and it is the number of times per second the condition of the electric signal on the line is changing. The *data rate* is the actual number of bits traveling at any point on the circuit per second. The baud rate describes the electrical property of the circuit while the data rate is a measure of data movement. The baud rate can also be defined as the modulation rate of change in the carrier signal. If we know the baud rate, then its reciprocal gives us the signaling time in seconds. If we can determine the number of bits sent during this interval, then the bit rate can be given as

$$B(\text{baud}) = \text{baud rate} \times \text{bits/s}$$

The throughput of a communication system can be defined as the number of bits transmitted over a period of time. Since we use this parameter as a measure in different areas of computer systems, there is no standard definition. It can be defined in various ways [8, 9].

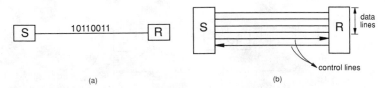

(a)   (b)

FIGURE 20.2   Mode of transmission. *(a)* Serial transmission. *(b)* Parallel transmission.

Parallel Transmission. In this transmission mode (Fig. 20.2*b*) each bit or packet is assigned to a data channel, and control channel signals (such as READY, BUSY, DE-MAND, and other types of control signals) are used to establish the connection between them. The number of bits or packets is equal to the number of channels. This type of mode can be used only for a short distance, typically for connecting peripheral devices or a big scientific setup. The speed of this mode is much larger than that of serial transmission.

20.3.6 Transmission Configurations

Depending on the type of data, two transmission configurations are asynchronous and synchronous. For example, the text data between terminals and the computer always use asynchronous transmission.

Asynchronous Transmission. In this configuration, each character contains a start pulse at the beginning of the character followed by a stop pulse (usually one or two) at the end. The start and stop pulses provide synchronization between sender and receiver and define the length or duration of the character. The transmission of a character takes place at random times. These characters (text data) are always sent from terminals or computers asynchronously. One start pulse is sent, followed by an 8-bit (ASCII) character which is further followed by one or two stop pulses. If we know the transmission bit rate, then we can determine the number of characters sent per second. For example, if we have a transmission speed of 2400 bits/s and we assume 1 bit for start and 2 bits for stop, then the number of ASCII characters in transmitted signals per second will be 2400/11 = 217 characters per second (Fig. 20.3). This transmission does not define a time relationship between consecutive characters or even between blocks of characters.

Synchronous Transmission. In this configuration, a regular time relationship between consecutive characters or a block of characters is defined. Here the characters are sent continuously on media one after another, from sender to receiver. No extra bits are required for each character for synchronization, but it is usually provided by a special control character pattern (SYN). This pattern is first sent to the receiver, informing him or her of the starting point of the character. Similarly, for digital data a unique bit pattern of 8 bits is sent to the receiver. When the communication medium is idle, it transmits logic 1s (marking) on the medium. Depending on the type of data and control pattern, the protocols are defined as character-oriented (for transmitting text data) or bit-oriented (bit data) protocols.

20.3.7 Multiplexing

To better utilize transmission media, multiplexing of several telephone channels on the physical medium is recommended. Combining different data streams and transmitting

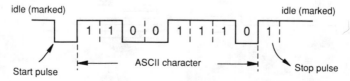

FIGURE 20.3 Asynchronous transmission of ASCII character.

them across a single line will not only increase the throughput of the communication system but also decrease the cost. Similarly, demultiplexing will regenerate the original signal separately. The primary techniques for multiplexing multiple signals onto a single physical medium are frequency-division and time-division multiplexing.

Frequency-Division Multiplexing (FDM). In this technique (Fig. 20.4*a*), the entire bandwidth of the medium is divided into smaller channels where each channel accommodates a voice-grade frequency (typically 4 kHz). Each user has exclusive control of one channel for sending data. For example, an AM radio station will divide the entire bandwidth (allocated to it by CCITT) into smaller channels. In each channel there is a bandwidth for a particular station, which uses it for broadcasting.

The FDM technique is officially not standardized, but it is being used as a universal technique for multiplexing a number of voice channels. It defines a 4000-Hz (4-kHz) bandwidth for each channel out of which 3000-Hz (3-kHz) bandwidth is useful (detected by the filters) for a voice-grade channel, while 1000-Hz (1 kHz) bandwidth is used to provide 500-Hz guard frequency on each side of the 3-kHz bandwidth. The reason for assigning a bandwidth of 1 kHz is to keep various channels separated from one another so as to avoid any electrical interference when the channels are multiplexed. A very popular and widely accepted standard for FDM is 12 4000-Hz multiplexed channels giving a bandwidth of 60–108 kHz and it is being used in a number of countries. Clearly there is a waste in frequency between channels. A 12-channel multiplexed signal in the range of 60 to 108 kHz is called a *group*. A group may have a frequency range from 48 to 60 kHz. Users may also request leased lines of 48K to 56K bits/s from the carriers. A *supergroup* is defined by multiplexing five groups to yield 60 voice channels. A *master group* is defined by multiplexing five supergroups (CCITT standard). The Bell System has defined its own standard of master group which multiplexes 10 supergroups. FDM is very useful when all input channels are busy, but it will not make efficient use of overall bandwidth. FDM finds application in increasing the number of voice channels for twisted-pair telephone lines, which in turn increases the number of telephone channels. It also is used in large-bandwidth coaxial cables. FDM can multiplex few communicating devices (terminals giving rates of 1200 to 4800 bits/s) because there is not enough voice-grade circuit.

Time-Division Multiplexing (TDM). In this multiplexing technique (Fig. 20.4*b*), a fixed time is allocated to each of the channels. Each channel gets a fixed time slot during which it can transmit a fixed number of bits such that the output data rate of the multiplexer is always equal to the sum of the input data rates across a TDM. The time slot is allocated by a round-robin technique. If a particular channel does not have data to transmit, that time slot is reserved for the channel, and after the elapsed fixed time, it will go to the next channel. TDM basically operates on digital signals, but it can also be used on analog signals where the output of the multiplexer has to be connected to a modem.

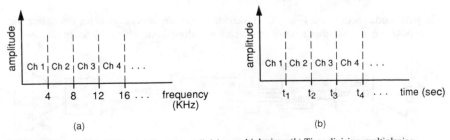

(a)   (b)

FIGURE 20.4   Multiplexing. *(a)* Frequency-division multiplexing. *(b)* Time-division multiplexing.

To avoid wasting a time slot, a variation of TDM known as *statistical time-division multiplexing* (STDM) has been defined. In STDM, no fixed time slot is assigned to any channel. The traffic on each channel is measured, and depending on the traffic, a variable time slot is allocated to the channel. If a particular channel does not have data to transmit, that channel is skipped and this time slot is used for other channels. In this technique buffers are used to store the data temporarily. This may become a major problem, especially during peak hours of traffic.

TDMs can be used on both synchronous and asynchronous transmissions. In synchronous multiplexing, the output generates a fixed sampling pattern and no input buffer is required; in asynchronous multiplexing, the output does not generate a fixed sampling pattern and usually requires an input buffer. Each sample from the input is usually represented by some pointer or identifier which is transmitted.

20.3.8 Telephone System

The local telephone network in the United States is operated and managed by seven *regional Bell holding companies* (RBHC) and other carriers such as AT&T, MCI, and Sprint. The main goal of RBHC is to maintain control of local networks in the region. The range of local networks is usually the same as for metropolitan-area networks, and as such, RBHC provides about 160 *local access and transport areas* (LATAs) for public packet-switched networks. RBHC also supports access to long-distance companies. The companies that use their backbone networks to provide communication services to users are known as *common carriers,* and the services offered by these carriers and the cost of services are specified in a document known as the tariff. All carriers, whether owned privately or owned by the government bodies of the countries, are controlled and managed by ITU, a United Nations treaty organization. The telephone network, which basically is a voice network, has multiple-level offices. The telephone voice network transmits voice signals in the frequency range of 20 Hz to 4 kHz. A voice voltage signal is transmitted over twisted-pair lines between the end or central office and the subscriber's (Fig. 20.5) telephone set. This distance is usually 1 to 7 mi and defines the subscriber end loop. A number belonging to the same end office can be connected by direct link. If that number belongs to another end office, then it will go through the toll office, which is connected to end offices by a toll trunk line. Further, if a number does not belong to the same toll office, it will go to intermediate switching offices (primary, sectional, and regional) which are connected to toll offices via high-bandwidth intertoll trunks (Fig. 20.5). All these offices provide switching paths for establishing connections between subscribers [1, 8, 13].

20.3.9 Bell System's T1 Carrier

In pulse code modulation (Fig. 20.6) a codec (*co*der-*dec*oder) digitalizes the analog dial number from a subscriber's set (if connected to a digital end office) by using the Nyquist

FIGURE 20.5   End-to-end communication on telephone hierarchical system.

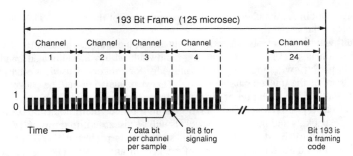

FIGURE 20.6   The Bell System T1 carrier (1.544 Mbits/s).

theorem [14]. Accordingly, codec generates 8000 samples per second, and these samples carry the complete information contained in a 4-kHz bandwidth. Bell's T1 carrier (non-standard), which is widely used, contains 24 voice channels which are multiplexed. Each channel contains 8 bits (7 bits are data and 1 bit is used for control). Each channel has 8000 samples and hence carries $8000 \times 7 = 56,000$ bits/s of data and $8000 \times 1 = 8000$ bits/s for control. A *frame* is defined as $24 \times 8 = 192$ bits to which 1 extra bit is attached for framing, making 193 bits every 125 μs. The data rate is 193 divided by 125 μs, or 1.544 Mbits/s [13].

20.3.10 Switching Techniques

The above section was a brief introduction to voice-grade channels (4 kHz) being multiplexed for better and efficient utilization of transmission media. The voice channel provides a conversation between two persons, and either multiplexing technique can be used for this purpose (provided that the output data rate equals the sum of the input rates across the multiplexer). In other words, we can say that multiplexing techniques can be used only for voice channels. If we want to provide communication between two computers, different types of switching techniques are employed such as circuit, message, and packet switching.

Circuit Switching.   In this technique, first the complete physical connection between two computers is established and then data are transmitted from the source computer to the destination computer. This technique provides end-to-end connection between computers. The setup time (for establishing end-to-end connection) in some applications may become a problem.

Message Switching.   The source computer sends data or the message to the switching office, which stores the data in its buffer. It then looks for a free link to another switching office and then sends the data to this office. This process is continued until the data are delivered to the destination computer. Due to its working principle, it is also known as *store-and-forward*. This method has no restriction on the size of the data, and, as a result, the computers, which want to send short messages, may have to starve. Also the switching offices should have enough buffer space to store long messages.

Packet Switching.   A fixed size of packet which can be transmitted across the network is specified. All the packets of fixed size are stored in main memory (instead of disk, as in message switching) which reduces the accessing time of the packets. This improves the throughput of the network.

Circuit switching controls the entire bandwidth of the medium in advance. Thus, once the connection is established, the unused bandwidth within the allocated bandwidth is wasted. In packet switching, after the bandwidth for packets is used, the bandwidth is released. Further the unused bandwidth in the network is also used. The packet switching does not establish a connection or circuit for transmitting a packet in advance. If a large number of packets arrive at a particular switching office, there could be a problem in storing these packets and maybe some packets will be discarded. In terms of delivering the packets in order to the destination, circuit switching is preferred to packet switching, which does not guarantee the delivery of packets in any order. The billing scheme is different for the two switching techniques. In circuit switching, the bill depends on distance and time while in packet switching it depends on the connect time and number of bytes transmitted [6, 12, 13].

20.4 LOCAL-AREA NETWORKS

Following is a brief description of some of these organizations, their needs, and their role in the standardization process during the evolution of local area networks.

20.4.1 Evolution of LAN

The first LAN report was described in Robert Metacalfe's Ph.D. dissertation from the Massachusetts Institute of Technology in 1973 (LANs will be used to increase employee productivity, efficiency, and resource sharing and to enable some of the obsolete equipment or resources to be used). Later Metacalfe along with David Boggs and others working at the Xerox Corporation defined the first LAN ETHERNET (a trademark of Xerox Corp.). This ETHERNET was adopted by various companies, and Intel built a single-chip controller for it. Thus, it became de facto standard for LANs. This LAN is characterized as nondeterministic.

During the same time, automobile industries, in particular General Motors (GM) in 1982, decided to increase productivity (through factory automation) and competitiveness. GM was looking for a network to connect all its factories, offices, and dealers. At the same time, this network needed to be able to provide a fixed rate of movement of various parts of the assembly by robots connected to the network. Since the first LAN (ETHERNET) was nondeterministic, GM defined its own LAN, known as the token-passing bus, which works on the basis of round-robin allocation to various machine robots, programmable devices, and resources, thus, giving a deterministic response to the machines. This LAN won acceptance from both vendors and customers. From the vendor's point of view, the LAN provided specifications to the network products (both hardware and software), and as such a protocol for factory use known as the manufacturing automation protocol (MAP) was defined. This protocol has been accepted by many manufacturing companies. MAP defined LAN standards for use in automobiles and an alternative within standards for the factory environment. Further, it offered a large market for products that comply with those standards. A large number of companies and organizations that have participated in the MAP environment have benefited in the mass production of their goods, particularly automobile parts.

A similar attempt (based on factory automation by GM) was made for office automation by Boeing Company. The main purpose of that LAN was to support office automation and engineering aspects in the real-time domain to Boeing 747 fleets. Boeing defined its own LAN and set of protocols for the office automation and called this a *technical office protocol* (TOP). GM and Boeing worked together to provide interoperability between their networks.

During the same time when GM was busy in selecting and defining the token-passing bus LAN for its factory automation, International Business Machines (IBM) defined its own LAN, the token ring LAN. The main purpose of the IBM token ring was to provide high reliability, availability, and maximum utilization of the resources, devices connected to the LAN.

Given this new trend of different organizations defining LANs as their standards, and because of the benefits of a high-performance, economical method of interconnection for resource sharing, it was felt that these LANs should be standardized by an international organization. IEEE was asked to form a committee for this purpose, and as a result the IEEE 802 committee came into existence. The main purpose of this committee was to define standards for all these LANs as well as the method of interconnection. Since each of the proposed LANs was defined for a specific environment and application, their architectures varied. A standard for each LAN was defined and assigned a specific number by the IEEE 802 committee. The standards defined for each of the LANs were based on the OSI reference model [1, 8, 9, 12, 13]. The standards define documents that discuss or describe protocols.

In early 1986, a nonprofit joint venture of more than 60 manufacturers and suppliers (of data processing and communication protocols) was formed, called the *Corporation for Open Systems* (COS). Its main objective was to provide interoperability for multivendor products and services offered by the OSI reference model, integrated services data network (ISDN), and related international standards, to convince customers and vendors to concentrate on an open-network architecture model. The COS also deals with the definition and development of a set of testing criteria, facilities, and certification procedures. Thus, vendors will be forced to certify that their products comply with international standards and hence are acceptable to customers [2, 7, 12, 14].

During the late 1980s, the OSI User Committee was formed by the U.S. government. Its main objective was to create OSI-related standards on the world market. This committee offers OSI requirements and specifications and works in coordination with government agencies and industries who are working for OSI-based standards.

All these organizations are working for a common objective: to promote OSI-based standards, widespread development, products, protocols for the OSI reference model, interoperability among various OSI-based incompatible products and between OSI and non-OSI network products.

20.4.2 LAN Architecture

To provide interoperability and interconnection between different types of LANs (incompatible layers, number of layers, different architectures, etc.), the International Standards Organization (ISO) set up a committee in 1977 to propose a common architecture for LANs, which can be used to connect various heterogeneous computers and other communicating devices. This is the first step in defining international standardization of various protocols to be used in the network layers. ISO published a document in 1984 covering specifications for architectures and protocols, ISO 7498, and defined it as the *open-system interconnection* (OSI) reference model. This term was used because it applies to systems that are open to interconnection with other vendor-customized or general systems. Another international standards organization, CCITT, also published a similar and compatible standard as X.200 [1, 6, 12].

One of the main intentions of the OSI reference model is to define and develop protocols which can perform the functions of each layer of the reference model. Thus, the majority of protocols being defined are based on the concept of the layered approach and hence are known as *layered protocols*. Any type of communication system can be defined by using the functional layering concept. It is important to know that the layered model is different from layered protocols in the sense that the model defines a logical framework on which protocols (that the sender and receiver agree to use) can be used to perform a specific application. Specific functions and services are defined through protocols for each layer and are implemented as a program segment on computer hardware by both the sender and the receiver. This approach of developing a layered protocol or functional layering of any communication process not only defines its specific application but also provides interoperability between vendor-specialized heterogeneous systems. These layers are, in fact, the foundation of many standards and products in the industry today.

Layered protocols using the same connections can allow different systems to communicate openly with each other without changing the logic of the layers. Thus, the systems that previously were unable to communicate with each other because of their "closeness" now could communicate by using layered protocols with slight changes in software and hardware.

20.4.3 Protocols, Layers, and Interfacing in LAN

There are a number of ways to define the communication system between the source and destination nodes. The usual approach is to define a communication system as a set of interacting processes (components) and then to define the functions and services offered by these processes. This approach is not useful because it describes the functions of a communication system which may be used in a limited environment and may not provide interoperability for different types of networks of different functionality. The second approach is rather abstract in the sense that the functions and services of the network are defined and described as a collection of processes at various levels. At each level, we can define one layer for a particular process(es). Each layer will correspond to a specific function(s) and service(s), and these layers are different for various networks. However, each of the layers and the implementation of these layers are totally hidden from the higher layers. The services offered by these layers are provided through protocols and are implemented by both source and destination on their respective computers. Protocols are defined in terms of rules (through syntax and semantics) describing the translation or conversion of services to an appropriate set of program segments. Each layer has an entity process and is different in different machines. It is this peer process through which other processes (corresponding to layers) communicate, using the protocols. Examples of entity processes are file transfer, application programs, and electronics facilities. These processes can be used by computers, terminals, PCs, and workstations. Protocols provide data formatting, various signal levels for data and control, flow control, synchronization, and appropriate sequencing for the data to be exchanged. Two networks will offer two-way communication for any specific application(s) if they use the same protocol. Implementing the protocols involves a lot of processing. To free the central processing unit (CPU) from the complexities of protocols, a specialized hardware chip can be used for data communication protocols. The mainframe computers (such as the IBM mainframe) use a separate specialized computer (known as the *front-end processor*). Many communication devices are known as terminals which are capable of communicating with a computer and which accept data from users, typically a keyboard. Terminals can be either dumb (little or no processing capability, e.g., VT100) or smart (local processing capability and local storage device). Many smart terminals employ synchronous communication.

A useful advantage of defining a peer entity is that these entities first establish connection in the OSI reference model prior to transfer of actual data. Depending on the type protocol under consideration, we can have different primitives; but for a typical pro-

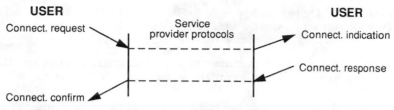

FIGURE 20.7   Peer-to-peer connection for network protocol.

tocol, Fig. 20.7 [10] shows the establishment of peer-to-peer connections using the primitives in the OSI reference model. Here the upper layer of the sender side issues a primitive command to the protocol of lower layers of the network for establishing a connection with its peer entity and sends it to the upper-layer entity of the receiver side. If the connection is approved (optional), the receiver side sends the response, using the confirmation primitive command of establishment of connection. Once the connection is established, the upper-layer entity of the sender will use a data set of primitives as a command to send the data to the receiver side which, in turn, using the same set of primitive commands, sends an acknowledgment of receipt of data.

20.4.4 OSI Reference Model

ISO defined the framework for the OSI reference model (Fig. 20.8) in terms of seven layers describing functions and services needed in international computer communication networks. By having defined layers for the framework, designers and developers can implement the layer's protocols independently since the functions and services of each layer are very specifically defined and accepted by the network community. The following section describes the functions and services of each layer of the OSI reference model. It is important to restate that the OSI reference model does not represent any specific architecture of the network; it simply provides a framework of layers and explains the purpose of the layers in it. Each layer has its own standards and protocols published as a separate international standard [1, 4, 6–8, 12].

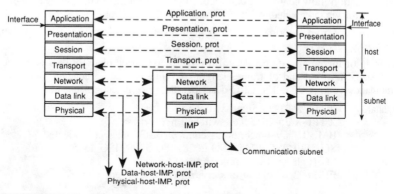

FIGURE 20.8   Network architecture, protocols, and layers.

Physical Layer.   The physical layer is the lowest layer of the OSI reference model, and it provides an interface between the data link and the transmission medium or circuit. This layer has the following characteristics:

- DTE/DCE is concerned with an interface between the data terminal equipment and data circuit terminating equipment where DTE is a computer or terminal and DCE is a modem.
- Mechanical characteristics comprise the physical properties of the interface to transmission media (size, configuration).
- Electrical characteristics relate to the representation of bits (voltage levels) and the data transmission rate in bits.
- Functional characteristics relate to the physical interface between a system and transmission media.
- Procedural characteristics are handled by protocol which determines bit streams that are exchanged across the transmission media.
- The activation/deactivation characteristic is concerned with the physical connection, control of the physical link, and preparation of transmission media to allow the bit stream to pass in both directions and termination of function at the end of transmission.
- Maintenance and management involve the transmission of bits and management of activities related to the physical link.
- The data link entities are notified of fault condition.
- The quality of service (QOS) is determined by characterization parameters of quality of transmission paths.
- Standards: EIA-232-D, EIA RS-49 (RS-422-A and RS-423-A), EIA-530, EIA-366
                 CCITT X.21-1 (circuit-switched network)
                 CCITT X.25-1 (packet-switched network)
                 CCITT V.24

Data Link Layer.   This layer provides the interface between the physical layer and the network layer. The following characteristics are defined for this layer:

- Manage the link connection and data interchange during transfer of data between source and destination.
- Provide synchronization, delimit, and reliable error-free transfer of data between source and destination: flow control for continuous flow of data across the physical layer; link flow control via acknowledgment.
- Error recovery from abnormal conditions in the event of lost frames or acknowledgment or bit-error recovery.
- Breaking of incoming data (in the form of packets) into a block of data or frames of fixed size, start and end of frame, length of frame, frame sequencing, and a cyclic redundancy code (CRC). The CRC describes the error detection scheme.
- Standards: CCITT X.21-2 (circuit-switched network)
                 CCITT X.25-2 (packet-switched network)
                 IBM's binary synchronous control (BSC), character-oriented
                 ISO 2110, ISO 1745, ISO 2628, ISO 3309, ISO 4335
                 ISO High-level data link protocol
                 IEEE 802.2 Logical link control (LLC), bit-oriented

Digital Equipment Corporation's digital data communication control, character count

Network Layer.   This layer provides the interface between the data link layer and transport layer. Following are the characteristics of the network layers.

- They establish, maintain, and terminate network connections.
- They serve as routing and switching circuits for the packets.
- Packet interface is achieved by segmenting and blocking the data information.
- They sequence and control flow at the packet level.
- They provide error recovery for lost packets in the network.
- They record the number of bits, packets, size of packets, etc., sent by each source station. This is required for billing purposes.
- They provide address sequencing of different networks.
- They support different types of communication links, e.g., point-to-point, multicasting, and broadcasting.
- Standards: CCITT X.21-3 (circuit-switched network)
     CCITT X.25-3 (packet-switched network)
     ISO connectionless-mode network

CCITT Standard X.25 is a very popular network layer protocol. In the documentation of X.25, the network layer is defined as the packet layer and the network protocol data unit (PDU) is defined as the packet. Two types of services in X.25 are called *switched virtual circuit* (SVC) and *permanent virtual circuit* (PVC). SVC is analogous to dialing a telephone for connection while PVC is analogous to services. Standard X.75 provides connection between various X.25 networks. Standard X.21 includes the lower three layers of the OSI reference model, and this is more popular in Europe than in the United States.

Transport Layer.   It provides an interface between the network and the transport layer. The following is a list of characteristics of this layer.

- Reliable, error-free, cost-effective communication link between source and destination for each application process in the application layer.
- Mapping between networks; management of concatenated network; transparent addressing to network addresses.
- End-to-end layer connection and error control; overseeing of lower-level controls.
- Breaking up of long messages or files into a smaller block of data (packets) at the source and reassembling packets into messages or a file at the destination.
- Supporting multiple connections; multiplexing; flow control of information (these parameters affect the cost of network connection, throughput, response time, etc.).
- Standards: ISO 8073, CCITT X.224

Both ISO and CCITT have defined multiple transport layer protocols. The type of transport protocol for a particular network depends on the type we select. Various types supported by transport protocol are A, B, and C. Type A offers the most reliable network service, which means simple implementation of the network layer. Type B offers a moderate network service while type C offers the lowest-quality service. The implementation of the network layer gets more complex when we choose type C protocol.

Session Layer. It provides interface between the transport and presentation layers. It has the following characteristics:

- Dialogue control, control of data exchange for priority, traffic, interaction, and synchronization for checkpoints.
- Administrative services (not well defined), e.g., binding/unbalancing connections, token management.
- Record of error statistics.
- Support of half duplex, full duplex transmitter and receiver requirements.
- Standards: Session services are defined in ISO 8327 and CCITT X.225 and protocols are defined in ISO 8327 and CCITT X.225. Various types of session layers, which are discussed in ISO 8073, are 0 through 4. Type 0 is used if we use type A transport layer while type 4 is used when we choose type C. Type 1 deals with error recovery, type 2 with multiplexing, type 3 with error and multiplexing, and type 4 with error detection and recovery.

Presentation Layer. It provides interface between the session and application layers. The layer possesses the following characteristics:

- Suitable syntax for data transformation.
- Data formatting (text compression), data encryption for security, privacy, and authentication.
- Establishment and termination of session between source and destination.
- Efficient transfer of data across the layers of the network.
- Standards: Presentation services are defined in ISO 8822 and CCITT X.216, protocols are defined in ISO 8823 and CCITT X.226, while both services and operations are defined in ISO 8822 and 8823. ISO 8824 defines a language called *Abstract Syntax Notation* (ASN.1) while ISO 8825 defines encoding rules for ASN.1. CCITT X.409 has defined a protocol as a part of the *message handling service* (MHS), which is a language for specifying the presentation syntax for electronic mail.

Application Layer. It provides interface between the presentation layer and user application. It is the highest layer of the OSI reference model. It possesses the following characteristics:

- Window for various tasks between application and OSI reference model.
- Mapping between incompatible terminals by using a virtual terminal software (VTS) containing network virtual terminal (NVT) software, editors, and other supporting software.
- Identification, availability of resources, authentication, agreement on syntax and quality of service, etc.
- Layer management function for cost-effective allocation strategy, agreement on error recovery, data integrity, data syntax protocols, etc.
- Applications, e.g., file transfer, electronic mail, access to remote resources (job entry, printing, accessing files, program databases, etc.), accessing of directory, user-oriented services, remote log-in, and many others.
- Standards: CCITT X.400 Message Handling System (MHS)
  ISO FTAM (file transfer access and management)
  ISO VTP (virtual terminal protocol)

A *private branch exchange* (PBX) offers some of the applications of a telephone network in a limited range. It can carry both analog and digital signals. It provides point-to-point transmission. We can transmit computer data (through modem) over PBX. *Data overvoice devices* (OVDs) can be used to send both telephone signals and computer data. In digital PBX, the digital switching is obtained through software, and so it is controlled. PBXs can offer speeds of 56K and 65K bits/s and supports both synchronous and asynchronous transmission. If we compare the PBX with LAN, in many cases we will support PBX over LANs.

20.4.5 Data Communication in the OSI Reference Model

Figure 20.9 shows how data transmit between source and destination by using the OSI reference model. Each OSI reference model is looked upon by a computer network as a collection of subprocesses with a specific layer of services and functions which are transformed into each of these subprocesses. Within each subprocess, a service or function of the layer is obtained through entities (segment of software, or a process, hardware I/O chips, etc.). Entities in the same layer on different systems are called *peer entities*. User data (for a particular application) are accepted by application layer. For each application, an entity carries on a dialogue with its peer entity on another side. An *application header* (AH) containing this dialogue and other control information is attached at the beginning of user data and is presented (AH along with original user data) as user data to the presentation layer.

The presentation layer selects appropriate syntax for data transformation, formatting, etc., and adds all this control information in its own presentation head (PH), which is attached at the beginning of user data. It presents this as user data to the session layer and so on. The original user data at the application layer move in this way through the physical layer. Note that the data link layer presents frames to the physical layer, where each frame contains both a data link header and a data link trailer (on each side of user data or packets received from the network layer); i.e., this is the only layer which includes both data link header (DLH) and data link trailer (DLT) pointers to the user data. The fourth layer (transport) breaks the user data into blocks of data or packets and passes them on to the network layer. The second layer (data link layer) converts these packets to frames which

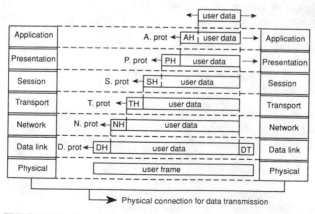

FIGURE 20.9 Data communication in OSI reference model.

are received by the physical layer. The physical layer accepts these frames from the data link layer and transmits over transmission media to the other side.

On the receiving side, these frames are received by the physical layer which presents them to its data link layer. The data link layer takes the header and trailer pointers from frames and presents them to its network layer. In this way, the original user data reach the application layer of the receiving side. Similarly, if the receiving side wants to send data or acknowledgment, it goes through its OSI reference model in the same way as the data from the sending side went through.

Higher layers are usually defined as the service user while lower layers are defined as the service provider. The services offered by higher layers are implemented by the entities of lower layers; i.e., presentation layer entities contain all the services provided by the application layer, and so on. The services offered by layers are available at *service access points* (SAPs). Each SAP has a unique address (either hardware or software). These SAPs are known as *sockets* and SAP addresses as *socket numbers* in Berkeley Unix. An operating system can also create sockets or ports for these SAPs in the model [1, 6, 8, 12, 13].

20.4.6 LAN Characterization

LAN is a data communication system which allows computers and devices to communicate with each other. The LANs are very localized; in most cases we find them in the office environment, linking several users. These networks are generally based upon protocols such as TCP/IP, Novell, or Appletalk (although others exist in this environment as well). The typical geographical area for LAN is a maximum of 1 mi and is useful in single or multiple buildings. LAN is owned by a single organization and is not regulated by the Federal Communications Commission (FCC). It offers a data (voice and video) rate between 1 and 10 Mbits/s with a low error rate. LANs can be characterized by the user computer (on which the user runs the application), protocol control (which maps user's application into a form acceptable to transmission media of LAN), medium interface (generation of electric signals for moving onto media), and physical path (transmission medium: twisted-pair, coaxial cable, fiber, etc.).

Based on architecture, switching techniques, interfaces, and applications, three categories of local networks can be defined. In the first category, for cheap resource sharing, twisted-pair LANs yielding a data transfer rate of 1 Mbit/s may be useful. In the second category, for high-speed devices and mass storage devices, sharing may require a bus topology using CATV coaxial cable and yielding a data transfer rate up to 50 Mbits/s, and the network is known as a *high-speed local network* (ANSI Standard X3T9.5). Both these categories of local network support packet switching for the transfer of data. In the third category, we have *computerized branch exchange* (CBX). It is a digital private exchange which provides connection to voice and data within the premises. It is based on star topology and provides end-to-end connection. For high-speed data transfer, coaxial cable or fiber may be used. It supports circuit switching [13].

Baseband LANs. This type of LAN uses digital signaling and accepts digital signals (as voltage pulses) using an encoding scheme (Manchester). A bus topology provides effective digital signaling. A transmission data rate up to 10 Mbits/s can be obtained. ETHERNET supports up to 10 Mbits/s while STARLAN supports up to 1 Mbit/s. Baseband LANs can be used up to a maximum distance of 1 mi (without repeaters). Various media being supported by baseband LANs are twisted-pair or coaxial cable. ETHERNET components include the transceiver, transceiver cable, 50-Ω coaxial cable, and 50-Ω terminator. In baseband LAN signals are carried on a network at their original frequency, called the *baseband*. The unmodulated data are pulsed in a single channel directly onto media.

Broadband LANs. These LANs use coaxial cable for analog signaling and frequency-division multiplexing (optional) for the transmission of signals on the media. The FDM divides the entire bandwidth of coaxial cable into a number of channels which can support data, voice, and video signals. The broadband LANs allow only unidirectional transmission of signals on coaxial cable. To use the same amplifier for signals moving in two directions, the signals are sent first to a common node (head end) of the LAN as the "inbound signal" on one data path, while the signals from the head end are sent to another station in the network as the "outbound signal" on a second data path. The inbound and outbound signals are distinguished by using dual-cable configuration (for two data paths) or single-cable configuration by splitting them on the basis of frequency. The components of broadband LANs include cable terminators, amplifiers, directional couplers, and controllers. It uses CATV cable (75-Ω) and provides a transmission rate up to 480 Mbits/s over a distance of thousands of miles. The broadband LANs use FDM, and multiplexed signals are transmitted within an allocated frequency range in one direction.

Topology. It defines the physical makeup of a network; i.e., endpoints or user stations attached to the network are interconnected. The network topology can be classified as LAN topology and WAN topology. A brief description of different types of topologies in each of the networks is given in the following paragraphs. Figure 20.10*a* shows LAN topologies.

1. *Star.* It is characterized by a central switching node (communication controller), a unique path (point-to-point link) for each of host (computer, terminal, peripheral devices, and other communication devices), ease in adding or removing host by upgrading centralized node, and vulnerability to failure. The central node is often backed up. The communication between any two hosts is controlled by the central node based on circuit switching. Depending on the application and the nature of the data, the star network could be either digital or voice and digital.

2. *Bus.* It is characterized by a common transmission medium shared by all connected hosts, managed by a dedicated node (communication controller), simultaneous flow of data and control, simplicity of adding or removing hosts from the network, extendability via repeaters, and the problem of contention. This problem can be solved by polling and selection of a high transfer rate. The advantage with this topology is that every device connected to it can communicate with every other device in the network.

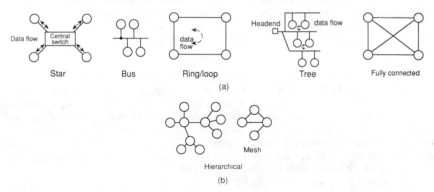

FIGURE 20.10 Network topologies. *(a)* Topologies for LANs. *(b)* Topologies for WANs.

3. *Ring or loop.*   It is characterized by data flow around the ring in one or two directions, sharing of ring through token (contention or taking turns), each node being connected to its neighboring nodes (direct link or point-to-point link), vulnerability to breaking of a link (i.e., ring), and poor survivability.

4. *Tree.*   A *tree* may be defined as a group of bus topologies put together and controlled by one node. From this node, one or more busses can send or receive data to or from the host connected to either the same bus or a different bus (i.e., two hosts which want to share data can be on different busses but the data will go through a common node known as the head end). Both bus and tree topologies can also be defined as multipoint communication to a single bus. Thus, the networks using these topologies are known as *multipoint networks*. For better utilization of tree networks, the functional modules can be defined such that each bus does a specific job. The advantage is that the entire network will not be down if one particular bus is down.

5. *Star-shaped ring.*   It is similar to the ring topology with a centralized communication controller. The topology supports the bypass of a faulty node or broken link.

6. *Bus-shaped ring.*   A typical topology is defined for IBM token ring compatible products by the company. The physical shape is like a Y connector, forming a daisy chain which preserves the ring by attaching a loop-back plug at the end of the chain.

7. *Logical ring.*   The heart of this topology is a bus topology around which a logical ring is defined for the hosts connected to the bus. The main advantage of this topology lies in its deterministic behavior to the network on bus topology.

8. *Fully connected topology.*   This is characterized by direct link between each host and a path of length 1 (or single hop) between every pair of hosts connected to the topology. There is no contention, a low queue delay, no routing (as already defined), high survivability, and high expense for large network size. The number of links is given by $N(N - 1)/2$, where N is the number of hosts connected.

Figure 20.10*b* shows the topologies for WANs:

Hierarchical Topology.   This topology uses different levels for connected hosts based on the parent-child relationship. This type of arrangement is useful as it helps in increasing the responsibility of data management. At each level, the hosts are connected to the root host until all hosts at the lowest level are connected directly to a single host for each level. The number of levels, the number of hosts to be connected, and other performance parameters depend on the particular application. This topology is very popular and common in different types of WANs.

Mesh.   This topology is usually defined on the basis of a number of parameters such as traffic, cost, throughput, etc. Each host is connected to more than one host to provide an alternative route in the case the host is either down or too busy. At each host the routing decision is made for the packets.

Transmission Media.   To transmit analog data (voice, video) and digital data (computers, terminals, or digitized signals) between the sending host transmitter and receiving host, a transmission medium defines a physical link between them. Various features offered by a medium to transmitting signals include being error-free, faster speed, and larger bandwidth. The bandwidth and quality depend on the components, such as resistance, capacitance, distance, and other parameters. The loss of the magnitude of a signal due to these is defined as *attenuation* (measured in decibels) while the quality of the signal is measured as the signal-to-noise ratio (in decibels).

Open-Wire Lines.   Open-wire lines consist of two uninsulated pairs of conductors or wires hung in air and supported by poles. Since wires are exposed to air, they are affected by atmospheric conditions, interference from high-power voltage lines, corrosion, etc., and these affect the quality of signals transmitted on it. Mutual interference of electromagnetic waves between two wires is significant and causes crosstalk. A number of techniques have been used to reduce crosstalk, e.g., transposition (crossing the wires of each line periodically), twisting the wires around each other, etc. Due to the second method of reducing crosstalk, these wires are known as twisted-pair wires. A pair of wires defines one channel. For long distance, cables containing a large number of wire pairs are used.

The open-wire lines are either shielded or unshielded. Unshielded wires are very cheap and are not covered by metal insulation. They provide an acceptable performance for long-distance signal transmission, but because they are uninsulated, they are affected by crosstalk, atmospheric conditions, etc. A majority of the twisted-pair telephone lines are unshielded and can transmit the signal up to 10 Mbits/s. Shielded open-wire lines are covered by metal insulation and hence are immune to crosstalk and atmospheric noises.

By putting a large number of pairs of insulated wire into one protective sheath (or insulating jacket), a cable is constructed. Insulated wires are twisted in such a way as to reduce the inductive coupling between the pairs. The wires are made of copper conductors, although aluminum (which is lighter and cheaper than copper) can also be used. The twisting of insulated wires is performed by considering four wires together to form a quad. The sheath provides external protection to these quads.

Coaxial Cable. The coaxial cable consists of two concentric copper conductors. The inner conductor is surrounded by insulating sheets to provide support, and both are then covered by another copper or aluminum conductor, which supports them through a cylindrical architecture. The whole set is then covered by protective sheath to prevent interference from signals from other media. The inner conductor is of very small gauge size and hence can be used for long-distance transmission, LANs, and a toll trunk carrier system (10,800 telephone channels per pair) at a maximum frequency of 60 MHz and a data rate of a few megabits per second. These are not useful in applications with frequencies lower than 60 kHz.

There are two types of coaxial cable used in LANs: 75-Ω cable (the same as CATV cable) and 50-Ω cable for digital signaling (baseband). Coaxial cables are immune to electrical interference (due to shielding), and the shielding is effective at higher frequencies (greater than 1 MHz). Voice, data, and video signals can be transmitted simultaneously.

A coaxial cable is used as an unbalanced circuit where the inner copper conductor carries the current while the outer shield (insulation) is grounded. Because of this imbalance, coaxial cable has more attenuation than balanced wire pairs, but they are cheaper, simpler to install, and very cheap to maintain. Further, coaxial cables offer larger bandwidth for long distance, and as such they are very popular and widely used. In particular, the advent of integrated digital networks (IDNs) and integrated services digital networks (ISDNs) has given a boost to coaxial cable as a medium for providing digital services to subscribers over a long distance.

Optical Fiber Cable. In early days, light was used as a carrier from one point to another. Atmospheric conditions attenuate the light, changing the direction of its transmission, and thus the signals were degraded. But if we can propagate light through a channel (free of atmospheric noise) which possesses known stable characteristics and provides controlled reflection along the channel to the light, then signals can be transmitted by pulses of light. In other words, it can be used to carry all the information (without any loss) from one point to another. The channel or tube or dielectric guide is known as *fiber,* which has a refractive index greater than that of the atmosphere. Light propagating through fiber channel can be used to carry different types of signals—data, voice, and video.

Optical fiber used as a transmission medium in telecommunication systems offers the following features:

- It supports very large bandwidth (50 to 80 MHz) in multimode fibers (several gigahertz in single-mode fiber), allowing a high bit rate. For example, 30,000 telephone voice channels can be transmitted simultaneously at a bandwidth of 500 MHz.
- Due to reflection inside the fiber, it has a minimal attenuation coefficient which requires fewer repeaters than coaxial cable for the same distance.
- Fiber has a very low error rate of 10^{-12} to 10^{-14}, compared to 10^{-5} to 10^{-7} in coaxial cable.
- It is impossible to detect or tap fiber-optic signals, and hence it is tightly secured communication.
- It possesses long life and long-term reliability.

In spite of these features, fiber suffers from the following problems:

- Development of optoelectronic transducers and their optical interface with fiber
- Electrical insulation between emitter, fiber, and receiver; also the difficulty of supplying dc power to intermediate repeater stations
- Impurities in fiber, mismatching, poor alignment of connectors, operating constraints, etc.
- Lack of standardization

Clearly, different media have different transfer capabilities, which are usually defined in terms of the frequency range or the number of bits per second. For example, coaxial cable has a bandwidth of 300 to 400 MHz while twisted-pair wires which are used in telephones provide a bandwidth of 1 to 2 MHz. The optic fiber yields between 2 and 6 GHz. LANs used coaxial cable to carry data, but they are shifting to twisted-pair and fiber systems. The bandwidth can be allocated by using FDM or TDM [1, 5, 6, 8, 12, 13].

Access Method.   Access to LANs is provided by two very common techniques: contention and token passing.

Contention.   There are two versions of this technique, namely, *carrier sense multiple access with collision avoidance* (CSMA/CA) and *with collision detection* (CSMA/CD). In CSMA/CA, each communication device (host) listens and transmits. Only one device is allowed to transmit at a time. After transmitting, it waits for the acknowledgment. In the case of CSMA/CD, the node first transmits and then listens for the collision. In the event of collision, both hosts pull out and wait for a random time. Again the node transmits and listens for collision. CSMA/CD is very useful for light-traffic interactive terminal sessions, but not useful for heavy traffic (because it will have more collisions, thus reducing throughput). It is a nondeterministic access method.

Token Passing.   A token (unique bit pattern) is used to allow multiple hosts to access a shareable LAN medium. The token moves around the ring to which hosts are connected. The token has to be grabbed by a host which wants to transmit data to another node. Once any node captures the token, it will attach its data to the token and release it in the ring. When the token carrying data passes over the destination host, it copies the contents and reverses a bit associated at the end of frame. This acknowledgment is recognized by the sending host which removes the data from the ring, and the token is released. This type of access method is most popular in ring topology, although it can also be implemented on another topology. The token is a 3-byte packet which is used for handling the requests for the token, assigning priorities, etc. The token-passing access method is deterministic, predictable, and very useful for heavy traffic and/or long data streams.

MAC and LLC Sublayers of IEEE LANs: Services and Standards. LANs transmit data over the physical medium with no intermediate routing; only the physical and data link layers need to be specified. The data link is divided into two sublayers: *medium access control* (MAC) and *logical link control* (LLC).

The MAC layer is concerned with the management of communication over the transmission media which includes frame formats and the media access method. Further, the MAC layer is concerned with sharing of media by different devices.

The LLC sublayer deals with the following services [13]:

- Assignment of service access points (SAPs) between the network layer and LLC.
- Receipt of packets from the network through SAPs and construction of frames with appropriate addressing and cyclic redundancy code (CRC) or frame check sequence (FCS) field.
- MAC of receiving side will pass the frames to its LLC which generates the packets and checks addressing and the CRC (or FCS) field.

IEEE 802 has defined standards for both MAC and LLC, as shown in Fig. 20.11. The following is a brief description of these standards:

1. Internetworking (IEEE 802.1). This standard describes other standards and also specifies the relationship between various layers of the OSI reference model in detail. Different aspects such as higher-layer protocols and management are also discussed.

2. Logical link protocol (IEEE 802.2). This standard defines a common interface between the network layer and MACs of all IEEE LANs. It describes control parameters and procedures for both connectionless (class 1) and connection-oriented (class 2) services.

3. Carrier-sense multiple access with collision detection (IEEE 802.3) LAN. This LAN uses bus topology and as such offers broadcasting communication. It offers a

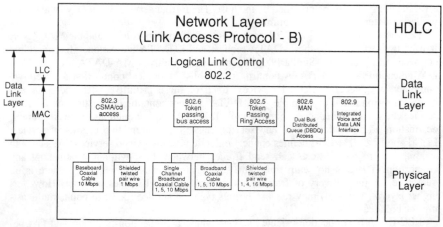

FIGURE 20.11 IEEE 802 and ISO model standards.

transmission speed of 10 Mbits/s with coaxial (baseband) and 150 Mbits/s with broadband coaxial cable. The unshielded twisted-pair wire offers 10 Mbits/s to its physical layer. If the network traffic is moderate (around 35 percent), the response time is good. For heavy traffic, more collisions occur and this means wasted bandwidth and poor throughput.

4. Token-passing bus (IEEE 802.4) LAN. It is based on bus topology and supports broadcasting communication. A control data token is used for controlling the data flow around a bus (logical ring connection between various devices). The token is passed from low-level to high-level address. This is mainly used in manufacturing automation protocol (MAP). It offers transmission speeds of 1, 5, and 10 Mbits/s to baseband coaxial cable; 1, 5, and 10 Mbits/s to broadband coaxial cable; and 5, 10, and 20 Mbits/s to optical fiber [8, 12].

5. Token ring (IEEE 802.5) LAN (IBM's LAN). The token-passing technique is used to control the flow of data around a loop or ring. This LAN is mainly used for connecting IBM computers. It supports point-to-point, multicasting, and broadcasting links. Since there is no collision, there is no wasted bandwidth and hence there is higher throughput and a lower response time. It offers 1, 4, and 16 Mbits/s to shielded twisted pairs.

6. Metropolitan-area network (IEEE 802.6) LAN: A large geographical area is covered by this LAN. It offers high speed and supports a large number of internetworked users. The private internetworked LANs (FDDI) offer a speed of 100 Mbits/s with optical fiber.

MAC and LLC Frame Formats.   The LLC sublayers provide an interface between the network layer and MAC sublayer. The connectionless service uses the services of MAC and defines the services it can offer to the network layer. The MAC sublayer provides connectionless service, and the LLC sublayer uses connectionless services offered by MAC to offer connection-oriented and connectionless services to the network layer. When LLC offers connection-oriented services to the network, it also defines a virtual connection between service access points (SAPs or peer entities) of source and destination nodes and provides flow control, error recovery, and sequencing. In the case of connectionless services, the frames go back and forth between two stations. The connectionless service supports different types of communication (point-to-point, multicasting, and broadcasting). Connection-oriented service is defined by three steps: Establish the connection, send data, and terminate the connection. In connectionless service, the destination address and error handling have to be provided by the host. The former service defines a virtual circuit while the latter defines a data gram.

LLC uses a set of primitives for interacting with its transport layer and the MAC layer. It uses two primitives—the L-DATA.request and L-DATA.indication—for providing connectionless services. Similarly, MAC uses the primitives MA-DATA.request, MA-DA.indication, and MA-DATA.confirm for establishing logical connection between two computers (connection-oriented service). Each of these primitives has addresses and control information. For example, MA-DATA.request contains the destination address, service class, and media access control while L-DATA.request contains the local address, destination address, data units, and service class. LLC offers two classes of service: LLC-I and LLC-II. LLC-I defines connectionless unacknowledged service. SAPs of both sending and receiving hosts can send frames between them without establishing any connection. There is no setup time, and call termination is not required. There is no guarantee for the delivery of frames, and it may not send frames in order. However, higher layers (transport) may request various types of service (point-to-point, multicasting, or broadcasting).

LLC-II offers connection-oriented service where a connection is established first before data can be sent. It provides point-to-point connection between SAPs. Error recovery and flow control are supported by it. Setup time and other related procedures ensure delivery of the frames in order at the receiving hosts. A complete list of primitives may be found [1, 8, 12, 13].

CSMA/CD Frame Format (Fig. 20.12). The preamble is a sequence of a particular bit pattern and is basically for allowing its physical layer to establish bit synchronization.

The start-frame delimiter is mainly used for synchronization and indicates the start of a frame of size 2 or a 6 octet (1 octet = 1 byte or 8 bits, the particular bit pattern for synchronization) address field for both source and destination field, which are defined by IEEE 802. If the destination address field has all 1s, this corresponds to broadcasting. The length field represents the number of octets in the data and pad fields. The user option field defines user data and pad. Finally, *frame check sequence* (FCS) is a 4 octet and is equivalent to a *cyclic redundancy check* (CRC).

Token-Passing Bus Frame Format (Fig. 20.13). The preamble is a minimum of 1 octet. The start delimiter of 1 octet defines the start of a frame. The frame control represents the type of frame (data or control). It has the same address field octets as CSMA/CD. The data field is 8191 octets. It has the same length of FCS as in IEEE 802.3.

Token Ring LAN Frame Format (Fig. 20.14). A token of 3 octet is used. The start delimiter defines the start of the frame. The 1 octet is used to define access control functions such as priority of the token, monitor bit, priority of a station, etc. The end delimiter defines the end of the frame and sends a bit to the sender in the case of error detection. The frame control differentiates between control and data. The source and destination addresses are the same as those of IEEE 802.3. The maximum limit for data

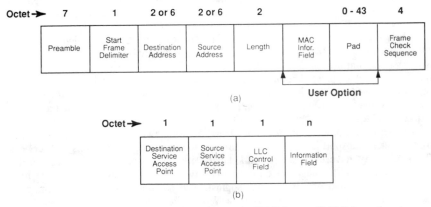

(a)

(b)

FIGURE 20.12 IEEE 802.3 CSMA/CD frame format. *(a)* MAC format. *(b)* LLC frame format.

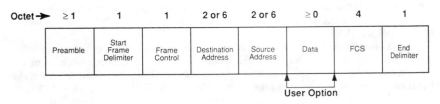

FIGURE 20.13 IEEE 802.4 token-passing bus frame format.

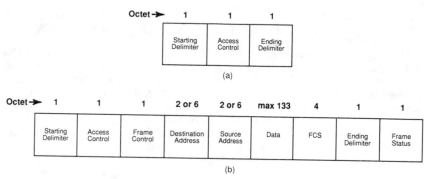

FIGURE 20.14   IEEE 802.5 token ring frame formats *(a)* and *(b)*.

is 133 octets. The frame status is a kind of acknowledgment to the sender that it has copied the data.

Hardware Devices for LAN Interconnection.   To obtain LAN-LAN interconnection and transfer of data between different LANs, high-performance hardware devices are available such as repeaters, bridges, routers, and gateways.

A repeater provides a direct physical link between two identical LANs, and it simply transfers the frame from one LAN to another one (i.e., frames are going from one medium to another). The repeater can only connect identical LANs, e.g., physical ETHERNET to backbone networks (ETHERNET). It does not have any idea about the contents of frames; it simply forwards frames to another LAN connected to it.

A bridge connects two different types of LANs at the MAC layer which decides the routing of the frames. This is against the OSI notion of having routing done at the network layer. Various stations on any OSI-based LAN can be easily determined by MAC rather than by the network layer. The bridge is a high-performance device which contains LAN interconnection hardware and a frame forwarding algorithm software module. These bridges have been used mainly for campus LAN interconnection and operate at a compatible MAC level.

A router (also known as an *internet router*) connects two LANs at the network level provided their transport layers have the same protocols and other functions and services. The LANs may have different network layers (i.e., different routing strategies). The routers provide end-to-end connection between two LANs. The routers have interconnection hardware and of course very sophisticated software modules for routing the packets. The routers can also be used in WANs and MANs. They also support the networks (LANs, WANs, MANs) having different protocols.

A gateway provides connection between two dissimilar networks at the application layer level. The networks are not OSI reference model and hence require the conversion right from the application layer so that application may be properly converted to that format. Further, the addressing schemes for non-OSI reference model networks are also different.

The selection of the bridge or router for any application seems to be difficult. Further, the problem becomes more complex when we decide to use a bridge because there are two types of bridges that the IEEE 802 committee is standardizing: the spanning tree bridge (IEEE 802.1) and source routing bridge (an addendum to IEEE 802.5) [10, 12, 13].

TCP/IP.   IEEE 802 has defined different types of LANs, which by using bridges and routers can be internetworked. This type of internetworking (based on OSI) is still a new

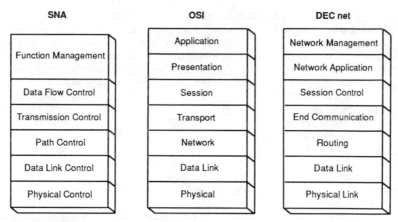

FIGURE 20.15 SNA, OSI, and DEC net models.

technology and somehow has not received widespread acceptance. The U.S. government has defined a national internetworked communication system through DARPA, which defined the standard for internetworking networks and routing as TCP/IP (transmission control protocol/internet protocol). TCP provides similar services as defined in ISO 8073 class 4. TCP is a connection-oriented protocol, and it provides reliable bidirectional transmission of data and corresponds to transport layer 4 protocol. IP represents a datagram protocol which uses globally assigned addresses and is equivalent to network layer 3 protocol. The protocol TCP/IP is being included in the BSD 4.2 version of the Unix operating systems. The interprocess communication within TCP/IP uses the socket concept of Unix, where socket represents bidirectional endpoint communication. The layers in different networks are shown in Fig. 20.15 [2].

20.5 METROPOLITAN-AREA NETWORK

A MAN is a standardized high-speed local wide-area network. MAN serves a metropolitan area (30- to 50-mi radius) and transmits data up to 200 Mbits/s. For the last two decades, IBM's *system network architecture* (SNA) and Digital Equipment Corporation's DECnet have been very popular as backbone networks in many organizations. As a result LAN has become an essential part in every corporation of the network industry. Due to the nature and understanding between LAN industry and users, LANs are considered multivendor, multiprotocol products. LANs provide various types of services to users; and as we can see, this LAN technology has generated a number of integrated technologies with a goal of transmitting data, voice, and video and a huge amount of data at very high speed. As a result, we can see a new technology, "internetworking," is emerging very rapidly. This has given a boost to develop high-speed communication networks. The *reduced instruction set computer* (RISC) has already helped the network industry to develop high-speed devices such as routers and internetworking nodal processors (INPs), to meet the ever-growing demand from users for high-speed transmission.

Looking at the demand of higher bandwidth and speed, regional Bell operating companies and other carriers are working toward an internetworking product vendor to adopt new technologies for high-speed data services, cheaper MANs, and wide-area bandwidth services. MAN is one breakthrough toward meeting that demand. MAN is defined to handle high-speed data requirements by the network industry. The network industry has said that data communication traffic is increasing at an alarming rate and until/unless this new concept of an internetworking product vendor is moved toward "real technology" which can support the amount of data, it will be very difficult for U.S. corporations to restructure their style of functioning. This is a new idea under consideration by a majority of corporations: restructure hierarchy to reduce cost. The purpose of MAN IEEE 802.6 is to provide integrated services (data, voice, and video) over a large geographical area. The access network need not be based on IEEE 802.6 protocol; it can be an extension of the user's own bus- or token-based LAN. IEEE 802.6 defines a high-speed shared MAC protocol for use over a dual unidirectional bus subnetwork. IEEE 802.6 specifies *distributed queue dual bus* (DQDB) subnetworks required to provide telecommunication service within metropolitan areas. Typical MAN consists of interconnected DQDB subnetworks where the interconnection can be via bridges, routers, or gateways. Various connectionless, connection-oriented, and isochronous data streams share the total capacity of subnetworks, flexibly and equitably [11, 15].

Bell Communication Research (Bellcore) defined a *switched multimegabit data service* (SMDS) which can transmit connectionless data packets within a metropolitan area. The basic philosophy behind SMDS (public MAN) is to connect LANs so that the interconnection gives the same performance to the user in the metropolitan range as the user gets on LAN. The user is working on the workstation and communications with such services as remote files, stations, file servers, and other remote devices provide transparency, i.e., make the user feel that these are local services. Due to this feature, the standard client-server relationship of LAN can be implemented on MANs and on WANs. The standard for SMDS has been defined by Bellcore's *technical advisories* (TAs) and *technical requirements* (TRs). An interface between MAN and the user's equipment is defined as the *subscriber network interface* (SNI). This requires users to send the packets following the SNI requirement. SMDS does provide the capability of validating the source address but does not support error recovery, since LAN services are connectionless. Further, error recovery and sequencing preservation are usually handled by the transport layer of the communicating station (TCP, ISO TP class 4). SNI TRs are based on IEEE 802.6 standard for MAN. This standard specifies a media access control sublayer and physical layer for each station and is known as the distributed queue dual bus (DQDB). On the user's premises, DQDB stations are connected to two unidirectional busses. To send data on one bus, a reservation control bit is sent on the other bus in the opposite direction. This standard supports four priorities, but at present only one for connectionless service is operational. SMDS specifies the DQDB access protocol between the user's access node and MAN switching system. The 802.6 MAC frame is defined as the MAC *protocol data unit* (PDU). SMDS offers 1.544 and 44.7 Mbits/s, and it is projected that SMDS over SONET [the standard for optical communication in the United States—other countries call this standard *synchronous digital hierarchy* (SDH)] may provide a rate of 155 Mbits/s by the end of 1995. For premises communication, no incentive is given to packet-switched LAN for voice communication because PBXs do a fairly good job. MANs can be used for interconnection of LANs, interconnection of mainframe (channel-to-channel), interconnection of PBXs for private network applications, medical imaging transfers, graphic and CAD/CAM, digital (compressed), and video applications for teleconferencing [11]. Many carriers now support the MAN concept. Work in defining the MAN standard is coordinated by IEEE 802.6 [11].

Bellcore has also defined TAs on SMDS maintenance, billing and accounting, interswitching system interfaces, exchange access, and customer network management.

MAN can also be used in a private (campus) application as a fiber distributed data interface (FDDI). FDDI is defined as a high-performance general-purpose multistation network which is basically a 100 Mbits/s version of IEEE 802.5. The FDDI offers a fiber backbone network which operates at 100 Mbits/s on pairs of fibers and uses token ring MAC. The FDDI provides interconnection for multiple LANs which use different protocols. ANSI committee X3T9.5 defined a standard for high-speed data networking. This standard offers a packet-switched LAN backbone that will transmit the data at very high throughput rates over a variety of fibers. As a result, FDDI became a useful standard for offering interconnection among mainframe, minicomputer, and peripheral devices. This standard includes lower layers of the OSI reference model and supports TCP/IP products. FDDI supports both synchronous and asynchronous transmissions and offers point-to-point connection; hence both star and ring topologies can be used. Dual fiber for connections up to 1.5 mi and support of 500-station single-mode fiber for connection up to 35 mi are some features of FDDI.

20.6 WIRELESS LANs

LANs have provided resource sharing, electronic mail, videoconferencing, electronic bulletin board, and many other services to users in the past few years. LANs have also been used for factory automation, office automation, and many real-time systems. These LANs are physically connected by physical transmission media (twisted-pair wires, cables, optical fiber). These media provide high data transmission with significantly large bandwidth, e.g., twisted pair (10 Mbits/s over a limited distance) and coaxial cable (300 to 400 MHz). Due to its high bandwidth, coaxial cable can carry data, voice, and video together. Optical fiber operates at 1 Gbit/s for a limited distance of 4 to 7 mi while FDDI which is fiber-based LAN operates at 100 Mbits/s. Due to physical media and their limited range coverage (without amplifiers and repeaters), we have very little flexibility in moving our system (PCs, workstations) beyond a certain range. Further, the installation effort and time required are really a big problem, particularly during office relocation. With the invention of wireless LANs, the installation problem will be completely eliminated, and user workstations can be easily moved. Users will still get all the same services as with physically connected LANs. Radio waves are currently being used in wireless LANs. The radio wave transceivers send data from one computer to another. The FCC has approved three shared frequency bands for the network. These frequencies are known as *industry, science,* and *medicine* (ISM), and bands are from 902 to 928 MHz, from 2400 to 2483.5 MHz, and from 5725 to 5850 MHz. The IEEE 802 committee has assigned the 802.11 standard for the wireless LAN working group. Currently this committee is working on defining specifications and requirements for MAC and physical layer services.

The services offered by wireless LANs proposed by the IEEE 802.11 committee are as follows [1]:

- Voice: same as conference PA system.
- File transfer: file distribution, file retrieval
- Database access: document register
- Off-site database access
- Electronic mail: both off-site and within conference
- File sharing
- Printing: printer sharing
- WAN access for databases, file transfer, electronic mail, etc.
- Voting

- Signaling to chairperson
- Image distribution

The users have their personal computers which may be portables, laptops, or notebooks.

20.7 WIDE-AREA NETWORK

In the preceding sections we discussed the use of circuit switching as a logical link to be established by physical media to connect two stations for the transfer of data between them. Another switching technique, which is based on store-and-forward switching, offers fast processing and other procedures for accepting, storing, and forwarding of packets, which usually require complex protocols on the switching sites (e.g., specialized computers). These switching computers are connected with large-bandwidth circuits and communication links defining a subnetwork which move the data from one switching node to another, retransmitting lost or corrupted data around the network. This type of store-and-forward network was called a *value-added network* (VAN) and has been renamed a *public data network* or *private data network* depending on whether it is owned and operated privately or by a common carrier.

A class of store-and-forward switching is packet switching, in which packets are forwarded and have to be stored for a very short time in the main memory. Thus access time is reduced, which also improves the throughput and response time. The only requirement of this technique is that the size of the packet (generated for the messages) has to be very small (maximum number of characters is 64 or 128). A *packet-switching network* (PSN) offers excellent support for interactive applications. Private PSNs can be built by installing switching computers interconnected by high-speed links (typically 56K bits/s); each computer can access others connected to this interconnected switching computer. The installation (basic communication and other services) is usually offered by common carriers, while the same services and connectivity can be obtained from public PSNs which offer other communication links (microwave link, satellite link) and are controlled by carriers (MCI, AT&T, Sprint). These carriers are regulated by the FCC.

The CCITT recommended X.25 as a standard interface between data terminal equipment (DTE) and data circuit (terminating) equipment (DCE) for terminals operating in the packet mode and connected to the public data networks by dedicated circuits. The terminals are basically defined as specially programmed computers. The network layer in the OSI reference model is also known as *subnet* (lower three layers), and it may run on different networks (X.25, ARPANET, NSFNET, and others). The network layer actually runs on IMP. The transport layer of the OSI reference model will run on hosts. The control and management of the network layer are provided by different organizations in different countries; the PTT seems to be very popular in many European and third world countries. Thus, the network layer provides services to the transport layer and interface between different hosts and different types of networks. An X.25 DCE is the point of interface and connection to the network which may or may not use RS-232 DCE (i.e., modem). The first version of X.25 was approved by CCITT in 1976, and since then it has been modified a number of times with a view to providing widespread implementation. A final version was approved in 1988 which includes several new features.

Standard X.25 does not describe the internal operation of the network (i.e., how data are formatted, moved, forwarded, etc.); it simply states that the network supports X.25. Public data networks will have different internal operations and are incompatible with each other (e.g., Telenet and Tymnet in the United States use X.25 for external interface, but their operations are totally different). The following paragraph discusses the standards for three lower layers which are defined for X.25.

CCITT defined the physical layer of X.21 specification for X.25. All three layers are described in Standard X.21 (physical layer). Due to the limited market at that time, CCITT defined another interim standard for the X.25 physical layer—the X.21bis. This standard supports RS-232 and V.24, which were physical-layer standards for slower-speed interface, and RS-449 for high-speed interfaces.

The standard for the data link layer was chosen from the second layer of X.25, a subset of HDLC called *link access procedure balance* (LAPB). All stations are considered as peer stations under LAPB. In other words, any station can issue a command or responses. In 1984, a new feature to support multiple physical connections between X.25 DTE and DCE was introduced in the latest version of X.25. The packet layer of X.25 has the same services as offered by the OSI reference model except it does not include a specification for how the network layer will interface with the transport layer. One of the valuable functions of X.25 is to multiplex multiple data exchange over a single X.25 interface. Standard X.25 allows for a maximum of 4095 logical channel numbers between each DTE-DCE pair.

CCITT defined *packet assembly and disassembly* (PAD) as an alternative for those who do not have CCITT X.25. The X.3 standard defines PAD which offers assembly of data into outgoing packets and disassembly of incoming packets into data and control information. Standard X.28 defines the interface between a PAD facility and an asynchronous device, while X.29 defines the interface between the PAD facility and packet-mode DTE.

Most microcomputers produce an asynchronous data stream which will be accepted by PAD through X.28. The data from PAD are accepted by DTE through X.29, whence the packets are sent to public packet networks through X.25. This is how the packets move from DTE microcomputers to a public packet network. The packets from one public network are transferred to another public network as well as across international boundaries via another CCITT standard: X.75. Thus, the public networks in the United States (e.g., Uninet, Tymnet, Telenet) will talk to each other through X.75. These public networks will talk to public network Datapac of Canada and PSS of the United Kingdom again through X.75.

A public network consists of switching nodes and links between those nodes. The nodes are communication processors which process incoming packets, their routing, and other related parameters in a routing table. Depending on the type of transmission media between various nodes, we can have different nodes; e.g., Tymnet consists of two types of nodes: Tymcom and Tymsat. Tymcom works with the host only while Tymsat works with asynchronous or synchronous terminals. The difference between these nodes is the speed of traffic; i.e., Tymcom generates high-speed traffic while Tymsat generates low-speed asynchronous traffic. Tymnet can be accessed through ports. These ports are either public access ports or private access ports. The public ports use public dial-up while private ports use either dial-up or leased lines. Figure 20.16 shows well-known protocols for various layers of the OSI reference model [2, 12, 14].

20.8 FUTURE TRENDS IN NETWORK TECHNOLOGY

One hopes that LAN architecture may eventually become an integral part of almost all companies for information processing and other operations in a very highly integrated framework for computing, communication resources and devices, their capabilities, etc.

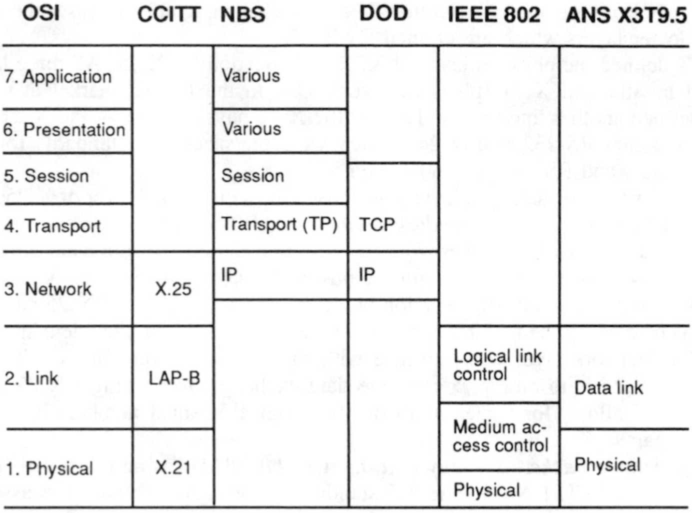

OSI	CCITT	NBS	DOD	IEEE 802	ANS X3T9.5
7. Application		Various			
6. Presentation		Various			
5. Session		Session			
4. Transport		Transport (TP)	TCP		
3. Network	X.25	IP	IP		
2. Link	LAP-B			Logical link control	Data link
				Medium access control	
1. Physical	X.21			Physical	Physical

FIGURE 20.16 Well-known layers.

It seems that LANs will be a central point for different types of "digital networks." In particular, fiber-optic LANs will be very useful in transferring large amounts of data across the networks quickly. This evolution of LANs in an integrated environment may have a great impact on various aspects of LAN technology including standards, bandwidth, transmission media, security, data integrity, customized services, and performance.

From the market point of view, in coming years various concepts in networking will be used, e.g., distributed computing, traffic capacity, connectivity, broadband data networks, etc. These concepts will dominate the network technology in the next decade. From the point of view of communications, three LANs [IEEE 802.3, IEEE 802.5, and FDDI (MAN)], WANs (X.25, ISDN, BISDN), and intelligent networks will dominate in the next decade. The concepts of broadband technology and frame relay have great potential in ISDNs, LAN-LAN, LAN-MAN, and LAN-WAN internetworking.

REFERENCES

1. R. Albrow, *Wireless LANs Meeting Ad-Hoc Group,* IEEE P802.11, Initial report, September 1991.

2. U. Black, *Data Networks, Concepts, Theory and Practices.* Englewood Cliffs, N.J.: Prentice-Hall, 1989.

3. P. Fontolliet, *Telecommunication System.* Dedham, Mass.: Artech House, 1986.

4. S. C. Helmers, *Data Communication: A Beginner's Guide to Concepts and Technology.* Englewood Cliffs, N.J.: Prentice-Hall, 1989.

5. T. Housley, *Data Communications and Teleprocessing System,* 2d ed. Englewood Cliffs, N.J.: Prentice-Hall, 1987.

6. G. S. Hura, "Local Area Networks: An Overview," tutorial, IEEE TENCON, the Region 10 Conference, Bombay, India, 1989.

7. G. S. Hura, "Network and Data Communication," tutorial, International Phoenix Conference on Computers and Communications, Scottsdale, Ariz., March 1991.

8. D. Hutchison, *Local Area Network Architecture*. Reading, Mass.: Addison-Wesley, 1988.

9. R. W. Markley, *Data Communication and Interoperability*. Englewood Cliffs, N.J.: Prentice-Hall, 1990.

10. P. V. Marney, *Networking and Data Communication*. Reston, Va.: Reston Publishing, 1986.

11. D. Minoli, *Telecommunication Technology Handbook*. Boston, Mass.: Artech, 1989.

12. W. Stallings, *Local Networks: An Introduction*. New York: Macmillan, 1984.

13. W. Stallings, *Handbook of Computer Communication Standards*, vol. 2, 2d ed. New York: Macmillan, 1990.

14. A. S. Tanenbaum, *Computer Networks*. Englewood Cliffs, N.J.: Prentice-Hall, 1988.

15. A. J. Weissberger, "Comparing Alternative Fast Packet Networking Technologies: Part I. Telecommunication," *Microwave,* 25(25): 58, September 1991.

INDEX

ABOUT THE EDITOR-IN-CHIEF

C. H. Chen, professor of electrical and computer engineering at the University of Massachusetts Dartmouth in North Dartmouth, Massachusetts, is the author or editor of more than fourteen books and numerous technical papers in the areas of pattern recognition, signal and image processing, artificial intelligence, time series analysis, and neural networks. He is also president and founder of Information Research Laboratory, Inc., a company dealing with research and development in signal/image processing, pattern recognition, and applications.